Lecture Notes in Computer Science

Lecture Notes in Artificial Intelligence 16688

Founding Editor

Jörg Siekmann

AF774399

Series Editors

Randy Goebel, *University of Alberta, Edmonton, Canada*
Wolfgang Wahlster, *DFKI, Berlin, Germany*
Zhi-Hua Zhou, *Nanjing University, Nanjing, China*

The series Lecture Notes in Artificial Intelligence (LNAI) was established in 1988 as a topical subseries of LNCS devoted to artificial intelligence.

The series publishes state-of-the-art research results at a high level. As with the LNCS mother series, the mission of the series is to serve the international R & D community by providing an invaluable service, mainly focused on the publication of conference and workshop proceedings and postproceedings.

Armin Biere · Carsten Lutz · Sara Negri
Editors

Automated Reasoning

13th International Joint Conference, IJCAR 2026
Lisbon, Portugal, July 26–29, 2026
Proceedings, Part I

Springer

Editors
Armin Biere
University of Freiburg
Freiburg, Germany

Carsten Lutz
Leipzig University
Leipzig, Germany

Sara Negri
University of Genoa
Genoa, Italy

ISSN 0302-9743 ISSN 1611-3349 (electronic)
Lecture Notes in Artificial Intelligence
ISBN 978-3-032-32588-4 ISBN 978-3-032-32589-1 (eBook)
https://doi.org/10.1007/978-3-032-32589-1

LNCS Sublibrary: SL7 – Artificial Intelligence

© The Editor(s) (if applicable) and The Author(s) 2026. This book is an open access publication.

Open Access This book is licensed under the terms of the Creative Commons Attribution 4.0 International License (http://creativecommons.org/licenses/by/4.0/), which permits use, sharing, adaptation, distribution and reproduction in any medium or format, as long as you give appropriate credit to the original author(s) and the source, provide a link to the Creative Commons license and indicate if changes were made.
The images or other third party material in this book are included in the book's Creative Commons license, unless indicated otherwise in a credit line to the material. If material is not included in the book's Creative Commons license and your intended use is not permitted by statutory regulation or exceeds the permitted use, you will need to obtain permission directly from the copyright holder.
The use of general descriptive names, registered names, trademarks, service marks, etc. in this publication does not imply, even in the absence of a specific statement, that such names are exempt from the relevant protective laws and regulations and therefore free for general use.
The publisher, the authors and the editors are safe to assume that the advice and information in this book are believed to be true and accurate at the date of publication. Neither the publisher nor the authors or the editors give a warranty, expressed or implied, with respect to the material contained herein or for any errors or omissions that may have been made. The publisher remains neutral with regard to jurisdictional claims in published maps and institutional affiliations.

This Springer imprint is published by the registered company Springer Nature Switzerland AG
The registered company address is: Gewerbestrasse 11, 6330 Cham, Switzerland

If disposing of this product, please recycle the paper.

Preface

These proceedings contain the articles accepted for presentation at the 13th International Joint Conference on Automated Reasoning (IJCAR), held in Lisbon, Portugal, July 26–29 2026. IJCAR 2026 was part of the Federated Logic Conference (FLoC 2026), which took place from July 13 to July 29, 2026.

IJCAR is the premier international joint conference on all aspects of automated reasoning, including foundations, implementations, and applications, bringing together several leading conferences and workshops. IJCAR 2026 comprised the Conference on Automated Deduction (CADE), the International Symposium on Frontiers of Combining Systems (FroCoS), and the International Conference on Automated Reasoning with Analytic Tableaux and Related Methods (TABLEAUX). Previous IJCAR conferences were held in Siena, Italy (2001), Cork, Ireland (2004), Seattle, USA (2006), Sydney, Australia (2008), Edinburgh, UK (2010), Manchester, UK (2012), Vienna, Austria (2014), Coimbra, Portugal (2016), Oxford, UK (2018), Paris, France (2020, virtual), Haifa, Israel (2022), and Nancy, France (2024).

IJCAR 2026 received 144 abstracts and 114 full submissions (93 regular and 19 short) out of which 112 went into review while two were desk-rejected. We accepted 41 regular papers and 8 short papers, resulting in acceptance rates of 44% for regular papers and 42% for short papers. Each submission was assigned to at least three Program Committee members for reviewing in single-blind mode. The review process included a feedback/rebuttal period, during which authors had the option to respond to reviewer comments.

The program included two invited talks by Viktor Kunčak and Brigitte Pientka; abstracts are provided in this volume. It also included a FLoC plenary talk by Leonardo de Moura, a FLoC keynote by Işıl Dillig, and a session in honor of the late Deepak Kapur. In addition to the main program, 10 FLoC workshops were affiliated with IJCAR 2026, as well as three system competitions (CASC, ProoVer, and termCOMP).

The Best Paper Award of IJCAR 2026 went to Florian Frohn and Jürgen Giesl for the paper "Accelerating Loops with Arrays" and the Best Student Paper Award went to Hongkai Yin for the single-authored paper "Saving Craig in the Fluted Fragment".

At IJCAR 2026, the 2026 Herbrand Award for Distinguished Contributions to Automated Reasoning was presented to Frank Pfenning (Carnegie Mellon University, USA) in recognition of "contributions to the foundations of type theory and logical frameworks, and the development of theory, automated tools, and applications for classical and non-classical logics."

The 2026 Bill McCune PhD Award was given to Jasper Nalbach for the PhD thesis "Cylindrical Algebraic Decomposition Based Methods in Satisfiability Modulo Nonlinear Real Arithmetic", completed at RWTH Aachen University, Germany. The committee decided to award an honorable mention to Joseph Reeves for his PhD thesis "Cardinality Constraints in Boolean Satisfiability Solving", completed at Carnegie Mellon University.

We would like to acknowledge the generous sponsorship of Springer, which was used to fund Woody Bledsoe student travel awards. In total, 7 such awards were given. We thank the FLoC 2026 organizing team, in particular Nuno Lopes, for assisting us with local organization and general conference management. Finally, we thank the chair of the IJCAR steering committee, Jürgen Giesl, and the IJCAR representative for FLoC, Franz Baader.

June 2026

Armin Biere
Carsten Lutz
Sara Negri

Organization

Conference Chair

Carlos Caleiro	University of Lisbon, Portugal

Program Committee Chairs

Armin Biere	University of Freiburg, Germany
Carsten Lutz	Leipzig University, Germany
Sara Negri	Università degli Studi di Genova, Italy

Workshop Chair

Mathias Fleury	University of Freiburg, Germany

Steering Committee

Franz Baader	TU Dresden, Germany
Carlos Caleiro	University of Lisbon, Portugal
Jürgen Giesl	RWTH Aachen University, Germany
Carsten Lutz	Leipzig University, Germany
Sara Negri	Università degli Studi di Genova, Italy
Lawrence Paulson	University of Cambridge, UK
Elaine Pimentel	University College London, UK
Christophe Ringeissen	Inria Loria, France

Program Committee

Clark Barrett	Stanford University, USA
Nikolaj Bjørner	Microsoft Research, USA
Jasmin Blanchette	LMU Munich, Germany
Maria Paola Bonacina	Università degli Studi di Verona, Italy
Agata Ciabattoni	TU Wien, Austria
Liron Cohen	Ben-Gurion University of the Negev, Israel

Mathias Fleury	University of Freiburg, Germany
Pascal Fontaine	University of Liège, Belgium
Didier Galmiche	University of Lorraine, CNRS LORIA, France
Silvio Ghilardi	Università degli Studi di Milano, Italy
Jürgen Giesl	RWTH Aachen University, Germany
Marianna Girlando	University of Amsterdam, Netherlands
Stefano Guerrini	Université Paris 13, France
Marijn Heule	Carnegie Mellon University, USA
Andrzej Indrzejczak	University of Lodz, Poland
Moa Johansson	Chalmers University of Technology, Sweden
Jean Christoph Jung	TU Dortmund University, Germany
Daniela Kaufmann	TU Wien, Austria
Patrick Koopmann	Vrije Universiteit Amsterdam, Netherlands
Konstantin Korovin	University of Manchester, UK
Laura Kovacs	TU Wien, Austria
Martin Lange	University of Kassel, Germany
Emiliano Lorini	CNRS IRIT, France
Tim Lyon	TU Dresden, Germany
Kuldeep S. Meel	Georgia Institute of Technology, USA, and University of Toronto, Canada
Stefan Mengel	Université d'Artois, CNRS, CRIL, France
Stephan Merz	Inria Loria, France
Tobias Nipkow	Technical University of Munich, Germany
Jakob Nordström	University of Copenhagen and Lund University, Denmark
Nicolas Peltier	CNRS LIG, France
Elaine Pimentel	University College London, UK
André Platzer	Karlsruhe Institute of Technology, Germany
Andrei Popescu	University of Sheffield, UK
Florian Rabe	FAU Erlangen-Nürnberg, Germany
Andrew Reynolds	University of Iowa, USA
Christophe Ringeissen	Inria Loria, France
Tanja Schindler	University of Basel, Switzerland
Renate Schmidt	University of Manchester, UK
Lutz Schröder	Friedrich-Alexander-Universität Erlangen-Nürnberg, Germany
Stephan Schulz	DHBW Stuttgart, Germany
Roberto Sebastiani	University of Trento, Italy
Martina Seidl	Johannes Kepler University Linz, Austria
Viorica Sofronie-Stokkermans	University of Koblenz, Germany
Martin Suda	Czech Technical University in Prague, Czech Republic

René Thiemann — University of Innsbruck, Austria
Cesare Tinelli — University of Iowa, USA
Sophie Tourret — Inria Loria, France
Josef Urban — AI4REASON, Czech Republic, University of Gothenburg and Chalmers University, Sweden
Uwe Waldmann — MPI for Informatics, Germany
Christoph Weidenbach — MPI for Informatics, Germany
Sarah Winkler — Free University of Bozen-Bolzano, Italy
Frank Wolter — University of Liverpool, UK
Yoni Zohar — Bar-Ilan University, Israel

Additional Reviewers

Eric Alsmann
Leni Aniva
Guy Axelrod
Lee A. Barnett
Bartosz Bednarczyk
Zvika Berger
Raven Beutner
Fernando Bobillo
Benjamin Bogø
Filippo Bonchi
Riccardo Borsetto
Tanguy Bozec
Marvin Brieger
Julia Butte
Julie Cailler
Jacques Carette
Davide Catta
David Cerna
Kaustuv Chaudhuri
Xin Chen
Wei-Ngan Chin
Karel Chvalovský
Robin Coutelier
Martin Desharnais-Schäfer
Francesco Di Cosmo
Sridhar Duggirala
Manuel Eberl
Clemens Eisenhofer
Matthew England
Ali Farjami
William Farmer
Thiago Felicissimo
Florian Frohn
Martin Fränzle
Carsten Fuhs
Ludovico Fusco
Mariami Gamsakhurdia
Milan Ganai
Francesco Gavazzo
Cigdem Gencer
Alessandro Gianola
Massin Guerdi
Thomas Hader
Jochen Hoenicke
Ullrich Hustadt
Swen Jacobs
Simon Jeanteur
Kevin Kappelmann
Jan-Christoph Kassing
Harun Khan
Lydia Kondylidou
Wietze Koops
Daniil Kozhemiachenko
Oliver Kullman
Satoshi Kura
Roman Kuznets
Nils Kürbis
Daniel Larraz
Quang Loc Le
David Lehnherr

Robert Lorch
Lorenzo Luperi
Alejandro Luque Cerpa
Luca Maio
Lars-Eric Marquardt
Andrew Marshall
Gabriele Masina
Andrea Masini
Jack McKeown
Aart Middeldorp
Mudathir Mohamed
Yoàv Montacute
Paolo Morettin
Jasper Nalbach
Johannes Niederhauser
Andy Oertel
Leonardo Pacheco
Promit Panja
Fabio Papacchini
Áron Ricardo Perez-Lopez
Liza Pertseva
Yaroslav Petrukhin
Dominik Pichler
Ian Pratt-Hartmann
Enguerrand Prebet
Revantha Ramanayake
Reuben Rowe
Sarah Sallinger
Johannes Schoisswohl
Borja Sierra
Nicholas Smallbone
Sam Speight
Fausto Spoto
Geoff Sutcliffe
Matteo Tesi
Balazs Toth
Guilherme Vicentin de Toledo
Laurent Vigneron
Arjun Viswanathan
Przemysław Wałega
Tjark Weber
Jack Widman
Lorenz Winkler
Hongkai Yin
Michał Zawidzki

Invited Talks

Polynomial-Time Deduction with Orthologic

Viktor Kunčak

School of Computer and Communication Sciences, EPFL, Switzerland
viktor.kuncak@epfl.ch

Abstract. Orthologic is a non-classical logic that supports arbitrary conjunction, disjunction and negation operators and is interpreted over ortholattices. If a formula is provable in orthologic, it is also provable in classical logic. I present a complete proof system (formalized in Rocq) and an efficient polynomial-time algorithm for provability in orthologic. We evaluated and deployed orthologic on boolean circuits, program verifiers, proof assistant kernels, and type systems. Joint work with Simon Guilloud.

A Type-Theoretic Framework for Meta-Programming: Lessons Learned from Writing Meta-Theoretic Proofs as Programs

Brigitte Pientka

McGill University, Montreal, Canada
brigitte.pientka@mcgill.ca

Abstract. Meta-programming is the practice of writing programs that generate and analyze code representations. It enables programmers to automate repetitive and error-prone tasks and to exploit domain-specific knowledge when generating code. As a result, meta-programming plays a central role across a wide range of applications, from splicing in optimized code that exploits memory layout, to generating representations of quantum circuits from classical programs, to writing meta-theoretic proofs as programs that transform derivation trees.

A fundamental question across all forms of meta-programming is how to design abstractions that support the correct generation, composition, and analysis of code representations. This question is challenging for two main reasons. First, it is important to distinguish between code as data (static structure) and the programs that generate and manipulate it (dynamic behavior). Second, representing code requires managing variables and scope, a task that is inherently error-prone and often exposes low-level implementation details.

In this talk, I discuss how advances in logical frameworks have informed the design of modern meta-programming languages. In particular, I revisit the development of the Beluga framework where formal systems are specified in the logical framework LF, using higher-order abstract syntax (HOAS) to represent binding constructs. On top of the LF layer sits a functional language where programmers write meta-theoretic proofs as transformations over HOAS representations. A key insight enabling recursive analysis and manipulation at the functional programming level is to treat HOAS objects together with their accompanying contexts–so-called contextual objects.

Over the past decade, this separation between static syntactic representations and dynamic program behaviour together with the use of contextual objects, has guided the development of a range of meta-programming systems. In particular, these ideas have informed the design of polymorphic and dependently typed meta-programming languages, and more recently, have been extended to support the generation, analysis, and evaluation of concurrent processes within a functional programming setting. These developments illustrate how ideas originating in automated reasoning–particularly techniques for representing and manipulating contextual objects–are having a broad impact beyond their original domain.

Contents

Theorem Proving and Automation

Tao's Equational Proof Challenge Accepted

Lydia Kondylidou[1(✉)], Jasmin Blanchette[1], and Marijn J.H. Heule[2]

[1] Ludwig-Maximilians-Universität München, Munich, Germany
{l.kondylidou,jasmin.blanchette}@lmu.de
[2] Carnegie Mellon University, Pittsburgh, USA
marijn@cmu.edu

Abstract. In the context of the Equational Theories Project, Terence Tao posed the challenge of finding alternatives to a complicated 62-step proof found by the Vampire superposition prover. We introduce a proof minimization tool called Krympa. Using a combination of brute force and heuristics, and exploiting both Vampire and the Twee equational prover, the tool reduces the 62-step proof to 20 steps, each corresponding to a rewrite. In an empirical evaluation, it also performs well on 1431 equational problems originating from the same project, reducing in particular a 151-step proof to only 10 steps.

Keywords: Theorem provers · Equational logic · Proof minimization

1 Introduction

The Equational Theories Project [6], launched in September 2024 by Fields medalist Terence Tao, aims at exploring the relations between different equational theories of magmas. A *magma* is a basic algebraic structure consisting of a set equipped with a single binary operation $\diamond$ closed on that set. The project's first phase, concluded in April 2025, focused on equational laws for magmas that contain at most four applications of $\diamond$.

The project uses the Lean [24] proof assistant to express proofs and counterexamples but depends on automatic theorem provers and other external tools. The problems explored in the project's first phase all fall within first-order logic's unit equality fragment: They consist of a universally quantified equation as the sole axiom and a universally quantified equation as the proof goal, or conjecture.

For the problem $650 \implies 448$, where 650 denotes the axiom $\forall x, y, z.\ x = x \diamond (y \diamond ((z \diamond x) \diamond y))$ and 448 denotes the conjecture $\forall x, y, z.\ x = x \diamond (y \diamond (z \diamond (x \diamond z)))$, the Vampire [4] superposition prover found a particularly complex proof, with 62 inference steps, excluding clausification and Skolemization. Given that the proof is unintelligible, Tao challenged the community to find "an alternate proof, by whatever means you wish—human, semi-automated, or automated" [30].

One idea was to run a specialized equational prover, Twee [26], instead of Vampire, but this results in a very long, 137-step proof. Another approach would

© The Author(s) 2026
A. Biere et al. (Eds.): IJCAR 2026, LNAI 16688, pp. 3–21, 2026.
https://doi.org/10.1007/978-3-032-32589-1_1

be to use Lean's automation, such as the `aesop` [21], `canonical` [25], `duper` [8], and `grind` [23] tactics and LeanHammer [32], to reconstruct and compress consecutive superposition steps, in the style of Sledgehammer's structured proof reconstruction [5, Sect. 6.3]. This would yield a shorter and more high-level proof, in which each step may combine multiple rewrites. Our approach is orthogonal. Our working hypothesis is that the 62-step Vampire proof, which emerged as the byproduct of a saturation process, is likely suboptimal. By mixing and matching proofs generated by different automatic provers, as proposed by Sutcliffe et al. [29], we hoped to achieve a shorter, simpler proof.

We introduce Krympa, a tool that minimizes equational proofs by decomposing them into independently provable parts and reassembling them into more concise, intelligible proofs. Specifically, starting from a Vampire-generated proof, the tool transforms it into a direct proof (Sect. 3) and analyzes its inferences to break it down into intermediate results that serve as candidate lemmas. Each of these lemmas is then proved independently using Vampire and Twee (Sect. 4), the two leading systems in the unit equality division of the 2025 edition of CASC [28]. The resulting proofs are then combined into a single proof using heuristics that favor shorter derivations (Sect. 5).

Given the 62-step Vampire proof of $650 \implies 448$, our tool produces a 20-step proof, where 13 steps are generated by Twee and 7 steps are generated by Vampire (Sect. 6). In a larger empirical evaluation, we applied the tool to 1431 provable implications from the Equational Theories Project and obtained positive results (Sect. 7). In particular, the tool reduced a 151-step Vampire proof to 10 steps.

Our tool is implemented in Rust, OCaml, and Python. Its source code is available at https://github.com/kondylidou/Krympa. The files associated with Tao's challenge and our empirical evaluation data are also available online [20].

An extended version of this paper is available online as a technical report at https://arxiv.org/abs/2605.21200.

2 Background

We briefly review the Vampire and Twee provers and their proof formats.

2.1 Vampire and Superposition Proofs

Vampire is a saturation-based theorem prover for first-order logic with equality based on the superposition calculus [3]. It implements highly optimized search strategies and data structures, and integrates techniques such as literal selection, term orders, redundancy elimination, strategy scheduling, and portfolios.

Superposition works on implicitly universally quantified clauses. A preprocessor performs clausification and Skolemization. For example, the axiom $\forall x.\ \mathsf{f}(x) = \mathsf{g}(x)$ is transformed into $\mathsf{f}(x) = \mathsf{g}(x)$, where x is a free variable, and the conjecture $\forall x.\ \mathsf{f}(x) = \mathsf{g}(x)$ is negated and transformed into $\mathsf{f}(\mathsf{sk}) \neq \mathsf{g}(\mathsf{sk})$, where sk is a Skolem constant. The objective is to derive the contradictory clause

$\bot$. For the unit equality fragment, the calculus's two relevant inference rules are as follows:

$$\frac{t \neq u}{\bot}\ \text{equality resolution} \qquad\qquad \frac{t = t' \quad s[u] \bowtie s'}{\mu(s[t'] \bowtie s')}\ \text{superposition}$$

The equality resolution rule has one premise, $t \neq u$, one conclusion, $\bot$, and one side condition: that t and u are unifiable. The superposition rule has two premises and one conclusion. The $\bowtie$ symbol denotes either $=$ or $\neq$ throughout the rule. The $=$ and $\neq$ operators are commutative; for example, the premise $t \neq u$ can match the disequation $\mathsf{f}(\mathsf{a}) \neq x$ either as is or as $x \neq \mathsf{f}(\mathsf{a})$. The premises are assumed to have mutually disjoint sets of variables, which can be achieved by renaming. The notation $s[\,]$ represents a term with a hole, the terms $s[u]$ and $s[t']$ are obtained by filling the hole in $s[\,]$ with u and t', and μ is a most general unifier of t and u. For example, the most general unifier of the terms $\mathsf{h}(\mathsf{a}, y)$ and $\mathsf{h}(x, \mathsf{b})$ is $\{x \mapsto \mathsf{a},\ y \mapsto \mathsf{b}\}$; applying it on both terms yields $\mathsf{h}(\mathsf{a}, \mathsf{b})$. Finally, the rule has further side conditions, not shown here, that restrict the search space.

Example 1. A subtle case of the superposition rule arises when both premises are the same clause. In the following, the variable in the second premise has been renamed to avoid a clash:

$$\frac{\mathsf{f}(\mathsf{f}(x)) = \mathsf{g}(x) \quad \mathsf{f}(\mathsf{f}(x')) = \mathsf{g}(x')}{\mathsf{f}(\mathsf{g}(x)) = \mathsf{g}(\mathsf{f}(x))}\ \text{superposition}$$

This instance is obtained by taking $t := \mathsf{f}(\mathsf{f}(x))$, $t' := \mathsf{g}(x)$, $\bowtie\ :=\ =$, $s[\,] := \mathsf{f}([\,])$, $u := \mathsf{f}(x')$, $s' := \mathsf{g}(x')$, and $\mu = \{x' \mapsto \mathsf{f}(x)\}$. Applying the unifier μ to both premises yields the equations $\mathsf{f}(\mathsf{f}(x)) = \mathsf{g}(x)$ and $\mathsf{f}(\mathsf{f}(\mathsf{f}(x))) = \mathsf{g}(\mathsf{f}(x))$. The inference replaces the subterm $\mathsf{f}(\mathsf{f}(x))$ in the second equation with $\mathsf{g}(x)$ using the first equation as a left-to-right rewrite rule, and derives the conclusion. ■

Example 2. Vampire implements *parallel superposition*, a variant of the superposition rule in which all subterms that match a term are replaced. For example:

$$\frac{\mathsf{b} = \mathsf{a} \quad \mathsf{h}(\mathsf{b}, \mathsf{a}, \mathsf{b}) \neq \mathsf{h}(\mathsf{a}, \mathsf{b}, \mathsf{a})}{\mathsf{h}(\mathsf{a}, \mathsf{a}, \mathsf{a}) \neq \mathsf{h}(\mathsf{a}, \mathsf{a}, \mathsf{a})}\ \text{parallel superposition}$$

■

Superposition proofs are expressed in a linear format. They are refutational and show how to derive $\bot$ from the input axioms and the negated conjecture.

Example 3. The following is a superposition proof from clauses 1–3:

1. $\mathsf{a} = \mathsf{b}$	axiom
2. $\mathsf{f}(x) = x$	axiom
3. $\mathsf{h}(\mathsf{f}(\mathsf{b}), \mathsf{a}) \neq \mathsf{h}(\mathsf{a}, \mathsf{f}(\mathsf{b}))$	negated conjecture
4. $\mathsf{h}(\mathsf{b}, \mathsf{a}) \neq \mathsf{h}(\mathsf{a}, \mathsf{b})$	by parallel superposition from 2 and 3
5. $\mathsf{h}(\mathsf{a}, \mathsf{a}) \neq \mathsf{h}(\mathsf{a}, \mathsf{a})$	by parallel superposition from 1 and 4
6. $\bot$	by equality resolution from 5

■

2.2 Twee and Structured Equational Chain Proofs

Twee is an automatic prover specialized for equational reasoning. It is based on the unfailing completion procedure [2], an extension of Knuth–Bendix completion [19]. As with superposition, quantifiers are eliminated by a preprocessor. In the DISCOUNT [10] and Waldmeister tradition [7], Twee's proofs are structured as a sequence of lemmas, where the lemmas and the conjecture are proved by chains of equalities. Twee introduces lemmas if they are needed more than once.

Example 4. The following is a Twee-style proof of goal 1 from axioms 1 and 2:

Axiom 1: $\mathsf{a} = \mathsf{b}$

Axiom 2: $\mathsf{f}(x) = x$

Lemma 3: $\mathsf{f}(\mathsf{b}) = \mathsf{a}$
Proof:
  $\mathsf{f}(\mathsf{b})$
$=$ { by axiom 1 right-to-left }
  $\mathsf{f}(\mathsf{a})$
$=$ { by axiom 2 }
  a
Goal 1: $\mathsf{h}(\mathsf{f}(\mathsf{b}), \mathsf{a}) = \mathsf{h}(\mathsf{a}, \mathsf{f}(\mathsf{b}))$
Proof:
  $\mathsf{h}(\mathsf{f}(\mathsf{b}), \mathsf{a})$
$=$ { by lemma 3 }
  $\mathsf{h}(\mathsf{a}, \mathsf{a})$
$=$ { by lemma 3 right-to-left }
  $\mathsf{h}(\mathsf{a}, \mathsf{f}(\mathsf{b}))$

■

3 Conversion to Direct Proofs

Vampire generates proofs by refutation, whereas our mix-and-match approach requires direct proofs. To bridge this gap, we transform Vampire proofs into direct proofs. In the following sections, we will always use direct proofs.

In equational logic, to produce a direct proof, we first introduce existential quantifiers for Skolem constants and universal quantifiers for variables. For example, $\mathsf{h}(x, \mathsf{sk}) \neq x$ is transformed into $\exists z.\ \forall x.\ \mathsf{h}(x, z) \neq x$. Then we apply the contrapositive to all inferences in which a premise and the conclusion are disequations to obtain positive equations. Thus, the inference

$$\frac{\mathsf{h}(\mathsf{a}, y) = \mathsf{b} \quad \mathsf{h}(x, \mathsf{sk}) \neq x}{\mathsf{b} \neq \mathsf{a}}\text{superposition}$$

becomes

$$\frac{\forall y.\ \mathsf{h}(\mathsf{a}, y) = \mathsf{b} \quad \mathsf{b} = \mathsf{a}}{\forall z.\ \exists x.\ \mathsf{h}(x, z) = x}$$

Notice that negating $\exists z.\ \forall x.\ \mathsf{h}(x, z) \neq x$ flips the quantifiers.

Equality resolution inferences from a premise $t \neq t$ are omitted since their contrapositives derive tautologies $t = t$. This reduces proof length by one.

Example 5. From Example 3's proof by refutation, we obtain this direct proof:

1. $\mathsf{a} = \mathsf{b}$	axiom
2. $\forall x.\ \mathsf{f}(x) = x$	axiom
3. $\mathsf{h}(\mathsf{b}, \mathsf{a}) = \mathsf{h}(\mathsf{a}, \mathsf{b})$	from 1 and the tautology $\mathsf{h}(\mathsf{a}, \mathsf{a}) = \mathsf{h}(\mathsf{a}, \mathsf{a})$
4. $\mathsf{h}(\mathsf{f}(\mathsf{b}), \mathsf{a}) = \mathsf{h}(\mathsf{a}, \mathsf{f}(\mathsf{b}))$	from 2 and 3 ■

We will refer to the statements of proof steps such as 3 and 4 above as *lemmas*. We will say that a lemma ℓ is a *direct dependency* of a lemma ℓ' if ℓ is used in the proof of ℓ', and that ℓ is an *indirect dependency*, or simply *dependency*, of ℓ' if it is transitively a dependency of ℓ'.

4 Proof Generation for Lemmas

Our approach starts by translating the main theorem into a TPTP [13] input problem and running Vampire to produce a baseline proof. This proof is turned into a direct proof. For each lemma in the direct proof, we generate corresponding problems, with the objective of proving them using Vampire and Twee. Three problem variants are generated:

1. *Big-step problems* contain the axioms together with the lemma as the conjecture, and nothing else. This allows us to investigate whether a radically new proof, with different intermediate steps, can be found.
2. *Small-step problems* contain the axioms together with the lemma as the conjecture, and all lemmas derived prior to this lemma in the baseline proof as additional axioms. This allows us to investigate whether a somewhat similar variant of the original derivation can be found.
3. *Abstracted problems* are variants of big-step problems that contain the axioms together with an abstracted, possibly unprovable version of the lemma as the conjecture. Specifically, selected subterms of the lemma—for example, terms such as $x \diamond y$ that do not contain nested applications—are replaced by fresh variables. This allows us to investigate whether a more general version of the lemma is provable, ideally with a shorter, more abstract proof.

Each problem is submitted to the two provers. If a proof is found for a small-step problem, we expand it to recursively include the shortest proofs of the lemmas used as axioms for the axioms referenced in the proof. Ties are broken arbitrarily.

Next, we compare the proofs of the three problem variants corresponding to the same lemma. If the abstracted problem has the shortest proof, the lemma it proves is replaced in all small-step problems where it appears as an axiom with the generalized lemma from the abstracted problem. Each updated small-step problem is then re-proved, and if the result has fewer steps, we replace the small-step problem's proof with it.

The length of a Vampire-generated proof is the number of steps of its direct proof, excluding preprocessing. For Twee, the length of a proof is the cumulative number of equalities in the equality chains. Thus, the Vampire proof in Example 5 has two steps, and the Twee proof in Example 4 has four steps.

5 Proof Construction for the Main Theorem

Based on the lemmas' proofs generated in the previous phase, our approach constructs a proof of the main theorem. The proof generally consists of three segments. The first segment starts with the axioms and ends with the derivation of a so-called *departure lemma*. The second segment derives a so-called *arrival lemma*. The third segment derives the conjecture. Different candidates are considered as the departure and arrival lemmas, yielding different proofs. The proof with the fewest steps is chosen.

Specifically, we first identify up to six lemmas that arise close to the end of the baseline proof, including the conjecture, and consider them as candidate arrival lemmas. For each candidate arrival lemma, we consider its dependencies as candidate departure lemmas. Then, for each candidate departure lemma, we construct a problem with the axioms and the departure lemma's dependencies as the axioms and the departure lemma itself as the conjecture. We run both provers and, if at least one succeeds, we use the shorter result as the proof of the first segment, unless an even shorter proof was generated in the previous phase.

Next, for each pair of candidate departure and arrival lemmas, we generate a new problem with the original axioms, the departure lemma, and its dependencies as axioms and the arrival lemma as the conjecture. We run both provers and, if at least one succeeds, we use the shorter result as the proof of the second segment, unless an even shorter proof was generated earlier. Finally, we generate a new problem with the original axioms, the departure lemma, its dependencies, and the arrival lemma as axioms and the original conjecture as the conjecture. We run both provers and, if at least one succeeds, we use the shorter result as the proof of the third segment, unless an even shorter proof was generated earlier.

Without the segmentation, proof minimization could be intractable due to combinatorial explosion. We chose to work with three segments, and six candidate arrival lemmas, as a trade-off between performance and flexibility. The number of candidate arrival lemmas is a parameter that can easily be adjusted.

Example 6. Before we review the three-segment proof construction approach in detail, let us look at an example. The following sketch represents a baseline seven-step Vampire direct proof of a theorem $A \implies C$, where A denotes the axiom and $L_1, \ldots, L_6$ are the lemmas used to derive the conjecture C:

A	axiom
L_1	from A
L_2	from A and L_1
L_3	from L_1 and L_2
L_4	from L_2 and L_3
L_5	from L_3 and L_4
L_6	from A and L_5
C	from L_5 and L_6

In the first phase, for each lemma $L_1, \ldots, L_6$ and the conjecture C, we construct big-step, small-step, and abstracted problems and try to prove them using Vampire and Twee, retaining the shortest proof for each lemma. Suppose the following: The shortest proof of L_1 has one step and is obtained from its big-step problem using Vampire; for L_2 and L_3, the shortest proofs are obtained from their small-step problems using Twee; for L_4, the shortest proof is obtained from its abstracted problem using Twee; and for L_5, L_6, and C, the shortest proofs are obtained from their small-step problems using Vampire.

In the next phase, the last five lemmas, $L_2, \ldots, L_6$, and the conjecture C are considered as candidate arrival lemmas. We focus on L_6. The proof below, found by Vampire for L_6's small-step problem, is the shortest proof for L_6:

A	axiom
L_1	from A
L_2	from A and L_1
L_3	from L_1 and L_2
L_4	from L_2 and L_3
L_5	from L_3 and L_4
L_6	from A and L_5

This proof happens to be identical to the first six steps of the baseline proof, but in general it could be different.

Next, lemmas L_1 to L_5 are considered as candidate departure lemmas. We focus on L_3. The proof of conjecture C is constructed by concatenating three segments. For the first segment, we create a new problem with A, L_1, and L_2 as axioms, since they are dependencies of the departure lemma L_3 in the above proof of L_6, and L_3 as the conjecture. We run both provers on this problem and obtain a two-step Vampire proof of L_3 from A, L_1, and a new lemma L'_2. Since L_1 is treated as an axiom, we must include its proof to obtain a complete proof of L_3. In the first phase, we found a one-step Vampire proof of L_1 from the axiom A, so we use it. In summary, the proofs of L_1 and L_3 form the first segment, which consists of one step for L_1 and two steps for L_3.

For the second segment, we create a new problem with A, L_1, L'_2, and L_3 as axioms and the arrival lemma L_6 as the conjecture. We run both provers on this problem and obtain a two-step Twee proof of L_6 from L_1 and L_3. Together with the first segment, this yields a five-step proof of L_6. Since this proof is shorter than the six-step proof of L_6 presented above, it is used as the second segment.

For the third segment, we create a new problem with A, L_1, L_2', the departure lemma L_3, and the arrival lemma L_6 as axioms and C as the conjecture. We run both provers on this problem and obtain a two-step Twee proof of C from L_2' and L_3. Since this proof does not use the arrival lemma L_6, the second segment is excluded from the result. Concatenating the first and third segments yields a new five-step proof of C, which is two steps shorter than the baseline proof:

A	axiom
L_1	from A
L_2'	from A and L_1
L_3	from L_1 and L_2'
C	by a two-step equality chain using L_2' and L_3

Finally, other combinations of candidate departure and arrival lemmas are considered, and the shortest proof is retained. ■

5.1 Construction of the Dependency Graph

We identify lemmas occurring close to the end of the derivation as candidate arrival lemmas. Different candidates typically depend on substantially different subsets of earlier lemmas. Each candidate therefore induces its own dependency chain, and different choices can lead to substantially different proof lengths. We consider six candidate arrival lemmas extracted from the baseline proof, including the conjecture itself, since our approach may produce a shorter proof of the conjecture by reproving it directly from a minimized dependency set. All six candidates can be processed in parallel.

For every candidate, we build a dependency graph that captures the lemmas required to derive it. Direct dependencies are determined from the shortest Vampire or Twee proof obtained for each lemma. Here, shortest means fewest inference steps, not fewest axioms. Given that we generate three problem variants and run two provers, up to six proofs per lemma are considered. A lemma ℓ is considered to directly depend on a lemma ℓ' if the shortest proof of ℓ uses ℓ' as an axiom. Thus, for big-step and abstracted problems, only the original axioms can be dependencies. For small-step problems, each step in a Vampire proof and each lemma in a Twee proof is considered a lemma.

The dependency graph associated with a candidate arrival lemma is a directed acyclic graph (DAG) whose nodes correspond to lemmas and whose edges express derivability between them. Formally, let V be a finite set of lemmas, each represented by an equation and a set of direct dependencies on other lemmas. We construct a DAG (V, E), where each vertex $\ell \in V$ corresponds to a lemma and each edge $(\ell, \ell') \in E$ indicates a direct dependency of ℓ on ℓ'. As an optimization, we merge lemmas that are identical up to the naming of variables, keeping the shortest proof.

5.2 Construction of the First Proof Segment

For each candidate arrival lemma, we investigate whether all lemmas included in its dependency graph are needed to derive it or whether a shorter proof can be obtained by choosing a departure lemma and recomputing parts of the derivation by combining proofs generated by the provers.

As candidate departure lemmas, we consider all lemmas in the DAG. Let ℓ be a candidate departure lemma. If ℓ depends only on the axioms, we take the shortest big-step, small-step, or abstracted proof previously found by Vampire or Twee. Otherwise, we build a problem that includes ℓ's dependencies in the DAG as axioms and the departure lemma as the conjecture, and we run Vampire and Twee. If at least one of them succeeds, we choose the shorter proof as ℓ's proof. This derivation, together with the shortest proofs of ℓ's dependencies generated for the big-step, small-step, or abstracted problems, forms the first segment of the final proof. However, if we found an even shorter proof for the big-step, small-step, or abstracted problem, we use that proof instead. For small-step proofs, we must also include the proofs of the lemmas encoded as axioms.

5.3 Construction of the Remaining Proof Segments

To construct the second segment, we generate a problem with the departure lemma and its dependencies as axioms and the arrival lemma as the conjecture, and run both provers. If at least one of them succeeds, we choose the shorter proof as the proof of the arrival lemma. As above, we fall back on the proof of a big-step, small-step, or abstracted problem if it is even shorter.

Finally, to construct the third segment, we generate a problem with the departure lemma, the arrival lemma, and their dependencies as axioms and the original conjecture as the conjecture, and invoke both provers. If at least one of them succeeds, we choose the shorter proof as the proof of the original conjecture. As above, we fall back on a previously derived proof if it is even shorter.

The final proof is obtained by concatenating the three segments. When we concatenate, lemmas from one segment are passed as axioms to subsequent segments. Twee equality chains used to prove lemmas are not visible in subsequent segments. The final proof might contain unreferenced lemmas; these are pruned.

5.4 Proof Output

Our tool generates the minimized proof in a native format, from which two Lean outputs are produced.

The first Lean output is a step-by-step formalization using the `calc` tactic to reconstruct equality chains. It applies the `duper` tactic to fill in the subproofs. For example, a proof of $t_1 = t_2 = t_3 = t_4$ becomes

```
calc
  t₁ = t₂ := by duper ...
  _ = t₃ := by duper ...
  _ = t₄ := by duper ...
```

where the ellipses stand for duper's arguments. The second Lean output is a more compact formalization in which each lemma is proved directly using Lean's automation without including the intermediate steps in equality chains.

6 Application to Tao's Challenge

We implemented our approach and tried the resulting tool, Krympa, on Tao's challenge theorem 650 $\Longrightarrow$ 448:

$$(\forall x, y, z.\ x = x \diamond (y \diamond ((z \diamond x) \diamond y))) \Longrightarrow \forall x, y, z.\ x = x \diamond (y \diamond (z \diamond (x \diamond z))).$$

Our tool first ran Vampire to obtain a baseline 62-step superposition proof. Then it constructed 62 problems of each variant (big-step, small-step, and abstracted) and tried to prove them using Vampire and Twee. Among the six candidate arrival lemmas, the shortest proof was found by selecting

$$\forall x, y, z.\ x = x \diamond ((y \diamond ((z \diamond y) \diamond y)) \diamond x). \qquad \text{(lemma 9)}$$

The coloring highlights repeating patterns. Next, our tool constructed the dependency graph for this lemma. The DAG contained 37 lemmas. It was based on big- and small-step proofs.

Among the 10 candidate departure lemmas, our tool found the shortest proof by selecting

$$\begin{aligned}&\forall x, y, z, w.\ (x \diamond ((y \diamond x) \diamond x)) \diamond z = \\ &\quad ((x \diamond ((y \diamond x) \diamond x)) \diamond z) \diamond (w \diamond ((x \diamond ((y \diamond x) \diamond x)) \diamond w)). \qquad \text{(lemma 7)}\end{aligned}$$

According to the DAG, the shortest proof of this lemma was found by running Vampire on the small-step problem consisting of the axiom and

$$\begin{aligned}&\forall x, y, z, w.\ x \diamond ((y \diamond ((z \diamond y) \diamond y)) \diamond x) = \\ &\quad (x \diamond ((y \diamond ((z \diamond y) \diamond y)) \diamond x)) \diamond \\ &\qquad (w \diamond ((y \diamond ((z \diamond y) \diamond y)) \diamond w)). \qquad \text{(lemma 5)}\end{aligned}$$

The shortest proof of lemma 5 was found by running Vampire on the corresponding big-step problem. The following lemmas were derived:

$$\begin{aligned}&\forall x, y, z, w.\ x \diamond ((y \diamond z) \diamond x) = \\ &\quad (x \diamond ((y \diamond z) \diamond x)) \diamond (w \diamond (z \diamond w)) \qquad \text{(lemma 1)}\\ &\forall x, y, z, w, v, u.\ x \diamond ((y \diamond ((z \diamond w) \diamond y)) \diamond x) = \\ &\quad (x \diamond ((y \diamond ((z \diamond w) \diamond y)) \diamond x)) \diamond (v \diamond ((u \diamond (w \diamond u)) \diamond v)) \qquad \text{(lemma 2)}\\ &\forall x, y, z, w, v.\ x \diamond (y \diamond x) = \\ &\quad (x \diamond (y \diamond x)) \diamond (z \diamond ((w \diamond ((v \diamond y) \diamond w)) \diamond z)) \qquad \text{(lemma 3)}\\ &\forall x, y, z, w, v.\ x \diamond (y \diamond x) = \\ &\quad (x \diamond (y \diamond x)) \diamond ((z \diamond (y \diamond z)) \diamond (w \diamond ((v \diamond y) \diamond w))) \qquad \text{(lemma 4)}\end{aligned}$$

Specifically, following the inference steps of the baseline Vampire proof, our tool derived lemma 1 by applying a superposition inference with the axiom $x = x \diamond (y \diamond ((z \diamond x) \diamond y))$ as the first premise and a renamed copy $x' = x' \diamond (y' \diamond ((z' \diamond x') \diamond y'))$ as the second premise. The most general unifier of the first premise's right-hand side and the subterm $z' \diamond x'$ of the second premise is $\{x' \mapsto y \diamond ((z \diamond x) \diamond y),\ z' \mapsto x\}$. Applying the unifier to both premises yields the equations $x = x \diamond (y \diamond ((z \diamond x) \diamond y))$ and $y \diamond ((z \diamond x) \diamond y) = (y \diamond ((z \diamond x) \diamond y)) \diamond (y' \diamond ((x \diamond (y \diamond ((z \diamond x) \diamond y))) \diamond y'))$. The superposition inference replaced the subterm $x \diamond (y \diamond ((z \diamond x) \diamond y))$ in the second equation with x using the first equation as a right-to-left rewrite rule, and thus derived lemma 1, up to the naming of variables. Lemmas 2 to 4 were derived similarly following the steps of the baseline Vampire proof.

Next, from the axiom and lemma 5 our tool proved the departure lemma (lemma 7) using Vampire. In the proof,

$$\begin{aligned}&\forall x, y, z, w.\ (x \diamond ((y \diamond x) \diamond x)) \diamond z = \\ &\quad ((x \diamond ((y \diamond x) \diamond x)) \diamond z) \diamond ((w \diamond ((x \diamond ((y \diamond x) \diamond x)) \diamond w)) \diamond \\ &\qquad (z \diamond ((x \diamond ((y \diamond x) \diamond x)) \diamond z)))\end{aligned} \qquad \text{(lemma 6)}$$

was derived by applying a superposition inference with the axiom as the first premise and lemma 5 as the second premise. Then, lemma 7 was derived by applying a superposition inference with lemma 6 as the first premise and lemma 5 as the second premise.

After, from the axiom and lemma 7, our tool proved the arrival lemma (lemma 9) using Twee. For this proof, Twee introduced the intermediate step

$$\begin{aligned}&\forall x, y, z, w.\ (y \diamond ((z \diamond y) \diamond y)) \diamond w = \\ &\quad ((y \diamond ((z \diamond y) \diamond y)) \diamond w) \diamond ((y \diamond ((z \diamond y) \diamond y)) \diamond x).\end{aligned} \qquad \text{(lemma 8)}$$

Finally, assuming all the lemmas derived so far, our tool proved the conjecture from lemmas 5 and 9 using Twee. The resulting proof has 20 steps, including three Twee-generated chains of equalities.

Below we present the final proof adapted from our tool's detailed Lean output. Instead of relying on proof automation, we use the `nth_rw` tactic, which performs a single rewrite step, where the numeric argument indicates which matching occurrence should be rewritten. In one case, two numbers are supplied, corresponding to a parallel rewrite.

```
theorem Equation650_implies_Equation448 (G : Type _) [Magma G]
      (op_law : ∀ x y z : G, x = x ◇ (y ◇ ((z ◇ x) ◇ y))) :
    ∀ x y z : G, x = x ◇ (y ◇ (z ◇ (x ◇ z))) :=
  have lemma1 (x y z w : G) :
      x ◇ ((y ◇ z) ◇ x) = (x ◇ ((y ◇ z) ◇ x)) ◇ (w ◇ (z ◇ w)) := by
    nth_rw 3 [op_law z x y]
```

```
  exact op_law (x ◇ ((y ◇ z) ◇ x)) w z

have lemma2 (x y z w v u : G) :
    x ◇ ((y ◇ ((z ◇ w) ◇ y)) ◇ x) =
    (x ◇ ((y ◇ ((z ◇ w) ◇ y)) ◇ x)) ◇ (v ◇ ((u ◇ (w ◇ u)) ◇ v)) := by
  nth_rw 1 2 [lemma1 y z w u]
  exact lemma1 x (y ◇ ((z ◇ w) ◇ y)) (u ◇ (w ◇ u)) v

have lemma3 (x y z w v : G) :
    x ◇ (y ◇ x) = (x ◇ (y ◇ x)) ◇ (z ◇ ((w ◇ ((v ◇ y) ◇ w)) ◇ z)) := by
  nth_rw 1 [lemma1 w v y x]
  exact op_law (x ◇ (y ◇ x)) z (w ◇ ((v ◇ y) ◇ w))

have lemma4 (x y z w v : G) :
    x ◇ (y ◇ x) = (x ◇ (y ◇ x)) ◇ ((z ◇ (y ◇ z)) ◇ (w ◇ ((v ◇ y) ◇ w))) := by
  nth_rw 1 [lemma1 w v y z]
  exact lemma3 x y (z ◇ (y ◇ z)) w v

have lemma5 (x y z w : G) :
    x ◇ ((y ◇ ((z ◇ y) ◇ y)) ◇ x) =
    (x ◇ ((y ◇ ((z ◇ y) ◇ y)) ◇ x)) ◇ (w ◇ ((y ◇ ((z ◇ y) ◇ y)) ◇ w)) := by
  nth_rw 1 [lemma2 w y z y x ((z ◇ y) ◇ y)]
  exact lemma4 x (y ◇ ((z ◇ y) ◇ y)) w x ((z ◇ y) ◇ y)

have lemma6 (x y z w : G) :
    (x ◇ ((y ◇ x) ◇ x)) ◇ z =
    ((x ◇ ((y ◇ x) ◇ x)) ◇ z) ◇ ((w ◇ ((x ◇ ((y ◇ x) ◇ x)) ◇ w)) ◇
      (z ◇ ((x ◇ ((y ◇ x) ◇ x)) ◇ z))) := by
  nth_rw 1 [lemma5 z x y w]
  exact op_law ((x ◇ ((y ◇ x) ◇ x)) ◇ z) (w ◇ ((x ◇ ((y ◇ x) ◇ x)) ◇ w)) z

have lemma7 (x y z w : G) :
    (x ◇ ((y ◇ x) ◇ x)) ◇ z =
    ((x ◇ ((y ◇ x) ◇ x)) ◇ z) ◇ (w ◇ ((x ◇ ((y ◇ x) ◇ x)) ◇ w)) := by
  nth_rw 1 [lemma5 w x y z]
  exact lemma6 x y z w

have lemma8 (x y z w : G) :
  ((x ◇ ((y ◇ x) ◇ x)) ◇ z) ◇ ((x ◇ ((y ◇ x) ◇ x)) ◇ w) =
  (x ◇ ((y ◇ x) ◇ x)) ◇ z := by
  let T := x ◇ ((y ◇ x) ◇ x)
  calc
    (T ◇ z) ◇ (T ◇ w) =
    ((T ◇ z) ◇ ((T ◇ w) ◇ ((T ◇ (T ◇ w)) ◇ ((w ◇ (T ◇ w)) ◇ (T ◇ (T ◇ w)))))) := by
      nth_rw 1 [←op_law]
    _ = ((T ◇ z) ◇ ((T ◇ w) ◇ ((T ◇ (T ◇ w)) ◇ ((w ◇ (T ◇ w)) ◇
          (T ◇ ((T ◇ w) ◇ (w ◇ (T ◇ w)))))))) := by
      nth_rw 1 [←lemma7]
    _ = ((T ◇ z) ◇ ((T ◇ w) ◇ ((T ◇ (T ◇ w)) ◇ ((w ◇ (T ◇ w)) ◇
          ((T ◇ ((T ◇ w) ◇ (w ◇ (T ◇ w)))) ◇ (((T ◇ w) ◇ (w ◇ (T ◇ w))) ◇
```

```
          (T ◇ ((T ◇ w) ◇ (w ◇ (T ◇ w))))))))) := by
      nth_rw 2 [←lemma7]
    _ = ((T ◇ z) ◇ ((T ◇ w) ◇ ((T ◇ (T ◇ w)) ◇ (w ◇ (T ◇ w))))) := by
      nth_rw 1 [←op_law]
    _ = ((T ◇ z) ◇ ((T ◇ w) ◇ (T ◇ (T ◇ w)))) := by
      nth_rw 1 [←lemma7]
    _ = ((x ◇ ((y ◇ x) ◇ x)) ◇ z) := by
      nth_rw 1 [←lemma7]

have lemma9 (x y z : G) :
    (x ◇ ((y ◇ ((z ◇ y) ◇ y)) ◇ x)) = x := by
  calc
    (x ◇ ((y ◇ ((z ◇ y) ◇ y)) ◇ x)) =
    (x ◇ (((y ◇ ((z ◇ y) ◇ y)) ◇ x) ◇ ((y ◇ ((z ◇ y) ◇ y)) ◇ x))) := by
      nth_rw 1 [lemma8]
    _ = (x ◇ (((y ◇ ((z ◇ y) ◇ y)) ◇ x) ◇ (((y ◇ ((z ◇ y) ◇ y)) ◇ x) ◇
          ((y ◇ ((z ◇ y) ◇ y)) ◇ x)))) := by
      nth_rw 2 [lemma8]
    _ = x := by
      nth_rw 1 [←op_law]

show _ by
  intros x y z
  calc
    x = x ◇ ((x ◇ ((y ◇ x) ◇ x)) ◇ x) := by
      nth_rw 1 [lemma9]
    _ = (x ◇ ((x ◇ ((y ◇ x) ◇ x)) ◇ x)) ◇ ((y ◇ (z ◇ (x ◇ z))) ◇
          ((x ◇ ((y ◇ x) ◇ x)) ◇ (y ◇ (z ◇ (x ◇ z))))) := by
      nth_rw 1 [←lemma5]
    _ = x ◇ ((y ◇ (z ◇ (x ◇ z))) ◇ ((x ◇ ((y ◇ x) ◇ x)) ◇
          (y ◇ (z ◇ (x ◇ z))))) := by
      nth_rw 1 [lemma9]
    _ = x ◇ (y ◇ (z ◇ (x ◇ z))) := by
      nth_rw 1 [lemma9]
```

7 Experiments on Other Equational Proofs

To assess the general potential of our approach, we evaluated our tool on a set of equational theorems obtained from the Equational Theories Project repository [6]. We selected all problems in the 13 Lean files `Proofs1` to `Proofs13` that have a proof and translated them to TPTP problem files, yielding 1431 benchmarks.

For each file, we invoked our tool's TPTP problem generator, which parses the Lean theorems and produces corresponding TPTP problem files. For each problem, our tool was given 600 s to produce a minimized proof using Vampire and Twee; on failure, the baseline Vampire proof was output. A time limit of 10 s was used for each prover invocation. The 600-second overall limit is generous; most proofs are minimized in well under a minute. The experiments were conducted on a server equipped with a dual-socket AMD EPYC 9965 system (384 cores, 768 threads) running at 2.25–3.70 GHz with 3 TiB of DDR5 ECC RAM, and running Debian GNU/Linux 13 (kernel 6.17.13+deb13-amd64).

Overall, proofs for the 13 Lean files have an average length of 6.6 steps before minimization and 4.5 steps after minimization using the combination of small-step and abstracted problems and both provers. This corresponds to a 31.5% decrease, showing that even short proofs can often be made shorter.

Table 1. Comparison of proof lengths before and after minimization for problems with baseline proofs of at least 15 steps

File	Num. problems	Avg. before	Avg. after			
			BA	SA	BS	BSA
`Proofs1`	9	17.3	16.0	**13.1**	13.3	13.3
`Proofs2`	8	16.9	14.4	**11.5**	**11.5**	**11.5**
`Proofs3`	7	19.3	15.6	10.9	**10.7**	10.9
`Proofs4`	11	19.1	14.3	**10.9**	11.4	11.4
`Proofs5`	9	20.1	17.6	12.8	**11.9**	**11.9**
`Proofs6`	11	25.6	18.9	**12.5**	12.6	12.6
`Proofs7`	11	37.2	19.7	**11.8**	11.9	11.9
`Proofs8`	7	24.4	15.6	**12.3**	13.1	13.1
`Proofs9`	14	39.8	29.0	**13.1**	14.1	14.1
`Proofs10`	2	21.5	16.0	**8.0**	11.0	11.0
`Proofs11`	5	25.4	22.4	**13.0**	14.0	14.0
`Proofs12`	13	24.6	16.5	**8.0**	8.5	8.5
`Proofs13`	10	35.3	27.7	**9.1**	10.1	10.1
Total	117	26.3	19.2	**11.4**	11.8	11.8

Since longer proofs present more opportunities for minimization, we now focus on the 117 benchmarks whose baseline proofs have at least 15 steps. Table 1 compares proof lengths before and after minimization. The "Avg. before" column shows the average number of steps in the baseline proofs. The "Avg. after" columns report the average proof length after minimization under four configurations, which differ in which problem variants are used: "BA" denotes the combination of the big-step and abstracted variants; "SA" denotes the combination of the small-step and abstracted variants; "BS" denotes the combination of the big- and small-step variants; and "BSA" denotes the combination of all three variants.

The results show an often substantial reduction in proof length. SA generally yielded the shortest proofs. Across all problems for the 13 Lean files, the average reduction with SA is 56.7%. BS and BSA also produced substantial reductions, whereas BA generally yielded the least improvements.

It might seem counterintuitive that SA, which does not consider big-step problems, outperforms BSA. However, the nonmonotonicity is to be expected.

Provers are nondeterministic, especially when invoked with a time limit; for example, a prover might sometimes find a proof after 9.98 s and sometimes time out after 10 s. Moreover, our approach makes different heuristic choices when constructing the three proof segments depending on which problem variants are used. As a result, SA might find a short proof that escapes BSA.

The reduction in proof length is especially noticeable in individual cases. The problem 2666 $\Longrightarrow$ 3460 has a Vampire proof with 51 inference steps, which our tool reduces to only 12 single rewrite steps, and 2923 $\Longrightarrow$ 2628 is reduced from 180 steps to only 34. The problem 3569 $\Longrightarrow$ 3957 is reduced from 92 to 23 steps and, even more dramatically, 3957 $\Longrightarrow$ 3971 is reduced from 141 steps to only 23. Furthermore, 2860 $\Longrightarrow$ 2660 is reduced from 44 to 14 steps, and 723 $\Longrightarrow$ 872 goes from 57 to 13 steps. Finally, 947 $\Longrightarrow$ 3897 underwent the largest reduction, from 151 to 10 steps. Overall, these results demonstrate that our approach produces shorter proofs across a diverse set of equational theorems.

8 Related Work

At least two other researchers took on Tao's challenge. Kinyon [18] found a 24-step proof (excluding preprocessing) of 650 $\Longrightarrow \forall x, y.\ x = x \diamond y$ using Prover9 [22], from which 650 $\Longrightarrow$ 448 follows by instantiation. Later, Le Floch [11] developed a pen-and-paper proof and translated it to Lean. The Lean proof relies on only 14 rewrite steps but includes additional reasoning as proof terms, and two of the rewrite steps are parallel, so the overall length is similar to ours. The proof is "loosely based" on the output of multiple Prover9 runs "with intermediate results thrown in as assumptions or as goals"—in essence, a manual approximation of our approach. Also in the context of the Equational Theories Project, Janota [16] evaluated Vampire on the project's problems and showed that combining superposition with finite model finding can solve almost all problems. One reason for this success might be the work on term ordering diagrams by Hajdu et al. [15].

We are aware of little work on automated proof minimization. Stachniak [27] designed an algorithm for constructing resolution proofs in propositional logics known as strongly finite logics. Amjad [1] and Cotton [9] introduced techniques for minimizing propositional resolution proofs. Vyskočil et al. [31] proposed to compress proofs by inventing new definitions using a heuristic based on substitution trees. Gu et al. [14] developed ProofOptimizer, which uses large language models to simplify Lean proofs.

Some SAT (satisfiability) and SMT (satisfiability modulo theories) solvers can minimize the number of axioms needed for a proof, but the result can be a longer proof. SAT solvers commonly interleave search, which can be expressed as resolution steps, with formula-rewriting techniques that go beyond resolution. This interleaving, known as inprocessing [17], is highly effective and often yields both faster solving times and shorter proofs than either approach in isolation.

The idea of automatically mixing and matching proofs is not new. Sutcliffe et al. [29] introduced a method for combining automatically generated proofs to generate new ones. Their proofs are represented as DAGs, enabling the identification and replacement of subproofs across different proofs. Proof combination is guided by heuristics that measure structural similarity, and a greedy search strategy is used to explore alternative combinations that yield proofs differing from the originals. In contrast to our approach, the main objective is to increase proof diversity rather than minimize proof length.

9 Conclusion

Historically, more research has gone into finding proofs automatically than into improving and presenting them. We introduced an approach for minimizing equational proofs by mixing and matching the output of separate runs of Vampire and Twee, and implemented it in a new tool, Krympa. We used the tool to minimize the proof of problem $650 \implies 448$ from the Equational Theories Project from 62 to 20 steps, thereby providing a fully automatic solution to a challenge posed by Tao. We also obtained remarkable reductions on other problems originating from the project. The shorter proofs are arguably easier to understand by humans and sometimes more general. Our work shows that proof automation and readability can go hand in hand.

Our approach could be extended in several ways. First, it could be generalized to support full first- or higher-order logic. Second, alternative lemma abstraction strategies could be explored. Third, proofs with four or more segments could be synthesized. Fourth, we might want to consider not only the number of steps but also term size when measuring proofs, as suggested by Le Floch [12]. Fifth, we could try to translate Vampire proofs to Twee's structured equality chain format.

Some possible extensions specifically concern the implementation. First, we could explore whether nondefault Vampire and Twee strategies can produce shorter proofs, following private suggestions by Martin Suda and Nicholas Smallbone. Second, since proof generation relies heavily on external provers, performance could benefit from better scheduling of prover invocations, using adaptive time limits. Finally, our approach is not tied to Vampire and Twee specifically. Vampire is representative of ATP systems that produce TSTP output, such as E and iProver, whereas Twee is representative of completion-based provers such as Waldmeister. Together, they cover most equational provers. Integrating further provers should be straightforward.

Acknowledgments. We thank Bruno Le Floch, Andrew Reynolds, Stephan Schulz, and Uwe Waldmann for fruitful discussions. We thank Laura Kovács, Luca Maio, Martin Suda, Mark Summerfield, and the anonymous reviewers for helpful textual suggestions.

Blanchette's research was cofunded by the European Union (ERC, Nekoka, 101083038). Views and opinions expressed are however those of the authors only and do not necessarily reflect those of the European Union or the European Research Council. Neither the European Union nor the granting authority can be held responsible for them.

Heule's research is supported by the NSF under grant DMS-2434625 and funding from AFRL and DARPA under Agreement FA8750-24-9-1000.

Disclosure of Interests. The authors have no competing interests to declare that are relevant to the content of this paper.

References

1. Amjad, H.: Compressing propositional refutations. In: Merz, S., Nipkow, T. (eds.) AVoCS 2006. Electronic Notes in Theoretical Computer Science, vol. 185, pp. 3–15. Elsevier (2006)
2. Bachmair, L., Dershowitz, N., Plaisted, D.A.: Completion without failure. In: Aït-Kaci, H., Nivat, M. (eds.) Rewriting Techniques, pp. 1–30. Academic Press (1989)
3. Bachmair, L., Ganzinger, H.: Strict basic superposition. In: Kirchner, C., Kirchner, H. (eds.) CADE 1998. LNCS, vol. 1421, pp. 160–174. Springer, Heidelberg (1998). https://doi.org/10.1007/BFb0054258
4. Bártek, F., et al.: The Vampire diary. In: Piskac, R., Rakamaric, Z. (eds.) CAV 2025. LNCS, vol. 15933, pp. 57–71. Springer (2025)
5. Blanchette, J.C., Böhme, S., Fleury, M., Smolka, S.J., Steckermeier, A.: Semi-intelligible Isar proofs from machine-generated proofs. J. Automated Reas. **56**, 155–200 (2016)
6. Bolan, M.: The Equational Theories Project (2025)
7. Buch, A., Hillenbrand, T.: WALDMEISTER: development of a high performance completion-based theorem prover. Tech. rep. (1996)
8. Clune, J., Qian, Y., Bentkamp, A., Avigad, J.: Duper: a proof-producing superposition theorem prover for dependent type theory. In: Bertot, Y., Kutsia, T., Norrish, M. (eds.) ITP 2024. LIPIcs, vol. 309, pp. 1–20. Leibniz-Zentrum für Informatik (2024)
9. Cotton, S.: Two techniques for minimizing resolution proofs. In: Strichman, O., Szeider, S. (eds.) SAT 2010. LNCS, vol. 6175, pp. 306–312. Springer, Heidelberg (2010). https://doi.org/10.1007/978-3-642-14186-7_26
10. Denzinger, J., Schulz, S.: Recording, analyzing and presenting distributed deduction processes. In: Hong, H. (ed.) PASCO 1994. Lecture Notes Series in Computing, vol. 5, pp. 114–123. World Scientific (1994)
11. Floch, B.L.: Zulip post in "Machine Learning for Theorem Proving: A (Semi)-Autoformalization Challenge (650 → 448)". Zulip (2025). https://leanprover.zulipchat.com/#narrow/channel/219941-Machine-Learning-for-Theorem-Proving/topic/A.20.28semi.29-autoformalization.20challenge.3A.20650.3D.3E448/near/518970125
12. Floch, B.L.: Zulip post in "Machine Learning for Theorem Proving: A (Semi)-Autoformalization Challenge (650 → 448)". Zulip (2025). https://leanprover.zulipchat.com/#narrow/channel/219941-Machine-Learning-for-Theorem-Proving/topic/A.20.28semi.29-autoformalization.20challenge.3A.20650.3D.3E448/near/568313777
13. Sutcliffe, G.: Stepping stones in the TPTP World. In: Benzmüller, C., Heule, M., Schmidt, R. (eds.) IJCAR 2024. LNCS, pp. 30–50 (2024)
14. Gu, A., Piotrowski, B., Gloeckle, F., Yang, K., Markosyan, A.H.: ProofOptimizer: training language models to simplify proofs without human demonstrations (2025). https://arxiv.org/abs/2510.15700

15. Hajdu, M., Coutelier, R., Kovács, L., Voronkov, A.: Term ordering diagrams. In: Barrett, C.W., Waldmann, U. (eds.) CADE-30. LNCS. Springer to appear
16. Janota, M.: Experimental results for vampire on the equational theories project (2025). https://arxiv.org/abs/2508.15856
17. Järvisalo, M., Heule, M.J.H., Biere, A.: Inprocessing Rules. In: Gramlich, B., Miller, D., Sattler, U. (eds.) IJCAR 2012. LNCS (LNAI), vol. 7364, pp. 355–370. Springer, Heidelberg (2012). https://doi.org/10.1007/978-3-642-31365-3_28
18. Kinyon, M.: Zulip post in "Machine Learning for Theorem Proving: A (Semi)-Autoformalization Challenge (650 → 448)". Zulip (2025). https://leanprover.zulipchat.com/#narrow/channel/219941-Machine-Learning-for-Theorem-Proving/topic/A.20.28semi.29-autoformalization.20challenge.3A.20650.3D.3E448/near/518961204
19. Knuth, D.E., Bendix, P.B.: Simple word problems in universal algebras. In: Leech, J. (ed.) Computational Problems in Abstract Algebra, pp. 263–297. Pergamon Press (1970)
20. Kondylidou, L., Blanchette, J., Heule, M.: Tao's equational proof challenge accepted. Zenodo (2026). https://doi.org/10.5281/zenodo.18624123
21. Limperg, J., From, A.H.: Aesop: white-box best-first proof search for Lean. In: CPP 2023, pp. 253–266. ACM (2023)
22. McCune, W.: Prover9 and Mace4 (2005–2010)
23. Morrison, K., de Moura, L.: `grind`: an SMT-inspired tactic for Lean 4 (short paper—system description). In: Biere, A., Lutz, C., Negri, S. (eds.) IJCAR 2026. LNCS, Springer
24. Moura, L., Ullrich, S.: The lean 4 theorem prover and programming language. In: Platzer, A., Sutcliffe, G. (eds.) CADE 2021. LNCS (LNAI), vol. 12699, pp. 625–635. Springer, Cham (2021). https://doi.org/10.1007/978-3-030-79876-5_37
25. Norman, C., Avigad, J.: Canonical for automated theorem proving in lean. In: ITP 2025. LIPIcs, vol. 352, pp. 1–20. Leibniz-Zentrum für Informatik (2025)
26. Smallbone, N.: Twee: an equational theorem prover. In: Platzer, A., Sutcliffe, G. (eds.) CADE 2021. LNCS (LNAI), vol. 12699, pp. 602–613. Springer, Cham (2021). https://doi.org/10.1007/978-3-030-79876-5_35
27. Stachniak, Z.: Minimization of resolution proof systems. Fundam. Inf. **14**(1), 129–146 (1991)
28. Sutcliffe, G.: The 12th IJCAR automated theorem proving system competition–CASC-J12. AI Commun. **38**, 3–20 (2025)
29. Sutcliffe, G., Chang, C., McGuinness, D., Lebo, T., Ding, L., da Silva, P.P.: Combining proofs to form different proofs. In: Fontaine, P., Stump, A. (eds.) PxTP 2011, pp. 60–73. LNCS (2011)
30. Tao, T.: Zulip thread "Machine Learning for Theorem Proving: A (Semi)-Autoformalization Challenge (650 → 448)". Zulip (2025). https://leanprover-community.github.io/archive/stream/219941-Machine-Learning-for-Theorem-Proving/
31. Vyskočil, J., Stanovský, D., Urban, J.: Automated proof compression by invention of new definitions. In: Clarke, E.M., Voronkov, A. (eds.) LPAR 2010. LNCS (LNAI), vol. 6355, pp. 447–462. Springer, Heidelberg (2010). https://doi.org/10.1007/978-3-642-17511-4_25
32. Zhu, T., Clune, J., Avigad, J., Jiang, A.Q., Welleck, S.: Premise selection for a Lean hammer (2026). https://arxiv.org/abs/2506.07477

Open Access This chapter is licensed under the terms of the Creative Commons Attribution 4.0 International License (http://creativecommons.org/licenses/by/4.0/), which permits use, sharing, adaptation, distribution and reproduction in any medium or format, as long as you give appropriate credit to the original author(s) and the source, provide a link to the Creative Commons license and indicate if changes were made.

The images or other third party material in this chapter are included in the chapter's Creative Commons license, unless indicated otherwise in a credit line to the material. If material is not included in the chapter's Creative Commons license and your intended use is not permitted by statutory regulation or exceeds the permitted use, you will need to obtain permission directly from the copyright holder.

Completeness of Synthesis Under Realizability Assumptions Using Superposition

Márton Hajdu, Petra Hozzová, Laura Kovács, and Eva Maria Wagner(✉)

TU Wien, Vienna, Austria
eva.maria.wagner@tuwien.ac.at

Abstract. Program synthesis is the task of automatically deriving a program that has been specified by a user in advance. Combining automated theorem proving with program synthesis enables the automated construction of proven-to-be-correct programs, thereby ensuring software reliability. In this paper, we consider the superposition-based calculus extended to support synthesis of recursion-free programs allowing reasoning with uncomputable symbols. We present cases where the calculus fails and refine it to solve them. We prove that the refined calculus is sound. Finally, we also prove completeness in the following sense: if at least one computable program satisfying the given specification exists, we show that the modified calculus finds one.

Keywords: Program Synthesis · Saturation · Superposition · Theorem Proving

1 Introduction

Program synthesis focuses on constructing programs from a given functional specification. There are many different approaches for solving different flavors of this problem, including ones that guarantee that the found program satisfies a logical specification [14,15,24]; techniques that synthesize a program based on a set of input-output examples [8,10,26]; and LLM-based methods which require external correctness checking [18]. In this paper, we focus on an automated deductive synthesis approach using a superposition-based theorem prover, in which a saturation-based framework proves a given specification while simultaneously generating code conforming to that specification.

Recent work in [15] extracts a recursion-free program from a superposition-based proof of a logical specification (requirement) on the program. Our approach explores and revises this framework and solves *program synthesis in the presence of uncomputable symbols* [14,15]. Doing so, we impose the following syntactic restrictions on the program to be synthesized: (i) the program should use only so-called *computable* symbols, while (ii) its functional specification may use

© The Author(s) 2026
A. Biere et al. (Eds.): IJCAR 2026, LNAI 16688, pp. 22–40, 2026.
https://doi.org/10.1007/978-3-032-32589-1_2

both computable and uncomputable symbols. Uncomputable symbols include, for example, symbols annotated as such by the user of the synthesis system, allowing for better control of what the output program should (not) use. Uncomputable symbols may, however, also include fresh symbols, such as Skolem functions, introduced during the proving process.

Motivating Example. We motivate our work using an example adapted from [12, 22]. Consider the following constraints from the FLoC 2026 workshop schedule:

1. On Friday (f), the Vampire (v) workshop is taking place. Using the unary predicate w for workshops, we assert $\mathsf{w(v)}$.
2. On Saturday (s), the PAAR (p) workshop is taking place (thus, $\mathsf{w(p)}$).
3. Today (x) is either Friday (f) or Saturday (s).

Our task for program synthesis is to infer what workshop y takes place depending on x, with the condition that w is uncomputable, i.e. the answer should not contain w.

We encode this instance of program synthesis as follows. For readability, we might omit parentheses in unary symbol applications throughout the paper, e.g. we might write wv instead of $\mathsf{w(v)}$. We are looking for a program that is a witness for y in the following formula:

$$\varphi: \quad \forall x \exists y.(((x \approx \mathsf{f} \vee x \approx \mathsf{s}) \wedge (x \approx \mathsf{f} \rightarrow \mathsf{wv}) \wedge (x \approx \mathsf{s} \rightarrow \mathsf{wp})) \rightarrow \mathsf{w}y). \qquad (1)$$

A program that is a witness for y in (1) is called a *solution of the synthesis problem* specified by (1); see Sect. 3 for precise formulation of program synthesis and its solution. In the case of (1), two possible programs found by our approach are **if** $x \approx \mathsf{f}$ **then** v **else** p and **if** $x \approx \mathsf{s}$ **then** p **else** v. ❑

Synthesis and Saturation. In our approach to program synthesis, we build on the saturation-based framework for program synthesis with uncomputable symbols using the superposition calculus, as introduced in [15]. While the approach was shown to be correct in [15], the question of completeness remained open until now. In this paper, we close this gap by investigating the *completeness of the calculus under the assumption of realizability*: if a computable program satisfying the specification exists, is the calculus guaranteed to derive it? We identify properties that make the calculus of [15] inherently incomplete. We adjust the calculus accordingly, resulting in our SUPRA framework (Sect. 5). We further prove completeness of SUPRA under the assumption of realizability (Sect. 5).

This paper starts with preliminaries in Sect. 2, summarizing necessary notions of first-order logic and automated reasoning. Section 3 defines our synthesis problem and presents a framework for solving it, by revising the setting of [15]. Following are *our main contributions*:

- We introduce a new superposition-based calculus for synthesis (Sect. 4). Our calculus is coined as Superposition with Realizability Assumptions, in short SUPRA. Motivated by examples that cannot be solved by [15], SUPRA includes tailored conditions for term orderings and selection functions.

- We prove completeness of our SUPRA calculus (Sect. 5). By completeness we mean that, if at least one computable program satisfying a given specification exists, our SUPRA calculus finds one such program.

We then review related work in Sect. 6, and conclude our paper in Sect. 7. The (omitted) proofs of our results from Sects. 4 and 5 are given in the extended version [11] of this paper.

2 Preliminaries

First-order Logic. We assume familiarity with standard multi-sorted first-order logic (FOL) with equality, where equality is denoted by $\approx$. We consider a fixed signature Σ consisting of a finite set of *function symbols* with associated arities and a set of *variables* $\mathcal{V}$; variables are not part of the signature. We define the set of *terms* $\mathcal{T}(\Sigma \cup \mathcal{V})$, or simply $\mathcal{T}$ when it is clear from the context, in the standard way over $\Sigma \cup \mathcal{V}$. We denote variables by x, y, z; terms by s, t, l, r, k; literals by L, K; clauses by C, D; and formulas by F, G, all possibly with indices. Further, we write α for Skolem constants. We denote lists of literals by $\mathcal{L}$ and $\mathcal{K}$. We denote the empty list of literals by ϵ. Let L be a literal and $\mathcal{L}$ a list of literals, then $L\mathcal{L}$ denotes the list of literals having L as a head and $\mathcal{L}$ as a tail. We write $\bar{a}$ for the tuple of variables or terms $a_1, \dots, a_n$. When a term t is of the form $f(\bar{t})$, we say that f is the *top-level symbol* of t. By $\mathsf{cnf}(F)$ we denote the *clausal normal form* (CNF) of the formula F. We reserve the symbol $\square$ for the *empty clause* which is logically equivalent to $\bot$. We write $\hat{L}$ for the literal complementary to L. We write $t \not\approx s$ as a shorthand for $\neg(t \approx s)$. We use the symbol $\dot{\approx}$ to denote either $\approx$ or $\not\approx$. An *expression* is a term, literal, clause, or formula. We write $E_1 = E_2$ to denote syntactic equality of two expressions. If an expression does not contain variables, we call it *ground*. We write $E[t]$ to denote all (possibly zero) occurrences of the term t. Then, $E[s]$ denotes the expression $E[t]$ where all occurrences of t are replaced by the term s. Formulas with free variables are considered implicitly universally quantified; that is, we consider closed formulas. A *substitution* σ is a mapping from variables to terms such that the set $\{x \mid \sigma(x) \neq x\}$ of variables is finite. A substitution σ is a *unifier* of two expressions E and E' if $E\sigma = E'\sigma$, and is a *most general unifier* (*mgu*) if for every unifier θ of E and E', there exists substitution τ such that $\theta = \sigma\tau$. We denote the mgu of expressions E_1, E_2, E_1', E_2' with $\mathsf{mgu}(E_1, E_1')$ and $\mathsf{mgu}((E_1, E_2), (E_1', E_2'))$ for the mgu of tuples.

Saturation-Based Proving and Superposition. A saturation-based prover works with clauses. To prove a theorem G from axioms $A_1, \dots, A_n$ (assumed to be clauses), the prover: (1) negates and clausifies G, obtaining clauses $\mathsf{cnf}(\neg G) = \{C_1, \dots, C_m\}$; (2) forms the *saturation set* $S = \{C_1, \dots, C_m, A_1, \dots, A_n\}$; (3) repeats the following: chooses clauses $D_1, \dots, D_k \in S$, uses an *inference rule* to derive a new clause D from $D_1, \dots, D_k$, and adds D into S. Deriving the empty clause $\square$ at any point in step (3) concludes the proof, because it means that $\neg G$ is inconsistent with the axioms, which is equivalent to G following from the axioms. A common *calculus* (a set of inference rules) used in saturation-based provers is the *superposition calculus* [20]. The calculus is parametrized by a *simplification order* $\succ$ on terms (see next paragraph) and a *selection function*, which selects in each non-empty clause some non-empty subset of literals. We denote selected literals by underlining them. An inference rule can be applied to the given premise(s) if the literals selected in the rule are also selected in the premise(s). For a certain class of selection functions, the superposition calculus is *sound* (if $\square$ is derived from F, then F is unsatisfiable) and *refutationally complete* (if F is unsatisfiable, then $\square$ can be derived from it).

Rewriting and Simplification Orders. A binary relation $\rightarrow$ over the set of terms is a *rewrite relation* if (i) $l \rightarrow r \Rightarrow l\theta \rightarrow r\theta$ and (ii) $l \rightarrow r \Rightarrow s[l] \rightarrow s[r]$ for any terms l, r, s and substitution θ. We write $\leftarrow$ to denote the inverse of $\rightarrow$. We call an ordered pair $l \rightarrow r$ a *rewrite rule* if (i) l is not a variable and (ii) l contains all variables that occur in r. A *rewrite system* R is a set of rewrite rules. We denote by $\rightarrow_R$ the smallest rewrite relation that contains R. A term l is *irreducible* in R if there is no r s.t. $l \rightarrow_R r \in R$. We denote with $\rightarrow_R^*$ the reflexive-transitive closure of $\rightarrow_R$. A term r is a *normal form* of a term l w.r.t R if $l \rightarrow_R^* r$ and r is irreducible in R. A *rewrite order* is a strict (irreflexive) rewrite relation. A *reduction order* is a well-founded rewrite order. We consider reduction orders which are total on ground terms; such orders are also called *simplification orders.* A *precedence relation*, denoted by $\gg$, is a total order on the signature Σ.

The *lexicographic path order (LPO)*, denoted by $\succ_{\mathsf{lpo}}$, is parameterized by a precedence relation $\gg$. Let s, t be terms with $s = f(s_1, ..., s_n)$ and $\succ_{\mathsf{lpo}}^{\mathsf{lex}}$ the standard lexicographic ordering extension of $\succ_{\mathsf{lpo}}$. We write $s \succ_{\mathsf{lpo}} t$ if:

1. t is a variable and a proper subterm of s, or
2. there is $i \in \{1, \ldots, n\}$ such that $s_i \succeq_{\mathsf{lpo}} t$, or
3. $t = f(t_1, ..., t_n)$, $(s_1, \ldots, s_n) \succ_{\mathsf{lpo}}^{\mathsf{lex}} (t_1, \ldots, t_n)$ and $s \succ_{\mathsf{lpo}} t_j$, for all $j \in \{1, \ldots, n\}$,or
4. $t = g(t_1, ..., t_m)$, $f \gg g$ and $s \succ_{\mathsf{lpo}} t_j$, for all $j \in \{1, \ldots, m\}$.

It is known that LPOs are simplification orders [20].

We view equalities as *bags*, finite multisets, and define and extend the term orderings on bags. The *bag extension* for an ordering $\succ$ on a set X is a binary relation on bags over X, denoted by $\succ^{\mathsf{bag}}$, defined as the smallest transitive relation on bags such that $\{x, y_1, \ldots, y_n\} \succ^{\mathsf{bag}} \{x_1, \ldots, x_m, y_1, \ldots, y_n\}$ if $x \succ x_i$ for all $i \in \{1, \ldots, m\}$ and $m \geq 0$. If $\succ$ is well-founded, then $\succ^{\mathsf{bag}}$ is too. We order equality literals by mapping each equality $s \approx t$ to the bag $\{s, t\}$ and each disequality $s \not\approx t$ to the bag $\{s, s, t, t\}$, and then using $\succ^{\mathsf{bag}}$ over these bags. Finally, we order clauses by taking the bag extension of the bag extension for literals. We only write $E_1 \succ E_2$ for two expressions E_1 and E_2 when it is clear from the context which ordering is used. We also write $E_1 \succeq E_2$ instead of $E_1 \succ E_2 \vee E_1 = E_2$.

3 The Synthesis Problem and How to Solve It

In this section, we adjust notions [15] to the purposes of our work. We assume a fixed signature Σ.

Definition 1 (Synthesis Specification). *Let Σ_c be a subset of Σ and φ a closed formula in first-order logic over Σ of the form:*

$$\forall \bar{x} \exists y. F[\bar{x}, y]. \tag{2}$$

We define a synthesis specification, *or simply* specification, *Λ as the pair $\langle \Sigma_c, \varphi \rangle$. We call any symbol in Σ_c* computable w.r.t. Λ, *or just* computable *when Λ is clear from the context. Further, any symbol in $\Sigma \setminus \Sigma_c$ is* uncomputable w.r.t. Λ, *or just* uncomputable. *We denote the set of uncomputable symbols by Σ_u.*

An expression containing an uncomputable symbol is called uncomputable. *Expressions that are not uncomputable are called* computable. ❑

To synthesize programs for specifications, we use an if-then-else term constructor, denoted by ite.

Definition 2 (ite and Program Terms). *We define the* conditional term constructor ite *as follows. Let F be a formula over Σ and p, q be terms. When F is true, then $\mathsf{ite}(F, p, q)$ is interpreted as the interpretation of p; otherwise, $\mathsf{ite}(F, p, q)$ is interpreted as the interpretation of q. We call F the* ite-condition.

We define program terms *as the smallest set $\mathcal{P}$ such that (i) $\mathcal{T} \subseteq \mathcal{P}$, and (ii) $\mathsf{ite}(l \approx r, p, q) \in \mathcal{P}$ for any $l, r \in \mathcal{T}$, and $p, q \in \mathcal{P}$. We denote program terms by p, q, possibly with indices. A term that does not contain a conditional term constructor is called a* simple term. ❑

We note that any term with the ite symbol containing arbitrary Boolean expressions as conditions can be translated into an equivalent program term in $\mathcal{P}$.

Definition 3 (Solution for a Specification). *Let $\Lambda = \langle \Sigma_c, \forall \bar{x} \exists y. F[\bar{x}, y]] \rangle$ be a specification. A computable $p[\bar{x}] \in \mathcal{P}$ is called a* solution *for the specification Λ if $\forall \bar{x}. F[\bar{x}, p[\bar{x}]\theta]$ is valid for an arbitrary substitution θ grounding $p[\bar{a}]$ for fresh constants $\bar{a}$.* ❑

Note that if $\bar{x}$ are the only variables in $p[\bar{x}]$, then the condition for $p[\bar{x}]$ being a solution reduces to $\forall \bar{x}. F[\bar{x}, p[\bar{x}]]$ being valid. On the other hand, if $p[\bar{x}]$ contains variables $\bar{z}$ other than $\bar{x}$, then $p[\bar{x}]$ represents a class of solutions, one for each grounding of $\bar{z}$.

Definition 4 (Realizable Specification). *Let Λ be a specification. We call Λ* realizable *if there exists a computable program term that is a solution to it.* ❑

We are now ready to state the problem that is the focus of the present paper.

The Synthesis Problem under Realizability Assumptions

Given a realizable specification Λ, the *synthesis problem under realizability assumptions* is the task of finding a solution to Λ.

In the following, we refer to the synthesis problem under realizability assumptions simply as *the synthesis problem.*

Saturation-based Synthesis Framework. One approach to solving synthesis problems is the saturation-based synthesis framework introduced in [15], which extends a saturation-based first-order theorem prover into a synthesizer. The framework constructs a program for specification Λ in parallel with searching for a proof that specification (2) holds. Intuitively, y in (2) represents the output for the inputs $\bar{x}$, and thus substitutions into y in the proof correspond to fragments of the sought program. To track these substitutions throughout the proof, the framework of [15] uses a mechanism called answer literals [7]. In this paper, we use constrained clauses, called *answer clauses*, rather than adding answer literals to clauses.

Definition 5 (Answer Clause). *Let C be a clause and p a program term. We call the expression $C[\![p]\!]$ an* answer clause. *We call p the* answer *for the answer clause $C[\![p]\!]$. We denote answer clauses with $\mathcal{C}$ and $\mathcal{D}$, possibly with indices. Given a substitution σ, we write $C[\![p]\!]\sigma$ to denote $C\sigma[\![p\sigma]\!]$.* ❑

W.l.o.g. we assume that axioms $A_1, \ldots, A_n$ are a part of specification (2); that is, $F[\bar{x}, y]$ is of the form $(A_1 \land \cdots \land A_n) \rightarrow G[\bar{x}, y]$. To derive a program, the framework first preprocesses (2) like a saturation-based prover would: the formula $\neg\forall\bar{x}\exists y.F[\bar{x}, y]$ is converted to the equivalent $\exists\bar{x}\forall y.\neg F[\bar{x}, y]$ and skolemized, obtaining the equisatisfiable $\forall y.\neg F[\bar{\alpha}, y]$,[1] which is then clausified, resulting into $\mathsf{cnf}(\neg F[\bar{\alpha}, y]) = \{C_1, \ldots, C_m\}$. The framework then extends the clauses $C_1, \ldots, C_m$, among which are also the axioms, into answer clauses $C_1[\![y]\!], \ldots, C_m[\![y]\!]$,[2] and initializes the saturation set $S = \{C_1[\![y]\!], \ldots, C_m[\![y]\!]\}$, called *the initial set from Λ*. We denote the consecutive steps of clausification and extending clauses into answer clauses by $\mathsf{cnf}(\neg F[\bar{\alpha}, y])[\![y]\!]$.

Definition 6 (Semantics of Answer Clauses). $C[\![p]\!]$ is true *with respect to a given specification $\Lambda = \langle \Sigma_c, \forall\bar{x}\exists y.F[\bar{x}, y]\rangle$, if the universal closure of $C \lor F[\bar{\alpha}, p]$ is true, where w.l.o.g. we assume $C[\![p]\!]$ and $F[\bar{\alpha}, y]$ to have disjoint sets of variables.*[3] ❑

To work with answer clauses, we use an extension of the superposition calculus [20]. Using this calculus, we *saturate* S like a saturation-based prover: we extend the set S by new clauses derived by rules from the calculus based on

---

1 Since the skolems $\bar{\alpha}$ represent the input of the sought program, they are computable.

2 In [15], only the clauses C containing y are extended into answer clauses $C[\![y]\!]$. In this paper we extend *all* clauses C in preprocessing, including axioms, into answer clauses $C[\![y]\!]$.

3 [15] uses analogous semantics while denoting $C[\![p]\!]$ by $C \lor \mathsf{ans}(p)$.

premises already present in the set. We call S the *set saturated from* Λ. The work [15] proves that the saturation approach is sound: it only derives valid answer clauses, and thus when the answer clause $\square[\![p[\bar{\alpha}]]\!]$ is derived, it is guaranteed that $p[\bar{x}]$ is a solution for Λ. However, [15] makes no completeness claims. In the following section, we show an example for which the approach fails to derive a program even though a computable program exists.

4 Superposition with Synthesis

In this section, we present our new calculus SUPRA, adapted from [15]. We discuss the orderings and selection constraints that guide SUPRA (Sect. 4.1). We also introduce an abstraction mechanism that separates computable and uncomputable terms via an inference rule, in addition to SUPRA (Sect. 4.2).

4.1 The SUPRA Calculus

Our new calculus for Superposition with Realizability Assumptions, in short SUPRA, is summarized in Fig. 1. Compared to [15], we do not use so-called computable unifiers (abstracting unifiers preventing uncomputable symbols from appearing in the answer term), but most general unifiers and only allow an inference when the answer term after applying σ is computable. Further, we include the rule Sup_U, which unifies the answer terms p, q from premises, while [15] included a superposition rule which did not unify p, q but rather added a constraint $p \not\approx q$ into the resulting clause. Finally, for simplicity, we work only with equality predicates; thus, we do not include binary resolution or factoring rules as in [15].

We next establish soundness of SUPRA; this result guarantees that the programs derived by SUPRA are solutions of the synthesis specification.[4]

Theorem 1 (Soundness). *The SUPRA calculus is sound with respect to the semantics of answer clauses.*

It follows from Theorem 1 that SUPRA derives solutions to synthesis specifications.

Corollary 1 (Solution to the Synthesis Problem). *Given a synthesis specification* $\Lambda = \langle \Sigma_c, \forall \bar{x} \exists y. F[\bar{x}, y] \rangle$, *if SUPRA derives* $\square[\![p[\bar{\alpha}]]\!]$ *from the initial set of* Λ, *then* $p[\bar{x}]$ *is a solution for* Λ.

The rules of SUPRA are, however, not the only ingredient necessary to guarantee that a solution for a realizable specification will be derived. The following example illustrates how a derivation can get stuck.

---

[4] We provide detailed proofs for all our results in the extended version [11] of this paper.

$$(\mathsf{Sup}_C)\ \frac{\underline{l \approx r} \vee C[\![p]\!] \qquad \underline{s[l'] \dot{\approx} t} \vee D[\![q]\!]}{s[r] \dot{\approx} t \vee C \vee D[\![\mathsf{ite}(l \approx r, q, p)]\!]\sigma} \quad \text{where} \begin{array}{l} (1)\ \sigma = \mathsf{mgu}(l, l') \\ (2)\ l' \text{ is not a variable} \\ (3)\ r\sigma \not\succeq l\sigma,\ t\sigma \not\succeq s[l']\sigma \\ (4)\ \mathsf{ite}(l \approx r, q, p)\sigma \text{ is computable} \end{array}$$

$$(\mathsf{Sup}_U)\ \frac{\underline{l \approx r} \vee C[\![p]\!] \qquad \underline{s[l'] \dot{\approx} t} \vee D[\![q]\!]}{s[r] \dot{\approx} t \vee C \vee D[\![p]\!]\sigma} \quad \text{where} \begin{array}{l} (1)\ \sigma = \mathsf{mgu}((l, p), (l', q)) \\ (2)\ l' \text{ is not a variable} \\ (3)\ r\sigma \not\succeq l\sigma,\ t\sigma \not\succeq s[l']\sigma \\ (4)\ p\sigma \text{ is a computable simple term} \end{array}$$

$$(\mathsf{EqRes})\ \frac{\underline{s \not\approx t} \vee C[\![p]\!]}{C[\![p]\!]\sigma} \quad \text{where} \begin{array}{l} (1)\ \sigma = \mathsf{mgu}(s, t) \\ (2)\ p\sigma \text{ is computable} \end{array}$$

$$(\mathsf{EqFac})\ \frac{\underline{s \approx t} \vee l \approx r \vee C[\![p]\!]}{s \approx t \vee t \not\approx r \vee C[\![p]\!]\sigma} \quad \text{where} \begin{array}{l} (1)\ \sigma = \mathsf{mgu}(s, l) \\ (2)\ t\sigma \not\succeq s\sigma,\ r\sigma \not\succ t\sigma \\ (3)\ p\sigma \text{ is computable} \end{array}$$

Fig. 1. Rules of SUPRA, where all maximal literals in a clause are selected (denoted underlined), and $C[\![p]\!]\sigma$ denotes the application of σ on $C[\![p]\!]$.

Example 1. Our motivating example corresponding to the specification (1) can be expressed as a synthesis specification with computable symbols f, s, p and v. That is, $\Lambda : \langle\{\mathsf{f}, \mathsf{s}, \mathsf{p}, \mathsf{v}\}, \varphi\rangle$. We consider predicate symbols as function symbols mapping values to $\{\top, \bot\}$ in a two-sorted logic. We will try to derive a solution for Λ using SUPRA. The initial set from Λ, where α is the Skolem constant introduced for x and numbers denote clause labels, is $\{(1)\ \alpha \approx \mathsf{f} \vee \underline{\alpha \approx \mathsf{s}}[\![y]\!], (2)\ \underline{\alpha \not\approx \mathsf{s}} \vee \mathsf{wp}[\![y]\!], (3)\ \underline{\alpha \not\approx \mathsf{f}} \vee \mathsf{wv}[\![y]\!], (4)\ \neg\underline{\mathsf{w}y}[\![y]\!]\}$. We use a selection function that selects either (i) all maximal literals or (ii) at least one negative literal.[5] Let $\succ$ be an LPO with the following symbol precedence: $\mathsf{s} \gg \mathsf{f} \gg \mathsf{p} \gg \mathsf{v} \gg \mathsf{w} \gg \alpha$. We obtain the following derivation, where we write SE for a Sup inference followed by an EqRes inference:

$$\dfrac{\dfrac{\dfrac{\dfrac{\overset{(1)}{\alpha \approx \mathsf{f} \vee \underline{\alpha \approx \mathsf{s}}[\![y]\!]} \qquad \overset{(2)}{\underline{\alpha \not\approx \mathsf{s}} \vee \mathsf{wp}[\![y]\!]}}{\underline{\alpha \approx \mathsf{f}} \vee \mathsf{wp}[\![y]\!]}(\mathsf{SE}) \qquad \overset{(3)}{\underline{\alpha \not\approx \mathsf{f}} \vee \mathsf{wv}[\![y]\!]}}{\underline{\mathsf{wp}} \vee \mathsf{wv}[\![y]\!]}(\mathsf{SE}) \qquad \overset{(4)}{\neg\underline{\mathsf{w}y}[\![y]\!]}}{\underline{\mathsf{wv}}[\![\mathsf{p}]\!]}(\mathsf{SE}) \qquad \overset{(4)}{\neg\underline{\mathsf{w}y}[\![y]\!]}}{\text{(inference not possible)}}$$

Here we get stuck, as no more inferences are possible. Superposition into (4) $\neg\mathsf{w}y[\![y]\!]$ with $\mathsf{wv}[\![\mathsf{p}]\!]$ cannot be applied, because v and p do not unify; moreover, we cannot create an ite with condition wv, because $\mathsf{w} \in \Sigma_u$. However, as mentioned before, Λ is realizable, e.g. by the solution $\mathsf{ite}(x \approx \mathsf{f}, \mathsf{v}, \mathsf{p})$. We did not derive a solution due to the selection of computable literals in clauses which also contained uncomputable literals. ❑

[5] Such a selection function is called *well-behaved* and is sufficient to achieve refutational completeness in standard superposition reasoning.

Remark 1. Since [15] does not restrict selection nor simplification orders in any way, the failed derivation from Example 1 can be replicated by the calculus of [15]. Therefore, the calculus [15] does not always find a solution if one exists – it is not complete under realizability assumptions. ❑

Based on Example 1, we observe that we have to select uncomputable literals before computable ones. To this end, we make uncomputable terms bigger than computable terms in the simplification order and restrict the selection functions admissible for SUPRA to always select all maximal literals. We formally refine the simplification order used by SUPRA as follows.

Definition 7 (Partitioned Ordering). *An ordering $\succ$ on terms is called* partitioned *if for any ground uncomputable term s and any ground computable term t it holds that $s \succ t$.* ❑

We require that the simplification order that parameterizes SUPRA is partitioned. In the rest of the paper, we will use an LPO with a precedence function where any uncomputable symbol is greater than any computable symbol. Not only can these types of LPOs be used for SUPRA, but also specific KBOs that are partitioned orderings, see [11] for further discussion.

Example 2. Let $\succ$ be an LPO based on $\mathsf{w} \gg \mathsf{v} \gg \mathsf{p} \gg \mathsf{s} \gg \mathsf{f}$. With a selection function selecting all maximal literals w.r.t. $\succ$, we find a solution for A from Example 1:

$$\text{(SE)}\,\dfrac{\text{(SE)}\,\dfrac{\text{(SE)}\,\dfrac{\overset{(2)}{\alpha \not\approx \mathsf{s} \vee \underline{\mathsf{wp}}\llbracket y \rrbracket} \quad \overset{(4)}{\neg \underline{\mathsf{w}y}\llbracket y \rrbracket}}{\underline{\alpha \not\approx \mathsf{s}}\llbracket \mathsf{p} \rrbracket} \quad \overset{(1)}{\alpha \approx \mathsf{f} \vee \underline{\alpha \approx \mathsf{s}}\llbracket y \rrbracket}}{\underline{\alpha \approx \mathsf{f}}\llbracket \mathsf{p} \rrbracket} \quad \dfrac{\overset{(4)}{\neg \underline{\mathsf{w}y}\llbracket y \rrbracket} \quad \overset{(3)}{\alpha \not\approx \mathsf{f} \vee \underline{\mathsf{wv}}\llbracket y \rrbracket}}{\underline{\alpha \not\approx \mathsf{f}}\llbracket \mathsf{v} \rrbracket}\,\text{(SE)}}{\square\llbracket \mathsf{ite}(\alpha \approx \mathsf{f}, \mathsf{v}, \mathsf{p}) \rrbracket}$$

❑

4.2 Abstraction of Computable Terms in Uncomputable Literals

While our motivating example (1) shows that inferences with uncomputable literals should be applied before inferences with computable literals, sometimes this cannot be enforced, as some uncomputable equations can only be used in a superposition inference after performing a superposition into them with a computable equation.

Example 3. Consider constants a, b, c, d, e, unary symbols f, g, h, and the specification:

$$\langle \{a, b, c, d, e\},\ \exists y.(fd \not\approx e \vee (d \not\approx c \wedge gy \approx ga) \vee (fc \approx e \wedge hy \approx hb))\rangle.$$

We perform the following derivation using an LPO $\succ$ with $h \gg g \gg f \gg e \gg d \gg c \gg b \gg a$. The leaves are obtained from the initial set of the above specification:

$$
(\mathsf{Sup}_C)\ \dfrac{(\mathsf{Sup}_U)\ \dfrac{\overset{(1)}{\underline{fd \approx e}\llbracket y \rrbracket} \qquad (\mathsf{ER})\ \dfrac{\overset{(2)}{d \approx c \vee \underline{gy \not\approx ga}\llbracket y \rrbracket}}{\underline{d \approx c}\llbracket a \rrbracket}}{\underline{fc \approx e}\llbracket \mathsf{ite}_{\approx}\ cya \rrbracket} \qquad (\mathsf{ER})\ \dfrac{\overset{(3)}{fc \not\approx e \vee \underline{hy \not\approx hb}\llbracket y \rrbracket}}{\underline{fc \not\approx e}\llbracket b \rrbracket}}{\text{(inference not possible)}}
$$

The last step of the derivation is not possible, because the answers b and $\mathsf{ite}_{\approx}\ cya$ do not unify, and we cannot construct an ite in the answer, because the condition $fc \approx e$ is uncomputable. ❑

The general observation we make from Example 3 is that we should resolve all uncomputable literals, even those containing computable subterms, before applying inferences with computable symbols. For this purpose, we *abstract the computable subterms of uncomputable literals*, thus separating reasoning with uncomputable and computable symbols. We do this by adding an auxiliary inference rule Abs, which replaces its premise by its consequence, indicated by the crossed-out premise. We *apply* Abs *exhaustively on each clause before we allow any further inferences*:

$$
(\mathsf{Abs})\ \dfrac{\cancel{\underline{s[k]} \mathrel{\dot{\approx}} t \vee C\llbracket p \rrbracket}}{s[x] \mathrel{\dot{\approx}} t \vee x \not\approx k \vee C\llbracket p \rrbracket}
$$

where
(1) $s \not\preceq t$
(2) there is a substitution θ s.t. $s[k]\theta$ is uncomputable and $k\theta$ is computable
(3) no proper superterm of k in $s[k]$ satisfies property (2)
(4) k is not a variable
(5) x is a fresh variable

Lemma 1. *The rule* Abs *is sound with respect to the semantics of answer clauses.*

To apply the rule in practice, we use the following syntactic conditions in place of condition (2) of Abs.

Lemma 2. *Condition (2) of rule* Abs *holds iff (2a) k is computable, and (2b) either $s[k]$ is uncomputable, or it contains a variable not contained in k, and there exists at least one uncomputable term.*

Example 4. The derivation from Example 3 changes as follows when using Abs:

$$
(\mathsf{SE})\ \dfrac{(\mathsf{ER})\ \dfrac{(\mathsf{ER})\ \dfrac{(\mathsf{Abs})\ \dfrac{\overset{(2)}{\cancel{d \approx c \vee \underline{gy \not\approx ga}\llbracket y \rrbracket}}}{d \approx c \vee \underline{gy \not\approx gx} \vee x \not\approx a\llbracket y \rrbracket}}{\underline{d \approx c} \vee \underline{x \not\approx a}\llbracket x \rrbracket}}{\underline{d \approx c}\llbracket a \rrbracket} \qquad (\mathsf{ER})\ \dfrac{(\mathsf{SE})\ \dfrac{(\mathsf{Abs})\ \dfrac{\overset{(1)}{\cancel{\underline{fd \approx e}\llbracket y \rrbracket}}}{\underline{fx \approx e} \vee x \not\approx d\llbracket y \rrbracket} \qquad (\mathsf{ER})\ \dfrac{(\mathsf{Abs})\ \dfrac{(\mathsf{ER})\ \dfrac{(\mathsf{Abs})\ \dfrac{\overset{(3)}{\cancel{fc \not\approx e \vee \underline{hy \not\approx hb}\llbracket y \rrbracket}}}{fc \not\approx e \vee \underline{hy \not\approx hx} \vee x \not\approx b\llbracket y \rrbracket}}{\cancel{\underline{fc \not\approx e} \vee \underline{x \not\approx b}\llbracket x \rrbracket}}}{\underline{fz \not\approx e} \vee z \not\approx c \vee \underline{x \not\approx b}\llbracket x \rrbracket}}{\underline{fz \not\approx e} \vee z \not\approx c\llbracket b \rrbracket}}{\underline{y \not\approx d} \vee y \not\approx c\llbracket b \rrbracket}}{\underline{d \not\approx c}\llbracket b \rrbracket}}{\square\llbracket \mathsf{ite}_{\approx}\ cba \rrbracket}
$$

Our new Abs rule allowed us to solve the specification of Example 3, deriving the program $\mathsf{ite}_{\approx}\ cba$.

❑

5 Completeness of SUPRA Under Realizability Assumptions

In this section, we prove that the SUPRA calculus is *complete with respect to realizability assumptions*. In particular, we show that if there exists a solution to the specification Λ, then SUPRA used exhaustively with the rule Abs is guaranteed to derive some (possibly different) computable program, which is also a solution for Λ since SUPRA is sound (see Sect. 4.1). Our main result is the following theorem.

Theorem 2 (Completeness Under Realizability). *Let $\Lambda = \langle \Sigma_c, \forall \bar{x} \exists y. F[\bar{x}, y] \rangle$ be a specification. If Λ is realizable, then SUPRA with* Abs *derives an answer clause of the form $\square [\![p[\bar{\alpha}]]\!]$ from Λ where $p[\bar{x}]$ is a computable program term that is a solution to Λ.*

We prove Theorem 2 similarly to the completeness proof of the superposition calculus [21], by contradiction. We assume that S is a set saturated from Λ up to redundancy and abstracted (Definition 12), and that $\square [\![p[\bar{\alpha}]]\!] \notin S$ for any $p[\bar{\alpha}]$. Yet, we assume that Λ is realizable and that $t[\bar{x}]$ is a solution to it – i.e., that $\forall \bar{x}. F[\bar{x}, t[\bar{x}]]$ is valid. W.l.o.g. we assume $t[\bar{x}]$ does not contain any variables except for $\bar{x}$. We then consider a grounding of S using $t[\bar{\alpha}]$ (Definition 15) and construct an interpretation for it (Definition 10). However, since the grounding of S is equisatisfiable with $\neg F[\bar{\alpha}, t[\bar{\alpha}]]$, which is unsatisfiable because $\forall \bar{x}. F[\bar{x}, t[\bar{x}]]$ is valid, the interpretation should not be a model of S. We then consider the smallest clause $\mathbb{C}$ in the grounding that is false in the interpretation. Based on it, we either find an even smaller clause in the grounding that is also false in the interpretation, or show that the clause in S, instance of which is $\mathbb{C}$, should have been removed by Abs, since S is abstracted. In either case, we obtain a contradiction. We split this part of the proof into two steps: first, in Lemma 4 we show that all computable clauses in the grounding of S are satisfied in the model; then in Lemma 6 we extend this property to all uncomputable clauses.

Our construction involves substituting program terms into clauses – the term $t[\bar{\alpha}]$ is substituted for y in $\mathsf{cnf}(\neg F[\bar{\alpha}, y])[\![y]\!]$. If $t[\bar{\alpha}]$ contains ite terms, we have to unroll them by creating multiple instances of the clause and adding the condition(s) from the ite into them. We collect the unrolled condition literals in lists and separate them from the original clause, using so-called conditional clauses, as defined below.

Definition 8 (Conditional Clause, c-clause). *Let C be a clause and $\mathcal{L}$ a list of literals. A* conditional clause, c-clause *for short, is an expression of the form $C \triangledown \mathcal{L}$. We call $\mathcal{L}$ the* condition *of the c-clause $C \triangledown \mathcal{L}$. The c-clause $C \triangledown \mathcal{L}$ is logically equivalent to the clause $C \vee \bigvee_{L \in \mathcal{L}} L$. We denote c-clauses with $\mathbb{C}$ and $\mathbb{D}$. We use the notation $C\blacktriangledown$ to denote the c-clause $C \triangledown \epsilon$.* ❏

We extend the ordering $\succ$ over clauses to c-clauses as follows.

Definition 9 (Ordering on c-clauses). *We define an* ordering $\succ$ over c-clauses *as follows. First, we extend* $\succ$ *to lists of literals. We have* $\mathcal{L} \succ \epsilon$ *for any non-empty* $\mathcal{L}$ *and* $L\mathcal{L} \succ K\mathcal{K}$ *if either (i)* $L \succ K$ *or (ii)* $L = K$ *and* $\mathcal{L} \succ \mathcal{K}$. *We have* $C \triangledown \mathcal{L} \succ D \triangledown \mathcal{K}$ *if either (i)* $C \succ D$, *or (ii)* $C = D$ *and* $\mathcal{L} \succ \mathcal{K}$.[6] ❑

We now define a model for sets of c-clauses. As usual in superposition completeness proofs, we use rewrite systems as interpretations, where any equation $s \approx t$ is true in a rewrite interpretation R, denoted $R \models s \approx t$, if s and t have the same normal form in R. As usual, when s, t are ground, $R \models s \not\approx t \iff R \not\models s \approx t$. A c-clause $C \triangledown \mathcal{L}$ is true in R if C or $\mathcal{L}$ contain at least one literal L such that $R \models L$.

Definition 10 (Model for c-clauses). *Let* S *be a set of ground c-clauses. For every c-clause* $\mathbb{C} \in S$, *we define in parallel two sets of term rewrite rules* $R_S^{\mathbb{C}}$ *and* $R_S^{\prec\mathbb{C}}$ *as* partial interpretations *by induction on the relation* $\succ$ *on ground c-clauses. First, we define:*

$$R_S^{\prec\mathbb{C}} := \bigcup_{\mathbb{D}\prec\mathbb{C}, \mathbb{D}\in S} R_S^{\mathbb{D}}.$$

A ground c-clause $\mathbb{C}$ *of the form* $\underline{l \approx r} \vee C \triangledown \mathcal{L}$ *is called* productive *if*

1. $\mathcal{L}$ *is computable,*
2. $l \approx r \vee C$ *is false in* $R_S^{\prec\mathbb{C}}$,
3. *if* $l \approx r \vee C$ *is not computable, then all literals in* $\mathcal{L}$ *are false in* $R_S^{\prec\mathbb{C}}$,
4. $l \approx r$ *is strictly maximal in* $\mathbb{C}$,
5. $l \succ r$,
6. C *is false in* $R_S^{\prec\mathbb{C}} \cup \{l \to r\}$,
7. l *is irreducible in* $R_S^{\prec\mathbb{C}}$.

In this case, we also say that $\mathbb{C}$ produces *the rule* $l \to r$. *Now we define*

$$R_S^{\mathbb{C}} := \begin{cases} R_S^{\prec\mathbb{C}} \cup \{l \to r\}, & \text{if } \mathbb{C} \text{ produces } l \to r; \\ R_S^{\prec\mathbb{C}}, & \text{otherwise.} \end{cases}$$

Finally, we define the total interpretation R_S for S *as* $\bigcup_{\mathbb{C}\in S} R_S^{\mathbb{C}}$. *As usual, an interpretation which satisfies a set of c-clauses* S *is called a model of* S. ❑

We state two standard properties about the model.

Lemma 3. *Let* S *be a set of ground c-clauses.*

1. R_S *is a convergent rewrite system.*
2. $R_S^{\mathbb{C}} \models \mathbb{C}$ *if and only if for all* $\mathbb{D} \succ \mathbb{C}$ *we have* $R_S^{\mathbb{D}} \models \mathbb{C}$, *if and only if* $R_S \models \mathbb{C}$.

We will construct a model for a set which is *saturated up to redundancy* and *abstracted*, with the following redundancy notions.

[6] This ordering preserves well-foundedness.

Definition 11 (Redundant Answer Clause/Inference). *An answer clause* $\mathcal{C}$ *is* redundant w.r.t. S *if every ground instance of* $\mathcal{C}$ *follows from smaller ground instances in* S. *Let* N *be the set of all ground instances of answer clauses in* S. *An inference* $\mathcal{C}_1, ..., \mathcal{C}_n \vdash \mathcal{D}$ *is* redundant w.r.t. S *if for each* θ *grounding for* $\mathcal{C}_1, \ldots, \mathcal{C}_n$ *and* $\mathcal{D}$ *either*

1. $\mathcal{D}\theta \succ \mathcal{C}_i\theta$ *for some* $1 \leq i \leq n$, *or*
2. $\mathcal{D}\theta$ *follows from the set* $\{C \mid C \in N \text{ and } \mathcal{C}_i\theta \succ C \text{ for some } 1 \leq i \leq n\}$. ❑

Definition 12 (Saturation Up to Redundancy, Abstracted Set). *A set of answer clauses* S *is* saturated up to redundancy *if, given non-redundant answer clauses* $\mathcal{C}_1, ..., \mathcal{C}_n \in S$, *any SUPRA inference* $\mathcal{C}_1, ..., \mathcal{C}_n \vdash \mathcal{D}$ *is redundant w.r.t.* S.
If there is no clause $\mathcal{C} \in S$ *on which* Abs *would apply, then we call* S abstracted.❑

In the remainder of this section, we assume $\Lambda = \langle \Sigma_c, \forall \bar{x}.\exists y.F[\bar{x}, y] \rangle$ to be a fixed but arbitrary specification, and S a set of answer clauses saturated up to redundancy from Λ and abstracted. We assume $\square[\![p]\!] \notin S$ for any $p \in \mathcal{P}$. Note that the set of all ground instances of S might be unsatisfiable even if there is no computable solution for the specification, just an uncomputable one. Therefore, we cannot show refutational completeness of SUPRA. Instead, we show that from S, we can construct a counter-model for any computable program being a solution to Λ. Formally, we show that given any ground computable program term $t[\bar{\alpha}]$ (possibly using ite), the formula $\mathsf{cnf}(\neg F[\bar{\alpha}, t])$ is satisfiable. Towards this, we first eliminate ite from answer clauses $C_1[\![t]\!], \ldots, C_m[\![t]\!]$ coming from preprocessing, resulting in c-clauses.

Definition 13 (ite Normal Form). *Let* $\mathcal{C} = C[y][\![y]\!]$ *be an answer clause and* t *a program term. The* ite normal form *of* $\mathcal{C}$ *w.r.t.* t, *denoted* $\mathsf{iteNF}(\mathcal{C}, t)$, *is the set of c-clauses defined inductively as follows:*

1. *If* $C[y]$ *contains* y *and* t *is of the form* $\mathsf{ite}(L, s_1, s_2)$, *then it is*

$$\{D \triangledown \hat{L}\mathcal{L} \mid D \triangledown \mathcal{L} \in \mathsf{iteNF}(\mathcal{C}, s_1)\} \cup \{D \triangledown L\mathcal{L} \mid D \triangledown \mathcal{L} \in \mathsf{iteNF}(\mathcal{C}, s_2)\},$$

2. *otherwise, it is* $\{C[t]\blacktriangledown\}$. ❑

Intuitively, we obtain a c-clause $C[s] \triangledown \mathcal{L}$ by elimination of ite from $C[\![t]\!]$ when $\mathcal{L}$ is the list of negations of ite-conditions needed to reach the branch term s in t.

For any ground computable program term t, we construct a set of ground c-clauses S' such that if S' is satisfiable, then $\mathsf{cnf}(\neg F[\bar{\alpha}, t])$ is also satisfiable. Then, we show that the total model R'_S satisfies S'. The computable part of S' is defined as follows.

Definition 14 (Computable Grounding). *We define the* computable grounding *of* S, *denoted* $\mathbf{cGr}(S)$, *as the set of c-clauses that contains:*

1. *all computable ground instances of c-clauses in* $\mathsf{iteNF}(\mathcal{C}, t')$ *for all* $\mathcal{C}$ *in the initial set of* Λ *and program terms* t', *and*

2. *all computable ground c-clause instances of answer clauses in S.* ❑

We prove that the model $R_{\mathbf{cGr}(S)}$ satisfies all computable clauses in $\mathbf{cGr}(S)$. The proof is very similar to standard completeness proofs, since the rules of SUPRA for computable clauses correspond to the standard superposition rules: we do not apply any extra restrictions to inferences between computable clauses, and any inference between them results in a computable clause. By induction on $\succ$ over c-clauses, we obtain the following.

Lemma 4. *If $\square[\![p]\!] \notin S$ for any computable $p \in \mathcal{P}$, then $R_{\mathbf{cGr}(S)} \models \mathbb{C}$ for all $\mathbb{C} \in \mathbf{cGr}(S)$.*

To obtain S', we extend the set $\mathbf{cGr}(S)$ with uncomputable ground clauses. This set also depends on a computable program term t, and is called a grounding of S w.r.t. t.

Definition 15 (Grounding w.r.t. a Program Term). *Let $t \in \mathcal{P}$ be ground and t' be the normal form of t w.r.t. $R_{\mathbf{cGr}(S)}$. We define the* grounding of S w.r.t. program term t, *denoted $\mathbf{Gr}(S,t)$. In parallel, we define the* derivation length *for each uncomputable $\mathbb{C}$ in $\mathbf{Gr}(S,t)$, denoted $\mathsf{dl}(\mathbb{C})$.*
We define $\mathbf{Gr}(S,t)$ as the minimal set of c-clauses containing $\mathbf{cGr}(S)$ such that:

1 *For any answer clause $\mathcal{C}$ in the initial set of Λ, the set $\mathbf{Gr}(S,t)$ contains all ground instances of c-clauses in $\mathsf{iteNF}(\mathcal{C},t')$.*
 For any $\mathbb{C}$ added to $\mathbf{Gr}(S,t)$ by this step, we define $\mathsf{dl}(\mathbb{C}) = 0$.
2 *For any inference $C_1[\![p_1]\!],\ldots,C_n[\![p_n]\!] \vdash C[\![p]\!]\sigma$ such that $C_i[\![p_i]\!] \in S$ for all $1 \leq i \leq n$, and $C[\![p]\!] \in S$, if there is a substitution θ such that $\sigma\theta = \theta$, $\mathbf{Gr}(S,t)$ contains uncomputable c-clauses $C_1\theta \triangledown \mathcal{L}_1,\ldots,C_n\theta \triangledown \mathcal{L}_n$, and there is j, $1 \leq j \leq n$, such that for all $1 \leq i \leq n$, either $\mathcal{L}_i = \epsilon$, or $\mathcal{L}_i = \mathcal{L}_j$, then $C\theta \triangledown \mathcal{L}_j$ is in $\mathbf{Gr}(S,t)$.*
 Take the inference and θ such that $\max(\mathsf{dl}(C_1\theta \triangledown \mathcal{L}_1),\ldots,\mathsf{dl}(C_n\theta \triangledown \mathcal{L}_n))$ is minimal. We define $\mathsf{dl}(C\theta \triangledown \mathcal{L}_j) = \max(\mathsf{dl}(C_1\theta \triangledown \mathcal{L}_1),\ldots,\mathsf{dl}(C_n\theta \triangledown \mathcal{L}_n)) + 1$. ❑

In the remainder of this section, we assume that t is an arbitrary but fixed ground computable program term. One key step in our main result is to show that inferences between uncomputable answer clauses with non-unifiable answers are not needed for a refutation that yields a computable answer. Towards this, we prove the following lemma about the grounding of S w.r.t. t, using induction on the derivation length of c-clauses.

Lemma 5. *There is a set of lists of computable ground literals Δ that satisfies the following properties:*

1. *Any uncomputable $\mathbb{C} \in \mathbf{Gr}(S,t)$ is of the form $C \triangledown \mathcal{L}$ where $\mathcal{L} \in \Delta \cup \{\epsilon\}$.*
2. *For any $\mathcal{L} \in \Delta \cup \{\epsilon\}$, there is a ground computable simple term $t_{\mathcal{L}}$ such that for any uncomputable $C' \triangledown \mathcal{L} \in \mathbf{Gr}(S,t)$, substitution θ, and clause $C[\![p]\!] \in S$ such that $C\theta = C'$, it holds that p is a simple term and $p\theta = t_{\mathcal{L}}$ or p is a variable not in C.*

3. If $\epsilon \notin \Delta$, then for any uncomputable $C'\blacktriangledown \in \mathbf{Gr}(S,t)$, substitution θ, and clause $C[\![p]\!] \in S$ such that $C\theta = C'$, it holds that p is a variable not in C.
4. For any $\mathcal{L}, \mathcal{K} \in \Delta$ such that $\mathcal{L} \neq \mathcal{K}$, $\mathcal{L}$ and $\mathcal{K}$ contain a complementary literal.

Intuitively, any list of literals $\mathcal{L}$ in Δ corresponds to the negation of ite-conditions needed to reach some branch term, i.e. a simple term s in t. The lemma states that:

(i) Any c-clause $\mathbb{C}$ in $\mathbf{Gr}(S,t)$ represents an instance of an answer clause $C[\![p]\!]$ in S with either the empty condition, meaning that p is any program term not depending on C, or with some conditions $\mathcal{L}$ in Δ such that s is an instance of p.
(ii) Any two lists of conditions in Δ contain a pair of complementary literals.

This ensures that inferences between uncomputable c-clauses corresponding to different branches from t are not needed, because if one of them is productive (Definition 10), the other one is necessarily satisfied by the model. Now we can prove that $R_{\mathbf{Gr}(S,t)}$, obtained by extending $R_{\mathbf{cGr}(S)}$ with uncomputable clauses, is a model of $\mathbf{Gr}(S,t)$, and thus also of $\neg F[\bar{\alpha}, t]$.

Lemma 6. *If $\square[\![p[\bar{\alpha}]]\!] \notin S$ for any computable program term $p[\bar{\alpha}]$, then the formula $\neg F[\bar{\alpha}, t]$ is satisfiable for any ground computable program term t.*

We conclude this section with the proof of our main result.

Proof (of Theorem 2). Since Λ is realizable, there is a program term $t[\bar{x}]$ with no variables except for $\bar{x}$, such that $\forall \bar{x}.F[\bar{x}, t[\bar{x}]]$ is valid. By contraposition of Lemma 6 it then follows that $\square[\![p[\bar{\alpha}]]\!] \in S$ for an abstracted set S saturated up to redundancy from Λ. Since SUPRA and Abs are sound (Theorem 1), $p[\bar{x}]$ is a solution to Λ. ❏

6 Related Work

Saturation-Based Synthesis. A saturation-based solution to the synthesis of recursion-free programs is introduced in [15]. We show that [15] is not complete. We introduce the SUPRA calculus to simplify the reasoning of [15], as (i) we assume all clauses to be answer clauses, and (ii) use most general unifiers instead of the arbitrary computable unifiers of [15] in inferences. Further, (iii) SUPRA implements a new abstraction rule Abs, needed for completeness under realizability assumptions.

Deductive Approaches to Synthesis. Our work, as well as [13,15], are based on the deductive synthesis approach of [19], adapted for resolution [17]. The mechanism in [28] restricts allowed programs, and subsumes our computability restrictions.

The work of [15] extends [13] with induction to support synthesis of recursive programs, with a proof of soundness and implementation, but without any completeness guarantees. Our notion of realizability does not cover recursive programs, as their construction requires a mechanism for defining new functions not included in the computable symbols we work with.

A practical approach for synthesis in the presence of uncomputable symbols uses quantifier elimination and SMT solving [14], and requires $F[\bar{x}, y]$ to be quantifier-free in (2) but may use linear arithmetic. The approach is complete only when $F[\bar{x}, y]$ uses theories that admit quantifier elimination, which excludes e.g. equalities or uninterpreted functions.

The SyGuS [2] format allows specifying programs in a fragment of first-order logic extended by theories and optionally a grammar for the sought programs. Some prominent SyGuS solvers are cvc5 [24] and DryadSynth [16], as evidenced by the SyGuS competition [3]. Component-based synthesis methods construct programs from logical specifications using a predefined set of functions. The approach of [27] is deductive, while [9,29] use SMT solving. The GAPT framework [6] synthesizes programs from proofs, by computing witnesses of second-order formulas with quantifier elimination [1], or by extracting programs from natural deduction proofs in classical logic [25].

Related Completeness Results. Our completeness proof is inspired by standard completeness proofs for superposition [21]. Yet, our model construction only works for groundings that substitute computable program terms into the specification due to realizability assumptions. This relates our work to [28]. Finally, [30] proved that a general synthesis system for recursive programs cannot exist. This does not contradict our findings, as we claim completeness *under the assumption that a program exists.*

Restricted Inferences. A rule similar to Abs is used in [4,21] to disallow superpositions into certain terms, while [5] introduces unification constraints to the clause level that are similar to abstracted terms. In [23], the unification algorithm is extended by abstraction to enhance theory reasoning within superposition, abstracting terms on demand to enable inferences while postponing expensive theory reasoning.

7 Summary and Outlook

We tackle program synthesis and introduce the SUPRA calculus for saturation-based proof search. Our calculus revises [15] by using an abstract unification rule, which unravels computable subterms from uncomputable literals such that uncomputable literals can be resolved without disobeying the computability constraint of the calculus. We also use specific simplification orders and selection functions in SUPRA, ensuring that uncomputable literals are always selected if there are any in a clause. SUPRA changes the notion of clauses with answer literals to constrained clauses to make reasoning simpler. Not only do these adaptions retain soundness of SUPRA, but they enable proving completeness of SUPRA under the assumption that synthesis specifications have a solution. A natural direction for future work is investigating completeness under realizability assumption for synthesis of recursive functions using calculi that make use of induction.

Acknowledgements. This research was funded in whole or in part by the ERC Consolidator Grant ARTIST 101002685, the Austrian Science Fund (FWF) 10.55776/DOC1345324, and the SBA Research COMET Center SBA-K1 NGC managed by the FFG.

Disclosure of Interests. The authors have no competing interests to declare that are relevant to the content of this article.

References

1. Achammer, F., Hetzl, S., Schmidt, R.: Computing witnesses using the SCAN algorithm. In: CADE (2025). https://doi.org/10.1007/978-3-031-99984-0_27
2. Alur, R., et al.: Syntax-guided synthesis. In: Dependable Software Systems Engineering. IOS Press (2015). https://doi.org/10.3233/978-1-61499-495-4-1
3. Alur, R., Fisman, D., Padhi, S., Reynolds, A., Singh, R., Udupa, A.: SyGuS-Comp (2019). https://sygus.org/comp/2019/
4. Bachmair, L., Ganzinger, H., Waldmann, U.: Refutational theorem proving for hierarchic first-order theories. In: AAECC 5, 193–212 (1994). https://doi.org/10.1007/BF01190829
5. Bhayat, A., Schoisswohl, J., Rawson, M.: Superposition with delayed unification. In: CADE (2023). https://doi.org/10.1007/978-3-031-38499-8_2
6. Ebner, G., Hetzl, S., Reis, G., Riener, M., Wolfsteiner, S., Zivota, S.: System description: GAPT 2.0. In: Olivetti, N., Tiwari, A. (eds.) IJCAR 2016. LNCS (LNAI), vol. 9706, pp. 293–301. Springer, Cham (2016). https://doi.org/10.1007/978-3-319-40229-1_20
7. Green, C.: Theorem-proving by resolution as a basis for question-answering systems. Mach. Intell. **4**, 183–205 (1969)
8. Gulwani, S.: Automating string processing in spreadsheets using input-output examples. In: POPL (2011). https://doi.org/10.1145/1926385.1926423
9. Gulwani, S., Jha, S., Tiwari, A., Venkatesan, R.: Synthesis of loop-free programs. In: PLDI (2011). https://doi.org/10.1145/1993498.1993506
10. Gulwani, S., Jojic, N.: Probabilistic inference of programs from input/output examples (2006). https://api.semanticscholar.org/CorpusID:59650668
11. Hajdu, M., Hozzová, P., Kovács, L., Wagner, E.M.: Completeness of synthesis under realizability assumptions using superposition (2026). https://arxiv.org/abs/2605.19683
12. Hozzová, P.: Integrating answer literals with AVATAR for program synthesis. In: Proceedings of the 7th and 8th Vampire Workshop (2024). https://doi.org/10.29007/vmn9
13. Hozzová, P., Amrollahi, D., Hajdu, M., Kovács, L., Voronkov, A., Wagner, E.M.: Synthesis of recursive programs in saturation. Automated Reas. (2024). https://doi.org/10.1007/978-3-031-63498-7_10
14. Hozzová, P., Bjørner, N.: Synthesiz3 This: an SMT-based approach for synthesis with Uncomputable symbols. In: FMCAD (2025). https://doi.org/10.34727/2025/isbn.978-3-85448-084-6_28

15. Hozzová, P., Kovács, L., Norman, C., Voronkov, A.: Program synthesis in saturation. In: CADE (2023). https://doi.org/10.1007/978-3-031-38499-8_18
16. Huang, K., Qiu, X., Shen, P., Wang, Y.: Reconciling enumerative and deductive program synthesis, p. PLDI (2020). https://doi.org/10.1145/3385412.3386027
17. Lee, R.C.T., Waldinger, R.J., Chang, C.L.: An improved program-synthesizing algorithm and its correctness. Commun. ACM (1974). https://doi.org/10.1145/360924.360967
18. Li, Y., Parsert, J., Polgreen, E.: Guiding enumerative program synthesis with large language models. In: CAV (2024). https://doi.org/10.1007/978-3-031-65630-9_15
19. Manna, Z., Waldinger, R.: A deductive approach to program synthesis. TOPLAS (1980). https://doi.org/10.1145/357084.357090
20. Nieuwenhuis, R., Rubio, A.: Paramodulation-based theorem proving. In: Handbook of Automated Reasonings. Elsevier and MIT Press (2001). https://doi.org/10.1016/B978-044450813-3/50009-6
21. Nieuwenhuis, R., Rubio, A.: Basic superposition is complete. In: Krieg-Brückner, B. (ed.) ESOP '92 (1992). https://doi.org/10.1007/3-540-55253-7_22
22. Reger, G.: Revisiting question answering in vampire. In: 4th Vampire Workshop (2018). https://doi.org/10.29007/fjc4
23. Reger, G., Suda, M., Voronkov, A.: Unification with abstraction and theory instantiation in saturation-based reasoning. In: TACAS (2018).https://doi.org/10.1007/978-3-319-89960-2_1
24. Reynolds, A., Kuncak, V., Tinelli, C., Barrett, C., Deters, M.: Refutation-based synthesis in SMT. Formal Methods Syst. Design **55**(2), 73–102 (2017). https://doi.org/10.1007/s10703-017-0270-2
25. Rietdijk, M.: Extracting programs from proofs using Friedman's A-translation and realizability (2018). https://repositum.tuwien.at/handle/20.500.12708/8452
26. Singh, R., Gulwani, S.: Synthesizing number transformations from input-output examples. In: CAV (2012). https://doi.org/10.1007/978-3-642-31424-7_44
27. Stickel, M., Waldinger, R., Lowry, M., Pressburger, T., Underwood, I.: Deductive composition of astronomical software from subroutine libraries. In: CADE (1994). https://doi.org/10.1007/3-540-58156-1_24
28. Tammet, T.: Completeness of resolution for definite answers with case analysis. Comput. Sci. Logic (1995). https://doi.org/10.1007/BFb0022265
29. Tiwari, A., Gascón, A., Dutertre, B.: Program synthesis using dual interpretation. In: CADE (2015). https://doi.org/10.1007/978-3-319-21401-6_33
30. Voronkov, A.: On completeness of program synthesis systems. In: Börger, E., Jäger, G., Kleine Büning, H., Richter, M.M. (eds.) CSL 1991. LNCS, vol. 626, pp. 411–418. Springer, Heidelberg (1992). https://doi.org/10.1007/BFb0023785

Open Access This chapter is licensed under the terms of the Creative Commons Attribution 4.0 International License (http://creativecommons.org/licenses/by/4.0/), which permits use, sharing, adaptation, distribution and reproduction in any medium or format, as long as you give appropriate credit to the original author(s) and the source, provide a link to the Creative Commons license and indicate if changes were made.

The images or other third party material in this chapter are included in the chapter's Creative Commons license, unless indicated otherwise in a credit line to the material. If material is not included in the chapter's Creative Commons license and your intended use is not permitted by statutory regulation or exceeds the permitted use, you will need to obtain permission directly from the copyright holder.

Generating Theorems by Generating Proof Structures

Christoph Wernhard(✉)

University of Potsdam, Potsdam, Germany
info@christophwernhard.com

Abstract. We address generating theorems from a given set of axioms, without proof goal, aiming at value from a mathematical point of view or as lemmas for automated proving. As benchmark, we convert a fragment of the Metamath database set.mm. Our techniques are centered on proof terms and condensed detachment. This ties in with automated first-order proving by proof structure enumeration, and links to Metamath and formulas-as-types. Our methods for generating theorems are based on partitioning the set of proof terms into inductively characterized levels. We study two ideas for improvement: Lemma synthesis by DAG compression of proof term sets, and incorporating combinators into proof terms. Our lemmas significantly improve solution rates of provers, e.g., of Vampire from 74% to 94%, and of leanCoP from 7% to 44%.

1 Introduction

We address generating theorems, together with proofs, from a given set of axioms, without proof goal, aiming at value from a mathematical point of view or as lemmas for automated proving. This occurs as subtask in automated proving and is on its own a classic objective of automated reasoning, e.g., with *Scott's challenge* [52]. Modern variations include lemma generation [32], premise selection, and, more generally, learning and AI methods for automated reasoning [6]. Given an ideal solution set T_{Ideal}, the task has two aspects: The *recall aspect*, finding a set of theorems that contains as much members of T_{Ideal} as possible, and the *precision aspect*, finding a set of theorems that has as few members as possible that are not in T_{Ideal}. We consider here mainly the recall aspect.

Our techniques are based on proof terms and condensed detachment. On the one hand this links to *Metamath* [27] and formulas-as-types; on the other hand it ties in with proof search through enumeration of proof structures, interwoven with formula unification, as in the connection method [4,5] and clausal tableaux [21]. Redundancies are avoided by having each structure (proof) only once in the enumeration, and by eliminating sets of structures early on through failure of unification for a substructure. Commonly, e.g., with *leanCoP* [28], this is employed "top-down", utilizing unifiability through a ground-instantiated goal theorem. Compared to saturation-based provers, a serious drawback is that proven subgoals are not re-used in *fresh copies*. However, proof structures can also be enumerated "bottom-up" without a given goal [32,37,44], and as DAGs with copying

© The Author(s) 2026
A. Biere et al. (Eds.): IJCAR 2026, LNAI 16688, pp. 41–61, 2026.
https://doi.org/10.1007/978-3-032-32589-1_3

Table 1. The axiom system of *set.mm* for classical propositional logic.

Identifier	*Axiom*	*Names* [40]
1	$x \Rightarrow (y \Rightarrow x)$	**K**, *Simp*
2	$(x \Rightarrow (y \Rightarrow z)) \Rightarrow ((x \Rightarrow y) \Rightarrow (x \Rightarrow z))$	**S**, *Frege*
3	$(\mathsf{n}(x) \Rightarrow \mathsf{n}(y)) \Rightarrow (y \Rightarrow x)$	*Transp*

formulas for each incoming edge [11,43]. We utilize this for generating theorems by generating proof terms, based on *inductive level characterizations.*

As a benchmark T_{Ideal}, we convert a fragment of 1,374 theorems from the *Metamath* database *set.mm* [25,26]. We identify 554 of these as easy to obtain by generating proof terms. With two novel techniques, we generate proofs for 180 further ones: (1) Lemma synthesis based on the hypothesis that a formula is a valuable lemma if it is proven by a proof term with significant compressing effect on a set of previously generated proof terms. (2) Incorporating combinators[1] into proof terms for their compressing effect. Several of our generated theorems are hard to prove for first-order provers. Supplied to provers, our lemmas significantly improve solution rates, e.g., for *Vampire* [19] from 74% to 94%, and for *leanCoP* [28] from 7% to 44%.

After preliminaries (Sect. 2), we describe our benchmark (Sect. 3) and develop our techniques for generating theorems/proof terms (Sect. 4). Then we identify the easy-to-generate theorems (Sect. 5), and study our improvements by lemma synthesis (Sect. 6) and incorporation of combinators (Sect. 7). Section 8 concludes the paper. Supplementary appendices are provided by [46]. The presented techniques are implemented in *SWI-Prolog* [51] with *CD Tools* [42]. Artifacts are accessible from a dedicated Web page [45].

2 Technical Framework: Condensed Detachment

Condensed detachment (CD), in essence modus ponens with unification, was introduced by Carew A. Meredith in the 1950s [31]. With proof terms, it can be viewed from the perspective of formulas-as-types [14,15,34]. In automated proving, it led to numerous advances up to the early 2000s [40], and recently its relevance for approaches based on proof structures was observed [47,48]. It is the basis of *Metamath* [27] with its database *set.mm* [26]. It is often applied to axiomatizations of propositional logics. From the first-order point of view, this involves a single unary predicate P ("*provable*"), whereas the propositional object-level formulas are represented as terms. We consider those defined by the grammar

$$f, g \ ::= \ x \mid f \Rightarrow g \mid \mathsf{n}(f),$$

where x ranges over a set of *variables* x, y, z, u, v, w, also with index subscript. From the first-order point of view, $\Rightarrow$ is a binary function symbol representing object-level implication, and n is a unary function symbol representing

[1] In the sense of combinatory logic [8,38]. For a practice-oriented introduction see [29].

object-level negation. Table 1 shows the axioms of classical propositional logic in *set.mm*, written as object-level formulas. From the first-order perspective, e.g., axiom 1 is $\forall x \forall y\, \mathsf{P}(x \Rightarrow (y \Rightarrow x))$. CD *proof terms* are defined by the grammar

$$d, e \;:=\; a \mid \mathsf{D}(d, e),$$

where a ranges over a finite set of constants, called *axiom identifiers*. With each axiom identifier a an object-level formula f_a is associated. The *most general theorem (MGT)* of a proof term is a positive unit clause defined as follows.

- $\mathsf{MGT}(a) \stackrel{\text{def}}{=} \mathsf{P}(f_a)$, if a is an axiom identifier;
- $\mathsf{MGT}(\mathsf{D}(d_1, d_2))$ is the unit clause resulting from the clause

$$\mathsf{P}(y) \leftarrow (\mathsf{P}(x \Rightarrow y) \wedge \mathsf{P}(x)) \qquad (Det)$$

  by two resolution steps: upon the body atom $\mathsf{P}(x \Rightarrow y)$ with $\mathsf{MGT}(d_1)$, and upon the obtained instance of the second body atom $\mathsf{P}(x)$ with $\mathsf{MGT}(d_2)$.

As usual, we assume that variables of resolved clauses are renamed such that they do not share variables. If $\mathsf{P}(f)$ is the MGT of some proof term, we sometimes also call just f the MGT. A proof term may have no MGT (w.r.t. a mapping of axiom identifiers to object-level formulas) since literals to be resolved upon may not unify. The MGT is then said to be *undefined.* If defined, the MGT of a proof term is unique up to renaming of variables. The MGT is the *most general* formula proven by a proof term since the formulas it proves are the MGT itself and all its substitution instances. For more precise discussions see [14,15,48,49].[2]

3 *POI*: A Benchmark Theorem Set from *set.mm*

As benchmark set for generating theorems we extract those theorems from the core part of *set.mm*[3] that are proven from its axioms for classical propositional logic (Table 1). We call this set of theorems*POI* (for *propositional-only implication form*). We start from the first two thirds of *set.mm* with 28,673 curated theorems about various topics, dropping the remainder of deprecated or unstable material, and select those theorems whose proof depends (aside of D) only on axioms 1, 2, 3[4] and special axioms introducing object-level symbols. To facilitate use with external systems, we canonicalize the theorem formulas as follows.

1. *Conversion to implication form.* From a first-order point of view, *Metamath* theorems are definite clauses $\mathsf{P}(g) \Leftarrow (\mathsf{P}(f_1) \wedge \ldots \wedge \mathsf{P}(f_n))$ [7,49], which we convert to unit clauses $\mathsf{P}(f_1 \Rightarrow (f_2 \Rightarrow \ldots (f_n \Rightarrow g)))$. Proofs for both forms can be linearly translated into one another [46, App. A].

---

[2] In the formulas-as-types view D is *application* and the MGT is the *principal type*.

[3] https://github.com/metamath/set.mm, from July 5, 2025 (commit 011fba3).

[4] Axioms 1,2,3 are `ax-1`, `ax-2`, `ax-3` in *set.mm*. D is `ax-mp` with switched arguments.

2. *Eliminating defined symbols.* In *set.mm* object-level symbols other than ⇒ and n are introduced with "definitional" axioms, recognizable by the name prefix `df-`. We unfold these definitions. In proofs of *set.mm*, the `df-` axioms can be replaced with proofs of associated theorems.
3. *Removing duplicates.* If, after these conversions, formulas for different theorems from *set.mm* are identical, we only record the name of the first encountered, comparing first with theorems that are unit clauses already in *set.mm*. We keep theorems that are strictly subsumed by others, since a subsumed theorem may be provable with a shorter proof.

As benchmark set *POI* we finally obtain a set of 1,374 theorems. Their object-level formulas are valid formulas of classical propositional logic. For 58% of them the source was a definite clause with nonempty body.

For each POI theorem we provide a *TPTP* [39] `FOF` problem. Its axioms are the universal closures of (*Det*) and, as first-order atoms with predicate P, the axioms from Table 1. The conjecture is the theorem formula, as universally closed atom with predicate P. To estimate difficulty for first-order provers, we tried *Vampire* [19], *E* [36], *Prover9* [24] (which stands out because its proofs can be converted to our proof terms), and *leanCoP* [28]. Table 2 shows how many of the 1,374 problems were solved in 3,600, 600, and 60 s[5] (details: App. I ch3appspsbigtable). We use the results of *Vampire*, *E* and *E-as* to assign a "difficulty rating" to each *POI* theorem, between 0 (most easy) and 1 (most hard): For *POI* theorems p we define $\texttt{rating}(p) \stackrel{\text{def}}{=} 1 - \sum_{s \in \{\textit{Vampire}, E, \textit{E-as}\}, t \in \{60,600,3600\}} \texttt{solved}(p,s,t)/9$, where $\texttt{solved}(p,s,t)$ is 1 if the proving problem for p was solved by prover s in our runs in at most t seconds, and 0 otherwise.

Table 2. Prover results.

Prover	*3,600 s*	*600 s*	*60 s*
Vampire	1,028	952	571
E	911	820	664
E-as	868	826	669
Prover9	314	303	258
leanCoP	92	84	76
Total	1,038	988	740

4 An Approach to Generating Proof Structures

We develop a systematic approach to generate theorems by generating, or enumerating, proof structures.

4.1 Inductive Level Characterizations

We assume a fixed finite set Ax of axiom identifiers, e.g., $\{1, 2, 3\}$ from Table 1. For a proof term d let $\mathsf{Subterms}(d)$ denote the (not necessarily proper) set of all subterms of d that are compound, i.e., not in Ax. Define *tree size*, *compacted size*, and *height* of a proof term as follows.

[5] Versions and settings: *Vampire* 5.0.0, `-mode casc`; *E* 3.2.5, `-auto`; *E-as* is *E* 3.2.5, `-auto-schedule`; *Prover9* `auto`; *leanCoP* 2.1b. Time limit: 3,600 s. Platform: Intel Xeon 9242 cluster. Best results of two runs, with RAM limits 3.77 GB and 15 GB.

- $\mathsf{tsize}(a) \stackrel{\text{def}}{=} 0$ if $a \in Ax$; $\mathsf{tsize}(\mathsf{D}(d,e)) \stackrel{\text{def}}{=} 1 + \mathsf{tsize}(d) + \mathsf{tsize}(e)$.
- $\mathsf{csize}(d) \stackrel{\text{def}}{=} |\mathsf{Subterms}(d)|$.
- $\mathsf{height}(a) \stackrel{\text{def}}{=} 0$ if $a \in Ax$; $\mathsf{height}(\mathsf{D}(d,e)) \stackrel{\text{def}}{=} 1 + \mathsf{max}(\mathsf{height}(d), \mathsf{height}(e))$.

The *compacted size* is also called *DAG-size* since it equals the number of inner nodes of the unique minimal DAG representing the proof term.

A *level characterization* L is a specification of a partition of the set of all proof terms into a series $L_0, L_1, L_2, \ldots$ of disjoint subsets, called *levels.* Each measure defined above can be taken as basis for a level characterization: $\mathcal{T}_i \stackrel{\text{def}}{=} \{d \mid \mathsf{tsize}(d) = i\}$, $\mathcal{C}_i \stackrel{\text{def}}{=} \{d \mid \mathsf{csize}(d) = i\}$, $\mathcal{H}_i \stackrel{\text{def}}{=} \{d \mid \mathsf{height}(d) = i\}$. Using level characterizations to organize proving or generating theorems is made possible by *inductive level characterizations*, which for $\mathcal{T}$ and $\mathcal{H}$ can be given as follows.

Definition 1 (Inductive Level Characterizations: Tree Size and Height).

$\mathcal{T}_0 \stackrel{\text{def}}{=} Ax$;

$\mathcal{T}_{n+1} \stackrel{\text{def}}{=} \{\mathsf{D}(d,e) \mid \exists i{\leq}n \,.\, d \in \mathcal{T}_i,\ e \in \mathcal{T}_{n-i}\}$.

$\mathcal{H}_0 \stackrel{\text{def}}{=} Ax$;

$\mathcal{H}_{n+1} \stackrel{\text{def}}{=} \{\mathsf{D}(d,e) \mid d \in \mathcal{H}_n,\ \exists i{\leq}n \,.\, e \in \mathcal{H}_i\} \cup \{\mathsf{D}(d,e) \mid e \in \mathcal{H}_n,\ \exists i{<}n \,.\, d \in \mathcal{H}_i\}$.

An inductive level characterization can be read in two ways as high-level specification of an algorithm to generate proof terms level-by-level, e.g., for T: (1) Top-down with iterative deepening: For increasing n, proof terms $\mathsf{D}(d,e)$ in $\mathcal{T}_{n+1}$ are generated by generating proof terms d in levels T_i for $i \leq n$, and, for each d, generating proofs e in level T_{n-i}. (2) Bottom-up: For increasing n, proofs in $\mathcal{T}_{n+1}$ are generated and cached. When generating proof terms $\mathsf{D}(d,e)$ in $\mathcal{T}_{n+1}$, suitable d and e are retrieved from cached levels T_i and T_{n-i} with $i \leq n$.

For proving or generating theorems, generation of levels is interwoven with MGT computation. Proof terms without defined MGT are excluded from computed levels. A proof term only has a defined MGT if all its subterms have one. Thus, if strict subterms of proof terms are in lower levels, the reducing effect of requiring defined MGTs transfers from lower to higher levels.

Bottom-up processing based on inductive level characterizations offers two key features of importance for proving and generating theorems. (1) *Caching* to avoid recomputations: When generating a level, proof terms that are subterms and in a lower level are retrieved from the cached lower level and not computed anew. Through copying MGTs of re-used subproofs, proof terms can be represented by DAGs instead of trees. (2) A certain *simple way to incorporate restrictions*: Computed levels can be restricted to proof terms that meet heuristic criteria. If strict subterms of proof terms are in lower levels, the reduction is passed on from lower to higher levels: a lower level with fewer proof terms makes fewer ones available as strict subterms of proof terms in higher levels. Useful heuristic restrictions can refer to MGTs, e.g., with a formula size limit. They may depend on the order in which proof terms are generated, e.g., if proof terms whose MGT is subsumed by that of a preceding one are to be excluded.

While these features are common for saturation-based provers, they are foreign to conventional structure-generating provers, which are proceeding top-down.

4.2 Considering Compacted Size

Level characterization by *compacted size* is appealing for two reasons. First, the compacted size of a proof term is often significantly smaller than its tree size. Let $d_1 \stackrel{\text{def}}{=} \mathsf{D}(\mathsf{D}(1,1),\mathsf{D}(\mathsf{D}(1,\mathsf{D}(1,1)),\mathsf{D}(1,\mathsf{D}(1,1))))$, which has tree size 7 and compacted size 4. DAG grammars[6] provide a term notation that respects compacted size:

$$\{4 \rightarrow \mathsf{D}(1,1),\ 5 \rightarrow \mathsf{D}(1,4),\ \mathit{Start} \rightarrow \mathsf{D}(4,\mathsf{D}(5,5))\}. \tag{1}$$

As nonterminals, we use *Start* and numbers larger than the axiom identifiers 1, 2, 3. In accord with compacted size, we find 4 occurrences of D in right-hand sides (RHSs) of the productions. Proofs in *set.mm* often have astronomical tree size but modest compacted size, e.g., 2.53×10^{22} versus 3, 647 for theorem `peano3`.

The second motive for level characterization by compacted size is incorporating *combinators* like axioms into proof term enumeration [43]. Combinators restructure proof terms such that new possibilities of factoring shared subterms emerge, reducing the compacted size. At the same time, they can be handled in determining MGTs like ordinary axioms, with their principal type as axiom formula. As example consider the proof term

$$d_2 \stackrel{\text{def}}{=} \mathsf{D}(\mathsf{D}(\mathsf{D}(\mathbf{B},1),1),\mathsf{D}(\mathsf{D}(\mathsf{D}(\mathbf{B},1),1),\mathsf{D}(\mathsf{D}(\mathsf{D}(\mathbf{B},1),1),1))). \tag{2}$$

We can write d_2 as DAG grammar, annotated with MGTs of the expanded subterms, headed by rows for 1 and **B**:

$$\begin{array}{rl}
1 & : x{\Rightarrow}(y{\Rightarrow}x)\\
\mathbf{B} & : (x{\Rightarrow}y){\Rightarrow}((z{\Rightarrow}x){\Rightarrow}(z{\Rightarrow}y))\\
4 \rightarrow \mathsf{D}(\mathsf{D}(\mathbf{B},1),1) & : x{\Rightarrow}(y{\Rightarrow}(z{\Rightarrow}x))\\
\mathit{Start} \rightarrow \mathsf{D}(4,\mathsf{D}(4,\mathsf{D}(4,1))) & : x{\Rightarrow}(y{\Rightarrow}(z{\Rightarrow}(u{\Rightarrow}(v{\Rightarrow}(w{\Rightarrow}(x_1{\Rightarrow}(y_1{\Rightarrow}x_1)))))))).
\end{array} \tag{3}$$

Counting D's in RHSs, we see that the compacted size of d_2 is 5. We can eliminate the **B** combinator from d_2 by rewriting with its reduction rule, i.e., $\mathsf{D}(\mathsf{D}(\mathsf{D}(\mathbf{B},V_1),V_2),V_3) \rightarrow \mathsf{D}(V_1,\mathsf{D}(V_2,V_3))$. The result is the proof term

$$d_3 \stackrel{\text{def}}{=} \mathsf{D}(1,\mathsf{D}(1,\mathsf{D}(1,\mathsf{D}(1,\mathsf{D}(1,\mathsf{D}(1,1)))))), \tag{4}$$

which has the same MGT as d_2 but the larger compacted size 6. Incorporating combinators can effect exponential reductions of compacted size [43]. Simulations of resolution by methods based on proof structures [10,11] can be understood as incorporating combinators and enumeration by compacted size [43].

[6] I.e., tree grammars [22] that are non-cyclic, have a single production for each nonterminal, and have only nonterminals without parameters.

Generation of proof terms in levels for increasing compacted size can be performed by an adaptation [43] of the *value-number method* for DAG enumeration [1,12]. Unfortunately, this does not provide an inductive characterization like those of Def. 1, which give way to caching and incorporating restrictions. However, if we give up completeness, i.e., accept that there are proof terms that are not in any L_i, the *PSP* (for *Proof-SubProof*) *level* [47,48] is a suitable inductive level characterization by compacted size:

Definition 2 (Inductive Characterization of the PSP Level).

$$\begin{aligned} \mathcal{P}_0 &\stackrel{\text{def}}{=} Ax; \\ \mathcal{P}_{n+1} &\stackrel{\text{def}}{=} \{\mathsf{D}(d,e) \mid d \in \mathcal{P}_n,\, e \in \mathsf{Subterms}(d) \cup Ax\} \\ &\quad \cup \{\mathsf{D}(d,e) \mid e \in \mathcal{P}_n,\, d \in \mathsf{Subterms}(e) \cup Ax\}. \end{aligned}$$

A proof term in PSP level i has compacted size i, in other words: $\mathcal{P}_i \subseteq \mathcal{C}_i$. For $i \leq 3$ it holds that $\mathcal{P}_i = \mathcal{C}_i$. Generating proofs by PSP level was inspired by proofs from logicians [47,48]. So far it has been applied [32,44,47] to single-axiom CD problems such as `LCL038-1` [30] and the hard problem `LCL073-1` [53].

4.3 Applying the *SGCD* System

The *SGCD* (*Structure-Generating theorem proving for Condensed Detachment*) prover [32,44], a part of *CD Tools*, implements methods based on inductive level characterizations. It is highly configurable, supporting interaction of top-down and bottom-up processing. Here we focus on bottom-up generation of theorems from given axioms. *SGCD* can be configured for level characterizations $L \in \{\mathcal{T}, \mathcal{H}, \mathcal{P}\}$ as given in Defs. 1 and 2. It then computes for increasing $i \in \{0, 1, 2, \ldots\}$ a *cached solution set* $M_i \subseteq \bigcup_0^i L_i$. $M_0 = Ax$. For $i \geq 1$, first a set $M_i' \subseteq L_i$ is generated on the basis of M_{i-1} such that whenever d is a subterm of a member of M_i' in a level L_j with $j < i$, then $d \in M_{i-1}$. Generation of M_i' can be constrained by configurable restrictions Rest, discussed below. M_i is formed from $M_i' \cup M_{i-1}$: the set is ordered according to configured criteria Ord, and the Trim (a natural number) top members are extracted and postprocessed as configured with Post, to yield M_i. *SGCD* maintains a further set of proof terms, *Abandoned*, that records for all considered i proof terms $(M_i' \cup M_{i-1}) \setminus M_i$.

SGCD terminates with `Exhausted` if no new proof terms are obtained for M_i', i.e., if $M_i' = M_{i-1}$. It terminates with `Stopped`, if M_i for a configured maximum i, MaxLevel, has been computed. The result of an *SGCD* run consists of two proof term sets, the last M_i and *Abandoned*. The cardinality of M_i is at most Trim. For theorem generation both sets are relevant. The following vector summarizes key parameters of *SGCD* for bottom-up theorem generation:

$$\langle L, \textsc{Rest}, \textsc{Ord}, \textsc{Trim}, \textsc{Post}, \textsc{MaxLevel} \rangle$$

For Rest, configurable settings include: `dup` (`subs`): exclude proof terms whose MGT is identical to (subsumed by) that of a proof term computed before for an M'_j with $j \leq i$; `lt_ft(`n`)` (`lt_fh(`n`)`): exclude proof terms whose MGT has tree size (height) larger than n;[7] `gen_max(`n`)`: Compute at most n members of M'_i. For Ord, configurable ordering criteria include lexical comparison by MGT size values, smallest preferred, specifically `f_th`: by tree size and then height, and `f_ht`: by height and then tree size. An option for Post is `subs`, subsumption reduction: remove members with the same MGT except one, and remove members whose MGT is strictly subsumed by that of another member.

5 *POI-Base*: An Easy-to-Generate Subset of *POI*

We define *POI-base* as the set of those theorems from *POI* for which proofs appear in outputs of a few specific runs of *SGCD* representing straightforward

Table 3. Legend for tables summarizing *SGCD* runs.

Column	*Explanation*
RunId	Identifier of the *SGCD* run.
L	Level characterization.
POI	Number of "solved" *POI* theorems, i.e., *POI* theorems for which a proof is in the result set $M_i \cup \mathit{Abandoned}$.
1	Number of "solved" *POI* theorems with rating 1.
NB	Number of "solved" *POI* theorems not in *POI-base* (defined below).
`lt_ft`	Configured value n of the `lt_ft(`n`)` restriction in Res.
GMax	Configured value of the `gen_max` restriction.
Trim	Configured value of the Trim parameter.
Ord	Configured value of the Ord parameter.
Lev	Level i of the final M_i. This was either configured as MaxLevel or *SGCD* terminated with `Exhausted`, indicated by suffix "e".
Time	Wall clock time of the run in seconds.
Mem	Peak value of heap use after computing an M'_i in GB.
$\lvert Gen \rvert$	Total number of generated proof terms, i.e., final value of $\lvert M_i \cup \mathit{Abandoned} \rvert$.

Table 4. Two runs of *SGCD* that contribute to *POI-base*. Rest is set to `dup` and Post to `subs`. The last row refers to the union of the results of both runs.

RunId	*L*	*POI*	*1*	Trim	Ord	*Lev*	*Time*	*Mem*	$\lvert Gen \rvert$
BP	$\mathcal{P}$	494	4	200k	`f_th`	64 e	17,124	53	13,108k
BT	$\mathcal{T}$	462	1	20k	`f_ht`	592 e	19,226	123	39,114k
BP, *BT*		544	4						

[7] Size measures analogous to those for proof terms, applied to object-level formulas.

Table 5. Five runs of *SGCD* that contribute to *POI-base*. RES is parameterized with `lt_ft(n)` for n between 8 and 12, and with `subs`. TRIM is unlimited. The last three rows refer to unions of runs.

RunId	*L*	*POI*	*1*	`lt_ft`	*Lev*	*Time*	*Mem*	*Gen*
BPF_8	$\mathcal{P}$	323	0	8	63 e	2,494	3	64,937
BPF_9	$\mathcal{P}$	377	0	9	25	7,500	2	27,3766
BPF_{10}	$\mathcal{P}$	232	0	10	17	5,555	2	325,454
BPF_{11}	$\mathcal{P}$	228	0	11	15	4,638	2	324,717
BPF_{12}	$\mathcal{P}$	201	0	12	14	4,602	2	352,928
BPF_{8-12}		426	0					
BPF_{8-12}, BP		507	4					
$B := BPF_{8-12}, BP, BT$		554	4					

proof term enumerations, constrained by straightforward heuristic restrictions, limited to a few hours on commodity hardware.[8] Table 4 summarizes a run with level characterization $\mathcal{P}$ and a run with $\mathcal{T}$. (For the legend of all tables summarizing *SGCD* runs see Table 3.) Values for TRIM were set to prevent a quick growth of the time spent for the levels.

Taken together, the two runs identify 544 *POI-base* problems. Table 5 summarizes a series of five further runs with level characterization $\mathcal{P}$, restricted by limiting the tree size of the MGT. We finally define *POI-base* as the set of the 554 *POI* theorems for which proofs are obtained in at least one of the *SGCD* runs BP, BT, and BPF_{8-12}. We declare B as identifier of a "virtual run" of *SGCD* that yields proofs for these 554 theorems.

Concerning the prover results from Sect. 3 we observe the following: Four *POI-base* theorems have rating 1, i.e., the corresponding proving problems are not easy for either *Vampire* or *E*. For all 92 problems proven by *leanCoP* and for all 314 proven by *Prover9* the theorem belongs to *POI-base*. For those proven by *leanCoP*, proofs were generated by just BT, by just BP, and by just BP_{8-12}.

6 Lemma Synthesis via Proof Term Compression

We now pursue the hypothesis that a formula is a valuable lemma if it is proven by a proof term with a significant compressing effect on some large set D_0 of proof terms with defined MGT.

6.1 Computing the Lemmas

As proof term compression we consider DAG compression, a special case of grammar-based tree compression [23, 49] with a unique best compression, the

[8] The platform for all *SGCD* runs described in the paper was *SWI-Prolog* 10.0.0 on a Linux server with four Intel Xeon E5-4640 processors and 256 GB RAM.

minimal DAG, which can be efficiently computed.[9] The size of a DAG grammar $G = \{a_i \rightarrow d_i \mid i \in \{1, \ldots, n\}\}$ is the sum of the tree sizes of its RHSs: $|G| \stackrel{\text{def}}{=} \sum_{i=1}^{n} \mathsf{tsize}(d_i)$.[10] The compressing effect of a production $a_k \rightarrow d_k$ in G is indicated by its *save-value* [23], the difference of the size of G after unfolding the production (i.e., removing it and replacing a_k by d_k in all other RHSs) and the original size of G. It can be calculated as $\mathsf{sav}_G(a_k \rightarrow d_k) \stackrel{\text{def}}{=} (\mathsf{ref}_G(a_k) - 1) * \mathsf{tsize}(d_k)$, where $\mathsf{ref}_G(a_k)$ is the number of occurrences of a_k in the RHSs of G.

Our workflow for lemma synthesis is as follows. A base set D_0 of proof terms is generated with *SGCD* and compressed into its minimal DAG, represented by a DAG grammar G. The productions of G are ordered according to lexical comparison of (1.) save-value (largest preferred), (2.) tree size of the MGT (smallest preferred), and (3.) height of the MGT (smallest preferred). The considered MGT for a production is the MGT of the full expansion of its RHS. An implementation can utilize the grammar representation to avoid actual expansion when computing these MGTs. Productions with save-value 0, i.e., "top-level" productions whose LHS does not occur in a RHS, are then deleted. The RHSs of the remaining productions are now fully expanded (efficiently through structure sharing) to get a sequence D'_{Lem} of proof terms, ordered by expected usefulness of their MGTs as lemmas. The final sequence of proof terms D_{Lem} is obtained from D'_{Lem} by subsumption reduction, i.e., removing members with the same MGT except one, and removing members whose MGT is strictly subsumed by that of another member. The MGTs of the prefix of D_{Lem} with a configured length NLEM are then given to applications as additional axioms in lemma role.

Table 6. SGCD runs used to compose base sets D_0 in our experiments.

RunId	*L*	*NB*	*POI*	*1*	TRIM	ORD	*Lev*	*Time*	$|Gen|$
SBP	$\mathcal{P}$	0	232	0	5k	`f_th`	55 e	175	161k
SBT	$\mathcal{T}$	0	277	0	1k	`f_ht`	161 e	138	256k
MBP	$\mathcal{P}$	1	366	1	20k	`f_th`	67 e	828	973k
MBT	$\mathcal{T}$	0	392	1	3k	`f_ht`	219 e	714	1,926k
LBP	$\mathcal{P}$	4	419	2	50k	`f_th`	103 e	4,565	2,574k
LBT	$\mathcal{T}$	0	433	1	10k	`f_ht`	438 e	6,265	13,734k

Base sets D_0 in our experiments were composed from results of the six *SGCD* runs summarized in Table 6. Configurations are as for *BP* and *BT* (Table 4) but with smaller TRIM values. *MBP* and *LBP* prove a few *POI* theorems not in *POI-base*: a larger TRIM value does not imply that the result is a superset. Based on the runs of Table 6 we synthesized different sequences D_{Lem}, shown in Table 7.

[9] *SWI-Prolog* supports this with the library predicate `term_factorized/3`.

[10] For general grammar-based tree compression the number of *edges* is more appropriate as basis [23,49]. For our full binary trees this is twice the number of inner nodes.

Table 7. Sequences D_{Lem} generated via DAG compression. D_0 is composed from results of *SGCD* runs *Base runs*, taking the components indicated in column D_0: M stands for the final M_i, A|n for n members from *Abandoned* (evenly distributed w.r.t. recording time). For *A50*, the 50k refer to each base run, amounting to a total of 100k proof terms. Column *Values of* NLEM lists prefix lengths with which the sequence was used in experiments. Further columns show cardinalities of intermediate results.

D_{Lem}-*Id*	*Base runs*	D_0	*Values of* NLEM	$\lvert D_0\rvert$	$\lvert D'_{Lem}\rvert$	$\lvert D_{Lem}\rvert$
LMS	*SBP*, *SBT*	M	500, 1k	5,974	2,722	2,455
LMM	*MBP*, *MBT*	M	100	22,870	10,830	9,877
LML	*LBP*, *LBT*	M	4k	59,835	27,412	24,970
LMT	*LBT*	M	200	9,998	3,840	3,806
A50	*LBT*, *LBP*	M, A|50k	1k	159,831	61,482	53,539
A100P	*LBP*	M, A|100k	800, 1k, 1.5k, 12k	150,000	69,493	66,637
A100T	*LBT*	M, A|100k	100	109,998	14,110	13,507

6.2 Lemma-Enhanced Theorem Generation with *SGCD*

Table 8 summarizes runs of *SGCD* with lemmas synthesized by our workflow supplied as additional axioms. In all runs, REST is set to `dup` and to `gen_max` with value *GMax*, ORD is `f_th`, and (except for S_{12}) POST is `subs`. Recall that our virtual run B defined the 554 *POI-base* theorems. Our experiments with lemma synthesis yield proofs of 143 further *POI* theorems. Thus, in total, we now have generated proofs for 697 *POI* theorems, including 10 with rating 1.

We "learned" from sets of proofs of easy problems (D_0) how to prove harder problems ("*NB* theorems", i.e., theorems in *POI* but not in *POI-base*). The D_0 may then be viewed as training data, and the number of proven *NB* theorems as evaluation criterion. Since the D_0 are computed similarly as the proofs used to define *POI-base*, the D_0 contain (with 5 exceptions) no proofs of *NB* theorems.

The runs of Table 8 were chosen from 100 test runs such that taken together they provide proofs for a large number of *NB* theorems. The median of the number of proven *NB* theorems in all 100 runs is 31.5. Runs not selected included those with fewer than 100 lemmas, and those with $\mathcal{T}$ as level characterization. Nevertheless, $\mathcal{T}$ proved useful for computing D_0. Also, both quickly obtained small sets as well as large sets of abandoned proof terms from long runs proved useful for D_0. Runs with many lemmas but low MAXLEVEL often give good results. Run S_{12} is extreme: with 12,000 lemmas it just generates level 1.

In the long term, lemma synthesis by compression should be integrated into *SGCD*. A naive approach fails due to an inherent mismatch with bottom-up level generation: The save-value of a proof term d is determined by proof terms that have d as strict subproofs, whereas for $\mathcal{T}$, $\mathcal{P}$, $\mathcal{H}$ the newly generated proof terms for M'_i never are strict subproofs of the available proofs in M_{i-1} and *Abandoned*.

Table 8. Lemma-enhanced runs of *SGCD*. D_{Lem} refers to Table 7. The first NLEM members of D_{Lem} are taken as lemmas, i.e., their MGTs are given as axioms, along with the three axioms from Table 1. Column *Inp* shows the number of *POI* theorems which are subsumed by an input lemma. The last four rows refer to unions of runs.

RunId	*L*	*NB*	*POI*	*1*	*Inp*	NLEM	D_{Lem}	*GMax*	TRIM	*Lev*	*Time*	*Mem*	$\|Gen\|$
S_1	$\mathcal{P}$	61	556	1	146	500	*LMS*	40,000k	80k	7	2,990	62	36,882k
S_2	$\mathcal{P}$	62	568	1	165	1,000	*LMS*	40,000k	80k	4	3,176	77	44,011k
S_3	$\mathcal{P}$	15	503	3	62	100	*LMM*	40,000k	80k	78	3,518	20	11,556k
S_4	$\mathcal{P}$	61	578	1	227	4,000	*LML*	40,000k	80k	2	3,117	117	46,219k
S_5	$\mathcal{P}$	28	514	1	70	200	*LMT*	30,000k	100k	26	3,269	38	22,737k
S_6	$\mathcal{P}$	43	558	5	70	200	*LMT*	30,000k	200k	7	2,901	52	31,848k
S_7	$\mathcal{P}$	22	502	1	131	1,000	*A50*	30,000k	50k	3	2,083	86	32,730k
S_8	$\mathcal{P}$	36	549	2	127	800	*A100P*	30,000k	100k	3	2,453	82	35,688k
S_9	$\mathcal{H}$	42	533	1	137	1,000	*A100P*	40,000k	80k	2	2,866	124	40,559k
S_{10}	$\mathcal{H}$	64	574	2	137	1,000	*A100P*	∞	20k	2	2,118	94	32,446k
S_{11}	$\mathcal{H}$	38	526	1	147	1,500	*A100P*	40,000k	20k	4	3,286	110	41,780k
S_{12}	$\mathcal{H}$	56	573	3	254	12,000	*A100P*	80,000k	∞	1	1,186	93	80,012k
S_{13}	$\mathcal{P}$	9	413	4	46	100	*A100T*	∞	100k	4	803	19	10,285k
S_{1-6}		115	655	5									
S_{7-13}		110	653	6									
S_{1-13}		143	692	8									
B, S_{1-13}		143	697	10									

6.3 Lemma-Enhanced First-Order Theorem Proving

Table 9 shows results of supplementing lemma sets used for the *SGCD* runs in Table 8 to first-order provers.[11] The provers were not involved in synthesis and selection of the lemmas. Significant improvements of the solution rates suggest that lemma synthesis with proof term compression makes a contribution that is orthogonal not just to top-down structure-generating provers, such as *leanCoP*, but also to the techniques in state-of-the-art provers, such as *Vampire*.

6.4 Precision Aspects

Our lemma synthesis provides an experimentally validated method to obtain sets of useful lemmas, suggesting to inspect these also from the "precision" perspective, assessing the proportion of members in the ideal solution set. As example, we consider the sequence *LMM* of proof terms specified in Table 7. Its members are already expected to have some "value", since they represent nodes with at least two incoming edges in the minimal DAG for some underlying D_0. To get

[11] Platform and provers as in footnote 5. Time limit: 3,600 s. RAM limit: 3.77 GB.

Table 9. Results of first-order provers on the 1,374 proving problems for the POI theorems (Sect. 3) with lemmas obtained by synthesis via proof term compression. Cells show the number of solved problems. *Base* refers to problems with just the three original axioms. The S_i columns refer to settings from Table 8: The axioms were enriched by the MGTs of the first NLEM proof terms from D_{Lem}. Best values are in bold.

Prover	*Base*	S_3	S_{13}	S_5	S_2	S_{10}	S_4	S_{12}
Vampire	1,023	**1,290**	1,284	1,250	1,180	1,179	1,091	1,064
E	906	893	873	936	865	**999**	969	935
Prover9	289	353	359	378	376	**438**	387	297
leanCoP	90	527	410	505	557	607	601	**609**

more fine-grained estimates, we compare three re-orderings of the sequence: by save-value from synthesis, by tree size of the MGT, and by height of the MGT. For prefixes of lengths 2^1–2^{11}, the percentage of members which prove a *POI* theorem then gives an idea of precision, as shown in Fig. 1. E.g., in the prefix of length $2^6 = 64$ of *LMM* ordered by save-value 50% (i.e., 32) of the proof terms prove a *POI* theorem. We see that MGT height gives the best result up to a prefix length 2^6–2^7, when MGT tree size and save-value become competitive.

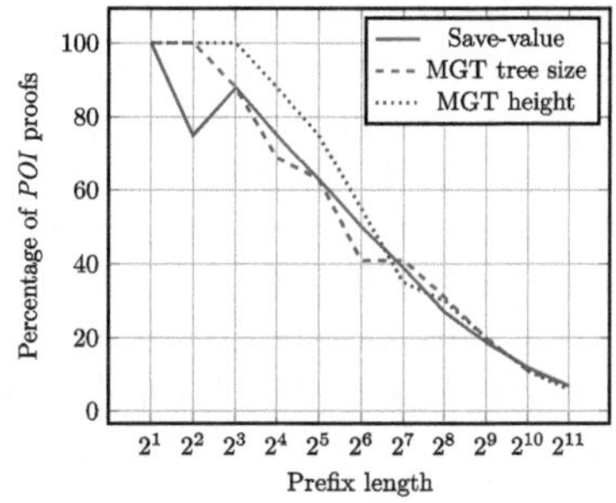

Fig. 1. Percentage of prefix members that prove a *POI* theorem.

7 Theorem Generation with Combinatory Proof Schemas

In Sect. 4.2 we outlined the incorporation of combinators into proof term construction [43]. We show how this can be utilized with generalizations of the PSP level and apply it for generating theorems with *SGCD*.

7.1 Proof Patterns with Combinatory Definitions

When enumerating proof terms, allowing arbitrary combinators in any position can excessively increase the number of proof terms. Thus, we consider mechanisms to allow only combinators from a given set, and only in given contexts.

A *proof pattern* p/k is characterized by a function symbol p with arity $k > 0$, and an associated combinator c, which determines semantics: For proof terms $d_1, \ldots, d_k$, the MGT of $p(d_1, \ldots, d_k)$ is the MGT of the corresponding instance $\mathsf{D}(\mathsf{D}(\mathsf{D}(c, d_1), d_2), \ldots, d_k)$ of the pattern's *combinatory definition*, taking as MGT of c its principal type. Proof terms are then formed from proof pattern functions instead of D. By rewriting patterns with their combinatory definition, they can be converted to proof terms with D as only function symbol and combinators in axiom position. E.g., let *Patterns* $= \{\mathsf{p}_1/2, \mathsf{p}_2/2\}$, where p_1 is associated with **B**, and p_2 with **I**. The following DAG grammar then represents a proof term.

$$\{4 \rightarrow \mathsf{p}_1(1,1),\ \mathit{Start} \rightarrow \mathsf{p}_2(4, \mathsf{p}_2(4, \mathsf{p}_2(4,1)))\} \tag{5}$$

By rewriting $\mathsf{p}_1(V_1, V_2)$ with $\mathsf{D}(\mathsf{D}(\mathbf{B}, V_1), V_2)$, the combinatory definition of p_1, and $\mathsf{p}_2(V_1, V_2)$ with $\mathsf{D}(V_1, V_2)$, we obtain (3) in Sect. 4.2. For rewriting p_2 we used $\mathsf{D}(V_1, V_2)$, obtained by combinator reduction from the longer combinatory definition $\mathsf{D}(\mathsf{D}(\mathbf{I}, V_1), V_2)$.

To convert a proof term with combinators to one with only original axioms, combinators can be rewritten with their reduction rules, as shown with (4), which may lead to exponential increase of compacted size. A possibility to eliminate combinators with linear increase opens up if their principal types can be proven from original axioms: occurrences of combinators in proof terms can then be replaced by proofs of their principal type. This holds for our axioms from Table 1, where proofs of **K** and **S** are directly available as axioms 1 and 2. E.g, the principal type of **B** is $(x \Rightarrow y) \Rightarrow ((z \Rightarrow x) \Rightarrow (z \Rightarrow y))$ and is the MGT of $\mathsf{D}(\mathsf{D}(2, \mathsf{D}(1,2)), 1)$. Or, in other words, **B** can be defined as **S**(**KS**)**K**. Hence, the production $4 \rightarrow \mathsf{D}(\mathsf{D}(\mathbf{B}, 1), 1)$ in (3) can be converted to $4 \rightarrow \mathsf{D}(\mathsf{D}(\mathsf{D}(\mathsf{D}(2, \mathsf{D}(1,2)), 1), 1), 1)$.

A third possibility for linearly eliminating combinators is by conversion to a tree grammar [22,23,49]. We do not pursue this here but note an observation: Since conversion of a tree grammar to a proof with combinators is essentially λ to SKI conversion, which can be performed in linear time and with linear size increase [17], it follows that if the principal types of the combinators can be proven from the original axioms, then the size of a tree grammar compression can improve at most linearly over the size of the minimal DAG compression.

7.2 The PSP Level for Proof Schemas

We assume a finite set Ax of axiom identifiers. For proof terms built from proof patterns, we generalize the inductive characterization of the PSP level as follows.

Definition 3 (The PSP Level for Proof Patterns). *Assume a finite set Patterns of proof patterns. Define the PSP level for proof patterns as*

$$\begin{aligned}
\mathcal{PP}_0 &\stackrel{\text{def}}{=} Ax;\\
\mathcal{PP}_{n+1} &\stackrel{\text{def}}{=} \{p(d_1, \ldots, d_{i-1}, d_i, d_{i+1} \ldots, d_k) \mid \\
&\qquad p/k \in \mathit{Patterns},\ i \in \{1, \ldots, k\},\ d_i \in \mathcal{PP}_n,\\
&\qquad \mathit{for}\ j \in \{1, \ldots, k\} \setminus \{i\}\ .\ d_j \in \mathsf{Subterms}(d_i) \cup Ax\}.
\end{aligned}$$

We also consider a second generalization, where, in addition to proof patterns, *direct proof schemas*, proof terms $\mathsf{D}(\mathsf{D}(\mathsf{D}(c, V_1), V_2), \ldots, V_k)$ representing combinatory definitions of patterns can be constituents of proof terms. A direct proof schema c/k is characterized by a combinator c and an arity $k > 0$. Direct subterms of a pattern instance $p(d_1, \ldots, d_k)$ are the arguments $d_1, \ldots, d_k$, while

Table 10. Runs of *SGCD* with level characterization $\mathcal{PP}$ for the specified patterns. The last three rows refer to unions of runs.

C_1	$\mathcal{PP}$	19	379	1	$\mathsf{I}/2, \mathsf{B_4}, \mathsf{C}, \mathsf{C_4}, \mathsf{S_4}$	133k	13k	20	540	7.00	2,280k
C_2	$\mathcal{PP}$	15	363	5	$\mathsf{I}/2, \mathsf{B_4}, \mathsf{C}, \mathsf{S}$	67k	10k	51	3,473	56.08	2,508k
C_3	$\mathcal{PP}$	14	397	2	$\mathsf{I}/2, \mathsf{B_4}, \mathsf{C_4}, \mathsf{B}$	133k	13k	27	1,166	14.30	2,976k
C_4	$\mathcal{PP}$	13	403	2	$\mathsf{I}/2, \mathsf{B_4}, \mathsf{C}, \mathsf{B}, \mathsf{S_4}$	133k	13k	48	1,609	31.96	2,651k
C_5	$\mathcal{PP}$	12	407	3	$\mathsf{I}/2, \mathsf{B_4}, \mathsf{C}, \mathsf{S}$	200k	20k	25	1,261	17.13	4,092k
C_6	$\mathcal{PP}$	10	397	3	$\mathsf{I}/2, \mathsf{B_4}, \mathsf{C}, \mathsf{C_4}$	533k	53k	14	1,162	15.62	5,783k
C_7	$\mathcal{PP}$	9	383	0	$\mathsf{I}/2, \mathsf{C_4}, \mathsf{S}$	133k	13k	20	603	8.96	2,234k
C_8	$\mathcal{PP}$	5	301	0	$\mathsf{I}/2, \mathsf{C}, \mathsf{S}$	200k	20k	20	317	3.16	1,453k
C_9	$\mathcal{PP}$	2	320	0	$\mathsf{I}/2, \mathsf{B_4}(\mathsf{C_4C})$	80k	8k	17	937	20.24	1,127k
C_{10}	$\mathcal{PP}$	26	213	0	$\mathsf{B_4}, \mathsf{C_4}$	267k	27k	21	1,348	19.38	4,462k
C_{11}	$\mathcal{PP}$	14	228	1	$\mathsf{B_4}, \mathsf{C_4}$	400k	40k	18	1,588	19.59	5,916k
C_{12}	$\mathcal{PP}$	12	182	0	B, C	200k	20k	20	261	2.78	1,319k
C_{13}	$\mathcal{PP}$	11	362	1	$\mathsf{B}, \mathsf{B_4}, \mathsf{C}, \mathsf{C_4C}$	133k	13k	19	513	7.83	2,125k
C_{14}	$\mathcal{PP}$	4	197	0	$\mathsf{B}, \mathsf{C_4}, \mathsf{S}, \mathsf{S_4}$	133k	13k	20	417	4.68	1,940k
C_{15}	$\mathcal{PP}$	3	263	0	$\mathsf{B_4B}$	100k	10k	12	185	3.12	882k
C_{1-9}		50	525	6							
C_{10-15}		46	443	1							
C_{1-15}		85	567	6							

for a direct schema instance $\mathsf{D}(\mathsf{D}(\mathsf{D}(c, d_1), d_2), \ldots, d_k)$ also c itself and applications of c to any prefix of the arguments, i.e., terms $\mathsf{D}(\mathsf{D}(\mathsf{D}(c, d_1), d_2), \ldots, d_i)$ for $i < k$, are strict subterms.

Definition 4 (Characterization by PSP Level with Proof Schemas). *Assume a finite set Schemas of proof patterns and direct proof schemas. Define the PSP level with proof schemas as*

$$\mathcal{PK}_0 \stackrel{def}{=} Ax;$$

$$\begin{aligned}\mathcal{PK}_{n+1} \stackrel{def}{=} & \{\mathsf{D}(d, e) \mid d \in \mathcal{PK}_n,\ e \in \mathit{Subterms}(d) \cup Ax\} \\ & \cup \{\mathsf{D}(d, e) \mid e \in \mathcal{PK}_n,\ d \in \mathit{Subterms}(e) \cup Ax\} \\ & \cup \{t[d_1, \ldots, d_k] \mid t/k \in \mathit{Schemas},\ \mathit{for}\ i \in \{1, \ldots, k\}\ .\ d_i \in \mathcal{PK}_n \cup Ax\},\end{aligned}$$

where if t/k is a proof pattern p/k, then $t[d_1, \ldots, d_k] = p(d_1, \ldots, d_k)$, and if t/k is a direct schema c/k, then $t[d_1, \ldots, d_k] = \mathsf{D}(\mathsf{D}(\mathsf{D}(c, d_1), d_2), \ldots, d_k)$.

7.3 Theorem Generation with *SGCD* and Proof Schemas

Table 11. Runs of *SGCD* with level characterization $\mathcal{PK}$ for the specified schemas. The last four rows refer to unions of runs, now also considering S_{1-13} from Table 8.

RunId	*L*	*NB*	*POI*	*1*	*Schemas*	*GMax*	TRIM	*Lev*	*Time*	*Mem*	*Gen*
C_{16}	$\mathcal{PK}$	6	209	0	**B**, **C**, **S**, $\mathbf{S_4}$	200k	20k	9	950	12.9	1,366k
C_{17}	$\mathcal{PK}$	5	190	0	**B**, $\mathbf{B_4}$, **S**	133k	13k	12	2,716	50.42	1,305k
C_{18}	$\mathcal{PK}$	17	223	0	*d* **B**, $\mathbf{B_4}$, $\mathbf{C_4}$, **S**	133k	13k	10	2,632	45.59	1,066k
C_{19}	$\mathcal{PK}$	6	235	0	*d* **B**, $\mathbf{S_4}$	44k	4k	12	1,482	28.29	403k
C_{20}	$\mathcal{PK}$	12	413	1	*d* **B**/1, **C**/1, $\mathbf{C_4}$/1, $\mathbf{S_4}$/1	400k	40k	20	341	3.47	1,685k
C_{21}	$\mathcal{PK}$	9	332	1	*d* $\mathbf{C_4}(\mathbf{C_4}(\mathbf{C_4}(\mathbf{C_4}\mathbf{C})))/1$	400k	40k	20	782	7.30	3,146k
C_{22}	$\mathcal{PK}$	7	360	0	*d* $\mathbf{B_4}(\mathbf{C_4}\mathbf{C})/1$	400k	40k	20	515	4.91	2,228k
C_{16-22}		45	503	1							
C_{1-22}		116	633	6							
B, C_{1-22}		116	670	10							
B, S_{1-13}, C_{1-22}		180	734	12							

To get initial sets of combinators that seem useful as proof schemas we analyzed *set.mm* [46, App. G]. Following [29], we considered as primitive combinators **S**, **K**, **I**, **B**, **C**, $\mathbf{S_4}$, $\mathbf{B_4}$, $\mathbf{C_4}$. The latter (called **S'**, $\mathbf{B^*}$, **C'** in [29]) are defined as follows.

	λ-Term	*Principal Type*
$\mathbf{S_4}$	$\lambda V_1 V_2 V_3 V_4 .\ \mathsf{D}(\mathsf{D}(V_1, \mathsf{D}(V_2, V_4)), \mathsf{D}(V_3, V_4))$	$(x \Rightarrow (y \Rightarrow z)) \Rightarrow ((u \Rightarrow x) \Rightarrow ((u \Rightarrow y) \Rightarrow (u \Rightarrow z)))$
$\mathbf{B_4}$	$\lambda V_1 V_2 V_3 V_4 . \mathsf{D}(V_1, \mathsf{D}(V_2, \mathsf{D}(V_3, V_4)))$	$(x \Rightarrow y) \Rightarrow ((z \Rightarrow x) \Rightarrow ((u \Rightarrow z) \Rightarrow (u \Rightarrow y)))$
$\mathbf{C_4}$	$\lambda V_1 V_2 V_3 V_4 . \mathsf{D}(\mathsf{D}(V_1, \mathsf{D}(V_2, V_4)), V_3)$	$(x \Rightarrow (y \Rightarrow z)) \Rightarrow ((u \Rightarrow x) \Rightarrow (y \Rightarrow (u \Rightarrow z)))$

Table 10 summarizes *SGCD* runs with level characterization $\mathcal{PP}$. Members of *Patterns* are specified by their defining combinator. As arity, by default the standard arity of the combinator minus one is taken, where the *standard arity* is the minimal k such that application of the combinator to k arguments reduces to a term without the combinator. E.g., the standard arity of **B** and **C** is 3, and that of $\mathbf{B_4}$, $\mathbf{C_4}$ and $\mathbf{S_4}$ is 4. Hence, e.g., the default arity for a pattern with defining combinator **B** is 2. The standard arity of **I** is 1. We use **I** as pattern with arity 2 to express D, as in (5) above. Both, runs with **I**/2 and without it, yield proofs of largely disjoint sets of *POI* theorems not in *POI-base*, 85 in total.

Table 11 summarizes *SGCD* runs with level characterization $\mathcal{PK}$. Members of *Schemas* are patterns as specified for Table 10, or, indicated by *d*, direct proof schemas, specified analogously by the combinator. In runs of Tables 10 and 11 REST is set to `dup` and to `gen_max` with value *GMax*, ORD is `f_th`, and POST is `subs`. As in the experiments described in Sect. 6.2, runs were chosen from a larger test set such that taken together they prove a large number of *POI* theorems not in *POI-base*. Runs with $\mathcal{PK}$ yield proofs of further such theorems, such that in total the runs with combinatory proof schemas contribute proofs for 116 *POI* theorems not in *POI-base*. Together with the results of lemma synthesis from Sect. 6.2, we finally have generated proofs for 734 of the 1,374 *POI* theorems, including 12 with rating 1. Those with rating 1 are re-inspected in [46, App. H]. Details for each *POI* theorem are given in [46, App. I].

8 Conclusion

To study generating theorems from given axioms, we extracted 1,374 theorems from *set.mm* as a benchmark, and developed techniques that could generate 734 of these. Our synthesized lemmas significantly improved solution rates of automated provers on proving problems for the benchmark theorems. Our approach is centered on proof structures as terms, which are enumerated and compressed, differently from most works with similar aims, which are centered on formulas, e.g., [2,3,13,41,52]. An early exception is work by Stephan Schulz [9,35], where, essentially, save-values in a proof DAG identify important steps. This and other measures based on proof graphs were later investigated with large *HOL light* corpora for lemma synthesis and premise selection [16].

Our uses of proof term compression call for further studies of DAGs vs. tree grammars, detecting combinatory schemas in *set.mm*, and investigating specific combinatory schemas. With *inductive level characterizations* we presented an abstract framework and a family of practical proving techniques, reimagining proving by proof enumeration, which seems worth further investigation. Follow-up tasks with the *SGCD* system include iteration and combination of presented techniques, automated parameter calibration, and experiments with it as prover, utilizing the interplay of top-down and bottom-up processing.

Although, so far, our experiments were limited to the fundamentals of *set.mm*, its axioms for propositional logic, our techniques and implementation are ready for other axioms, arbitrary first-order Horn formulas. Predicate logic in *set.mm* would require more: a second function in proof terms [27], and axioms that seem to benefit from adapting equality handling of saturation-based provers.

Essential for our approach are proof terms with a most general theorem. For resolution, this seems possible if proofs are constrained [20] or transformed [18, Lemma 4.1.3] such that final steps are for goals. Another path to resolution would be simulation by combinators in proof terms [43], related to [11].

For automated proving that involves machine learning with proof structures [32,33,50], our work provides a foundation, an implemented infrastructure, and a yardstick for comparison with capabilities of symbolic techniques.

Acknowledgments. The author would like to thank Zsolt Zombori for the fruitful exchange during work on this project, Tim Richter for technical support, and anonymous reviewers for helpful suggestions to improve the presentation.

Funded by the Deutsche Forschungsgemeinschaft (DFG, German Research Foundation) – Project-ID 457292495. The author gratefully acknowledges the computing time granted by the Resource Allocation Board and provided on the supercomputer Emmy/Grete at NHR-Nord@Göttingen as part of the NHR infrastructure. The calculations for this research were conducted with computing resources under the project `nhr_bb_test_proof_structures`.

References

1. Aho, A.V., Sethi, R., Ullman, J.D.: Compilers – Principles, Techniques, and Tools. Addison-Wesley (1986)
2. Alhessi, Y., et al.: Lemmanaid: neuro-symbolic lemma conjecturing. CoRR abs/2504.04942 (2025). https://doi.org/10.48550/ARXIV.2504.04942
3. Axelrod, G., Dubhashi, D., Johansson, M., Silvi, A., Smallbone, N., Stucki, S.: Learning to generate abstractions for an equational solver. In: Douglas, M.R., Hales, T.C., Kaliszyk, C., Schulz, S., Urban, J. (eds.) AITP 2025 (Informal Book of Abstracts) (2025). https://aitp-conference.org/2025/abstract/AITP_2025_paper_18.pdf. Accessed 8 May 2026
4. Bibel, W.: Automated Theorem Proving. Vieweg (1987). First edition 1982
5. Bibel, W., Otten, J.: From Schütte's formal systems to modern automated deduction. In: Kahle, R., Rathjen, M. (eds.) The Legacy of Kurt Schütte, chap. 13, pp. 215–249. Springer (2020). https://doi.org/10.1007/978-3-030-49424-7_13
6. Blaauwbroek, L., et al.: Learning guided automated reasoning: a brief survey. In: Capretta, V., Krebbers, R., Wiedijk, F. (eds.) Logics and Type Systems in Theory and Practice - Essays Dedicated to Herman Geuvers on The Occasion of His 60th Birthday. LNCS, vol. 14560, pp. 54–83. Springer (2024). https://doi.org/10.1007/978-3-031-61716-4_4
7. Carneiro, M., Brown, C.E., Urban, J.: Automated theorem proving for Metamath. In: Naumowicz, A., Thiemann, R. (eds.) ITP 2023. LIPIcs, vol. 268, pp. 9:1–9:19. Schloss Dagstuhl – Leibniz-Zentrum für Informatik (2023). https://doi.org/10.4230/LIPIcs.ITP.2023.9
8. Curry, H., Feys, R.: Combinatory Logic, vol. I. North-Holland (1958)
9. Denzinger, J., Schulz, S.: Analysis and Representation of Equational Proofs Generated by a Distributed Completion Based Proof System. Seki-Report SR-94-05, Universität Kaiserslautern (1994). http://wwwlehre.dhbw-stuttgart.de/~sschulz/PAPERS/DS94-SR-94-05.ps.gz. Revised September 1997
10. Eder, E.: Relative Complexities of First Order Calculi. Vieweg, Braunschweig (1992). https://doi.org/10.1007/978-3-322-84222-0
11. Eder, E.: A comparison of the resolution calculus and the connection method, and a new calculus generalizing both methods. In: Börger, E., Büning, H.K., Richter, M.M. (eds.) CSL 1988. LNCS, vol. 385, pp. 80–98. Springer, Heidelberg (1989). https://doi.org/10.1007/BFb0026296
12. Genitrini, A., Gittenberger, B., Kauers, M., Wallner, M.: Asymptotic enumeration of compacted binary trees of bounded right height. J. Comb. Theory, Ser. A **172**, 105177 (2020). https://doi.org/10.1016/j.jcta.2019.105177
13. Hetzl, S.: Applying tree languages in proof theory. In: Dediu, A.H., Martín-Vide, C. (eds.) LATA 2012. LNCS, vol. 7183, pp. 301–312 (2012) .https://doi.org/10.1007/978-3-642-28332-1_26
14. Hindley, J.R.: Basic simple type theory. Cambridge University Press (1997). https://doi.org/10.1017/CBO9780511608865
15. Hindley, J.R., Meredith, D.: Principal type-schemes and condensed detachment. J. Symb. Log. **55**(1), 90–105 (1990). https://doi.org/10.2307/2274956
16. Kaliszyk, C., Urban, J.: Learning-assisted theorem proving with millions of lemmas. J. Symb. Comput. **69**, 109–128 (2015). https://doi.org/10.1016/J.JSC.2014.09.032
17. Kiselyov, O.: λ to SKI, Semantically. In: Gallagher, J.P., Sulzmann, M. (eds.) FLOPS 2018. LNCS, vol. 10818, pp. 33–50. Springer, Cham (2018). https://doi.org/10.1007/978-3-319-90686-7_3

18. Kleine Büning, H., Lettmann, T.: Propositional Logic – Deduction and Algorithms. Cambridge University Press (1999)
19. Kovács, L., Voronkov, A.: First-order theorem proving and Vampire. In: Sharygina, N., Veith, H. (eds.) CAV 2013. LNCS, vol. 8044, pp. 1–35. Springer (2013). https://doi.org/10.1007/978-3-642-39799-8_1
20. Lee, R.C.T.: A completeness theorem and computer program for finding theorems derivable from given axioms. Ph.D. thesis, University of California, Berkeley, CA (1967)
21. Letz, R.: Tableau and Connection Calculi. Structure, Complexity, Implementation. Habilitationsschrift, TU München (1999). https://web.archive.org/web/20230604101128/https://www2.tcs.ifi.lmu.de/~letz/habil.ps. Accessed 8 May 2026
22. Lohrey, M.: Grammar-based tree compression. In: Potapov, I. (ed.) DLT 2015. LNCS, vol. 9168, pp. 46–57. Springer, Cham (2015). https://doi.org/10.1007/978-3-319-21500-6_3
23. Lohrey, M., Maneth, S., Mennicke, R.: XML tree structure compression using RePair. Inf. Syst. **38**(8), 1150–1167 (2013). https://doi.org/10.1016/j.is.2013.06.006
24. McCune, W.: Prover9 and Mace4 (2005–2010). http://www.cs.unm.edu/~mccune/prover9
25. Megill, N., Wheeler, D.A.: Metamath: A Computer Language for Mathematical Proofs. lulu.com, second edn. (2019). https://us.metamath.org/downloads/metamath.pdf
26. Megill, N.D.: Metamath Proof Explorer Home Page. https://us.metamath.org/mpeuni/mmset.html. Accessed 8 May 2026
27. Megill, N.D.: A finitely axiomatized formalization of predicate calculus with equality. Notre Dame J. of Formal Logic **36**(3), 435–453 (1995). https://doi.org/10.1305/ndjfl/1040149359
28. Otten, J.: Restricting backtracking in connection calculi. AI Commun. **23**(2–3), 159–182 (2010). https://doi.org/10.3233/AIC-2010-0464
29. Peyton Jones, S.L.: The Implementation of Functional Programming Languages. Prentice Hall (1987). https://simon.peytonjones.org/slpj-book-1987/
30. Pfenning, F.: Single axioms in the implicational propositional calculus. In: Lusk, E., Overbeek, R. (eds.) CADE 1988. LNCS, vol. 310, pp. 710–713. Springer, Heidelberg (1988). https://doi.org/10.1007/BFb0012869
31. Prior, A.N.: Logicians at play; or Syll, Simp and Hilbert. Australas. J. Philos. **34**(3), 182–192 (1956). https://doi.org/10.1080/00048405685200181
32. Rawson, M., Wernhard, C., Zombori, Z., Bibel, W.: Lemmas: Generation, selection, application. In: Ramanayake, R., Urban, J. (eds.) TABLEAUX 2023. LNAI, vol. 14278, pp. 153–174 (2023). https://doi.org/10.1007/978-3-031-43513-3_9
33. Rawson, M., Zombori, Z., Doré, M., Wernhard, C.: Project proposal: forward reasoning in hindsight. In: Douglas, M.R., Hales, T.C., Kaliszyk, C., Schulz, S., Urban, J. (eds.) AITP 2024 (Informal Book of Abstracts) (2024). https://aitp-conference.org/2024/abstract/AITP_2024_paper_6.pdf. Accessed 8 May 2026
34. Rezus, A.: Witness Theory - Notes on λ-Calculus and Logic, Studies in Logic, vol. 84. College Publications, London (2020)
35. Schulz, S.: Analyse und Transformation von Gleichheitsbeweisen. Projektarbeit in informatik, Fachbereich Informatik, Universität Kaiserslautern (1993). http://wwwlehre.dhbw-stuttgart.de/~sschulz/PAPERS/Sch93-project.ps.gz. (German Language)

36. Schulz, S., Cruanes, S., Vukmirović, P.: Faster, higher, stronger: E 2.3. In: Fontaine, P. (ed.) CADE 27, pp. 495–507. no. 11716 in LNAI, Springer (2019). https://doi.org/10.1007/978-3-030-29436-6_29
37. Schumann, J.M.P.: DELTA — A bottom-up preprocessor for top-down theorem provers. In: CADE-12. LNCS (LNAI), vol. 814, pp. 774–777. Springer (1994). https://doi.org/10.1007/3-540-58156-1_58
38. Schönfinkel, M.: Über die Bausteine der mathematischen Logik. Math. Ann. **92**(3–4), 305–316 (1924). https://doi.org/10.1007/BF01448013
39. Sutcliffe, G.: The TPTP problem library and associated infrastructure. From CNF to TH0, TPTP v6.4.0. J. Autom. Reasoning **59**(4), 483–502 (2017). https://doi.org/10.1007/S10817-009-9143-8
40. Ulrich, D.: A legacy recalled and a tradition continued. J. Autom. Reasoning **27**(2), 97–122 (2001). https://doi.org/10.1023/A:1010683508225
41. Vyskocil, J., Stanovský, D., Urban, J.: Automated proof compression by invention of new definitions. In: Clarke, E.M., Voronkov, A. (eds.) LPAR-16. LNCS, vol. 6355, pp. 447–462. Springer (2010). https://doi.org/10.1007/978-3-642-17511-4_25
42. Wernhard, C.: CD Tools. http://cs.christophwernhard.com/cdtools/. Accessed 8 May 2026
43. Wernhard, C.: Generating compressed combinatory proof structures — an approach to automated first-order theorem proving. In: Konev, B., Schon, C., Steen, A. (eds.) PAAR 2022. CEUR Workshop Proc., vol. 3201. CEUR-WS.org (2022). https://arxiv.org/abs/2209.12592
44. Wernhard, C.: Structure-generating first-order theorem proving. In: Otten, J., Bibel, W. (eds.) AReCCa 2023. CEUR Workshop Proceeding, vol. 3613, pp. 64–83. CEUR-WS.org (2024). https://ceur-ws.org/Vol-3613/AReCCa2023_paper5.pdf
45. Wernhard, C.: Generating theorems by generating proof structures – supplementary artifacts (2026). http://cs.christophwernhard.com/cdtools/exp-thgen/
46. Wernhard, C.: Generating theorems by generating proof structures (extended version). CoRR abs/2602.15511 (2026). https://arxiv.org/abs/2602.15511
47. Wernhard, C., Bibel, W.: Learning from Łukasiewicz and Meredith: investigations into proof structures. In: Platzer, A., Sutcliffe, G. (eds.) CADE 2021. LNCS (LNAI), vol. 12699, pp. 58–75. Springer, Cham (2021). https://doi.org/10.1007/978-3-030-79876-5_4
48. Wernhard, C., Bibel, W.: Investigations into proof structures. J. Autom. Reasoning **68**(24) (2024). https://doi.org/10.1007/s10817-024-09711-8
49. Wernhard, C., Zombori, Z.: Mathematical knowledge bases as grammar-compressed proof terms: exploring Metamath proof structures. CoRR abs/2505.12305 (2025). https://doi.org/10.48550/arXiv.2505.12305
50. Wernhard, C., Zombori, Z.: Are proof structures machine-learnable? a study with Dag-structured proof terms (2026). In preparation
51. Wielemaker, J., Schrijvers, T., Triska, M., Lager, T.: SWI-Prolog. Theory Pract. Logic Program. **12**(1–2), 67–96 (2012). https://doi.org/10.1017/S1471068411000494
52. Wos, L.: The resonance strategy. Comput. Math. Applic. **29**(2), 133–178 (1995). https://doi.org/10.1016/0898-1221(94)00220-F
53. Wos, L.: Conquering the Meredith single axiom. J. Autom. Reasoning **27**(2), 175–199 (2001). https://doi.org/10.1023/A:1010691726881

Open Access This chapter is licensed under the terms of the Creative Commons Attribution 4.0 International License (http://creativecommons.org/licenses/by/4.0/), which permits use, sharing, adaptation, distribution and reproduction in any medium or format, as long as you give appropriate credit to the original author(s) and the source, provide a link to the Creative Commons license and indicate if changes were made.

The images or other third party material in this chapter are included in the chapter's Creative Commons license, unless indicated otherwise in a credit line to the material. If material is not included in the chapter's Creative Commons license and your intended use is not permitted by statutory regulation or exceeds the permitted use, you will need to obtain permission directly from the copyright holder.

Twitch: Learning Abstractions for Equational Theorem Proving

Guy Axelrod[1,2], Moa Johansson[1,2], and Nicholas Smallbone[1,2](✉)

[1] Chalmers University of Technology, Göteborg, Sweden
{guya,jomoa,nicsma}@chalmers.se
[2] University of Gothenburg, Göteborg, Sweden

Abstract. Automated theorem provers often perform better when told what shapes of terms are interesting. In this paper we discover interesting term shapes automatically, in the form of *abstractions*, term patterns that occur over and over again in proofs. Our tool *Twitch* produces abstractions automatically and can do so in two ways: (1) from a partial, failed proof of a conjecture; (2) from successful proofs of other theorems in the same domain. Twitch is built on top of Stitch, a tool designed for discovering reusable library functions in program synthesis tasks. We have also extended Twee, an equational theorem prover, to use the generated abstractions. We evaluate Twitch on a set of unit equality (UEQ) problems from TPTP, and show that it proves problems previously unsolved by Twee, as well as yielding speed-ups on many other problems.

Keywords: automated theorem proving · equational theorem proving · completion · abstraction learning · proof-guided search

1 Introduction

Automated theorem provers must navigate a massive search space, choosing the useful inferences and discarding the useless ones. Modern provers therefore rely on sophisticated guidance mechanisms, including finely-tuned clause-selection heuristics [29], strategy portfolios [6], and learning-based guidance [11,17].

A complementary approach, popularized by Otter [22], is to inject human guidance about which *shapes* of terms or clauses are interesting. The user specifies a set of interesting shapes, and generated clauses that match these shapes are preferred over ones that do not. This idea originated in the *weighting strategy* [24] and was later refined by the *resonance strategy* [7,14,37] and *hint strategy* [33,34]. We are attempting to automate this by discovering interesting shapes automatically. We focus on equational reasoning, in particular, the equational prover Twee [30]. Compared with the highly tuned guidance mechanisms available in other ATPs, Twee's heuristics are rather simplistic, relying mostly on the size of the critical pair. This makes Twee a good setting in which to study whether automatically discovered term patterns can provide useful guidance.

© The Author(s) 2026
A. Biere et al. (Eds.): IJCAR 2026, LNAI 16688, pp. 62–79, 2026.
https://doi.org/10.1007/978-3-032-32589-1_4

To find interesting term shapes *automatically*, we analyse failed proof attempts and proofs of related conjectures to find term shapes which occur often, which we call *abstractions*. We have added support for abstractions to Twee, and with the help of automatically generated abstractions we are able to prove 12 rating-1[1] problems from the TPTP [32], as well as several other problems that Twee previously could not solve (see Sect. 5). Our contributions are:

- A method for automatically generating abstractions from an *unsuccessful attempt* to prove a conjecture (see Sect. 3.1). The idea is to pick out interesting lemmas from the proof attempt, and find patterns of terms that occur repeatedly in the proofs of those lemmas. To find the patterns we use the tool STITCH [10], which attempts to *compress* a set of terms (here from proofs) by introducing auxiliary function definitions as abbreviations.
- A method for generating abstractions from a corpus of successful proofs in the same domain, again using STITCH (see Sect. 3.2). The hypothesis is that patterns of terms that occur repeatedly in the proofs are often good abstractions for other conjectures in the same domain. The aim here is to create a methodology inspired by curriculum learning [8] for proving difficult equational problems: first prove some simpler problems in the same domain, abstract out common patterns appearing in those proofs, and use those abstractions to guide the proof of the difficult problem.
- An implementation of abstractions in the equational theorem prover Twee [30], inspired by the weighting strategy [24] (see Sect. 4).

The code for Twitch as well as all data and experimental results are supplied in the associated repository [1].

1.1 Motivating Example

Let us consider the problem `LAT075-1` from the TPTP, a problem about modular ortholattices in a language with a single function symbol f representing the Sheffer stroke (or NAND operator). The details of this problem are not important here, but what is relevant is that the same kind of term appears repeatedly in

[1] From the TPTP Technical Manual [31, Problem Presentation], the rating "gives the difficulty of the problem, measured relative to state-of-the-art ATP systems [...] The rating is a real number in the range 0.0 to 1.0, where 0.0 means that all state-of-the-art ATP systems can solve the problem [...] and 1.0 means no state-of-the-art ATP system can solve the problem".

the proof that Twee finds. Here is a short fragment of the proof:

$$\begin{aligned}
\ldots &= f(x, f(y, \boxed{f(f(z, \boxed{f(x,x)}), f(z, \boxed{f(x,x)}))}))\\
&= f(x, f(y, f(f(z, \boxed{f(x,x)}), f(\boxed{f(x,x)}, z))))\\
&= f(x, f(y, \boxed{f(f(\boxed{f(x,x)}, z), f(\boxed{f(x,x)}, z))}))\\
&= f(\boxed{f(\boxed{f(x,x)}, \boxed{f(x,x)})}, f(y, \boxed{f(f(\boxed{f(x,x)}, z), f(\boxed{f(x,x)}, z))}))
\end{aligned}$$

As we can see, terms of the form $f(t,t)$, which we have marked with a box above, appear over and over in the proof.[2] Our hypothesis is that *the same term shape* is likely to be common in proofs of other theorems about the Sheffer stroke.

This suggests the following basic approach to proving a difficult theorem. First we analyse a proof of a related theorem to find commonly occurring term patterns. Then, hoping that these term patterns might also occur in the proof of the difficult theorem, we ask the theorem prover to prefer inferences involving those term patterns. The remaining questions are, how can we find these commonly-occurring term patterns, and how can the prover exploit them?

To formalize the notion of *common patterns* in a proof, we imagine *compressing* the proof by introducing new definitions to abbreviate certain terms. For example, if we were to define $g(x) := f(x,x)$, then the proof above could be written more compactly; e.g. the first term could be written as $f(x, f(y, g(f(z, g(x)))))$. Then we ask: what is a *maximally compressive* set of abbreviations, that is, a set of definitions that allows us to express the proof terms as compactly as possible?

The tool STITCH [10] (see Sect. 2) is designed to answer exactly this question. Given a set of terms, it searches for the maximally compressive function definitions. Henceforth, we will call such function definitions *abstractions*. In this case, STITCH would find that $g(x) := f(x,x)$ is a maximally compressive abstraction (and when given the full proof, it also finds other useful abstractions, such as the AND operator $h(x,y) := f(f(x,y), f(x,y))$).

Once we have these abstractions, how can we use them to influence proof search? The simplest option is to add the function definition as an axiom, in this case $\forall x.\, g(x) = f(x,x)$. This allows the prover to rewrite terms of the form $f(t,t)$ to $g(t)$, making the term smaller, so that critical pairs containing the term are more likely to be selected. For `LAT075-1` this approach works well, and reduces the runtime of Twee from $\sim 250s$ to $\sim 10s$.

Adding definitional axioms that abbreviate useful term patterns is a known and useful technique.[3] However, adding new axioms also allows new inferences between them, thus expanding the search space. As we show in Sect. 5.3, adding more than a few such axioms harms the prover's performance.

[2] This is perhaps not so surprising as $f(t,t)$ represents the negation of t.

[3] For example, see the Robbins problem variant `ROB033-1` in the TPTP. Definitional axioms are also used in Twee's goal direction heuristic [30].

Instead, we have extended Twee to natively support abstractions (see Sect. 4). The abstractions influence the heuristic function of the prover, so that inferences matching them are more likely to be selected, but they do not alter the search space itself. Because of this, we can provide many more abstractions, but the individual abstractions may have a smaller effect. In this case, passing $f(x, x)$ as an abstraction reduces the runtime of Twee from $\sim 250s$ to $\sim 130s$.

2 Background: Stitch

STITCH [10] is a system originally designed for library learning in program synthesis – automatically discovering reusable function abstractions from an existing collection of programs. Given a set of terms as input, it constructs functions which generalize parts of the terms, and uses those functions to abbreviate the terms. STITCH attempts to construct *maximally compressive* abstractions; specifically, it maximizes the product of the size of the function and the number of places where the function can be used.

Although STITCH was designed to work on program code, it accepts as input any set of terms. Hence, given a Twee proof, we can give STITCH the set of all terms occurring in the proof and it will find abstractions for it.[4]

STITCH's input language is a higher-order λ-calculus. Thus, we need to translate proof terms into λ-terms, which we do by treating function symbols as constants, and λ-abstracting all free variables. For example, the term $f(x,\ f(y,\ f(f(z, f(x,x)),\ f(z, f(x,x)))))$ from our example is translated into $\lambda x.\lambda y.\lambda z.\ (f\ x\ (f\ y\ (f\ (f\ z\ (f\ x\ x))\ (f\ z\ (f\ x\ x)))))$. In this case, STITCH will return the abstraction $g(\alpha) := (f\ \alpha\ \alpha)$, where α is a *schematic parameter* standing for an arbitrary subterm, which can be used to compress the input term to $\lambda x.\lambda y.\lambda z.\ (f\ x\ (f\ y\ g(f\ z\ g(x))))$. Because the body of g has a first-order shape, it can be translated back directly, yielding the abstraction $f(x, x)$.

In general, STITCH abstractions are arbitrary λ-terms and can be higher-order. In practice, STITCH rarely generates higher-order abstractions in our setting since the input terms are first-order. If it does, we discard the abstraction.

3 Twee + Stitch = Twitch

In this section we present the implementation of Twitch: a system for automating the discovery of reusable abstractions that can be used to help solve hard problems in a given domain. Twitch has two modes of usage: abstractions can be discovered from partial proof attempts as described in Sect. 3.1, or from easier proofs in the same domain, as described in Sect. 3.2. The abstractions found by Twitch are used to adjust the search heuristics in the Twee prover, as described in Sect. 4.

Henceforth, we denote a given input problem – which consists of a set of equations (axioms) and a goal/conjecture equation to prove – by P.

[4] The terms given to STITCH are the top-level terms from Twee proof steps, but STITCH's compression procedure searches for repeated structure inside these terms.

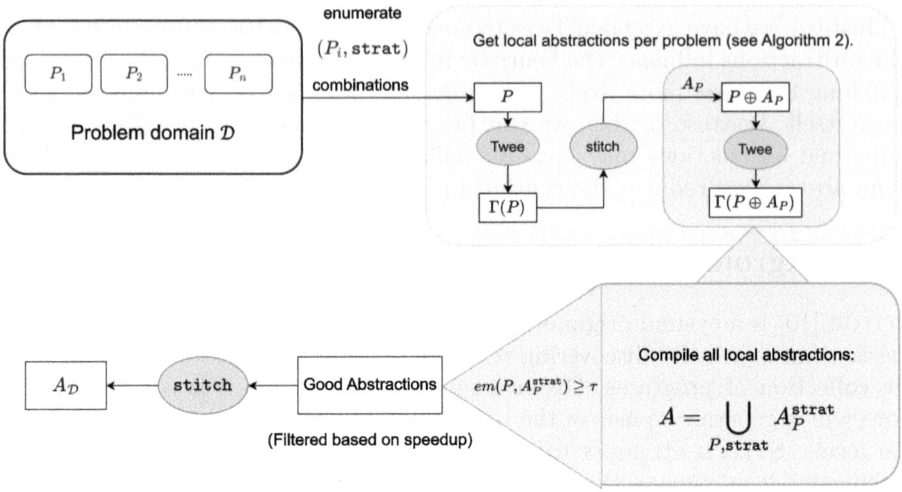

Fig. 1. Overview of domain abstraction generation via Twitch (Algorithm 1 and its subroutine Algorithm 2).

3.1 Abstractions from Partial Proofs

The first approach we explore discovers abstractions given as input a single hard problem P_h, and can be used when we do not have examples of related problems to learn from. We start by running Twee (without abstractions) on P_h for a fixed amount of time. When it times out, even though it has not proved the goal, it will have derived a large collection of rewrite rules. Each of these derived rules $l \to r$ corresponds to an equation $l = r$ about the theory we are exploring. Many of these equations will be quite boring, but some will represent interesting lemmas. Our idea is to learn abstractions from only the most interesting lemmas.

In order to define interestingness, we first need some auxiliary definitions. For any lemma $l = r$, we shall denote by $T(l = r)$ the set of terms occurring in its proof, including the proofs of any sub-lemmas used in the proof. More precisely, the proof of $l = r$ is a chain $l = t_1 = \ldots = t_n = r$, where each step may be justified by a lemma $l_i = r_i$ having its own proof. We then define $T(l = r) = \{l, t_1, \ldots, t_n, r\} \cup \bigcup_i T(l_i = r_i)$.

For a term t, we define its weight $|t|$ as the number of function applications plus the number of unique variables occurring in t. We extend this to equations by defining $|l = r| = |l| + |r|$, and to sets of terms T by defining $|T| = \sum_{t \in T} |t|$. We then define the "interestingness" $s(l = r)$ of a lemma as follows:

$$s(l = r) := \frac{|T(l = r)|}{|l = r|^2}.$$

The intuition is that lemmas with higher scores are those that are simple statements requiring a long proof. Of course this does not necessarily coincide with what a human would consider interesting or useful, but we take it as a rough heuristic towards measuring these notions.

Given a partial proof of P_h, we pick out the k lemmas with the greatest interestingness score, $l_1 = r_1, \ldots, l_k = r_k$. We then generate what we call *partial proof abstractions* by running STITCH on $\bigcup_{1 \leq i \leq k} T(l_i = r_i)$. We can then rerun Twee on P_h augmented with these abstractions.

3.2 Domain Abstractions

The goal of this approach is to learn abstractions that are useful for proving problems in a particular domain $\mathcal{D}$. We require a set of problems, some of which are already proved (the "easy" problems) and some of which are not (the "hard" problems). The algorithm works as follows:

1. First, we use STITCH on the proofs of the easy problems to find abstractions for each problem. These abstractions are *local*, i.e. specific to one problem.
2. Then, we augment each problem with its local abstractions and re-run Twee to test if the abstractions are *good*, i.e. allow us to reprove the problem faster.
3. Finally, we build a set of all the good local abstractions, and compress it with STITCH to find commonalities and derive higher-level *domain abstractions.*

This process is illustrated in Fig. 1, with pseudocode in Algorithm 1. There, we use $T(\Gamma(P))$ to denote the set of terms occurring in the proof $\Gamma(P)$ of problem P found by Twee. The set of abstractions derived by running STITCH on $T(\Gamma(P))$ (where $\Gamma(P)$ was found using a specific Twee strategy `strat`) is denoted by $A_P^{\texttt{strat}}$. We use $P \oplus A$ to denote P augmented with abstractions A. Finally, the local abstractions are filtered by an effect metric *em* which measures the speedup obtained by augmenting the problem with the abstraction. More precisely,

$$em(P, A) = \frac{t(\Gamma(P))}{t(\Gamma(P \oplus A))},$$

where $t(\Gamma(P))$ denotes the time taken by Twee to find proof $\Gamma(P)$. Only those abstractions that lead to a speedup above some threshold τ are added to the set of good abstractions.

We see that growing the good abstraction set relies on running the LOCAL-ABSTRACTIONS subroutine for a collection of different *strategies.* This simply refers to an assignment of specific values to parameters that influence the working of Twee. In particular, the strategy parameters are (1) whether to run Twee with or without its *goal flattening* option [30] and (2) the abstraction weight factor (see Sect. 4.1). By iterating over combinations of these parameters, we increase the pool of good abstractions to derive domain abstractions from later.

We can then use these domain abstractions to augment hard problems in the same domain, with one caveat: some abstractions may mention functions that do not occur in the hard problem, and these are removed.

Algorithm 1.

procedure DomainAbstractions($\mathcal{D}$)
  good_absts ← empty set
  for all combinations of $P \in \mathcal{D}$ and strat $\in$ strategies **do**
    $A_P^{\texttt{strat}}, em(P, A_P^{\texttt{strat}}) \leftarrow$ LocalAbstractions(P, strat)
    if $em(P, A_P^{\texttt{strat}}) \geq \tau$ **then**
      Add the alpha-normalized $A_P^{\texttt{strat}}$ to good_absts
    end if
  end for
  $\mathcal{D} \leftarrow$ Run Stitch over good_absts
  Return $\mathcal{D}$
end procedure

Algorithm 2.

procedure LocalAbstractions(P, strat)
  Run Twee on P with strat.
  If it fails to terminate within the time limit, return failure.
  Else we get proof $\Gamma(P)$.
  Extract terms from $\Gamma(P)$ as strings to get list $T(\Gamma(P))$.
  Run Stitch on $T(\Gamma(P))$ to get abstractions $A_P^{\texttt{strat}}$.
  Run Twee on $P \oplus A_P^{\texttt{strat}}$ with strat.
  Compute $em(P, A_P^{\texttt{strat}})$. If Twee timed out on $P \oplus A_P^{\texttt{strat}}$, set $em(P, A_P^{\texttt{strat}}) = 0$.
  Return $A_P^{\texttt{strat}}$, $em(P, A_P^{\texttt{strat}})$.
end procedure

4 Supporting Abstractions in Twee

Twee's architecture is based on *unfailing completion* [5,21], which works by treating the input equations as rewrite rules and then deriving new rules that cannot be proved by forward rewriting. For example, given some axioms about group theory, Twee might orient them into the following rules:

$$e \cdot x \to x \qquad x^{-1} \cdot x \to e \qquad (x \cdot y) \cdot z \to x \cdot (y \cdot z)$$

We can observe that the term $(x^{-1} \cdot x) \cdot y$ has two normal forms:

$$(x^{-1} \cdot x) \cdot y \to e \cdot y \to y \qquad (x^{-1} \cdot x) \cdot y \to x^{-1} \cdot (x \cdot y),$$

hence the equation $x^{-1} \cdot (x \cdot y) = y$ is true but cannot be proved by forward rewriting, since both sides are normal forms (this is called a *critical pair*). Twee therefore adds the new rewrite rule $x^{-1} \cdot (x \cdot y) \to y$. This process of deriving new rewrite rules continues until the rule set is saturated or the goal is proved.

The number of critical pairs is typically quadratic in the number of rewrite rules [16, Section 2.2], and may reach $\sim 10^{10}$ in a longer proof attempt. Hence, rather than turning all critical pairs into rules, Twee repeatedly picks the "best" critical pair and turns it into a rule (following a DISCOUNT loop [4]). To judge the goodness of a critical pair, Twee first normalizes it with respect to the existing rewrite rules, then computes a score for the resulting equation. The score has several components (see [30]) but the most important one is the equation's *weight*, defined as the number of symbols in the equation:

$$w(t = u) = w(t) + w(u)$$
$$w(x) = 1, \text{ if } x \text{ is a variable}$$
$$w(F(t_1, \ldots, t_n)) = 1 + \sum_{i=1}^{n} w(t_i), \text{ if } F \text{ is a function symbol}$$

Our approach to abstractions is inspired by the *weighting strategy* [24]: whenever a term or subterm in a critical pair matches an abstraction, reduce its computed weight. Specifically, we extend w with the following clause:

$$w(A\sigma) = w_A + \sum_{x \in dom(\sigma)} w(x\sigma), \text{ if } A \text{ is an abstraction and } \sigma \text{ is a substitution}$$

Here, w_A is a constant representing the weight of the abstraction. We come back to this in Sect. 4.1, but for now, let us assume that $w_A = 1$.

For example, suppose we are studying two functions *times* and *plus*. To encourage the prover to reason about distributivity, we might give the following abstraction A, representing a term in which distributivity can be applied.

$$\mathit{plus}(\mathit{times}(x, y), \mathit{times}(x, z))$$

Now suppose that the following equation occurs as a critical pair:

$$\mathit{times}(c, \underline{\mathit{plus}(\mathit{times}(g(f(a), b), f(x)), \mathit{times}(g(f(a), b), g(y, z)))}) = g(a, b)$$

Without the abstraction A, this equation would have a weight of 21. With A, the underlined term can be matched as $A\sigma$, where $\sigma = \{x \mapsto g(f(a), b),\ y \mapsto f(x), z \mapsto g(y, z)\}$. Hence the total weight is $1 + w(c) + w(A\sigma) + w(g(a, b)) = 2 + w_A + w(g(f(a), b)) + w(f(x)) + w(g(y, z)) + 3 = 15$. The lesser weight means that this critical pair will be selected sooner.

Note that A reduces the equation's weight in two ways: (1) the abstraction's "skeleton", $\mathit{plus}(\mathit{times}(\_, \_), \mathit{times}(\_, \_))$, only counts for weight 1 instead of 3; (2) although x occurs twice in the abstraction, $x\sigma$ is only counted once, hence the repeated subterm $g(f(a), b)$ is only counted once. Property (2) is vital in order for abstractions to act like *abbreviations*. For example, in Sect. 1.1 we define the abstraction $f(x, x)$, where f is the Sheffer stroke, which represents the negation of x. Property (2) ensures that $f(t, t)$ has the same weight as a hypothetical term $\mathit{not}(t)$.

As an aside, we have also implemented term-level *resonators* [37] in Twee. These work just the same as abstractions, except that they only match if every variable in σ is mapped to a variable (not a compound term).

4.1 The Cost of an Abstraction

Above we assumed that the weight w_A of an abstraction was 1. In fact, we allow the user to choose how w_A is computed. There are two strategies, both parametrized on a user-specified constant k: *(1) Constant weight:* Every abstraction A has the same weight, $w_A = k$. *(2) Weight factor:* We set $w_A = k\, w_{skel}(A)$, where $w_{skel}(A)$ is the weight of A if all variables are counted as weight 0. In the example above, $w_{skel}(A) = 3$. This gives larger abstractions greater weight.

4.2 Implementing Hints using Rewriting

We can implement w efficiently using ideas from term rewriting. Let us call the original weighting function, without the $w(A\sigma)$ clause, w_0. First, for each abstraction $A := t[x_1, \ldots .x_n]$, we introduce a fresh function symbol $A_t(x_1, \ldots, x_n)$. Then, to weigh a critical pair, we first *replace* any term of the form $t[u_1, \ldots, u_n]$ with $A_t(u_1, \ldots, u_n)$, and then weigh the result using w_0. For the example above, if we call the abstraction function A, replacement produces the following term:

$$\mathit{times}(c, A(g(f(a), b), f(x), g(y, z))) = g(a, b)$$

and we can see that its weight according to w_0 is indeed 15. We can see this as *normalizing* the critical pair with respect to the following rewrite rule:

$$\mathit{plus}(\mathit{times}(x, y), \mathit{times}(x, z)) \to A(x, y, z)$$

and this is in fact how Twee implements it. The function w transforms the abstractions into a set of rules like the one above, and normalizes the critical pair with respect to those rules before weighing it.[5] Hence we can use Twee's term indexing machinery to efficiently handle large numbers of abstractions.

We have not specified what happens if a term matches multiple abstractions. This is determined by the particulars of Twee's normalization algorithm. This uses outermost reduction, and prefers more specific to more general matches.

5 TPTP Experiments

We have evaluated Twitch on a set of unsatisfiable unit equality (UEQ) problems from TPTP v9.2.1 [32]. The problems are drawn from nine TPTP domains, summarized in Table 1. The main purpose is to measure whether the abstractions discovered by Twitch help in solving problems from the TPTP.

Section 5.1 measures whether partial proof abstractions and domain abstractions improve Twee's runtime. For domain abstractions, the user must define which problems make up the domain; in our experiments (with one exception

[5] Note that these rules are purely internal to w and are not added to the clause set. The normalized term is thrown away after w is done with it.

mentioned in Sect. 5.2), we considered the domain to be the set of problems in a given TPTP domain (e.g. Group Theory (GRP), Lattice Theory (LAT), etc.)

Section 5.2 reports on the hard problems solved using abstractions from Twitch. We define a problem as hard if it has TPTP rating at least 0.9 (i.e. 90% of ATPs cannot solve it within 300 s) and Twee (without abstractions) cannot solve it within 1000 s. There are 70 such problems from Table 1.

Section 5.3 considers various ablations testing some aspects of Twitch's architecture and strategies.

Table 1. Unsatisfiable UEQ problems per TPTP domain, TPTP v9.2.1

Domain	Count
ALG (General Algebra)	20
BOO (Boolean Algebra)	56
COL (Combinatory Logic)	120
GRP (Group Theory)	481
LAT (Lattice Theory)	126
LCL (Logic Calculi)	84
REL (Relation Algebra)	81
RNG (Ring Theory)	48
ROB (Robbins Algebra)	25
Total	1041

5.1 Overall Runtime Improvements

Figs. 2a and 2b include cactus plots of runtimes of Twee on the TPTP problems listed in Table 1. We benchmark Twee both with and without its *goal flattening* strategy [30], in order to see how this strategy interacts with abstractions. In both figures, the 'Twee (flat)' and 'Twee (no flat)' plots show Twee running without abstractions (with and without goal flattening respectively) for the full time limit of 1000 s. We have plotted a line at 300 s, a typical timeout for ATP benchmarking, but continue the evaluation until 1000 s.

Figure 2a shows the results for partial proof abstractions. Here, we first run Twee (without goal flattening) for 150 s, then if it times out, extract partial proof abstractions from the failed proof, and rerun Twee (with goal flattening) augmented with these abstractions for the remaining time.

Figure 2b shows the results when using domain abstractions. The 'Twee (flat)' and 'Twee (no flat)' show the performance of Twee without abstractions. 'Absts. (flat)' and 'Absts. (no flat)' show the performance of Twee once the abstractions are added. Unlike with partial proof abstractions, there is no time-slicing. The plot does not include the time to learn the abstractions for a given domain, as this is shared between all problems in the domain.

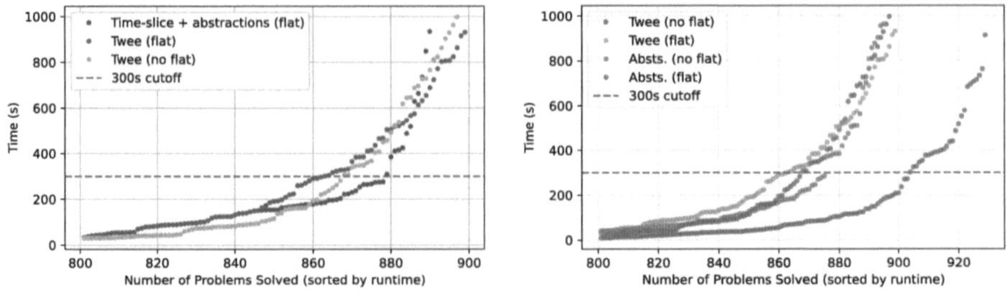

(a) Using partial proof abstractions. (b) Using domain abstractions.

Fig. 2. Cactus plots of Twee runtimes for TPTP problems. A given point in these plots corresponds to a particular problem P from Table 1. The y-value of a point indicates the time taken by Twee to find a proof of P (possibly augmented with Twitch domain abstractions), and the corresponding x-value is the index of P when the problems are sorted in increasing order of runtime.

We see that applying just domain abstractions to a problem results in a modest speedup, but also applying goal flattening leads to a large speedup, with roughly 25 more problems solved inside of 300 s. When comparing only the problems that baseline Twee could solve within 300 s, adding domain abstractions with goal flattening roughly halves the runtime. Hence domain abstractions seem to interact particularly well with goal flattening.

Partial proof abstractions provide some improvement in runtimes, and solve more problems after 300 s, but are not as effective as domain abstractions. However, they are still useful in many cases since they do not require any preprocessing to find the abstractions. They also have the advantage of being available for any problem, even those for which we have no other proofs to learn from.

5.2 Solving Hard Problems

Along with general runtime improvements, we find that adding Twitch abstractions allows us to prove 18 hard problems. As an additional baseline, we ran Vampire 5.0.1 on the 12 rating-1 problems solved by Twitch, using the same 1000 s timeout. Vampire solved only three of them—LCL375-10, LCL304-10, and LCL395-10—and was slower than Twitch in each case; the other nine timed out. We summarise the Twitch results here, and highlight some interesting cases.

Partial Proof Abstractions. Given a hard problem, we run Twee on it for at most 500 s. We then generate abstractions from the top lemmas of the partial proof, and supply these to Twee. This allowed us to solve 11 hard problems – each with a total time limit of 1000 s, including the partial proof run. The majority of these (6 out of the 11) are LCL problems that contain translations of Horn clauses into equational logic (using the technique introduced in [12]). In these cases, we find that partial proof abstractions of the form $ifeq(x, true, y, true)$

are always discovered – encodings of implication in terms of the $ifeq$ function. And through manual testing, we find that these are the abstractions that make the real difference in helping solve the hard problems.

Domain Abstractions. Domain abstractions solved 18 hard problems within 1000 s, including every hard problem solved by partial proof abstractions. For instance, problem `LAT075-1` (Rating: 1.00) was solved in 32 s (without goal flattening) by providing the following domain abstractions:

- $f(A, A)$
- $f(f(B, A), f(B, A))$
- $f(f(A, B), f(A, C))$
- $f(f(D, C), f(B, A))$
- $f(f(f(C, f(C, f(f(A, A), B))), B), A)$

Checking manually, we found that the first and third abstractions were crucial to finding a proof in a reasonable amount of time.

Note that the first three abstractions are semantically meaningful. The first one corresponds to the *not* operator, the second one to *and*, and the third to one side of a kind of self-distributivity law satisfied by the Sheffer stroke.

Further inspection of the full results (supplied in the source repository) shows that the abstraction lists are quite long in three cases. These cases highlight that it is sometimes helpful to skip abstracting over the good abstractions (line 10 of Procedure 1) and simply take $A_{\mathcal{D}}$ to be the set of all good abstractions.

In addition to the 18 problems, Problem `GRP677-1.p` was also solved (in 180 s) using domain abstractions. However, this required constraining the domain $\mathcal{D}$ to only include problems that share very similar axioms to the hard problem being solved. So, we see that a larger domain is not necessarily better. This suggests that, when aiming to solve a particular hard problem, curation of the domain we provide Twitch may be a useful direction for future work.

5.3 Abstractions vs Definitional Axioms

There are two ways one might use STITCH abstractions to augment a problem P – by giving them to Twee as abstractions, or by adding them as definitional axioms (as described in Sect. 1.1). Twitch uses the abstractions approach. We here present experiments that aim to validate this choice, by comparing the two approaches. The experiments involved running Algorithm 2 on the TPTP problems listed in Table 1.

Figure 3a depicts cactus plots of runtimes obtained in line 7 of Algorithm 2 for each problem. The different colours correspond to different approaches in augmenting P with A. The 'top k' in the figure legends refers to taking the top k abstractions found by STITCH in line 6 of Algorithm 2.[6].

[6] Note that we do not necessarily actually use all k abstractions to augment the problem, as some may not be back-translatable (see Sect. 2). Nonetheless, the comparison remains informative as the actual number of abstractions used for a given problem was the same for both the abstraction and axiom approaches.

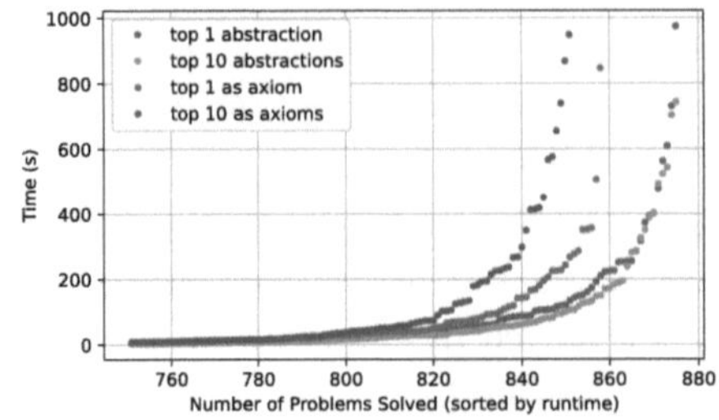

(a) Cactus plot of runtimes for varying number of abstractions and ways of providing them to Twee – as axioms or abstractions.

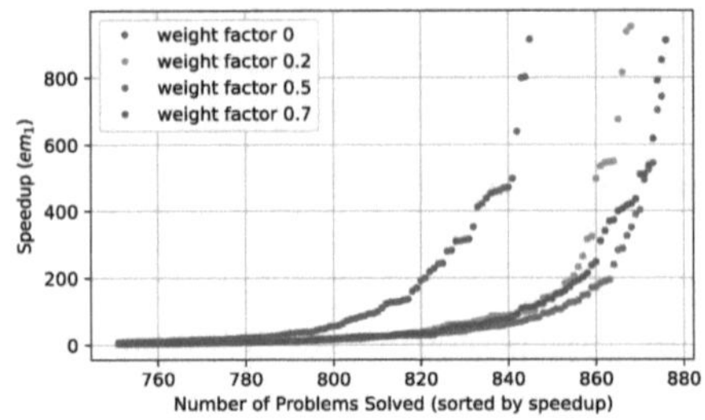

(b) Cactus plot of runtimes for varying weight factors (see Section 4).

Fig. 3. The effect of local abstractions. Each point corresponds to a particular problem P from Table 1. The y-value of a point corresponds to the time taken by Twee to find a proof of P when augmented with local abstractions, i.e. abstractions derived from an existing proof of P by default Twee. The x-value corresponds to the index of the problem when the problems are sorted by increasing runtime of Twee P augmented with the local abstractions. In other words, the points correspond to runtimes from line 7 of Algorithm 2.

We see that overall abstractions lead to lower runtimes compared to definitional axioms, and in particular, fewer cases in which Twee times out as a result of the augmentation. As such, the abstractions approach provides a larger pool of good abstractions for Twitch to derive domain abstractions from. Furthermore, we see that increasing from 1 to 10 abstractions leads to a significant increase in timeouts when using axioms, while the abstractions approach is much more robust to this increase. Hence, using the domain abstractions derived from Twitch as Twee abstractions to augment some hard problem allows us to provide more abstractions with a lesser chance of incurring substantial slowdowns.

However, there are still some problems where providing abstractions as axioms lead to more significant speedups compared to using Twee's abstraction mechanism. For example, our earlier motivating `LAT075-1` problem illustrates such a case.[7] This suggests that there may be room for combining the two approaches in future work.

Finally, we include Fig. 3b which shows a cactus plot of abstraction-augmented runtimes with varying weight factors. A weight factor of about 0.5 (halving the cost of terms matching abbreviations) seems to work best. This aligns with the intuition that low weight factors are more aggressive and hence

[7] There are also 15 problems where axioms lead to speedups while abstractions lead to slowdowns. For LAT141-1, we get a proof $\Gamma(P)$ from default Twee (without goal-flattening) in $\sim$ 160 seconds. The top abstraction found by STITCH on this proof is $f(X, Y, Z) = meet(X, join(Y, Z))$. Adding this as an axiom leads to a proof in $\sim$ 12 seconds, while with the abstraction mechanism, it leads to a proof in $\sim$ 260 seconds.

lead to more slowdowns (in particular, timeouts). However, some individual problems have the greatest speed-ups with lower weight factors.

6 Related Work

Our implementation of abstractions in Twee is an automatically controlled instance of the *weighting strategy* [24]. Weighting later influenced the work of Wos on the *resonance strategy* [37]. Resonators are clause patterns that bias clause selection toward shapes deemed promising by a human expert. This approach proved effective in difficult domains [7,14]. At around the same time Veroff introduced the *hint strategy* [33] as well as the *proof sketches* method [34], in which a prover first establishes an easier or related theorem and then reuses clauses from that proof as hints to guide the search for the harder goal. Our abstractions are in spirit the opposite of Veroff's hints: hint clauses are key clauses which might be derived only once, whereas our abstractions are key term structures which appear over and over again.

Our symbolic learning of domain structure in proofs is very related in spirit to the work of Schulz on pattern-learning and term space mapping [13,27,28].

Closely related to (and inspiration for) our use of STITCH is previous work on automated proof compression. Urban et al. [35] propose introducing new definitions to shorten proofs found by saturation provers. Their goal is proof refactoring and compression, whereas we use compression primarily as a mechanism for discovering search-guiding patterns. Similarly, recent work by Wernhard and Zombori [36] explores grammar-based compression of Metamath proofs.

Related to the idea that internal proof structure can be mined to improve future search is work on learning-based guidance for saturation provers, such as ENIGMA [11,17]. However, these approaches rely on statistical models for clause selection, whereas our method extracts explicit syntactic abstractions that provide lightweight and interpretable guidance tailored to equational completion.

The automatic ranking of interesting derived results has been studied by Puzis et al. [26], who use automated reasoning to generate and filter potentially interesting theorems. Their work inspired our simple heuristic for ranking lemmas extracted from partial Twee proofs, and further exploration of their measures in our setting is an interesting direction for future work.

Other approaches to learning from related problems have been explored in automated reasoning. For example, the *Octopus* system [23] combines learning and parallel search, using information from easier problems to guide proofs of harder ones. This aligns with our domain abstraction approach, which is inspired by curriculum learning [8]: simpler problems in a domain provide reusable structural patterns for harder ones.

Automated theorem provers and finite-model finders have long been used as research tools in algebra [20,25]. Recent examples include work on semigroup, ring, loop, and magma varieties, as well as Tao's Equational Theories Project, which used ATPs and Lean to map implications between small equational laws of magmas [2,3,9,15,18,19]. In such settings, the usefulness of ATPs depends on finding proofs that can be understood and reformulated in standard mathematical terms. Techniques such as proof sketches and proof simplification address this need. Our abstractions are related in spirit: the recurring term patterns identified by Twitch would ideally correspond to algebraically meaningful constructions, and guiding proof search toward these patterns may help produce proofs that are more structured and easier to analyse.

7 Limitations and Future Work

The system we have presented is in many ways quite simple-minded, and there are many ways in which it can be refined. Firstly, our domain construction is quite crude: we restrict to problems within the same TPTP theory sharing concrete symbols, and we do not attempt to automatically generate related or weakened conjectures in the style of proof sketches. Likewise, lemma scoring and term extraction from proofs are based on simple heuristics that could likely be refined as a path to more useful abstractions.

Further, abstraction selection is treated as a single-objective optimization problem focused primarily on runtime speedup. Alternative or multi-objective criteria—such as proof length reduction or robustness across strategies—may yield better guidance. It may also be fruitful to learn abstraction proposals directly from accumulated (problem, abstraction) training data, potentially via language models. Despite these simplifications, we believe our results demonstrate that even a relatively simple abstraction pipeline can produce abstractions yielding substantial improvements and solve previously intractable problems, and that this suggests that automated, structure-based abstraction discovery is a promising direction for future research in equational theorem proving. We also note that for some problems, the best runtimes were obtained by providing both domain and partial proof abstractions. In particular, one more hard problem – `LCL351-10` – was solved this way, where all other approaches failed, indicating potential of further benefits through such combination.

Also, the implementation of abstractions in Twee is currently quite brittle. The problem is that we only give bonuses to critical pairs that contain instances of the abstraction terms. However, Twee demodulates critical pairs, simplifying them using the generated rewrite rules. Thus a term matching an abstraction may well get rewritten to a term that does not match. For example, consider the abstraction $f(x, x)$. If f is also associative $(f(f(x, y), z) \rightarrow f(x, f(y, z)))$ then the term $f(f(x, x), y)$ (which matches the abstraction) will be rewritten to $f(x, f(x, y))$ (which does not). We are experimenting with a critical pair-like mechanism for generating extra *derived abstractions* in these cases. We can generate many extra abstractions this way, but they look very different from the user-provided abstractions and it is not clear if they respect the user's intent.

Finally, we would like to explore generating not only abstractions but also hints. These are key steps that are needed in a proof, but may be difficult for the prover to find. An example of a good hint might be a rewrite rule which is large (hence is unlikely to be selected by Twee) but leads to a proof of a conjecture or important lemma.

8 Conclusion

We have shown that abstractions, automatically generated via compression of existing proofs, are a promising strategy for equational proving. Augmenting Twee with pre-learned domain abstractions allows us to prove several difficult conjectures and roughly halves the prover's runtime for more typical conjectures.

Creating high-quality abstractions currently requires a supply of simpler problems within the same domain. In cases where these do not exist, we can also generate abstractions from a failed proof attempt, which are currently lower quality. Since typically only a few simple domain abstractions are needed, we hope that a more sophisticated extraction mechanism can solve this problem.

There is clearly much potential to refine the method, both how the abstractions are found and how they are exploited by the prover. Even so, we believe the results are promising and motivate further exploration of this idea.

Acknowledgments. This work was partially supported by the Wallenberg AI, Autonomous Systems and Software Program (WASP) funded by the Knut and Alice Wallenberg Foundation, and by the Swedish Research Council (VR) grant 2025-06153, Semantically-guided theorem proving for mathematics.

References

1. Twitch Experiment Repository. https://github.com/WeAreDevo/ijcar26-twee_abstractions
2. Araújo, J., Ferreira, F., Janota, M., Kinyon, M.: Forbidden substructure theorems: a computational tool applied to varieties of lazy magmas. Math. Comput. (2026). https://doi.org/10.1090/mcom/4169
3. Araújo, J., Kinyon, M., Robert, Y.: Varieties of regular semigroups with uniquely defined inversion. Port. Math. **76**(2), 205–228 (2019)
4. Avenhaus, J., Denzinger, J., Fuchs, M.: Discount: a system for distributed equational deduction. In: Proceedings of the International Conference on Rewriting Techniques and Applications, pp. 397–402. Springer (1995)
5. Bachmair, L., Dershowitz, N., Plaisted, D.A.: Completion without failure. In: Proceedings of the Rewriting Techniques, pp. 1–30. Academic Press (1989). https://doi.org/10.1016/B978-0-12-046371-8.50007-9
6. Bártek, F., Chvalovský, K., Suda, M.: Regularization in spider-style strategy discovery and schedule construction. In: Benzmüller, C., Heule, M.J., Schmidt, R.A. (eds.) Automated Reasoning, pp. 194–213. Springer Nature Switzerland, Cham (2024)
7. Beeson, M., Wos, L.: Finding proofs in Tarskian geometry. J. Autom. Reason. **58**(1), 181–207 (2017). https://doi.org/10.1016/B978-0-12-046371-8.50007-9
8. Bengio, Y., Louradour, J., Collobert, R., Weston, J.: Curriculum learning. In: Proceedings of the 26th Annual International Conference on Machine Learning, pp. 41–48. ICML '09, Association for Computing Machinery, New York, NY, USA (2009). https://doi.org/10.1145/1553374.1553380
9. Bolan, M., et al.: The equational theories project: advancing collaborative mathematical research at scale. arXiv preprint arXiv:2512.07087 (2025)

10. Bowers, M., et al.: Top-down synthesis for library learning. Proc. ACM Program. Lang. **7**(POPL), 1182–1213 (2023). https://doi.org/10.1145/3571234
11. Chvalovský, K., Jakubův, J., Suda, M., Urban, J.: ENIGMA-NG: efficient neural and gradient-boosted inference guidance for E. In: Proceedings of the Automated Deduction - CADE 27: 27th International Conference on Automated Deduction, Natal, Brazil, August 27–30, 2019, Proceedings, pp. 197–215. Springer, Heidelberg (2019). https://doi.org/10.1007/978-3-030-29436-6_12
12. Claessen, K., Smallbone, N.: Efficient encodings of first-order Horn formulas in equational logic. In: Galmiche, D., Schulz, S., Sebastiani, R. (eds.) Automated Reasoning, pp. 388–404. Springer, Cham (2018)
13. Denzinger, J., Schulz, S.: Learning domain knowledge to improve theorem proving. In: McRobbie, M.A., Slaney, J.K. (eds.) CADE 1996. LNCS, vol. 1104, pp. 62–76. Springer, Heidelberg (1996). https://doi.org/10.1007/3-540-61511-3_69
14. Fitelson, B., Wos, L.: Missing proofs found. J. Autom. Reason. **27**(2), 201–225 (2001)
15. Hemmila, D., Phillips, J.D., Rowe, D., White, R.: The varieties of rings of Bol-Moufang type. J. Algebra Appl. **23**(11), 2450177 (2024). https://doi.org/10.1142/S0219498824501779
16. Hillenbrand, T., Löchner, B.: The next Waldmeister loop. In: Voronkov, A., (ed.) Automated Deduction–CADE-18, pp. 486–500. Springer, Heidelberg (2002)
17. Jakubův, J., Urban, J.: Enigma: Efficient learning-based inference guiding machine. In: Geuvers, H., England, M., Hasan, O., Rabe, F., Teschke, O. (eds.) Intelligent Computer Mathematics, pp. 292–302. Springer, Cham (2017)
18. Kinyon, M., Phillips, J.: Loops with Squares in Two Nuclei (2025). arXiv preprint arXiv:2510.19961
19. Kinyon, M., Stanovskỳ, D.: Abelianness and centrality in inverse semigroups. Proc. Edinb. Math. Soc. **69**(1), 160–176 (2026)
20. Kinyon, M., Phillips, J.: Rectangular quasigroups and rectangular loops. Comput. Math. Appl. **49**(11), 1679–1685 (2005). https://doi.org/10.1016/j.camwa.2005.01.018. https://www.sciencedirect.com/science/article/pii/S0898122105001896
21. Knuth, D.E., Bendix, P.B.: Simple Word Problems in Universal Algebras, pp. 342–376. Springer, Heidelberg (1983). https://doi.org/10.1007/978-3-642-81955-1_23
22. McCune, W.: OTTER 3.3 reference manual. Tech. rep. (2003)
23. Newborn, M., Wang, Z.: Octopus: combining learning and parallel search. J. Autom. Reason. **33**(2), 171–218 (2004)
24. Overbeek, R., McCharen, J., Wos, L.: Complexity and related enhancements for automated theorem-proving programs. Comput. Math. Appl. **2**(1), 1–16 (1976). https://doi.org/10.1016/0898-1221(76)90002-X. https://www.sciencedirect.com/science/article/pii/089812217690002X
25. Phillips, J.D., Stanovský, D.: Automated theorem proving in quasigroup and loop theory. AI Commun. **23**(2–3), 267–283 (2010)
26. Puzis, Y., Gao, Y., Sutcliffe, G.: Automated generation of interesting theorems. FLAIRS, pp. 49–54 (2006)
27. Schulz, S.: Term Space Mapping for DISCOUNT. In: Denzinger, J., Spencer, B. (eds.) Proceedings of the CADE-15 Workshop on Using AI methods in Deduction, Lindau (1998)
28. Schulz, S., Brandt, F.: Using term space maps to capture search control knowledge in equational theorem proving. In: Kumar, A.N., Russell, I., (eds.) Proceedings of the 12th FLAIRS, pp. 244–248. AAAI Press, Orlando (1999)

29. Schulz, S., Möhrmann, M.: Performance of clause selection heuristics for saturation-based theorem proving. In: Proceedings of the International Joint Conference on Automated Reasoning, pp. 330–345. Springer (2016)
30. Smallbone, N.: Twee: An Equational Theorem Prover, pp. 602–613. CADE (2021)
31. Sutcliffe, G.: The TPTP Problem Library. https://tptp.org/UserDocs/ProblemLibraryManual/TPTPTR.shtml (2025)
32. Sutcliffe, G., Suttner, C.: The TPTP problem library. J. Autom. Reason. **21**(2), 177–203 (1998)
33. Veroff, R.: Using hints to increase the effectiveness of an automated reasoning program: case studies. J. Autom. Reason. **16**(3), 223–239 (1996)
34. Veroff, R.: Solving open questions and other challenge problems using proof sketches. J. Autom. Reason. **27**(2), 157–174 (2001)
35. Vyskočil, J., Stanovský, D., Urban, J.: Automated proof compression by invention of new definitions. In: Proceedings of the International Conference on Logic for Programming Artificial Intelligence and Reasoning, pp. 447–462. Springer (2010)
36. Wernhard, C., Zombori, Z.: Mathematical knowledge bases as grammar-compressed proof terms: exploring metamath proof structures (2025). https://arxiv.org/abs/2505.12305
37. Wos, L.: The resonance strategy. Comput. Math. Appl. **29**(2), 133–178 (1995). https://doi.org/10.1016/0898-1221(94)00220-F. https://www.sciencedirect.com/science/article/pii/089812219400220F

Open Access This chapter is licensed under the terms of the Creative Commons Attribution 4.0 International License (http://creativecommons.org/licenses/by/4.0/), which permits use, sharing, adaptation, distribution and reproduction in any medium or format, as long as you give appropriate credit to the original author(s) and the source, provide a link to the Creative Commons license and indicate if changes were made.

The images or other third party material in this chapter are included in the chapter's Creative Commons license, unless indicated otherwise in a credit line to the material. If material is not included in the chapter's Creative Commons license and your intended use is not permitted by statutory regulation or exceeds the permitted use, you will need to obtain permission directly from the copyright holder.

Towards Fast Automatic Verification of Textbook Proof Steps

Adam Dingle(✉)

Charles University, Prague, Czech Republic
adam.dingle@mff.cuni.cz

Abstract. Natural-language proof assistants such as Naproche and our own system Natty can translate a mathematical text in controlled natural language into a series of logical formulas to be verified. Natty also contains an automatic prover that is designed to quickly verify formulas representing proof steps. Natty's prover is based on superposition, but uses a variety of techniques that are unusual for superposition-based provers, including commutative unification and a form of rewriting that sometimes preserves the rewritten clause. To evaluate this prover and others, we have produced a test suite called TextbookMath containing over 150 theorems and their proofs, which we transcribed from a classic number systems textbook by Mendelson into N, the controlled natural language of Natty. Natty can read this text and generate a set of over 900 conjectures of higher-order logic, each corresponding to a single proof step in the original Mendelson text. We find that established high-order provers such as E and Vampire can prove only about 85% of these conjectures using a single strategy with a 5-second timeout. Surprisingly, some of the conjectures they fail to prove look relatively easy and should be provable with only a few superposition steps. Natty's automatic prover can prove about 91% of these conjectures under a similar time restriction. If we expand the Mendelson text with various intermediate proof steps and lemmas, Natty can completely verify a textbook development of the natural numbers, integers and rationals including 5 of Wiedijk's well-known list of 100 theorems.

Keywords: Theorem proving · Higher-order logic · Superposition

1 Introduction

In many interactive proof systems such as Isabelle [35], Lean [33] and Rocq [9], the user works with the system to build a proof that may look more like a computer program than textbook mathematics. By contrast, in a style of interactive proving pioneered by Naproche [10] and also used by our own prover Natty [12], the user instead enters proof text in a controlled natural language [26] that looks much like ordinary mathematical English. If the system cannot verify all the steps in a proof, the user must expand the proof by adding intermediate

© The Author(s) 2026
A. Biere et al. (Eds.): IJCAR 2026, LNAI 16688, pp. 80–97, 2026.
https://doi.org/10.1007/978-3-032-32589-1_5

steps. For this form of proving to be practical, we would like the system to be able to verify steps of a size typically found in textbook mathematics. Because we want the system to be interactive, ideally we would like this verification to be fast, taking no more than a few seconds per proof step.

We have developed an automatic prover based on higher-order superposition that is an integral part of Natty. The primary design goal for this prover is to be able to prove conjectures that represent typical proof steps reliably and quickly. The architecture of Natty's prover is unusual in some ways: its unification, term ordering, given clause selection, heuristics for pruning inferences, and rewriting mechanism work somewhat differently from most other automatic provers such as E [38] and Vampire [37].

We have constructed a test suite called TextbookMath containing problems transcribed directly from proof steps in a mathematics textbook, namely a classic work by Mendelson [31] that develops the number systems starting from the Peano postulates. To construct the TextbookMath suite, we transcribed several sections of the Mendelson text as literally as possible into N, the controlled natural language of the Natty proof assistant. Natty can read this text and generate a set of over 900 conjectures in the standard THF format [22] for higher-order logic, each corresponding to a single proof step in the original text.

We have evaluated the higher-order provers E, Vampire and Zipperposition [44] on the TextbookMath suite with a 5-second timeout per problem, reflecting our desire for fast interactive verification. We found that each of these systems can prove only about 80-85% of the conjectures in the suite. Natty can prove about 91% of the conjectures with a 5-second time limit, or 93% if we allow it to use *reasons* with which some proof steps are annotated. Furthermore, its average time per problem solved is less than half of the next faster prover, even though Natty does not yet implement term indexing.

Natty has a standard mathematics library called Natlib [13]. Like TextbookMath, Natlib is written in N, is based on the Mendelson text and develops the number systems beginning with the Peano postulates. However Natlib follows the Mendelson text more loosely than TextbookMath, and includes additional proof steps and lemmas which allow Natty to prove 100% of theorems in the library. Even though the proof steps in Natlib are smaller than those in TextbookMath, we find that Vampire and Zipperposition are only able to verify about 75%-80% of conjectures in Natlib within a 5-second time limit.

In the following sections we explain this work in more detail. We first give a high-level overview of the Natty system and the N language. We then describe the architecture of Natty's automatic prover in some detail. After that, we describe the TextbookMath suite and the Natlib library, and use them to evaluate E, Vampire, Zipperposition, and Natty's own automatic prover.

We previously described Natty and its automatic prover in a workshop paper two years ago [12], however the prover's architecture has evolved since then and its performance has improved dramatically. This paper brings the high-level description of the prover up to date.

2 The Natty Proof Assistant

Natty is a proof assistant based on controlled natural language and higher-order logic. The system has been in development for two years, and presently consists of about 6,000 lines of OCaml code. It is freely available online. [14]

Natty implements a controlled natural language called N for writing mathematics. A text in N looks much like ordinary mathematical writing, but with a restricted vocabulary and grammar. In N an input file may include axioms, definitions, and theorems with or without proofs. The TextbookMath suite [15] and Natty's standard library Natlib [13] contain many source files written in N.

In N every variable has a type, which the user must usually declare explicitly. The core system includes a base type $\mathbb{B}$, the booleans. An input file may declare additional base types and assert axioms about them. For example, in TextbookMath the file `nat.n` declares the type $\mathbb{N}$ and asserts the Peano postulates. The file `int.n` declares the type $\mathbb{Z}$ and asserts axiomatically that $\mathbb{Z}$ is isomorphic to an equivalence class of pairs of natural numbers. N also includes function types $\sigma \to \tau$ and product types $\tau_1 \times \cdots \times \tau_n$. The type system includes let-polymorphism [32] as found in ML-like programming languages, as well as overloading: for example, an input text may define both an operator $+ : \mathbb{N} \to \mathbb{N} \to \mathbb{N}$ and an operator $+ : \mathbb{Z} \to \mathbb{Z} \to \mathbb{Z}$.

Each axiom or theorem in an N source file may be given a number and/or a name. Inside a proof, any step may be annotated with *reasons*, which are references to one or more axioms or theorems to be used in proving that step (e.g. "`By [transitivity of` $<$ `on` $\mathbb{N}$`], x` $<$ `z`").

In N each source file represents a single module, and may begin with a `using` declaration that declares its dependency on other modules.

2.1 Translating N into Logical Conjectures

Natty can translate an N source file into a series of formulas of polymorphic higher-order logic [1,16] as standardized by the TH1 format [22] from the TPTP project [41]. This is essentially the same logic used by higher-order proof assistants such as Isabelle/HOL [34] and HOL Light [19].

When Natty is invoked on an N source file, it recursively reads all dependent modules, then performs parsing and type checking. Natty then generates a series of *conjectures*, each of which is a formula representing a proof step in one of the input theorems. (If an input theorem does not include a proof, then Natty generates just a single conjecture representing the theorem.)

Each generated conjecture is paired with a set of *premises* that may be used in proving it. Each of these premises is classified as one of the following:

- an **axiom**, **definition**, or **theorem** that appeared earlier in the input file or one of its dependent modules, or
- a **hypothesis** indicating an assumption that is active at the current position in the proof, or a fact that was proven earlier in the proof.

By default, Natty will use its internal prover to attempt to prove all the conjectures generated from the specified module. Alternatively, Natty can write each generated conjecture along with its premises to a separate output file in the THF format [22]. The premise types mentioned above are all valid *roles* in THF, and Natty will faithfully record each premise's role in the THF output.

If a proof step in the input text is annotated with reasons, then Natty will record these reasons in the THF file that is output for the corresponding conjecture. To achieve this, Natty outputs syntax such as "`[by([thm_2_3_2, thm_2_3_4])]`" in the *useful_info* field of the conjecture's annotated formula. This allows these reasons to be preserved when Natty later reads the THF file. (This `by` syntax is of our own invention.)

3 Natty's Automatic Prover

Natty contains an automatic prover for higher-order logic, intended to be able to quickly prove conjectures representing typical textbook proof steps. As such, the prover is pragmatic and incomplete, and is unlikely to be able to verify conjectures whose proofs require long chains of inferences.

In designing the prover we have been guided by three main principles. First, we want to restrict superposition inferences to those that seem "natural", in the sense that a human reading a proof might make similar judgments. For example, someone reading a proof would certainly not write down commutative variations of all known theorems, e.g. swapping $x + y$ for $y + x$ in the statement of every theorem because $+$ is known to be commutative. And yet many provers based on superposition will do basically this. By excluding these and other "unnatural" inferences we have attempted to "humanize" superposition to some degree.

Our second principle is our observation that many short proofs consist of one or more "expanding" steps, in which we apply a theorem or expand a definition, followed by a series of "contracting" steps in which the term size decreases. As we will see, Natty essentially requires every proof to be of this form. After an initial "expanding" phase in a proof, Natty only allows contracting superpositions in which the term weight (after rewrites are complete) has not increased.

The third principle is our observation that in many proofs, each step is a direct or indirect consequence of the immediately preceding step. For this reason, Natty treats the *last hypothesis* as special and treats superpositions with it more liberally than with other premises.

4 Proof Calculus

Natty's proof calculus is based on a pragmatic subset of the higher-order superposition calculus oλSup recently developed by Bentkamp et al. [5].

A *type* is either the predefined Boolean type $\mathbb{B}$, a user-defined base type, a function type $\sigma \to \tau$, a product type $\tau_1 \times \cdots \times \tau_n$, or a type variable α. A *term* is either a typed constant $c : \tau$, a typed variable $x : \tau$, an application st, a lambda term $\lambda x : \tau \,.\, t$, or an equality $t \approx u$, where τ is any type and s, t are any terms. The logic includes the Boolean constants $\top, \bot, \neg, \wedge, \vee, \rightarrow$, and $\leftrightarrow$ with their usual types, as well as the constants $\forall$ and $\exists$ which are ad hoc polymorphic. We require that all terms be well-typed; we omit the usual typing rules here.

The TH1 logic additionally has the Π-types $\Pi\alpha : * \, . \, \tau$ and allows types to be terms, as in System F [17]. For example, in TH1 it is possible to define a constant $\mathbf{id} : \Pi\alpha : * \, . \, \alpha \rightarrow \alpha$, and apply it in a term such as $\mathbf{id}(\mathbb{B})(\bot)$. Before invoking its automatic prover, Natty finds all terms in which a constant with a Π-type is applied to one or more types, and replaces these terms with new constants without Π-types. For example, $\mathbf{id}(\mathbb{B})$ is replaced with a new constant $\mathbf{id}_{\mathbb{B}} : \mathbb{B} \rightarrow \mathbb{B}$. Because TH1 has only rank-1 polymorphism, this eliminates all terms with Π-types, and the automatic prover never sees such types.

A *literal* is a term of the form $t \approx u$ or $t \not\approx u$. A *clause* is a disjunction $L_1 \vee \cdots \vee L_n$ of literals. As in Bentkamp [5] we distinguish the symbol $\vee$, which separates literals in a clause, from the boldface symbol $\boldsymbol{\vee}$, a logical constant. The *weight* of a literal is the count of its subterms that are constants, variables, or lambdas, with the exception that the constants $\bot$, $\neg$, $\forall$ and $\exists$ have a weight of 0. The weight of a clause is the sum of the weights of its literals.

A *substitution* is a mapping from type variables to types and term variables to terms. $t\rho$ denotes the result of applying the substitution ρ to t. A substitution θ *unifies* terms t and u if $t\theta = u\theta$. We require that all substitutions produce well-typed terms, so Natty's unification algorithm will only unify two terms if they have compatible types. Because types may contain type variables, the algorithm must unify types as well. We use $\mathrm{csu}(t, u)$ to denote the complete set of unifiers [21,45] of terms t and u.

4.1 Subterms, Term Ordering, and Eligibility

oλSup defines the notion of a *green subterm* of a λ-term. Essentially a green subterm is at a position where a first-order inference could take place; see Bentkamp [5], Sect. 3 for a definition. As in oλSup, we write $C\langle t\rangle$ to denote a clause C with a green subterm t.

As in oλSup, Natty's calculus is parameterized by a *strict term order* $\prec$ that must be well-founded and total on ground terms. $\preceq$ is the reflexive closure of $\prec$. The term order $\prec$ is lifted to literals and clauses via the multiset encoding described in Bachmair [3], Sect. 2.4.

oλSup also defines which positions are *eligible* in a clause with respect to a substitution σ. Essentially a green position is eligible in C with respect to σ if it can be reached by descending the term structure of a maximal literal while never passing through a term s in an equation $s \approx t$ where $s\sigma \preceq t\sigma$. See Bentkamp for a precise definition.

As in oλSup, a *fluid term* is either a variable applied to one or more arguments, or a λ-expression t such that for some substitution σ, $t\sigma$ is no longer a λ-expression due to η-reduction. As suggested in Bentkamp, Natty assumes that any non-ground λ-expression is fluid.

4.2 Inference Rules

Natty performs superposition inferences using the following rule:

$$\frac{\overbrace{D' \vee t \approx t'}^{D} \quad C\langle u\rangle}{(D' \vee C\langle t'\rangle)\sigma}\ \textsc{Sup} \qquad \sigma \in \mathrm{csu}(t, u)$$

(i) u is not fluid
(ii) u is not a variable
(iii) $t\sigma \not\preceq t'\sigma$ (*)
(iv) the position of u is eligible in C w.r.t. σ (*)
(v) $t \approx t'$ is maximal in D w.r.t. σ (*)
(vi) if $t'\sigma = \bot$, u is in a literal of the form $u \approx \top$
(vii) if $t'\sigma = \top$, u is in a literal of the form $u \approx \bot$

Most differences between this rule and the corresponding rule in oλSup are minor. One notable difference is that we have excluded the condition $C\sigma \not\preceq D\sigma$ found in oλSup. We found that removing this restriction lets Natty prove a few more theorems in the standard library, at only a small performance cost.

In some situations to be described below, Natty will perform a *lenient superposition* in which the term ordering restrictions marked with a (*) above are disregarded.

Natty classifies each superposition inference as a *resolution* if $t'\sigma = \bot$ or $t'\sigma = \top$, otherwise as a *paramodulation*. Informally, a resolution inference could be made by the classic first-order resolution rule, whereas a paramodulation inference involves an equality substitution. As described below, Natty avoids paramodulations in some situations because they can be extremely productive.

Natty's proof calculus also contains rules for equality resolution, for clausifying and simplifying formulas, and for destructive rewriting and subsumption. These rules are generally similar to those in other provers such as E.

5 Term Ordering

Unusually among automatic provers, Natty uses the lexicographic path order [2,23] (LPO) for term ordering. Most other systems such as E and Vampire will use the Knuth-Bendix order [24] (KBO) by default.

The lexicographic path order requires a total ordering on constant symbols. We say that symbol c has higher *precedence* than symbol d if $c > d$. Natty assigns the lowest precedences to logical constants such as $\neg$ and $\wedge$. Above those, constants are given precedences according to their declaration order in the N or THF source file, with symbols appearing later having higher precedence.

We have chosen the LPO and this particular term ordering so that rewrites will expand definitions and algebraic expressions. Ground terms are always rewritten in a decreasing direction in the term ordering. If a symbol c is defined in terms of a symbol d, then c will appear after d in the input, so Natty will assign c a higher precedence and a term involving c will be rewritten to use d when possible. For example, in the file `nat.n` in TextbookMath, the multiplication operator $\cdot$ is defined in terms of the addition operator $+$. This input file asserts the theorem $\forall x, y, z : \mathbb{N} \,.\, x \cdot (y + z) = x \cdot y + x \cdot z$, a left distributive law on $\mathbb{N}$. As a consequence, a term of the form $x \cdot (y + z)$ will be rewritten to $x \cdot y + x \cdot z$, because the top-level operator $\cdot$ on the left has a higher precedence than the top-level operator $+$ on the right. The Knuth-Bendix order would not allow this rewrite since it does not allow the term weight to increase.

The lexicographic path order is normally defined only on first-order terms, but Natty uses higher-order logic. In Sect. 3.9 of their paper describing the oλSup calculus, Bentkamp et al. [5] present a term ordering for higher-order terms via a transformation to untyped first-order terms, on which they then apply the transfinite Knuth-Bendix order [28]. We have adapted this ordering in a straightforward way for the lexicographic path order.

6 Unification

When unifying terms Natty will perform commutative unification [40], which is unusual among current automatic provers. To achieve this, the prover notices any axioms or theorems that state that a binary operation is commutative. If $\oplus$ is known to be commutative, then Natty will unify $s_1 \oplus t_1$ with $s_2 \oplus t_2$ if the pair (s_1, t_1) unifies with either (s_2, t_2) or (t_2, s_2). As one consequence of this, for any terms s, t the terms $s \oplus t$ and $t \oplus s$ will unify with an empty substitution. Accordingly Natty will treat these terms as equivalent.

Because Natty performs commutative unification, it does not need to perform any superposition or rewrite between a commutative axiom or theorem C and another clause D, since that would just produce a clause considered redundant with D. So the automatic prover removes commutative axioms/theorems during its initial scan before beginning the main loop.

Commutative unification may generate many possible unifiers for a single pair of terms, so the prover code must handle multiple results whenever it performs unification, but this is not a major complication. The problem of deciding whether two terms can be commutatively unified is NP-complete [2], but in practice we have not found our unification to be particularly expensive.

We have not experimented with full associative-commutative (AC) unification. We believe it might be too expensive, though some past provers such as EQP [30] have implemented it in some form.

Natty's unification procedure is almost entirely first-order. As one limited form of higher-order unification, Natty will unify two lambda terms if the variables bound by the lambdas appear in the same positions in the terms, and if the remaining subterms of the lambda terms can be unified. For example, $\lambda x \,.\, f(x, y)$ and $\lambda z \,.\, f(z, 4)$ are unifiable. Despite these limitations, a variable can unify with a higher-order term, which is often adequate for applying a higher-order induction axiom via superposition. Our earlier workshop paper [12] presents a specific example of this behavior.

7 Proof Procedure

Natty's prover takes as input a *conjecture* (also called a *goal*) to be proven, plus a set of *premises* that are available for proving it. As described in Sect. 2.1, each premise is classified as an axiom, definition, theorem, or hypothesis. Natty notes the order in which hypotheses appear in the input, and in particular marks the last hypothesis as special as we noted above. Some of these premises may be additionally marked as *reasons*, which as described in Sect. 2 the user has explicitly said should be used in proving the conjecture.

Like most provers based on superposition, Natty negates the conjecture and searches for a refutation, i.e. a proof of $\bot$. Natty uses a variant of the DISCOUNT loop [11] found in E and other automatic provers. The prover keeps two sets of clauses called the *used* and *unused* sets. Initially all premises are placed in the unused set, which is stored in a priority queue, ordered using a cost function to be described shortly. In each iteration, the prover removes the lowest-cost clause (the *given clause*) from the unused set, adds it to the used set and generates new formulas via superposition between the given clause and all other used clauses. Most clauses in the used set are always in a mutually rewritten form, though as we will see Natty also protects some clauses from rewriting.

7.1 Initial Inferences

Natty considers certain superposition steps at the beginning of a clause's derivation to be *initial inferences*, which are treated more liberally than any following inferences in the derivation. Every derivation begins with 0 or more initial inferences, followed by any number of inferences that are not treated specially.

There are three classes of initial inferences. A *reason application* is an initial superposition between a premise marked as a reason and either the goal or the last hypothesis. A *definition expansion* is an initial superposition between a premise marked as a definition and either the goal or any hypothesis. A *hypothesis substitution* is an initial superposition between any hypothesis and either the goal or the last hypothesis. We treat initial inferences specially because they commonly form part of an initial expansive phase of short proofs, as we noted in Sect. 3 above.

Once any non-initial inferences have occurred in a clause's derivation, all subsequent inferences are considered to be non-initial, even if they are superpositions of the nature described in the previous paragraph.

7.2 Superposition Restrictions

To reduce the branching factor, Natty restricts superpositions in various ways. Most fundamentally, in all superpositions at least one premise must be derived from a hypothesis or the goal. This is essentially a set of support strategy [49] in which the hypotheses plus the goal constitute the set of support. A set of support strategy is not refutationally complete in the presence of ordered resolution or paramodulation rules [3] but Natty is not a complete prover anyway.

Additionally, as we noted in Sect. 4.2 above, Natty does not always allow superpositions that are classified as paramodulations. Specifically, paramodulations are allowed only in these circumstances:

- The inference is a definition expansion or hypothesis substitution.
- At least one of the two premises is a unit equality.
- One of the premises is a *conditioned equality* of the form $P_1 \to \cdots \to P_n \to X = Y$, and the other is the last hypothesis or the goal.
- The two premises are the last hypothesis and the goal.

As also noted in Sect. 4.2, Natty performs some superpositions *leniently*. Specifically, all definition expansions and hypothesis substitutions are performed leniently. In addition, reason applications and all superpositions with a goal clause are performed leniently if they are resolution (not paramodulation) steps.

We recognize that some of the restrictions described in this section have an arbitrary nature, and we hope to simplify them in future work.

7.3 Cost Function

Unlike many automatic provers, Natty has only a single priority queue of clauses, ordered by *cost*. Every inference in the prover is assigned a cost, as described below. The cost of a clause is the total cost of all inferences in its derivation.

Suppose that a superposition inference produces the clause C from premises A and B. We say that the inference is *increasing* if C (after simplification and rewriting) has a weight that is larger than the weight of some premise that is in the set of support, i.e. is derived from a hypothesis or the goal.

Only initial superposition inferences are allowed to increase. If any non-initial superposition is increasing, its cost is ∞ (and so it will be discarded). Otherwise, every superposition inference has a cost of 0.01, except for a non-increasing reason application which has a cost of 0.[1]

The cost of an equality resolution inference is 0.01. The cost of all other inferences, notably including rewrite steps and clausification inferences, is 0.

7.4 Non-destructive Rewriting

Destructive rewrites are essential for efficient term simplification, but also carry a certain risk. Suppose that a clause C may be rewritten with either of two identities A or B. It may be that a rewrite with A will yield a quick refutation, possibly even in a single superposition step, whereas a rewrite with B will destroy that opportunity, specifically if the identities A and B have a non-joinable critical pair [2,24]. In this situation, a superposition between A and B will typically yield a new identity that can be used for a refutation even after a rewrite with B.

[1] As another exception, a superposition with a clause that has the form of a higher-order induction axiom (such as Peano induction on $\mathbb{N}$) has a cost of 1.0. This seems a bit arbitrary, and we would to remove this rule from our system if possible.

However in Natty a superposition between A and B may never occur due to its set of support strategy. In a complete prover a superposition between A and B will occur, however computing all superpositions between all available premises may be expensive. Furthermore, deriving a refutation after several rewrites in the "wrong direction" may require an identity that was derived via superposition from several premises; generating all such identities is more expensive still.

As an example, in the Natlib library the proof of the commutativity of multiplication in $\mathbb{N}$ contains a step $(y + 1) \cdot x = s(y) \cdot x$, where s is the successor function. The negated goal to be refuted is thus $(y+1)\cdot x \neq s(y)\cdot x$. The premises $1 = s(0), \forall x, y \,.\, x + s(y) = s(x + y)$ and $\forall x \,.\, x + 0 = x$ are all available, so the goal may be refuted by rewriting the left side to $(y + s(0)) \cdot x$, then to $s(y+0)\cdot x$, and finally to $s(y) \cdot x$. However the premise $\forall x, y, z \,.\, x \cdot (y + z) = x \cdot y + x \cdot z$ is also available, a left distributive law. If the left side of the goal is rewritten with this premise, the clause becomes $y \cdot x + 1 \cdot x \neq s(y) \cdot x$, and now no further rewrites using these premises are possible.

To prevent an unfortunate rewrite from spoiling an easy refutation attempt, Natty implements a technique that we call *non-destructive rewriting.* To minimize its performance cost, it is used only for clauses derived from the goal or the last hypothesis. When such a clause is first created, Natty marks it as only *partially rewritable.* A partially rewritable clause is only rewritten with certain identities deemed to be *safe*, as defined below. After these safe rewrites are complete, if any non-safe rewrites are possible then Natty creates a copy of the clause called a *rewrite child* and marks it as *fully rewritable.* A fully rewritable clause may be rewritten with any identity.

In the current implementation, a rewrite with an identity I is classified as *safe* if I is of the form $\forall x_1, \ldots, x_n \,.\, f(t_1, \ldots, t_j) \leftrightarrow g(u_1, \ldots, u_k)$, where f and g are constants and t_i, u_i are any terms. For example, the identity $\forall x, y . x > y \leftrightarrow y < x$ is safe. We believe that safe identities are unlikely to have non-joinable critical pairs with other identities; for example, replacing $x > y$ with $y < x$ in every clause should do no harm. In future work, we would like to give a more principled definition of safe rewrites.

7.5 Premise Selection

Before entering the main loop, Natty performs a form of premise selection that is roughly like a simplified form of SInE [20], but also uses type information. When verifying a conjecture derived from a proof step, the prover first forms a set C of all constant symbols already seen in previous steps in the proof, as well as a set T of base types already seen in previous steps. For every defining formula D of any symbol in C, the prover then add D's symbols to the set C unless the formula D uses some base type not found in T. Finally, the prover selects only premises whose symbols are all in C.

Our motivation for using types in this mechanism is to exclude premises involving types that have not been mentioned in a proof. For example, if a proof has used only the base type $\mathbb{Z}$ but not $\mathbb{N}$, then the premise selection will not pull in axioms that define $\mathbb{Z}$ in terms of $\mathbb{N}$, which could in turn cause numerous axioms and theorems about $\mathbb{N}$ to be used as premises.

8 Evaluation

8.1 The TextbookMath Test Suite

We have built a test suite called TextbookMath derived from a textbook by Mendelson that develops the number systems $\mathbb{N}$, $\mathbb{Z}$, $\mathbb{Q}$ and $\mathbb{R}$. We translated definitions, theorems and proofs from the Mendelson text into a set of N source files found in the TextbookMath repository, including

- `nat.n`: definition of $\mathbb{N}$, addition, ordering, multiplication on $\mathbb{N}$ (2.1, 2.3-2.5)
- `int.n`: definition of $\mathbb{Z}$, addition, multiplication, ordering on $\mathbb{Z}$ (3.1-3.4)
- `div.n`: division, greatest common divisors (3.5)
- `prime.n`: relative primality, prime numbers (3.5)

We attempted to perform this translation as literally as possible, though some changes were necessary for various practical and foundational reasons. For example, Mendelson's foundation is ZFC set theory, which is fundamentally untyped: every value is a set. However N is based on higher-order logic, in which every variable has a type. In particular, Mendelson defines $\mathbb{Z}$ to be a *set* of equivalence classes of $\mathbb{N} \times \mathbb{N}$. We want $\mathbb{N}$ and $\mathbb{Z}$ to be distinct types in N, so we translated Mendelson's definition into a set of axioms that declare that $\mathbb{Z}$ is a *type* that is *isomorphic to* a set of equivalence classes of $\mathbb{N} \times \mathbb{N}$.

Despite these differences, we believe that our translation is faithful to the Mendelson text in the sense that individual proof steps have almost always been preserved. Furthermore, in our translation we have annotated proof steps with reasons to be used in proving them exactly whenever such reasons appeared in the original textbook.

The suite currently contains 151 theorems, from which Natty generates 962 conjectures that can be used for evaluating higher-order provers. TextbookMath contains two versions of the test suite, each of which contains all of the N source files listed above. The `nums` directory contains a version in which polymorphism is freely used. The `nums_mono` directory contains a version of the suite in which we have avoided polymorphism, so that we can test with all provers including E, which does not support polymorphism.

8.2 Natlib

Natty includes a standard library of mathematics called Natlib [13] that is more loosely based on the Mendelson text, and in which we have freely added intermediate proof steps and lemmas so that Natty can verify all theorems in the library with a 5-second time limit per step. Natlib contains more mathematics than TextbookMath: it also develops the rational numbers, and includes proofs of 5 of Wiedijk's famous list [47,48] of 100 challenge theorems for interactive proof systems. Currently Natlib contains 235 theorems with 1597 proof steps to be verified.

8.3 Performance Comparison

In this section we compare Natty to E, Vampire, and Zipperposition, which have been the top 3 higher-order provers in the last several years of the CASC competition [42]. Tables 1 and 2 below show the performance of these systems in proving the conjectures from the TextbookMath suite (version 0.1) and the Natlib library. We used a 5-second time limit per conjecture, reflecting our desire for fast interactive verification of proof steps. We used the monomorphic version of TextbookMath so that we could evaluate E, which does not support polymorphism. Natlib is polymorphic, so the Natlib comparison does not include E.

We built Natty from tag `0.0.3` (commit `818c9aea`). We tested with E version `3.3.1-ho`, built with the `-enable-ho` option from commit `8f999d07`. We used Vampire 4.8, built from the `hol` branch from commit `7b44b1c2f`. We ran Zipperposition built from git master (commit `050072e0`). When invoking all provers we specified a timeout on the command line. When running E we also passed the `-auto` option for automatic strategy selection, and we ran Zipperposition with `-mode best`. We passed no additional options to Vampire.

In these tables the column entitled "Natty + by" shows Natty's performance when it is given the reasons that were indicated for each proof step. The column "Natty" shows the performance when those reasons are hidden. The other provers have no way to follow reasons, so arguably a comparison with the numbers in the latter column is fairest. In many modules Natty's performance in the "Natty + by" column shows only a modest increase, for the simple reason that only a small number of steps are annotated with reasons. For example, the `div` module in TextbookMath has 141 proof steps, but only 2 of these are annotated with reasons in the source file `div.n`. When these reasons are given to Natty it is able to prove both steps.

In the TextbookMath suite Natty substantially outperforms all other provers in the large `int` module, which contains many proofs involving large algebraic expressions. On the other hand, Natty lags far behind the other provers in the `prime` module, which appears later in the textbook and has some substantially larger proof steps. In the Natlib library the opposite is true: we have added proof steps and lemmas that allow Natty (when using reasons) to prove 100% of conjectures, but the other provers perform much more poorly especially in the later modules `div`, `prime`, `rat` and `real`. We currently do not have an adequate explanation for this discrepancy, and intend to investigate it in future work.

Some conjectures in TextbookMath that E, Vampire and/or Zipperposition fail to prove look like they should be very easy. For example, the proof of Theorem 3.2.4.e contains a step $n \cdot (i+j)+ji = (ni+nj)+ji$ that should be provable by a single application of a distributive axiom, yet E and Zipperposition fail to prove this conjecture within 5 s. As another example, the proof of Theorem 3.4.1.b contains a step in which $u < v$ is already known, and the goal is $y + u < y + v$. This should be easily provable by applying the known theorem $\forall x, y, z \,.\, x < y \rightarrow x + z < y + z$ plus the commutativity of addition, yet none of E, Vampire,

Table 1. Prover performance on TextbookMath

module		Natty + by	Natty	E	Vampire	Zipperpos.
div	proved (of 141)	115 (82%)	113 (80%)	114 (81%)	111 (79%)	101 (72%)
	avg time	0.13 sec	0.14 sec	0.28 sec	0.47 sec	0.69 sec
int	proved (of 483)	456 (94%)	451 (93%)	373 (77%)	390 (81%)	384 (80%)
	avg time	0.05 sec	0.04 sec	0.10 sec	0.50 sec	0.32 sec
nat	proved (of 301)	299 (99%)	290 (96%)	285 (95%)	280 (93%)	261 (87%)
	avg time	0.02 sec	0.02 sec	0.01 sec	0.16 sec	0.14 sec
prime	proved (of 37)	23 (62%)	23 (62%)	37 (100%)	37 (100%)	36 (97%)
	avg time	0.07 sec	0.07 sec	0.68 sec	0.08 sec	1.24 sec
total	proved (of 962)	893 (93%)	877 (91%)	809 (84%)	818 (85%)	782 (81%)
	avg time	0.05 sec	0.05 sec	0.12 sec	0.36 sec	0.35 sec

Table 2. Prover performance on Natlib

module		Natty + by	Natty	Vampire	Zipperposition
card	proved (of 23)	23 (100%)	23 (100%)	14 (61%)	14 (61%)
	avg time	0.08 sec	0.08 sec	0.71 sec	0.71 sec
div	proved (of 259)	259 (100%)	253 (98%)	172 (66%)	187 (72%)
	avg time	0.11 sec	0.11 sec	0.63 sec	0.87 sec
int	proved (of 648)	648 (100%)	637 (98%)	549 (85%)	526 (81%)
	avg time	0.04 sec	0.04 sec	0.57 sec	0.43 sec
nat	proved (of 264)	264 (100%)	259 (98%)	240 (91%)	239 (91%)
	avg time	0.01 sec	0.02 sec	0.17 sec	0.25 sec
prime	proved (of 130)	130 (100%)	120 (92%)	75 (58%)	38 (29%)
	avg time	0.11 sec	0.10 sec	0.82 sec	0.54 sec
rat	proved (of 257)	257 (100%)	252 (98%)	163 (63%)	123 (48%)
	avg time	0.09 sec	0.08 sec	1.09 sec	1.42 sec
real	proved (of 16)	16 (100%)	14 (88%)	11 (69%)	6 (38%)
	avg time	0.08 sec	0.08 sec	0.81 sec	0.48 sec
total	proved (of 1597)	1597 (100%)	1558 (98%)	1224 (77%)	1133 (71%)
	avg time	0.06 sec	0.06 sec	0.59 sec	0.58 sec

Table 3. Effect of removing prover features

suite		Full prover	No CU	No NDR	No PS	No SR
TM	proved (of 962)	893 (93%)	874 (91%)	884 (92%)	886 (92%)	893 (93%)
	avg time	0.05 sec	0.06 sec	0.05 sec	0.19 sec	0.12 sec
Natlib	proved (of 1597)	1597 (100%)	1561 (98%)	1544 (97%)	1560 (98%)	1555 (97%)
	avg time	0.06 sec	0.08 sec	0.07 sec	0.29 sec	0.16 sec

or Zipperposition can prove this within 5 s. We suspect that in these provers a destructive rewrite is causing trouble as we described in 7.4 above, but would like to investigate this more.

8.4 Performance Benefit of Individual Features

We have performed a simple ablation study to investigate the effect of removing individual prover features that we have described in this work. The result appears in Table 3, which uses the following abbreviations: TM = Textbook-Math, CU = commutative unification, NDR = non-destructive rewriting, PS = premise selection, SR = superposition restrictions. We see that removing any individual feature decreases the fraction of successful proofs by only a few percent at most, however removing either premise selection or the superposition restrictions has a dramatic effect on the average time per successful proof.

9 Related Work

Naproche [10] can also translate a text in controlled natural language to a series of logical conjectures to be verified, though it uses first-order rather than higher-order logic. Naproche uses E as an external prover and has had some success in verifying textbook mathematics including 10 of the Wiedijk theorems [25]. However this verification assumes the existence of the number system $\mathbb{R}$ including all the axioms of a real ordered field. By contrast, TextbookMath and Natlib assume only the existence of the number system $\mathbb{N}$ satisfying the Peano postulates, a significantly lower-level foundation. Naproche will sometimes invoke E several times while proving a single conjecture, which may take several seconds; Natty seems to be much faster.

The Verbose Lean [29] and Waterproof [46] systems add a controlled natural language syntax to the proof assistants Lean and Rocq, with a focus on writing proofs in an educational setting. This syntax may help ease the learning curve for users of these systems, though it is not nearly as freeform as the textbook mathematical English that Natty and Naproche attempt to imitate.

Other provers have formally verified mathematics from textbooks. In fact as early as 1977 Landau's Foundations of Analysis [27], which also develops the number systems, was verified in AUTOMATH [4].

In recent years large language models have become enormously more capable, and can now often translate natural-language textbook mathematics into proof languages such as Isabelle/Isar in a fully or semi-automated fashion [8,43]. These capabilities are impressive, but we believe there is still value in having a proof language such as N that is deterministically checkable and also highly readable.

Premise selection and clause selection heuristics have a fundamental impact on the performance of saturation-based provers. SinE [20] has been the most influential premise selection heuristic in recent years, though unlike Natty's premise selection it does not use type information. Schulz and Möhrmann [39] have compared a variety of clause selection heuristics. All of their heuristics consider only the attributes of a clause itself, not of the clause's derivation as in Natty. Many researchers have attempted to use machine learning to improve premise and clause selection heuristics, as described in a survey by Blaauwbroek et al. [6].

Sledgehammer and similar systems [7,36] have become standard tools for applying automated provers to proof obligations encountered in interactive theorem proving work. In Natty every proof step must be verified by an automatic prover, which is like using Sledgehammer as a universal tactic. Hammer tools must translate between the logics of a proof assistant and an automated prover, which is not always trivial [7]. Natty uses an internal automatic prover whose logic is nearly identical to the logic of the controlled language N, reducing the burden of this translation.

10 Conclusions and Future Work

As far as we know our TextbookMath suite is the first transcription of a significant body of textbook mathematics into a series of logical conjectures that correspond more or less precisely with the proof steps in the original text. No existing prover seems to be able to prove all of these conjectures automatically, at least not with a short timeout. We hope that this suite will serve as a useful benchmark for automatic provers in general.

A fundamental limitation of Natty today is that the user has no control over premise selection. A user may provide a reason for a proof step, but that does not exclude any other premises from consideration. By contrast, a proof in systems such as Isabelle/HOL may explicitly specify the set of premises to be passed to a saturation-based prover. We intend to enhance the N language so that the user may restrict the set of premises to be used in proving a step. We hope this will allow Natty to verify steps that currently seem beyond the reach of its automatic prover.

As a soundness check, it is possible to run Natty with an option that asks it to try to prove the converse of all proof steps. That reveals no unsoundness when run on the TextbookMath and Natlib suites. However, Natty does not have a small kernel and its output proofs are not in a format that can be easily checked by another prover. We would like to add a trusted LCF-style kernel [18] to Natty, though it may be a significant project if the kernel allows only low-level inferences such as those of the HOL Light calculus [19].

Acknowledgments. Thanks to Martin Suda for helpful discussions and for reviewing drafts of this paper. This research was supported by the Grant Agency of Charles University (grant 128524).

Disclosure of Interests. The authors have no competing interests to declare that are relevant to the content of this article.

References

1. Andrews, P.B.: An introduction to mathematical logic and type theory: to truth through proof, vol. 27. Springer Science & Business Media (2013)
2. Baader, F., Nipkow, T.: Term rewriting and all that. Cambridge University Press (1998)

3. Bachmair, L., Ganzinger, H.: Rewrite-based equational theorem proving with selection and simplification. J. Log. Comput. **4**(3), 217–247 (1994)
4. van Benthem Jutting, L.S.: Checking Landau's "Grundlagen" in the AUTOMATH system (1977)
5. Bentkamp, A., Blanchette, J., Tourret, S., Vukmirović, P.: Superposition for higher-order logic. J. Autom. Reason. **67**(1) (2023)
6. Blaauwbroek, L., et al.: Learning guided automated reasoning: a brief survey. Logics and Type Systems in Theory and Practice: Essays Dedicated to Herman Geuvers on The Occasion of His 60th Birthday, pp. 54–83 (2024)
7. Blanchette, J.C., Kaliszyk, C., Paulson, L.C., Urban, J.: Hammering towards QED. J. Formalized Reasoning **9**(1), 101–148 (2016)
8. Bryant, D., Kaliszyk, C., Urban, J.: Munkres' general topology auto-formalized in Isabelle/HOL. arXiv preprint arXiv:2604.07455 (2026)
9. Chlipala, A.: Certified programming with dependent types: a pragmatic introduction to the Coq proof assistant. MIT Press (2013)
10. Cramer, M., et al.: The Naproche project: controlled natural language proof checking of mathematical texts. In: Proceedings of the International Workshop on Controlled Natural Language, pp. 170–186. Springer (2009)
11. Denzinger, J., Kronenburg, M., Schulz, S.: DISCOUNT-a distributed and learning equational prover. J. Autom. Reason. **18**, 189–198 (1997)
12. Dingle, A.: A natural-language proof assistant for higher-order logic (work in progress). In: Brown, C.W., Kaufmann, D., Nalon, C., Steen, A., Suda, M., (eds.) Proceedings of the 9th Workshop on Practical Aspects of Automated Reasoning (PAAR), 2024 co-located with the 12th International Joint Conference on Automated Reasoning (IJCAR 2024), Nancy, France. CEUR Workshop Proceedings, vol. 3717, pp. 57–73. CEUR-WS.org (2024)
13. Dingle, A.: Natlib: Natty standard library (2026). https://github.com/medovina/natty/tree/main/math
14. Dingle, A.: Natty code repository (2026). https://github.com/medovina/natty
15. Dingle, A.: TextbookMath Test Suite (2026). https://github.com/medovina/textbook_math/tree/main
16. Farmer, W.M.: The seven virtues of simple type theory. J. Appl. Log. **6**(3), 267–286 (2008)
17. Girard, J.Y.: The system f of variable types, fifteen years later. Theoret. Comput. Sci. **45**, 159–192 (1986)
18. Gordon, M.J., Milner, A.J., Wadsworth, C.P.: Edinburgh LCF: a mechanised logic of computation. Springer (1979)
19. Harrison, J.: Hol light: an overview. In: Proceedings of the International Conference on Theorem Proving in Higher Order Logics, pp. 60–66. Springer (2009)
20. Hoder, K., Voronkov, A.: Sine qua non for large theory reasoning. In: Proceedings of the International Conference on Automated Deduction, pp. 299–314. Springer (2011)
21. Jensen, D.C., Pietrzykowski, T.: Mechanizing ω-order type theory through unification. Theoret. Comput. Sci. **3**(2), 123–171 (1976)
22. Kaliszyk, C., Sutcliffe, G., Rabe, F.: TH1: The TPTP typed higher-order form with rank-1 polymorphism, pp. 41–55. PAAR@ IJCAR (2016)
23. Kamin, S.: Two generalizations of the recursive path ordering. Unpublished Manuscript (1980)
24. Knuth, D.E., Bendix, P.B.: Simple word problems in universal algebras. In: Proceedings of the Computational problems in abstract algebra, pp. 263–297. Elsevier (1970)

25. Koepke, P., Marcol, M., Schäfer, P.: Formalizing sets, numbers, and some "Wiedijk theorems" in Naproche (2023), talk at the NatFoM workshop at CICM (2023), Cambridge, UK
26. Kuhn, T.: A survey and classification of controlled natural languages. Comput. Linguist. **40**(1), 121–170 (2014)
27. Hahn, H.: Grundlagen der Analysis. Monatshefte für Mathematik und Physik **37**(1), A35–A36 (1930). https://doi.org/10.1007/BF01696844
28. Ludwig, M., Waldmann, U.: An extension of the Knuth-Bendix ordering with LPO-like properties. In: Proceedings of the International Conference on Logic for Programming Artificial Intelligence and Reasoning, pp. 348–362. Springer (2007)
29. Massot, P.: Teaching mathematics using lean and controlled natural language. In: Proceedings of the 15th International Conference on Interactive Theorem Proving (ITP 2024), pp. 27–1. Schloss Dagstuhl–Leibniz-Zentrum für Informatik (2024)
30. McCune, W.: 33 basic test problems: a practical evaluation of some paramodulation strategies. Autom. Reasoning Appl. Essays Honor Larry Wos, 71–114 (1997)
31. Mendelson, E.: Number Systems and the Foundations of Analysis. Academic Press, Inc (1973)
32. Milner, R.: A theory of type polymorphism in programming. J. Comput. Syst. Sci. **17**(3), 348–375 (1978)
33. Moura, L., Ullrich, S.: The Lean 4 Theorem Prover and Programming Language. In: Platzer, A., Sutcliffe, G. (eds.) CADE 2021. LNCS (LNAI), vol. 12699, pp. 625–635. Springer, Cham (2021). https://doi.org/10.1007/978-3-030-79876-5_37
34. Nipkow, T., Wenzel, M., Paulson, L.C.: Isabelle/HOL: a proof assistant for higher-order logic. Springer (2002)
35. Paulson, L.C.: Isabelle: A generic theorem prover. Springer (1994)
36. Paulson, L.C., Susanto, K.W.: Source-level proof reconstruction for interactive theorem proving. In: Proceedings of the International Conference on Theorem Proving in Higher Order Logics, pp. 232–245. Springer (2007)
37. Riazanov, A., Voronkov, A.: The design and implementation of vampire. AI Commun. **15**(2–3), 91–110 (2002)
38. Schulz, S.: E-a brainiac theorem prover. AI Commun. **15**(2–3), 111–126 (2002)
39. Schulz, S., Möhrmann, M.: Performance of Clause Selection Heuristics for Saturation-Based Theorem Proving. In: Olivetti, N., Tiwari, A. (eds.) IJCAR 2016. LNCS (LNAI), vol. 9706, pp. 330–345. Springer, Cham (2016). https://doi.org/10.1007/978-3-319-40229-1_23
40. Siekmann, J.: Unification of commutative terms. In: Ng, E.W., (ed.) Symbolic and Algebraic Computation. LNCS, vol. 72, p. 22. Springer, Heidelberg (1979). https://doi.org/10.1007/3-540-09519-5_53
41. Sutcliffe, G.: The TPTP problem library and associated infrastructure. J. Autom. Reason. **59**(4), 483–502 (2017)
42. Sutcliffe, G., Suttner, C.: The state of CASC. AI Commun. **19**(1), 35–48 (2006)
43. Urban, J.: 130k lines of formal topology in two weeks: simple and cheap autoformalization for everyone? arXiv preprint arXiv:2601.03298 (2026)
44. Vukmirovic, P., et al.: Making higher-order superposition work, pp. 415–432. CADE (2021)
45. Vukmirović, P., Bentkamp, A., Nummelin, V.: Efficient full higher-order unification. Logical Methods Comput. Sci. **17** (2021)
46. Wemmenhove, J., et al.: Waterproof: educational software for learning how to write mathematical proofs. arXiv preprint arXiv:2211.13513 (2022)
47. Wiedijk, F.: Formal proof-getting started. Not. Am. Math. Soc. **55**(11), 1408–1414 (2008)

48. Wiedijk, F.: Formalizing 100 theorems (2026). https://www.cs.ru.nl/~freek/
49. Wos, L., Robinson, G.A., Carson, D.F.: Efficiency and completeness of the set of support strategy in theorem proving. J. ACM (JACM) **12**(4), 536–541 (1965)

Open Access This chapter is licensed under the terms of the Creative Commons Attribution 4.0 International License (http://creativecommons.org/licenses/by/4.0/), which permits use, sharing, adaptation, distribution and reproduction in any medium or format, as long as you give appropriate credit to the original author(s) and the source, provide a link to the Creative Commons license and indicate if changes were made.

The images or other third party material in this chapter are included in the chapter's Creative Commons license, unless indicated otherwise in a credit line to the material. If material is not included in the chapter's Creative Commons license and your intended use is not permitted by statutory regulation or exceeds the permitted use, you will need to obtain permission directly from the copyright holder.

Pgeon: Generating Tableau-Based Provers from Declarative Specifications of Logical Calculi

Romain Sidhoum(✉), Simon Robillard, and David Delahaye

LIRMM, Univ Montpellier, CNRS, Montpellier, France
{Romain.Sidhoum,Simon.Robillard,David.Delahaye}@lirmm.fr

Abstract. This paper introduces Pgeon, a meta-prover framework that generates tableau-based automated theorem provers from declarative specifications. In Pgeon, the syntax of a given calculus, its tableau inference rules, and the proof-search strategy are described in a small domain-specific language that closely follows textbook presentations. From such a specification, Pgeon instantiates a fully functional prover, handling tableau construction, rule instantiation, branching, and backtracking in a logic-agnostic manner. Proof-search is driven by a strategy engine that gives users explicit control over exploration order while keeping logical content separate from operational concerns. Pgeon supports first-order reasoning through binders, capture-avoiding substitution, and extensible term generators required for Skolemization and free variable introduction. We describe the design of the specification language, the execution model of the tool, and the strategy mechanism, and illustrate the approach on case studies covering classical first-order tableau calculus and intuitionistic propositional calculus.

Keywords: Tableau Calculi · Automated Prover Generation · Logical Framework

1 Introduction

Many Automated Theorem Provers (ATPs) have been implemented, covering a broad range of techniques (resolution, tableaux, superposition, DPLL, etc.), as well as a variety of target logics. These systems are usually highly specialized and optimized with implementations that often intertwine proof rules and search control, resulting in code that is difficult to reuse. The development of a new prover is a challenge that requires a deep understanding of the implemented calculus, as well as practical programming skills. As a result theoretical developments in deductive systems are not always implemented.

Pgeon (short for Prover GEneratiON) is a tool designed to help quickly develop an ATP. It offers a DSL that allows the user to specify the syntax of a logic, proof production rules, and the proof-search strategy that controls those

© The Author(s) 2026
A. Biere et al. (Eds.): IJCAR 2026, LNAI 16688, pp. 98–105, 2026.
https://doi.org/10.1007/978-3-032-32589-1_6

rules. From that description, Pgeon generates an executable prover able to handle term management, branch expansion, and backtracking. Pgeon is equipped with features to handle quantified logics, including the ability to specify binders in the syntax, rules with unification and substitution, and proof-search strategies with fine-tuned control over the application of rule instances and backtracking. Although logic-agnostic, Pgeon is primarly intended to generate tableau-based provers. More generally, the rules describe transformation steps on proof trees and their nodes. The description language of Pgeon is meant to resemble textbook notation and provide a natural framework for researchers to prototype or experiment with new deduction techniques.

This paper presents the design and current implementation of Pgeon. We describe the specification language and the proof-search engine. Along the way, we report on case studies ranging from classical first-order tableau calculus to intuitionistic propositional calculus, outlining what makes Pgeon[1] a versatile framework for automated proving research.

Related Work. For background on tableau methods we refer to the Handbook of Tableau Methods [5]. This work is inspired by previous tableau prover generators, in particular LoTREC [4], Tableau workbench [1] and MetTeL [10]. Unlike Pgeon, these systems are limited to propositional logics. Prolog has been used to provide elegant and concise implementations of provers for first-order logic, based on semantic tableaux [3], as well as connection tableaux [8], although in both cases the evaluation strategy is largely constrained by the semantics of Prolog. A different approach is taken by the first-order tableau prover KeY, namely allowing users to extend the calculi with new rules through a dedicated description language [2]. Sequoia [9] is another system with a dedicated description language for (propositional) logical calculi, intended for meta-logical analysis rather than execution. Our strategy language is also related to tactic languages in interactive theorem proves, such as Ltac, the tactic language of Rocq, which provides combinators and constructs for composing proof-search procedures [6].

2 Specification Language and Usage

Pgeon generates tableau provers from a declarative specification consisting of a file that defines the syntax, inference rules and a proof-search strategy of a given logic. Problems are defined in separate files that extend the syntax with the symbols occurring in the problem, and provide the formulas from which the proof is started. Listing 1.1 shows the specification of a tableau calculus for classical first-order logic, from which Pgeon generates an executable prover. We refer to this specification as a running example throughout this section.

Syntax. This file starts with type declarations, corresponding to syntactic categories (here: `formula` and `term`). Types are used to enforce well-formedness in symbol declarations and rules. One type must be prefixed with the keyword `main`, thereby designating it as the type of elements in the proof tree nodes.

[1] Pgeon is an open source tool, available at https://gite.lirmm.fr/rsidhoum/pgeon.

```
main type formula
type term

function not  : formula -> formula
function and  : formula formula -> formula
function or   : formula formula -> formula
function impl : formula formula -> formula

binder forall : term. formula
binder exists : term. formula

rule rAxiom   : P ; not(P) ==X
rule rAnd     : and(P, Q)       ==> P ; Q
rule rOr      : or(P, Q)        ==> P | Q
rule rImpl    : impl(P, Q)      ==> not(P) | Q
rule rNotNot  : not(not(P))     ==> P
rule rNotAnd  : not(and(P, Q))  ==> not(P) | not(Q)
rule rNotOr   : not(or(P, Q))   ==> not(P) ; not(Q)
rule rNotImpl : not(impl(P, Q)) ==> P ; not(Q)
tree rule rClosure : (P0 ; not(P1) ; ...B) | ...T --> ...T'
where {
  T' = ((P0; not(P1); ...B) | ...T)[mgu(P0, P1)]
}
rule rForall : forall x. P --> Q
where {
  Q = P[x <- @fresh()]
}
rule rNotForall : not(forall x. P) ==> not(Q)
where {
  Q = P[x <- @skolem()]
}
rule rNotExists : not(exists x. P) --> not(Q)
where {
  Q = P[x <- @fresh()]
}
rule rExists : exists x. P ==> Q
where {
  Q = P[x <- @skolem()]
}

strategy closure : rAxiom || (rClosure; rAxiom)
strategy alpha : rAnd || rNotNot || rNotOr || rNotImpl
strategy beta : rOr || rImpl || rNotAnd
strategy delta : rExists || rNotForall
strategy gamma : rForall!? ; rNotExists!?
main strategy prove :
    (closure || alpha || delta || beta || gamma)*
```

Listing 1.1. Classical First-Order Tableau Calculus Specification in Pgeon

The syntactic constructors of the object language are declared with the keyword `function`, with their type signature (`not`, `and`, `or`, `impl` map formulas to formulas). The syntax may also include `binders` (here `forall`, `exists`, that build `formulas` with a bound `term`), allowing the definition of quantified logics.

Rules. Rules describe admissible transformations on tableau branches. Closure rules (`==X`) mark a branch as closed, invertible rules (`==>`) remove matched nodes in a branch to extend it with new nodes, and non-invertible rules (`-->`) extend the branch with new nodes, without removing the matched nodes. Each rule has a name, a left-hand side pattern, and (except for closure rules) a right-hand side that specifies the generated nodes. Patterns use meta-variables (e.g., `P`, `Q`) that match nodes occurring on a branch. Some rules may require the presence of multiple nodes in the branch (separated by the operator `;` on the left-hand side), e.g., the rule `rAxiom`. For such patterns, the order of nodes is irrelevant, i.e., a branch is treated as a multiset of nodes. On the right-hand side, the semicolon (`;`) adds formulas to the same branch, and the vertical bar (`|`) denotes branching. Here, the rule `rAnd` decomposes a conjunction on the same branch, whereas `rOr` creates a branching point. For inferences that require global tableau information, `tree rules` match and modify the tableau, rather than a single branch. The ellipses "`...`" denote patterns that match an arbitrary number of formulas or branches. Here, the `rClosure` rule implements unification-based closure: it searches for complementary formulas up to unification and applies the most general unifier to the whole tableau. Rules can have side-conditions and computational definitions in a block `where`. The notation `t[x <- e]` is used to perform capture-avoiding substitution, and calls to external Ocaml functions are indicated with `@`. We provide utility functions for first-order logic, such as `fresh` (that generates a fresh free variable) and `skolem` (that generates a Skolem term parameterized by the free variables in the current branch). Additional external functions can be defined by the user to perform complex operations outside the scope of Pgeon's description language.

Strategies. Strategies define how rules are applied during proof-search. One strategy must be prefixed with the keyword `main`, designating it as the strategy executed by the evaluation engine. A rule call is interpreted as a function from proof states to a sequence of successor states. The sequence may be empty, when no instance of the rule is applicable, or may contain several states, when the rule has several possible matches. Strategy operators combine such state transformers:

- `S1 || S2` is left-biased choice: `S1` is tried first, and `S2` is tried only if `S1` produces no successor.
- `S1 ; S2` is sequential composition: `S2` is applied to each successor produced by `S1`.
- `S?` is optional execution: it behaves as `S` when `S` succeeds, and as the identity strategy otherwise.
- `S*` denotes repeated application of the strategy `S`. It explores states reachable by zero or more applications of `S`
- `R!` applies every currently available instance of the rule `R` once. Unlike `*`, `!` takes a rule as argument, not an arbitrary strategy. It does not recursively apply to the states it produces.

The strategy definitions in Listing 1.1 group non-branching rules, branching rules, quantifier rules, and closure rules, and compose them in the main strategy.

3 Engine Architecture and Execution Model

Pgeon builds proofs by interpreting user-defined strategies over an evolving tableau. A tableau is represented as a tree structure whose nodes are individual formulas. Each branch corresponds to a multiset of formulas. A branch is considered closed if a closure rule has been applied to it. The tableau is closed when each of its branch is closed. Proof search is implemented by interpreting strategies over proof states. A proof state consists of a tableau together with a strategy that remains to be executed. Strategy evaluation may fail, produce one successor state, or produce several alternatives. These alternatives are stored as continuations and explored by backtracking. Thus, non-determinism arises both from explicit strategy operators and from the possible instantiations of a rule.

Rule Instantiation. Rule application proceeds by searching for matches of the rule's left-hand side pattern in the current tableau. For ordinary rules, matching is performed on individual branches, viewed as multisets of formulas. For tree rules, matching is performed on the whole tableau, allowing transformations that depend on several branches or on the global shape of the proof tree. Once a match is found, the rule body and its side-conditions are evaluated under the computed substitution. The tableau is then updated according to the kind of rule: closure rules mark branches as closed, invertible rules replace matched formulas by their conclusions, non-invertible rules add conclusions while preserving the matched formulas, and tree rules may rewrite the tableau globally. Each successful instantiation yields a new proof state. When several matches are possible, the engine schedules the corresponding states as alternatives, thereby integrating rule-level non-determinism into the global search.

Backtracking. Backtracking arises from explicit choice points and alternative rule matches. When a rule has several admissible instances, each instance produces a successor state, and the resulting stream represents the corresponding choice points. The default exploration order is depth-first, following the order in which successor states are produced. Consequently, termination and fairness are not guaranteed for arbitratry strategies. This is expected for first-order proof search, where rules such as quantifier instantiation may generate infinitely many successors. The purpose of the strategy language is therefore not to guarantee termination automatically, but to make the search policy explicit.

For example, iterative deepening can be expressed by combining repetition with sequential composition. If `gamma` denotes quantifier instantiation and `sat` a saturation phase for the remaining rules, then `(gamma* ; sat)*` schedules saturation after zero, one, two, and progressively more applications of over `gamma`. Provided that the results of `gamma` are enumerated fairly, this prevents an infinite sequence of quantifier instantiations from starving the other rules.

4 Description of Another Use-Case

Section 2 already provides a complete calculus example, namely tableaux for classical first-order logic with Skolemization and free variables, in a destructive version, i.e., the use of the closure rule generates a substitution that is applied to the entire tree. In this section, we will look at a less straightforward example, namely intuitionistic propositional logic. While this logic remains decidable, expressing the corresponding sequent calculus in an automation-friendly system presents some difficulties. The first difficulty lies in the intuitionistic semantics of the sequent, where there is a single formula on the right. It is not possible to put this formula on the left (with a negation) because that would amount to applying the excluded middle. This means that the formulas need to be tagged (left or right) in order to emulate a sequent, which Pgeon allows us to do.

$$\frac{}{\Gamma, A \vdash A}\ \mathsf{ax}$$

$$\frac{\Gamma, A, B \vdash C \qquad A \text{ atomic}}{\Gamma, A \Rightarrow B, A \vdash C}\ \Rightarrow_{\mathsf{left1}} \qquad \frac{\Gamma, A \Rightarrow (B \Rightarrow C) \vdash D}{\Gamma, (A \wedge B) \Rightarrow C \vdash D}\ \Rightarrow_{\mathsf{left2}}$$

$$\frac{\Gamma, A \Rightarrow C, B \Rightarrow C \vdash D}{\Gamma, (A \vee B) \Rightarrow C \vdash D}\ \Rightarrow_{\mathsf{left3}} \qquad \frac{\Gamma, B \Rightarrow C \vdash A \Rightarrow B \qquad \Gamma, C \vdash D}{\Gamma, (A \Rightarrow B) \Rightarrow C \vdash D}\ \Rightarrow_{\mathsf{left4}}$$

$$\frac{\Gamma, A \vdash B}{\Gamma \vdash A \Rightarrow B}\ \Rightarrow_{\mathsf{right}} \qquad \frac{\Gamma, A, B \vdash C}{\Gamma, A \wedge B \vdash C}\ \wedge_{\mathsf{left}} \qquad \frac{\Gamma \vdash A \qquad \Gamma \vdash B}{\Gamma \vdash A \wedge B}\ \wedge_{\mathsf{right}}$$

$$\frac{\Gamma, A \vdash C \qquad \Gamma, B \vdash C}{\Gamma, A \vee B \vdash C}\ \vee_{\mathsf{left}} \qquad \frac{\Gamma \vdash A}{\Gamma \vdash A \vee B}\ \vee_{\mathsf{right1}} \qquad \frac{\Gamma \vdash B}{\Gamma \vdash A \vee B}\ \vee_{\mathsf{right2}}$$

Fig. 1. LJT Rules for Intuitionistic Propositional Logic

The other difficulty lies in the use of contraction (on the left). While contraction (on the left or right) can be removed in classical propositional logic, this is not the case in intuitionistic logic. Left contraction can be removed everywhere except for the left implication rule. Since the goal is to automate the search for proof, this rule is problematic because it is a source of non-termination. Roy Dyckhoff proposed a system, called LJT [7], which replaces this rule with four other rules $\Rightarrow_{\mathsf{lefti}}$ with $i = 1, \ldots, 4$, allowing contraction to be eliminated completely. The entire LJT system is presented in Fig. 1. Note that to simplify the presentation, we adhere to Dyckhoff's original system by not considering top, bottom, negation, and equivalence. It should also be noted that all rules are reversible except for the rules $\vee_{\mathsf{right1}}$, $\vee_{\mathsf{right2}}$, and $\Rightarrow_{\mathsf{left4}}$.

The specification in Pgeon of the LJT rules is given in Listing 1.2. Note the existence of the two tags left and right, which allow us to emulate the intuitionistic sequent as mentioned above. Furthermore, since contraction is no longer necessary, we use "==>" for all rules (except the axiomatic rule), which allows us to produce new sequents without the matched formulas. In addition to the problem of contraction, this type of rule allows for the management of potential weakening, as in rule $\Rightarrow_{\mathsf{left4}}$, where D in the conclusion of the rule is removed from the left branch of the premises. This allows the rules of the LJT system to be written almost directly without transforming the system. Non-reversible rules are handled by Pgeon's backtracking mechanism, described earlier in Sect. 3.

```
type prop
main type formula

function and : prop prop -> prop
function or  : prop prop -> prop
function imp : prop prop -> prop
function left  : prop -> formula
function right : prop -> formula

rule ax : left(P0) ; right(P0) ==X
rule and_right : right(and(P0, P1)) ==> right(P0) | right(P1)
rule and_left : left(and(P0, P1)) ==> left(P0) ; left(P1)
rule or_right1 : right(or(P0, P1)) ==> right(P0)
rule or_right2 : right(or(P0, P1)) ==> right(P1)
rule or_left : left(or(P0, P1)) ==> left(P0) | left(P1)
rule imp_right : right(imp(P0, P1)) ==> left(P0) ; right(P1)
rule imp_left1 : left(imp(P0, P1)) ; left(P0) ==>
  left(P0) ; left(P1)
rule imp_left2 : left(imp(and(P0, P1), P2)) ==>
  left(imp(P0, imp (P1, P2)))
rule imp_left3 : left(imp(or(P0, P1), P2)) ==>
  left(imp(P0, P2)) ; left(imp(P1, P2))
rule imp_left4 : left(imp(imp(P0, P1), P2)) ; right(P3) ==>
  left(imp(P1, P2)) ; right(imp(P0, P1))
| left(P2) ; right(P3)

strategy reduce_once : ax || and_right || and_left
  || or_right1 || or_right2 || or_left || imp_right
  || imp_left1 || imp_left2 || imp_left3 || imp_left4
strategy reduce_all : reduce_once*
strategy reduce_fixed : (reduce_once ; reduce_fixed)?
main strategy prove : reduce_all ; reduce_fixed?
```

Listing 1.2. LJT Specification in Pgeon

5 Conclusion and Future Work

This paper introduces Pgeon, a framework designed to generate tableau-based provers from declarative logical specifications. By separating logical content from implementation, users can describe syntax, inference rules, and proof strategies in a lightweight DSL that mirrors textbook presentations. Specifications are compiled into executable provers via a logic-agnostic engine.

Case studies covering classical first-order tableau calculus and intuitionistic propositional calculus show that Pgeon enables rapid prototyping and experimentation, with strategies providing compositional control over proof-search. While flexible, Pgeon prioritizes clarity over efficiency: termination is not ensured and empirical evaluation remains to be carried out.

Future work includes improving efficiency through optimized indexing and term-sharing structures, supporting associative and associative-commutative operators, adding proof trace generation, and exploring additional logics such as modal logic. We would also like to introduce the concept of sequent in a primitive way (we have seen that this concept can already be encoded in the LJT example), which would increase the versatility of the tool by offering the possibility of directly implementing sequent calculi (in particular systems that do not have an associated tableau calculus that is easy to implement).

Disclosure of Interest. The authors have no competing interests to declare.

References

1. Abate, P., Goré, R.: The tableau workbench. Electron. Notes Theor. Comput. Sci. **231**, 55–67 (2009)
2. Beckert, B., et al.: Taclets: a new paradigm for constructing interactive theorem provers. RACSAM **98**(1), 17–53 (2004)
3. Beckert, B., Posegga, J.: leanTAP: lean tableau-based deduction. J. Autom. Reason. **15**(3), 339–358 (1995)
4. del Cerro, L.F., Fauthoux, D., Gasquet, O., Herzig, A., Longin, D., Massacci, F.: Lotrec: the generic tableau prover for modal and description logics. In: Goré, R., Leitsch, A., Nipkow, T. (eds.) Automated Reasoning. IJCAR 2001. Lecture Notes in Computer Science, vol. 2083, pp. 453–458. Springer, Berlin, Heidelberg (2001). https://doi.org/10.1007/3-540-45744-5_38
5. D'Agostino, M., Gabbay, D.M., Hähnle, R., Posegga, J.: Handbook of Tableau Methods. Springer Science & Business Media (2013)
6. Delahaye, D.: A tactic language for the system coq. In: Parigot, M., Voronkov, A. (eds.) LPAR 2000. LNAI, vol. 1955, pp. 85–95. Springer, Heidelberg (2000). https://doi.org/10.1007/3-540-44404-1_7
7. Dyckhoff, R.: Contraction-free sequent calculi for intuitionistic logic. J. Symb. Logic **57**, 795–807 (1992)
8. Otten, J., Bibel, W.: leanCoP: lean connection-based theorem proving. J. Symb. Comput. **36**(1–2), 139–161 (2003)
9. Reis, G., Naeem, Z., Hashim, M.: Sequoia: a playground for logicians. In: Peltier, N., Sofronie-Stokkermans, V. (eds.) IJCAR 2020. LNCS (LNAI), vol. 12167, pp. 480–488. Springer, Cham (2020). https://doi.org/10.1007/978-3-030-51054-1_32
10. Tishkovsky, D., Schmidt, R.A., Khodadadi, M.: The tableau prover generator MetTeL2. In: del Cerro, L.F., Herzig, A., Mengin, J. (eds.) JELIA 2012. LNCS (LNAI), vol. 7519, pp. 492–495. Springer, Heidelberg (2012). https://doi.org/10.1007/978-3-642-33353-8_41

Open Access This chapter is licensed under the terms of the Creative Commons Attribution 4.0 International License (http://creativecommons.org/licenses/by/4.0/), which permits use, sharing, adaptation, distribution and reproduction in any medium or format, as long as you give appropriate credit to the original author(s) and the source, provide a link to the Creative Commons license and indicate if changes were made.

The images or other third party material in this chapter are included in the chapter's Creative Commons license, unless indicated otherwise in a credit line to the material. If material is not included in the chapter's Creative Commons license and your intended use is not permitted by statutory regulation or exceeds the permitted use, you will need to obtain permission directly from the copyright holder.

grind: An SMT-Inspired Tactic for Lean 4 (Short Paper – System Description)

Kim Morrison[1(✉)] and Leonardo de Moura[1,2]

[1] Lean FRO, Washington, USA
{kim,leo}@lean-fro.org
[2] Amazon Web Services, Washington, USA
leomoura@amazon.com

Abstract. We describe `grind`, an SMT-inspired proof automation tactic for Lean 4. Unlike hammer-style tools that translate proof obligations into external logics and invoke external ATP and SMT solvers, `grind` works natively in the Calculus of Inductive Constructions, producing kernel-checkable proof terms without any soundness compromises. At its core, `grind` combines congruence closure for dependent type theory with E-matching and a suite of satellite solvers for linear integer arithmetic, linear arithmetic over ordered modules, polynomial equations over commutative (semi)rings, and associative-commutative operators. Each satellite solver is parameterized by Lean's typeclasses, enabling it to operate over any type that implements the appropriate algebraic interface—not just hardcoded numeric types. Users can extend `grind` with new theory solvers through a plugin API, control theorem instantiation through instantiation constraints on E-matching patterns, and inspect the internal state through an interactive DSL. An annotation system, including automatic pattern selection, enables libraries to declare how their theorems should be used by `grind`. The tactic is distributed as part of Lean and is used extensively in Lean's Mathlib [19] and CSLib [2] libraries.

1 Introduction

Proof assistants based on dependent type theory—Coq [18] and Lean 4 [12]—provide strong guarantees: every accepted proof is checked by a small trusted kernel. The price is that constructing proofs often requires substantial manual effort.

Two families of automation dominate current practice. *Rewriting-based* tactics such as `simp` apply oriented equations exhaustively. *Hammer-style* tools translate goals into first-order or higher-order logic, invoke external provers, and reconstruct proofs internally. Sledgehammer [14] pioneered this approach for Isabelle/HOL; CoqHammer [3] adapted it for Coq; lean-auto [15] and LeanHammer [20] bring it to Lean 4. Translation introduces a gap: not every feature of dependent type theory has a counterpart in the target logic, and reconstruction can fail even when the external prover succeeds.

© The Author(s) 2026
A. Biere et al. (Eds.): IJCAR 2026, LNAI 16688, pp. 106–114, 2026.
https://doi.org/10.1007/978-3-032-32589-1_7

grind takes a different approach. Inspired by the architecture of SMT solvers [1,11], it combines congruence closure, E-matching, and theory solvers into a single tactic operating directly on Lean expressions in the Calculus of Inductive Constructions. There is no translation step and no external tool: every proof term is checked by Lean's kernel. The congruence closure procedure handles the full Calculus of Inductive Constructions, extending earlier work [17].

Each satellite solver in grind is parameterized by Lean's typeclass mechanism. The linear arithmetic solver operates over any type equipped with a module structure over a semiring, and becomes incrementally more powerful over a ring or field. This design enables grind to handle the rich algebraic hierarchy found in mathematical libraries, without hardcoding specific types.

grind is open source,[1] distributed as part of Lean 4 with no external dependencies, and has been available since Lean 4.22 (August 2025). We recommend the reader consult the reference manual.[2] The implementation comprises approximately 40 000 lines of Lean.

Contributions. This paper describes grind with a focus on the following contributions. (1) *Native operation in the CIC.* grind combines congruence closure, E-matching, and theory solvers in a single framework that operates directly on Lean expressions—including dependent types, dependent pattern matching, universe polymorphism, and proof irrelevance—producing kernel-checkable proof terms without translation to an external logic. (2) *Typeclass-parametrized solvers.* Each satellite solver is parameterized by Lean typeclasses, activating automatically for any type with the required algebraic structure. This contrasts with traditional SMT solvers that hardcode specific types. (3) *Annotation and instantiation control.* An annotation system with automatic pattern selection lets library authors declare how their theorems should be used by grind, and a constraint language on E-matching patterns restricts when theorems are instantiated (Sect. 2). (4) *Extensibility.* All built-in solvers are implemented through the same plugin API available to users, who can register new theory solvers and constraint propagators without leaving Lean. (5) *Proof stability and diagnostics.* grind? outputs self-contained invocations listing the theorems actually used, an interactive mode (grind =>) exposes the solver's execution step by step, and comprehensive failure diagnostics report equivalence classes, satellite solver states, and resource limits reached.

2 grind by Example

All examples here can be explored interactively at https://live.lean-lang.org/.

Congruence closure. At the core of grind is a congruence closure algorithm for dependent type theory [17]. It maintains equivalence classes over the terms. When two terms are known to be equal, congruence closure automatically deduces equalities between larger expressions built from them.

[1] https://github.com/leanprover/lean4/tree/master/src/Lean/Meta/Tactic/Grind.

[2] https://lean-lang.org/doc/reference/latest/The--grind--tactic.

```
example (f : Nat → Nat) (h : a = b) : f (f b) = f (f a) := by grind
```

Here `grind` notices the `a = b` hypothesis, applies congruence to obtain `f a = f b`, and then concludes `f (f a) = f (f b)`. A contradiction is detected when the equivalence classes containing `True` and `False` are merged. Before adding terms to the E-graph, `grind` normalizes them: β-reduction, canonicalization of instances and implicit arguments, and hash-consing so that structural equality reduces to pointer equality.

E-Matching and Annotations. While the Lean `simp` tactic uses theorems as rewriting rules, `grind` instantiates theorems using E-matching. Each theorem annotated for `grind` carries one or more *patterns*. Whenever the E-graph contains terms that match a pattern modulo known equalities, `grind` instantiates the theorem and asserts the result as a new fact.

```
@[grind =] theorem fg : f (g x) = x
example : f a = b → a = g c → b = c := by grind
```

The attribute `[grind =]` selects the left-hand side of the equation, `f (g x)`, as the E-matching pattern. Although the goal does not contain a literal instance of `f (g x)`, the hypothesis `a = g c` allows `grind` to match `f a` by substituting `a` with `g c` modulo the known equality.

Library authors typically do not want to specify patterns manually for every theorem. `grind` provides a family of annotations that capture commonly used idioms. For equational theorems, `[grind =]` selects the left-hand side as the pattern, `[grind _=_]` selects both sides, and the bare `[grind]` attribute invokes an algorithm that traverses the conclusion and hypotheses left to right, collecting the minimal set of indexable subexpressions—those with a constant at the head—that cover all universally quantified variables. For implications, `[grind →]` extracts patterns from the hypotheses (forward reasoning) and `[grind ←]` from the conclusion (backward reasoning).

As an example of forward reasoning, consider annotating transitivity and symmetry lemmas for a relation `R`:

```
def R : Nat → Nat → Prop
@[grind →] theorem Rtrans : R x y → R y z → R x z
@[grind →] theorem Rsymm  : R x y → R y x
example : R a b → R c b → R d c → R a d := by grind
```

When `grind` discovers that `R a b` and `R c b` hold, E-matching triggers `Rsymm` to derive `R b c`, then `Rtrans` chains the results. For theorems that do not fit any built-in idiom, the `grind_pattern` command allows manual specification of patterns, including *multi-patterns* that require all components to match simultaneously before the theorem is instantiated.

Instantiation Constraints. Consider the theorem stating that left-shift distributes over addition in the exponent:

```
theorem shiftLeft_add (m n : Nat) : ∀ k, m <<< (n + k) = (m <<< n) <<< k
grind_pattern shiftLeft_add => m <<< (n + k) where m ≠ 0
```

The constraint `m ≠ 0` prevents instantiation when `m` is definitionally equal to zero, since the separate theorem `zero_shiftLeft` (stating $0 \lll n = 0$) already covers that case. Without the constraint, `grind` would generate redundant instances. Other available constraints include generation bounds, instance count limits, structural conditions on matched terms (e.g., requiring a term to be ground or a value), and guards that postpone instantiation until a proposition is known to hold.

Case Splitting and Inductive Predicates. `grind` does not case-split over arbitrary Boolean variables like a SAT solver. Instead, it follows structure: splitting on `if-then-else` expressions, `match` expressions, and inductive predicates. For inductive predicates, the annotation `[grind]` enables both case analysis on hypotheses and introduction using the constructors. As an example, we define big-step operational semantics for a simple imperative language.

```
attribute [grind] BigStep

theorem if_iff {B S T s t} : (ifThenElse B S T, s) ==>
    t ↔ (B s ∧ (S, s) ==> t) ∨ (¬ B s ∧ (T, s) ==> t) := by grind
```

Here `grind` case-splits on the `BigStep` constructors to decompose the hypothesis, propagates the condition `B s` or its negation into the congruence closure module, and applies the `if_true` and `if_false` constructors to close each branch.

Dependent Pattern Matching. When match-expressions involve indexed inductive families, the Calculus of Inductive Constructions requires unifying type indices and inserting cast operations—features with no counterpart in first-order or higher-order logic. Consider a function on length-indexed vectors:

```
inductive Vec (α : Type u) : Nat → Type u
  | nil : Vec α 0
  | cons : α → Vec α n → Vec α (n+1)

@[grind =] def Vec.head : Vec α (n+1) → α
  | .cons a _ => a

example (as bs : Vec Int (n+1)) : as.head = bs.head
    → (match as, bs with
        | .cons a _, .cons b _ => a + b) = 2 * as.head := by grind
```

Because the index is `n+1`, both arguments must be `.cons`—the `.nil` case is ruled out by the type—so `Vec.head` and the inline `match` each have a single branch instead of two and four respectively. When `grind` splits on the `match`, it generates heterogeneous equalities and cast operations that the E-graph tracks automatically. With only one case surviving, the E-graph learns `as = .cons a as'` and `bs = .cons b bs'`; E-matching then instantiates the equation for `Vec.head`, yielding `as.head = a` and `bs.head = b`. Combined with the hypothesis `as.head = bs.head`, the linear arithmetic solver closes the goal.

3 Typeclass-Parametrized Solvers

SMT solvers such as CVC5 [1] and Z3 [11] ship built-in theories for a fixed set of types—typically the integers, rationals, and reals, with fixed signatures for $+$, $\times$, $\leq$. Extending them to new types requires modifications to the solver's source code. In `grind`, each satellite solver is parameterized by Lean typeclasses. The solver activates automatically for any type that provides the required instances—no source-code changes are needed.

The Ring Solver. The ring solver reduces polynomial equalities using Gröbner bases. It activates for any type that is at least a commutative semiring, with extensions for commutative rings and fields. The following example derives the value of the fourth power sum from the first three:

```
example [CommRing α] (a b c : α) :
    a + b + c = 3 →
    a^2 + b^2 + c^2 = 5 →
    a^3 + b^3 + c^3 = 7 →
    a^4 + b^4 + c^4 = 9 := by grind
```

Because the solver is parameterized by a typeclass rather than hardcoded for a specific type, the same reasoning applies to any commutative ring. When the ring has a known characteristic p, the solver performs coefficient arithmetic modulo p via the IsCharP typeclass. For example, `BitVec 8` is a commutative ring of characteristic 256, and `grind` handles it without any bitvector-specific theory:

```
example (x : BitVec 8) : (x - 16) * (x + 16) = x^2 := by grind
```

This holds because $16 \times 16 = 256 \equiv 0 \pmod{256}$. The ring solver also handles commutative semirings—where subtraction is not available—by constructing the Grothendieck completion to obtain a ring:

```
example [CommSemiring α] [AddRightCancel α] (x y : α) :
    x^2*y = 1 → x*y^2 = y → y*x = 1 := by grind
```

Linear Arithmetic and Orders. The linear arithmetic solver handles any type equipped with a `NatModule` (an additive commutative monoid with scalar multiplication by natural numbers) or an `IntModule` (an additive commutative group with scalar multiplication by integers). It extends naturally to ordered settings—supporting preorders, partial orders, and linear orders—and has further extensions for semirings, rings, and fields. A second solver, `lia`, implements a CutSat-style [8] decision procedure for linear integer arithmetic. It operates over any type that admits an injection into $\mathbb{Z}$ via the `ToInt` typeclass. For example, `UInt32` maps into $[0, 2^{32})$:

```
example (a b : UInt32) : a ≤ 2 → b ≤ 3 → a + b ≤ 5 := by grind
```

A dedicated solver for partial and linear orders propagates transitivity, antisymmetry, and totality. It activates for any type with at least a preorder:

```
example [LE α] [Std.IsLinearPreorder α] (a b c d : α) :
```

```
      a ≤ b → ¬ (c ≤ b) → ¬ (d ≤ c) → a ≤ d := by grind
```

Theory Combination. The satellite solvers do not operate in isolation. They share information through the congruence closure core: when one solver reports an equality, all solvers see it. The following example requires the ring solver and congruence closure to cooperate. The typeclass `NoNatZeroDivisors` provides the property that $k \neq 0 \wedge k \cdot a = 0 \implies a = 0$, which the ring solver uses for equality propagation:

```
  example [CommRing α] [NoNatZeroDivisors α]
      (a b c : α) (f : α → Nat) :
      a + b + c = 3 → a^2 + b^2 + c^2 = 5 → a^3 + b^3 + c^3 = 7 →
      f (a^4 + b^4) + f (9 - c^4) ≠ 1 := by grind
```

Here the ring solver derives $a^4 + b^4 = 9 - c^4$. Congruence closure then deduces `f (a^4 + b^4) = f (9 - c^4)`, reducing the goal to $2 \cdot f(9 - c^4) \neq 1$, which is discharged by the linear integer arithmetic solver.

Extensibility. Built-in solvers are implemented through the same plugin interface that is available to users. A solver extension declares an *internalizer* (called when new terms enter the E-graph), and *equality handlers* (called when new equalities and disequalities are discovered). Because the interface is defined in Lean, users can add domain-specific solvers without leaving the language and without any privileged access to `grind`'s internals.

4 Interactive Mode and Diagnostics

When `grind` fails, or when a user wants to understand or control its behavior, the syntax `grind =>` exposes a domain-specific language for stepping through the solver's execution. Users can invoke individual solver steps, trigger E-matching, perform case splits, inspect equivalence classes, and add new hypotheses—all inside Lean, freely mixing `grind` steps with ordinary tactic proofs.

`grind?`] outputs a self-contained tactic script containing the exact steps used to close the goal. The generated script does not depend on the annotations from the environment, improving proof stability across library updates. In the following example, `grind?` generated a script with two steps. The first step instantiates only the theorem `trig_identity`, and the second applies the ring solver.

```
example : (cos x + sin x)^2 = 2 * cos x * sin x + 1 := by
  grind =>
    instantiate only [trig_identity]
    ring
```

5 Related Work

External Provers. Sledgehammer [14] pioneered the hammer approach for Isabelle/HOL, translating goals to first-order logic and invoking external ATPs

(E, Vampire) and SMT solvers (CVC5, Z3). CoqHammer [3] adapted this for Coq. In Lean 4, lean-auto [15] translates goals to monomorphic higher-order logic and dispatches to external ATPs, while LeanHammer [20] adds neural premise selection. lean-smt [10] and SMTCoq [4] integrate external SMT solvers with Lean 4 and Coq respectively, reconstructing proofs from solver certificates. These tools benefit from mature premise selection and highly optimized solver backends, making them more scalable when large numbers of lemmas are available. The cost is a translation gap: not every feature of the Calculus of Inductive Constructions has a counterpart in the target logic, reconstruction can fail even when the external prover succeeds, and the round-trip adds latency. `grind` avoids all three costs by operating directly on Lean expressions and producing kernel-checkable proof terms incrementally. Because it runs inside the Lean elaborator, verification frameworks built in Lean—such as Aeneas [6] and Velvet [5]—can share state across `grind` calls: E-graph contents, resolved instances, and asserted facts carry over when multiple verification conditions share a common proof context.

In Lean 4, the `simp` tactic performs equational rewriting. The `omega` tactic decides Presburger arithmetic over `Nat` and `Int`. Aesop [9] performs best-first search over tactic scripts. Canonical [13] is a type inhabitation solver that exhaustively searches for proof terms in a canonical form. The `egg` tactic [16] uses equality saturation to explore the space of equivalent terms via e-graphs, similar to `grind`'s directed congruence closure. `grind` complements these: it combines theory reasoning with E-matching in a single framework, handles algebraic structures through typeclasses, and supports user extensibility through the plugin API and the constraint propagator interface.

6 Evaluation and Conclusion

`grind` was released in August 2025 and has been rapidly adopted. As of February 2026, Mathlib uses `grind` approximately 3 400 times across 2 400 theorems. Of these, around 1 200 were initially authored using `grind`, while the other 1 200 were refactored after `grind` became available. These refactors averaged a reduction of 28% in lines of code, with ~50 theorems seeing proofs reduced by 10 lines or more.[3] CSLib [2], the Prime Number Theorem[4] project and Terence Tao's Analysis I[5] repository each also uses `grind` around 500 times.

The most immediate opportunities lie in scaling premise selection to large unannotated libraries. We already have a configurable premise selection engine (`grind +suggestions`), which uses trigger-based relevance filtering inspired by [7] to rank unannotated library theorems by relevance to the current goal, but it needs tuning for Lean's libraries, and we anticipate integrating external neural premise selection engines. We also plan to scale better when very large (>1000)

---

[3] https://github.com/leanprover/lean4/blob/master/doc/examples/IJCAR2026/analyze_grind_loc.py.

[4] https://github.com/AlexKontorovich/PrimeNumberTheoremAnd.

[5] https://github.com/teorth/analysis.

numbers of lemmas are available for instantiation, and have initial linting tools to help users design good annotations.

Disclosure of Interests. The authors have no competing interests to declare that are relevant to the content of this article.

References

1. Barbosa, H., et al.: Cvc5: a versatile and industrial-strength SMT solver. Presented at the (2022). https://doi.org/10.1007/978-3-030-99524-9_24
2. Barrett, C., et al.: CSLib: the Lean computer science library. arXiv preprint arXiv:2602.04846 (2026). https://doi.org/10.48550/arXiv.2602.04846
3. Czajka, Ł, Kaliszyk, C.: Hammer for Coq: automation for dependent type theory. J. Autom. Reason. **61**, 423–453 (2018)
4. Ekici, B., et al.: SMTCoq: a plug-in for integrating SMT solvers into Coq. In: Majumdar, R., Kunčak, V. (eds.) CAV 2017. LNCS, vol. 10427, pp. 126–133. Springer, Cham (2017). https://doi.org/10.1007/978-3-319-63390-9_7
5. Gladshtein, V., Pîrlea, G., Zhao, Q., Kurin, V., Sergey, I.: Foundational multimodal program verifiers. Proc. ACM Program. Lang. **10**(POPL) (2026). https://doi.org/10.1145/3776719
6. Ho, S., Protzenko, J.: Aeneas: rust verification by functional translation. Proc. ACM Program. Lang. **6**(ICFP), 711–741 (2022).https://doi.org/10.1145/3547647
7. Hoder, K., Voronkov, A.: Sine Qua non for large theory reasoning. In: Bjørner, N., Sofronie-Stokkermans, V. (eds.) CADE 2011. LNCS (LNAI), vol. 6803, pp. 299–314. Springer, Heidelberg (2011). https://doi.org/10.1007/978-3-642-22438-6_23
8. Jovanović, D., de Moura, L.: Cutting to the chase: solving linear integer arithmetic. J. Autom. Reason. **51**(1), 79–108 (2013). https://doi.org/10.1007/s10817-013-9281-x
9. Limperg, J., From, A.H.: Aesop: white-box best-first proof search for Lean. In: Proceeding CPP 2023, pp. 253–266. ACM (2023)
10. Mohamed, A., et al.: lean-SMT: an SMT tactic for discharging proof goals in Lean. In: Proceeding CAV 2025. LNCS, vol. 15933, pp. 197–212. Springer (2025). https://doi.org/10.1007/978-3-031-98682-6_11
11. de Moura, L., Bjørner, N.: Z3: an efficient SMT solver. In: Ramakrishnan, C.R., Rehof, J. (eds.) TACAS 2008. LNCS, vol. 4963, pp. 337–340. Springer, Heidelberg (2008). https://doi.org/10.1007/978-3-540-78800-3_24
12. Moura, L., Ullrich, S.: The lean 4 theorem prover and programming language. In: Platzer, A., Sutcliffe, G. (eds.) CADE 2021. LNCS (LNAI), vol. 12699, pp. 625–635. Springer, Cham (2021). https://doi.org/10.1007/978-3-030-79876-5_37
13. Norman, C., Avigad, J.: Canonical for automated theorem proving in Lean. In: Proc. ITP 2025. LIPIcs, vol. 352, pp. 14:1–14:20. Schloss Dagstuhl – Leibniz-Zentrum für Informatik (2025). https://doi.org/10.4230/LIPIcs.ITP.2025.14
14. Paulson, L.C., Blanchette, J.C.: Three years of experience with Sledgehammer, a practical link between automatic and interactive theorem provers. In: Proceeding IWIL 2010. EPiC Series in Computing, vol. 2, pp. 1–11. EasyChair (2010). https://doi.org/10.29007/36dt
15. Qian, Y., Clune, J., Barrett, C., Avigad, J.: Lean-auto: an interface between lean 4 and automated theorem provers. In: Piskac, R., Rakamarić, Z. (eds.) Computer Aided Verification, pp. 175–196. Springer Nature Switzerland, Cham (2025)

16. Rossel, M., Schneider, R., Koehler, T., Steuwer, M., Goens, A.: Towards pen-and-paper-style equational reasoning in interactive theorem provers by equality saturation. Proc. ACM Program. Lang. **10**(POPL), 718–747 (2026). https://doi.org/10.1145/3776667
17. Selsam, D., de Moura, L.: Congruence closure in intensional type theory. In: Olivetti, N., Tiwari, A. (eds.) IJCAR 2016. LNCS (LNAI), vol. 9706, pp. 99–115. Springer, Cham (2016). https://doi.org/10.1007/978-3-319-40229-1_8
18. The Coq Development Team: The Coq proof assistant (2024). https://coq.inria.fr/
19. The Mathlib Community: The Lean mathematical library. In: Proceeding CPP 2020, pp. 367–381. ACM (2020). https://doi.org/10.1145/3372885.3373824. https://github.com/leanprover-community/mathlib4
20. Zhu, T., Clune, J., Avigad, J., Jiang, A.Q., Welleck, S.: Premise selection for a Lean hammer (2025)

Open Access This chapter is licensed under the terms of the Creative Commons Attribution 4.0 International License (http://creativecommons.org/licenses/by/4.0/), which permits use, sharing, adaptation, distribution and reproduction in any medium or format, as long as you give appropriate credit to the original author(s) and the source, provide a link to the Creative Commons license and indicate if changes were made.

The images or other third party material in this chapter are included in the chapter's Creative Commons license, unless indicated otherwise in a credit line to the material. If material is not included in the chapter's Creative Commons license and your intended use is not permitted by statutory regulation or exceeds the permitted use, you will need to obtain permission directly from the copyright holder.

SAT, SMT, and Verification

Formally Verified Graph Generation with SAT Modulo Symmetries and Lean

Markus Kirchweger, Pablo Manrique(✉), and Stefan Szeider

Algorithms and Complexity Group, TU Wien, Vienna, Austria
{mk,pmanriqu,sz}@ac.tuwien.ac.at

Abstract. In this paper, we present the first proof-of-concept framework for end-to-end formally verified graph generation. Our approach integrates SAT modulo symmetries with the Lean proof assistant, providing a unified, machine-checked verification pipeline that spans high-level graph-theoretic specifications, propositional encodings, symmetry-breaking mechanisms, and solver-based search. By formalizing graph invariance and symmetry reasoning within Lean, we eliminate common trust assumptions and obtain fully certified non-existence results. We evaluate the framework on three benchmark classes of graph-generation problems, showing practical feasibility on nontrivial unsatisfiable instances.

Keywords: graph generation · formal verification · SAT solving · Lean · symmetry breaking

1 Introduction

Graph generation, i.e., the systematic construction of graphs satisfying specific structural properties, is a fundamental task in combinatorial search. To navigate the vast search space of all possible graphs, research typically focuses on generating graphs *up to isomorphism*, treating relabeled versions of the same structure as identical to avoid redundant computations. For example, Fig. 1 shows two isomorphic graphs.

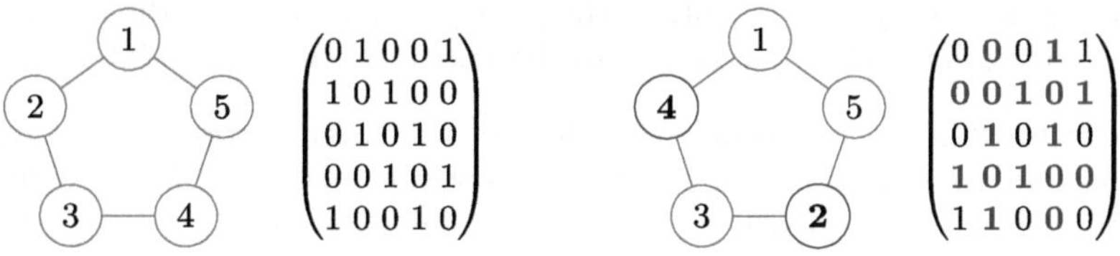

Fig. 1. Two ways to label C_5, and their corresponding adjacency matrices.

The applications of graph generation are broad, spanning practical domains such as chemical informatics [38] as well as theoretical pursuits in extremal

© The Author(s) 2026
A. Biere et al. (Eds.): IJCAR 2026, LNAI 16688, pp. 117–135, 2026.
https://doi.org/10.1007/978-3-032-32589-1_8

graph theory [23,37] and the search for counterexamples to long-standing conjectures [27,29,48]. Historically, one of the most successful approaches is the *canonical construction path* method, exemplified by tools like `geng` (part of the `nauty` package) [36]. These tools are often employed in a *generate-and-test* framework: first, all non-isomorphic graphs up to a certain order are enumerated, and subsequently, these candidates are filtered according to the desired property.

In recent years, the use of Boolean Satisfiability (SAT) and Constraint Programming (CP) solvers has gained prominence for graph generation. Early approaches relied on adding static, often incomplete, symmetry-breaking constraints to the encoding [10]. However, because no polynomial-sized encoding for complete symmetry breaking is known, recent research has shifted toward *dynamic* symmetry breaking via specialized propagators. Notable examples include the authors' previous work SAT modulo Symmetries (SMS) [28,29], SAT+CAS [30], and techniques based on canonical codes in CP solvers [41].

Despite these algorithmic advances, the *formal verification* of graph generation remains an open challenge. Verification is particularly critical when a search yields a "null result", for example when proving the non-existence of a graph with certain properties to settle a conjecture. Currently, the reliability of tools based on the canonical construction path method relies on independent replication of results rather than formal proof. It is common practice to compare the outputs of different independent implementations; if the resulting sets of graphs are identical, it is taken as strong evidence of correctness. For example, in the study of snarks, Brinkmann et al. noted: "Since all results were in complete agreement, we believe that this provides strong evidence for the correctness of our implementations and results" [6].

Modern SAT solvers offer a higher degree of confidence by producing certificates (e.g., DRAT [25] or LRAT [13] proofs) that can be formally checked externally. However, this does not constitute a full end-to-end verification of the graph generation process. Two significant "trust gaps" remain:

1. **Encoding Correctness:** There is no formal guarantee that the CNF formula accurately captures the intended graph-theoretic property.
2. **Symmetry Breaking:** In tools like SMS or SAT+CAS, the symmetry-breaking clauses are introduced by an external propagator. While these clauses can be verified independently, the verification usually assumes the property is a graph invariant. If the user provides an encoding that is not invariant under vertex permutation, the entire proof is invalidated.

The latter issue is compounded by the fact that many properties are encoded using cardinality constraints or other auxiliary variables that "hide" symmetries from the solver. Consequently, standard techniques for breaking *syntactic* symmetries [1,3,14,44] often fail, as the symmetries are *semantic* in nature (see Sect. 3).

Lean 4 is a proof assistant and functional programming language based on dependent type theory; together with its community library `mathlib`, it provides a large and rapidly growing foundation for formalized mathematics [12,40]. Its increasing role in mainstream mathematical formalization is reflected by recent large-scale community efforts [5,11,34,35].

In the SAT community specifically, recent Lean-based work includes machine-checked verification of SAT encodings [9] and end-to-end formal verification of SAT-driven combinatorial results such as the Empty Hexagon Number [26,45].

Building on this line of work, we present a proof-of-concept for end-to-end formal verification of graph generation using the Lean proof assistant [40]. Our approach ensures that the encoding, the symmetry-breaking constraints, and the search itself are all part of a single, formally verified chain of reasoning. We demonstrate the efficacy of our method on three distinct problems:

(i) The **Murty-Simon Conjecture** regarding the maximum number of edges in diameter-2-critical graphs;
(ii) The computation of exact **Turán numbers**, which define the maximum number of edges in graphs forbidding specific subgraphs;
(iii) The search for **Cages**, identifying the minimum number of vertices required for a graph with a given girth and degree.

2 Preliminaries

For a positive integer n, we write $[n] = \{1, 2, \ldots, n\}$. We assume familiarity with fundamental notions of propositional logic [42]. Readers unfamiliar with Lean 4 syntax may consult the official Lean Language Reference [46] for the notation used in the code snippets throughout the paper.

Graphs. All considered graphs are undirected and simple (i.e., without parallel edges or self-loops). A *graph* G consists of a set $V(G)$ of vertices and a set $E(G)$ of edges; we denote the edge between vertices $u, v \in V(G)$ by uv or equivalently vu. The *order* of a graph G is the number of its vertices, $|V(G)|$. We write $\mathcal{G}_n$ to denote the class of all graphs with $V(G) = [n]$. The *adjacency matrix* of a graph $G \in \mathcal{G}_n$, denoted by A_G, is the $n \times n$ matrix where the element at row u and column v, denoted by $A_G(u, v)$, is 1 if $uv \in E$ and 0 otherwise.

Two graphs $G, H \in \mathcal{G}_n$ are *isomorphic* if there exists a bijection $\pi : V(G) \to V(H)$ such that $uv \in E(G)$ if and only if $\pi(u)\pi(v) \in E(H)$. For a permutation π of $[n]$, we write $\pi(G)$ for the graph obtained from G by relabelling each vertex v by $\pi(v)$; its adjacency matrix $A_{\pi(G)}$ is obtained from A_G by simultaneously permuting rows and columns according to π.

We compare graphs in $\mathcal{G}_n$ by the lexicographic order of their adjacency matrices, viewed as binary strings obtained by concatenating rows from top to bottom. A graph $G \in \mathcal{G}_n$ is *canonical* if A_G is lexicographically minimal among $\{A_{\pi(G)} \mid \pi \in S_n\}$, where S_n is the symmetric group over $[n]$.

Partially Defined Graphs. A *partially defined graph* [28] is a graph G where $E(G)$ is split into two disjoint sets $D(G)$ and $U(G)$. $D(G)$ contains the *defined* edges, $U(G)$ contains the *undefined* edges. A (*fully defined*) graph is a partially defined graph G with $U(G) = \emptyset$. Similarly to $\mathcal{G}_n$, we write $\mathcal{P}_n$ to denote the class of all partially defined graphs with vertex set $[n]$. A partially defined graph G can be *extended* to a graph H if $D(G) \subseteq E(H) \subseteq D(G) \cup U(G)$. The set of all extensions of a partially defined graph G is denoted by $\mathcal{X}(G)$. A partially defined graph $G \in \mathcal{P}_n$ is *canonical* if $\mathcal{X}(G)$ contains a canonical graph.

SAT Modulo Symmetries (SMS). SMS is a framework that augments a CDCL SAT solver [21,33] with a custom propagator that can reason about symmetries, allowing to search modulo isomorphisms for graphs in $\mathcal{G}_n$ which satisfy constraints described by a propositional formula using variables $e_{v,u}$ indicating whether an edge is present or not. During search the SMS propagator can trigger additional conflicts on top of ordinary CDCL and consequently learn *symmetry-breaking clauses*, which exclude isomorphic copies of graphs. More precisely, only those copies are kept which are lexicographically minimal (*canonical*). A key component is a minimality check, which decides whether a partially defined graph can be extended to a minimal graph; if it cannot, a corresponding blocking clause is learned. For a full description of SMS, we refer to the original work where the framework was introduced [29].

DRAT and LRAT. To certify unsatisfiability results produced by SAT solvers, we rely on proof formats based on clause addition and deletion. The *DRAT* (Deletion Resolution Asymmetric Tautology) format [47] allows a solver to record learned clauses whose addition preserves satisfiability, together with clause deletions that simplify the formula. DRAT proofs are expressive and well-suited for modern CDCL solvers, but checking them requires nontrivial reasoning. The *LRAT* format is a variant of DRAT that augments each clause addition with explicit hints, making proofs more efficient. In particular, LRAT proofs are amenable to verification in proof assistants such as Lean, which makes them suitable for certified unsatisfiability results.

Lean 4. Interactive proof assistants support the development of machine-checked proofs, but do not automatically prove theorems on their own. Lean 4 is both a proof assistant and a functional programming language, based on the calculus of constructions with inductive types [40]. Combined with automation through tactics and the large reusable library `mathlib` [12], Lean enables the formalization of graph-theoretic properties, correctness proofs for our SAT encodings and symmetry arguments, and checking of solver-generated LRAT certificates. This keeps the full chain of reasoning in one system and yields an end-to-end certification argument whose trusted base is the Lean kernel. In addition, a growing ecosystem of tooling helps develop Lean proofs in practice [15,22,39].

3 Formal Verification Pipeline

In this section, we now describe our framework for the *end-to-end formal verification* for the non-existence of graphs with given properties. The entire pipeline

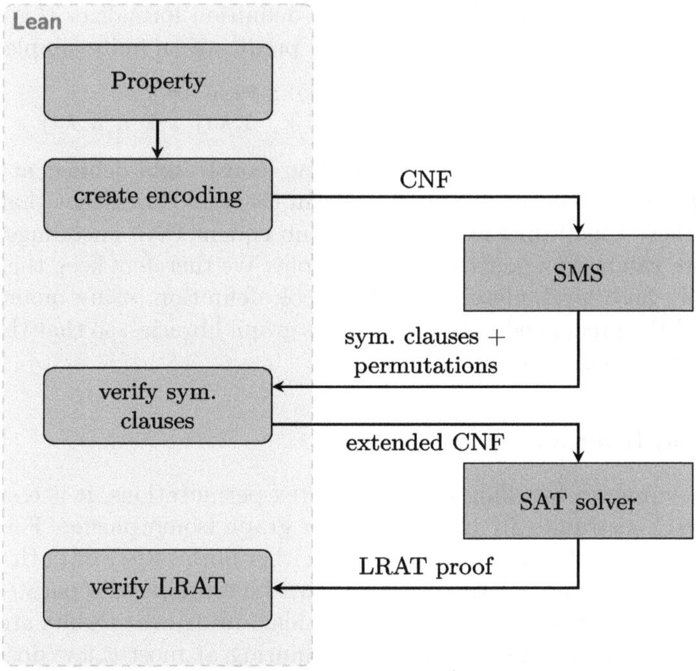

Fig. 2. Basic workflow of verified graph generation with Lean

is implemented and verified in Lean 4, with calls to SAT modulo Symmetries to generate symmetry-breaking clauses and to a SAT solver to produce checkable LRAT proofs for specific problem instances. Figure 2 provides a high-level overview of the workflow. Our implementation is publicly available at

https://github.com/leansolving/leansms.

3.1 Constraint Definition

In order to be able to verify the non-existence of a graph meeting a certain property or constraint (we will use these two terms indistinguishably), the first step is to define the semantics of these properties at a graph-theoretic level. Our definitions are made upon the `SimpleGraph` formalization of `mathlib`. Typical examples include constraints on the number of vertices and edges, forbidding specific subgraphs (e.g., triangles), degree constraints, or girth conditions. Note that we might want to combine multiple constraints into one using conjunctions (e.g., having degree at most 3 *and* not containing any cycle of length 4, etc.).

Example. A graph has diameter at most 2 if and only if for every pair of distinct vertices, either the vertices are adjacent or they share a common neighbor. As an illustrative example, the following Lean definition formalizes this equivalent characterization of diameter at most 2 as a predicate on finite simple graphs:

```
def IsDiameter2 (G : SimpleGraph (Fin n)) : Prop :=
  ∀ i j : Fin n, i ≠ j → G.Adj i j ∨ ∃ k, G.Adj i k ∧ G.Adj k j
```

Since our goal is a fully verified pipeline, constraints defined at this stage are the *reference specification*: the final Lean theorem establishes that no graph satisfying these constraints exists, and all subsequent CNF encodings and proof checking are validated against these definitions. We therefore keep the statement intentionally high level, close to the textbook definition, using quantifiers over vertices and the predefined notions of Lean's graph libraries, so that the intended meaning is transparent and easy to audit.

3.2 Graph Invariance Verification

To enable symmetry breaking based on vertex permutations, it is essential that the specified constraints are invariant under graph isomorphisms. Formally, one must prove in Lean that isomorphic graphs either both satisfy or both violate the constraint, and such an invariance result must be established separately for each graph constraint considered. These isomorphism-invariance results are generally straightforward to establish in practice, requiring at most a few dozen lines of Lean code.

Example. Continuing the example from above, we have to show in Lean that the predicate `IsDiameter2` is invariant under graph isomorphism (denoted by $\cdot \simeq$g $\cdot$):

```
theorem IsDiameter2_iso_invariant {G H : SimpleGraph (Fin n)}
    (e : G ≃g H) :
  IsDiameter2 G ↔ IsDiameter2 H
```

3.3 Encoding Implementation and Proof of Correctness

We encode graph properties as propositional CNF formulas over Boolean edge variables $e_{u,v}$, where $e_{u,v}$ is true exactly when the edge $\{u, v\}$ is present.

Each encoding is implemented in Lean as a function parameterized by the graph order n and by problem-specific parameters (e.g., degree, girth, or edge bounds). The generated CNF instance depends on concrete parameter values, but the correctness results are proved uniformly for all possible values, and then reused across different instances.

The resulting CNF need not preserve syntactic symmetries. For instance, to encode that a graph has at least m edges, we may use a sequential counter encoding. Given a list of literals $[x_1, \ldots, x_s]$ and a threshold k, auxiliary variables $y_{i,j}$ are introduced, where $y_{i,j}$ intuitively expresses that at least j of the first i literals are true. Such encodings break the syntactic interchangeability of the original literals by imposing an implicit ordering via the auxiliary variables, even though the underlying graph property remains invariant under vertex permutations.

To obtain certified non-existence results, we prove *completeness* of the encoding: for every graph G satisfying the target property, there exists an assignment that represents G on the edge variables and satisfies the corresponding CNF. In our pipeline, this direction is the essential one for unsatisfiability-based arguments; the converse direction is not required.

Establishing these links between high-level graph definitions and low-level CNF encodings is typically the most labor-intensive part of the development. However, these proofs are done once per constraint family and are independent of concrete parameter values, so the effort amortizes across many runs.

Example: As a concrete illustration of our approach, we sketch the encoding of the property that a graph on a fixed number of vertices n has diameter at most 2. This means that for every pair of distinct vertices i, j, either they are adjacent, or there exists a third vertex k adjacent to both i and j.

The encoding introduces auxiliary variables for common neighbors. For each unordered pair i, j with $i < j$, and each vertex $k \neq i, j$, we introduce an auxiliary variable that is intended to be true exactly when both edges (i, k) and (j, k) are present. The clauses enforcing this relation are omitted here for brevity.

For each pair (i, j), the diameter constraint is encoded by one clause: either i and j are adjacent, or at least one corresponding common-neighbor auxiliary variable is true. In Lean, this is implemented as follows.

```
def encodeDiameter2Pair (n : Nat) (i j : Fin n) (hij : i < j)
    (auxOffset : Nat) : Clause (PropVar n) :=
  let edgeIJ := PropVar.edge i j hij
  let commonNeighborLits := (otherVertices n i j).map fun k =>
    let cnVar := PropVar.aux (auxOffset + commonNeighborIndex n i j k
    hij)
    Literal.pos cnVar
  Literal.pos edgeIJ :: commonNeighborLits

def encodeDiameter2 (n : Nat) (auxOffset : Nat) : CNF (PropVar n) :=
  (allPairs n).filterMap fun (i, j) =>
    if hij : i < j then
      some (encodeDiameter2Pair n i j hij auxOffset)
    else none
```

The function `encodeDiameter2Pair` constructs the clause corresponding to a single vertex pair (i, j). The first literal represents the edge (i, j) itself, while the remaining literals correspond to the auxiliary variables for all possible common neighbors. The full encoding `encodeDiameter2` is obtained by iterating over all unordered vertex pairs.

Finally, the encoding must be accompanied by a proof that it faithfully captures the intended graph property. As noted above, we show completeness: if a graph has diameter at most 2, then there exists an assignment that satisfies all clauses produced by the encoding. Formally, given an assignment σ whose associated graph (`(PropGraph.fromAssignment σ).toSimpleGraph`) has diameter at most 2, we prove that there exists another assignment that agrees with σ on edge variables and makes the encoding evaluate to true.

```
lemma encodeDiameter2_complete {n : Nat} (σ : Assignment n)
    (auxOffset : Nat)
    (hD2 : IsDiameter2 (PropGraph.fromAssignment σ).toSimpleGraph) :
  ∃ σ', Assignment.agreeOnEdges σ' σ ∧
        CNF.eval σ' (encodeDiameter2 n auxOffset) = true
```

3.4 DIMACS Translation

The abstract CNF encoding is then translated into the DIMACS CNF format expected by SAT solvers using a simple Lean function. Variables are mapped to integers, with the first $\binom{n}{2}$ variables representing the edge variables $e_{u,v}$. Following the convention used by SMS, these variables correspond to the upper triangle of the adjacency matrix, ordered row by row. For example, for $n = 5$ the mapping is shown below.

-	1	2	3	4
-	-	5	6	7
-	-	-	8	9
-	-	-	-	10
-	-	-	-	-

3.5 SMS Execution: Generation of Symmetry Clauses

Symmetry-breaking clauses prune non-canonical graphs from the search space: for each graph isomorphism class, at least one canonical representative is preserved, so equisatisfiability is maintained.

The resulting DIMACS file is then processed by the SAT Modulo Symmetries (SMS) solver, which generates such clauses dynamically during search. Although SMS may already conclude unsatisfiability at this stage, our goal here is not to certify unsatisfiability yet, but to extract the generated symmetry-breaking clauses and their justifications. There exist incremental proof formats, such as LIDRUP [20], that would allow SMS to produce a checkable certificate directly, avoiding the need for a second solver run, but a LIDRUP checker does not yet exist in Lean. Since Lean already supports LRAT, and the SMS-generated clauses are not in general RAT-derivable while LRAT itself is non-incremental, we defer proof production to a later stage.

This is also the first step outside Lean, so every generated symmetry-breaking clause is subsequently checked independently in Lean; for this purpose, we record, for each clause, the permutation witnessing the corresponding symmetry.

3.6 Symmetry-Breaking Clauses Verification

Each symmetry-breaking clause is verified in Lean to eliminate only non-canonical graphs from the search space.

A clause c is interpreted as a partially defined graph $P \in \mathcal{P}_n$ by $A_P(u, v) = 1$ if $\neg e_{u,v} \in c$, $A_P(u, v) = 0$ if $e_{u,v} \in c$, and $A_P(u, v) = \star$ otherwise. Thus, c excludes exactly all fully defined graphs in $\mathcal{X}(P)$.

Given a clause c and a permutation π, Lean computes the lexicographically smallest vertex pair (u, v) such that $A_P(u, v) = 1$ and $A_{\pi(P)}(u, v) = 0$ via `firstDefinedDiff`, and then checks (in `verifyPrefix`) that for every $(u', v') \prec_{\text{lex}} (u, v)$, either $\{u', v'\} = \{\pi(u'), \pi(v')\}$, or $A_P(u', v') = 1$, or $A_{\pi(P)}(u', v') = 0$.

This establishes (u, v) as a strong (P, π)-indicator pair, which implies that P and all its extensions are non-canonical [29, Proposition 2]. In Lean, we define a `SymBreakClause` as a list of literals together with its associated permutation. The main function `verifyDominationFull` returns `true` if and only if, for the given symmetry clause and permutation, every extension $G \in \mathcal{X}(P)$ is strictly lexicographically greater than its permuted graph $\pi(G)$.

```
def verifyDominationFull (c : SymBreakClause n) : Bool :=
  if c.literals.isEmpty then false
  else
    let P := c.toPartialWhenFalse
    let π := c.permutation
    let πP := P.permute π.symm
    match firstDefinedDiff P πP with
    | none => false
    | some (i, j) =>
      verifyPrefix π P πP (i, j) &&
      P.edge i j == some true && πP.edge i j == some false
```

3.7 LRAT Proof Generation and Verification.

After extending the original CNF with all verified symmetry-breaking clauses, the formula is passed to a SAT solver to produce an LRAT proof of unsatisfiability. Lean's existing LRAT checker is then used to verify the proof against the extended CNF.

3.8 Combination of All Components

Finally, the certified non-existence result is obtained by combining the following verified components:

- **Isomorphism invariance of the property:** the target graph property is preserved under vertex relabeling.
- **Encoding correctness (completeness):** every graph satisfying the target property can be represented by an assignment that satisfies the generated CNF.

- **Symmetry-breaking validity:** each added symmetry-breaking clause removes only non-canonical graphs and preserves satisfiability for canonical representatives.
- **LRAT proof correctness:** the final CNF (base encoding plus symmetry-breaking clauses) is proven unsatisfiable by a checker-validated LRAT proof.

Together, these imply that any satisfying graph could be mapped to a canonical representative that satisfies the extended CNF, contradicting LRAT-certified unsatisfiability. Hence, no graph satisfying the specified property exists.

In Lean, we proved a general theorem that verifies the entire workflow assuming that we have already run the entire pipeline:

```
theorem trustModel_impossibility
    (n : Nat) (spec : EncodingSpec n) (cert : SymBreakCertificate n)
    (combinedCNF : CNF Nat)
    (hcombined : combinedCNF = propCNFToNatCNF n (spec.encoding ++
    cert.toPropCNF))
    (lratProof : Array Std.Tactic.BVDecide.LRAT.IntAction)
    (hLRAT : LRAT.checkProof lratProof combinedCNF = true) :
  ∀ G : SimpleGraph (Fin n), [DecidableRel G.Adj] → ¬spec.property G
```

Here, `spec` is what we have defined in Lean as an encoding specification, which captures a property P on graphs, a proof that P is isomorphism-invariant, a CNF encoding of P, and a completeness proof of the encoding. Also, `cert` contains clauses that have passed the computational verification (`verifyDominationFull`). `combinedCNF` is the property CNF encoding plus the symmetry-breaking clauses, and `lratProof` is the checked LRAT proof. The sketch of the theorem proof is as follows: by contradiction, assume there is a graph G that satisfies the property P. Since P is invariant under isomorphism, we can find the lexicographically minimal graph G' that satisfies P. By completeness, G' gives an assignment that makes all the encoding CNF clauses true, and since G' is lex-minimal, all symmetry clauses are satisfied as well. So we found an assignment that satisfies `combinedCNF`, but the LRAT proof ensures that this formula is unsatisfiable. Contradiction.

In the following sections, we will demonstrate that this general theorem can be applied to formally prove the non-existence of graphs that have certain properties.

4 Applications

We now present three representative graph generation problems that serve as case studies for our framework. The purpose of these examples is not to resolve long-standing open problems, but to demonstrate that our verification pipeline is broadly applicable across different classes of graph-theoretic constraints and that the additional overhead introduced by formal verification remains practical.

For all examples, we implement SAT encodings in Lean, which are proven to be complete with respect to the high-level graph-theoretic properties that define each problem.

4.1 Murty-Simon Conjecture

The *diameter* of a graph G is the largest distance over all vertex pairs in G, where the *distance* of two vertices is the length of a shortest path between them. A disconnected graph has diameter ∞. A graph is *diameter-d-critical* if its diameter is d, but the deletion of any edge increases the diameter. The study of extremal properties of graphs with prescribed diameter has been initiated by Erdős and Rényi in the early 1960s [16] and has been the subject of intensive research. An important topic in the field is the characterization of diameter-d-critical graphs [7,8,24,31]. An intriguing open problem is whether the Murty-Simon Conjecture [7] holds, which states that if G is a diameter-2-critical graph with n vertices and m edges, then $m \leq \lfloor n^2/4 \rfloor$, with equality precisely for the complete bipartite graph $K_{\lceil n/2 \rceil, \lfloor n/2 \rfloor}$ (analogous to Mantel's Theorem [32]). Using the list of non-isomorphic graphs generated with `nauty` [36], Radosavljević and Živković [43] computed all diameter-2-critical graphs with up to 10 vertices. Using SMS, one can enumerate all diameter-2-critical graphs up to 13 vertices [29]. We use the same encoding for this property, and additionally assert a lower bound on the number of edges and add a constraint that forbids bipartite graphs in order to exclude $K_{\lceil n/2 \rceil, \lfloor n/2 \rfloor}$; every other bipartite graph has strictly fewer edges.

In Lean, we define the following property on graphs to later formally confirm the Murty Simon conjecture for specific values of n. Here, `cfg` contains the parameter n, and `edgeThreshold` computes $\lfloor n^2/4 \rfloor$.

```
def murtySimonViolationProperty (cfg : MurtySimonConfig)
    (G : SimpleGraph (Fin cfg.vertices)) [DecidableRel G.Adj] : Prop :=
  Constraint.IsDiameter2Critical G ∧
  Constraint.IsNonBipartite G ∧
  edgeCountAssignment cfg.vertices (PropGraph.fromSimpleGraph
    G).toAssignment >= edgeThreshold cfg
```

4.2 Turán Numbers for Forbidden Cycles

Given a graph H, the *Turán number* $\mathrm{ex}(n, H)$ is the maximum number of edges in an n-vertex graph that does not contain H as a subgraph. Determining $\mathrm{ex}(n, H)$ is one of the central problems of extremal graph theory. The area began with Turán's 1941 theorem for cliques and was further developed by Erdős and collaborators [17,18].

A particularly important and challenging class of Turán problems arises when H is a cycle. For even cycles C_{2k}, Erdős conjectured in the 1960s that $\mathrm{ex}(n, C_{2k}) = O(n^{1+1/k})$. Bondy and Simonovits [4] proved that $\mathrm{ex}(n, C_{2k}) \leq c_k n^{1+1/k}$ for a constant c_k depending only on k, establishing the correct order of magnitude. In contrast, forbidding odd cycles leads to a different behavior: a graph with no odd cycle is bipartite, so $\mathrm{ex}(n, C_{2k+1}) = \lfloor n^2/4 \rfloor$, achieved by the complete bipartite graph $K_{\lceil n/2 \rceil, \lfloor n/2 \rfloor}$. Thus, odd cycles reduce to Mantel's theorem, while even cycles remain substantially harder.

To express these constraints in Lean and prove upper bounds of $\text{ex}(n, C_k)$, we use the following definition (note that here `cfg` provides the parameters n (`vertices`), k (`cycleSize`) and m (`minEdges`); the required minimum number of edges of the graph):

```
def turanViolationProperty (cfg : TuranConfig)
    (G : SimpleGraph (Fin cfg.vertices)) [DecidableRel G.Adj] : Prop :=
  Constraint.NoCycleOfLength G cfg.cycleSize ∧
  edgeCountAssignment cfg.vertices (PropGraph.fromSimpleGraph
    G).toAssignment >= cfg.minEdges
```

4.3 Cages

A (k, g)-*graph* is a k-regular graph with girth g, where the *girth* is the length of a shortest cycle. A (k, g)-*cage* is a (k, g)-graph with the minimum possible number of vertices. The study of cages is a classical topic in graph theory that lies at the intersection of extremal graph theory, algebraic graph theory, and combinatorial design theory.

The problem of determining the order of a (k, g)-cage was introduced by Tutte in the 1940s and 1950s. A fundamental lower bound on the number of vertices of a (k, g)-graph is given by the *Moore bound*, which depends only on k and g and is attained only in very few cases.

For many values of k and g, the exact order of the corresponding cage is known through explicit constructions, often relying on algebraic or geometric methods. In other cases, only bounds are known, and the determination of the smallest possible order remains open. The currently accepted values for small degrees and girths are typically summarized in tables compiled from a combination of theoretical arguments and extensive computer searches (see, e.g., [19]).

The Lean property used for this example is the following, where `cfg` contains the parameters n, k and g:

```
def cagesViolationProperty (cfg : CagesConfig)
    (G : SimpleGraph (Fin cfg.vertices)) [DecidableRel G.Adj] : Prop :=
  (∀ v, G.degree v ≤ cfg.regularity) ∧
  (∀ v, cfg.regularity ≤ G.degree v) ∧
  Constraint.GirthAtLeast G cfg.girth
```

5 Experiments

For each of the three examples we are considering, we define CNF encodings in Lean that are proven to satisfy the reference specification properties, in the sense of completeness we introduced above. Table 1 summarizes the proof effort in terms of lines of code, divided by the different scripts in our Lean formalization. Column *Spec* gives the number of lines for defining the CNF encoding functions and *Proof* gives the number of lines to prove the completeness of the encoding. Note that this is done only once parametrically, regardless of graph

Table 1. Encoding completeness Lean proof effort (in lines of code).

Encoding	Spec	Proof
SequentialCounter	131	1406
CliqueFree	22	418
DegreeConstraints	67	1295
GirthConstraints	220	4195
Cages	23	578
MurtySimon	249	4226

size. The *SequentialCounter* file encodes cardinality constraints using a sequential counter, *CliqueFree* defines and verifies a clique-free constraint encoding, *DegreeConstraints* depends on *SequentialCounter* to encode minimum and maximum degree on a graph, and *GirthConstraints* defines and proves the completeness of a cycle-free encoding and two minimum-girth encodings (simple and compact, being the latter more efficient). The completeness of the *Turan* property encoding is almost trivial to prove using the completeness results of cycle-free and cardinality constraints encodings. However, for the *Cages* property encoding, auxiliary variable allocation requires more attention, so we include its completeness proof in a separate file. Finally, we define and verify an *ad hoc* optimized encoding for the *MurtySimon* violation property, which assumes the non-bipartiteness, diameter-2-criticality, and minimum number of edges $\lfloor n^2/4 \rfloor$ of the graph at the same time. The general idea behind the completeness proofs is the following: first, given a graph satisfying the property, we construct an explicit assignment that is "semantically correct", i.e., "agrees" with the graph in the edge variables, and extends to auxiliary variables by assigning values based on the graph properties directly (for instance, in the compact girth encoding, we use variables that are true if a vertex i is reachable from j avoiding k in the graph); and then we verify that all clauses of the CNF encoding are satisfied by this assignment.

In total, our formalization comprises roughly 18000 lines of Lean code, with around 500 theorems and lemmas and 300 definitions across 33 files, carried out over roughly 10 weeks by three contributors. Of this, 61% is reusable infrastructure (graph-constraint encodings and core definitions), 10% is the SMS verification framework, and 29% is problem-specific. About 75% of the codebase lies in the encoding-correctness proofs, where aligning high-level graph properties with CNF auxiliary variables is the main source of difficulty. Isomorphism-invariance results are lightweight (a few tens of lines each) and the central `trustModel_impossibility` theorem is about 500 lines. Because the correctness proofs are parameterised on graph size, the effort amortises across pipeline runs and is reusable for future graph classes.

Once the completeness of the encodings is formally verified and the properties are proven to be isomorphism-invariant, we can evaluate our approach across three representative benchmark families on a range of graph sizes and parameter

Table 2. Experimental results for different graph instances. 'CNF' denotes the encoding generation time, 'SMS' the time spent generating symmetry-breaking clauses using SAT modulo symmetries, 'SC' denotes the symmetry-breaking clauses checking time, and 'LRAT-g' and 'LRAT-c' denote the LRAT proof generation and checking times, respectively. '#LRAT' denotes the size of the LRAT proof, measured in proof steps, and '#SC' shows the number of symmetry-breaking clauses generated and checked for each instance. In the Murty-Simon benchmark, $m = \lfloor n^2/4 \rfloor$.

Murty-Simon										
params			times (s) and metrics							
n	m		total	CNF	SMS	SC	LRAT-g	LRAT-c	#LRAT	#SC
9	20		0.20	0.00	0.07	0.00	0.06	0.02	5113	90
10	25		0.77	0.00	0.29	0.01	0.31	0.12	28327	186
11	30		2.96	0.01	1.19	0.02	1.12	0.43	70319	586
12	36		15.11	0.01	6.14	0.05	6.71	2.16	289289	1443
13	42		123.85	0.01	49.53	0.25	58.17	15.83	1457551	4843
Turán Numbers										
params			times (s) and metrics							
n	C_k	m	total	CNF	SMS	SC	LRAT-g	LRAT-c	#LRAT	#SC
14	4	28	2.00	0.02	0.77	0.03	0.82	0.32	72637	703
15	4	31	6.26	0.02	2.37	0.07	2.80	0.95	179412	1270
16	4	34	20.52	0.04	8.07	0.17	8.94	3.07	454014	2347
17	4	37	79.73	0.05	25.79	0.37	41.08	12.38	1597838	4108
18	4	40	274.81	0.08	104.54	1.45	133.33	35.15	4202467	9850
Cages										
params			times (s) and metrics							
n	k	g	total	CNF	SMS	SC	LRAT-g	LRAT-c	#LRAT	#SC
22	3	7	2.6	0.54	0.97	0.04	0.27	0.71	27002	451
28	3	8	22.42	7.25	4.23	0.22	2.68	7.88	403891	1209
18	4	5	0.26	0.04	0.07	0.01	0.05	0.06	8368	120
25	4	6	3.31	0.63	1.05	0.06	0.65	0.84	110364	566
28	5	5	3.59	0.62	1.12	0.14	0.78	0.86	124887	868
40	5	6	273.35	34.79	87.18	3.29	96.21	51.52	2674873	6710
39	6	5	231.46	11.88	169.21	5.47	24.96	19.69	1338016	9515

settings. The results are summarized in Table 2. All experiments ran on an AMD Ryzen 5 PRO 8540U CPU at 4.979GHz with 32GB of memory under Ubuntu 24.04.3, and all considered instances are unsatisfiable. We use the CaDiCaL [2] SAT solver to generate the LRAT proofs.

For the Murty–Simon problem, we confirm the conjecture up to 13 vertices. In the case of the Turán-type benchmarks, we consider graphs with $m = \mathrm{ex}(n, C_4) + 1$ edges, thereby certifying that no graph with these parameters can exist. For each of the (k, g)-cages considered in the Cages benchmarks, we verify the order of these graphs by running our pipeline for graphs with $i < n$ vertices, where n is the order of the (k, g)-cage. For space reasons, in the table, we show results only for graphs with $n-1$ vertices for even degrees and $n-2$ vertices for odd degrees (in this case, $n-1$ is trivially impossible since odd-degree regular graphs cannot have an odd order). In any case, times are always shorter for smaller graphs.

For each instance, we report the total verification time, as well as a breakdown of the main components of the pipeline. Overall, the dominant costs arise from computing the symmetry-breaking clauses and from generating and checking the LRAT proofs. Other parts of the pipeline, such as checking the symmetry-breaking clauses themselves or constructing the encoding, contribute only marginally to the total runtime.

Across the benchmark set, the total runtime is generally on the order of three times the SMS runtime. While some instances deviate from this pattern, the results indicate that the additional cost of full certification remains moderate, and the pipeline is computationally practical on challenging cases.

Finally, we can use the generated SMS clauses and LRAT proofs to prove non-existence results in Lean for specific parameter values, as shown below for some of them. Their proofs consist of a direct application of the general `trustModel_imposibility` theorem, instantiated with the corresponding verified encodings, symmetry clauses and LRAT proofs.

```
theorem murtySimon13_no_exists :
    ¬∃ (G : SimpleGraph (Fin 13)), murtySimonViolationProperty cfg G
theorem turan18C4Free_no_exists :
    ¬∃ (G : SimpleGraph (Fin 18)), turanViolationProperty cfg G
theorem cages6_5_39_no_exists :
    ¬∃ (G : SimpleGraph (Fin 39)), cagesViolationProperty cfg G
```

6 Conclusion

We presented a proof-of-concept framework for end-to-end formally verified graph generation by combining SAT modulo symmetries with the Lean proof assistant. The framework connects high-level graph-theoretic specifications, verified encodings, certified symmetry breaking, and proof-producing SAT solving into a single machine-checked pipeline. In this way, we address key trust gaps that remain in standard SAT-based workflows, in particular at the interface between mathematical modeling and low-level solver reasoning.

Our case studies on diameter-2-critical graphs (Murty–Simon), Turán numbers, and cages show that the approach is expressive across distinct families of graph-generation problems and practically feasible on nontrivial unsatisfiable instances. The experimental results indicate that verification overhead is moderate relative to the core symmetry and SAT phases, supporting the viability of formally certified computational search.

Future work includes extending the framework from non-existence proofs to certified enumeration up to isomorphism, integrating and verifying additional domain-specific propagators, and parallel proof-producing search, including cube-and-conquer.

Acknowledgments. This research was funded in whole or in part by the Austrian Science Fund (FWF) 10.55776/COE12 and 10.55776/P36688.

Disclosure of Interests. The authors have no competing interests to declare that are relevant to the content of this article.

References

1. Anders, M., et al.: Faster certified symmetry breaking using orders with auxiliary variables. CoRR abs/2511.16637 (2025). https://doi.org/10.48550/ARXIV.2511.16637
2. Biere, A., Faller, T., Fazekas, K., Fleury, M., Froleyks, N., Pollitt, F.: CaDiCaL 2.0. In: Gurfinkel, A., Ganesh, V. (eds.) 36th International Conference on Computer Aided Verification, CAV 2024, Proceedings, Part I. LNCS, Montreal, QC, Canada, 24–27 July 2024, vol. 14681, pp. 133–152. Springer, Heidelberg (2024). https://doi.org/10.1007/978-3-031-65627-9_7
3. Bogaerts, B., Gocht, S., McCreesh, C., Nordström, J.: Certified symmetry and dominance breaking for combinatorial optimisation. In: Thirty-Sixth AAAI Conference on Artificial Intelligence, AAAI 2022, Thirty-Fourth Conference on Innovative Applications of Artificial Intelligence, IAAI 2022, The Twelveth Symposium on Educational Advances in Artificial Intelligence, EAAI 2022 Virtual Event, 22 February–1 March 2022, pp. 3698–3707. AAAI Press (2022). https://doi.org/10.1609/AAAI.V36I4.20283
4. Bondy, J.A., Simonovits, M.: Cycles of even length in graphs. J. Combin. Theor. Ser. B **16**(2), 97–105 (1974). https://doi.org/10.1016/0095-8956(74)90052-5
5. Brasca, R., Birkbeck, L., Boidi, P., Best, T., Velde, A.V., Yang, S.: Fermat's last theorem for regular primes in Lean. Ann. Formalized Math. (2025). https://doi.org/10.46298/afm.16046, https://afm.episciences.org/16046
6. Brinkmann, G., Goedgebeur, J.: Generation of cubic graphs and snarks with large girth. J. Graph Theor. **86**(2), 255–272 (2017). https://doi.org/10.1002/jgt.22125
7. Caccetta, L., Häggkvist, R.: On diameter critical graphs. Discrete Math. **28**(3), 223–229 (1979). https://doi.org/10.1016/0012-365X(79)90129-8
8. Chen, Y.C., Füredi, Z.: Minimum vertex-diameter-2-critical graphs. J. Graph Theor. **50**(4), 293–315 (2005). https://doi.org/10.1002/jgt.20111
9. Codel, C.R., Avigad, J., Heule, M.: Verified encodings for SAT solvers. In: 2023 Formal Methods in Computer-Aided Design (FMCAD), pp. 141–151 (2023). https://api.semanticscholar.org/CorpusID:265859217
10. Codish, M., Miller, A., Prosser, P., Stuckey, P.J.: Constraints for symmetry breaking in graph representation. Constraints **24**(1), 1–24 (2018). https://doi.org/10.1007/s10601-018-9294-5
11. Commelin, J., Massot, P., Mehta, B., Affeldt, R., Baanen, A., et al.: The liquid tensor experiment, July 2022. https://leanprover-community.github.io/blog/posts/lte-final/, lean community project completion post
12. The mathlib Community: The Lean mathematical library (2020). https://github.com/leanprover-community/mathlib4
13. Cruz-Filipe, L., Heule, M.J.H., Hunt, W.A., Kaufmann, M., Schneider-Kamp, P.: Efficient certified RAT verification. In: de Moura, L. (ed.) CADE 2017. LNCS (LNAI), vol. 10395, pp. 220–236. Springer, Cham (2017). https://doi.org/10.1007/978-3-319-63046-5_14

14. Devriendt, J., Bogaerts, B., Bruynooghe, M.: Symmetric explanation learning: effective dynamic symmetry handling for SAT. In: Gaspers, S., Walsh, T. (eds.) 20th International Conference on Theory and Applications of Satisfiability Testing, SAT 2017, Proceedings. LNCS, Melbourne, VIC, Australia, 28 August–1 September 2017, vol. 10491, pp. 83–100. Springer, Heidelberg (2017). https://doi.org/10.1007/978-3-319-66263-3_6
15. Dressler, O.: Lean LSP MCP: tools for agentic interaction with the Lean theorem prover, March 2025. https://github.com/oOo0oOo/lean-lsp-mcp
16. Erdős, P., Rényi, A.: On a problem in the theory of graphs. A Magyar Tudományos Akadémia Matematikai Kutató Intézetének Közleményei **7**(4), 623–641 (1963) (1962)
17. Erdős, P., Simonovits, M.: A limit theorem in graph theory. Stud. Sci. Math. Hung. **1**, 51–57 (1966)
18. Erdős, P., Stone, A.H.: On the structure of linear graphs. Bull. Am. Math. Soc. **52**(12), 1087–1091 (1946). https://doi.org/10.1090/S0002-9904-1946-08715-7
19. Exoo, G., Jajcay, R.: Dynamic cage survey. Electron. J. Comb. Dyn. Surv. **16**, 1–95 (2008)
20. Fazekas, K., Pollitt, F., Fleury, M., Biere, A.: Certifying incremental SAT solving. In: Bjørner, N., Heule, M., Voronkov, A. (eds.) Proceedings of 25th Conference on Logic for Programming, Artificial Intelligence and Reasoning. EPiC Series in Computing, vol. 100, pp. 321–340. EasyChair (2024). https://doi.org/10.29007/pdcc, /publications/paper/TbPs
21. Fichte, J.K., Hecher, M., Berre, D.L., Szeider, S.: The silent (r)evolution of SAT. Commun. ACM **66**(6), 64–72 (2023). https://doi.org/10.1145/3560469
22. GasStationManager: LeanTool: Helping LLMs be better at Lean, February 2025. https://github.com/GasStationManager/LeanTool
23. Goedgebeur, J.: On minimal triangle-free 6-chromatic graphs. J. Graph Theor. **93**(1), 34–48 (2020). https://doi.org/10.1002/jgt.22467
24. Haynes, T.W., Henning, M.A., van der Merwe, L.C., Yeo, A.: Progress on the Murty–Simon Conjecture on diameter-2 critical graphs: a survey. J. Comb. Optim. **30**(3), 579–595 (2013). https://doi.org/10.1007/s10878-013-9651-7
25. Heule, M.J.H.: The DRAT format and DRAT-trim checker. CoRR abs/1610.06229 (2016). http://arxiv.org/abs/1610.06229
26. Heule, M.J.H., Scheucher, M.: Happy ending: an empty hexagon in every set of 30 points. In: 30th International Conference on Tools and Algorithms for the Construction and Analysis of Systems, TACAS 2024, Held as Part of the European Joint Conferences on Theory and Practice of Software, ETAPS 2024, Proceedings, Part I, Luxembourg City, Luxembourg, 6-11 April 2024, pp. 61–80 (2024). https://doi.org/10.1007/978-3-031-57246-3_5
27. Kirchweger, M., Peitl, T., Szeider, S.: A SAT solver's opinion on the Erdős-Faber-Lovász conjecture. In: 26th International Conference on Theory and Applications of Satisfiability Testing, SAT 2023. LIPIcs, 4–8 July 2023, Alghero, Italy, vol. 271, pp. 13:1–13:17. Schloss Dagstuhl - Leibniz-Zentrum für Informatik (2023). https://doi.org/10.4230/LIPIcs.SAT.2023.13
28. Kirchweger, M., Szeider, S.: SAT modulo symmetries for graph generation. In: 27th International Conference on Principles and Practice of Constraint Programming, CP 2021, pp. 39:1–39:17. LIPIcs, Dagstuhl (2021). https://doi.org/10.4230/LIPIcs.CP.2021.34
29. Kirchweger, M., Szeider, S.: SAT modulo symmetries for graph generation and enumeration. ACM Trans. Comput. Log. **25**(3), 1–30 (2024). https://doi.org/10.1145/3670405

30. Li, Z., Bright, C., Ganesh, V.: A SAT solver + computer algebra attack on the minimum Kochen–Specker problem. Tech. rep., School of Computer Science at the University of Windsor, November 2022. https://cbright.myweb.cs.uwindsor.ca/reports/nmi-ks-preprint.pdf
31. Loh, P.S., Ma, J.: Diameter critical graphs. J. Combin. Theor. Ser. B **117**, 34–58 (2016). https://doi.org/10.1016/j.jctb.2015.11.004
32. Mantel, W.: Solution to problem 28, by H. Gouwentak, W. Mantel, J. Teixeira de Mattes, F. Schuh, and WA Wythoff. Wiskundige Opgaven **10**, 60–61 (1907)
33. Marques-Silva, J., Lynce, I., Malik, S.: Conflict-driven clause learning SAT solvers. In: Biere, A., Heule, M., van Maaren, H., Walsh, T. (eds.) Handbook of Satisfiability - Second Edition, Frontiers in Artificial Intelligence and Applications, vol. 336, pp. 133–182. IOS Press (2021). https://doi.org/10.3233/FAIA200987
34. Massot, P., et al.: Sphere eversion in Lean (2022). https://github.com/leanprover-community/sphere-eversion, lean formalization project
35. Math Inc.: Strong prime number theorem in Lean (2025). https://github.com/math-inc/strongpnt, public Lean formalization repository
36. McKay, B.D., Piperno, A.: Practical graph isomorphism. II. J. Symbolic Comput. **60**, 94–112 (2014). https://doi.org/10.1016/j.jsc.2013.09.003
37. McKay, B.D., Radziszowski, S.P.: R(4, 5) = 25. J. Graph Theor. **19**(3), 309–322 (1995). https://doi.org/10.1002/jgt.3190190304
38. McKay, B.D., Yirik, M.A., Steinbeck, C.: Surge: a fast open-source chemical graph generator. J. Cheminformatics **14**(1), 24 (2022). https://doi.org/10.1186/S13321-022-00604-9
39. Mohamed, A., et al.: LEAN-SMT: an SMT tactic for discharging proof goals in lean. In: Piskac, R., Rakamaric, Z. (eds.) Computer Aided Verification. LNCS, vol. 15398, pp. 263–286. Springer, Cham (2025). https://doi.org/10.1007/978-3-031-98682-6_11
40. Moura, L., Ullrich, S.: The Lean 4 theorem prover and programming language. In: Automated Deduction – CADE 28: 28th International Conference on Automated Deduction, Virtual Event, 12–15 July 2021, Proceedings, pp. 625–635. Springer-Verlag, Berlin, Heidelberg (2021). https://doi.org/10.1007/978-3-030-79876-5_37
41. Peng, X., Solnon, C.: BFS-based canonical codes for generating graphs with constraint programming. In: de la Banda, M.G. (ed.) 31st International Conference on Principles and Practice of Constraint Programming, CP 2025, Glasgow, Scotland, 10–15 August 2025. LIPIcs, vol. 340, pp. 32:1–32:16. Schloss Dagstuhl - Leibniz-Zentrum für Informatik (2025). https://doi.org/10.4230/LIPICS.CP.2025.32
42. Prestwich, S.D.: CNF encodings. In: Biere, A., Heule, M., van Maaren, H., Walsh, T. (eds.) Handbook of Satisfiability - Second Edition, Frontiers in Artificial Intelligence and Applications, vol. 336, pp. 75–100. IOS Press (2021). https://doi.org/10.3233/FAIA200985
43. Radosavljević, J., Živković, M.: The list of diameter-2-critical graphs with at most 10 nodes. IPSI Trans. Adv. Res. **16**(1), 1–5 (2020). http://ipsitransactions.org/journals/papers/tar/2020jan/p9.pdf
44. Sakallah, K.A.: Symmetry and satisfiability. In: Biere, A., Heule, M., van Maaren, H., Walsh, T. (eds.) Handbook of Satisfiability, vol. 185, pp. 289–338. IOS Press (2009)
45. Subercaseaux, B., Nawrocki, W., Gallicchio, J., Codel, C.R., Carneiro, M., Heule, M.J.H.: Formal verification of the empty hexagon number. In: Bertot, Y., Kutsia, T., Norrish, M. (eds.) 15th International Conference on Interactive Theorem Proving, ITP 2024, Tbilisi, Georgia, 9–14 September 2024. LIPIcs, vol. 309, pp.

35:1–35:19. Schloss Dagstuhl - Leibniz-Zentrum für Informatik (2024). https://doi.org/10.4230/LIPICS.ITP.2024.35

46. The Lean Developers: The Lean Language Reference (2026). https://lean-lang.org/doc/reference/latest/, lean version 4.30.0-rc2
47. Wetzler, N., Heule, M.J.H., Hunt, W.A.: DRAT-trim: efficient checking and trimming using expressive clausal proofs. In: Theory and Applications of Satisfiability Testing – SAT 2014. LNCS, vol. 8561, pp. 422–429. Springer, Heidelberg (2014). https://doi.org/10.1007/978-3-319-09284-3_31
48. Zhang, T., Szeider, S.: The 3-decomposition conjecture: a SAT-based approach with specialized propagators. In: de la Banda, M.G. (ed.) 31st International Conference on Principles and Practice of Constraint Programming, CP 2025. Leibniz International Proceedings in Informatics (LIPIcs), vol. 340, pp. 39:1–39:19. Schloss Dagstuhl – Leibniz-Zentrum für Informatik (2025). https://doi.org/10.4230/LIPIcs.CP.2025.39

Open Access This chapter is licensed under the terms of the Creative Commons Attribution 4.0 International License (http://creativecommons.org/licenses/by/4.0/), which permits use, sharing, adaptation, distribution and reproduction in any medium or format, as long as you give appropriate credit to the original author(s) and the source, provide a link to the Creative Commons license and indicate if changes were made.

The images or other third party material in this chapter are included in the chapter's Creative Commons license, unless indicated otherwise in a credit line to the material. If material is not included in the chapter's Creative Commons license and your intended use is not permitted by statutory regulation or exceeds the permitted use, you will need to obtain permission directly from the copyright holder.

Accelerating Loops with Arrays

Florian Frohn(✉) and Jürgen Giesl(✉)

RWTH Aachen University, Aachen, Germany
{florian.frohn,giesl}@informatik.rwth-aachen.de

Abstract. We propose a novel *acceleration technique* for loops operating on arrays. The goal of acceleration is to characterize the transitive closure of loops in a logic which is suitable for automated reasoning. Using the new notion of *inductive lvalues*, our technique can handle loops where previous techniques fail, and it *unifies* acceleration for arrays and scalar variables by regarding scalars as arrays of dimension 0. Moreover, our approach uses λs instead of quantifiers. Then the resulting SMT problems can be solved via *lemmas on demand*. An empirical evaluation of our implementation in the tool LoAT shows the power of our approach.

1 Introduction

Model checking programs operating on arrays is notoriously difficult. One reason is that interesting properties of array programs often involve quantifiers, but reasoning about quantifiers is still challenging for SMT solvers. In particular, they can hardly find models for such formulas, but models are crucial for model checking algorithms that use them to prove unsafety and for abstraction refinement.

Alternatives to abstraction refinement are based on *acceleration techniques* [5,9–11,15,18,31,32] that try to characterize the transitive closure of a single-path loop. Then algorithms like Acceleration Driven Clause Learning [20] or Accelerated Bounded Model Checking (ABMC) [22] can lift acceleration from single-path loops to full programs. As acceleration does not over-approximate, it is particularly useful for finding counterexamples, but it can also be used for proving safety [12].

We present a new acceleration technique for loops operating on arrays. In contrast to earlier approaches [1–3,28,34], it applies to a broader class of loops, due to the novel notion of *inductive lvalues*. The core idea of inductive lvalues is that the effect of assignments like $a[i+1] \leftarrow a[i]+1; i \leftarrow i+1$ in loop bodies can be summarized by recurrence equations. Here, the value $a[i]$ that is read is equal to the value that has been written to $a[i+1]$ in the previous iteration.

Another benefit of inductive lvalues is that they allow us to *unify* loop acceleration for arrays and scalar variables by regarding scalar variables as arrays of dimension 0. In contrast, earlier approaches treat arrays and scalars differently.

One more key difference to earlier approaches is that we use λs and a specialized quantifier elimination technique to avoid quantifiers. Even though

© The Author(s) 2026
A. Biere et al. (Eds.): IJCAR 2026, LNAI 16688, pp. 136–155, 2026.
https://doi.org/10.1007/978-3-032-32589-1_9

most SMT solvers have very limited support for λs, the resulting SMT problems can usually be solved with a refinement loop in the spirit of *lemmas on demand* [13,37,38].

2 Overview and Contributions

```
int i = 0;
int k = 10000;
while(i < k) {
    a[i+1] = a[i];
    i = i + 1;
}
int j = nondet(0, k);
assert(a[j] != a[0]);
```

We start with an informal overview, where we illustrate our pipeline for verifying array programs, and explain which parts are contributions of this paper. Consider the C program on the right, which writes $a[0]$ to $a[1], \ldots, a[k]$. Here, nondet(0, k) returns some integer between 0 and k. So the final assertion always fails. There exist various techniques to transform imperative programs into more formal representations like *transition systems*, resulting in:

$$
\begin{aligned}
\mathsf{init}(a) &\to \mathsf{while}(a, 0, 10000) \\
\mathsf{while}(a, i, k) &\to \mathsf{while}(\lambda j.\ \textbf{if}\ (j = i+1)\ a[i]\ \textbf{else}\ a[j], i+1, k) && \textbf{if}\ i < k \quad (\textsc{Loop}) \\
\mathsf{while}(a, i, k) &\to \mathsf{check}(a, j) && \textbf{if}\ i \geq k \wedge 0 \leq j \leq k \\
\mathsf{check}(a, j) &\to \mathsf{err} && \textbf{if}\ a[j] = a[0]
\end{aligned}
$$

In our evaluation (see Sect. 7), this step is done by our tool HornKlaus that transforms C programs into linear Constrained Horn Clauses, which are equivalent to transition systems. In the transition (Loop), "$\lambda j.$ **if** $(j = i + 1)$ $a[i]$ **else** $a[j]$" denotes the array that results from writing $a[i]$ to $a[i + 1]$.

To prove unsafety, one has to show that the location err can be reached from init. The core idea of acceleration is to replace loops like (Loop) with transitions like the one below that can simulate arbitrarily many iterations in a single step:

$$
\begin{aligned}
\mathsf{while}(a, i, k) \to \mathsf{while}(a', i+n, k) \quad \textbf{if}\ & n > 0 \wedge i + n \leq k \wedge \forall j \in \mathbb{Z} && (\textsc{Accel}) \\
& (i < j \leq i + n \implies a'[j] = a[i]) \wedge \\
& (j \leq i \vee i + n < j \implies a'[j] = a[j])
\end{aligned}
$$

It simulates n iterations, where n is chosen non-deterministically.

For this step, two ingredients are needed: First, one needs a *closed form* for each variable x that expresses the value of x after n iterations. For scalar variables like i, *closed form expressions* are computed by solving recurrence equations, resulting in the closed form $i + n$. So a closed form expression for a variable x involves program variables and the additional variable n, and its value is equal to the value of x after n iterations, for all instantiations of the occurring variables.

For arrays, existing acceleration techniques characterize closed forms via quantified formulas of the form "$\forall j \in \mathbb{Z}.\ \varphi$" instead of expressions, where j

is used as array index, as in (ACCEL). The reason is that the standard theory of arrays [35] is not expressive enough to admit suitable closed form expressions.

In this paper, we propose to use λ-expressions as a suitable language to express closed forms for arrays. In our example, instead of (ACCEL), our approach yields:

$$\begin{array}{l}\mathsf{while}(a, i, k) \to \\ \mathsf{while}'\,(\lambda j.\ \textbf{if}\ (i < j \leq i + n)\ a[i]\ \textbf{else}\ a[j], i + n, k)\end{array}\ \textbf{if}\ n > 0 \wedge i + n \leq k. \qquad (\lambda)$$

Moreover, our approach can characterize closed forms exactly in cases where earlier approaches fail or approximate. To achieve this, we introduce *inductive lvalues*. An lvalue is an expression like i or $a[i]$ that refers to a memory location. We call an lvalue like $a[i]$ in (LOOP) *inductive*, as the value that is read from $a[i]$ is equal to the value that has been written to $a[i{+}1]$ in the previous iteration. Thus, the value that is referenced by $a[i]$ in the nth iteration can be defined recursively, which gives rise to recurrence equations, as in the case of scalars. This allows us to accelerate loops like (LOOP) where earlier approaches fail, and to handle arrays and scalars uniformly by regarding scalars as arrays of dimension 0.

While λs can replace the outermost universal quantifier (as in the step from (ACCEL) to (λ)), in general, nested quantifiers are needed to characterize closed forms for arrays. As most acceleration based verification techniques rely on SMT solvers, and SMT solvers still struggle with quantifiers, our goal is to also eliminate the remaining quantifiers. To this end, we identify an important class of loops where all quantifiers can indeed be eliminated, see Sect. 5.

The second ingredient for acceleration is a formula which guarantees that the loop can be executed n times. In our example, this is ensured by the constraint $i + n \leq k$. In our implementation, such formulas are synthesized using the technique from [18]. The details are beyond the scope of this paper, but one core idea is to exploit monotonicity: In our example, if $i < k$ holds after executing the loop body, then it also held before. So if $i < k$ holds before the nth iteration, then the loop can be executed n times. At this point, the value of i is $i + n - 1$, so we obtain $i + n \leq k$. While originally developed for integer loops, the approach from [18] immediately carries over to our setting.
Now our verification problem can be encoded into an SMT formula with λs:

$$\begin{array}{ll}\overbrace{i = 0 \wedge k = 10000}^{\text{initialization}} \wedge \overbrace{n > 0 \wedge i + n \leq k}^{\text{guard of } (\lambda)} \wedge & \\ i' = i + n \wedge a' = \lambda j.\ \textbf{if}\ (i < j \leq i + n)\ a[i]\ \textbf{else}\ a[j] \wedge & \big\}\text{update of } (\lambda) \\ \underbrace{i' \geq k \wedge 0 \leq j \leq k}_{\text{transition to check}} \wedge \underbrace{a'[j] = a'[0]}_{\text{transition to err}} & \end{array}$$

Unfortunately, the major SMT solvers usually fail if λs cannot be β-reduced (i.e., evaluated). However, SMT problems with λs can often be solved via *lemmas on demand* [13,37,38]. Here, the main idea is to abstract λs with uninterpreted functions, and refine this abstraction with suitable *lemmas* whenever a model for the abstraction cannot be lifted to the original problem. In this way, we can prove satisfiability of the formula above, which implies unsafety of our example.

To summarize, our main contributions are: **(1)** *inductive lvalues* that allow for accelerating loops where existing techniques fail, **(2)** the first *uniform* approach for handling scalars and arrays in acceleration, **(3)** the use of λs to accelerate arrays, where the resulting SMT problems can be solved via *lemmas on demand*, **(4)** a quantifier elimination technique which often yields quantifier-free closed forms (with λs) for arrays, and **(5)** a competitive implementation in our tool LoAT.

Outline: After introducing preliminaries in Sect. 3, our main contributions are presented in Sects. 4 and 5. Related work is discussed in Sect. 6, and we evaluate our approach empirically and conclude in Sect. 7. The extended version [23] explains how we handle λs in SMT, and it contains all proofs.

3 Preliminaries

We write $\vec{v}$ and $\mathbf{v}$ for column and row vectors, and v_i is the ith element of $\vec{v}$ or $\mathbf{v}$.

Arrays and Expressions: Let $\mathcal{V}$ be a countably infinite set of variables, where each $x \in \mathcal{V}$ has a designated *arity* $\mathsf{arity}(x) \in \mathbb{N}$. Then x ranges over $\mathbb{Z}^{\mathbb{Z}^{\mathsf{arity}(x)}}$, i.e., over all functions with domain $\mathbb{Z}^{\mathsf{arity}(x)}$ and codomain $\mathbb{Z}$ (i.e., x maps row vectors to integers). Intuitively, x represents an integer array of dimension $\mathsf{arity}(x)$, i.e., we only consider integer valued arrays. So x represents a scalar if $\mathsf{arity}(x) = 0$, and a 1-dimensional array which is infinite in both directions if $\mathsf{arity}(x) = 1$. Considering infinite arrays is in line with SMT-LIB [6]. To model finite arrays, array-accesses must be guarded with suitable constraints. Note that we interpret arrays as uncurried functions, i.e., $x[\mathbf{i}]$ is not a valid expression if $|\mathbf{i}| \neq \mathsf{arity}(x)$. So if a is a 2-dimensional array, then $a[0]$ is undefined. In contrast, $a[0]$ would be a 1-dimensional array in, e.g., C. Handling "curried arrays" is future work.

We use c, i, j, k, m, n for scalar variables and integer constants, a, b for non-scalars (i.e., for arrays of dimension > 0), and x, y can represent both scalars and non-scalars. For any entity e, $\mathcal{V}(e)$ denotes the variables that occur freely in e.

An expression of the form $x[\mathbf{c}]$ where $\mathbf{c} \in \mathbb{Z}^{\mathsf{arity}(x)}$ refers to a *cell*, where each cell stores an integer value. The set *Rval* of *rvalues* is defined by the grammar

$$Rval ::= c \mid Rval \circ Rval \mid x[\mathbf{r}]$$

where $c \in \mathbb{Z}$, $\circ$ is an arithmetic operator,[1] $x \in \mathcal{V}$, and $\mathbf{r} \in Rval^{\mathsf{arity}(x)}$. The set *Lval* of *lvalues* is defined as

$$Lval := \{x[\mathbf{r}] \mid x \in \mathcal{V}, \mathbf{r} \in Rval^{\mathsf{arity}(x)}\}.$$

[1] We use $+, -, \cdot$, and div (for integer division), but other operators are possible as well.

So an rvalue (lvalue) is an expression that may occur on the right-hand (left-hand) side of an assignment. We write i instead of $i[\,]$ if $i \in \mathcal{V}$ has arity 0. For rvalues $r \in \mathit{Rval}$ we define $\mathit{Lval}(r)$ to be the set of r's "top-level" lvalues, i.e.,

$$\mathit{Lval}(r) := \begin{cases} \{r\} & \text{if } r \in \mathit{Lval} \\ \mathit{Lval}(r_1) \cup \mathit{Lval}(r_2) & \text{if } r = r_1 \circ r_2 \\ \varnothing & \text{if } r \in \mathbb{Z} \end{cases}$$

So we have $\mathit{Lval}(a[i] + 7) = \{a[i]\}$ and, importantly, $i \notin \mathit{Lval}(a[i] + 7)$, i.e., $\mathit{Lval}(r)$ only contains the lvalues occurring in r that are not nested below other lvalues.

An *array expression* is a variable from $\mathcal{V}$, or of the form $\lambda \mathbf{i}.\ e$, where $\mathbf{i}$ is a vector of scalar variables, and $e \in \mathit{Expr}$ is an *expression*. We define $\mathsf{arity}(\lambda\mathbf{i} \ldots) := |\mathbf{i}|$. Expressions are generated by the grammar

$$\mathit{Expr} ::= c \mid \mathit{Expr} \circ \mathit{Expr} \mid p[\mathbf{e}] \mid \textbf{if } (\mu)\ \mathit{Expr} \textbf{ else } \mathit{Expr}$$

where $c \in \mathbb{Z}$, $\circ$ is again an arithmetic operator, p is an array expression, $\mathbf{e} \in \mathit{Expr}^{\mathsf{arity}(p)}$, and μ is a first-order formula over expressions involving the relations $>, \neq, \ldots$, and $|$, and the usual Boolean connectives. Here, $|$ denotes divisibility, i.e., $c \mid i$ is true iff c divides i. So "$\textbf{if } (j = i)\ a[i-1] \textbf{ else } a[j]$" is an expression, and "$\lambda j.\ \textbf{if } (j = i)\ a[i-1] \textbf{ else } a[j]$" is an array expression of arity 1. We use r for rvalues, ℓ for lvalues, p, q for array expressions, and e for expressions.

Loops: We consider single-path loops (without branching in their body):

$$\textbf{while } \varphi \textbf{ do } \vec{\ell} \leftarrow \vec{r} \textbf{ done} \qquad (\mathcal{T}_{loop})$$

Here, φ is a conjunction of (in)equations over rvalues, $\vec{\ell} = \begin{pmatrix} x_1[\mathbf{r}_1] \\ \cdots \\ x_m[\mathbf{r}_m] \end{pmatrix}$ is a vector of lvalues such that[2]

$$\forall i, j \in [1 \mathinner{..} m].\ i \neq j \implies x_i \neq x_j \vee \mathbf{r}_i \neq \mathbf{r}_j \qquad (\text{DISTINCT})$$

holds, and $\vec{r} \in \mathit{Rval}^m$. Here, $[1 \mathinner{..} m]$ denotes the closed integer interval $\{1, \ldots, m\}$ (and "$[1 \mathinner{..} m)$" denotes a half-open integer interval). Intuitively, the body of $\mathcal{T}_{loop}$ updates all lvalues $\vec{\ell}$ simultaneously[3] by overwriting each $x_i[\mathbf{r}_i] \in \vec{\ell}$ with r_i, which is the ith component of $\mathbf{r}$. We also use the notation $\mathsf{rhs}(x_i[\mathbf{r}_i]) := r_i$. Such loops correspond to recursive transitions like (LOOP) in Sect. 2. (DISTINCT) ensures that two different lvalues cannot refer to the same cell, which prevents loops like

$$\textbf{while } a[j] = 0 \textbf{ do } \begin{pmatrix} a[i] \\ a[j] \end{pmatrix} \leftarrow \begin{pmatrix} 0 \\ 1 \end{pmatrix} \textbf{ done.}$$

As $a[i]$ and $a[j]$ are written simultaneously, here it is unclear if $a[j]$ is 0 or 1 after

[2] A less restrictive definition would require $\varphi \implies$ (DISTINCT). We use the definition above instead to simplify the presentation.

[3] Considering sequential updates instead requires additional technicalities, so we restrict our attention to simultaneous updates for the sake of simplicity.

the loop body if $i = j$. In the sequel, $\mathcal{T}_{loop}$ denotes an arbitrary but fixed loop.

Example 1 (Running Example). We use the following loop as running example:

$$\textbf{while } i < k \textbf{ do } \begin{pmatrix} i \\ a[i+1] \\ a[i] \end{pmatrix} \leftarrow \begin{pmatrix} i+1 \\ a[i] \\ a[i+1] \end{pmatrix} \textbf{ done} \qquad \boxed{\mathcal{T}_{swap}}$$

It swaps the values of $a[i]$ and $a[i+1]$ in each iteration. So if the initial value of $a[i]$ is c, then after n iterations the value of $a[i+n]$ is c, and the initial values of $a[i+1], \ldots, a[i+n]$ have been shifted one position to the left.

For each $x \in \mathcal{V}$, $\mathsf{up}_x(\vec{\ell})$ is an array expression that describes the array x after one iteration of the loop body. More precisely, we define $\mathsf{up}_x(\vec{\ell})$ inductively as follows:

$$\mathsf{up}_x(\vec{\ell}) := \begin{cases} x & \text{if } \vec{\ell} \text{ is empty} \\ \lambda \mathbf{i}.\ \textbf{if } (\mathbf{i} = \mathbf{r})\ \mathsf{rhs}(x[\mathbf{r}])\ \textbf{else } \mathsf{up}_x(\vec{\ell'})[\mathbf{i}] & \text{if } \vec{\ell} = \begin{pmatrix} x[\mathbf{r}] \\ \vec{\ell'} \end{pmatrix} \\ \mathsf{up}_x(\vec{\ell'}) & \text{if } \vec{\ell} = \begin{pmatrix} y[\mathbf{r}] \\ \vec{\ell'} \end{pmatrix} \text{ where } x \neq y \end{cases} \qquad \boxed{\substack{read \\ write}}$$

Here, the scalars $\mathbf{i} \in \mathcal{V}^{\mathsf{arity}(x)}$ do not occur freely in $\mathbf{r}, \mathsf{rhs}(x[\mathbf{r}])$, or $\mathsf{up}_x(\vec{\ell'})$. Moreover, we define $\mathsf{up} := [x/\mathsf{up}_x(\vec{\ell}) \mid x \in \mathcal{V}]$, i.e., up is the substitution that replaces each variable x with the result of updating x according to the body of the loop.

Example 2 (up*).* For $\mathcal{T}_{swap}$, we have

$$\mathsf{up}_i \begin{pmatrix} i \\ a[i+1] \\ a[i] \end{pmatrix} \quad = \quad \lambda.\ \textbf{if } ([] = [])\ i+1 \textbf{ else } \mathsf{up}_i \begin{pmatrix} a[i+1] \\ a[i] \end{pmatrix} \quad = \quad i+1$$

where $\lambda.\ \ldots$ denotes a function of arity 0, and:

$$\begin{aligned} \mathsf{up}_a \begin{pmatrix} i \\ a[i+1] \\ a[i] \end{pmatrix} &= \mathsf{up}_a \begin{pmatrix} a[i+1] \\ a[i] \end{pmatrix} = \lambda j.\ \textbf{if } (j = i+1)\ a[i] \textbf{ else } \mathsf{up}_a(a[i])[j] \\ &= \lambda j.\ \textbf{if } (j = i+1)\ a[i] \textbf{ else if } (j = i)\ a[i+1] \textbf{ else } \mathsf{up}_a()[j] \\ &= \lambda j.\ \textbf{if } (j = i+1)\ a[i] \textbf{ else if } (j = i)\ a[i+1] \textbf{ else } a[j] \end{aligned}$$

The definition of $\boxed{\substack{read \\ write}}$ corresponds to the *read-over-write axioms* [35]:

$$\mathbf{i} = \mathbf{r} \implies \mathsf{up}_x(x[\mathbf{r}])[\mathbf{i}] = \mathsf{rhs}(x[\mathbf{r}]) \qquad\qquad \mathbf{i} \neq \mathbf{r} \implies \mathsf{up}_x(x[\mathbf{r}])[\mathbf{i}] = x[\mathbf{i}]$$

So our notion of arrays is compatible with the standard first-order theory of arrays. However, our array expressions are more expressive than expressions in the standard theory. As an example, consider the array expression

$$\lambda i.\ \textbf{if } (0 \leq i \leq j)\ 0 \textbf{ else } a[i]. \qquad (1)$$

Here, the number of elements where a and (1) differ is not fixed (it depends on j). Expressions for such arrays do not exist in the standard theory.

A *state* s maps each $x \in \mathcal{V}$ to a function of arity $\mathsf{arity}(x)$. The semantics $[\![e]\!]_s$ of an (array) expression e w.r.t. a state s is defined in the obvious way (see [23]), and it is lifted to formulas over (array) expressions as usual. In particular, the semantics of an array expression is a function. Given a first-order formula ψ, we often say that "ψ holds" or "ψ is valid", which means that $[\![\psi]\!]_s = \mathsf{true}$ for all states s. Now we can define the *transition relation* of $\mathcal{T}_{loop}$.

Definition 3 (Transition Relation). *We define the relation $\rightarrow_{\mathcal{T}_{loop}}$ on states as follows: We have $s \rightarrow_{\mathcal{T}_{loop}} s'$ if $[\![\varphi]\!]_s = \mathsf{true}$ and $s'(x) = [\![\mathsf{up}(x)]\!]_s$ for all $x \in \mathcal{V}$.*

Example 4 (Transition Relation). Let $s(i) = 0$, $s(k) = 5$, and $s(a) = \lambda j.\ j$. Then $s \rightarrow_{\mathcal{T}_{swap}} s'$ with $s'(i) = [\![\mathsf{up}(i)]\!]_s = [\![i+1]\!]_s = s(i) + 1 = 1$, $s'(k) = s(k) = 5$, and:

$$\begin{aligned} s'(a) = [\![\mathsf{up}(a)]\!]_s &= [\![\lambda j.\ \mathbf{if}\ (j = i+1)\ a[i]\ \mathbf{else\ if}\ (j = i)\ a[i+1]\ \mathbf{else}\ a[j]]\!]_s \\ &= \lambda j.\ \mathbf{if}\ (j = 1)\ 0\ \mathbf{else\ if}\ (j = 0)\ 1\ \mathbf{else}\ j \end{aligned}$$

Acceleration: Our goal is to *accelerate* loops like $\mathcal{T}_{loop}$.

Definition 5 (Acceleration). *Let $\rightarrow^n_{\mathcal{T}}$ denote the n-fold closure of $\rightarrow_{\mathcal{T}}$. An* acceleration technique *is a partial function* accel*, mapping loops to first-order formulas over $\mathcal{V}$, $\mathcal{V}' := \{x' \mid x \in \mathcal{V}\}$, and a designated variable n such that*

$$\mathsf{accel}(\mathcal{T})\ [x/s(x), x'/s'(x) \mid x \in \mathcal{V}] \iff s \rightarrow^n_{\mathcal{T}} s'$$

holds for all $\mathcal{T} \in \mathrm{dom}(\mathsf{accel})$, $n \in \mathbb{N}_{>0}$, and all states s, s'. Here, $[x/s(x), x'/s'(x) \mid x \in \mathcal{V}]$ is the substitution that replaces x by $s(x)$ and x' by $s'(x)$, for all $x \in \mathcal{V}$.

So acceleration yields a formula over $\mathcal{V}$ and $\mathcal{V}'$, representing the values of the program variables before and after n loop iterations, and a dedicated loop counter n. This formula characterizes the n-fold closure of $\mathcal{T}_{loop}$ precisely.[4]

Example 6 (Acceleration). Consider the loop

$$\mathbf{while}\ i > 0\ \mathbf{do}\ i \leftarrow i - 1\ \mathbf{done}$$

Here, an acceleration technique may yield the formula $i - n \geq 0 \land i' = i - n$.

As explained in Sect. 2, many acceleration techniques rely on *closed form expressions* that characterize the values of the variables after n iterations of the loop.

Definition 7 (Closed Forms). *We call an expression $x^{(n)}$ over $\mathcal{V} \cup \{n\}$ a* closed form *for $x \in \mathcal{V}$ if $x^{(n)} = \mathsf{up}^n(x)$ holds for all $n \in \mathbb{N}$.*

---

[4] Some acceleration techniques also construct under-approximations, but since we show how to accelerate certain loops precisely, Definition 5 does not allow approximations.

For integers, closed forms are usually computed via *recurrence solving*.

Example 8 (Closed Forms). For Example 6, a closed form for i is computed by solving the recurrence equation $i^{(n)} = i^{(n-1)} - 1$ with the initial condition $i^{(0)} = i$.

Given closed forms for each $x \in \mathcal{V}$, an acceleration technique can return

$$\left(\forall k \in [0\,..\,n).\ \varphi[x/x^{(k)} \mid x \in \mathcal{V}]\right) \wedge \bigwedge_{x \in \mathcal{V}(\mathcal{T}_{loop})} x' = x^{(n)}.$$

However, most acceleration techniques try to avoid quantifiers, as they are challenging for automated reasoning. Instead, the calculus from [18] can be used (see Sect. 2), which can often compute suitable quantifier-free formulas. Therefore, in the sequel, we focus on computing closed forms for loops involving arrays.

4 Closed Forms for Lvalues

We now show how to compute closed forms for array loops. To this end, we impose mild restrictions. First, we require that the indices in $\vec{\ell}$ behave monotonically w.r.t. the lexicographic order (where we have $\mathbf{r} < \mathbf{r}'$ if there is an $i \in [1\,..\,|\mathbf{r}|]$ such that $r_i < r'_i$ and $r_j = r'_j$ hold for all $j \in [1\,..\,i)$). $\mathcal{T}_{loop}$ is *x-increasing* if the indices $\mathbf{r}$ where x is updated by the loop increase their values weakly in each iteration.

Definition 9 (Monotonic Loop). *$\mathcal{T}_{loop}$ is* x-increasing *or* x-decreasing *if*

$$\bigwedge_{x[\mathbf{r}] \in \vec{\ell}} \mathbf{r} \leq \mathsf{up}(\mathbf{r}) \qquad \text{or} \qquad \bigwedge_{x[\mathbf{r}] \in \vec{\ell}} \mathbf{r} \geq \mathsf{up}(\mathbf{r})$$

is valid, respectively. If $\mathcal{T}_{loop}$ is x-increasing or x-decreasing, then it is x-monotonic. *If $\mathcal{T}_{loop}$ is x-monotonic for each $x \in \mathcal{V}$, then $\mathcal{T}_{loop}$ is* monotonic.

Example 10. Reconsider $\mathcal{T}_{swap}$, where a is accessed via the indices i and $i+1$ in $\vec{\ell}$. Since we have $i \leq \mathsf{up}(i) = i + 1$, $\mathcal{T}_{swap}$ is a-increasing and thus a-monotonic. As i is a scalar variable, $\mathcal{T}_{swap}$ is also i-monotonic. Thus, $\mathcal{T}_{swap}$ is monotonic.

For simplicity, in the sequel we assume that x-monotonic loops are x-increasing. Lifting our approach to arbitrary monotonic loops is straightforward.

A monotonic loop $\mathcal{T}_{loop}$ is *array-solvable*, or *a-solvable* for short, if each set $Lval(r_i)$ only refers to array cells that have been written in the previous iteration, or only to array cells that have not been written yet.

Definition 11 (A-Solvable Loop). *Let $\mathcal{L}$ be the smallest set such that:*

$$Lval(\vec{r}) \subseteq \mathcal{L} \qquad \text{and} \qquad \text{if } x[\mathbf{r}] \in \mathcal{L}, \text{ then } Lval(\mathbf{r}) \subseteq \mathcal{L}$$

An lvalue $x[\mathbf{r}] \in \mathcal{L}$ is

- trivial *if for all $y[\mathbf{r}'] \in \vec{\ell}$, we have $y \notin \mathcal{V}(x[\mathbf{r}])$*
- inductive *if $x[\mathsf{up}(\mathbf{r})] \in \vec{\ell}$*
- displacing *if for all $\mathbf{r}'$ such that $x[\mathbf{r}'] \in \vec{\ell}$, we have $\mathbf{r}' < \mathsf{up}(\mathbf{r})$*

$\mathcal{T}_{loop}$ *is* a-solvable *if it is monotonic, each element of* $\mathcal{L}$ *is trivial, inductive, or displacing, and one of the following holds for each* $i \in [1 .. |\vec{r}|]$:

(a) all lvalues in $Lval(r_i)$ *are trivial or inductive*
(b) all lvalues in $Lval(r_i)$ *are displacing*

So $x[\mathbf{r}]$ is trivial if none of the variables occurring in $x[\mathbf{r}]$ are changed by $\mathcal{T}_{loop}$. Inductive lvalues $x[\mathbf{r}]$ give rise to inductive definitions, as reading $x[\mathbf{r}]$ in the nth iteration yields the value that has been written to the same cell (i.e., to $x[\mathsf{up}(\mathbf{r})]$) in the $(n-1)^{th}$ iteration. In contrast, the cell that is referenced by a displacing lvalue $x[\mathbf{r}]$ has not been written before it is being read, as all (increasing) indices that were used for write accesses to x in earlier iterations are smaller than $\mathbf{r}$ in the nth iteration. Note that trivial lvalues are a special case of displacing lvalues. For x-decreasing loops, the inequation $\mathbf{r}' < \mathsf{up}(\mathbf{r})$ becomes $\mathbf{r}' > \mathsf{up}(\mathbf{r})$.

Example 12 (A-Solvable). For $\mathcal{T}_{swap}$, we have $r_1 = i+1$, $r_2 = a[i]$, $r_3 = a[i+1]$, and $\mathcal{L} = \{i, a[i], a[i+1]\}$. For $Lval(r_1) = \{i\}$, we have $i \in \vec{\ell}$, i.e., i is inductive. For $Lval(r_2) = \{a[i]\}$, we have $a[\mathsf{up}(i)] = a[i+1] \in \vec{\ell}$, so $a[i]$ is inductive, too. For $Lval(r_3) = \{a[i+1]\}$, we have $a[\mathsf{up}(i+1)] = a[i+2]$. So $a[i+1]$ is displacing, as $i < i+2$ and $i+1 < i+2$ hold for the accesses $a[i]$ and $a[i+1]$ to a in $\vec{\ell}$. Hence, $\mathcal{T}_{swap}$ is a-solvable.

Earlier acceleration techniques for arrays could essentially only handle displacing lvalues without approximations, i.e., loops where each cell is written at most once, see Sect. 6. Moreover, they treated arrays and scalars differently. Our new notion of inductive lvalues allows us to also handle examples like $\mathcal{T}_{swap}$, and to unify the treatment of arrays and scalars (by regarding them as arrays of dimension 0). Example 13 shows why we disallow mixing inductive and displacing lvalues in $Lval(r_i)$.

Example 13 (Mixing Inductive and Displacing Lvalues). Consider the loop

$$\textbf{while } i < k \textbf{ do } \left(\begin{smallmatrix} i \\ a[i+1] \end{smallmatrix}\right) \leftarrow \left(\begin{smallmatrix} i+1 \\ a[i]+a[i+1] \end{smallmatrix}\right) \textbf{ done}$$

where $a[i]$ is inductive and $a[i+1]$ is displacing. We have $\mathsf{up}^n(a[i]) = \sum_{j=i}^{i+n} a[j]$, which is not an expression as defined in Sect. 3. For such loops, extensions of the underlying theory are required, see, e.g., [29]. We leave that to future work.

We first show how to compute closed forms for all lvalues in $\mathcal{L}$.

Definition 14 (Closed Forms for Lvalues). *We call an expression* $\ell^{(n)}$ *over* $\mathcal{V} \cup \{n\}$ *a* closed form *for* $\ell \in Lval$ *if* $\ell^{(n)} = \mathsf{up}^n(\ell)$ *holds for all* $n \in \mathbb{N}$.

For trivial lvalues, computing closed forms is straightforward.

Lemma 15 (Closed Forms for Trivial Lvalues). *If* $\ell \in \mathcal{L}$ *is trivial, then* $\ell^{(n)} := \ell$ *is a closed form for* ℓ.

Theorem 16 yields closed forms for displacing lvalues $x[\mathbf{r}]$ if closed forms for all $\ell \in Lval(\mathbf{r})$ are known. Here, we use the notation $\mathbf{r}^{(n)} := \mathbf{r}[\ell/\ell^{(n)} \mid \ell \in Lval(\mathbf{r})]$.[5]

Theorem 16 (Closed Forms for Displacing Lvalues). *If $\mathcal{T}_{loop}$ is monotonic and $x[\mathbf{r}] \in \mathcal{L}$ is displacing, then $x[\mathbf{r}]^{(n)} := x[\mathbf{r}^{(n)}]$ is a closed form for $x[\mathbf{r}]$.*

Example 17. Reconsider $\mathcal{T}_{swap}$, where the only displacing lvalue is $a[i+1]$. Indeed,

$$\mathsf{up}^n(a[i+1]) = a[(i+1)^{(n)}] = a[i+n+1]$$

holds for all $n \in \mathbb{N}$, i.e., the value that is referenced by the lvalue $a[i+1]$ after n iterations is equal to the value that is referenced by $a[i+n+1]$ initially.

For inductive lvalues, a-solvable loops give rise to systems of recurrence equations.[6]

Definition 18 (Recurrence Equations). *Let $\mathcal{R}$ be a set of symbols with $n \notin \mathcal{R}$. A* recurrence equation *(over $\mathcal{R}$) is an equation $\mathsf{rec}' = e$ where $\mathsf{rec} \in \mathcal{R}$ and e is an arithmetic expression over $\mathcal{R}$. A substitution θ which maps symbols from $\mathcal{R}$ to arithmetic expressions over $\mathcal{R} \cup \{n\}$ is a* solution *for $\mathsf{rec}' = e$ if*

$$\theta(\mathsf{rec})[n/n+1] = \theta(e) \qquad \text{and} \qquad \theta(\mathsf{rec})[n/0] = \mathsf{rec}$$

are valid. A set of recurrence equations is also called a system*, and θ is a solution for such a system if it is a solution for each of its elements.*

Example 19. Consider the recurrences $i' = i + 1$ and $j' = j + i$. Then θ with $\theta(i) = i + n$ and $\theta(j) = j + \frac{1}{2} \cdot n^2 + n \cdot i - \frac{1}{2} \cdot n$ is a solution, as we have:

$$\theta(i)[n/n+1] = i + n + 1 = \theta(i) + 1 = \theta(i+1) \qquad \theta(i)[n/0] = i + 0 = i$$
$$\theta(j)[n/n+1] = j + \tfrac{1}{2} \cdot n^2 + \tfrac{1}{2} \cdot n + n \cdot i + i = \theta(j) + n + i = \theta(j) + \theta(i) = \theta(j+i)$$
$$\theta(j)[n/0] = j + \tfrac{1}{2} \cdot 0^2 + 0 \cdot i - \tfrac{1}{2} \cdot 0 = j$$

To construct such systems, we apply the *lvalue-substitution* $\sigma_{\mathsf{rec}} := [\ell/\mathsf{rec}_\ell \mid \ell \in Lval]$, which replaces every top-level occurrence of an lvalue ℓ by a fresh symbol rec_ℓ. Now we define the recurrences that yield closed forms for inductive lvalues.

Definition 20 (Rec). Rec *is the system of recurrence equations that contains $\mathsf{rec}'_{x[\mathbf{r}]} = r\sigma_{\mathsf{rec}}$ where $r = \mathsf{rhs}(x[\mathsf{up}(\mathbf{r})])$ for each inductive $x[\mathbf{r}] \in \mathcal{L}$.*

So Rec is a system of recurrences over $\{\mathsf{rec}_\ell \mid \ell \in \mathcal{L}\}$. As the lvalues in $\mathbf{r}$ are updated simultaneously, the value of $x[\mathbf{r}]$ in the *next* iteration corresponds to the value that is written to $x[\mathsf{up}(\mathbf{r})]$ in the current iteration, so we have $r = \mathsf{rhs}(x[\mathsf{up}(\mathbf{r})])$. This is in line with Definition 11, which ensures $x[\mathsf{up}(\mathbf{r})] \in \vec{\ell} = \mathrm{dom}(\mathsf{rhs})$.

[5] A similar observation has been used in [33] to deduce invariants.

[6] Our definition of recurrence equations is less general than usual, as we only need recurrences of order 1, and the initial conditions are always the same in our setting.

Example 21 (Rec). For $\mathcal{T}_{swap}$, we get $\mathsf{Rec} = \{\mathsf{rec}'_i = \mathsf{rec}_i + 1, \mathsf{rec}'_{a[i]} = \mathsf{rec}_{a[i]}\}$. Note that we indeed have $\mathsf{rhs}(i) = i + 1$ and $\mathsf{rhs}(a[\mathsf{up}(i)]) = \mathsf{rhs}(a[i+1]) = a[i]$. Then θ with $\theta(\mathsf{rec}_i) = \mathsf{rec}_i + n$ and $\theta(\mathsf{rec}_{a[i]}) = \mathsf{rec}_{a[i]}$ is a solution of Rec, as:

$$\theta(\mathsf{rec}_i)[n/n+1] = (\mathsf{rec}_i + n)[n/n+1] = \mathsf{rec}_i + n + 1 = \theta(\mathsf{rec}_i + 1)$$
$$\theta(\mathsf{rec}_{a[i]})[n/n+1] = \mathsf{rec}_{a[i]}[n/n+1] = \mathsf{rec}_{a[i]} = \theta(\mathsf{rec}_{a[i]})$$
$$\theta(\mathsf{rec}_i)[n/0] = (\mathsf{rec}_i + n)[n/0] = \mathsf{rec}_i \qquad \theta(\mathsf{rec}_{a[i]})[n/0] = \mathsf{rec}_{a[i]}[n/0] = \mathsf{rec}_{a[i]}$$

To solve Rec, standard techniques for recurrence solving can be used (see, e.g. [4]). While these techniques are very powerful, there are of course cases where Rec cannot be solved, so that our approach cannot accelerate $\mathcal{T}_{loop}$. In the sequel, we assume that Rec can be solved. For inductive lvalues $\ell \in \mathcal{L}$, the following theorem shows that a solution of Rec allows us to construct a closed form.

Theorem 22 (Closed Forms for Inductive Lvalues). *Let $\mathcal{T}_{loop}$ be a-solvable and let θ be a solution for* Rec. *Then for each inductive $\ell \in \mathcal{L}$, $\ell^{(n)} := \theta(\mathsf{rec}_\ell)\sigma_{\mathsf{rec}}^{-1}$ is a closed form for ℓ. Here, $\sigma_{\mathsf{rec}}^{-1}$ is the inverse of σ_{rec}.*

Example 23. Continuing Example 21, we get:

$$i^{(n)} = \theta(\mathsf{rec}_i)\sigma_{\mathsf{rec}}^{-1} = (\mathsf{rec}_i + n)\sigma_{\mathsf{rec}}^{-1} = i + n \qquad a[i]^{(n)} = \theta(\mathsf{rec}_{a[i]})\sigma_{\mathsf{rec}}^{-1} = \mathsf{rec}_{a[i]}\sigma_{\mathsf{rec}}^{-1} = a[i]$$

Indeed, we have $i + n = \mathsf{up}^n(i)$ and $a[i] = \mathsf{up}^n(a[i])$ for all $n \in \mathbb{N}$, i.e., the value that is referenced by $a[i]$ after n iterations is equal to the initial value of $a[i]$.

Lemma 15, Theorem 16, and Theorem 22 give rise to an algorithm for computing closed forms for *all* lvalues in $\mathcal{L}$ (as defined in Definition 11) whenever $\mathcal{T}_{loop}$ is a-solvable:

1. compute closed forms for all trivial lvalues via Lemma 15
2. compute closed forms for all inductive lvalues via Theorem 22
3. while there is an lvalue whose closed form has not yet been computed
   (a) pick an $x[\mathbf{r}] \in \mathcal{L}$ where the closed forms for all $\ell \in Lval(\mathbf{r})$ are known
   (b) compute the closed form for $x[\mathbf{r}]$ as in Theorem 16

For Step (3a), if $x[\mathbf{r}] \in \mathcal{L}$ is displacing and the closed form for $\ell \in Lval(\mathbf{r})$ has not yet been computed, then ℓ is displacing, too, and thus one can consider ℓ instead. As ℓ is a subterm of $x[\mathbf{r}]$, this yields a terminating approach for picking $x[\mathbf{r}]$.

5 Closed Forms for Arrays

We now show how to compute closed forms for arrays, given closed forms for all relevant lvalues, i.e., for all $\ell \in \mathcal{L}$ (as defined in Definition 11). The following theorem is an important step towards closed forms for arrays.

Lemma 24 (Towards Closed Forms for Arrays). *Let $\mathcal{T}_{loop}$ be a-solvable and let $x \in \mathcal{V}$. For each $x[\mathbf{r}] \in \vec{\ell}$, we define the following auxiliary predicates:*

$$\begin{aligned}
\mathsf{written}_{\mathbf{r}}(m, \mathbf{c}) &\iff \mathbf{r}^{(m-1)} = \mathbf{c} \\
!\mathsf{written}_{x}(m, n, \mathbf{c}) &\iff \bigwedge_{x[\mathbf{r}] \in \vec{\ell}} \forall m' \in [m \mathinner{..} n].\ \neg\mathsf{written}_{\mathbf{r}}(m', \mathbf{c}) \\
\mathsf{last_write}_{x[\mathbf{r}]}(m, n, \mathbf{c}) &\iff \mathsf{written}_{\mathbf{r}}(m, \mathbf{c}) \land !\mathsf{written}_{x}(m+1, n, \mathbf{c})
\end{aligned}$$

Then the following holds for all $x[\mathbf{r}] \in \vec{\ell}$ and all $\mathbf{c} \in \mathbb{Z}^{\mathsf{arity}(x)}$:

$$\forall m \in [1 \mathinner{..} n].\ \mathsf{last\_write}_{x[\mathbf{r}]}(m, n, \mathbf{c}) \implies \mathsf{up}^n(x)[\mathbf{c}] = \mathsf{rhs}(x[\mathbf{r}])^{(m-1)} \qquad \text{(QUANT)}$$

Intuitively, $\mathsf{written}_{\mathbf{r}}(m, \mathbf{c})$ checks whether the write access $x[\mathbf{r}] \leftarrow \ldots$ modifies the cell $x[\mathbf{c}]$ in the mth iteration. The predicate $!\mathsf{written}_x(m, n, \mathbf{c})$ is true if $x[\mathbf{c}]$ does not change between the mth and the nth iteration. The predicate $\mathsf{last\_write}_{x[\mathbf{r}]}(m, n, \mathbf{c})$ holds if the last write access to $x[\mathbf{c}]$ (up until the nth iteration) takes place in the mth iteration via the assignment $x[\mathbf{r}] \leftarrow \ldots$. Note that we have $x[\mathbf{r}] \in \vec{\ell}$, so $\mathsf{rhs}(x[\mathbf{r}])$ is well defined. As the final value of $x[\mathbf{c}]$ is written by $x[\mathbf{r}] \leftarrow \mathsf{rhs}(x[\mathbf{r}])$ in the mth iteration, the final value of $x[\mathbf{c}]$ is equal to the value of the right-hand side after the $(m-1)^{th}$ iteration, i.e., $\mathsf{rhs}(x[\mathbf{r}])^{(m-1)}$.

Example 25 (Towards Closed Forms for Arrays). Continuing Example 23, we obtain the following definitions for written and !written due to the lvalues $a[i]$ and $a[i+1]$:

$$\begin{aligned}
\mathsf{written}_i(m, c) &\iff i + m - 1 = c \qquad \mathsf{written}_{i+1}(m, c) \iff i + m = c \\
!\mathsf{written}_a(m, n, c) &\iff \forall m' \in [m \mathinner{..} n].\ \neg\mathsf{written}_i(m', c) \land \neg\mathsf{written}_{i+1}(m', c)
\end{aligned}$$

Here, we combined two universal quantifiers to simplify !written. The definition of last_write is as in Lemma 24. Then by Lemma 24, for all $c \in \mathbb{Z}$ we have:

$$\begin{aligned}
\forall m \in [1 \mathinner{..} n].\ \mathsf{last_write}_{a[i]}(m, n, c) &\implies \mathsf{up}^n(a)[c] = (a[i+1])^{(m-1)} = a[i+m] \\
\forall m \in [1 \mathinner{..} n].\ \mathsf{last_write}_{a[i+1]}(m, n, c) &\implies \mathsf{up}^n(a)[c] = (a[i])^{(m-1)} = a[i]
\end{aligned} \qquad (2)$$

Lemma 24 indicates that a closed form for x might have the form

$$\begin{aligned}
x^{(n)} := \lambda \mathbf{c}.\ &\mathbf{if}\ (1 \leq m \leq n \land \mathsf{last_write}_{x[\mathbf{r}_1]}(m, n, \mathbf{c}))\ \mathsf{rhs}(x[\mathbf{r}_1])^{(m-1)}\ \mathbf{else\ if}\ \ldots \\
&\mathbf{else\ if}\ (1 \leq m \leq n \land \mathsf{last_write}_{x[\mathbf{r}_k]}(m, n, \mathbf{c}))\ \mathsf{rhs}(x[\mathbf{r}_k])^{(m-1)}\ \mathbf{else}\ x[\mathbf{c}]
\end{aligned}$$

where the value of m is uniquely determined by last_write. However, due to the additional free variable m, such an expression is not a closed form in the sense of Definition 7, and thus it is not suitable for acceleration. Moreover, last_write is defined in terms of !written, and the latter contains universal quantifiers, which complicates subsequent automated reasoning.

Thus, we now show how to eliminate both the variable m and the universal quantifiers in !written in the important special case that for every $x[\mathbf{r}] \in \vec{\ell}$, $\mathsf{up}(\mathbf{r}) - \mathbf{r} = \mathbf{d}$ is a vector of constants (which may differ for each $x[\mathbf{r}] \in \vec{\ell}$). Note that if $\mathbf{d}$ is a vector of constants, then we have $\mathbf{r}^{(n)} = \mathbf{r} + \mathbf{d} \cdot n$.

Eliminating the Quantifier from !written: For !written, we get:

$$
\begin{aligned}
& \forall m' \in [m \mathinner{..} n].\ \neg \mathsf{written}_{\mathbf{r}}(m', \mathbf{c}) \\
\iff & \forall m' \in [m \mathinner{..} n].\ \mathbf{r}^{(m'-1)} \neq \mathbf{c} && \text{(by def. of written)} \\
\iff & \forall m' \in [m \mathinner{..} n].\ \mathbf{r} + \mathbf{d} \cdot (m' - 1) \neq \mathbf{c} && \text{(as } \mathbf{r}^{(n)} = \mathbf{r} + \mathbf{d} \cdot n) \\
\iff & \forall m' \in [m \mathinner{..} n].\ \bigvee_{i \in [1..|\mathbf{r}|]} r_i + d_i \cdot (m' - 1) \neq c_i \\
\iff & \bigvee_{\substack{i \in [1..|\mathbf{r}|] \\ d_i \geq 0}} c_i < r_i + d_i \cdot (m-1) \vee r_i + d_i \cdot (n-1) < c_i \quad \vee \\
& \bigvee_{\substack{i \in [1..|\mathbf{r}|] \\ d_i < 0}} c_i < r_i + d_i \cdot (n-1) \vee r_i + d_i \cdot (m-1) < c_i \quad \vee \quad \bigvee_{\substack{i \in [1..|\mathbf{r}|] \\ |d_i| > 1}} d_i \nmid (c_i - r_i)
\end{aligned}
\tag{qe}
$$

Again, "|" denotes divisibility, so $d_i \nmid (c_i - r_i)$ is true iff d_i does not divide $c_i - r_i$. In the last step, the first two sub-formulas $\bigvee \ldots$ cover the case that

$$
c_i \notin \left[\min_{m' \in [m,n]} (r_i + d_i \cdot (m' - 1)),\ \max_{m' \in [m,n]} (r_i + d_i \cdot (m' - 1)) \right], \tag{3}
$$

which immediately implies $r_i + d_i \cdot (m' - 1) \neq c_i$. Here, we consider the cases $d_i \geq 0$ (first $\bigvee \ldots$) and $d_i < 0$ (second $\bigvee \ldots$) separately. If (3) does not hold, then we have $\forall m' \in [m \mathinner{..} n].\ r_i + d_i \cdot (m' - 1) \neq c_i$ iff $c_i - r_i$ is not divisible by d_i.

Eliminating the Quantifier from (QUANT): Next, we eliminate m from the negated matrix of (QUANT), i.e., from

$$
m \in [1 \mathinner{..} n] \wedge \mathsf{last\_write}_{x[\mathbf{r}]}(m, n, \mathbf{c}) \wedge \mathsf{up}^n(x)[\mathbf{c}] \neq \mathsf{rhs}(x[\mathbf{r}])^{(m-1)}, \tag{!QUANT}
$$

by deriving an instantiation $e_{x[\mathbf{r}]}$ so that $\exists m.$ (!QUANT) $\iff$ (!QUANT)$[m/e_{x[\mathbf{r}]}]$ and thus (QUANT) $\iff$ $\neg$(!QUANT)$[m/e_{x[\mathbf{r}]}]$ holds. We get:

$$
\begin{aligned}
\mathsf{last\_write}_{x[\mathbf{r}]}(m, n, \mathbf{c}) \iff & \mathsf{written}_{\mathbf{r}}(m, \mathbf{c}) \wedge \ldots && \text{(by def. of last\_write)} \\
\iff & \mathbf{r}^{(m-1)} = \mathbf{c} \wedge \ldots && \text{(by def. of written)} \\
\iff & \mathbf{r} + \mathbf{d} \cdot (m-1) = \mathbf{c} \wedge \ldots && \text{(by def. of } \mathbf{r}^{(n)}) \\
\iff & \bigwedge_{\substack{i \in [1..|\mathbf{r}|] \\ d_i = 0}} r_i = c_i \wedge \bigwedge_{\substack{i \in [1..|\mathbf{r}|] \\ d_i \neq 0}} d_i | (c_i - r_i) \wedge m = (c_i - r_i) \operatorname{div} d_i + 1 \wedge \ldots
\end{aligned}
$$

The last step results from solving the equation $\mathbf{r} + \mathbf{d} \cdot (m-1) = \mathbf{c}$ for m. More explicitly, this equation means $\bigwedge_{i=1}^{|\mathbf{r}|} r_i + d_i \cdot (m-1) = c_i$. So for each conjunct, we obtain $m = \frac{c_i - r_i}{d_i} + 1$ if $d_i \neq 0$, or $r_i = c_i$ if $d_i = 0$. As m is an integer, the former is equivalent to $m = (c_i - r_i) \mathsf{div}\ d_i + 1 \wedge d_i | (c_i - r_i)$. So if there is a $d_i \neq 0$, then m can be eliminated by propagating the equality $m = (c_i - r_i) \mathsf{div}\ d_i + 1$.

If *all* elements of $\mathbf{d}$ are 0, then $\mathbf{r}$ does not change at all, and we obtain:

$$\begin{aligned} \mathsf{last\_write}_{x[\mathbf{r}]}(m, n, \mathbf{c}) &\iff \mathsf{written}_{\mathbf{r}}(m, \mathbf{c}) \wedge \mathsf{!written}_x(m+1, n, \mathbf{c}) \quad \text{(def. of } \mathsf{last\_write}\text{)} \\ &\iff \mathsf{written}_{\mathbf{r}}(m, \mathbf{c}) \wedge m \geq n \end{aligned}$$

The reason for the last step is that, in this case, the write access $x[\mathbf{r}] \leftarrow \ldots$ overwrites the same cell in every iteration. So $\mathsf{written}_{\mathbf{r}}(m, \mathbf{c})$ implies $\mathsf{written}_{\mathbf{r}}(m+1, \mathbf{c})$, which contradicts $\mathsf{!written}_x(m+1, n, \mathbf{c})$, unless we have $m + 1 > n$. In the latter case, $\mathsf{!written}_x(m+1, n, \mathbf{c})$ is trivially true. As m ranges over $[1, n]$ in (!QUANT), $m + 1 > n$ implies $m = n$, so we can instantiate m with n if $\mathbf{d} = [0, \ldots, 0]$.

Hence, if the indices of all array accesses only change by constants in every iteration, then all quantifiers that occur in Lemma 24 can be eliminated.

Example 26 (Quantifier Elimination). For $\mathcal{T}_{swap}$, we have $\mathbf{d} = 1$ for both $a[i]$ and $a[i+1]$. As explained above, we can simplify $\mathsf{!written}_a(m, n, c)$ from Example 25:

$$(c < i + m - 1 \vee i + n - 1 < c) \wedge (c < i + m \vee i + n < c) \qquad ④$$

Moreover, the final formulas ② from Example 25 can be simplified to:

$$\left.\begin{aligned} 1 \leq c - i + 1 \leq n \wedge \mathsf{last\_write}_{a[i]}(c - i + 1, n, c) &\implies \mathsf{up}^n(a)[c] = a[c+1] \\ 1 \leq c - i \leq n \wedge \mathsf{last\_write}_{a[i+1]}(c - i, n, c) &\implies \mathsf{up}^n(a)[c] = a[i] \end{aligned}\right. \qquad ⑤$$

Here, we propagated the equality $m = c - i + 1$ (implied by $\mathsf{last\_write}_{a[i]}(m, n, c)$) in the first line, and the equality $m = c - i$ (implied by $\mathsf{last\_write}_{a[i+1]}(m, n, c)$) in the second line. For the first occurrence of $\mathsf{last\_write}$ in ⑤, we get:

$$\begin{aligned} &\mathsf{last\_write}_{a[i]}(c - i + 1, n, c) \\ \iff\ & i^{(c-i)} = c \wedge \mathsf{!written}_a(c - i + 2, n, c) \qquad \text{(by def. of } \mathsf{last\_write} \text{ and } \mathsf{written}\text{)} \\ \iff\ & i + c - i = c \wedge \mathsf{!written}_a(c - i + 2, n, c) \iff \mathsf{!written}_a(c - i + 2, n, c) \overset{④}{\iff} \mathsf{true} \end{aligned}$$

Similarly, for the second occurrence of $\mathsf{last\_write}$ in ⑤, we get:

$$\mathsf{last\_write}_{a[i+1]}(c - i, n, c) \iff \mathsf{!written}_a(c - i + 1, n, c) \overset{④}{\iff} i + n - 1 < c$$

Thus, ⑤ simplifies to:

$$0 \leq c - i < n \implies \mathsf{up}^n(a)[c] = a[c+1] \qquad 1 \leq c - i = n \implies \mathsf{up}^n(a)[c] = a[i] \quad ⑥$$

The left implication states that $a[i+1], \ldots, a[i+n]$ are shifted to the left by one position, and the right implication states that $a[i]$ gets moved to index $i+n$.

Putting it all Together: Now we can finally compute closed forms for arrays. Recall that the quantified variable m from (QUANT) was eliminated via instantiation. For each $x[\mathbf{r}] \in \vec{\ell}$, let $e_{x[\mathbf{r}]}$ be the corresponding instantiation of m, i.e., the expression such that

$$\begin{aligned} & \forall m \in [1\,..\,n].\ \mathsf{last\_write}_{x[\mathbf{r}]}(m, n, \mathbf{c}) \implies \mathsf{up}^n(x)[\mathbf{c}] = \mathsf{rhs}(x[\mathbf{r}])^{(m-1)} \\ \text{iff} \quad & 1 \leq e_{x[\mathbf{r}]} \leq n \land \mathsf{last\_write}_{x[\mathbf{r}]}(e_{x[\mathbf{r}]}, n, \mathbf{c}) \implies \mathsf{up}^n(x)[\mathbf{c}] = \mathsf{rhs}(x[\mathbf{r}])^{(e_{x[\mathbf{r}]}-1)}. \end{aligned}$$

Then we obtain our main theorem:

Theorem 27 (Closed Forms for Arrays). *Let $x \in \mathcal{V}$, let $\mathcal{T}_{loop}$ be a-solvable, assume that* Rec *can be solved, and let $x[\mathbf{r}_1], \ldots, x[\mathbf{r}_k]$ be all elements of $\vec{\ell}$ of the form $x[\ldots]$. If $\mathsf{up}(\mathbf{r}_i) - \mathbf{r}_i$ is a vector of constants for every $i \in [1\,..\,k]$, then*

$$\begin{aligned} x^{(n)} := \lambda \mathbf{c}.\ & \\ & \textbf{if } (1 \leq e_{x[\mathbf{r}_1]} \leq n \land \mathsf{last\_write}_{x[\mathbf{r}_1]}(e_{x[\mathbf{r}_1]}, n, \mathbf{c}))\ \mathsf{rhs}(x[\mathbf{r}_1])^{(e_{x[\mathbf{r}_1]}-1)} \ \textbf{else if} \ldots \quad ⑦ \\ \textbf{else if } & (1 \leq e_{x[\mathbf{r}_k]} \leq n \land \mathsf{last\_write}_{x[\mathbf{r}_k]}(e_{x[\mathbf{r}_k]}, n, \mathbf{c}))\ \mathsf{rhs}(x[\mathbf{r}_k])^{(e_{x[\mathbf{r}_k]}-1)} \ \textbf{else } x[\mathbf{c}] \end{aligned}$$

is a closed form for x.

So the closed form $x^{(n)}$ is the array that maps every index $\mathbf{c}$ to the updated right-hand side $\mathsf{rhs}(x[\mathbf{r}_i])^{(e_{x[\mathbf{r}_i]}-1)}$ (which is constructed using the closed forms for lvalues from Sect. 4), where the last write access to the cell $x[\mathbf{c}]$ took place in the $e_{x[\mathbf{r}_i]}{}^{th}$ iteration via an assignment to $x[\mathbf{r}_i]$. As shown when deriving (qe), all quantifiers can be eliminated from the definition of !written (and thus last_write), so Theorem 27 gives rise to *quantifier-free* closed forms for arrays.

Example 28 In Example 26, we instantiated m with $e_{a[i]} := c-i+1$ and $e_{a[i+1]} := c - i$, respectively. Thus, similar to ⑤, we obtain the closed form

$$\begin{aligned} a^{(n)} = \lambda c.\ & \textbf{if } (1 \leq c - i + 1 \leq n \land \mathsf{last\_write}_{a[i]}(c - i + 1, n, c))\ a[c+1] \quad \textbf{else} \\ & \textbf{if } (1 \leq c - i \leq n \land \mathsf{last\_write}_{a[i+1]}(c - i, n, c))\ a[i] \qquad \textbf{else } a[c] \end{aligned}$$

since $(a[i+1])^{(c-i+1-1)} = a[c+1]$ and $(a[i])^{(c-i-1)} = a[i]$. By eliminating all remaining quantifiers and applying simplifications, analogously to ⑥, we obtain:

$$a^{(n)} = \lambda c.\ \textbf{if } (0 \leq c - i < n)\ a[c+1] \ \textbf{else if } (1 \leq c - i = n)\ a[i] \ \textbf{else } a[c] \quad ⑧$$

At this point, we obtained closed form expressions in the sense of Definition 7, i.e., they are suitable for acceleration. As they are quantifier-free, they are also suitable for automation via SMT by handling λs with *lemmas on demand*, see [23].

6 Related Work

Acceleration techniques for arrays were already studied in [1,28,34], where [28] is restricted to loops where arrays are partitioned into read- and write-only arrays.

The technique from [34] does not require such a partitioning, but if the same array cell is written more than once (as in $\mathcal{T}_{swap}$, where $a[i] \leftarrow \ldots$ overwrites a cell that has already been written by $a[i+1] \leftarrow \ldots$ in the previous iteration), then [34] approximates. Moreover, to compute a closed form for an array a, [34] requires that the closed forms for right-hand sides of updates $a[i] \leftarrow \ldots$ are already known. This means that a itself must not occur on the right-hand side.

In [1], it is shown how to accelerate *local ground assignments*. Their definition imposes certain restrictions that are not required in our setting. In particular, the loop body must only update each array a at a single index i. So their approach does not apply to, e.g., $\mathcal{T}_{swap}$. In contrast to [34], restricted forms of occurrences of the array a are possible on the right-hand side of $a[i] \leftarrow \ldots$

A similar approach to our elimination of the quantifiers from !written in Sect. 5 is also used in [1], but our technique for eliminating the quantifier from (QUANT) is specific to our approach. Moreover, [1] also uses λs for the result of acceleration, but only to simplify the presentation. In their implementation, they use quantifiers instead, whereas we use SMT solving with λs.

Subsequently, the results from [1] have been used in [2] to show decidability of safety for a certain class of array programs. In an orthogonal line of research, [3] describes a framework to combine acceleration techniques.

7 Implementation and Evaluation

We implemented our approach in LoAT [19], where we use it in our model checking algorithm ABMC [22], which integrates acceleration into Bounded Model Checking (BMC). ABMC lifts acceleration from single-path loops to systems with complex control flow, i.e., it also supports multi-path loops, nested loops, etc. LoAT uses our SMT solver SwInE [21], which is built on top of Z3 [36]. The input format of LoAT are Constrained Horn Clauses (CHCs) [14], where (un)safe verification tasks correspond to (un)satisfiable CHCs.

We used our novel tool HornKlaus [24] to transform the C benchmarks from the category `ReachSafety-Arrays` of the Software Verification Competition (SV-COMP [7]) to CHCs. HornKlaus does not (yet) aim to preserve (un)safety in all cases, as it does not take all intricacies of the C standard into account. Instead, its purpose is to generate CHCs that mirror the given *algorithm* as closely as possible. Thus, HornKlaus cannot yet be used to compare CHC solvers with C verifiers, but it has certain advantages over other tools that convert C to CHCs: SeaHorn [27] converts multi-dimensional arrays to one-dimensional arrays, resulting in a larger gap between the C program and the CHCs, and Korn [16] often yields non-linear CHCs (which are not yet supported by LoAT) when HornKlaus does not.

		✓	unsat	sat
SV (201 ex.)	LoAT	25	24	1
	Eldarica	2	0	2
	LoAT BL	2	2	0
	Z3	1	0	1
	Golem	0	0	0
$\mathsf{SV}_{\neg}$ (201 ex.)	LoAT	129	120	9
	Eldarica	78	68	10
	LoAT BL	65	65	0
	Z3	62	62	0
	Golem	30	30	0

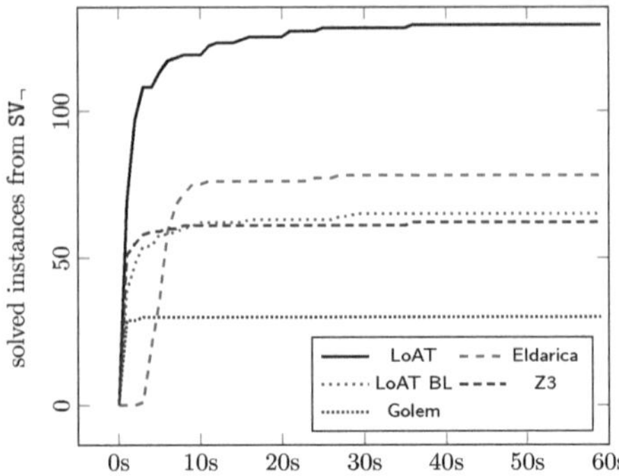

Currently, HornKlaus supports a fragment of C that corresponds to the CHCs handled by LoAT (e.g., it does not support pointers, structs, or bit-wise operations). Thus, it can only transform 201 of the 439 SV-COMP benchmarks into CHCs, resulting in our first collection of benchmarks, called SV. However, most of these benchmarks are satisfiable, but ABMC's main purpose is proving unsat. To obtain unsatisfiable instances, we modified HornKlaus so that it negates the assertions that characterize the error states, resulting in our second set of benchmarks $\mathsf{SV}_{\neg}$.

We compared LoAT with the state-of-the-art CHC solvers Eldarica [30], Golem [8], and Z3 [36]. We tested several configurations, and used the most powerful ones for proving unsat: The default configuration of Eldarica 2.2.1, the symbolic execution engine of Golem 0.9.0, and the BMC implementation of Z3 4.15.4. Additionally, we compared with a baseline variant LoAT BL without the contributions from Sects. 4 and 5, i.e., it can only accelerate loops without arrays.

Note that some SV-COMP benchmarks contain non-linear arithmetic, which is not supported by Golem, and sometimes prevents Eldarica from computing interpolants. Moreover, each of our benchmark collections contains 13 examples with "curried" arrays (see Sect. 3), which are not supported by LoAT.

We could not compare with MCMT [1–3], a state-of-the-art model checker that supports array acceleration. The reason is that MCMT's array acceleration introduces quantifiers, which are then handled via over-approximations (see [26] for details), and thus they cannot be used for proving unsafety. This shows the importance of our quantifier elimination technique from Sect. 5 and the use of λs, as these two ingredients allow us to use acceleration for proving unsatisfiability.

We used CLAIX-2023-HPC nodes of the RWTH University High Performance Computing Cluster with 10560 MiB memory limit and 60 s timeout per example.

The results of our experiments are shown in the table above. On SV, all tools perform quite badly, which confirms the observation from Sect. 1 that model checking array programs is notoriously difficult. LoAT is the only tool that can prove unsat in some cases. On $\mathsf{SV}_{\neg}$, all tools can prove unsat sometimes, but LoAT is significantly ahead of its closest competitors. Whenever another tool can prove unsatisfiability, LoAT can do so as well (apart from 3 of the examples with "curried" arrays). The fact that LoAT outperforms LoAT BL shows that its good results are indeed due to our novel contributions. For $\mathsf{SV}_{\neg}$, the plot on the right depicts the runtimes for solved instances. It shows that LoAT solves most instances quickly, i.e., our approach is not only competitive in terms of solved instances, but it is also quite efficient. See [17,25] for more details on LoAT and our evaluation.

Conclusion: We presented a new loop acceleration technique for array loops. By using the novel notion of *inductive lvalues*, it can accelerate more classes of loops than earlier techniques, and it handles arrays and scalars uniformly. Due to the use of λ-expressions and our technique for eliminating quantifiers from Sect. 5, it improves over previous SMT-based model checking algorithms for array programs, in particular for proving unsafety, as demonstrated by our evaluation.

Acknowledgments. We thank Matthias Heizmann for vital initial discussions.

Disclosure of Interests. The authors have no competing interests to declare that are relevant to the content of this article.

References

1. Alberti, F., Ghilardi, S., Sharygina, N.: Definability of accelerated relations in a theory of arrays and its applications. In: Fontaine, P., Ringeissen, C., Schmidt, R.A. (eds.) FroCoS 2013. LNCS (LNAI), vol. 8152, pp. 23–39. Springer, Heidelberg (2013). https://doi.org/10.1007/978-3-642-40885-4_3
2. Alberti, F., Ghilardi, S., Sharygina, N.: Decision procedures for flat array properties. J. Autom. Reason. **54**(4), 327–352 (2015). https://doi.org/10.1007/S10817-015-9323-7
3. Alberti, F., Ghilardi, S., Sharygina, N.: A new acceleration-based combination framework for array properties. In: Lutz, C., Ranise, S. (eds.) FroCoS 2015. LNCS (LNAI), vol. 9322, pp. 169–185. Springer, Cham (2015). https://doi.org/10.1007/978-3-319-24246-0_11
4. Bagnara, R., Pescetti, A., Zaccagnini, A., Zaffanella, E.: PURRS: towards computer algebra support for fully automatic worst-case complexity analysis. CoRR arxiv:cs/0512056 (2005). https://doi.org/10.48550/arXiv.cs/0512056
5. Bardin, S., Finkel, A., Leroux, J., Petrucci, L.: FAST: acceleration from theory to practice. Int. J. Softw. Tools Technol. Transf. **10**(5), 401–424 (2008). https://doi.org/10.1007/s10009-008-0064-3
6. Barrett, C., Fontaine, P., Tinelli, C.: The Satisfiability Modulo Theories Library (SMT-LIB) (2016). https://smt-lib.org/
7. Beyer, D., Strejček, J.: Improvements in software verification and witness validation: SV-COMP 2025. In: Gurfinkel, A., Heule, M. (eds.) TACAS 2025. LNCS, vol. 15698, pp. 151–186. Springer, Heidelberg (2025). https://doi.org/10.1007/978-3-031-90660-2_9. https://sv-comp.sosy-lab.org
8. Blicha, M., Britikov, K., Sharygina, N.: The Golem Horn solver. In: Enea, C., Lal, A. (eds.) CAV 2023. LNCS, vol. 13965, pp. 209–223. Springer, Heidelberg (2023). https://doi.org/10.1007/978-3-031-37703-7_10

9. Boigelot, B.: On iterating linear transformations over recognizable sets of integers. Theor. Comput. Sci. **309**(1–3), 413–468 (2003). https://doi.org/10.1016/S0304-3975(03)00314-1
10. Bozga, M., Gîrlea, C., Iosif, R.: Iterating octagons. In: Kowalewski, S., Philippou, A. (eds.) TACAS 2009. LNCS, vol. 5505, pp. 337–351. Springer, Heidelberg (2009). https://doi.org/10.1007/978-3-642-00768-2_29
11. Bozga, M., Iosif, R., Konečný, F.: Fast acceleration of ultimately periodic relations. In: Touili, T., Cook, B., Jackson, P. (eds.) CAV 2010. LNCS, vol. 6174, pp. 227–242. Springer, Heidelberg (2010). https://doi.org/10.1007/978-3-642-14295-6_23
12. Bozga, M., Iosif, R., Konečný, F.: Relational analysis of integer programs. Technical Report TR-2012-10, VERIMAG (2012). https://www-verimag.imag.fr/TR/TR-2012-10.pdf
13. Brummayer, R., Biere, A.: Lemmas on demand for the extensional theory of arrays. J. Satisf. Boolean Model. Comput. **6**(1–3), 165–201 (2009). https://doi.org/10.3233/SAT190067
14. CHC Competition Input Format. https://chc-comp.github.io/format.html
15. Comon, H., Jurski, Y.: Multiple counters automata, safety analysis and Presburger arithmetic. In: Hu, A.J., Vardi, M.Y. (eds.) CAV 1998. LNCS, vol. 1427, pp. 268–279. Springer, Heidelberg (1998). https://doi.org/10.1007/BFb0028751
16. Ernst, G.: Loop verification with invariants and contracts. In: Finkbeiner, B., Wies, T. (eds.) VMCAI 2022. LNCS, vol. 13182, pp. 69–92. Springer, Cham (2022). https://doi.org/10.1007/978-3-030-94583-1_4
17. Frohn, F.: LoAT website (2018). https://loat-developers.github.io/LoAT/
18. Frohn, F.: A calculus for modular loop acceleration. In: Biere, A., Parker, D. (eds.) TACAS 2020. LNCS, vol. 12078, pp. 58–76. Springer, Cham (2020). https://doi.org/10.1007/978-3-030-45190-5_4
19. Frohn, F., Giesl, J.: Proving non-termination and lower runtime bounds with LoAT (system description). In: Blanchette, J., Kovács, L., Pattinson, D. (eds.) IJCAR 2022. LNCS, vol. 13385, pp. 712–722. Springer, Heidelberg (2022). https://doi.org/10.1007/978-3-031-10769-6_41
20. Frohn, F., Giesl, J.: ADCL: acceleration driven clause learning for constrained horn clauses. In: Hermenegildo, M.V., Morales, J.F. (eds.) SAS 2023. LNCS, vol. 14284, pp. 259–285. Springer, Heidelberg (2023). https://doi.org/10.1007/978-3-031-44245-2_13
21. Frohn, F., Giesl, J.: Satisfiability modulo exponential integer arithmetic. In: Benzmüller, C., Heule, M.J.H., Schmidt, R.A. (eds.) IJCAR 2024. LNCS, vol. 14739, pp. 344–365. Springer, Heidelberg (2024). https://doi.org/10.1007/978-3-031-63498-7_21
22. Frohn, F., Giesl, J.: Integrating loop acceleration into bounded model checking. In: Platzer, A., Rozier, K.Y., Pradella, M., Rossi, M. (eds.) FM 2024. LNCS, vol. 14933, pp. 73–91. Springer, Heidelberg (2024). https://doi.org/10.1007/978-3-031-71162-6_4
23. Frohn, F., Giesl, J.: Accelerating loops with arrays. CoRR arxiv:2605.19499 (2026). https://doi.org/10.48550/arXiv.2605.19499
24. Frohn, F.: HornKlaus (2026). https://github.com/LoAT-developers/HornKlaus
25. Frohn, F., Giesl, J.: Evaluation of "Accelerating Loops with Arrays" (2026). https://loat-developers.github.io/arrays-eval/
26. Ghilardi, S.: MCMT v. 3.0 - User Manual (2020). http://users.mat.unimi.it/users/ghilardi/mcmt/UM_MCMT_3.0.pdf
27. Gurfinkel, A., Kahsai, T., Komuravelli, A., Navas, J.A.: The SeaHorn verification framework. In: Kroening, D., Păsăreanu, C.S. (eds.) CAV 2015. LNCS, vol. 9206,

pp. 343–361. Springer, Cham (2015). https://doi.org/10.1007/978-3-319-21690-4_20
28. Henzinger, T.A., Hottelier, T., Kovács, L., Rybalchenko, A.: Aligators for arrays (tool paper). In: Fermüller, C.G., Voronkov, A. (eds.) LPAR 2010. LNCS, vol. 6397, pp. 348–356. Springer, Heidelberg (2010). https://doi.org/10.1007/978-3-642-16242-8_25
29. Herrmann, R., Rümmer, P.: What's decidable about arrays with sums? In: Barrett, C., Waldmann, U. (eds.) CADE 2025. LNCS, vol. 15943, pp. 56–74. Springer, Heidelberg (2025). https://doi.org/10.1007/978-3-031-99984-0_4
30. Hojjat, H., Rümmer, P.: The Eldarica Horn solver. In: Bjørner, N.S., Gurfinkel, A. (eds.) FMCAD 2018, pp. 1–7 (2018). https://doi.org/10.23919/FMCAD.2018.8603013
31. Konečný, F.: PTIME computation of transitive closures of octagonal relations. In: Chechik, M., Raskin, J.-F. (eds.) TACAS 2016. LNCS, vol. 9636, pp. 645–661. Springer, Heidelberg (2016). https://doi.org/10.1007/978-3-662-49674-9_42
32. Kovács, L.: Reasoning algebraically about P-solvable loops. In: Ramakrishnan, C.R., Rehof, J. (eds.) TACAS 2008. LNCS, vol. 4963, pp. 249–264. Springer, Heidelberg (2008). https://doi.org/10.1007/978-3-540-78800-3_18
33. Kovács, L., Voronkov, A.: Finding loop invariants for programs over arrays using a theorem prover. In: Chechik, M., Wirsing, M. (eds.) FASE 2009. LNCS, vol. 5503, pp. 470–485. Springer, Heidelberg (2009). https://doi.org/10.1007/978-3-642-00593-0_33
34. Kroening, D., Lewis, M., Weissenbacher, G.: Under-approximating loops in C programs for fast counterexample detection. Formal Methods Syst. Des. **47**(1), 75–92 (2015). https://doi.org/10.1007/s10703-015-0228-1
35. McCarthy, J.: Towards a mathematical science of computation. In: Program Verification - Fundamental Issues in Computer Science, Studies in Cognitive Systems, vol. 14, pp. 35–56. Springer, Dordrecht (1993). https://doi.org/10.1007/978-94-011-1793-7_2
36. de Moura, L., Bjørner, N.: Z3: an efficient SMT solver. In: Ramakrishnan, C.R., Rehof, J. (eds.) TACAS 2008. LNCS, vol. 4963, pp. 337–340. Springer, Heidelberg (2008). https://doi.org/10.1007/978-3-540-78800-3_24
37. Preiner, M., Niemetz, A., Biere, A.: Lemmas on demand for lambdas. In: Proceedings of 2nd International Workshop on Design and Implementation of Formal Tools and Systems. CEUR Workshop Proceedings, vol. 1130 (2013). https://ceur-ws.org/Vol-1130/paper_7.pdf
38. Preiner, M.: Lambdas, Arrays and Quantifiers. Ph.D. thesis, Johannes Kepler Universität Linz (2017). https://epub.jku.at/obvulihs/content/titleinfo/1915381

Open Access This chapter is licensed under the terms of the Creative Commons Attribution 4.0 International License (http://creativecommons.org/licenses/by/4.0/), which permits use, sharing, adaptation, distribution and reproduction in any medium or format, as long as you give appropriate credit to the original author(s) and the source, provide a link to the Creative Commons license and indicate if changes were made.

The images or other third party material in this chapter are included in the chapter's Creative Commons license, unless indicated otherwise in a credit line to the material. If material is not included in the chapter's Creative Commons license and your intended use is not permitted by statutory regulation or exceeds the permitted use, you will need to obtain permission directly from the copyright holder.

A General Approach for SMT Proof Skeletons

Joseph E. Reeves[1(✉)], Haniel Barbosa[2], Andrew Reynolds[3,4], and Marijn J. H. Heule[1,4]

[1] Carnegie Mellon University, Pittsburgh, PA, USA
{jereeves,mheule}@cs.cmu.edu
[2] Universidade Federal de Minas Gerais, Belo Horizonte, Brazil
hbarbosa@dcc.ufmg.br
[3] The University of Iowa, Iowa City, USA
andrew-reynolds@uiowa.edu
[4] Amazon Web Services, Seattle, WA, USA

Abstract. SMT solvers increasingly produce proof certificates to meet the trust requirements of safety-critical applications. However, eagerly justifying learned theory lemmas during solving constitutes a major performance bottleneck. Recent work mitigates this cost by emitting proof skeletons that record only SAT reasoning and unannotated theory lemmas, though existing approaches depend on new proof formats and specialized theory-specific tooling. We present a general approach that restricts SMT proof skeletons to core SMT reasoning: preprocessing, clausification, and unannotated theory lemmas. We develop external tools for SAT reasoning and proof trimming that reduce the number of theory lemmas requiring justification. An experimental evaluation using the SMT solver CVC5 on SMT-LIB benchmarks across the UF, LIA and LRA theories, with and without quantifiers, demonstrates faster solving and competitive checking performance compared to eager proof production, particularly on quantifier-free problems.

Keywords: Satisfiability Modulo Theories · Proof Logging · Proof Skeletons

1 Introduction

Automated reasoning tools, particularly satisfiability modulo theories (SMT) solvers [6], are widely used in applications requiring high levels of trust including cloud security [2] and hardware and software verification [15,23–25,28]. Because SMT solvers are large and complex pieces of software, some tools now produce proof certificates [3] that justify solver reasoning thereby increasing confidence for *unsatisfiable* results.

To derive unsatisfiability, an SMT solver performs: i) *preprocessing*—rewriting and simplification; ii) *clausification*—transforming the preprocessed input into clauses forming the Boolean abstraction; iii) *propositional satisfiability (SAT) reasoning* over the clauses; and iv) *theory reasoning*—using theory solvers to learn *theory lemmas* constructed as clauses that refine the Boolean abstraction; eventually deriving a contradiction when no solution exists. An SMT proof certificate contains the information necessary to verify reasoning underlying the SAT refutation, including both the SAT

© The Author(s) 2026
A. Biere et al. (Eds.): IJCAR 2026, LNAI 16688, pp. 156–174, 2026.
https://doi.org/10.1007/978-3-032-32589-1_10

reasoning steps used to derive a contradiction and the preprocessing, clausification, and theory reasoning proof steps used to justify the relevant clauses and theory lemmas that appear in the SAT reasoning. Each proof step is accompanied by a *justification* with sufficient details for efficient validity checking. While justifications for SAT reasoning and clausification are straightforward to log, those for preprocessing and theory lemmas can be substantially more complex, as they must capture the intricate reasoning of rewriting engines and theory solvers.

The standard *eager* approach has the preprocessing module and theory solvers produce justifications online during solving [3]. For example, each time a theory solver implementing congruence closure for the theory of uninterpreted functions (QF_UF) is called, the theory solver will record the series of inferences used to deduce a theory lemma [29]. Once the SMT solver derives a conflict, the solver traces its SAT reasoning and emits all relevant theory lemmas and their justifications to the proof certificate. Any justifications for theory lemmas that are ultimately unused represent wasted computation; this overhead can be substantial for certain theories [5, Sect. 6], and is exacerbated in high-throughput applications processing up to a billion queries a day [35].

An alternative *lazy* approach has the SMT solver produce a *proof skeleton*— a subset of the full reasoning steps that omits e.g. theory lemma justifications— thereby reducing proof-logging overhead during solving. Existing frameworks support skeletons containing clausification steps, unjustified theory lemmas, and SAT reasoning [14,18,31]. To check such a skeleton, the SAT refutation is extracted, optionally *trimmed* to remove redundant reasoning steps, and the theory lemmas retained in the trimmed refutation are then justified by a dedicated *elaborator* and verified by a *proof checker*.

We present a more general approach for SMT proof skeletons (Sect. 3) that logs only core SMT reasoning: preprocessing (pre_i), clausification (C_i) and theory lemmas (T_i). Such a skeleton is accessible to SMT solvers without prior proof support for theories or SAT reasoning. Our skeleton extends the Alethe proof format [37], which supports preprocessing and quantifier reasoning beyond the scope of existing skeleton formats. The skeleton contains justifications J_i^{type} for the preprocessing and clausification steps but omits theory lemma justifications:

$$(pre_1, J_1^{\text{pre}}), \ldots, (pre_m, J_m^{\text{pre}}), (C_1, J_1^{\text{C}}), \ldots, (C_r, J_r^{\text{C}}), (T_1, \_), \ldots, (T_k, \_)$$

Rather than recording the SMT solver's SAT refutation, our skeleton contains only the information needed to extract the unsatisfiable propositional formula $F = C_1 \wedge \cdots \wedge C_r \wedge T_1 \wedge \cdots \wedge T_k$. We developed separate tools for SAT reasoning and trimming that produce an unsatisfiable core $U = C_1 \wedge \cdots \wedge C_r \wedge T'_1 \wedge \cdots \wedge T'_j$ with $U \subseteq F$. By performing SAT reasoning externally, we can apply trimming strategies specifically targeting theory lemma removal, reducing the number of theory lemmas in the core. Finally, we produce justifications for the remaining theory lemmas in the core: $(T'_1, J_1^T), (T'_2, J_2^T), \ldots, (T'_j, J_j^t)$.

While other skeleton checking tools used hand-crafted elaborators and checkers for each supported theory to improve performance, we use a general elaborator, cvc5 [5], that can produce Alethe justifications [22] for lemmas from the quantified and quantifier-free theories of equality and uninterpreted functions (UF), linear integer and real arithmetic (LIA and LRA), and theory combinations therein (Sect. 4.2). We mitigate the overhead of using a general-purpose elaborator by i) organizing justification in *batches*, meaning several theory lemmas can be justified and checked at once, and ii) parallelizing theory lemma justifications.

In summary, our contributions are:

- a generic framework for production and checking of SMT proof skeletons that relies on external SAT reasoning tools, based on the Alethe proof format, implemented in the SMT solver CVC5 and proof checker CARCARA;
- iterative proof-trimming techniques for minimizing theory lemma counts in cores, together with batched and parallelized lemma justification;
- a large-scale evaluation on SMT-LIB benchmarks that demonstrates the effectiveness of our lazy approach on the quantifier-free logics QF_UF, QF_LIA, QF_LRA, and QF_UFLIA and its limitations on the quantified logics UF and UFLIA.[1]

2 Background

2.1 Proof Production in SAT

We represent formulas for the Boolean satisfiability problem (SAT) in propositional logic using *conjunctive normal form* (CNF), i.e., conjunctions of *clauses* where each clause is a disjunction of *literals*. A literal ℓ is either a Boolean variable x or a negated variable $\overline{x}$. A *unit* clause contains a single literal. *Unit propagation* applies the following operation to formula F until a fixed point is reached: for all units α, remove clauses from F containing a literal in α and remove from the remaining clauses all literals negated in α. If unit propagation yields the empty clause ($\perp$) we say it derived a *conflict*. An *unsatisfiable core* (core) of a formula is a subset of the formula that is unsatisfiable, and is *minimal* if removing any clause from the core will make it satisfiable.

The dominant SAT algorithm, conflict-driven clause-learning (CDCL), produces a *clausal proof* for unsatisfiable problems. A clausal proof is a sequence of clause additions and deletions, where each subsequent clause addition step must meet the criteria of a chosen proof system, e.g., $F, C_1, C_2, \ldots, C_m$ is a clausal proof of C_m. The case of $C_m = \perp$ serves as a refutation for F. We will refer to clauses in the proof as *clausal lemmas* to avoid confusion with theory lemmas. CDCL solvers and proof checkers commonly use the resolution asymmetric tautology with deletions (DRAT) proof system [20], but when used within SMT solvers they are restricted to a subset of DRAT, the reverse unit propagation with deletions (DRUP) proof system, to prevent unsound reasoning. A clause C is RUP w.r.t. formula F if unit propagation on F and the units $\overline{\ell}$ for $\ell \in C$ derives a conflict.

A DRUP proof is transformed into a linear RUP (LRUP) proof by adding *hints* to proof steps, i.e., identifiers that denote clauses propagated in each RUP check, used to speed up checking with a formally verified tool [39]. The proof trimming tool DRAT-TRIM simultaneously trims unnecessary clausal lemmas from the proof and transforms RUP steps into LRUP steps through a process called *backward checking* (Sect. 4.1).

[1] Code and data available at https://github.com/jreeves3/SMT-Skeleton-Check.

2.2 Proof Production in SMT

SMT solvers generally follow the CDCL($\mathcal{T}$) architecture [30], combining a *CDCL SAT solver* and *a set of specialized theory solvers*. The SAT solver searches for satisfying assignments for the Boolean abstraction of the input, in which the theory atoms are abstracted as propositional variables. The theory solvers determine whether these literals are also satisfiable modulo the combination of theories $\mathcal{T}$. If they are not, a $\mathcal{T}$-valid disjunction of literals, a *lemma*, is learned to capture the inconsistency, which will force the SAT solver to search for a new assignment, if any exists. The other key solving components include a *preprocessing module*, which simplifies the input formulas as much as possible; and a *clausifier*, which converts the preprocessed formulas into a conjunction of *clauses* over theory literals, whose abstraction is the initial clause set for the SAT solver. Given the differences in these components, and the varying ways solvers simplify formulas and reason about theories, SMT solvers can differ significantly in how they produce proofs [8,19,21,27], and a standard proof system or format is yet to emerge in SMT. Here we focus on the proof production architecture of cvc5, the Alethe proof format [37] and its checker CARCARA [1], which we extend for this work, and the proof system relevant to the logical fragment we consider: formulas involving any of quantifiers, equality, uninterpreted functions, and linear integer or real arithmetic.[2]

Given an SMT input φ, cvc5 can produce a refutation in the Alethe proof system with the form $\pi : \varphi \rightarrow \bot$, i.e., deriving $\bot$ from the assumption φ. This proof is produced modularly, with each solving component producing individual proofs that are merged together into this refutation. The preprocessing module produces proofs $\pi_i^{\text{pp}} : \varphi \rightarrow \phi_i$, for each ϕ_i generated during the simplification of φ. Different simplifications may require different sets of rules, such as constant folding in different theories or if-then-else elimination. The clausifier produces proofs $\pi^{\text{cnf}} : \phi \rightarrow C_j$ for each clause C_j generated from the preprocessed formulas. The rules in each π^{cnf} are a combination of Boolean transformations and introductions of Boolean formulas representing the definition of Tseytin variables, used to ensure that the CNF conversion is polynomial. The combination of theory solvers produce proofs $\pi^{\text{t}} : L$ for each theory lemma L derived. The rules in each π^{t} depend on the respective theory. For example, the UF theory reasoning is modeled with rules to describe congruence reasoning [17], whereas the LRA theory reasoning is modeled with a rule capturing Farkas' lemma [13,36], which guarantees that there exists a linear combination of these inequalities equivalent to $\bot$, that can be checked polynomially. For LIA, rules for branching and integer bound tightening are used in addition to the Farkas' lemma. The SAT solver produces a resolution proof $\pi^{\text{res}} : C_1 \wedge \cdots \wedge C_m \wedge T_1 \wedge \cdots \wedge T_l \rightarrow \bot$ for the refutation of the clause set corresponding to the subset of the clausified preprocessed input and the theory lemmas needed to derive $\bot$. Note that π^{res} is in terms of the first-order clauses, as are the derivation rules that conclude $\bot$ from them, since the inferences on the propositional abstraction are

[2] Internally cvc5 produces proofs in the Cooperating Proof Calculus (CPC) (https://cvc5.github.io/docs-ci/docs-main/proofs/output_cpc.html), which are then translated into Alethe. The Alethe format, together with a complete list of the proof rules, is described at https://verit.gitlabpages.uliege.be/alethe/specification.pdf. Extensions of Alethe to other theories, such as the theories of fixed-width bit-vectors and of strings, are under active development.

lifted to the original literals. By connecting the assumptions of each of these proofs, the final refutation of the input φ is generated. For more details see e.g. [5, 19].

Alethe proofs are a series of steps represented as an indexed list of `step` commands referencing their premises and justified by a given inference rule, concluding a clause, represented as a list of theory literals. The command `assume` is analogous but used only for introducing assumptions. The indexed steps induce a directed acyclic graph rooted on the step concluding $\bot$ and with $\varphi_1, \ldots, \varphi_n$ as the only assumption leaves (the input φ is generally given as multiple assertions $\varphi_1, \ldots, \varphi_n$). The format supports subproofs, which simulate the effect of the $\Rightarrow$-introduction rule of Natural Deduction, where local assumptions are put in context and the last step in a subproof represents its conclusion and the closing of its context. The overall proof may be seen as preprocessing and a ground first-order resolution refutation with theory lemmas justified by closed subproofs. Alethe proofs can be reconstructed in several proof assistants [11, 12, 22, 38] and it has a dedicated high-performance checker and elaborator, CARCARA.

Example 1. This QF_UF query requiring simple congruence reasoning is used throughout the paper, labelled CONGEX. The query can be found in the Github repository.

```
(assert (= a b))
(assert (= b d))
(assert (and p1 true))
(assert (or (not p1) (and p2 p3)))
(assert (or (not p3) (not (= (f a b) (f b d)))))
(assert (or (not p3) (not (= a d))))
```

3 The Alethe SMT Proof Skeleton Framework

Our SMT proof skeleton framework, shown in Fig. 1, is divided into solving, checking, and a *theory oracle* for the new proof rule `prop_unsat`. The oracle computes and trims a SAT refutation, then justifies and checks the core theory lemmas.

In CVC5, the existing eager approach [5] computes and stores all preprocessing and theory lemma justifications during solving, then after solving trims the SAT refutation and prints the relevant proof steps.[3] We instrumented CVC5 to produce an Alethe proof skeleton by logging inferences as they were derived. The skeleton includes fully justified preprocessing and clausification steps transforming the preprocessed input query into clauses $C_1, \ldots, C_r$, plus two new step types: unjustified theory lemma additions (`hole`) producing the set $T_1, \ldots, T_k$, and a claim of propositional unsatisfiability (`prop_unsat`). An example `hole` step from CONGEX derived via transitivity is:

```
step t7 (cl (or (= a d) (not (= a b)) (not (= b d)))) :rule hole :args ("LEMMA")
```

[3] Hitarth et al. [18] instrumented CVC5 to log SAT clauses and theory lemmas as they are derived, but their tool is not open source. Moreover it did not support preprocessing nor other formats than their *e*DRAT proof format, whose validation toolchain VALIDO is also not open source.

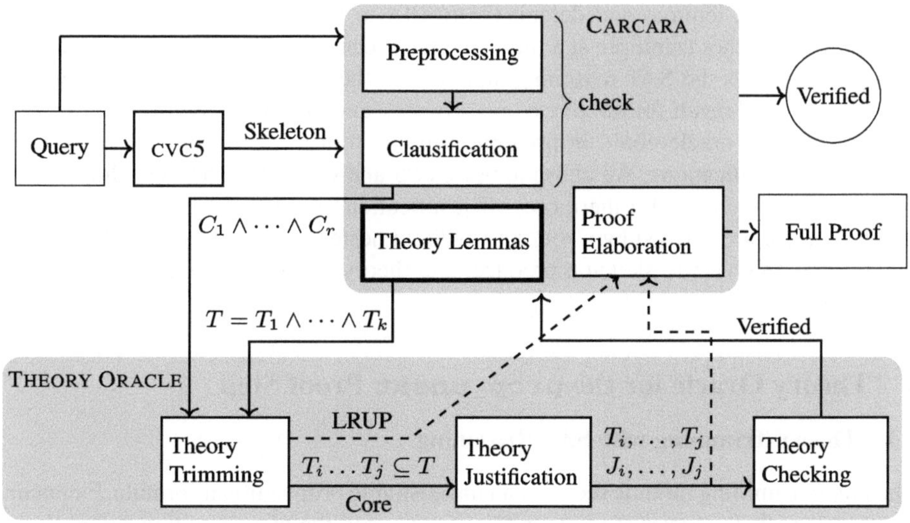

Fig. 1. SMT solving and proof checking. CARCARA checks preprocessing and clausification steps normally. Then, the theory oracle produces, trims, and checks SAT reasoning and justifies and checks core theory lemmas. LRUP proof production and theory justifications can optionally be used for proof elaboration (dashed lines).

Unlike the default eager approach, proof logging within theory solvers is disabled when producing theory lemma holes, speeding up solving. Furthermore, the skeleton omits SAT reasoning and instead concludes with the `prop_unsat` step containing an unsatisfiable set of premises $C_1, \ldots, C_r, T_1, \ldots, T_k$. A `prop_unsat` step for CONGEX would, e.g., be

```
(step t9 (cl) :rule prop_unsat :premises (C1 C2 C3 C4 C5 C6 C7 C8 C9 T1 T2))
```

which uses 9 justified premises and 2 unjustified theory lemmas (`T1` and `T2`). Their conjunction (each interpreted in their clausified format) forms an unsatisfiable propositional formula.

The checker, CARCARA, accepts the resulting skeleton and verifies the preprocessing and clausification steps normally, skipping the theory lemma hole steps. Upon reaching the `prop_unsat` step, it calls the external theory oracle with a propositional representation of the premises (F) and an SMT-LIB representation of the theory lemmas. The oracle verifies F's unsatisfiability by computing a refutation, then justifies and checks the relevant theory lemmas. An optional elaborator replaces the `prop_unsat` step by a fine-grained proof using theory lemma justifications and the LRUP proof from the oracle, enabling independent checking outside our framework. The elaborator's detailed description and evaluation can be found in the tool's Github repository.

The oracle operates in two phases: (1) *theory trimming*, using a SAT solver and proof trimmer to verify SAT reasoning and reduce the number of theory lemmas in the core; and (2) *theory lemma justification and checking*, using cvc5 to compute justifications for core lemmas and default CARCARA to verify them. Theory lemmas are processed in batches (multiple at a time) and the process can be parallelized. If the theory oracle verifies the SAT reasoning and verifies the justifications of core lemmas it returns a verified result for the `prop_unsat` step and otherwise returns a not verified result. Note, the oracle could in principle use any tool to justify theory lemmas and check those justifications. We chose to use CVC5 and CARCARA because they already support many theories. Furthermore, all justifications produced by CVC5 within the external oracle are verified by CARCARA without nested calls to the external oracle, so the reliance on CVC5 as skeleton producer and theory lemma elaborator introduces no unsoundness.

4 Theory Oracle for the `prop_unsat` Proof Step

4.1 Theory Trimming with SAT Reasoning

The theory trimming module receives an unsatisfiable propositional formula F containing the clausified preprocessed input $C_1, \ldots, C_r$ and the clausified unjustified theory lemmas $T_1, \ldots, T_k$, together with a mapping from theory lemma clauses to their SMT-LIB representation. It first computes a clausal proof $(P_1, \ldots, P_n)$ of F using the SAT solver CADICAL [7], then applies our *theory-last* proof trimmer to both verify the SAT reasoning and produce a core $U \subseteq F$. Only the theory lemmas in U are subsequently justified and checked.

Theory-Last Proof Trimming. Theory-last trimming modifies the *backward trimming* algorithm of DRAT-TRIM [40]. Standard backward trimming processes the clausal proof in reverse, performing RUP checks on active steps and using conflict analysis to mark (activate) the clauses (reasons) that contributed to each conflict (see Example 2); all marked input clauses then constitute the core. Specifically, a RUP check on step P_i will add all clauses in F and clauses $P_1, \ldots, P_{i-1}$ to the propagation engine, then propagate the units $\overline{P}_i$ to derive a conflict. Conflict analysis marks reasons for the conflict, where a *reason* is the clause that propagated a specific unit. Given a conflicting clause C, conflict analysis starts from the list of negated unit literals $\{\ell_1, \ldots, \ell_k\} = C$, then for each ℓ_i in the list the reason clause $R(\ell_i)$ will be marked and the literals $R(\ell_i) \setminus \ell_i$ will be added to the unit list. The procedure continues until only unit literals without reasons (unit clauses from the original formula or unit clauses from $\overline{P}_i$) remain.

Example 2. Given a formula $F = C_1 : (\overline{x}_1 \vee x_4 \vee x_6) \wedge C_2 : (\overline{x}_2 \vee \overline{x}_3) \wedge C_3 : (x_1 \vee x_3 \vee x_4) \wedge C_4 : (\overline{x}_2 \vee x_7) \wedge C_5 : (\overline{x}_2 \vee \overline{x}_4)$, to show that a clause $D = (\overline{x}_2 \vee x_6)$ is RUP w.r.t. F, we propagate $F \wedge (x_2 \wedge \overline{x}_6)$.

Propagation derives the corresponding units and corresponding reason clauses: $(\overline{x}_3, C_2), (x_7, C_4), (\overline{x}_4, C_5), (\overline{x}_1, C_1)$, then C_3 is in conflict.

Analysis of the conflict on C_3 yields reasons C_2, C_5, C_1. Note, C_4 is absent because the unit x_7 is not used to derive the conflict on C_3.

The proof is verified once all marked proof steps have been checked. During each RUP check, *core-first* propagation can be used to minimize the core by partitioning

Algorithm 1. Theory-Last Trimming

1.	$Level_1 \leftarrow Level_2 \leftarrow \emptyset$	// *initialize propagation levels*
2.	$Level_1 \leftarrow \{C_1, \dots, C_r\}$	// *add input clauses*
3.	$Level_2 \leftarrow \{T_1, \dots, T_k\}, \{P_1, \dots, P_n\}$	// *add theory lemmas and proof steps*
4.	**for** $i = n$ down to 1:	// *iterate proof steps backwards*
5.	$Delete(P_i, Level_1); Delete(P_i, Level_2)$	// *remove from future propagation*
6.	**if** $marked(P_i)$:	// *skip unmarked proof steps*
7.	$C \leftarrow clause(P_i)$	// *clause representing proof step*
8.	$Units \leftarrow \{\bar{\ell} \mid \ell \in C\}$	// *negate clause*
9.	**while** $propagate(Level_1, Units) \neq \bot$:	// *propagate in level 1*
10.	$propagatePartial(Level_2, Units)$	// *propagate in level 2*
11.	**if** no new unit literals:	// *nothing new derived*
12.	**return** UNVERIFIED	// *proof check failed*
13.	$Reasons \leftarrow analyze$(conflict)	// *analyze conflict*
14.	**for each** $D \in Reasons$:	
15.	$mark(D)$	// *mark reason clause*
16.	**if** $D \in Level_2$: move D to $Level_1$	// *promote clause*
17.	**return** $filter(marked, \{T_1, \dots, T_k\})$	// *return marked theory lemmas*

propagation into two levels: $Level_1$ (marked core clauses) and $Level_2$ (unmarked clauses). Initially, $Level_1$ is empty while $Level_2$ contains input clauses and proof steps. During a RUP check, the propagation engine alternates between $Level_1$ and $Level_2$ as follows. First, propagation is performed on $Level_1$. If a conflict is derived, conflict analysis proceeds immediately. Otherwise, $Level_2$ is *partially propagated* until the first new unit is derived, at which point control returns to $Level_1$ to propagate that learned unit. During conflict analysis, any reason clauses originating from $Level_2$ are marked and promoted to $Level_1$ for subsequent RUP checks. This approach attempts to minimize the number of newly marked clauses in each RUP check, thereby reducing the size of the core.

Theory-last trimming (Algorithm 1) modifies core-first trimming by initializing $Level_1$ with all input clauses (line 2) and $Level_2$ with theory lemmas and proof steps (line 3). Consequently, the initial propagations during a RUP check prioritize input clauses (line 9). Only when propagation on $Level_1$ fails to derive a conflict does propagation proceed on $Level_2$; thus, theory lemmas are propagated last. The function $propagatePartial$ propagates until a new unit literal is derived, after which control returns to $Level_1$. Lines $13 - 16$ mark reason clauses, and the marked (core) theory lemmas are returned on line 17. Example 3 illustrates theory-last propagation.

The resulting core may be larger because it always contains all input clauses, but it often contains fewer theory lemmas. Theory-last trimming always produces a valid core for a valid RUP proof because the propagation engine still has access to all relevant clauses across $Level_1$ and $Level_2$. In the worst case, backward trimming is quadratic in the size of the proof; however, in practice, its runtime is often comparable to the time required to generate the proof.

Example 3. Given F from Example 2, let C_4 and C_5 be theory lemmas. To show D is RUP, theory-last propagation would proceed as follows:

1. Propagate $Level_1$: (C_1, C_2, C_3) with units $x_2, \overline{x}_6$, giving $(\overline{x}_3, C_2)$.
2. No conflict was derived, so partially propagate $Level_2$: (C_4, C_5) with units $x_2, \overline{x}_6, \overline{x}_3$ giving (x_7, C_4).
3. Return to $Level_1$ propagating the new unit x_7.
4. Again, no conflict is derived so partially propagate $Level_2$, giving $(\overline{x}_4, C_5)$.
5. Return to $Level_1$ propagating $\overline{x}_4$ giving $(\overline{x}_1, C_1)$ then a conflict.
6. Analysis gives reasons C_2, C_5, C_1, so theory lemma C_5 would be marked and promoted from $Level_2$ to $Level_1$, with C_4 remaining in $Level_2$.

Iterative Theory Trimming. The theory trimming algorithm does not guarantee optimality; algorithms for finding a minimal core require many calls to a SAT solver, in the worst case removing only one clause from the core at a time. Small reductions to the size of the core provide diminishing returns for theories where theory lemmas are easy to justify. *Iterative trimming* feeds the output core back into the trimming pipeline as the new input formula, repeating until the number of core theory lemmas stabilizes. Subsequent iterations benefit from fresh SAT proofs and can remove additional theory lemmas, though the first iteration typically achieves the largest reduction. This approach achieves moderate reductions with fewer calls to a SAT solver and trimming tool.

4.2 Theory Lemma Justification and Checking

Each core theory lemma $l_1 \vee \cdots \vee l_n$ is justified by proving the unsatisfiability of $\neg l_1 \wedge \cdots \wedge \neg l_n$ via CVC5. The justification is checked with CARCARA and optionally returned for proof elaboration. The input to CVC5 is an SMT-LIB query using the original problem's preamble, which contains the declaration of sorts and functions symbols, along with the assertion that negates the lemma. The query below, for example, would be used to justify theory lemma t_7 from CONGEX.

```
<Preamble>
(assert (not (or (= a d) (not (= a b)) (not (= b d)))) )
(check-sat)
```

Rather than justifying lemmas individually, we can process them in batches, similar to the work on propositional proof skeletons [33]. Given a batch $T_1, \ldots, T_k$, their joint validity is established by proving the unsatisfiability of $\overline{T}_1 \vee \cdots \vee \overline{T}_k$. This is constructed as a single SMT-LIB query with the original problem's preamble and an assertion forming a disjunction of the negation of the set of theory lemmas, for example:

```
(assert ( or ( not (t_1)) (not (t_2)) ... (not (t_k)))))
```

A single CARCARA call checks the validity of the entire batch. The batch quality—the difficulty of solving and checking the batch—depends on the number of lemmas in the batch, the relationship between lemmas in the batch, and the underlying theory. Smaller batch sizes can lead to significant overhead when executing CVC5 and CARCARA on thousands of trivial queries, but larger batches can grow increasingly more difficult to prove. Through experimentation, a batch size of 50 was found to balance solver overhead against per-batch difficulty. Lemmas are batched in the order they were learned by the SMT solver, keeping related theory lemmas together and enabling the SMT solver to reuse intermediate results.

Batches may be distributed across multiple cores to parallelize justification. However, the effectiveness of parallelization will still depend on the batch quality, as much harder batches can create a bottleneck. While a similar issue is recurring in parallel SMT solving [41], we did not experience this much.

In our evaluation the majority of theory lemmas were justified quickly, motivating the batch size of 50. However, initial experimentation for other theories, including the theory of bitvectors which require more complex justifications, suggest that smaller batch sizes may lead to faster verification.

4.3 Lemmas Containing Fresh Symbols

Preprocessing in quantified logics may introduce fresh symbols via Skolemization, and these symbols can appear in theory lemmas. Therefore when applying the process above to check lemmas with such symbols, the problem's preamble has to be extended to declare them. This however is not sufficient because the fresh symbol is not unconstrained. For example, in the case of Skolemization, the introduced symbol is a witness for a particular Skolemized quantifier. So these constraints may be required in the query to justify the lemma. This is a general issue that limits e.g. validating Skolemization inferences via external solvers [32, Sec. 1.2].

We can circumvent the problem in our approach because Skolemization in Alethe is justified in an equivalence-preserving way via Hilbert's choice operator $\epsilon x.\, \varphi$, which is characterized via the axiom $\exists x. \varphi[x] \rightarrow \varphi[\epsilon x.\, \varphi]$, i.e., the operator yields a term that makes its bound formula hold [4]. Therefore, CARCARA can use the formulas in the choice operators to constrain the fresh symbols appearing in lemmas. So the validity of a lemma $L[\epsilon x.\, \varphi]$ in the Alethe skeleton is justified by proving the unsatisfiability of the SMT formula $(\exists x. \varphi[x] \rightarrow \varphi[k]) \wedge \neg L[k]$, where k is a fresh symbol of the same type of the choice term.

In full generality symbols introduced via Skolemization may depend on other fresh symbols. For example, when Skolemizing $\exists x_1 x_2. \varphi$, first $\exists x_2.\, \varphi[\epsilon x_1.\, \exists x_2.\, \varphi]$ is derived, and the Skolemization of x_2 will be defined by a formula containing the choice term for x_1. Checking the validity of lemmas containing such choice terms, i.e., $L[k]$ where k is $\epsilon x.\, \varphi[\epsilon_1, \dots, \epsilon_n]$, with $\epsilon_1, \dots, \epsilon_n$ being choice terms, requires the constraint to validate L to also characterize k accounting for all possible values that $\epsilon_1, \dots, \epsilon_n$ may assume. Thus the formula that we generate for such lemmas is $(\forall y_1 \dots y_n.\, \exists x. \varphi[y_1, \dots, y_n] \rightarrow \varphi[k]) \wedge \neg L[k]$, requiring quantifier reasoning by the backend solver.

5 Experimental Evaluation

All experiments were performed in the Pittsburgh Supercomputing Center on nodes with 128 cores and 256 GB RAM [9]. We used a 5,000 second timeout for solving and a 5,000 second timeout for proof checking, and 64 experiments were run in parallel per node so each process held approximately 4GB of memory. We report the *penalized*

Table 1. Solving time comparison on unsatisfiable formulas that cvc5 solves within the timeout (number of formulas shown beneath each theory).

Theory	Config	Timeouts	PAR2	Theory	Config	Timeouts	PAR2
QF_UF	cvc5	–	5	QF_LIA	cvc5	–	42
4,356	cvc5-pr	14	47	2,757	cvc5-pr	127	483
	t-5	1	12		t-5	47	221
QF_LRA	cvc5	–	118	QF_UFLIA	cvc5	–	10
696	cvc5-pr	3	205	190	cvc5-pr	3	161
	t-5	1	141		t-5	2	108

average runtime (PAR2). PAR2 is the average runtime with a two times penalty for timeouts, e.g., a timeout on 5,000 seconds is counted as a 10,000 second runtime.

We considered benchmarks from the 2023 release of the SMT-LIB logics QF_UF, QF_LIA, QF_LRA, and QF_UFLIA , UF, and UFLIA which are representative of the fragment supported by cvc5's Alethe proof production. We exclude benchmarks from the `nec-smt` family in QF_LIA, for which cvc5 introduces fresh terms during preprocessing in a way not yet supported by the Alethe translation. We first present the results for the quantifier-free logics, and then for quantified logics in Sect. 5.4.

For the evaluation, we first solved each formula using cvc5 without proof production. Unsatisfiable formulas without a timeout were used to compare solving times in Table 1. Next, we further filtered away formulas for which the proof did not include a `prop_unsat` step, i.e., cvc5 solved them purely via preprocessing. These problems for which trimming can occur were used to compare checking times in Table 2.

While we only consider the UF, LIA, and LRA theories, our approach is theory agnostic and can be readily extended to other theories once an Alethe-producing SMT solver is available for it. Extensions of cvc5 to produce Alethe proofs for example for bitvectors and strings are ongoing work, and we expect the impact of our approach to be significant in these theories, where theory reasoning is more expensive.

We used the following configurations in our main experiments, with all proofs checked by Carcara as described in Sect. 3:

- cvc5 - Default cvc5 without proof production.
- cvc5-proof - Default eager proof production in cvc5.
- cvc5-theory-trim5 - Proof skeleton framework with 5 iterations of theory trimming and lemma justification performed in batches of 50. Summarized as t-5. Optionally, we could use a single trimming iteration (t-1), use a single lemma per batch (t-5-s), or use standard DRAT-trim instead of our theory-trim tool (d-5).

5.1 Solving Time

Solving results (Table 1) show the expected ordering: cvc5-theory-trim5 is faster on average than cvc5-proof but slower than uninstrumented cvc5. Scatter plots

Table 2. Solving and checking comparison on formulas with a `prop_unsat` step. Solving timeouts count towards the checking PAR2. Average lemma count reports core theory lemmas from solved formulas. Best Core is the number of formulas for which a unique configuration among CVC5-PR, D-5, and T-5 found a core with the fewest theory lemmas, with no values reported for T-1 which has at least as many lemmas as T-5 and T-5-S which has exactly as many lemmas as T-5. *CVC5-PR times out on harder QF_LIA instances with many lemmas, making the average incomparable because the number of theory lemmas for unsolved problems are not included. Excluding the 75 CVC5-PR timeouts, T-5 has an average of 599.

Theory Formulas	Config	# Timeouts Solve	# Timeouts Check	PAR2 Solve	PAR2 Check	Avg. Lemmas	# Best Core
QF_UF	CVC5	–	–	4	–	–	–
4,154	CVC5-PR	13	0	46	33	2,510	17
	T-1	–	9	10	44	1,662	–
	D-5	–	10	10	45	1,562	604
	T-5-S	–	78	10	543	1,549	–
	T-5	–	10	10	43	1,549	3,011
QF_LRA	CVC5	–	–	129	–	–	–
639	CVC5-PR	2	0	207	38	4,057	10
	T-1	–	5	138	209	2,212	–
	D-5	–	5	138	194	1,698	99
	T-5-S	–	27	138	871	1,686	–
	T-5	–	5	138	191	1,686	239
QF_LIA	CVC5	–	–	27	–	–	–
1,843	CVC5-PR	75	0	440	414	*672	6
	T-1	–	31	69	250	4,903	–
	D-5	–	32	69	258	4,895	94
	T-5-S	–	94	69	573	4,894	–
	T-5	–	32	69	256	4,894	162
QF_UFLIA	CVC5	–	–	6	–	–	–
106	CVC5-PR	0	0	6	0	1,105	0
	T-1	–	0	6	6	589	–
	D-5	–	0	6	6	470	15
	T-5-S	–	0	6	236	462	–
	T-5	–	0	6	5	462	29

(Fig. 2) show results for a set of hard problems, with the benchmark selection criteria described below in the parallel checking section. The solving benefit is most pronounced on a group of hard problems in QF_LIA where CVC5-PROOF times out at 5,000 seconds but CVC5-THEORY-TRIM5 solves them in one to two hundred seconds.

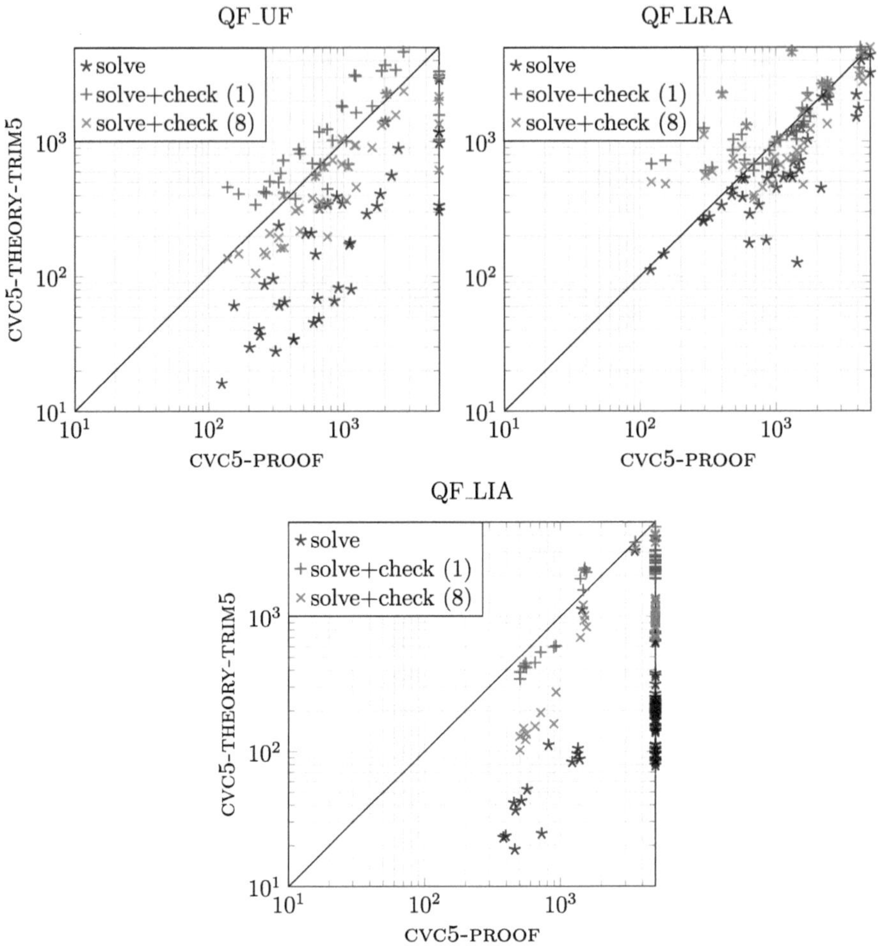

Fig. 2. Scatter plots showing the solving times and the full solving + checking times comparing CVC5-PROOF with a single core and CVC5-THEORY-TRIM5 with (1) or (8) cores. Benchmarks are the filtered set described in the parallel checking evaluation.

5.2 Sequential Checking

Table 2 compares solving times, checking times, and core theory lemma counts for configurations with proof support. For QF_UF and QF_LIA, the combined solving and checking time under CVC5-THEORY-TRIM5 is often lower than under CVC5-PROOF, demonstrating that iterative trimming and batched justification can rival eager proof production while also providing faster solving. Iterative trimming (CVC5-THEORY-TRIM5) often produces cores with fewer theory lemmas than non-iterative (T-1) or standard DRAT-TRIM (D-5), with CVC5-PROOF cores almost never containing fewer theory lemmas than our configurations. Mean lemma reduction rates with CVC5-THEORY-TRIM5 are 54% (QF_UF), 18% (QF_LRA), 21% (QF_LIA), 39% (QF_UFLIA). On average, between 30 $\sim$ 45% of the propositional formula prior to trimming consists of theory lemmas.

The benefit of iterative trimming varies by theory. In QF_LIA, iterative trimming produces smaller cores yet higher checking times, suggesting the trimming cost exceeds the savings from fewer justifications. In QF_UF, QF_LRA, or QF_UFLIA iterative trimming reduces total checking time. Sequential single lemma elaboration (T-5-S) performs poorly across all theories, underscoring the importance of batching.

5.3 Parallel Checking

We applied parallel batch justification across 8 cores to formulas with at least a 300 seconds checking time and at least 400 core theory lemmas when using the sequential version of CVC5-THEORY-TRIM5 . We chose the value of 400 so that each core can process at least one batch of size 50. No formula in QF_UFLIA met this criterion.

Table 3. Number of formulas successfully checked for CVC5-PR on a single core, CVC5-THEORY-TRIM5 on a single core (1-core) and CVC5-THEORY-TRIM5 on 8 cores (8-core), and PAR2 scores for checking time and the speedup on CVC5-THEORY-TRIM5.

		# Checked			Checking PAR2			
Theory	Formulas	CVC5-PR	1-core	8-core	CVC5-PR	1-core	8-core	Speedup
QF_UF	40	34	38	39	1,565	1,596	722	2.2
QF_LRA	40	38	39	40	560	1,067	584	1.8
QF_LIA	70	15	62	65	7,883	2,819	1,487	1.9

Table 3 shows for both QF_UF and QF_LIA, CVC5-THEORY-TRIM5 with 8 cores achieves faster solving-plus-checking than CVC5-PROOF, in addition to faster sequential solving. For QF_LRA, solving-time gains are moderate, resulting in a combined solving-plus-checking time that is often slightly worse than CVC5-PROOF. Note, there is no implementation for parallelizing CARCARA without our proof skeleton framework, so the CVC5-PROOF configuration can only be run on a single core. These results highlight the benefit of skeleton checking on difficult problems containing many theory lemmas for which proof logging is computationally expensive.

5.4 Theories with Quantifiers

Results for UF and UFLIA are summarized in Table 4. The large difference in checking PAR2 is mostly due to timeouts. As discussed in Sect. 4.2, in quantified logics, justifying some lemmas may require solving quantified problems, and SMT solvers are well known to be incomplete and unstable in quantified logics [42]. So unfortunately timeouts in lemma checking with CVC5 can be expected.

Furthermore, there is less gain in the solving time, or no gain. This is explained by theory reasoning for quantified lemmas in SMT being done mostly via instantiation [34], for which the overhead of proof production is minimal (how the instance was found is irrelevant; only that it is a sound instantiation needs to be justified). Moreover, SMT solvers, and CVC5 is no different, generate instances mostly in a non-goal oriented way, i.e., they are not derived to refine the search directly, but rather on the expectation that they *may* be useful. As a result, solvers generate very large numbers of useless instances, which in our approach are all logged in the skeleton, and this overhead may be one reason our solving is often slightly slower than CVC5-PR. Finally, we observe that problems in UF/UFLIA mostly do not have as deep a ground structure as problems in the quantifier-free logics, and with less ground reasoning less overhead is added by producing proofs, which we would have saved.

Table 4. Timeouts, PAR2 scores, and number of core lemmas for quantified theories UF and UFLIA comparing CVC5, CVC5-PR, and T-5. Description of PAR2, Avg. Lemmas, and Best Core found in caption of Table 2.

Theory	Config	# Timeouts		PAR2		Avg. Lemmas	# Best Core
Formulas		Solve	Check	Solve	Check		
UF	CVC5	–	–	57	–	–	–
679	CVC5-PR	0	0	53	0	38	15
	T-5	–	14	53	210	33	659
UFLIA	CVC5	–	–	14	–	–	–
1,411	CVC5-PR	1	0	21	7	91	224
	T-5	–	12	14	88	82	1,133

6 Related Work

Several works have used clausal proofs for SMT with varying success [14,31]. The work on the *extended* DRAT (*e*DRAT) proof system [18] most closely relates to our work. They modified CVC5 to produce *e*DRAT proofs for QF_UF and QF_LRA consisting of the SAT proof steps as well as unjustified theory lemma steps. Then, after trimming the SAT proof with DRAT-TRIM, their VALIDO toolchain elaborated proof steps and checked them with theory-specific RUST and Lean [26] tools respectively. One key difference is that we leverage existing tools, avoiding the cost of developing theory-specific elaborators and checkers. This also allows us to support preprocessing proofs, a crucial component missing in *e*DRAT. Next, we focus on iterative proof trimming using our modified DRAT-TRIM with theory-last propagation. Finally, our relaxed approach with batch justification facilitates parallelization in checking. The VALIDO toolchain is not open source so we cannot compare our tools directly.

Proof skeleton frameworks have also been explored in other domains including constraint programming [16], with the focus of reducing proof logging overhead during solving.

Core extraction has also been explored in the context of SMT, with early ideas stemming from work on lemma-lifting [10]. Notably, these approaches use off-the-shelf core extractors, whereas our approach attempts to minimize theory lemmas in the core.

7 Conclusion and Future Work

We presented a general approach for producing and checking SMT proof skeletons. External SAT reasoning enables improved theory trimming, and batched parallel theory justification improves runtimes on quantifier-free logics. This framework requires only that an SMT solver logs preprocessing and clausification proofs together with theory lemma holes, making it accessible to solvers beyond cvc5 that lack full proof support.

Future work will explore harder theories including bit-vectors and mechanisms for incorporating preprocessing steps into the trimming and skeleton checking procedures. In addition, the skeleton format may be extended to support partial or fully justified theory lemmas when including such information does not compromise solver runtime.

Acknowledgments. This work was partially supported by a gift from Amazon Web Services, the National Science Foundation (NSF) under grant CCF-2415773, and by the Defense Advanced Research Projects Agency (DARPA) under contracts FA8750-24-9-1000 and FA8750-24-2-1001. Any opinions, findings, and conclusions or recommendations expressed here are those of the authors and do not necessarily reflect the views of DARPA. Joseph E. Reeves was supported by a fellowship award under contract FA9550-21-F-0003 through the National Defense Science and Engineering Graduate (NDSEG) Fellowship Program, sponsored by the Air Force Research Laboratory (AFRL), the Office of Naval Research (ONR) and the Army Research Office (ARO).

Disclosure of Interests. The authors have no competing interests to declare that are relevant to the content of this article.

References

1. Andreotti, B., Lachnitt, H., Barbosa, H.: Carcara: an efficient proof checker and elaborator for SMT proofs in the alethe format. In: Sankaranarayanan, S., Sharygina, N. (eds.) Tools and Algorithms for Construction and Analysis of Systems (TACAS), Part I. Lecture Notes in Computer Science, vol. 13993, pp. 367–386. Springer (2023). https://doi.org/10.1007/978-3-031-30823-9_19
2. Backes, J., et al.: Semantic-based automated reasoning for AWS access policies using SMT. In: Bjørner, N., Gurfinkel, A. (eds.) Formal Methods in Computer-Aided Design (FMCAD), pp. 1–9. IEEE (2018). https://doi.org/10.23919/FMCAD.2018.8602994
3. Barbosa, H., et al.: Generating and exploiting automated reasoning proof certificates. Commun. ACM **66**(10), 86–95 (2023). https://doi.org/10.1145/3587692
4. Barbosa, H., Blanchette, J.C., Fleury, M., Fontaine, P.: Scalable fine-grained proofs for formula processing. J. Autom. Reason. **64**(3), 485–510 (2019). https://doi.org/10.1007/s10817-018-09502-y

5. Barbosa, H., et al.: Flexible proof production in an industrial-strength SMT solver. In: Blanchette, J., Kovács, L., Pattinson, D. (eds.) International Joint Conference on Automated Reasoning (IJCAR). Lecture Notes in Computer Science, vol. 13385, pp. 15–35. Springer (2022). https://doi.org/10.1007/978-3-031-10769-6_3
6. Barrett, C.W., Sebastiani, R., Seshia, S.A., Tinelli, C.: Satisfiability modulo theories. In: Biere, A., Heule, M., van Maaren, H., Walsh, T. (eds.) Handbook of Satisfiability - Second Edition, Frontiers in Artificial Intelligence and Applications, vol. 336, pp. 1267–1329. IOS Press (2021). https://doi.org/10.3233/FAIA201017
7. Biere, A., Faller, T., Fazekas, K., Fleury, M., Froleyks, N., Pollitt, F.: Cadical 2.0. In: Computer Aided Verification (CAV), pp. 133–152. Springer (2024). https://doi.org/10.1007/978-3-031-65627-9_7
8. Bouton, T., Caminha B. de Oliveira, D., Déharbe, D., Fontaine, P.: veriT: an open, trustable and efficient SMT-solver. In: Schmidt, R.A. (ed.) CADE 2009. LNCS (LNAI), vol. 5663, pp. 151–156. Springer, Heidelberg (2009). https://doi.org/10.1007/978-3-642-02959-2_12
9. Brown, S.T., Buitrago, P., Hanna, E., Sanielevici, S., Scibek, R., Nystrom, N.A.: Bridges-2: a platform for rapidly-evolving and data intensive research, pp. 1–4. Association for Computing Machinery, New York, NY, USA (2021). https://doi.org/10.1145/3437359.3465593
10. Cimatti, A., Griggio, A., Sebastiani, R.: Computing small unsatisfiable cores in satisfiability modulo theories. J. Artif. Int. Res. **40**(1), 701–728 (2011). https://dl.acm.org/doi/abs/10.5555/2016945.2016964
11. Coltellacci, A., Merz, S., Dowek, G.: Reconstruction of SMT proofs with lambdapi. In: Reger, G., Zohar, Y. (eds.) Proceedings of the 22nd International Workshop on Satisfiability Modulo Theories co-located with the Computer Aided Verification (CAV), Montreal, Canada, 22–23 July 2024. CEUR Workshop Proceedings, vol. 3725, pp. 13–23. CEUR-WS.org (2024). https://ceur-ws.org/Vol-3725/paper8.pdf
12. Ekici, B., et al.: SMTCoq: a plug-in for integrating SMT solvers into Coq. In: Majumdar, R., Kunčak, V. (eds.) CAV 2017. LNCS, vol. 10427, pp. 126–133. Springer, Cham (2017). https://doi.org/10.1007/978-3-319-63390-9_7
13. Farkas, G.: A Fourier-féle mechanikai elv alkamazásai. Mathematikaiés Természettudományi Értesítö **12**, 457–472 (1894), reference from Schrijver's Combinatorial Optimization textbook (Hungarian)
14. Feng, N., et al.: DRAT proofs of unsatisfiability for SAT modulo monotonic theories. In: Finkbeiner, B., Kovács, L. (eds.) Tools and Algorithms for the Construction and Analysis of Systems (TACAS), pp. 3–23. Springer, Cham (2024). https://doi.org/10.1007/978-3-031-57246-3_1
15. Filliâtre, J.-C., Paskevich, A.: Why3 — where programs meet provers. In: Felleisen, M., Gardner, P. (eds.) ESOP 2013. LNCS, vol. 7792, pp. 125–128. Springer, Heidelberg (2013). https://doi.org/10.1007/978-3-642-37036-6_8
16. Flippo, M., Sidorov, K., Marijnissen, I., Smits, J., Demirović, E.: A multi-stage proof logging framework to certify the correctness of CP solvers. In: Shaw, P. (ed.) Constraint Programming (CP). Leibniz International Proceedings in Informatics (LIPIcs), vol. 307, pp. 11:1–11:20. Schloss Dagstuhl – Leibniz-Zentrum für Informatik, Dagstuhl, Germany (2024). https://drops.dagstuhl.de/entities/document/10.4230/LIPIcs.CP.2024.11
17. Fontaine, P., Marion, J.-Y., Merz, S., Nieto, L.P., Tiu, A.: Expressiveness + automation + soundness: towards combining SMT solvers and interactive proof assistants. In: Hermanns, H., Palsberg, J. (eds.) TACAS 2006. LNCS, vol. 3920, pp. 167–181. Springer, Heidelberg (2006). https://doi.org/10.1007/11691372_11
18. Hitarth, S., Codel, C., Lachnitt, H., Dutertre, B.: Extending DRAT to SMT (2024). https://www.amazon.science/publications/extending-drat-to-smt

19. Hoenicke, J., Schindler, T.: A simple proof format for SMT. In: Déharbe, D., Hyvärinen, A.E.J. (eds.) International Workshop on Satisfiability Modulo Theories (SMT). CEUR Workshop Proceedings, vol. 3185, pp. 54–70. CEUR-WS.org (2022). http://ceur-ws.org/Vol-3185/paper9527.pdf
20. Järvisalo, M., Heule, M.J.H., Biere, A.: Inprocessing rules. In: Gramlich, B., Miller, D., Sattler, U. (eds.) IJCAR 2012. LNCS (LNAI), vol. 7364, pp. 355–370. Springer, Heidelberg (2012). https://doi.org/10.1007/978-3-642-31365-3_28
21. Katz, G., Barrett, C.W., Tinelli, C., Reynolds, A., Hadarean, L.: Lazy proofs for DPLL(T)-based SMT solvers. In: Piskac, R., Talupur, M. (eds.) Formal Methods in Computer-Aided Design (FMCAD), pp. 93–100. IEEE (2016). https://doi.org/10.1109/FMCAD.2016.7886666
22. Lachnitt, H., et al.: Improving the SMT proof reconstruction pipeline in Isabelle/HOL. In: Forster, Y., Keller, C. (eds.) Interactive Theorem Proving (ITP). LIPIcs, vol. 352, pp. 26:1–26:22. Schloss Dagstuhl - Leibniz-Zentrum für Informatik (2025). https://doi.org/10.4230/LIPICS.ITP.2025.26
23. Lattuada, A., et al.: Verus: a practical foundation for systems verification. In: Proceedings of the ACM SIGOPS 30th Symposium on Operating Systems Principles, SOSP 2024, pp. 438–454. Association for Computing Machinery, New York, NY, USA (2024). https://doi.org/10.1145/3694715.3695952
24. Leino, K.R.M.: Dafny: an automatic program verifier for functional correctness. In: Clarke, E.M., Voronkov, A. (eds.) LPAR 2010. LNCS (LNAI), vol. 6355, pp. 348–370. Springer, Heidelberg (2010). https://doi.org/10.1007/978-3-642-17511-4_20
25. Mann, M., et al.: `Pono`: a flexible and extensible SMT-based model checker. In: Silva, A., Leino, K.R.M. (eds.) CAV 2021. LNCS, vol. 12760, pp. 461–474. Springer, Cham (2021). https://doi.org/10.1007/978-3-030-81688-9_22
26. Moura, L., Ullrich, S.: The lean 4 theorem prover and programming language. In: Platzer, A., Sutcliffe, G. (eds.) CADE 2021. LNCS (LNAI), vol. 12699, pp. 625–635. Springer, Cham (2021). https://doi.org/10.1007/978-3-030-79876-5_37
27. de Moura, L.M., Bjørner, N.: Proofs and refutations, and Z3. In: Rudnicki, P., Sutcliffe, G., Konev, B., Schmidt, R.A., Schulz, S. (eds.) Logic for Programming, Artificial Intelligence, and Reasoning (LPAR) Workshops. CEUR Workshop Proceedings, vol. 418. CEUR-WS.org (2008)
28. Mukherjee, R., Kroening, D., Melham, T.: Hardware verification using software analyzers. In: 2015 IEEE Computer Society Annual Symposium on VLSI, pp. 7–12 (2015). https://doi.org/10.1109/ISVLSI.2015.107
29. Nieuwenhuis, R., Oliveras, A.: Proof-producing congruence closure. In: Giesl, J. (ed.) RTA 2005. LNCS, vol. 3467, pp. 453–468. Springer, Heidelberg (2005). https://doi.org/10.1007/978-3-540-32033-3_33
30. Nieuwenhuis, R., Oliveras, A., Tinelli, C.: Solving SAT and SAT modulo theories: from an abstract Davis-Putnam-Logemann-Loveland procedure to DPLL(T). J. ACM **53**(6), 937–977 (2006). https://doi.org/10.1145/1217856.1217859
31. Otoni, R., Blicha, M., Eugster, P., Hyvärinen, A.E.J., Sharygina, N.: Theory-specific proof steps witnessing correctness of SMT executions. In: ACM/IEEE Design Automation Conference (DAC), pp. 541–546 (2021). https://doi.org/10.1109/DAC18074.2021.9586272
32. Rawson, M., Voronkov, A., Schoisswohl, J., Komel, A.P.: Ground truth: checking vampire proofs via satisfiability modulo theories. In: Barrett, C.W., Waldmann, U. (eds.) Proceedings of Conference on Automated Deduction (CADE). Lecture Notes in Computer Science, vol. 15943, pp. 136–149. Springer (2025). https://doi.org/10.1007/978-3-031-99984-0_8
33. Reeves, J.E., Kiesl-Reiter, B., Heule, M.J.H.: Propositional proof skeletons. In: Tools and Algorithms for the Construction and Analysis of Systems (TACAS), pp. 329–347. Springer (2023). https://doi.org/10.1007/978-3-031-30823-9_17

34. Reynolds, A., Barbosa, H., Fontaine, P.: Revisiting enumerative instantiation. In: Beyer, D., Huisman, M. (eds.) TACAS 2018. LNCS, vol. 10806, pp. 112–131. Springer, Cham (2018). https://doi.org/10.1007/978-3-319-89963-3_7
35. Rungta, N.: A billion SMT queries a day (invited paper). In: Shoham, S., Vizel, Y. (eds.) Computer Aided Verification (CAV), Part I. Lecture Notes in Computer Science, vol. 13371, pp. 3–18. Springer (2022). https://doi.org/10.1007/978-3-031-13185-1_1
36. Schrijver, A.: Theory of Linear and Integer Programming. Wiley (1998)
37. Schurr, H., Fleury, M., Barbosa, H., Fontaine, P.: Alethe: towards a generic SMT proof format (extended abstract). CoRR abs/2107.02354 (2021). https://arxiv.org/abs/2107.02354
38. Schurr, H.-J., Fleury, M., Desharnais, M.: Reliable reconstruction of fine-grained proofs in a proof assistant. In: Platzer, A., Sutcliffe, G. (eds.) CADE 2021. LNCS (LNAI), vol. 12699, pp. 450–467. Springer, Cham (2021). https://doi.org/10.1007/978-3-030-79876-5_26
39. Tan, Y.K., Heule, M.J.H., Myreen, M.O.: cake_lpr: verified propagation redundancy checking in CakeML. In: Tools and Algorithms for the Construction and Analysis of Systems (TACAS), Part II. LNCS, vol. 12652, pp. 223–241 (2021). https://doi.org/10.1007/s10009-022-00690-y
40. Wetzler, N., Heule, M.J.H., Hunt, W.A.: DRAT-trim: efficient checking and trimming using expressive clausal proofs. In: Sinz, C., Egly, U. (eds.) SAT 2014. LNCS, vol. 8561, pp. 422–429. Springer, Cham (2014). https://doi.org/10.1007/978-3-319-09284-3_31
41. Wilson, A., Nötzli, A., Reynolds, A., Cook, B., Tinelli, C., Barrett, C.W.: Partitioning strategies for distributed SMT solving. In: Nadel, A., Rozier, K.Y. (eds.) Formal Methods In Computer-Aided Design (FMCAD), pp. 199–208. IEEE (2023). https://doi.org/10.34727/2023/ISBN.978-3-85448-060-0_28
42. Zhou, Y., Bosamiya, J., Takashima, Y., Li, J., Heule, M., Parno, B.: Mariposa: measuring SMT instability in automated program verification. In: Nadel, A., Rozier, K.Y. (eds.) Formal Methods In Computer-Aided Design (FMCAD), pp. 178–188. IEEE (2023). https://doi.org/10.34727/2023/ISBN.978-3-85448-060-0_26

Open Access This chapter is licensed under the terms of the Creative Commons Attribution 4.0 International License (http://creativecommons.org/licenses/by/4.0/), which permits use, sharing, adaptation, distribution and reproduction in any medium or format, as long as you give appropriate credit to the original author(s) and the source, provide a link to the Creative Commons license and indicate if changes were made.

The images or other third party material in this chapter are included in the chapter's Creative Commons license, unless indicated otherwise in a credit line to the material. If material is not included in the chapter's Creative Commons license and your intended use is not permitted by statutory regulation or exceeds the permitted use, you will need to obtain permission directly from the copyright holder.

Avoiding Big Integers: Parallel Multimodular Algebraic Verification of Arithmetic Circuits

Clemens Hofstadler[1(✉)], Daniela Kaufmann[2], and Chen Chen[3]

[1] Johannes Kepler University, Linz, Austria
clemens.hofstadler@jku.at
[2] TU Wien, Vienna, Austria
daniela.kaufmann@tuwien.ac.at
[3] Hong Kong University of Science and Technology (Guangzhou), Guangzhou, China
cchen099@connect.hkust-gz.edu.cn

Abstract. Word-level verification of arithmetic circuits with large operands typically relies on arbitrary-precision arithmetic, which can lead to significant computational overhead as word sizes grow. In this paper, we present a hybrid algebraic verification technique based on polynomial reasoning that combines linear and nonlinear rewriting. Our approach relies on multimodular reasoning using homomorphic images, where computations are performed in parallel modulo different primes, thereby avoiding any large-integer arithmetic. We implement the proposed method in the verification tool TalisMan2.0 and evaluate it on a suite of multiplier benchmarks. Our results show that hybrid multimodular reasoning significantly improves upon existing approaches.

Keywords: Computer Algebra · Hardware Verification · Homomorphic Images · Linear Extractions · Guess and Prove

1 Introduction

Word-level reasoning using computer algebra has proven to be an effective approach for the formal verification of arithmetic circuits, especially for circuits encoding nonlinear operations, such as multiplier and divider circuits [13,20,22, 27,28], as it avoids the combinatorial blow-up caused by bit-blasting. In this line of work, circuits are translated into systems of polynomial equations whose solutions characterize all valid circuit behaviors. Verification then reduces to proving that a given specification polynomial is implied by the circuit encoding.

A major limitation of existing word-level algebraic reasoning approaches is their reliance on large-integer arithmetic. For arithmetic circuits with word sizes of 64 bits and beyond, the resulting polynomial systems contain coefficients whose bit-widths exceed native machine word sizes by orders of magnitude. For instance, the specification of 64-bit multipliers contains coefficients up to

© The Author(s) 2026
A. Biere et al. (Eds.): IJCAR 2026, LNAI 16688, pp. 175–193, 2026.
https://doi.org/10.1007/978-3-032-32589-1_11

2^{127}. As a result, state-of-the-art reasoning tools typically depend on arbitrary-precision arithmetic, e.g., the implementations of [12,21,26,27] all rely on the GMP library [9], which incurs computational overhead and limits scalability in practice.

In this paper, we address this limitation by introducing a verification framework based on *parallel multimodular reasoning.* Our approach avoids large-integer arithmetic entirely by computing *homomorphic images* of the polynomial system modulo multiple machine-word-sized prime numbers. Rather than reasoning over $\mathbb{Z}$ or $\mathbb{Q}$, all computations are carried out modulo those primes in parallel, ensuring that coefficients remain within machine word sizes. The Chinese remainder theorem (Theorem 1) ensures the correctness, provided that sufficiently many primes are used (Theorem 2). While homomorphic images are a classical tool in computer algebra, see e.g., [8, Ch. 5], to the best of our knowledge this is the first work to employ them for word-level circuit verification.

To exploit multimodular reasoning effectively, we combine it with a *hybrid rewriting framework* that integrates both linear and nonlinear algebraic reasoning. Linearization-based techniques [13,20] extract linear relations from the algebraic encoding of the circuit to enable a fast linear rewriting of the previously linearized circuit specification. We build upon the guess-and-prove strategy presented in [13]. The core idea is to sample valid assignments for extracted subcircuits, from which linear relations are guessed using linear algebra. The correctness of these guesses is proved using satisfiability (SAT) solving. In this paper, we significantly improve, parallelize, and adapt this approach to our multimodular setting. In particular, we apply a structure-aware subcircuit selection, weighted sampling for more targeted assignments, and dedicated linear algebra routines to better handle a large number of samples. All of these optimizations significantly improve the guess-and-prove strategy.

When linear reasoning becomes computationally infeasible due to the size of the selected subcircuit, our framework switches to nonlinear rewriting, using the nonlinear circuit encoding to continue rewriting the specification until completion. This combination yields the efficiency of linearization together with the robustness of nonlinear reasoning. Additionally, this procedure allows us to always produce counterexamples in case of faulty circuits, which is not always possible in purely linear approaches.

We implement the proposed approach in our novel verification tool TalisMan2.0 [15], and evaluate it on a suite of multiplier benchmarks. The results demonstrate that parallel multimodular reasoning combining linear and nonlinear rewriting is able to efficiently solve a large set of benchmarks while remaining robust.

2 Preliminaries

In Sect. 2.1, we review fundamental concepts from polynomial algebra that are required throughout this work. For a more comprehensive introduction, we refer to the standard textbooks [6,7]. In Sect. 2.2, we recall And-Inverter Graphs (AIGs) and describe how they can be represented by polynomial encodings.

2.1 Algebra

Let $X = \{x_1, \dots, x_n\}$ be a finite set of indeterminates and let R be a commutative ring with unity. A *monomial* (in X) is a product of the form $x_1^{\alpha_1} \dots x_n^{\alpha_n}$, where $\alpha_1, \dots, \alpha_n \in \mathbb{N}$. The set of all monomials in X is denoted by $[X]$.

A *polynomial* f (over R) is a finite R-linear combination of monomials, i.e., $f = c_1m_1 + \dots + c_sm_s$, with *coefficients* $c_1, \dots, c_s \in R$ and monomials $m_1, \dots, m_s \in [X]$. The product c_im_i is called a *term*. The set of all polynomials is denoted by $R[X] = R[x_1, \dots, x_n]$.

The *degree* $\deg(m)$ of a monomial $m = x_1^{\alpha_1} \dots x_n^{\alpha_n} \in [X]$ is defined as the sum of its exponents, that is, $\deg(m) = \alpha_1 + \dots + \alpha_n$. A polynomial f is called *linear* if every monomial m in f has $\deg(m) \leq 1$, otherwise f is called *nonlinear*.

A *monomial order* is a total order $\prec$ on $[X]$ such that $1 \prec m$ for all $m \neq 1$, and $m_1 \prec m_2$ implies $mm_1 \prec mm_2$ for all $m, m_1, m_2 \in [X]$. Typical examples are the *lexicographic order*, which compares exponent vectors componentwise, and the *degree lexicographic order*, which first compares degrees and breaks ties lexicographically. An order is *degree-compatible* if smaller degree implies smaller order. With respect to a fixed monomial order, every nonzero polynomial $f \in R[X]$ has a unique maximal monomial, called its *leading monomial*.

A nonempty subset $I \subseteq R[X]$ is an *ideal* if $f + g \in I$ and $hf \in I$ for all $f, g \in I$ and $h \in R[X]$. A finite set of polynomials $F = \{f_1, \dots, f_r\} \subseteq R[X]$ can be interpreted as a system of equations $f_1 = \dots = f_r = 0$. The set of all polynomials h whose equation $h = 0$ can be derived algebraically from this system forms an ideal, denoted by $\langle F \rangle$. It is given explicitly by

$$\langle F \rangle = \{h_1f_1 + \dots + h_rf_r \mid h_1, \dots, h_r \in R[X]\}.$$

2.2 And-Inverter Graphs and Their Polynomial Encodings

An *And-Inverter Graph* (AIG) [29] is a directed acyclic graph representing a Boolean circuit C. Internal nodes correspond to logical conjunctions, while edge annotations encode negation. Primary inputs correspond to Boolean variables.

A *specification* of an AIG is a polynomial $\mathcal{S} \in R[X]$, where R is a chosen coefficient domain (typically $\mathbb{Z}$) and X contains all input, gate, and output variables of the circuit. The specification relates the outputs of the circuit to its primary inputs. Although AIGs operate on Boolean signals, the specification is not restricted to the Boolean ring $\mathbb{B}[X]$. For instance, the specification of multipliers with inputs $a_{n-1}, \dots, a_0, b_{n-1}, \dots, b_0$ and outputs $s_{2n-1}, \dots, s_0$ can be represented as $\sum_{i=0}^{2n-1} 2^i s_i - \left(\sum_{i=0}^{n-1} 2^i a_i\right) \cdot \left(\sum_{i=0}^{n-1} 2^i b_i\right)$ over $\mathbb{Z}[X]$ or $\mathbb{Q}[X]$.

To relate the behavior of gates in the circuit to polynomial equations, we map $\top \mapsto 1$ and $\bot \mapsto 0$, yielding the correspondences $x \wedge y \simeq xy$ and $\neg x \simeq 1 - x$ between logic and algebra. Based on these relations, we define the following *gate polynomials* for gates in a circuit.

Definition 1. *The* gate polynomial *of an AIG node g with inputs x, y is:*

Logical constraint		*Gate polynomial*
$g = x \wedge y$	$\Rightarrow$	$g - xy$
$g = \neg x \wedge y$	$\Rightarrow$	$g - (1-x)y$
$g = x \wedge \neg y$	$\Rightarrow$	$g - x(1-y)$
$g = \neg x \wedge \neg y$	$\Rightarrow$	$g - (1-x)(1-y)$

We denote by $G(C) \subseteq R[X]$ the set of all gate polynomials of a circuit C.

To enforce Boolean semantics when working over coefficient domains $R \neq \mathbb{B}$, we introduce *Boolean value polynomials.* For each primary input x_i of the AIG, we define the constraint $x_i^2 - x_i = 0$. We denote the set of all such polynomials by $B(C)$. Boolean constraints propagate through the circuit, and it therefore suffices to introduce Boolean value polynomials only for the primary inputs [23].

Gate Polynomials $G(C)$	Logical constraints
$s_3 - g_{24}$	$s_3 = g_{24}$
$s_2 - g_{28}$	$s_2 = g_{28}$
$s_1 - g_{20}$	$s_1 = g_{20}$
$s_0 - g_{10}$	$s_0 = g_{10}$
$g_{28} - (1 - g_{26})(1 - g_{24})$	$g_{28} = \neg g_{26} \wedge \neg g_{24}$
$g_{26} - (1 - g_{22})(1 - g_{16})$	$g_{26} = \neg g_{22} \wedge \neg g_{16}$
$g_{24} - g_{22}g_{16}$	$g_{24} = g_{22} \wedge g_{16}$
$g_{22} - b_1 a_1$	$g_{22} = b_1 \wedge a_1$
$g_{20} - (1 - g_{18})(1 - g_{16})$	$g_{20} = \neg g_{18} \wedge \neg g_{16}$
$g_{18} - (1 - g_{14})(1 - g_{12})$	$g_{18} = \neg g_{14} \wedge \neg g_{12}$
$g_{16} - g_{14}g_{12}$	$g_{16} = g_{14} \wedge g_{12}$
$g_{14} - b_1 a_0$	$g_{14} = b_1 \wedge a_0$
$g_{12} - b_0 a_1$	$g_{12} = b_0 \wedge a_1$
$g_{10} - b_0 a_0$	$g_{10} = b_0 \wedge a_0$

$B(C)$: $a_1^2 - a_1, a_0^2 - a_0, b_1^2 - b_1, b_0^2 - b_0$

Spec $\mathcal{S}$: $8s_3 + 4s_2 + 2s_1 + s_0 - 4a_1b_1 - 2a_1b_0 - 2a_0b_1 - a_0b_0$

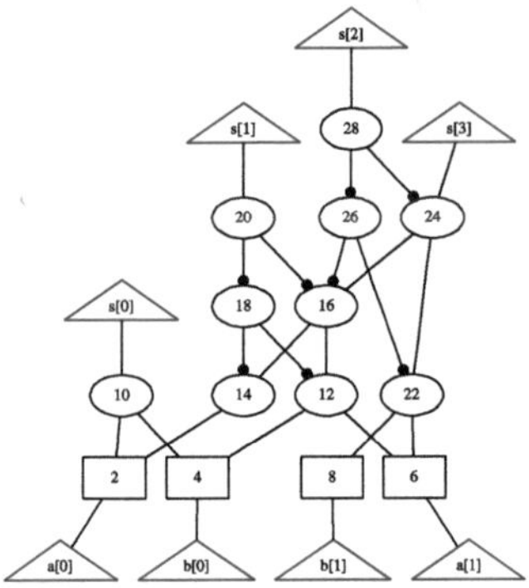

Fig. 1. AIG and polynomial encoding of a 2-bit multiplier.

Example 1. Figure 1 shows an AIG representing a 2-bit multiplier and its corresponding polynomial encoding. We denote the primary inputs by a_0, a_1, b_0, b_1 and outputs by s_0, s_1, s_2, s_3. The internal nodes are denoted by g_i, where i corresponds to the respective AIG node. The specification $\mathcal{S}$ expresses that the weighted sum of output bits (= output bit-vector) is equal to the product of the weighted sum of input bits (= input bit-vectors).

To relate a circuit to its specification, we recall the notion of models from [22]. First, recall that a *(Boolean) assignment* is a function $\varphi \colon X \to \{0,1\} \subseteq R$ that maps the variables in X to the values 0 and 1. Any assignment φ can be extended to an evaluation of polynomials by substituting $\varphi(x)$ for each variable $x \in X$. For a polynomial $p \in R[X]$, we denote the evaluation under φ by $\varphi(p) \in R$.

Definition 2. *Let $P \subseteq R[X]$ be a set of polynomials. A (Boolean) assignment φ is a* model *of P (over R) if $\varphi(p) = 0$ for all $p \in P$. Moreover, for $q \in R[X]$, we write $P \models_R q$ if every model for P is also a model for $\{q\}$, i.e., whenever $\varphi(p) = 0$ for all $p \in P$, then also $\varphi(q) = 0$.*

We say that a circuit C *fulfills* a specification $\mathcal{S}$ (over R) if $G(C) \models_R \mathcal{S}$. Note that, since we consider only Boolean assignments, this is equivalent to $G(C) \cup B(C) \models_R \mathcal{S}$. By [24, Thm. 2,3], this holds if and only if the specification polynomial $\mathcal{S}$ lies in the ideal $\langle G(C) \cup B(C)\rangle$. Hence, correctness of C can be verified algebraically by checking whether $\mathcal{S} \in \langle G(C) \cup B(C)\rangle$. Classically, this computation is performed over $R = \mathbb{Z}$ (or $R = \mathbb{Q}$ when a field is required). In Sect. 4, we present a multimodular approach that reduces verification over $\mathbb{Z}$ to verification over sufficiently many finite rings $\mathbb{Z}_{m_i}$.

3 Related Work

The ideal membership $\mathcal{S} \overset{?}{\in} \langle G(C) \cup B(C)\rangle$ is decidable using Gröbner basis theory [5]. The set $G(C) \cup B(C)$ needs to be transformed into a Gröbner basis, which can be of double exponential complexity in the number of variables [32]. However, if a lexicographic monomial order is chosen such that variables follow a reverse topological order of the circuit, the set $G(C) \cup B(C)$ already forms a Gröbner basis [24]. Thus, correctness of the circuit can be decided by computing the remainder of $\mathcal{S}$ under multivariate polynomial division with respect to $G(C) \cup B(C)$, see [6, Ch. 2.3]. We refer to this approach as *nonlinear rewriting.*

For multiplier verification, nonlinear rewriting with respect to a lexicographic order is known to suffer from severe *monomial blow-up.* Since the leading monomial of gate polynomials typically has lower degree than the remaining terms (cf. Definition 1), the degree of intermediate results may increase substantially. This frequently produces intermediate results with millions of monomials [30] and drastically slows down computations. To mitigate this effect, several advanced rewriting engines have been proposed in recent years. Early work employed dedicated preprocessing and incremental reasoning [22], where syntactically identified parts of the multiplier are rewritten using SAT solving prior to applying a column-wise verification algorithm [21]. Subsequent refinements eliminated the reliance on an external SAT solver by introducing a syntactic algebraic encoding that incorporates literal polarities [19]. However, the dependence on syntactic heuristics remains a major limitation of these approaches, as they are often not robust for unseen circuit architectures, such as those generated by logic synthesis.

Orthogonal to this line of work, dynamic rewriting determines the rewrite order on the fly and backtracks if intermediate results exceed a predefined threshold [31]. This idea was further extended by incorporating literal polarities into the encoding [27]. While this approach is more robust across different circuit architectures, it remains infeasible for certain multiplier designs.

Recent approaches depart from the lexicographic ordering and instead employ *degree-compatible* orderings to prevent degree growth during rewriting [13,20].

By linearizing the specification, rewriting is restricted to linear polynomials, which avoids the monomial blow-up. We refer to this approach as *linear rewriting.*

Linear rewriting comes at the cost of having to extract suitable linear relations from the circuit. To address this, on-the-fly techniques have been proposed that identify subcircuits and compute Gröbner bases locally to derive the required linear relations [20], as well as approaches based on algebraic transformations and guess-and-prove techniques [13]. Among these, the guess-and-prove approach has shown particular promise, as it can handle comparatively large subcircuits ($>$ 1000 nodes). In this technique, a subcircuit is selected and valid assignments for that subcircuit are generated. Linear algebra is then used to derive candidate linear relations ("guesses"), which subsequently need to be proven, for instance, using SAT solving. If a candidate relation is invalid, a counterexample returned by the SAT solver can be used to refine the guess. If no suitable relation is found, the subcircuit is expanded and the process is repeated, see [13, Sec. 3.2, 4] for a more in-depth discussion.

Despite its effectiveness, the guess-and-prove approach has notable limitations. First, performance degrades significantly once the extracted subcircuit exceeds a certain size ($>$ 5000 nodes). Second, due to large coefficients in guessed polynomials, the SAT-based proofs can become infeasible in practice, as the coefficients of the derived polynomials must be encoded at the bit level.

Our work addresses these shortcomings by applying linear rewriting via the guess-and-prove approach using *multimodular* computations, which impose explicit bounds on coefficients. Moreover, whenever linear extraction becomes too costly we propose to switch to nonlinear rewriting, thereby combining the strengths of both paradigms in a hybrid approach.

4 Multimodular Verification via Homomorphic Images

Algebraic word-level verification of arithmetic circuits with real-world input sizes of 64 bits and beyond faces a fundamental scalability bottleneck: intermediate coefficients arising during symbolic reasoning may become extremely large. As a consequence, verification procedures must rely on arbitrary-precision arithmetic, which is significantly slower than native machine-word operations that can exploit fast hardware arithmetic.

Such *expression swell* is a well-known challenge in computer algebra. Classic examples include linear system solving and Gröbner basis computations over the integers or rationals. To address this issue, computer algebra systems often employ *homomorphic images* [1,4,16,36]. The central idea of homomorphic images is to map computations from an unbounded domain, such as $\mathbb{Z}$ or $\mathbb{Q}$, into finite algebraic structures, typically into $\mathbb{Z}_m$, the integers modulo m, where all elements have a fixed-size representation and no expression swell can occur. Typically, m is chosen to be a prime number, such that $\mathbb{Z}_m$ is a finite field, ensuring desirable algebraic properties for reasoning and computation.

Concretely, we translate the idea into the following multimodular verification strategy: Instead of verifying that a circuit C fulfills a specification $\mathcal{S}$ over $\mathbb{Z}$, we perform the verification modulo several integers $m_1, \ldots, m_k$ (typically primes). Working in $\mathbb{Z}_{m_i}$ ensures that coefficients remain bounded, and when the moduli m_i are chosen to fit within machine words, we can rely on fast native arithmetic. The Chinese remainder theorem ensures the correctness of the circuit over the integers, provided that sufficiently many moduli are used. We recall the Chinese remainder theorem below and refer to, e.g., [35, Thm. 4.12] for a proof.

Theorem 1 (Chinese Remainder Theorem). *Let $m_1, \ldots, m_k \in \mathbb{N}$ be pairwise coprime positive integers. For any $a_1, \ldots, a_k \in \mathbb{Z}$, the system of linear congruences $x \equiv a_i \bmod m_i$ for $i = 1, \ldots, k$ has a unique solution modulo $\prod_{i=1}^{k} m_i$.*

To formally justify our approach, we first observe that the set of models of a circuit does not depend on whether computations are carried out over the integers or modulo an integer $m \geq 2$ before proving our main result in Theorem 2.

Lemma 1. *Let C be an AIG and $m \geq 2$. A Boolean assignment φ is a model of $G(C)$ over $\mathbb{Z}$ if and only if it is a model of $G(C)$ over $\mathbb{Z}_m$.*

Proof. If $\varphi(p) = 0$ over $\mathbb{Z}$, then clearly $\varphi(p) \equiv 0 \bmod m$. Thus, any model over $\mathbb{Z}$ is also a model over $\mathbb{Z}_m$. Conversely, assume that φ is not a model of $G(C)$ over $\mathbb{Z}$, i.e., there exists $p \in G(C)$ such that $\varphi(p) \neq 0$. Since p is a gate polynomial, $\varphi(p) \in \{-1, 1\}$. For $m \geq 2$, both values remain nonzero modulo m, implying that $\varphi(p) \not\equiv 0 \bmod m$. So, φ is also not a model of $G(C)$ over $\mathbb{Z}_m$.

Theorem 2. *Let C be an AIG and let $\mathcal{S} \in \mathbb{Z}[X]$ be a specification of C. Further, let $m_1, \ldots, m_k \in \mathbb{N} \setminus \{0, 1\}$ be pairwise coprime positive integers such that $|\varphi(\mathcal{S})| < \prod_{i=1}^{k} m_i$ for all Boolean assignments φ. Then*

$$G(C) \models_{\mathbb{Z}} \mathcal{S} \qquad \textit{iff} \qquad \forall i \in \{1, \ldots, k\} : G(C) \models_{\mathbb{Z}_{m_i}} \mathcal{S}.$$

Proof. First, assume that $G(C) \models_{\mathbb{Z}} \mathcal{S}$ holds. Let $i \in \{1, \ldots, k\}$ be arbitrary and let φ be a model of $G(C)$ over $\mathbb{Z}_{m_i}$. By Lemma 1, φ is also a model of $G(C)$ over $\mathbb{Z}$. Thus, by assumption $\varphi(\mathcal{S}) = 0$ over $\mathbb{Z}$, which implies $\varphi(\mathcal{S}) \equiv 0 \bmod m_i$, showing that φ is also a model of $\mathcal{S}$ over $\mathbb{Z}_{m_i}$.

Conversely, assume that $G(C) \models_{\mathbb{Z}_{m_i}} \mathcal{S}$ holds for all $i = 1, \ldots, k$. Let φ be a model of $G(C)$ over $\mathbb{Z}$. Again by Lemma 1, φ is also a model of $G(C)$ over each $\mathbb{Z}_{m_i}$. Hence, $\varphi(\mathcal{S}) \equiv 0 \bmod m_i$ for all i by assumption. By the Chinese remainder theorem, this implies $\varphi(\mathcal{S}) \equiv 0 \bmod \prod_{i=1}^{k} m_i$. Since $|\varphi(\mathcal{S})| < \prod_{i=1}^{k} m_i$, we have $\varphi(\mathcal{S}) = 0$ over $\mathbb{Z}$, showing that φ is also a model of $\mathcal{S}$ over $\mathbb{Z}$.

Theorem 2 establishes the correctness of the multimodular verification approach, but it is deliberately agnostic about how the modular verifications of $G(C) \models_{\mathbb{Z}_{m_i}} \mathcal{S}$ are performed. In particular, this could be done by purely algebraic methods, but also using SAT-based reasoning, or any combination thereof. In the following Sect. 5, we will discuss how to perform the modular verification using our hybrid algebraic reasoning approach.

Note that Theorem 2 does not require the moduli m_i to be prime numbers. It suffices that they are pairwise coprime. Nevertheless, it is beneficial to choose the m_i to be primes, so that each $\mathbb{Z}_{m_i}$ forms a finite field, which simplifies subsequent computations that rely on field properties. By using word-sized primes, all coefficients fit into native machine words, avoiding arbitrary-precision arithmetic altogether. In particular, as witnessed by implementations of other multimodular algorithms [11,33], it can be beneficial to use 32-bit (resp. 16-bit) prime moduli while storing intermediate results in 64-bit (resp. 32-bit) integers. This way several arithmetic operations can be accumulated before applying a modular reduction, thereby reducing the number of expensive modulo operations.

The required number of moduli depends on an upper bound for the absolute value of the evaluation of $\mathcal{S}$ on all Boolean assignments φ. Such a bound can be easily obtained directly from $\mathcal{S}$: since we consider only Boolean assignments, each monomial in $\mathcal{S}$ evaluates to either 0 or 1. Hence, $|\varphi(\mathcal{S})|$ is bounded by the maximum of the sum of all positive coefficients of $\mathcal{S}$ and the absolute value of the sum of all negative coefficients of $\mathcal{S}$. For example, if $\mathcal{S}$ is the specification of an n-bit signed or unsigned multiplier, then $|\varphi(\mathcal{S})| < 2^{2n}$ for all φ.

Consequently, for 64-bit multipliers, five 32-bit primes suffice to meet the condition of Theorem 2. Since the verification tasks for different moduli are completely independent, they can be run in parallel, yielding near-linear speedups on modern multicore machines.

Finally, we note that the multimodular approach also supports the computation of *witnesses* of faulty circuits. By Lemma 1, any counterexample discovered during verification over a modulus $\mathbb{Z}_{m_i}$, that is, any model of $G(C)$ that violates $\mathcal{S}$ modulo m_i, also forms a valid counterexample over $\mathbb{Z}$, and thus directly witnesses incorrect circuit behavior.

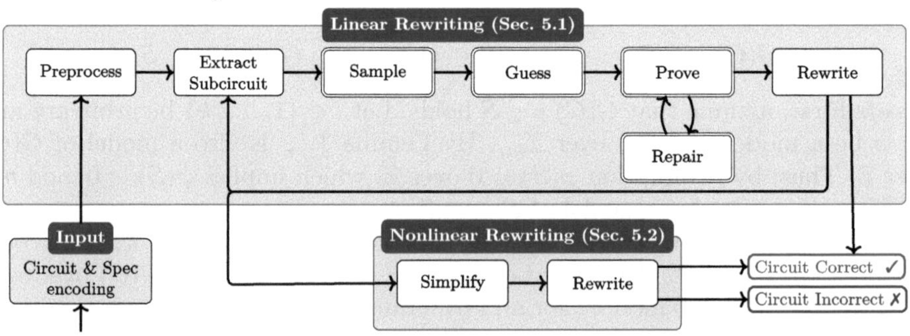

Fig. 2. Overview of the TalisMan2.0 workflow. Double-edged boxes are computations that are run in parallel in TalisMan2.0.

5 Hybrid Algebraic Circuit Verification

In the following, we combine the complementary strengths of linear and nonlinear rewriting in a hybrid algebraic verification framework that also makes use of the multimodular approach presented in Sect. 4. We also discuss implementation details of this hybrid approach in our tool TalisMan2.0 [15] that targets verification of multiplier circuits.

The overall workflow is shown in Fig. 2. Given an input AIG C, let X be the set of all input, output and internal gate variables of C. We encode the gate constraints $G(C)$ and the Boolean value polynomials $B(C)$ as described in Sect. 2.2. A given specification $\mathcal{S} \in \mathbb{Z}[X]$ is linearized using extension variables [13,20]: for every nonlinear monomial m in $\mathcal{S}$, we introduce a new variable $v \notin X$ that acts as a placeholder. The corresponding constraints $E(C) = \{v - m \mid m \in \mathcal{S} \wedge \deg(m) > 1 \wedge v \notin X\}$ are added to the circuit encoding $G(C) \cup B(C) \cup E(C)$.

Verification then proceeds in two phases. We first apply linear rewriting as long as linear relations can be derived efficiently. Once this becomes ineffective, we switch to nonlinear rewriting. Crucially, both phases are executed over multiple prime fields using homomorphic images, ensuring that all arithmetic remains word-sized and that candidate relations can be validated efficiently. The internal structure of both phases is explained in the following sections.

We note that the approach also works with non-prime moduli, since correctness ultimately relies on Theorem 2, which only requires pairwise coprime moduli. However, we use primes in practice as they ensure that each residue ring is a field. This is particularly useful in the linear rewriting phase, where systems of linear equations are solved to detect candidate relations (see the following section). While this can also be done over composite moduli (e.g., via Hermite or Smith normal form), Gaussian elimination over prime fields is more efficient.

5.1 Linear Rewriting

Linear rewriting aims to simplify the specification polynomial by iteratively deriving and applying linear relations implied by the circuit. After encoding and linearizing the specification, we first perform a preprocessing step to identify recurring arithmetic structures that induce linear constraints. The resulting relations are collected for subsequent use in rewriting.

The main procedure then iteratively considers the current leading monomial of the specification polynomial. To determine the leading monomial we use a reverse topological ordering of the variables. If a previously derived linear relation is applicable, it is used to rewrite the monomial. Otherwise, we select a suitable subcircuit and guess a candidate linear relation suggested by its structure. The guessed relation is then formally proved correct with respect to the circuit semantics before it is applied for rewriting. If no suitable relation can be found efficiently, we fall back to nonlinear rewriting.

Preprocessing. Many linear relations in arithmetic circuits originate from small building blocks such as half adders (HA) or full adders (FA). For example, a FA with inputs x, y, z, sum s, and carry c satisfies the linear relation $2c + s - x - y - z = 0$. Our first goal is to identify all half and full adders in the AIG. Instead of relying on syntactic pattern matching like in previous work [19,22], which may be obscured by synthesis, we detect arithmetic structure semantically using cut enumeration (up to three leaves) and local truth tables, which we have implemented in our own modified version of ABC [2]. For each detected HA/FA, the corresponding linear polynomial is constructed and cached for use during linear rewriting.

Beyond local half and full adders, verification based on linear rewriting also requires us to identify higher-level adder blocks that are used to sum bit-vectors, such as the final-stage adder (FSA) in multipliers. Since the linear relations of the FSA generally depend on its global structure, it is necessary to identify a subcircuit that captures the FSA in its entirety. During preprocessing, we use our modified version of ABC to identify an approximate FSA subcircuit by traversing the circuit backwards from the outputs until reaching previously detected HA/FA blocks, which form a structural boundary between the FSA and the remaining circuit. Deriving a topological closure ensures that the resulting boundary forms a valid cut. Since the input size of the FSA easily exceeds 64 nodes, we do not attempt to derive its linear relations using truth tables as we did for FA/HA. Instead, they are derived later in the guess-and-prove phase, where we treat the FSA as a single extracted subcircuit. Hence, this approximation may safely over-approximate the FSA.

Extract Subcircuit. During rewriting, we consider the leading monomial of the current specification. If a cached linear polynomial with matching leading monomial exists, we immediately apply it for a rewrite step. Otherwise, we attempt to derive such a relation via guess-and-prove on a suitable subcircuit. If the corresponding gate is part of the FSA approximation, we consider the entire FSA subcircuit. If not, we extract a depth-bounded subcircuit rooted at that gate. Notably, all nodes whose children are contained in the subcircuit will also be added to the subcircuit. Hence, the subcircuit may have more than one output node. If no suitable linear relation is found, we increase the depth bound and repeat the procedure with an enlarged subcircuit. In the worst case we would need to increase the subcircuit until it covers the whole circuit.

Sample. To infer candidate relations in a suitable subcircuit, we generate samples of assignments to the subcircuit variables. In our previous work [13], we relied on uniform sampling over the inputs, with the values of internal gate variables being determined by propagation through the circuit structure. While this approach is simple and fast, it can miss rare but semantically relevant behaviors. This limitation becomes apparent in subcircuits that include long sequences of AND gates. The output of an n-ary AND gate $x = x_0 \wedge \cdots \wedge x_{n-1}$ is 1 if and only if all n inputs x_i are set to 1. Under uniform input sampling, this assignment occurs with probability 2^{-n}. As a result, the guessing procedure most likely observes only assignments for which $x = 0$, leading to incorrect guesses.

To address this issue, we replace uniform input sampling with the weighted uniform-like sampler CMSGen [10]. Unlike uniform sampling over subcircuit inputs, CMSGEN constructs uniformly sampled assignments over *all* circuit variables. It does this incrementally by propagating implications from the current assignment and learning from encountered conflicts. This significantly improves coverage of rare behaviors as the results in Sect. 6 show. We typically generate three times as many samples as the subcircuit size.

Guess. After sampling, the candidate linear relations modulo a prime p are computed by solving the linear system $Ax \equiv 0$ over $\mathbb{Z}_p$, where the columns of the matrix A correspond to variables and the rows to samples, cf. [13, Alg. 2].

In TALISMAN2.0, we now apply a trick to speed up this linear algebra step. The matrices arising in our context have a special structure: they contain only entries from $\{0, 1\}$ and they have a lot more rows than columns. We exploit this structure by solving the system $(BA)x \equiv 0$ instead of $Ax \equiv 0$, where B is a randomly chosen $\{0, 1\}$-matrix. Since both A and B have entries in $\{0, 1\}$, the product BA can be computed efficiently (over $\mathbb{Z}_p$) using bitwise operations. By choosing B to have fewer rows than A, the resulting system becomes smaller and thus easier to solve. In our implementation, B is chosen so that BA is a square matrix. The resulting (square) systems are solved using the number theory library FLINT [37]. Every solution of the original system $Ax \equiv 0$ is also a solution of $(BA)x \equiv 0$, and if B is chosen randomly, then the two solution spaces coincide with high probability. Any spurious solutions introduced by the projection would be eliminated during the subsequent prove step. In our experiments, we never encountered such spurious solutions.

Prove and Repair. We prove the correctness of the linear guesses using SAT solving. To establish that a linear guess f is correct over $\mathbb{Z}_p$, we must show that for all models φ of the extracted subcircuit, $\varphi(f) \equiv 0 \bmod p$. We translate each gate of the extracted subcircuit into conjunctive normal form (CNF) using Tseitin transformation, and encode $f \neq 0$ in CNF using PBLIB [34]. We then prove that the formula is unsatisfiable using the SAT solver CADICAL [3].

However, encoding $f \neq 0$ alone is actually too weak in our modular setting, since f may evaluate to a non-zero multiple of p. Therefore, whenever the SAT solver returns a satisfying assignment φ, we explicitly check whether $\varphi(f) \equiv 0 \bmod p$. If this is the case, the assignment is excluded from the search space and the SAT call is repeated. We have experimented with directly encoding $f \neq 0 \wedge f \neq p \wedge \cdots \wedge f \neq lp$ for a suitable upper bound l. However, this caused a significant overhead, even for $l = 2$. Additionally, we also experimented with mixed-integer programming, but did not observe any significant difference.

Only if we obtain a satisfying assignment with $\varphi(f) \not\equiv 0 \bmod p$ do we accept it as a witness that the guess f is incorrect. We add φ as a new sample to the matrix BA to repair the linear guesses and re-solve the updated linear system $(BA)x \equiv 0$. The resulting refined guesses must then be verified again.

Rewrite. Once all correct guesses have been collected, we use them to rewrite the specification as far as possible. In TALISMAN2.0, we perform rewriting steps modulo different primes simultaneously by representing each coefficient of a multimodular polynomial f as a vector, where the ith entry stores the coefficient of f modulo the ith prime. Thus, monomials have to be stored only once and coefficient arithmetic can be efficiently vectorized using SIMD instructions.

Example 2. Suppose we want to rewrite the specification $\mathcal{S} = -5x+4b+3a$ using the linear polynomial $f = 3x+b-a$ over the three prime moduli $\mathcal{M} = (7, 11, 13)$. We first represent $\mathcal{S}$ componentwise as $\mathcal{S} = (2,6,8)x+(4,4,4)b+(3,3,3)a$, since $-5 \equiv (2,6,8) \bmod \mathcal{M}$. Say x is the leading monomial of $\mathcal{S}$ and f. Then we first normalize f by inverting its x-coefficient modulo each prime. Multiplying f componentwise by $(5,4,9)$ yields $f' = (1,1,1)x + (5,4,9)b + (2,7,4)a$. Finally, we compute the following difference to cancel the x-term from $\mathcal{S}$:

$$\mathcal{S} - (2,6,8) \cdot f' \equiv (1,2,10)b + (6,5,10)a \mod \mathcal{M}.$$

If the result of such a linear rewriting step is zero, the circuit satisfies the specification and the procedure terminates. Otherwise, we consider the leading monomial of the simplified specification and start the next iteration of the linear rewriting loop. If we fail to retrieve a linear relation whose leading monomial matches that of the specification, we increase the depth of the subcircuit to be extracted. To prevent the subcircuit from growing excessively, we switch to nonlinear rewriting if no suitable linear relation is found after increasing the subcircuit depth a fixed number of times. In TalisMan2.0, we set this threshold to three, as determined empirically.

Parallelization. A key property of our multimodular framework is that computations for different prime moduli are independent. Although this would allow the entire workflow in Fig. 2 to be executed in parallel, such a coarse-grained strategy would duplicate substantial work, since several phases (e.g., preprocessing, subcircuit extraction, and sampling) are identical across primes. Hence, we apply a more fine-grained parallelization scheme. Circuit encoding, preprocessing, and subcircuit extraction are done in serial and shared across primes, while the guess, prove, and repair steps are parallelized across moduli, with each thread handling one prime. Sampling is parallelized as well, but independently of the primes. Here we use multiple threads to generate samples for the same subcircuit and aggregate them for guessing. Linear and nonlinear rewriting are executed serially, as further parallelization did not yield any speedups.

5.2 Nonlinear Rewriting

Once we switch from linear to nonlinear rewriting, we fix a lexicographic monomial order that orders the variables following a reverse topological order of the circuit, starting from the output variables and progressing toward the inputs. Under this ordering, each gate polynomial has a leading monomial consisting of a unique variable. This implies that $G(C) \cup B(C)$ forms a Gröbner basis [23].

Simplify. We first simplify the AIG to reduce the number of rewriting steps. To this end, we eliminate intermediate nodes that have single fanouts. Specifically, if a node g only has one parent, we directly substitute the gate constraint of g into that of its parent. We repeat this process until no such nodes remain. The gate polynomials of the rewritten AIG still form a Gröbner basis [23].

Rewrite. We iteratively rewrite the specification polynomial using the simplified gate polynomials, thereby computing the unique normal form modulo the circuit ideal. The fact that $G(C) \cup B(C)$ forms a Gröbner basis establishes the soundness and completeness of nonlinear rewriting for deciding ideal membership. If the normal form of $\mathcal{S}$ is the zero polynomial, then the circuit fulfills the specification and is therefore correct.

Otherwise, $\mathcal{S} \notin \langle G(C) \cup B(C) \rangle$. In this case, the normal form consists only of primary inputs of the AIG. A counterexample can therefore be extracted by choosing an input assignment for which the normal form does not evaluate to zero. Deriving counterexamples is not immediately possible in purely linear rewriting approaches [13,20], as the normal form with respect to a degree-compatible order may still contain internal circuit variables.

Nonlinear rewriting is performed analogously to the linear case by representing coefficients modulo different primes by coefficient vectors (cf. Example 2).

6 Experiments

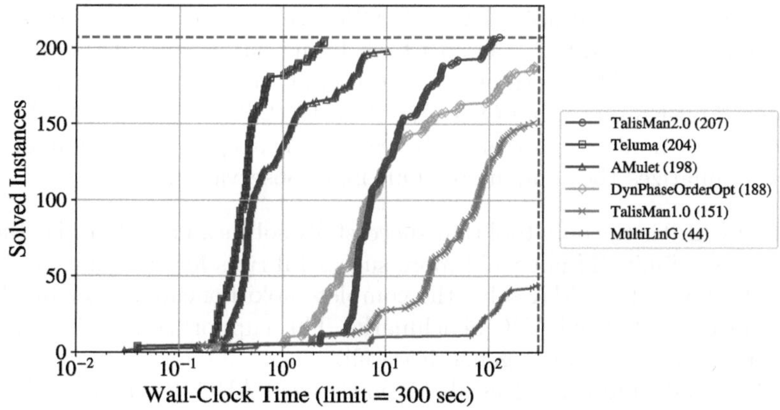

Fig. 3. Comparison of TALISMAN2.0 and related work. For each tool the number of solved instances is added in parentheses.

We have implemented the presented hybrid multimodular approach in our tool called TALISMAN2.0 [15], which acts as an improved successor of TALISMAN1 [13]. In the following, we evaluate TALISMAN2.0 and compare it to related work [13,19–21,27] using a total of 207 *correct* integer multiplier benchmarks.

We consider two types of benchmarks: *structured circuits*, where the components of a multiplier (partial product generation (PPG), partial product accumulation (PPA), and the final stage adder (FSA)) are clearly separable, and *synthesized circuits*, where gates are merged and rewritten to optimize the circuit, blurring component boundaries and complicating direct verification. We consider the following sets:

1. *Structured aoki-multipliers* [18]: This set of 64-bit multipliers is generated by combining different architectures for PPG, PPA, and FSA (see Appendix A in [14]) yielding 192 structured multiplier architectures.
2. *Synthesized* ABC-*multipliers* [2]: We generate 32-, 64-, 128-bit multipliers of type *sp-ar-rc* and optimize them with ABC using four standard synthesis scripts (resyn, resyn2, resyn3, dc2) and a complex optimization script[1]. These 15 optimized benchmarks showcase the robustness of our approach.

In our experiments, we use primes of approximately 16 bits, which provide a good trade-off between keeping the number of required moduli small and enabling efficient coefficient encoding in the SAT solver. Verifying 64-bit multipliers requires 8 such primes, while 128-bit multipliers require 16. All parallel computations use as many threads as we have primes.

The experiments were run on dual-socket AMD EPYC 7313 @3.7GHz machines running Ubuntu 24.04. Reported times are rounded wall-clock seconds. The time limit was 300 s and the memory limit was 32 GB to ensure sufficient resources for all tools. Notably, TalisMan2.0 itself only required at most 5 GB.

We compare TalisMan2.0 against tools from related work: TalisMan1 [12, 13] and MultiLinG [20], both of which also apply linear rewriting. In addition, we consider DynPhaseOrderOpt [27], AMulet2 [21,22], and TeluMA [19], all of which use nonlinear rewriting based on a lexicographic monomial order. Figure 3 summarizes the comparison. Our main observations are:

- TalisMan2.0 is the only tool that successfully solves all benchmarks. Increasing the time limit did not yield more successful runs for the other tools.
- AMulet2 and TeluMA solve the complete aoki benchmark set but fail on some of the synthesized ABC benchmarks. This supports our claim that their syntactic heuristics do not generalize well.
- DynPhaseOrderOpt solves all 15 synthesized ABC benchmarks, but only 173 out of 192 aoki benchmarks. Notably, among the 19 benchmarks it fails on, 14 contain a carry look-ahead adder (cl) as FSA, indicating that this structure is hard for purely nonlinear rewriting approaches.

We highlight the runtimes of the different phases of TalisMan2.0 from Fig. 2 in Table 1. A complete table is contained in Appendix B in [14]. Notably, we only

[1] `-c "logic; mfs2 -W 20; ps; mfs; st; ps; dc2 -l; ps; resub -l -K 16 -N 3 -w 100; ps; logic; mfs2 -W 20; ps; mfs; st; ps; iresyn -l; ps; resyn; ps; resyn2; ps; resyn3; ps; dc2 -l; ps;".`

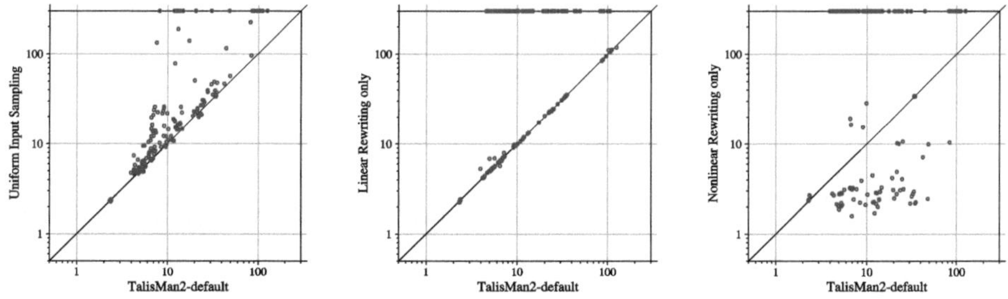

Fig. 4. Comparing the default setting when either uniform input sampling (left), only linear rewriting (middle), or only nonlinear rewriting is used (right).

had to enter the repair phase in 36 out of 207 benchmarks. In all other cases the guesses were immediately correct. Almost all of those benchmarks have either a carry look-ahead (cl) or a conditional sum adder (cn) as the FSA.

To assess the contribution of individual components of TalisMan2.0, we conducted an ablation study in which selected improvements were disabled. The results are shown in Fig. 4. When disabling CMSGen-based sampling and instead using uniform input sampling as in TalisMan1 (left plot), TalisMan2.0 fails to solve 24 benchmarks and exhibits increased runtimes on almost all remaining instances. Restricting the approach to linear rewriting only (middle plot) reduces the number of solved benchmarks to 98. Conversely, when only nonlinear rewriting is applied (right plot), 79 benchmarks can be solved; however, within this subset, TalisMan2.0 is faster than the hybrid configuration in 63 cases, indicating that nonlinear rewriting is particularly effective on selected instances but lacks overall robustness when used in isolation.

We evaluated the impact of replacing our custom linear algebra routines by FLINT, which increases the overall runtime by 34% on average. We also investigated whether using (pseudo-)Mersenne primes, i.e., primes of the form $2^k - c$ with small c, improves performance in the proving phase. Our intuition was that guessed linear relations often contain coefficients that are powers of two. Modulo (pseudo-)Mersenne primes, such coefficients map to small residues, which could simplify the SAT-based verification as smaller integers lead to smaller propositional encodings. To test this conjecture, we compared the default configuration of TalisMan2.0 using only pseudo-Mersenne primes in the range $2^{16} \pm 50$ with a configuration using randomly selected primes from the interval $[2^{15}, 2^{17}]$. The latter exhibited only a negligible average slowdown of 1.2%. We have also evaluated the impact of different prime sizes. Using 8-bit primes results in an average slowdown of 27% compared to the 16-bit default, likely due to increased memory traffic from more parallel threads. In contrast, 31-bit primes lead to a slowdown of 394%, with only 161 out of 207 benchmarks solved within the 300 s time limit. This significant degradation is caused by substantially higher SAT verification costs due to larger coefficients in the guesses.

Table 1. Per-phase runtime (rounded to tenths of seconds) of TalisMan2.0. In columns marked with '*' we report the average time per prime modulus. Entries '–' indicate that this phase was not entered.

Name	Total	TalisMan2.0 — Phase Times (s)								
		Linear							Nonlinear	
		Prepr.	Extract	Sample	Guess*	Prove*	Repair*	Rewrite	Simplify	Rewrite
abc64-cmp	2.3	2.1	<0.05	<0.05	<0.05	<0.05	-	<0.05	-	-
bp-ar-cl	44.0	1.4	0.7	0.9	9.7	26.6	3.0	0.1	<0.05	0.2
bp-ba-cn	42.0	1.6	<0.05	2.3	23.0	3.6	5.3	<0.05	4.8	0.4
bp-bd-cl	86.2	1.4	0.9	1.6	21.6	50.1	8.3	0.2	<0.05	0.2
bp-cn-cs	13.5	1.5	<0.05	1.4	7.9	1.6	-	<0.05	0.2	0.4
bp-ct-hc	9.0	0.9	2.1	0.2	3.9	1.1	-	0.1	<0.05	0.2
bp-dt-lf	7.1	1.3	0.5	0.2	3.3	1.3	-	0.1	<0.05	0.2
bp-wt-rc	4.8	1.4	0.5	0.1	1.1	1.2	-	0.1	<0.05	0.2
sp-ar-cl	19.7	2.2	0.1	0.4	3.1	12.6	0.6	0.1	-	-
sp-ba-cn	48.6	2.7	0.1	2.8	25.0	7.1	2.8	<0.05	6.7	0.3
sp-bd-cl	88.1	2.3	0.3	1.6	19.8	54.4	7.0	0.2	-	-
sp-cn-cs	21.4	2.7	<0.05	1.3	7.9	1.8	-	<0.05	0.3	6.8
sp-ct-hc	11.9	1.6	4.2	0.2	4.1	1.3	-	0.2	-	-
sp-dt-lf	6.8	2.1	<0.05	0.2	2.8	1.4	-	0.1	-	-
sp-wt-rc	5.0	2.3	<0.05	0.2	0.9	1.4	-	0.1	-	-

7 Conclusion and Future Work

We presented a hybrid multimodular framework for word-level verification of arithmetic circuits that completely avoids arbitrary-precision arithmetic. By performing algebraic reasoning in parallel over word-sized prime fields and combining linear with nonlinear rewriting, our approach achieves both efficiency and robustness. Our implementation in TalisMan2.0 shows that this design significantly improves performance in practice.

An important next step is the integration of proof logging techniques such as [24,25] into our framework. In particular, recycling proof steps as proposed in [25] appears especially promising in the multimodular setting. We also plan to investigate methods for generating short proofs of ideal membership [17]. Beyond circuit verification, we expect that our techniques can be applied also to related problems such as equivalence checking.

Acknowledgments. C.H. was supported by the LIT AI Lab funded by the state of Upper Austria and by the Austrian Science Fund (FWF) [10.55776/COE12]. D.K. was supported by the Austrian Science Fund (FWF) under grant [10.55776/ESP666].

Disclosure of Interests. The authors have no competing interests to declare that are relevant to the content of this article.

References

1. Arnold, E.A.: Modular algorithms for computing Gröbner bases. J. Symb. Comput. **35**(4), 403–419 (2003)
2. Berkeley Logic Synthesis and Verification Group: ABC: a system for sequential synthesis and verification (2019). http://www.eecs.berkeley.edu/~alanmi/abc/, bitbucket Version 1.01
3. Biere, A., Faller, T., Fazekas, K., Fleury, M., Froleyks, N., Pollitt, F.: CaDiCaL 2.0. In: Gurfinkel, A., Ganesh, V. (eds.) Proceedings of the 36th International Conference on Computer Aided Verification (CAV) 2024, Part I. Lecture Notes in Computer Science, vol. 14681, pp. 133–152. Springer, Cham (2024). https://doi.org/10.1007/978-3-031-65627-9_7
4. Brown, W.S.: On Euclid's algorithm and the computation of polynomial greatest common divisors. J. ACM **18**(4), 478–504 (1971)
5. Buchberger, B.: Ein Algorithmus zum Auffinden der Basiselemente des Restklassenringes nach einem nulldimensionalen Polynomideal. Ph.D. thesis, University of Innsbruck (1965)
6. Cox, D.A., Little, J., O'Shea, D.: Ideals, Varieties, and Algorithms - An Introduction to Computational Algebraic Geometry and Commutative Algebra, 2nd edn. Undergraduate Texts in Mathematics, Springer, New York, NY (1997). https://doi.org/10.1007/978-1-4757-2693-0
7. Cox, D.A., Little, J., O'Shea, D.: Using Algebraic Geometry. Springer, New York, NY (2005). https://doi.org/10.1007/b138611
8. Gerhard, J., Von zur Gathen, J.: Modern Computer Algebra, 3rd edn. Cambridge University Press (2013)
9. GMP: The GNU multiple precision arithmetic library. https://gmplib.org
10. Golia, P., Soos, M., Chakraborty, S., Meel, K.S.: Designing samplers is easy: the boon of testers. In: Proceedings of 2021 Formal Methods in Computer Aided Design (FMCAD), pp. 222–230 (2021). https://doi.org/10.34727/2021/isbn.978-3-85448-046-4_31
11. Heisinger, M., Hofstadler, C.: f4ncgb: high performance Gröbner basis computations in free algebras. In: Boulier, F., Mou, C., Sadykov, T.M., Vorozhtsov, E.V. (eds.) Proceedings of the International Workshop on Computer Algebra in Scientific Computing (CASC) 2025, pp. 79–97. Springer, Cham (2025). https://doi.org/10.1007/978-3-032-09645-6_5
12. Hofstadler, C., Kaufmann, D.: TalisMan. https://doi.org/10.4230/artifacts.23376, https://github.com/d-kfmnn/talisman/tree/be8187d, software, version 1.0., swhId: swh:1:dir:8af022a61661d2b7fb281abbdc2f18d51f221c20 (visited on 2025-08-08)
13. Hofstadler, C., Kaufmann, D.: Guess and prove: a hybrid approach to linear polynomial recovery in circuit verification. In: Proceedings of the 31st International Conference on Principles and Practice of Constraint Programming (CP) 2025. Leibniz International Proceedings in Informatics (LIPIcs), vol. 340, pp. 14:1–14:22 (2025). https://doi.org/10.4230/LIPIcs.CP.2025.14

14. Hofstadler, C., Kaufmann, D., Chen, C.: Avoiding big integers: parallel multimodular algebraic verification of arithmetic circuits. arXiv:2603.09501 (2026), extended version with appendices
15. Hofstadler, C., Kaufmann, D., Chen, C.: TalisMan2.0 - Artifact (2026). https://doi.org/10.5281/zenodo.20019348
16. Hofstadler, C., Levandovskyy, V.: Modular algorithms for computing Gröbner bases in free algebras. J. Symb. Comput. **137**, 102581 (2026)
17. Hofstadler, C., Verron, T.: Short proofs of ideal membership. J. Symb. Comput. **125**, 102325 (2024)
18. Homma, N., Watanabe, Y., Aoki, T., Higuchi, T.: Formal design of arithmetic circuits based on arithmetic description language. IEICE Trans. Fundam. Electron. Commun. Comput. Sci. **89-A**(12), 3500–3509 (2006). https://doi.org/10.1093/ietfec/e89-a.12.3500
19. Kaufmann, D., Beame, P., Biere, A., Nordström, J.: Adding dual variables to algebraic reasoning for gate-level multiplier verification. In: Proceedings of 2022 Design, Automation & Test in Europe Conference & Exhibition (DATE), pp. 1431–1436. IEEE (2022). https://doi.org/10.23919/DATE54114.2022.9774587
20. Kaufmann, D., Berthomieu, J.: Extracting linear relations from Gröbner bases for formal verification of and-inverter graphs. In: Gurfinkel, A., Heule, M. (eds.) Proceedings of Tools and Algorithms for the Construction and Analysis of Systems (TACAS), vol. 15696, pp. 355–374. Springer, Cham (2025). https://doi.org/10.1007/978-3-031-90643-5_19
21. Kaufmann, D., Biere, A.: AMulet 2.0 for verifying multiplier circuits. In: Proceedings of Tools and Algorithms for the Construction and Analysis of Systems (TACAS). LNCS, vol. 12652, pp. 357–364. Springer, Cham (2021). https://doi.org/10.1007/978-3-030-72013-1_19
22. Kaufmann, D., Biere, A., Kauers, M.: Verifying large multipliers by combining SAT and computer algebra. In: Proceedings of Formal Methods in Computer Aided Design (FMCAD), pp. 28–36. IEEE (2019). https://doi.org/10.23919/FMCAD.2019.8894250
23. Kaufmann, D., Biere, A., Kauers, M.: Incremental column-wise verification of arithmetic circuits using computer algebra. Formal Methods Syst. Des. **56**(1), 22–54 (2020). https://doi.org/10.1007/s10703-018-00329-2
24. Kaufmann, D., Fleury, M., Biere, A., Kauers, M.: Practical algebraic calculus and Nullstellensatz with the checkers Pacheck and Pastèque and Nuss-Checker. Formal Methods Syst. Des. **64**(1), 73–107 (2024). https://doi.org/10.1007/s10703-022-00391-x
25. Kaufmann, D., Hofstadler, C.: Recycling algebraic proof certificates. In: Proceedings of the 10th International Workshop on Satisfiability Checking and Symbolic Computation (SC-Square) 2025, vol. 4116, pp. 35–40. Ceur (2025). https://ceur-ws.org/Vol-4116/
26. Konrad, A., Scholl, C.: FastPoly: an efficient polynomial package for the verification of integer arithmetic circuits. In: Proceedings of Formal Methods in Computer Aided Design (FMCAD), pp. 139–144 (2025). https://doi.org/10.34727/2025/isbn.978-3-85448-084-6_20
27. Konrad, A., Scholl, C.: Symbolic computer algebra for multipliers revisited - It's all about orders and phases. In: Proceedings of Formal Methods in Computer-Aided Design (FMCAD), pp. 261–271. IEEE (2024). https://doi.org/10.34727/2024/isbn.978-3-85448-065-5_32

28. Konrad, A., Scholl, C., Mahzoon, A., Große, D., Drechsler, R.: Divider verification using symbolic computer algebra and delayed don't care optimization. In: Proceedings of Formal Methods in Computer-Aided Design (FMCAD), pp. 1–10. IEEE (2022). https://doi.org/10.34727/2022/isbn.978-3-85448-053-2_17
29. Kuehlmann, A., Paruthi, V., Krohm, F., Ganai, M.K.: Robust boolean reasoning for equivalence checking and functional property verification. IEEE Trans. Comput. Aided Des. Integr. Circ. Syst. **21**(12), 1377–1394 (2002). https://doi.org/10.1109/TCAD.2002.804386
30. Mahzoon, A., Große, D., Drechsler, R.: Polycleaner: clean your polynomials before backward rewriting to verify million-gate multipliers. In: Proceedings of International Conference on Computer-Aided Design (ICCAD). ACM (2018). https://doi.org/10.1145/3240765.3240837
31. Mahzoon, A., Große, D., Scholl, C., Drechsler, R.: Towards formal verification of optimized and industrial multipliers. In: Proceedings of Design, Automation & Test in Europe Conference & Exhibition (DATE), pp. 544–549. IEEE (2020). https://doi.org/10.23919/DATE48585.2020.9116485
32. Mayr, E.W., Meyer, A.R.: The complexity of the word problems for commutative semigroups and polynomial ideals. Adv. Math. **46**(3), 305–329 (1982)
33. Monagan, M., Pearce, R.: A compact parallel implementation of F4. In: Proceedings of the 2015 International Workshop on Parallel Symbolic Computation, pp. 95–100 (2015)
34. Philipp, T., Steinke, P.: PBLib - A library for encoding pseudo-boolean constraints into CNF. In: Heule, M., Weaver, S. (eds.) Proceedings of 18th International Conference on Theory and Applications of Satisfiability Testing (SAT) 2015. LNCS, vol. 9340, pp. 9–16. Springer, Cham (2015). https://doi.org/10.1007/978-3-319-24318-4_2
35. Rosen, K.H.: Elementary Number Theory and Its Applications, Pearson Education London (2011)
36. Stein, W.A.: Modular Forms: A Computational Approach, vol. 79. American Mathematical Society (2007)
37. The FLINT team: FLINT: fast library for number theory (2025). https://flintlib.org, version 3.4.0

Open Access This chapter is licensed under the terms of the Creative Commons Attribution 4.0 International License (http://creativecommons.org/licenses/by/4.0/), which permits use, sharing, adaptation, distribution and reproduction in any medium or format, as long as you give appropriate credit to the original author(s) and the source, provide a link to the Creative Commons license and indicate if changes were made.

The images or other third party material in this chapter are included in the chapter's Creative Commons license, unless indicated otherwise in a credit line to the material. If material is not included in the chapter's Creative Commons license and your intended use is not permitted by statutory regulation or exceeds the permitted use, you will need to obtain permission directly from the copyright holder.

Bringing Closure to Theory Combination Properties

Guilherme V. Toledo[1(✉)], Benjamin Przybocki[2], and Yoni Zohar[1]

[1] Bar-Ilan University, Ramat Gan, Israel
guivtoledo@gmail.com
[2] Carnegie Mellon University, Pittsburgh, USA

Abstract. We consider the closure of three classical combination properties, namely, stable infiniteness, gentleness and shininess (or, equivalently for decidable theories, strong politeness), under intersection and combinability. We compute every possible intersection, and then compute the maximal set of theories that can be combined with each resulting intersection. We iterate this process until no new sets are identified. How many properties will we end up with?

1 Introduction

Theory combination in Satisfiability Modulo Theories [1,2] studies how to combine decision procedures of two theories into a decision procedure for their combination (or, axiomatically, their union). Most research in this field focuses on *disjoint* combination, where the theories share no symbols other than equality.

Nelson and Oppen proved [8,9] that any pair of decidable stably infinite[1] theories can be disjointly combined. Tinelli and Zarba [12] proved that every decidable shiny theory can be disjointly combined with any decidable theory.[2] Fontaine [5] proved that every decidable gentle theory can be disjointly combined with a general class of theories that includes gentle theories.

Recently, we studied the other directions of these results [10]. We have shown that the first two results are *sharp*: every decidable theory that can be disjointly combined with all decidable stably infinite theories must be stably infinite; and every decidable theory that can be disjointly combined with all decidable theories must be shiny. As for gentleness, we proved in [10,14] that the result of [5] can be made sharp, by introducing the notion of theories with *computable finite spectra*.

All these results are summarized in Table 1 and Fig. 1a, using the notations of Table 2. They also employ a function, denoted G, that takes a set X of decidable theories, and returns the set $G(X)$ of all decidable theories that can be disjointly combined with every theory of X. For example, the Nelson–Oppen theorem is phrased as $\mathfrak{T}_{\mathrm{SI}} \subseteq G(\mathfrak{T}_{\mathrm{SI}})$ and its sharpened version as $\mathfrak{T}_{\mathrm{SI}} = G(\mathfrak{T}_{\mathrm{SI}})$.

In Fig. 1a, an edge between two sets of theories means that the lower is a subset of the upper (all inclusions were proven in [10]). $G(X)$ is the mirror of

[1] All technical notions in the introduction will be formally defined in Sect. 2.

[2] Following [3,6,11], the same can be said about decidable strongly polite theories.

© The Author(s) 2026
A. Biere et al. (Eds.): IJCAR 2026, LNAI 16688, pp. 194–211, 2026.
https://doi.org/10.1007/978-3-032-32589-1_12

X against the dashed line. This structure is contained in the lattice of sharp theory combination properties, introduced in [10]: the order is $\subseteq$, the meet is the intersection, and the join (which is not as useful in our context) is defined in terms of the meet and G. But, Fig. 1a itself is not a lattice. For example, the intersection of gentleness and stable infiniteness is not there. The main motivating question of this paper is: **what is the smallest lattice, closed under G, containing Fig. 1a?** The answer, as we prove in Sect. 3, is Fig. 1b.

Table 1. Classical theory combination results and their sharpened versions

Source	Original Result	Sharpness Results [10]
[8]	$\mathfrak{T}_{\mathrm{SI}} \subseteq G(\mathfrak{T}_{\mathrm{SI}})$	$\mathfrak{T}_{\mathrm{SI}} = G(\mathfrak{T}_{\mathrm{SI}})$
[12]	$\mathfrak{T}_{\mathbf{shiny}} \subseteq G(\mathfrak{T})$	$\mathfrak{T}_{\mathbf{shiny}} = G(\mathfrak{T})$, $G(\mathfrak{T}_{\mathbf{shiny}}) = \mathfrak{T}$
[5]	$\mathfrak{T}_{gen} \subseteq G(\mathfrak{T}_{gen})$	$\mathfrak{T}_{\mathrm{CFS}} = G(\mathfrak{T}_{gen})$, $G(\mathfrak{T}_{\mathrm{CFS}}) = \mathfrak{T}_{gen}$

As a practical outcome, we introduce two new combination methods in Sect. 4, that allow combinations absent from Fig. 1a. We improve the understanding of theory combination properties at a general, abstract level; in the future, when theories are considered for implementation, researchers will have a larger suite of tests they can perform to determine the theories' combinability properties. And, if a pair of theories cannot be combined, researchers will have a more precise understanding of how the expressiveness of one of the theories needs to be weakened to allow combination. Following [10], we focus on one-sorted logic, leaving the generalization to many-sorted logic to future work.

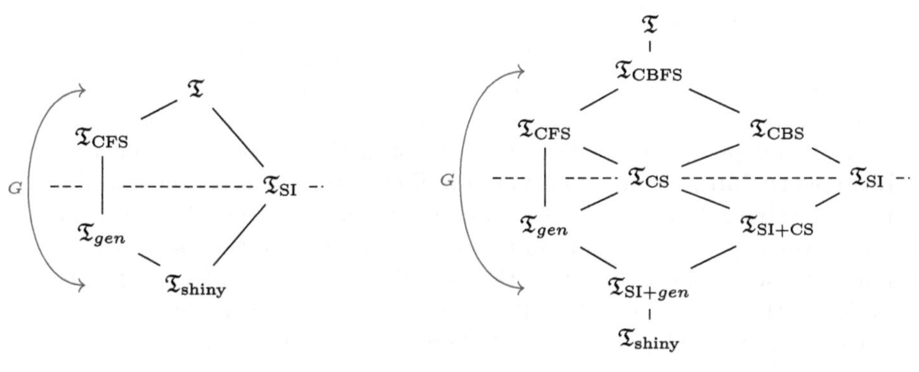

(a) Before this paper (not a lattice) (b) After this paper (a lattice)

Fig. 1. Diagrams of theory combination properties

Outline. In Sect. 2 we present preliminaries, from first-order logic, through theory combination, to the Galois connection of theory combination. Section 3 presents the process through which we close the lattice; Sect. 3.2 gives relationships between properties and may be skipped in a first reading, being quite technical, much like the new theories of Table 6, which are useful only for proofs. Section 4 gives further details on new combination methods. Section 4.1 shows sharpness. Section 5 introduces a separating property that we call *self-combinability*, roughly meaning the ability of a theory to be combined with (a copy of) itself. Section 6 concludes and sketches directions for future work.

$$\neq(x_1,\ldots,x_n) = \bigwedge_{i=1}^{n-1}\bigwedge_{j=i+1}^{n} \neg(x_i = x_j) \qquad \psi_{\leq n} = \exists\, x_1,\ldots,x_n.\,\forall\, y.\, \bigvee_{i=1}^{n} y = x_i$$

$$\psi_{\geq n} = \exists\, x_1,\ldots,x_n.\, \neq(x_1,\ldots,x_n) \qquad \psi_{=n} = \psi_{\geq n} \wedge \psi_{\leq n}$$

Fig. 2. Cardinality formulas

2 Preliminaries

2.1 First-Order Logic

We review standard definitions regarding first-order logic [4]. A **signature** Σ is a set of function and predicate symbols, each equipped with an arity, that includes $=$ as a binary predicate symbol. We only consider signatures that are at most countably infinite. Two signatures are **disjoint** if they share only the equality symbol. We define terms, formulas, literals, and sentences (formulas with no free variables) in the standard way; $QF(\Sigma)$ is the set of quantifier-free Σ-formulas.

A Σ**-structure** $\mathbb{A}$ is a non-empty set $dom(\mathbb{A})$ (its domain) equipped with functions $f^{\mathbb{A}} : dom(\mathbb{A})^n \rightarrow dom(\mathbb{A})$ and predicates $P^{\mathbb{A}} \subseteq dom(\mathbb{A})^m$, for all function symbols f and predicate symbols P in Σ, of arities n and m, respectively. A Σ**-interpretation** $\mathcal{A}$ is an extension of a Σ-structure, where each variable x is assigned a value $x^{\mathcal{A}} \in dom(\mathcal{A})$. We define the value $\tau^{\mathcal{A}} \in dom(\mathcal{A})$ of a term, and the truth-value $\varphi^{\mathcal{A}}$ of a formula in an interpretation $\mathcal{A}$ in the usual way; if φ is true in $\mathcal{A}$ we write $\mathcal{A} \vDash \varphi$. In Fig. 2 the formula $\neq(x_1,\ldots,x_n)$ for $n \geq 2$ states the variables x_1 through x_n all take different values (for $n = 1$ it is simply *true*). The formulas $\psi_{\geq n}$, $\psi_{=n}$ and $\psi_{\leq n}$ state that there are at least, exactly, and at most n elements in the domain, respectively.

A Σ**-theory** is a set of Σ-sentences (**axioms**). A Σ-interpretation that satisfies all axioms of $\mathcal{T}$ is called a $\mathcal{T}$**-interpretation**, or a **model of** $\mathcal{T}$. A formula is $\mathcal{T}$**-satisfiable** if there is a $\mathcal{T}$-interpretation that satisfies it, and a set of formulas is $\mathcal{T}$-satisfiable if there is a $\mathcal{T}$-interpretation that satisfies all formulas in the set simultaneously. A Σ-theory is **decidable** when there is an algorithm that takes a quantifier-free Σ-formula and returns whether or not it is $\mathcal{T}$-satisfiable. $\mathcal{T}_{Eq}$ is the theory over the empty signature (that only has $=$ as a symbol) having no axioms. Given signatures Σ_1 and Σ_2, $\Sigma_1 \sqcup \Sigma_2$ is their **disjoint union**, that is, if there are any symbols in common between the two, we rename them in Σ_2 before adding them to the symbols of Σ_1. Given a Σ_1-theory $\mathcal{T}_1$ and a Σ_2-theory $\mathcal{T}_2$, their **disjoint combination** $\mathcal{T}_1 \sqcup \mathcal{T}_2$ is the $\Sigma_1 \sqcup \Sigma_2$-theory whose axiomatization is the union of $\mathcal{T}_1$ and $\mathcal{T}_2$ (after renaming the symbols in Σ_2 occurring in $\mathcal{T}_2$).

We denote $\mathbb{N} \cup \{\aleph_0\}$ by $\mathbb{N}_\omega$, and $\{n \in \mathbb{N}_\omega : p \leq n \leq q\}$ by $[p, q]$. The **spectrum** of a formula φ in a theory $\mathcal{T}$, denoted $Spec_{\mathcal{T}}(\varphi)$, is the subset of $\mathbb{N}_\omega$ of those elements n such that there exists a $\mathcal{T}$-interpretation $\mathcal{A}$ that satisfies φ with $|dom(\mathcal{A})| = n$. Our restriction from the class of all cardinals to $\mathbb{N}_\omega$ in this definition is possible thanks to the downward Löwenheim–Skolem theorem, and the assumption that all signatures we deal with are countable. We state the Löwenheim–Skolem theorem as well as the compactness theorem:

Theorem 1 (**[7, Theorems 2.3.4 and 2.3.7]**). *Let Δ be a set of formulas over a countable signature, and let $\kappa \geq \aleph_0$. Then, Δ is satisfied by an interpretation of size κ if and only if it is satisfied by an interpretation of size $\aleph_0$.*

Theorem 2 (**[7, Theorem 2.1.4]**). *A set of formulas is satisfiable if and only if every finite subset of it is satisfiable.*

Corollary 1. *Let Σ be a countable signature, $\mathcal{T}$ a Σ-theory, and ϕ a Σ-formula. Suppose ϕ is $\mathcal{T}$-satisfiable but $\aleph_0 \notin Spec_{\mathcal{T}}(\phi)$. Then $Spec_{\mathcal{T}}(\phi)$ is finite.*

2.2 Theory Combination Properties

In Table 2, we summarize the theory combination properties of the paper: essentially, we shall denote the set of decidable theories with property X by $\mathfrak{T}_X$.

Table 2. Notations for sets of theories

Symbol	Description (decidable and ...)	Definition
$\mathfrak{T}$	—	Sect. 2.1
$\mathfrak{T}_{\mathrm{SI}}$	Stably infinite	Sect. 2.2
$\mathfrak{T}_{\mathrm{shiny}}$	Shiny	
$\mathfrak{T}_{gen}$	Gentle	
$\mathfrak{T}_{\mathrm{SI}+gen}$	Stably infinite and Gentle	
$\mathfrak{T}_{\mathrm{CFS}}$	Computable finite spectra	
$\mathfrak{T}_{\mathrm{CS}}$	Computable spectra	
$\mathfrak{T}_{\mathrm{SI+CS}}$	Stably infinite and computable spectra	
$\mathfrak{T}_{\mathrm{CBFS}}$	Computable bounded finite spectra	Definition 1
$\mathfrak{T}_{\mathrm{CBS}}$	Computable bounded spectra	Definition 2

Let $\mathcal{T}$ be a theory, and let us denote $\mathbb{N} \setminus \{0\}$ by $\mathbb{N}^*$. $\mathcal{T}$ is **stably infinite** [8] if $Spec_{\mathcal{T}}(\phi) \neq \varnothing$ implies $\aleph_0 \in Spec_{\mathcal{T}}(\phi)$. $\mathcal{T}$ has **computable finite spectra** [14] if there is an algorithm that takes a quantifier-free formula ϕ and $n \in \mathbb{N}^*$, and returns whether $n \in Spec_{\mathcal{T}}(\phi)$; $\mathcal{T}$ is **infinitely decidable** [14] if there is an algorithm that takes a quantifier-free formula ϕ and returns whether $\aleph_0 \in Spec_{\mathcal{T}}(\phi)$; a theory with both these properties is said to have **computable spectra**.

$\mathcal{T}$ is **smooth** when, given a quantifier-free formula ϕ, a $\mathcal{T}$-interpretation $\mathcal{A}$ that satisfies ϕ, and any cardinal $\kappa \geq |dom(\mathcal{A})|$, there exists a $\mathcal{T}$-interpretation $\mathcal{B}$ that satisfies ϕ with $|dom(\mathcal{B})| = \kappa$. $\mathcal{T}$ has the **finite model property** when, $Spec_{\mathcal{T}}(\phi) \neq \varnothing$ implies $Spec_{\mathcal{T}}(\phi) \cap \mathbb{N}^* \neq \varnothing$, for every quantifier-free formula ϕ. And, if $\mathcal{T}$ is decidable, its **minimal model function** is the function $\text{minmod}_{\mathcal{T}}$ that takes a quantifier-free formula ϕ and returns, if ϕ is $\mathcal{T}$-satisfiable, the least element in $Spec_{\mathcal{T}}(\phi)$. $\mathcal{T}$ is **shiny** [12] when it is smooth, has the finite model property, and its minimal model function is computable.

Denote $\mathbb{N}_\omega \setminus \{0\}$ by $\mathbb{N}_\omega^*$. $\mathcal{T}$ is **gentle** [5,14] when there is an algorithm that takes a quantifier-free formula ϕ and returns a pair (S, b), where $S \subset \mathbb{N}^*$ is finite and b is a Boolean, such that: if b is true, $Spec_{\mathcal{T}}(\phi) = S$; and if b is false, $Spec_{\mathcal{T}}(\phi) = \mathbb{N}_\omega^* \setminus S$. The original definition of gentleness, however, is a bit different. It says that, for every quantifier-free formula ϕ: $Spec_{\mathcal{T}}(\phi)$ is either a finite subset of $\mathbb{N}^*$ or a cofinite subset of $\mathbb{N}_\omega^*$ containing $\aleph_0$; there is an algorithm that tells us which is the case (corresponding to our Boolean b); and there is an algorithm that, given ϕ, returns $Spec_{\mathcal{T}}(\phi)$ if this set is finite, and $\mathbb{N}_\omega^* \setminus Spec_{\mathcal{T}}(\phi)$ otherwise. We prefer the former one, as it merges both algorithms into one.

Proposition 1 ([10]). *$\mathfrak{T}_{shiny} \subseteq \mathfrak{T}_{gen} \cap \mathfrak{T}_{SI}$ and $\mathfrak{T}_{gen} \subseteq \mathfrak{T}_{CFS}$; the theories of $\mathfrak{T}_{SI}$ are all infinitely decidable; and $\mathfrak{T}_{SI} \cap \mathfrak{T}_{CS} = \mathfrak{T}_{SI} \cap \mathfrak{T}_{CFS}$.*

We call the following result *Fontaine's lemma*. Its "if" direction was proved in [5], while its "only if" direction was proved in [10]. We could state it for arbitrary quantifier-free formulas, but we follow its original formulation.

Lemma 1 (Fontaine's lemma). *The disjoint combination $\mathcal{T}_1 \sqcup \mathcal{T}_2$ is decidable if and only if the following problem is decidable: given conjunctions of literals ϕ_1 and ϕ_2, determine whether $Spec_{\mathcal{T}_1}(\phi_1) \cap Spec_{\mathcal{T}_2}(\phi_2) = \varnothing$.*

2.3 The Lattice of Theory Combination Properties

We review the main definitions of [10]. Two theories are **combinable** if their disjoint combination is decidable. Two sets of theories are combinable if every theory of one is combinable with every theory of the other. We may identify an element with the singleton containing it. Let $\mathfrak{T}$ be the set of decidable theories.[3] For each $X \subseteq \mathfrak{T}$, $G(X)$ is the set of all decidable theories combinable with X.

[3] This, in principle, would not constitute a set, but a proper class, but we can just select all symbols for our (countable) signatures from a countable pool of symbols.

Table 3. Analogy between lattice-theoretic notions and theory combination

Notion	Lattice Theory	Theory Combination
G	A Galois connection	A function that maps X to the set of all decidable theories combinable with X
G is antitone	$X \subseteq Y \Rightarrow G(Y) \subseteq G(X)$	If $\mathcal{T}$ is combinable with Y, then it is combinable with every subset of Y
G is a Galois connection	$X \subseteq G(Y) \Leftrightarrow Y \subseteq G(X)$	Combinability is symmetric
$G \circ G$	$X \subseteq G(G(X))$	There is always a combination theorem between X and $G(X)$
X is closed	$X = G(G(X))$	The combination theorem between X and $G(X)$ is sharp
Closing a set under $\cap$ and G	Finding the minimal containing lattice	Finding the minimal set of properties with sharp combination theorems

If $X \subseteq Y$ then every theory combinable with Y is also combinable with X. Hence, $X \subseteq Y$ implies $G(Y) \subseteq G(X)$. Further, combinability is symmetric: $X \subseteq G(Y)$ iff $Y \subseteq G(X)$. Thus, G is an **antitone Galois connection**. A **combination theorem** has the form $X \subseteq G(Y)$. We always have a combination theorem between X and $Y = G(X)$. Such a theorem is **sharp** if, moreover, $X = G(Y)$. In this case, X is called **closed under** G, or just **closed**.

Take any set of closed sets of theories and for every X and Y in it, add infimum $G(G(X \cap Y))$ and supremum $G(G(X \cup Y))$, until fixpoint. The result is a **lattice** ordered by $\subseteq$. If X and Y are closed, then the infimum and supremum are $X \cap Y$ and $G(G(X) \cap G(Y))$, resp. Thus it suffices to compute closure under $\cap$ and G. Table 3 summarizes the lattice-theoretic view of theory combination.

Algorithm 1 Pseudocode for closure under $\cap$ and G.

```
1: function. GENERATE(S)
2:     while true do
3:         S∩ ← {X ∩ Y | X, Y ∈ S}
4:         SG ← {G(X) | X ∈ S}
5:         if S = S ∪ S∩ ∪ SG then return S
6:         S ← S ∪ S∩ ∪ SG
```

Table 4. Execution of Algorithm 1

Iteration	Line	Computation	Result	Proof
0	—	—	$\mathfrak{T}_{\text{SI}}$ $\mathfrak{T}_{\text{shiny}}$ $\mathfrak{T}_{gen}$	—
1	3	$\mathfrak{T}_{\text{SI}} \cap \mathfrak{T}_{gen}$	$\mathfrak{T}_{\text{SI}+gen}$	—
	4	$G(\mathfrak{T}_{\text{shiny}})$	$\mathfrak{T}$	Table 1
	4	$G(\mathfrak{T}_{gen})$	$\mathfrak{T}_{\text{CFS}}$	Table 1
2	3	$\mathfrak{T}_{\text{SI}} \cap \mathfrak{T}_{\text{CFS}}$	$\mathfrak{T}_{\text{SI+CS}}$	Proposition 1
	4	$G(\mathfrak{T}_{\text{SI}+gen})$	$\mathfrak{T}_{\text{CBFS}}$	Corollary 2
3	4	$G(\mathfrak{T}_{\text{SI+CS}})$	$\mathfrak{T}_{\text{CBS}}$	Corollary 2
4	3	$\mathfrak{T}_{\text{CFS}} \cap \mathfrak{T}_{\text{CBS}}$	$\mathfrak{T}_{\text{CS}}$	Proposition 4

3 So, How Many Combination Properties?

Algorithm 1 takes a set S of properties, and closes it under G and intersection. As seen in Sect. 2.3, this suffices for computing the minimal lattice that contains S. A priori, this process does not have to terminate.

Remarkably, it terminates when the input set is $\{\mathfrak{T}_{\text{SI}}, \mathfrak{T}_{\text{shiny}}, \mathfrak{T}_{gen}\}$. The resulting set is presented in Fig. 1b as a Hasse diagram. It mostly contains properties defined in Sect. 2, though it also involves two new properties, namely *computable bounded finite spectra* and *computable bounded spectra.* These give rise to two new combination theorems that we introduce in Sect. 4.

Theorem 3. GENERATE*($\{\mathfrak{T}_{SI}, \mathfrak{T}_{shiny}, \mathfrak{T}_{gen}\}$) terminates, and its output consists of the 10 properties that appear in Fig. 1b.*

Proof. The proof has two parts: First, we show that each property in Fig. 1b must indeed be in the resulting set, by justifying inclusion. Second, we prove that there are no other added properties: after 4 iterations of the loop of Algorithm 1, we reach a fixed-point.

Addition of Properties: We justify the addition of each property in Fig. 1b to the resulting set, by specifying in which step of Algorithm 1 it is added, and explaining why. A tabular representation of this process is available in Table 4.

Iteration 0: Clearly, $\mathfrak{T}_{\mathrm{SI}}$, $\mathfrak{T}_{\mathrm{shiny}}$ and $\mathfrak{T}_{gen}$ must be included, as they are the input to the algorithm, and the algorithm never removes a property.

Iteration 1: The intersections of $\mathfrak{T}_{\mathrm{SI}}$, $\mathfrak{T}_{\mathrm{shiny}}$ and $\mathfrak{T}_{gen}$ are added in line 3 of the first iteration of the loop. Every shiny theory is stably infinite and gentle from Proposition 1, and thus we only have to add $\mathfrak{T}_{\mathrm{SI}} \cap \mathfrak{T}_{gen}$, denoted $\mathfrak{T}_{\mathrm{SI}+gen}$.

Also, $G(X)$ must be added for each property X in the input set, which is done in line 4. By Table 1, $G(\mathfrak{T}_{\mathrm{shiny}}) = \mathfrak{T}$, $G(\mathfrak{T}_{\mathrm{SI}}) = \mathfrak{T}_{\mathrm{SI}}$, and $G(\mathfrak{T}_{gen}) = \mathfrak{T}_{\mathrm{CFS}}$. Thus, $\mathfrak{T}$ and $\mathfrak{T}_{\mathrm{CFS}}$ are added ($\mathfrak{T}_{\mathrm{SI}}$ is already included).

Iteration 2: Now we close the 6 properties collected so far under intersection. Most of the resulting intersections are already within these 6 properties: $\mathfrak{T}_{\mathrm{shiny}} \subseteq \mathfrak{T}_{\mathrm{SI}+gen} \subseteq \mathfrak{T}_{gen} \subseteq \mathfrak{T}_{\mathrm{CFS}} \subseteq \mathfrak{T}$, and also $\mathfrak{T}_{\mathrm{shiny}} \subseteq \mathfrak{T}_{\mathrm{SI}+gen} \subseteq \mathfrak{T}_{\mathrm{SI}} \subseteq \mathfrak{T}$ (see Proposition 1), and the intersections of every two properties in the same sequence of inclusions is just the smaller one. Thus, we only add a single property, namely the intersection of $\mathfrak{T}_{\mathrm{SI}}$ and $\mathfrak{T}_{\mathrm{CFS}}$, that is, $\mathfrak{T}_{\mathrm{SI}} \cap \mathfrak{T}_{\mathrm{CFS}}$. By Proposition 1, $\mathfrak{T}_{\mathrm{SI}} \cap \mathfrak{T}_{\mathrm{CFS}} = \mathfrak{T}_{\mathrm{SI}} \cap \mathfrak{T}_{\mathrm{CS}}$, and we choose to denote this property by $\mathfrak{T}_{\mathrm{SI}+\mathrm{CS}}$ because, as will be seen below, in the last iteration of the loop we will add $\mathfrak{T}_{\mathrm{CS}}$, and the notation $\mathfrak{T}_{\mathrm{SI}+\mathrm{CS}}$ will then better reflect the placing of this property in Fig. 1b.

The next addition is due to the closure under G computed in iteration 2. We have already closed the three initial properties under G in iteration 1. Also, $G(\mathfrak{T}) = \mathfrak{T}_{\mathrm{shiny}}$ and $G(\mathfrak{T}_{\mathrm{CFS}}) = \mathfrak{T}_{gen}$, as shown in Table 1. Thus in this iteration, we only add $G(\mathfrak{T}_{\mathrm{SI}+gen})$. This requires a new combination theorem, based on a new property of theories, that we call *computable bounded finite spectra*, denoted $\mathfrak{T}_{\mathrm{CBFS}}$: a theory has this property when it has an algorithm that, given a quantifier-free ϕ and $m, n \in \mathbb{N}^*$, returns whether n is in $Spec_{\mathcal{T}}(\phi)$ as long as $\phi \wedge \neq(x_1, \ldots, x_m)$ (for fresh variables x_i) is not $\mathcal{T}$-satisfiable. It is formally defined in Definition 1, and its sharp combination theorem is proven in Corollary 2.

Iteration 3: The set obtained by the end of iteration 2 is already closed under intersection (see Propositions 1 and 4). Thus, we close it under G. From Table 1, $G(\mathfrak{T}) = \mathfrak{T}_{\mathrm{shiny}}$ and $G(\mathfrak{T}_{\mathrm{CFS}}) = \mathfrak{T}_{gen}$. By Corollary 2, $G(\mathfrak{T}_{\mathrm{CBFS}}) = \mathfrak{T}_{\mathrm{SI}+gen}$. Thus, we only need to add $G(\mathfrak{T}_{\mathrm{SI}+\mathrm{CS}})$, which requires yet another new combination theorem, based on a new property, which we call *computable bounded spectra*, denoted $\mathfrak{T}_{\mathrm{CBS}}$: fortunately, it can be defined as being infinitely decidable and having computable bounded finite spectra. Its formal definition is in Definition 2, and a sharp combination theorem for it is proven in Corollary 2.

Iteration 4: In addition to the inclusions specified in Iteration 2, we also have $\mathfrak{T}_{\mathrm{CFS}} \subseteq \mathfrak{T}_{\mathrm{CBFS}} \subseteq \mathfrak{T}$ and $\mathfrak{T}_{\mathrm{SI}} \subseteq \mathfrak{T}_{\mathrm{CBS}} \subseteq \mathfrak{T}_{\mathrm{CBFS}}$ from Proposition 4, and the intersection of every two properties in each resulting inclusion path is the smaller of the two. The only missing intersection is that of $\mathfrak{T}_{\mathrm{CFS}}$ and $\mathfrak{T}_{\mathrm{CBS}}$, which we prove in Proposition 4 to be equal to $\mathfrak{T}_{\mathrm{CS}}$, which we now add.

There are no Other Properties: Denote by S_0 the set of 10 properties listed in Fig. 1b. This set is $S_\cap$ after line 3 of the fourth iteration of Algorithm 1. From Corollary 2 and Table 1, we have that after line 4 of the fourth iteration, we get $S_G = S_0$ as well, that is, that $G(S_0) = S_0$. Going to the fifth iteration of the loop, we have already seen that S_0 is closed under intersection. Thus, in the fifth iteration, after lines 3 and 4 are executed, we have $S_\cap = S_G = S_0 = S$, and so in line 6 we return S_0.

3.1 Other Resulting Sets

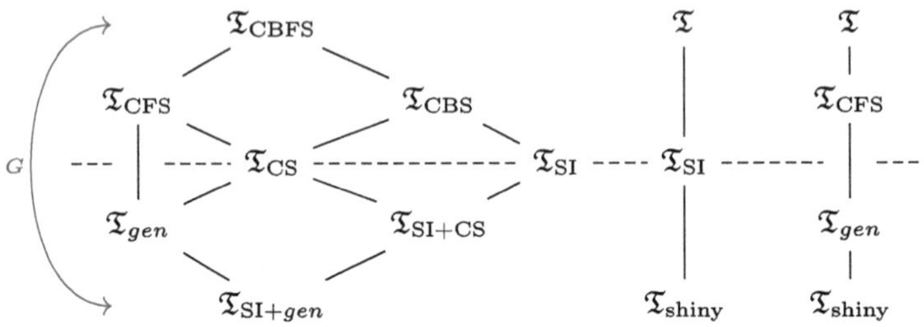

Fig. 3. The Hasse diagrams for the resulting sets given different inputs

We have generated a lattice from the three properties of stable infiniteness, gentleness and shininess. What would happen if we were to restrict ourselves to only two among these properties instead?

Stable infiniteness and gentleness are enough to generate most of Fig. 1b: a reasoning similar to the one found at the proof of Theorem 3 shows we only miss $\mathfrak{T}$ and $\mathfrak{T}_{\mathrm{shiny}}$. For shininess and stable infiniteness, we only get $\mathfrak{T}$, $\mathfrak{T}_{\mathrm{SI}}$ and $\mathfrak{T}_{\mathrm{shiny}}$. For gentleness and shininess the situation is similar, except that we must add $G(\mathfrak{T}_{gen}) = \mathfrak{T}_{\mathrm{CFS}}$. The resulting lattices are shown in Fig. 3. Formally:

Theorem 4.

1. Generate$(\{\mathfrak{T}_{SI}, \mathfrak{T}_{gen}\})$ *terminates, and its output consists of the 8 properties that appear in the left diagram of Fig. 3.*
2. Generate$(\{\mathfrak{T}_{SI}, \mathfrak{T}_{shiny}\})$ *terminates, and its output consists of the 3 properties that appear in the middle diagram of Fig. 3.*
3. Generate$(\{\mathfrak{T}_{gen}, \mathfrak{T}_{shiny}\})$ *terminates, and its output consists of the 4 properties that appear in the right diagram of Fig. 3.*

3.2 The Relationships Between the Properties

To conclude this section, we prove that the properties are correctly situated in Fig. 1b. That is, if there is a line between two properties, the lower one is stronger than the upper one. Most of these relationships are already captured by Proposition 1. Relationships that involve the new properties, $\mathfrak{T}_{\mathrm{CBS}}$ and $\mathfrak{T}_{\mathrm{CBFS}}$, are proven in Proposition 4 below. We just need two more connections:

Table 5. Signatures

Sig.	Functions	Predicates
Σ_1	$\varnothing$	$\varnothing$
Σ_P	$\varnothing$	$\{P\}$
$\Sigma_P^{\mathbb{N}}$	$\varnothing$	$\{P_n : n \in \mathbb{N}^*\}$
$\Sigma_P^{\mathbb{N}\times\mathbb{N}}$	$\varnothing$	$\{P_{m,n} : m, n \in \mathbb{N}^*\}$

Table 6. Theories defined over signatures from Table 5. L.S. stands for the least set the theory belongs to. $P_{\neq}=\{P_i\rightarrow\neg P_j : i\neq j\}$, $P_\infty=\{P_1\rightarrow\psi_{\geq k} : k\in\mathbb{N}\}$, and $P_U(n)=\{P_n\rightarrow\neg\psi_{=k} : k\notin U\}$.

Sig.	Name	Axiomatization	Source	L.S.
$\Sigma_P^{\mathbb{N}}$	$\mathcal{T}_{\langle si\rangle}$	$\{P_n \rightarrow \psi_{\geq m} : n \in U, m \in \mathbb{N}^*\} \cup P_{\neq}$	[10]	$\mathfrak{T}_{\mathrm{SI}}$
Σ_P	$\mathcal{T}_{\langle cs\rangle}$	$\{P \rightarrow \psi_{=1}\} \cup \{\neg P \rightarrow \psi_{\geq m} : m \in \mathbb{N}\}$	[10]	$\mathfrak{T}_{\mathrm{CS}}$
Σ_1	$\mathcal{T}_{\leq n}$	$\{\psi_{\leq n}\}$	[13]	$\mathfrak{T}_{gen}$
Σ_1	$\mathcal{T}_{\infty}$	$\{\psi_{\geq k} : k \in \mathbb{N}^*\}$	[13]	$\mathfrak{T}_{\mathrm{SI+CS}}$
Σ_1	$\mathcal{T}_{\geq n}$	$\{\psi_{\geq n}\}$	[13]	$\mathfrak{T}_{\mathrm{shiny}}$
Σ_1	$\mathcal{T}^{=n}_{\geq n+2}$	$\{\psi_{=n} \vee \psi_{\geq n+2}\}$	New	$\mathfrak{T}_{\mathrm{SI}+gen}$
$\Sigma_P^{\mathbb{N}}$	$\mathcal{T}(m,n)$	$\{\psi_{=m} \vee \psi_{=n}\} \cup \{P_k \rightarrow \psi_{=m} : k \in U\} \cup \{P_1 \rightarrow \psi_{=n}\} \cup P_{\neq}$	New	$\mathfrak{T}$
$\Sigma_P^{\mathbb{N}}$	$\mathcal{T}_{\langle cbfs\rangle}$	$P_\infty \cup P_U(2) \cup \{P_k \rightarrow \psi_{\leq F(k)} : k > 2, F(k) \in \mathbb{N}\} \cup P_{\neq}$	New	$\mathfrak{T}_{\mathrm{CBFS}}$
$\Sigma_P^{\mathbb{N}}$	$\mathcal{T}_{\langle cfs\rangle}$	$P_\infty \cup \{P_k \rightarrow \psi_{\leq F(k)} : k > 1, F(k) \in \mathbb{N}\} \cup P_{\neq}$	New	$\mathfrak{T}_{\mathrm{CFS}}$
$\Sigma_P^{\mathbb{N}}$	$\mathcal{T}_{\langle cbs\rangle}$	$P_U(1) \cup \{P_k \rightarrow \psi_{=k} : k > 1\} \cup P_{\neq}$	New	$\mathfrak{T}_{\mathrm{CBS}}$

Proposition 2. *$\mathfrak{T}_{SI} \cap \mathfrak{T}_{CFS} = \mathfrak{T}_{SI+CS}$ and $\mathfrak{T}_{gen} \cap \mathfrak{T}_{SI+CS} = \mathfrak{T}_{SI+gen}$.*

Proof. By Proposition 1, stable infiniteness implies being infinitely decidable (for decidable theories), and by appealing to the definition of having computable spectra we get $\mathfrak{T}_{\mathrm{SI}} \cap \mathfrak{T}_{\mathrm{CFS}} = \mathfrak{T}_{\mathrm{SI+CS}}$.

By Proposition 1, gentleness implies having computable spectra, so the conjunction of gentleness, stable infiniteness and computable spectra is the same as that of gentleness and stable infiniteness, that is, $\mathfrak{T}_{gen} \cap \mathfrak{T}_{\mathrm{SI+CS}} = \mathfrak{T}_{\mathrm{SI}+gen}$.

We also prove that all inclusions in Fig. 1b are strict. For this, we present theories that separate between the different sets. The signatures for these theories can be found in Table 5. Σ_1 is empty, Σ_P includes a single nullary predicate symbol P, and $\Sigma_P^{\mathbb{N}}$ includes a nullary predicate symbol P_n for every $n \in \mathbb{N}^*$. Table 5 includes one more signature, with predicate symbols for each pair of natural numbers, to be used in Sect. 4 below.

The axiomatizations of the separating theories are found in Table 6. In it, $F : \mathbb{N}^* \rightarrow \mathbb{N}^* \cup \{\aleph_0\}$ is a function such that: (i) $\{(m,n) \in \mathbb{N}^* \times \mathbb{N}^* : F(m) \geq n\}$ is decidable; and (ii) $\{n : F(n) = \aleph_0\}$ is undecidable.[4] Also, $U \subset \mathbb{N}^*$ is an undecidable set such that $1 \notin U$.

[4] Uses and explicit examples of such functions may be found in [2,14].

The upper part of Table 6 includes theories that were defined in previous works (whose axiomatizations we present for completeness' sake). Briefly, a $\mathcal{T}_{\langle si \rangle}$-interpretation that satisfies a P_n, for $n \in U$, must be infinite; a $\mathcal{T}_{\langle cs \rangle}$-interpretation either satisfies P and has a single element, or $\neg P$ and is infinite; $\mathcal{T}_\infty$ has only infinite interpretations, $\mathcal{T}_{\leq n}$ only interpretations of size at most n, and $\mathcal{T}_{\geq n}$ interpretations of size at least n.

The last five theories will also be used in Sect. 5 below and are brand new. $\mathcal{T}^{=n}_{\geq n+2}$ is easy to understand: it has models of cardinality exactly n, or strictly greater than $n + 1$. $\mathcal{T}(m, n)$ has models of cardinality m or n; if P_k is true, for some $k \in U$, then the cardinality must be m; but if P_1 is true (and we assumed $1 \notin U$), then the cardinality must be n. In $\mathcal{T}_{\langle cbfs \rangle}$ the truth of: P_1 implies a model is infinite; P_2 implies a model has cardinality in U; and P_k, for $k > 2$, implies a model has cardinality at most $F(k)$, whenever $F(k)$ is finite. $\mathcal{T}_{\langle cfs \rangle}$ is similar to $\mathcal{T}_{\langle cfbs \rangle}$, except that the truth of P_2 now implies a model has cardinality at most $F(2)$, if this value is finite. And, finally, in $\mathcal{T}_{\langle cbs \rangle}$ the truth of P_1 implies a model has cardinality in U, while the truth of P_k for $k > 1$ implies a model has cardinality precisely k.

Indeed, the theories in Table 6 separate the properties of Fig. 1b, meaning that each has a property without having any of the properties below it. This is represented in Table 6 by column L.S., which stands for the "least set" of Fig. 1b the theory belongs to.

Proposition 3. *The last column of Table 6 correctly identifies the least set (L.S.) the theories belong to.*

Example 1. Theory $\mathcal{T}_{\langle si \rangle}$ is stably infinite but does not have computable spectra. Thus, it shows that the inclusion $\mathfrak{T}_{\mathrm{SI+CS}} \subseteq \mathfrak{T}_{\mathrm{SI}}$ observed in Fig. 1b is strict.

4 Two New Combination Methods

In this section, we introduce two new combination methods. While they were tailored precisely for "running" Algorithm 1 in search of the smallest lattice that contains Fig. 1a, they are interesting in their own right, and allow combinations of theories that other methods do not support (see Example 2 below).

The new methods are inspired by gentleness and, in particular, Fontaine's lemma (Lemma 1) plays a crucial role in their correctness proofs.

Recall that having computable finite spectra amounts to the existence of an algorithm that decides whether a given natural number is in the spectrum of a given formula. We here weaken this requirement by allowing the algorithm to return arbitrary values in case the spectra is unbounded: if it is bounded, however, it must answer correctly whether an element n is or not in the spectra, given an adequate upper bound m.

Definition 1. *A theory $\mathcal{T}$ is said to have* computable bounded finite spectra *if there is an algorithm that takes a quantifier-free formula ϕ and two $m, n \in \mathbb{N}^*$, and adheres to the following specification: if ϕ is not $\mathcal{T}$-satisfiable by an interpretation with at least m elements, then the algorithm must return whether $n \in Spec_{\mathcal{T}}(\phi)$. Otherwise, the algorithm can return any Boolean value.*

Algorithm 2 Determining non-emptiness of $Spec_{\mathcal{T}_1}(\phi_1) \cap Spec_{\mathcal{T}_2}(\phi_2)$, assuming $\mathcal{T}_1 \in \mathfrak{T}_{\mathrm{CBFS}}$ and $\mathcal{T}_2 \in \mathfrak{T}_{\mathrm{SI}+gen}$.

function. CBFS+(SI+GEN)(ϕ_1, ϕ_2)
  if ϕ_2 is not $\mathcal{T}_2$-satisfiable **then return** false
  $m \leftarrow \max(\mathbb{N}_\omega \setminus Spec_{\mathcal{T}_2}(\phi_2))$.
  if $\phi_1 \wedge \neq(x_1, \dots, x_{m+1})$ is $\mathcal{T}_1$-satisfiable **then** ▷ $x_1, \dots, x_{m+1}$ are fresh
    return true
  $X \leftarrow Spec_{\mathcal{T}_1}(\phi_1) \setminus (\mathbb{N}_\omega \setminus Spec_{\mathcal{T}_2}(\phi_2))$
  for $n \leftarrow [1, m-1]$ **do**
    if $n \in X$ **then**
      return true
  return false

Algorithm 3 Determining non-emptiness of $Spec_{\mathcal{T}_1}(\phi_1) \cap Spec_{\mathcal{T}_2}(\phi_2)$, assuming $\mathcal{T}_1 \in \mathfrak{T}_{\mathrm{SI+CS}}$ and $\mathcal{T}_2 \in \mathfrak{T}_{\mathrm{CBS}}$.

function. (SI+CS)+CBS(ϕ_1, ϕ_2)
  if ϕ_1 is $\mathcal{T}_1$-satisfiable and $\aleph_0 \in Spec_{\mathcal{T}_2}(\phi_2)$ **then**
    return true
  $m \leftarrow 1$
  while $\phi_2 \wedge \neq(x_1, \dots, x_m)$ is $\mathcal{T}_2$-satisfiable **do** ▷ $x_1, \dots, x_m$ are fresh
    $m \leftarrow m + 1$
  for $n \leftarrow [1, m-1]$ **do**
    if $n \in Spec_{\mathcal{T}_1}(\phi_1) \cap Spec_{\mathcal{T}_2}(\phi_2)$ **then**
      return true
  return false

Just like computable spectra adds infinite decidability to computable finite spectra, a similar change to computable bounded finite spectra is pivotal:

Definition 2. *A theory $\mathcal{T}$ is said to have* computable bounded spectra *if it is infinitely decidable and has computable bounded finite spectra.*

We now examine the relations between these properties and others we have met so far. The result is formalized in the next theorem, depicted in Fig. 4.

Proposition 4. *$\mathfrak{T}_{SI} \subseteq \mathfrak{T}_{CBS} \subseteq \mathfrak{T}_{CBFS}$, $\mathfrak{T}_{CFS} \subseteq \mathfrak{T}_{CBFS}$, and $\mathfrak{T}_{CFS} \cap \mathfrak{T}_{CBS} = \mathfrak{T}_{CS}$.*

Proof. To see that $\mathfrak{T}_{\mathrm{SI}} \subseteq \mathfrak{T}_{\mathrm{CBS}}$, given a quantifier-free ϕ and $m, n \in \mathbb{N}^*$, our algorithm may return an arbitrary boolean, as a stably infinite theory is infinitely decidable by [10] and ϕ always has models of cardinality greater than m.

To see that $\mathfrak{T}_{\mathrm{CFS}} \subseteq \mathfrak{T}_{\mathrm{CBFS}}$, given a quantifier-free formula ϕ and $m, n \in \mathbb{N}^*$, we can define the algorithm that proves $\mathcal{T}$ has computable bounded finite spectra by simply ignoring m and feeding ϕ and n to the algorithm that guarantees $\mathcal{T}$ has computable finite spectra.

That $\mathfrak{T}_{\mathrm{CBS}} \subseteq \mathfrak{T}_{\mathrm{CBFS}}$ follows from the definition of the latter. Finally, as a theory with computable bounded spectra is infinitely decidable by definition, and computable spectra is defined as being infinitely decidable and having computable finite spectra, $\mathfrak{T}_{\mathrm{CBS}} \cap \mathfrak{T}_{\mathrm{CFS}} = \mathfrak{T}_{\mathrm{CS}}$.

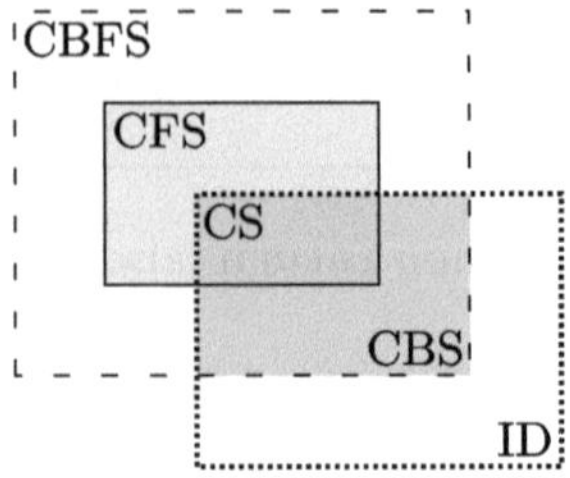

Fig. 4. Relationships between having computable bounded finite spectra (CBFS, dashed box), having computable finite spectra (CFS, red), having computable bounded spectra (CBS, blue), having computable spectra (CS, purple), and being infinitely decidable (ID, dotted box) (Color figure online)

The next theorem provides a new combination method between theories with computable bounded finite spectra, and theories both stably infinite and gentle.

Theorem 5. *If* $\mathcal{T}_1 \in \mathfrak{T}_{CBFS}$ *and* $\mathcal{T}_2 \in \mathfrak{T}_{SI+gen}$*, then* $\mathcal{T}_1 \sqcup \mathcal{T}_2$ *is decidable. That is,* $\mathfrak{T}_{CBFS} \subseteq G(\mathfrak{T}_{SI+gen})$ *(and* $\mathfrak{T}_{SI+gen} \subseteq G(\mathfrak{T}_{CBFS})$*).*

Proof (sketch). By Lemma 1, it suffices to show a decision procedure that decides, given ϕ_1 and ϕ_2 whether $Spec_{\mathcal{T}_1}(\phi_1) \cap Spec_{\mathcal{T}_2}(\phi_2)$ is empty. We present such a decision procedure in Algorithm 2. It relies on the properties of $\mathcal{T}_1$ and $\mathcal{T}_2$ in order to determine whether the models of the two formulas share a cardinality, by iterating over all possible cardinalities. Termination is guaranteed by Corollary 1. Notice that in line 3, $m \in \mathbb{N}^*$: since $\mathcal{T}_2$ is stably infinite we have $\aleph_0 \in Spec_{\mathcal{T}_2}(\phi_2)$, and since $\mathcal{T}_2$ is also gentle the set $Spec_{\mathcal{T}_2}(\phi_2)$ must be cofinite, making of $\mathbb{N}^*_\omega \setminus Spec_{\mathcal{T}_2}(\phi_2)$ a finite subset of $\mathbb{N}^*$.

A similar yet distinct combination theorem is obtained between theories that are stably infinite and have computable spectra, and theories with computable bounded spectra. It is proved in a similar fashion to Theorem 5. In particular, it relies on Lemma 1 and Algorithm 3.

Theorem 6. *If* $\mathcal{T}_1 \in \mathfrak{T}_{SI+CS}$ *and* $\mathcal{T}_2 \in \mathfrak{T}_{CBS}$*, then* $\mathcal{T}_1 \sqcup \mathcal{T}_2$ *is decidable. That is,* $\mathfrak{T}_{CBS} \subseteq G(\mathfrak{T}_{SI+CS})$ *(and* $\mathfrak{T}_{SI+CS} \subseteq G(\mathfrak{T}_{CBS})$*).*

Examples of theories with computable bounded finite spectra include all of those in Table 6 but $\mathcal{T}(m,n)$, and examples of theories with computable bounded spectra include all of those in Table 6 but $\mathcal{T}(m,n)$, $\mathcal{T}_{\langle cbfs\rangle}$ and $\mathcal{T}_{\langle cfs\rangle}$. More importantly, $\mathcal{T}_{\langle cbfs\rangle}$ is an example of a theory with computable bounded finite spectra but neither computable bounded spectra or computable finite spectra; and $\mathcal{T}_{\langle cbs\rangle}$ is an example of a theory with computable bounded spectra but that neither is stably infinite nor has computable spectra. Such examples may seem artificial but finding a theory with a given property, and none of the stronger ones, can be non-trivial; if we relax these restrictions, any stably infinite theory, for example, has both forms of bounded spectra. The following example shows a combination made possible by Theorem 6 not known to be possible by existing methods, in particular those in Fig. 1a.

Example 2. The combination of $\mathcal{T}_{\langle cbs \rangle}$ and $\mathcal{T}_{\infty}$ from Table 6 is decidable by Theorem 6, because the former has computable bounded spectra, and the latter is stably infinite and has computable spectra. We don't get this from any of the combination methods that correspond to Fig. 1a: not from Nelson–Oppen (as $\mathcal{T}_{\langle cbs \rangle}$ is not stably infinite), nor from the shiny combination method (as neither of the theories is shiny), nor from the gentle combination method (as $\mathcal{T}_{\langle cbs \rangle}$ does not have computable finite spectra).

4.1 Sharpness

We now prove that Theorems 5 and 6 are, in fact, sharp. For Theorem 5, this means that every decidable theory that can be combined with all decidable theories that are both stably infinite and gentle, must have computable bounded finite spectra, and vice-versa. A similar result holds for Theorem 6.

$$\{P_{m,n} \rightarrow (\psi_{=n} \vee \psi_{\geq m+1}) : 1 \leq n \leq m\} \cup \{P_{m,n} \rightarrow \neg P_{p,q} : (m,n) \neq (p,q)\}$$

Fig. 5. Axiomatization of $\mathcal{T}_{=}^{>}$

Theorem 7. *$G(\mathfrak{T}_{SI+gen}) \subseteq \mathfrak{T}_{CBFS}$ and $G(\mathfrak{T}_{CBFS}) \subseteq \mathfrak{T}_{SI+gen}$.*

Theorem 8. *$G(\mathfrak{T}_{CBS}) \subseteq \mathfrak{T}_{SI+CS}$ and $G(\mathfrak{T}_{SI+CS}) \subseteq \mathfrak{T}_{CBS}$.*

As a consequence, we obtain the following equalities, which are especially useful for the execution of Algorithm 1:

Corollary 2. *$G(\mathfrak{T}_{SI+gen}) = \mathfrak{T}_{CBFS}$, $G(\mathfrak{T}_{CBFS}) = \mathfrak{T}_{SI+gen}$, $G(\mathfrak{T}_{SI+CS}) = \mathfrak{T}_{CBS}$, and $G(\mathfrak{T}_{CBS}) = \mathfrak{T}_{SI+CS}$.*

The proofs of Theorems 7 and 8 are carried out using the technique of *test theories*, introduced in [10]. The idea is, given a reference set, to define a family of *test theories* that is, in a sense, "maximally difficult" to combine: then, if a theory is combinable with these test theories, it must be combinable with the entire reference set. We mostly use the test theories introduced in [10]. For them, we have to prove that they can indeed serve as test theories for the two new properties that we introduce. We also introduce one new theory, denoted $\mathcal{T}_{=}^{>}$, which is axiomatized in Fig. 5 over signature $\Sigma_{P}^{\mathbb{N}\times\mathbb{N}}$ from Table 5. Essentially, in a $\mathcal{T}_{=}^{>}$-interpretation $\mathcal{A}$, if $P_{m,n}$ holds true then either $|dom(\mathcal{A})| = n$ or $|dom(\mathcal{A})| > m$. It has the following properties:

Proposition 5. *The theory $\mathcal{T}_{=}^{>}$ is decidable, stably infinite, gentle, and for $\aleph_0 \notin Spec_{\mathcal{T}}(\phi)$, $m = \max Spec_{\mathcal{T}}(\phi)$ finite, and $n \leq m$, we have that $\phi \wedge P_{m,n}$ is $\mathcal{T} \sqcup \mathcal{T}_{=}^{>}$-satisfiable if and only if $n \in Spec_{\mathcal{T}}(\phi)$.*

With this theory, and its properties as listed in Proposition 5, we can provide a sketch for the proof of Theorem 7. The proof of Theorem 8 is similar.

Proof (of Theorem 7, sketch). We show that $G(\mathfrak{T}_{\mathrm{SI}+gen}) \subseteq \mathfrak{T}_{\mathrm{CBFS}}$. The second part can be done in a similar fashion, but requires further test theories from [10].

Suppose that $\mathcal{T}$ is decidable and can be combined with every decidable, gentle and stably infinite theory. We prove that $\mathcal{T}$ has computable bounded finite spectra. Take a quantifier-free ϕ, and $m, n \in \mathbb{N}^*$: our algorithm simply returns whether $\phi \wedge P_{m,n}$ is $\mathcal{T} \sqcup \mathcal{T}_=^>$-satisfiable; in case $\phi \wedge \neq(x_1, \ldots, x_m)$ is not $\mathcal{T}$-satisfiable this happens iff $n \in Spec_{\mathcal{T}}(\phi)$, for $1 \leq n \leq m$, so the algorithm has the required properties. We are then done as $\mathcal{T} \sqcup \mathcal{T}_=^>$ is indeed decidable, given that $\mathcal{T}_=^>$ is decidable, gentle and stably infinite, see Proposition 5.

5 Theories that Cannot be Combined with Themselves

In Fig. 1b, G behaves as a reflection over the dashed line. For each set of theories $\mathfrak{T}_{\mathrm{X}}$ in the diagram, either $\mathfrak{T}_{\mathrm{X}}$ sits above $G(\mathfrak{T}_{\mathrm{X}})$ (and so $G(\mathfrak{T}_{\mathrm{X}}) \subseteq \mathfrak{T}_{\mathrm{X}}$), or $G(\mathfrak{T}_{\mathrm{X}})$ sits above $\mathfrak{T}_{\mathrm{X}}$ (and so $\mathfrak{T}_{\mathrm{X}} \subseteq G(\mathfrak{T}_{\mathrm{X}})$). This is true for all combination properties we studied so far in this paper, and for all those found in [10], but is it true in general? In other words, must G look like a reflection? The answer, surprisingly, is no, as we proceed to show.

We first introduce the notion of self-combinable theories, and prove that all theories up to the dashed line of Fig. 1b are self-combinable. This is an interesting property, and to our knowledge it was not studied so far. We will use it below to prove that G does not have to be a reflection.

Definition 3. *A decidable theory $\mathcal{T}$ is* self-combinable *if $\mathcal{T} \sqcup \mathcal{T}$ is decidable.*

Recall that $\sqcup$ makes the signatures disjoint before joining the axiomatizations, and so this definition, while strange, is acceptable. We show below examples of both self-combinable and non self-combinable theories.

Proposition 6. *If $\mathcal{T} \in \mathfrak{T}_X$ for $\mathfrak{T}_X \in \{\mathfrak{T}_{shiny}, \mathfrak{T}_{SI+gen}, \mathfrak{T}_{gen}, \mathfrak{T}_{SI+CS}, \mathfrak{T}_{CS}, \mathfrak{T}_{SI}\}$ then it is self-combinable.*

Proof. $\mathfrak{T}_{\mathrm{X}} \subseteq G(\mathfrak{T}_{\mathrm{X}})$, and so $\mathcal{T} \in \mathfrak{T}_{\mathrm{X}} \cap G(\mathfrak{T}_{\mathrm{X}})$, hence $\mathcal{T} \sqcup \mathcal{T}$ is decidable.

Example 3. We show the theory $\mathcal{T}(m,n)$ from Table 6, with $m > n$, is not self-combinable. For simplicity, let $\Sigma_{P'}^{\mathbb{N}}$ be a disjoint copy of $\Sigma_P^{\mathbb{N}}$, with predicates P'_k instead of P_k. Consider the quantifier-free formulas $P_k \wedge P'_1$: they are $\mathcal{T}(m,n) \sqcup \mathcal{T}(m,n)$-satisfiable if and only if $k \notin U$. Indeed, if $k \in U$ then P_k implies $\psi_{=m}$, while P'_1 implies $\psi_{=n}$; and if $k \notin U$, define a $\mathcal{T}(m,n) \sqcup \mathcal{T}(m,n)$-interpretation $\mathcal{A}_k$ with n elements, where P_k is true, all other P_i are false, P'_1 is true, and all other P'_i are false; of course it satisfies $P_k \wedge P'_1$. Thus, if $\mathcal{T}(m,n) \sqcup \mathcal{T}(m,n)$ is decidable, we get a decision procedure for the undecidable set U, a contradiction.

Now, $\mathcal{T}(m,n)$ is decidable, but has none of the other properties. We show that for each property strictly above the dashed line of Fig. 1b there is a theory that exhibits it but is not self-combinable. We actually already defined these theories in the bottom part of Table 6:

Proposition 7. *$\mathcal{T}_{\langle cbfs \rangle}$ $\mathcal{T}_{\langle cfs \rangle}$, and $\mathcal{T}_{\langle cbs \rangle}$ from Table 6 are not self-combinable.*

Returning to the reflection principle, we obtain the following negative result:

Proposition 8. *There is a closed set $\mathfrak{T}_X$ with $\mathfrak{T}_X \not\subseteq G(\mathfrak{T}_X)$ and $G(\mathfrak{T}_X) \not\subseteq \mathfrak{T}_X$.*

Proof. Take $\mathfrak{T}_X$ to be $G(\{\mathcal{T}(m,n)\})$ for some $m > n$: it is not in Fig. 1b due to Proposition 6. It is closed because every output of G is closed, thus $G(G(\mathfrak{T}_X)) = \mathfrak{T}_X$. Notice that for any $p > q$ with $\{m,n\} \cap \{p,q\} = \emptyset$, $\mathcal{T}(m,n)$ is combinable with $\mathcal{T}(p,q)$, as the models of one do not share cardinalities with models of the other.

By Example 3, $\mathcal{T}(m,n)$ is not in $\mathfrak{T}_X$ but $\mathcal{T}(p,q)$ is, and because of that $\mathcal{T}(m,n)$ is in $G(\mathfrak{T}_X)$ but $\mathcal{T}(p,q)$ is not. Therefore $\mathfrak{T}_X \not\subseteq G(\mathfrak{T}_X)$ and $G(\mathfrak{T}_X) \not\subseteq \mathfrak{T}_X$.

6 Conclusion

We have computed the minimal lattice of theory combination properties that contains the classical properties of stable infiniteness, shininess, and gentleness. This process generated two new sharp combination methods, based on the novel notions of theories with computable bounded (finite) spectra.

Going forward, we notice that [10] showed the feasibility of proving sharpness of combination theorems. We here adhere to this raised standard: the two new combination theorems that we present are proven sharp. However, the sharpness proofs both here and in [10] require tailored test theories. We plan to streamline this process, looking for more general sufficient conditions for sharpness, and study the completeness of test theories, as defined in [10], for the new properties shown here.

Acknowledgments. This research was supported in part by Defense Advanced Research Projects Agency (DARPA) contract FA875024-2-1001, Israel Science Foundation (ISF) grant number 209/25, and the Binational Science Foundation (BSF) grant number 2024049. Przybocki was supported by the NSF Graduate Research Fellowship Program under Grant No. DGE-2140739.

References

1. Barrett, C., Sebastiani, R., Seshia, S., Tinelli, C.: Satisfiability modulo theories. In: Biere, A., Heule, M.J.H., van Maaren, H., Walsh, T. (eds.) Handbook of Satisfiability, Second Edition, volume 336 of Frontiers in Artificial Intelligence and Applications, chapter 33, pp. 825–885. IOS Press (2021). http://www.cs.stanford.edu/~barrett/pubs/BSST21.pdf

2. Bonacina, M.P., Fontaine, P., Ringeissen, C., Tinelli, C.: Theory combination: beyond equality sharing. In: Lutz, C., Sattler, U., Tinelli, C., Turhan, A.-Y., Wolter, F. (eds.) Description Logic, Theory Combination, and All That. LNCS, vol. 11560, pp. 57–89. Springer, Cham (2019). https://doi.org/10.1007/978-3-030-22102-7_3
3. Casal, F., Rasga, J.: Revisiting the equivalence of shininess and politeness. In: McMillan, K., Middeldorp, A., Voronkov, A. (eds.) LPAR 2013. LNCS, vol. 8312, pp. 198–212. Springer, Heidelberg (2013). https://doi.org/10.1007/978-3-642-45221-5_15
4. Herbert Bruce Enderton: A Mathematical Introduction to Logic. Academic Press, New York (1972)
5. Fontaine, P.: Combinations of theories for decidable fragments of first-order logic. In: Ghilardi, S., Sebastiani, R. (eds.) FroCoS 2009. LNCS (LNAI), vol. 5749, pp. 263–278. Springer, Heidelberg (2009). https://doi.org/10.1007/978-3-642-04222-5_16
6. Jovanović, D., Barrett, C.: Polite theories revisited. In: Fermüller, C.G., Voronkov, A. (eds.) LPAR 2010. LNCS, vol. 6397, pp. 402–416. Springer, Heidelberg (2010). https://doi.org/10.1007/978-3-642-16242-8_29
7. Marker, D.: Model Theory: An Introduction, volume 217 of Graduate Texts in Mathematics. Springer-Verlag, New York (2002). https://doi.org/10.1007/b98860
8. Nelson, G., Oppen, D.C.: Simplification by cooperating decision procedures. ACM Trans. Program. Lang. Syst. **1**(2), 245–257 (1979). https://doi.org/10.1145/357073.357079
9. Oppen, D.C.: Complexity, convexity and combinations of theories. Theoret. Comput. Sci. **12**(3), 291–302 (1980). https://doi.org/10.1016/0304-3975(80)90059-6
10. Przybocki, B., Toledo, G.V., Zohar, Y.: Characterizing sets of theories that can be disjointly combined. In: 53rd ACM SIGPLAN Symposium on Principles of Programming Languages, POPL 2026 (2026)
11. Ranise, S., Ringeissen, C., Zarba, C.G.: Combining data structures with nonstably infinite theories using many-sorted logic. In: Gramlich, B. (ed.) FroCoS 2005. LNCS (LNAI), vol. 3717, pp. 48–64. Springer, Heidelberg (2005). https://doi.org/10.1007/11559306_3
12. Tinelli, C., Zarba, C.: Combining decision procedures for theories in sorted logics. Technical Report 04-01, Department of Computer Science, The University of Iowa (2004). ftp://ftp.cs.uiowa.edu/pub/tinelli/papers/TinZar-RR-04.pdf
13. Toledo, G.V., Zohar, Y., Barrett, C.: Combining combination properties: an analysis of stable infiniteness, convexity, and politeness. In: Pientka, B., Tinelli, C. (eds.) Automated Deduction – CADE 29, pp. 522–541. Springer, Cham (2023). https://doi.org/10.1007/978-3-031-38499-8_30
14. Toledo, G.V., Przybocki, B., Zohar, Y.: Being polite is not enough (and other limits of theory combination). In: Automated Deduction – CADE 30: 30th International Conference on Automated Deduction, Stuttgart, Germany, July 28–31, 2025, Proceedings, pp. 17–34. Springer, Berlin, Heidelberg (2025). https://doi.org/10.1007/978-3-031-99984-0_2

Open Access This chapter is licensed under the terms of the Creative Commons Attribution 4.0 International License (http://creativecommons.org/licenses/by/4.0/), which permits use, sharing, adaptation, distribution and reproduction in any medium or format, as long as you give appropriate credit to the original author(s) and the source, provide a link to the Creative Commons license and indicate if changes were made.

The images or other third party material in this chapter are included in the chapter's Creative Commons license, unless indicated otherwise in a credit line to the material. If material is not included in the chapter's Creative Commons license and your intended use is not permitted by statutory regulation or exceeds the permitted use, you will need to obtain permission directly from the copyright holder.

Automatically Translating Proof Systems for SMT Solvers to the λΠ-Calculus

Ciarán Dunne[1,3(✉)] and Guillaume Burel[2,3]

[1] INRIA, ENS Paris-Saclay,Gif-sur-Yvette, France
cciaranddunne@gmail.com
[2] ensIIE, Évry-Courcouronnes, France
[3] SAMOVAR, Télécom SudParis, Institut Polytechnique de Paris, 91120 Palaiseau, France

Abstract. Eunoia is a logical framework designed for specifying the proofs and proof systems of SMT solvers, namely cvc5. We present a translation from a core fragment of Eunoia to the λΠ-*calculus modulo rewriting* as implemented by the LambdaPi proof assistant. The translation is implemented by our tool `eo2lp`, which we use for generating LambdaPi encodings of (a) a large fragment of the *Cooperating Proof Calculus* (CPC), the Eunoia signature defining cvc5's proof system, and (b) proofs produced by cvc5 on `unsat` problems from various fragments of SMT-LIB.

1 Introduction

The area of automated reasoning known as *satisfiability modulo theories* (SMT) focuses on the development of tools for checking the satisfiability of first-order formulas over combinations of mathematical theories [9]. Such tools (known as SMT *solvers*) are increasingly used as back-ends for various tasks: hardware [27] and software verification [6,24,30], model checking [15], cyber-security [4,31], and to improve automation in proof assistants [1,10]. Because these applications demand a high level of confidence in the results produced by the solver, many solvers are capable of generating *proof certificates* that witness the unsatisfiability of formulas reported as such by the solver.

The *SMT-LIB standard* [8] specifies the syntax and semantics of a common language used for interacting with solvers. Proof generation is however not covered by the standard, leading to the development of various proof formats, namely LFSC [33], Alethe [32], and recently Eunoia [19]. Eunoia is both a proof output language and a logical framework for specifying the constants, side-condition programs, and inference rules of an SMT solver (e.g., cvc5). The *Cooperating Proof Calculus* (CPC) is the Eunoia signature encoding cvc5's proof system, and Eunoia proof scripts may be checked by the C++ tool Ethos [19].

The λΠ-calculus modulo rewriting [18] and its implementations in the tools Dedukti [3] and LambdaPi [20] provide trustworthy proof checking with an emphasis on interoperability of proof systems. This paper presents a translation from Eunoia to LambdaPi and an OCaml tool `eo2lp` that implements the

© The Author(s) 2026
A. Biere et al. (Eds.): IJCAR 2026, LNAI 16688, pp. 212–229, 2026.
https://doi.org/10.1007/978-3-032-32589-1_13

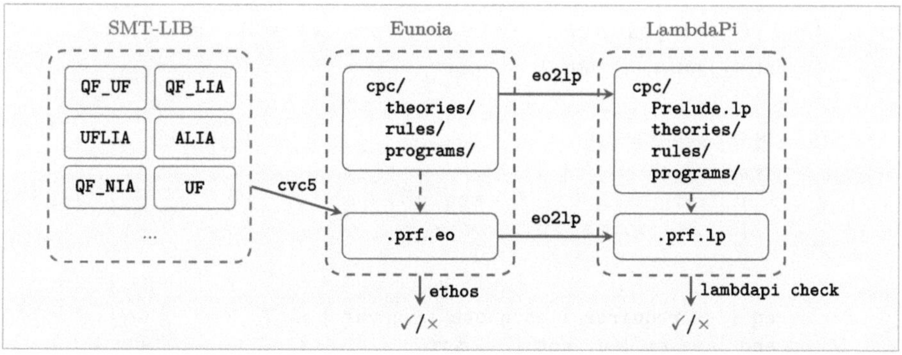

Fig. 1. Overview of the translation pipeline. cvc5 produces Eunoia proof scripts using rules from the CPC signature, which may be checked by Ethos. `eo2lp` translates both the signature and the proofs to LambdaPi, which independently verifies them.

translation. We used our tool to translate *CPC-MINI*, a fragment of CPC covering 14 SMT-LIB logic fragments (Fig. 1), and to further translate and typecheck over 1,000 proof scripts produced by running cvc5 on `unsat` problems from those fragments.

Related Work. The reduction of SMT proof checking to type checking originates with LFSC [33]; Eunoia inherits this approach and extends it with higher-order features similar to those of the speculative SMT-LIB 3 proposal [5,7,21]. Brown [12] compares the prospects of interpreting the proposed type system within type-theoretic and set-theoretic frameworks; our encoding realizes the former via the $\lambda\Pi$-calculus modulo rewriting.

The Dedukti/LambdaPi ecosystem is an interoperability hub for proof assistants (Rocq [11], Isabelle [22], HOL Light [2], Matita [25], Lean [35]) and automated provers (iProverModulo [13], ArchSAT [14], Vampire [23], TPTP [34]). Coltellacci et al. [16,17] reconstruct cvc5 proofs in LambdaPi via hand-written soundness lemmas for each rule of the Alethe [32] proof format. Similarly, LEAN-SMT [28] reconstructs Eunoia proofs in Lean 4 using lemmas that encode a subset of CPC's rules. Our work instead targets Eunoia at the framework level to allow encoding arbitrary Eunoia signatures and proof scripts in a type-theoretic framework.

Outline Section 2 introduces the fragment of Eunoia targeted by our translation and its elaboration step; Sect. 3 defines the translation into the $\lambda\Pi$-calculus modulo rewriting uniformly across rules, programs, and proof scripts; Sect. 4 describes `eo2lp` and reports the benchmark results.

2 Eunoia

This section presents the fragment of Eunoia targeted by our translation, together with the elaboration step that resolves n-ary applications to normal

$$t ::= s \mid \ell \mid (s\ \vec{t}) \mid (s\ (\vec{\rho})\ t) \quad \text{(terms)} \qquad \rho ::= (s\ t\ \langle\nu\rangle_?) \quad \text{(parameters)}$$
$$\ell ::= \mathsf{int}(n) \mid \mathsf{rat}(n,m) \mid \mathsf{str}(s) \quad \text{(literals)} \qquad c ::= (t\ t') \quad \text{(cases)}$$

$$\nu ::= \texttt{:implicit} \mid \texttt{:list} \quad \text{(prm. attributes)}$$
$$\begin{aligned}\alpha ::=\ & \texttt{:right-assoc} \mid \texttt{:right-assoc-nil}\ t \quad \text{(const. attributes)}\\ \mid\ & \texttt{:left-assoc} \mid \texttt{:left-assoc-nil}\ t\\ \mid\ & \texttt{:chainable}\ s \mid \texttt{:pairwise}\ s\\ \mid\ & \texttt{:binder}\ s \mid \texttt{:arg-list}\ s\end{aligned}$$

$$\begin{aligned}\beta ::=\ & \mathsf{eo::}\mathbf{eq} \mid \mathsf{eo::}\mathbf{requires} \mid \mathsf{eo::}\mathbf{quote} \mid \mathsf{eo::}\mathbf{var} \mid \ldots && \text{(core)}\\ \mid\ & \mathsf{eo::}\mathbf{and} \mid \mathsf{eo::}\mathbf{or} \mid \mathsf{eo::}\mathbf{not} \mid \mathsf{eo::}\mathbf{xor} && \text{(boolean)}\\ \mid\ & \mathsf{eo::}\mathbf{add} \mid \mathsf{eo::}\mathbf{mul} \mid \mathsf{eo::}\mathbf{neg} \mid \mathsf{eo::}\mathbf{zdiv} \mid \ldots && \text{(arithmetic)}\\ \mid\ & \mathsf{eo::}\mathbf{nil} \mid \mathsf{eo::}\mathbf{cons} \mid \mathsf{eo::}\mathbf{list\_concat} \mid \mathsf{eo::}\mathbf{list\_len} \mid \ldots && \text{(list)}\end{aligned}$$

$$\begin{aligned}\delta ::=\ & (\texttt{declare-const}\ s\ t\ \langle\alpha\rangle_?) \qquad \text{(std. commands)}\\ \mid\ & (\texttt{declare-parameterized-const}\ s\ (\vec{\rho})\ t\ \langle\alpha\rangle_?)\\ \mid\ & (\texttt{declare-consts}\ \ell\ t)\\ \mid\ & (\texttt{define}\ s\ (\vec{\rho})\ t\ \langle\texttt{:type}\ t'\rangle_?)\\ \mid\ & (\texttt{program}\ s\ (\vec{\rho})\ \texttt{:signature}\ (\vec{t})\ t'\ (\vec{c}))\\ \mid\ & (\texttt{declare-rule}\ s\ (\vec{\rho})\\ & \quad \langle\texttt{:assumption}\ t_{\text{assm}}\rangle_?\\ & \quad \langle\texttt{:premises}\ (\vec{t}_{\text{prem}}) \mid \texttt{:premise-list}\ t_{\text{prem}}\ t_{\text{op}}\rangle_?\\ & \quad \langle\texttt{:args}\ (\vec{t}_{\text{args}})\rangle_?\\ & \quad \langle\texttt{:requires}\ (\vec{c})\rangle_?\\ & \quad \texttt{:conclusion}\ t_{\text{conc}})\\ \mid\ & (\texttt{include}\ \mu)\end{aligned}$$

$$\begin{aligned}\pi ::=\ & (\texttt{assume}\ s\ \varphi) \qquad \text{(prf. commands)}\\ \mid\ & (\texttt{assume-push}\ s\ \varphi)\\ \mid\ & (\texttt{step}\ s\ \varphi\ \texttt{:rule}\ s'\ \langle\texttt{:premises}\ \vec{\psi}\rangle_?\ \langle\texttt{:args}\ \vec{t}\rangle_?)\\ \mid\ & (\texttt{step-pop}\ s\ \varphi\ \texttt{:rule}\ s'\ \langle\texttt{:premises}\ \vec{\psi}\rangle_?\ \langle\texttt{:args}\ \vec{t}\rangle_?)\end{aligned}$$

Fig. 2. Eunoia syntax: terms, attributes, built-in symbols, commands, proof commands.

form. Eunoia currently has no published formal semantics: its meaning is defined operationally by Ethos. The presentation here was informed by the Ethos user manual [19], the Ethos source, and through discussions with the cvc5/Eunoia developers.

2.1 Syntax, Commands, and Signatures

Figure 2 defines the concrete syntax for Eunoia, where the metavariable s ranges over a set of *symbols*. A term is either a symbol s, a literal ℓ (integer, rational, or string), an *application* $(s\ \vec{t})$, or a *binder application* $(s\ (\vec{\rho})\ t)$. A *parameter* $(s\ t\ \langle\nu\rangle_?)$ declares a symbol s of type t with an optional *parameter attribute*

Table 1. Declarations produced by each Eunoia command. Parts in $\langle\cdot\rangle_?$ are present only when the corresponding attribute is supplied. Each program case $c_i = (l_i\ r_i)$ contributes one rewrite rule.

Command	Declarations
(declare-const $s\ t\ \langle\alpha\rangle_?$)	$\{s : t\}\ \langle\cup\{s :: \alpha\}\rangle_?$
(declare-parameterized-const s ($\vec{\rho}$) $t\ \langle\alpha\rangle_?$)	$\{s(\vec{\rho}) : t\}\ \langle\cup\{s :: \alpha\}\rangle_?$
(declare-consts $\ell\ t$)	binds the literal class ℓ to type t
(define s ($\vec{\rho}$) t $\langle$:type $t'\rangle_?$)	$\{s(\vec{\rho}) \hookrightarrow t\}\ \langle\cup\{s(\vec{\rho}) : t'\}\rangle_?$
(program s ($\vec{\rho}$) :signature ($\vec{t}$) t' ($c_1 \dots c_m$))	$\{s(\vec{\rho})$: (-> $\vec{t}\ t'$)$\} \cup \{l_i \hookrightarrow r_i \mid c_i = (l_i\ r_i)\}$
(declare-rule s ($\vec{\rho}$) ...)	$\{s(\vec{\rho}) : \tau^\star\}$ (Section 2.2)
(include μ)	declarations of module μ
(assume $s\ \varphi$) / (assume-push $s\ \varphi$)	$\{s$: (Proof φ)$\}$
(step $s\ \varphi$:rule r $\langle$:args ($\vec{t}$)$\rangle_?$ $\langle$:premises ($\vec{p}$)$\rangle_?$)	$\{s$: (Proof φ), $s \hookrightarrow$ ($r\ \vec{t}\ \vec{p}$)$\}$

ν. Similarly, a symbol may have a *constant attribute* α that specifies how its n-ary applications are elaborated to binary form. Eunoia provides a fixed set of *built-in symbols* β that operate on the syntactic structure of terms; their role is explained alongside the constructs that use them (rule declarations in Sect. 2.2 and elaboration in Sect. 2.3). Commands are divided into *standard commands* and *proof commands.*

A *signature* Σ is a set of *declarations*, where each declaration is either a *typing* $s(\vec{\rho}) : t$, an *attribution* $s(\vec{\rho}) :: \alpha$, or a *rewrite rule* $\ell \hookrightarrow r$ with parameters $\vec{\rho}$. Table 1 maps each command to the set of declarations it contributes. Any sequence of standard commands $\vec{\delta}$ thus determines a signature: the union of the declarations contributed by each command. A *proof script* $\Upsilon = (\vec{\delta}\,;\vec{\pi})$ pairs a sequence of standard commands $\vec{\delta}$ (the *preamble*) with a sequence of proof commands $\vec{\pi}$ (the *body*); Υ likewise determines a signature, which we call a *proof.*

2.2 Rule Declarations and Proofs

Two of the core built-in symbols play a role specific to rule declarations. The guard (eo::**requires** $t_1\ t_2\ t_3$) evaluates to t_3 only when t_1 and t_2 are syntactically identical, and is otherwise stuck; it lets a rule make its conclusion conditional on a side-condition. The marker (eo::**quote** t) flags t as a *quoted argument* whose value may appear in the return type of the rule, giving Eunoia's mechanism for object-level dependent types. Given an inference rule declaration (declare-rule s ($\vec{\rho}$) ... :conclusion φ), the derivation of its contributed type declaration $s(\vec{\rho}) : \tau^\star$ is given thus:

1. Given :requires (($l_1\ r_1$) ... ($l_k\ r_k$)), define $\varphi^\star$ below. Otherwise, $\varphi^\star := \varphi$.
   $\varphi^\star$:= (eo::**requires** $l_1\ r_1$ (... (eo::**requires** $l_k\ r_k\ \varphi$)))
2. If the declaration provides no premises, let $\tau^\star$:= (Proof $\varphi^\star$). Otherwise, define $\tau^\star$ thus:

(a) Given :premises $(\psi_1 \ldots \psi_m)$, let:

$$\tau^\star := \texttt{(-> (Proof } \psi_1\texttt{) ... (Proof } \psi_m\texttt{) (Proof } \varphi^\star\texttt{))}$$

(b) Given :premise-list ψ f for some associative symbol f, redefine:

$$\varphi^\star := \texttt{(eo::requires (eo::is\_list } f\ \psi\texttt{) true } \varphi^\star\texttt{)}$$

and let $\tau^\star := \texttt{(-> (Proof } \psi\texttt{) (Proof } \varphi^\star\texttt{))}$.

3. If the declaration provides :args $(t_1 \ldots t_n)$, then the type contributed for s is:

$$s(\vec{\rho}) : \texttt{(-> (eo::quote } t_1\texttt{) ... (eo::quote } t_n\texttt{) } \tau^\star\texttt{)}$$

Otherwise, $s(\vec{\rho}) : \tau^\star$.

Example 1. Consider four rule declarations from cpc/rules/Booleans.eo.

```
(declare-rule modus_ponens ((F1 Bool) (F2 Bool))
  :premises (F1 (=> F1 F2))
  :conclusion F2)
```

```
(declare-rule cnf_implies_pos ((F1 Bool) (F2 Bool))
  :args ((=> F1 F2))
  :conclusion (or (not (=> F1 F2)) (not F1) F2))
```

```
(declare-rule reordering ((C1 Bool) (C2 Bool))
  :premises (C1)
  :args (C2)
  :requires (((eo::list_minclude or C1 C2) true))
  :conclusion C2)
```

```
(declare-rule and_intro ((F Bool))
  :premise-list F and
  :conclusion F)
```

The modus_ponens rule has only :premises and :conclusion, so item 2a gives:

$$\texttt{modus\_ponens}(\vec{\rho}) : \texttt{(-> (Proof F1) (Proof (=> F1 F2)) (Proof F2))}$$

The cnf_implies_pos rule has :args ((=> F1 F2)); item 3 makes this an eo::quote-typed parameter that pattern-matches at the point of use, where φ is the term given by its :conclusion attribute:

$$\texttt{cnf\_implies\_pos}(\vec{\rho}) : \texttt{(-> (eo::quote (=> F1 F2)) (Proof } \varphi\texttt{))}$$

The reordering rule combines :args with :requires: item 1 builds the guarded conclusion $\varphi^\star :=$ (eo::requires (eo::list_minclude or C1 C2) true C2), item 2a adds the premise C1, and item 3 wraps the eo::quote-typed argument C2:

$$\texttt{reordering}(\vec{\rho}) : \texttt{(-> (eo::quote C2) (Proof C1) (Proof } \varphi^\star\texttt{))}$$

The and_intro rule has :premise-list F and, so item 2b guards the conclusion with $\varphi^\star :=$ (eo::requires (eo::is_list and F) true F) and takes the premise list as a single (Proof F) argument:

$$\texttt{and\_intro}(\vec{\rho}) : \texttt{(-> (Proof F) (Proof } \varphi^\star\texttt{))}$$

2.3 Elaboration

Unlike standard LF-style frameworks, Eunoia supports n-ary applications of binary symbols, with the unrolling determined by a *constant attribute* α (Fig. 2) assigned to the symbol at its declaration. After elaboration, every application of a declared constant s uses the built-in higher-order application operator $\_$, so that $(s\ t_1\ t_2)$ becomes $(\_\ (\_\ s\ t_1)\ t_2)$; only built-in and program symbols are applied directly. For example, given f with attribute `:right-assoc-nil` t_{nil}, the *f-list* with elements $t_1 \ldots t_n$ is the nested application $(\_\ (\_\ f\ t_1)\ (\_\ (\_\ f\ \ldots)\ (\_\ (\_\ f\ t_n)\ t_{\text{nil}})))$. The built-in symbols `eo::nil`, `eo::cons`, and `eo::list_concat` construct and combine such f-lists from within programs and rule conclusions.

A second elaboration strategy targets binder applications. Eunoia provides a built-in *heterogeneous list* type `eo::List`, with constructors `eo::List::nil` and `eo::List::cons`, whose entries may have different types, and a built-in symbol `eo::var` that constructs variable-like terms $(\texttt{eo::var}\ "x"\ t)$. The attribute `:binder` t_{cons} specifies that a binder application $(s\ (\vec{\rho})\ t)$ is elaborated so that each parameter $(x_i\ t_i)$ in $\vec{\rho}$ becomes an `eo::var` term, and these terms are gathered with the list constructor t_{cons} (typically `eo::List::cons`, with terminator `eo::List::nil`).

The **elab** operator below captures both strategies uniformly. It is parameterized by a signature Σ and a local parameter context $\vec{\rho}$; we write $\mathsf{progs}(\Sigma)$ for the set of symbols introduced by `program` commands in Σ.

Definition 1. For any signature Σ and parameter context $\vec{\rho}$, let $\mathbf{elab}_{(\Sigma,\vec{\rho})}$ be the least operator such that:

1. For any symbol s, $\mathbf{elab}_{(\Sigma,\vec{\rho})}[s] = s$.
2. For a binder application $(s\ (\vec{v})\ t)$ where $(s :: \texttt{:binder}\ t_{\text{cons}}) \in \Sigma$, each parameter $(x_i\ t_i) \in \vec{v}$ is reified as $X_i := (\texttt{eo::var}\ "x_i"\ t_i)$, and the X_i are gathered with the list constructor t_{cons}:
$$\mathbf{elab}_{(\Sigma,\vec{\rho})}[(s\ (\vec{v})\ t)] = (s\ t_{\text{vars}}\ t_{\text{body}}) \quad \text{where} \quad \begin{array}{l} t_{\text{vars}} := \mathbf{elab}_{(\Sigma,\vec{\rho})}[(t_{\text{cons}}\ X_1 \ldots X_n)] \\ t_{\text{body}} := \mathbf{elab}_{(\Sigma,\vec{\rho})}[\mathbf{subst}_{(\vec{x},\vec{X})}[t]] \end{array}$$
3. For an application $(s\ \vec{t})$, let $t'_i := \mathbf{elab}_{(\Sigma,\vec{\rho})}[t_i]$ in:
   (a) If s is a built-in or $s \in \mathsf{progs}(\Sigma)$, then then $\mathbf{elab}_{(\Sigma,\vec{\rho})}[(s\ \vec{t})] = (s\ \vec{t}')$.
   (b) If $s \in \vec{\rho}$, then $\mathbf{elab}_{(\Sigma,\vec{\rho})}[(s\ \vec{t})] = (\_\ \ldots\ (\_\ (\_\ s\ t'_1)\ \ldots)\ t'_n)$.
   (c) If $(s :: \alpha) \in \Sigma)$ for an associative α, the result is one of:
$$\begin{cases} \mathbf{foldr}(G, t_{\text{nil}}, \vec{t}') & (\alpha = \texttt{:right-assoc-nil}\ t_{\text{nil}}) \\ \mathbf{foldl}(G, t_{\text{nil}}, \vec{t}') & (\alpha = \texttt{:left-assoc-nil}\ t_{\text{nil}}) \\ \mathbf{foldr}(G, t'_n, t'_1 \ldots t'_{n-1}) & (\alpha = \texttt{:right-assoc}) \\ \mathbf{foldl}(G, t'_1, t'_2 \ldots t'_n) & (\alpha = \texttt{:left-assoc}) \end{cases}$$
   where the combining function $G(x, y)$ is $(\texttt{eo::list\_concat}\ s\ x\ y)$ if $(x :: \texttt{:list}) \in \vec{\rho}$ and $(\_\ (\_\ s\ x)\ y)$ otherwise.
   (d) If $(s :: \alpha) \in \Sigma)$ for a non-associative α, then $\mathbf{elab}_{(\Sigma,\vec{\rho})}[(s\ \vec{t})] = \mathbf{elab}_{(\Sigma,\vec{\rho})}[(t_{\text{cons}}\ \vec{u})]$ where:

$$\vec{u} := \begin{cases} (s\ t_1 t_2)\ (s\ t_2 t_3)\ \ldots\ (s\ t_{n-1} t_n) & (\alpha = \texttt{:chainable}\ t_{\text{cons}}) \\ (s\ t_i t_j) \text{ for all } i < j & (\alpha = \texttt{:pairwise}\ t_{\text{cons}}) \\ \vec{t} & (\alpha = \texttt{:arg-list}\ t_{\text{cons}}) \end{cases}$$

Example 2. The constants `or`, `=`, and `forall` carry attributes that drive each of the elaboration cases:

```
(declare-const or (-> Bool Bool Bool) :right-assoc-nil false)
(declare-parameterized-const =
  ((A Type :implicit))
  (-> A A Bool) :chainable and)
```

```
(declare-const forall (-> eo::List Bool Bool) :binder)
```

Since `or` has attribute `:right-assoc-nil false`, item 3c applies with $G(x, y) =$ (_ (_ `or` x) y) and the right fold gives:

$$\mathbf{elab}_{(\Sigma,\vec{\rho})}[(\texttt{or x y z})] = (\_\ (\_\ \texttt{or x})\ (\_\ (\_\ \texttt{or y})\ (\_\ (\_\ \texttt{or z})\ \texttt{false})))$$

Since `=` has attribute `:chainable and`, item 3d first chains the equalities and then recurses through `and`'s `:right-assoc-nil false` attribute:

$$\mathbf{elab}_{(\Sigma,\vec{\rho})}[(\texttt{= a b c d})] = \mathbf{elab}_{(\Sigma,\vec{\rho})}[(\texttt{and (= a b) (= b c) (= c d)})]$$

Since `forall` has attribute `:binder eo::List::cons`, item 2 reifies each parameter as an `eo::var` term inside an `eo::List` and elaborates the body under the substitution $\sigma := (\texttt{x} \mapsto X)$, where $X :=$ (`eo::var` "x" `Int`):

$$\begin{aligned} \mathbf{elab}_{(\Sigma,\vec{\rho})}[(\texttt{forall ((x Int)) F})] &= (\texttt{forall}\ t_{\text{vars}}\ t_{\text{body}}) \\ t_{\text{vars}} &= (\texttt{eo::List::cons}\ X\ \texttt{eo::List::nil}) \\ t_{\text{body}} &= \mathbf{elab}_{(\Sigma,\vec{\rho})}[\sigma\texttt{F}] \end{aligned}$$

3 Encoding Eunoia in the λΠ-Calculus

Figure 3 provides syntax and typing rules for the *λΠ-calculus modulo rewriting.* Each term is either a *variable* x, a *constant* κ, a *universe* from $\{\texttt{TYPE}, \texttt{KIND}\}$, an *application* of two terms $(t\,t')$, or an *abstraction* $(\mathscr{B}\,x : t.\,t')$ where $\mathscr{B}$ is a *binder* from $\{\lambda, \Pi\}$. Terms are identified up to α-conversion (i.e., renaming of bound variables), and we assume appropriate definitions for *substitution* $(t[x \mapsto t'])$ and *β-reduction* $(t \rightsquigarrow_\beta t')$. Hereinafter, we may write $(t_1 \to t_2')$ for the term $(\Pi\,(x : t_1).\,t_2)$, where x does not occur free in t_2.

A *typing* is an expression of the form $(t : t')$, and a *context* is a list of typings each of the form $x : t$. A *rewrite rule* is an expression of the form $(t \hookrightarrow t')$, where t has the form $((\kappa t_1) \ldots t_n)$. A *signature* is a list of typings $(\kappa : t)$ (with t closed) and rewrite rules. For any signature Σ, let R_Σ be the smallest binary relation such that:

$$\mu ::= \texttt{TYPE} \mid \texttt{KIND} \qquad \text{(universes)}$$
$$t ::= x \mid \kappa \mid \mu \mid (t\,t') \mid (\lambda x : t.\, t') \mid (\Pi x : t.\, t') \qquad \text{(terms)}$$

$$(\text{WF}\emptyset)\ \frac{}{\mathsf{wf}\,\emptyset} \qquad (\text{WF}+)\ \frac{\Gamma \vdash_\Sigma t : \mu}{\mathsf{wf}\,(\Gamma, (x : t))}\ x \notin \mathbf{dom}(\Gamma)$$

$$(\text{VAR})\ \frac{\mathsf{wf}\,\Gamma}{\Gamma \vdash_\Sigma x : t}\ (x : t) \in \Gamma \qquad (\text{CON})\ \frac{\mathsf{wf}\,\Gamma \quad \Gamma \vdash_\Sigma t : \mu}{\Gamma \vdash_\Sigma \kappa : t}\ (\kappa : t) \in \Sigma$$

$$(\text{UNIV})\ \frac{\mathsf{wf}\,\Gamma}{\Gamma \vdash_\Sigma \texttt{TYPE} : \texttt{KIND}} \qquad (\text{PROD})\ \frac{\Gamma \vdash_\Sigma t : \texttt{TYPE} \quad \Gamma, (x : t) \vdash_\Sigma t' : \mu'}{\Gamma \vdash_\Sigma (\Pi x : t.\, t') : \mu'}$$

$$(\text{FUN})\ \frac{\Gamma, (x : t) \vdash_\Sigma e : t' \quad \Gamma \vdash_\Sigma (\Pi x : t.\, t') : \mu}{\Gamma \vdash_\Sigma (\lambda x : t.\, e) : (\Pi x : t.\, t')}$$

$$(\text{APP})\ \frac{\Gamma \vdash_\Sigma e : (\Pi x : t.\, t') \quad \Gamma \vdash_\Sigma e' : t}{\Gamma \vdash_\Sigma (e\,e') : t'[x \mapsto e']}$$

$$(\text{CONV})\ \frac{\Gamma \vdash_\Sigma e : t \quad \Gamma \vdash_\Sigma t' : \mu}{\Gamma \vdash_\Sigma e : t'}\ (t \equiv_{\beta\Sigma} t')$$

Fig. 3. Syntax and typing rules for the λΠ-calculus modulo rewriting.

1. for any rule $(\ell \hookrightarrow r) \in \Sigma$ and substitution σ, $(\ell\sigma, r\sigma) \in R_\Sigma$, and
2. R_Σ is *congruent* under application and abstraction.

Then, *equality modulo rewriting* $(\equiv_{\beta\Sigma})$ is defined as the least equivalence relation containing R_Σ and the β-reduction relation. The rules in Fig. 3 provide a (mutually inductive) definition of a *well-formedness* relation (wf_Σ) on contexts and a *typing relation* ($\vdash_\Sigma$) between contexts and typings, where ($\Gamma \vdash_\Sigma e : t$) may be read as "$e$ has type t with respect to signature Σ and context Γ".

3.1 Translating Eunoia Terms

The typing rules of the λΠ-calculus disallow abstractions on types (i.e., there are no expressions of type $\texttt{TYPE} \to t$ in any context). Eunoia's types are therefore encoded as λΠ-terms of type Set, using the Tarski-style universe of LambdaPi's standard library: an injective symbol $\tau : \mathsf{Set} \to \texttt{TYPE}$ lifts a Set-term to a λΠ-type, and the (infix) function-space symbol $(\leadsto) : \mathsf{Set} \to \mathsf{Set} \to \mathsf{Set}$ satisfies $\tau\,(A \leadsto B) \hookrightarrow \tau\,A \to \tau\,B$. The dependent types arising from `eo::quote` arguments are not expressible with $(\leadsto)$ alone, so we additionally introduce a dependent function space $(\leadsto^{\mathsf{d}}) : \Pi T : \mathsf{Set}.\, (\tau\,T \to \mathsf{Set}) \to \mathsf{Set}$ with the rule $\tau\,(T \leadsto^{\mathsf{d}} F) \hookrightarrow \Pi x : \tau\,T.\, \tau\,(F x)$; the non-dependent case is recovered by taking $F := \lambda\,\_.\, B$. We keep $(\leadsto)$ as a first-class operator rather than defining it from $(\rightsquigarrow^{\mathsf{d}})$ because programs need a matchable function-space head: pattern variables cannot bind under a Π, but they can under $(\rightsquigarrow)$.

The translation $[\![\cdot]\!]_{\mathsf{tm}}$ on Eunoia terms below produces $\lambda\Pi$-terms in the abstract calculus of Fig. 3 and assumes all terms have already been processed by the **elab** operator of Sect. 2.3. Because some Eunoia symbols are not valid LambdaPi identifiers, the translation on symbols uses LambdaPi syntax for escaping: $\bar{s} := \{\!|s|\!\}$ iff s contains forbidden characters, and $\bar{s} := s$ otherwise.

Definition 2. Let $[\![\cdot]\!]_{\mathsf{tm}}$ be the least operator such that:

1. For any symbol s or literal ℓ, the following hold:

$$[\![s]\!]_{\mathsf{tm}} = \begin{cases} \texttt{eo.Type} & \text{if } s = \texttt{Type}, \\ \bar{s} & \text{otherwise.} \end{cases} \qquad [\![\ell]\!]_{\mathsf{tm}} = \begin{cases} \texttt{of\_Z}\ [\![n]\!]_{\mathsf{tm}} & \text{if } \ell = \mathsf{int}(n), \\ \texttt{of\_Q}\ [\![n]\!]_{\mathsf{tm}}\ [\![m]\!]_{\mathsf{tm}} & \text{if } \ell = \mathsf{rat}(n, m), \\ \texttt{"}s\texttt{"} & \text{if } \ell = \mathsf{str}(s). \end{cases}$$

   The symbols `of_Z` and `of_Q` are defined in our prelude (Sect. 4) and embed the integer and rational literals of LambdaPi's standard library into the carrier type of Eunoia's arithmetic sorts.
2. For arrow types, the following hold, where $(x\ T) \in \vec{\rho}$:
$$[\![\texttt{(-> (eo::quote } x\texttt{) } \vec{t}\texttt{)}]\!]_{\mathsf{tm}} = [\![T]\!]_{\mathsf{tm}} \rightsquigarrow^{\mathsf{d}} \lambda x.\ [\![\texttt{(-> } \vec{t}\texttt{)}]\!]_{\mathsf{tm}}$$
$$[\![\texttt{(-> } t'\ \vec{t}\texttt{)}]\!]_{\mathsf{tm}} = [\![t']\!]_{\mathsf{tm}} \rightsquigarrow [\![\texttt{(-> } \vec{t}\texttt{)}]\!]_{\mathsf{tm}}$$
$$[\![\texttt{(-> } t\texttt{)}]\!]_{\mathsf{tm}} = [\![t]\!]_{\mathsf{tm}}$$
3. For binary and n-ary applications, the following hold:
$$\begin{aligned} [\![\texttt{(\_ } t_1\ t_2\texttt{)}]\!]_{\mathsf{tm}} &= \texttt{eo.app}\ [\![t_1]\!]_{\mathsf{tm}}\ [\![t_2]\!]_{\mathsf{tm}} \\ [\![\texttt{(Proof } t\texttt{)}]\!]_{\mathsf{tm}} &= \texttt{eo.Proof}\ [\![t]\!]_{\mathsf{tm}} \\ [\![\texttt{(}s\ \vec{t}\texttt{)}]\!]_{\mathsf{tm}} &= \bar{s}\ [\![t_1]\!]_{\mathsf{tm}} \cdots [\![t_n]\!]_{\mathsf{tm}} \end{aligned}$$
4. After elaboration, every other binder application is unfolded by item 2 of Definition 1; only `eo::define` survives because it is a let-binder rather than a binding form. It is translated using LambdaPi's standard let binder:
$$[\![\texttt{(eo::define (}\vec{v}\texttt{) } t'\texttt{)}]\!]_{\mathsf{tm}} = (\mathsf{let}\ \vec{w}\ \mathsf{in}\ [\![t']\!]_{\mathsf{tm}})$$
   where $w_i = (\bar{x}_i := [\![t_i]\!]_{\mathsf{tm}})$ for each $v_i = (x_i\ t_i)$.

3.2 The LambdaPi Proof Assistant

Figure 4 defines the fragment of LambdaPi required for encoding Eunoia. It is sugar over the calculus of Fig. 3: implicit binders $[x : t]$ and placeholders _ are elaborated to Π-binders and metavariables during type inference, and each declaration extends Σ.

A *symbol declaration* $\langle m\rangle_?$ `symbol` $s\ \vec{\rho} : t\ \langle := t'\rangle_?$ introduces s with the typing $(@s : \Pi\,\vec{\rho}.\,t)$, where parameters $\vec{\rho}$ are either *explicit* $(x : t)$ or *implicit* $[x : t]$.

$m ::=$ `constant` | `sequential`	(modifiers)	$\theta ::= \$\mathrm{x} \mid s\ \langle\theta\rangle_*$	(patterns)
$\rho ::= (s : t) \mid [s : t]$	(parameters)	$r ::= (s\ \langle\theta\rangle_* \hookrightarrow \theta')$	(rewrite rules)

$c ::= \langle m\rangle_?$ `symbol` $s\ \langle\rho\rangle_*\ : t\ \langle := t'\rangle_?;$ (commands)
$\mid$ `rule` $r\ \langle$`with` $r'\rangle_*;$
$\mid$ `assert` $\vdash\ t : t';$
$\mid$ `require open` $\langle\mu\rangle_+;$

Fig. 4. Syntax for a fragment of the LambdaPi proof assistant.

We write `@`s (with an @) for the *fully-explicit* form; an unprefixed s inserts a placeholder for each leading implicit, to be filled by higher-order unification. The optional `constant` modifier forbids rewrite rules with s at the head; `sequential` matches rewrite rules with head s in their textual order; and a definition $(:= t')$ adds the rewrite rule $(s \hookrightarrow \lambda\vec{\rho}.\, t')$. A *rewrite rule declaration* $\theta \hookrightarrow \theta'$ adds the rule $(\theta \hookrightarrow \theta')$ to the signature, where θ and θ' are *patterns*—either a *pattern variable* \$x (written \$x) or a *pattern application* $(s\ \langle\theta\rangle_*)$. The rule is valid when θ is a pattern application and every pattern variable in θ' also occurs in θ. LambdaPi additionally verifies *subject reduction* at declaration time: for every typed substitution of the pattern variables, both sides must have the same type. An *assertion* `assert` $\vdash\ t : t'$ checks $t : t'$ without extending the signature.

3.3 Translating Eunoia Commands and Proofs

We extend the term translation $[\![\cdot]\!]_{\mathsf{tm}}$ (Definition 2) to parameter contexts and to both standard and proof commands. Table 2 summarises the full Eunoia-to-LambdaPi encoding; the remainder of this section formalises the operators on contexts (Definition 3), standard commands (Definition 4), and proof commands (Definition 5).

Translating Commands. Parameter contexts and two auxiliary notations support the command translation that follows.

Definition 3. Given $\vec{\rho} = (x_1\ t_1\ \langle\nu_1\rangle_?) \ldots (x_n\ t_n\ \langle\nu_n\rangle_?)$, define:

$$[\![\vec{\rho}]\!]_{\mathsf{ctx}} := \rho_1^\star \ \ldots\ \rho_n^\star \quad \text{where} \quad \rho_i^\star = \begin{cases} [\bar{x}_i : \tau\, [\![t_i]\!]_{\mathsf{tm}}] & \text{if } \nu_i = \texttt{:implicit}, \\ (\bar{x}_i : \tau\, [\![t_i]\!]_{\mathsf{tm}}) & \text{otherwise.} \end{cases}$$

We further write $[\![t]\!]_{\mathsf{tm}}^{\$}$ for the result of applying $[\![\cdot]\!]_{\mathsf{tm}}$ to t and replacing each free variable x with the pattern variable \$x; and $\mathbf{impl}(\vec{\rho}, t)$ for the sublist of $[\![\vec{\rho}]\!]_{\mathsf{ctx}}$ containing each $x_i \in \vec{\rho}$ that occurs free in t, marked as implicit.

Definition 4. Let δ be a standard Eunoia command. Then $[\![\delta]\!]_{\mathsf{cmd}}$ is the list of LambdaPi commands described as follows:

Table 2. Eunoia-to-LambdaPi encoding. Symbols prefixed with eo. are defined in our hand-written prelude (Sect. 4); $\rightsquigarrow$ and are the function-space symbols introduced in Sect. 3.

Eunoia feature	LambdaPi encoding
Type universe `Type`	term T : Set, carrier $\tau\, T$
Function type `(->` A B`)`	$A \rightsquigarrow B$, with $\tau\,(A \rightsquigarrow B) \hookrightarrow \tau\, A \to \tau\, B$
Dependent type from `(eo::quote` x`)`	$A \rightsquigarrow^{\mathsf{d}} \lambda x. B$ (matchable head, unlike Π)
Parameter attribute `:implicit`	implicit binder $[x : \tau\, T]$
Macro `define`	`symbol` $s\, \vec{\rho} := t$
Higher-order application `(_` t_1 t_2`)`	eo.app t_1 t_2
n-ary `(`$f\, \vec{t}$`)` with attribute	nested binary application; nil terminator via rewrite rule
Binder variables `(eo::var)`	reified into the list type `eo.List`
Program (`program`)	`sequential symbol` + one rewrite rule per case (SR-checked)
Inference rule (`declare-rule`)	`constant symbol` + auxiliary symbol with quote-pattern rewrite when `:args` present
Built-in arithmetic	prelude rules delegating to $\mathbb{Z}, \mathbb{Q}$
Conclusion guard `(eo::requires` l r ψ`)`	ψ applies only when $l \equiv r$ syntactically
Proof command `assume`	`constant symbol` of type `eo.Proof` φ
Proof command `step`	defined symbol + `assert`

1. If δ is a constant declaration, $\delta \vdash s(\vec{\rho}) : t$, the head of $[\![\delta]\!]_{\mathsf{cmd}}$ is `symbol` $\bar{s}$ $[\![\vec{\rho}]\!]_{\mathsf{ctx}} : \tau\, [\![t]\!]_{\mathsf{tm}}$;. If $\delta \vdash s :: \alpha$ and α is `:right-assoc-nil` t_{nil} or `:left-assoc-nil` t_{nil}, the following rewrite rule is also produced, where `eo.nil` returns the nil-terminator of an associative symbol and `eo.as` performs type ascription:
$$\texttt{rule (eo.nil}\ \bar{s}\ \texttt{\$T)} \hookrightarrow \texttt{(eo.as}\ [\![t_{\text{nil}}]\!]_{\mathsf{tm}}\ \texttt{\$T)}$$
2. If δ is a macro definition, $\delta \vdash s(\vec{\rho}) := t$, then $[\![\delta]\!]_{\mathsf{cmd}}$ is `symbol` $\bar{s}$ $[\![\vec{\rho}]\!]_{\mathsf{ctx}}$: $\tau\, [\![t']\!]_{\mathsf{tm}} := [\![t]\!]_{\mathsf{tm}}$ (with the typing omitted if no t' is supplied).
3. If δ is a program declaration with $\delta \vdash s(\vec{\rho})$: `(->` $t_1 \ldots t_n\, t'$`)` and cases `(`l_1 r_1`)` ... `(`l_m r_m`)`, then $[\![\delta]\!]_{\mathsf{cmd}}$ declares $\bar{s}$, where $T := \tau\, [\![$`(->` $t_1 \ldots t_n\, t'$`)`$]\!]_{\mathsf{tm}}$:
$$\begin{aligned}&\texttt{sequential symbol}\ \bar{s}\ \vec{\rho}^{\star} : T;\\ &\texttt{rule}\ [\![l_1]\!]^{\$}_{\mathsf{tm}} \hookrightarrow [\![r_1]\!]^{\$}_{\mathsf{tm}}\\ &\ldots\\ &\texttt{with}\ [\![l_m]\!]^{\$}_{\mathsf{tm}} \hookrightarrow [\![r_m]\!]^{\$}_{\mathsf{tm}}\ ;\end{aligned}$$
where $\vec{\rho}^{\star} := \mathbf{impl}(\vec{\rho}, T)$ binds all of the free parameters in T as implicits.
4. If δ is a rule declaration with `:args` `(`$t_1 \ldots t_n$`)` of type $\tau_1 \ldots \tau_n$, then $\delta \vdash s(\vec{\rho})$: `(-> (eo::quote` t_1`)` ... `(eo::quote` t_n`)` $\tau^{\star}$`)` where $\tau^{\star}$ encodes the premises and conclusion (Sect. 2.1). An auxiliary symbol $s^{\star}$ eliminates the `eo.quote` types by rewriting to $[\![\tau^{\star}]\!]_{\mathsf{tm}}$ on terms matching the argument pat-

terns; s then takes the arguments explicitly and uses $s^\star$ for its return type:
symbol $\bar{s}^\star\ \vec{\sigma} : [\![\tau_1]\!]_{\mathsf{tm}} \to \dots \to [\![\tau_n]\!]_{\mathsf{tm}} \to$ TYPE;
rule $\bar{s}^\star\ [\![t_1]\!]^{\$}_{\mathsf{tm}} \dots [\![t_n]\!]^{\$}_{\mathsf{tm}} \hookrightarrow [\![\tau^\star]\!]^{\$}_{\mathsf{tm}}$;
constant symbol $\bar{s}\ (\alpha_1 : [\![\tau_1]\!]_{\mathsf{tm}}) \dots (\alpha_n : [\![\tau_n]\!]_{\mathsf{tm}}) : (\bar{s}^\star\ \alpha_1 \dots \alpha_n)$

Example 3. We illustrate $[\![\delta]\!]_{\mathsf{cmd}}$ on the four declarations from Example 1:

```
constant symbol = [A : Set] : τ (A ↝ (A ↝ Bool));
constant symbol or : τ (Bool ↝ (Bool ↝ Bool));
rule eo.nil or $T ↪ eo.as false $T;
```

```
constant symbol modus_ponens [F1 F2 : τ Bool]
  : eo.Proof F1
  → eo.Proof (eo.app (eo.app => F1) F2)
  → eo.Proof F2;
```

```
symbol cnf_implies_pos_aux : τ Bool → TYPE;
rule @cnf_implies_pos_aux
  (eo.app (eo.app => $F1) $F2)
  ↪ eo.Proof
     (eo.app (eo.app or (eo.app not (eo.app (eo.app => $F1) $F2)))
        (eo.app (eo.app or (eo.app not $F1)) (eo.app (eo.app or $F2) false)));
constant symbol cnf_implies_pos
  (x1 : τ Bool) : cnf_implies_pos_aux x1;
```

The polymorphic equality = and the associative or translate by case 1, the latter also producing a nil-terminator rewrite rule. modus_ponens has no :args, so case 1 yields its derived type directly. cnf_implies_pos has the compound argument :args((=> F1 F2)), triggering case 4: an auxiliary symbol matches the argument pattern and rewrites to the translated conclusion under eo.Proof.

Translating Proofs

Definition 5. Let Π be a proof command. Then $[\![\Pi]\!]_{\mathsf{cmd}}$ is the list of LambdaPi commands such that:

1. If π is an assumption, then $\pi \vdash s : (\mathtt{Proof}\,\varphi)$:

   constant symbol $\bar{s}$: eo.Proof $[\![\varphi]\!]_{\mathsf{tm}}$;

2. If π is a step, then $\pi \vdash s : (\mathtt{Proof}\ \varphi)$ and $\pi \vdash s := (r\ t_1 \dots t_m\ p_1 \dots p_n)$:

   symbol $\bar{s} := \bar{r}\ \ [\![t_1]\!]_{\mathsf{tm}}\ \dots\ [\![t_m]\!]_{\mathsf{tm}}\ \bar{p}_1\ \dots\ \bar{p}_n$;
   assert $\vdash\ \bar{s}$: eo.Proof $[\![\varphi]\!]_{\mathsf{tm}}$;

   The body applies rule $\bar{r}$ to its arguments then premises. The type is checked separately via assert, which uses LambdaPi's type inference to fill implicit arguments.

Example 4. A QF_UF proof script (top) deriving **false** from (= x0 x0) via **eq-refl** and **eq_resolve** (CPC uses both - and _ in rule names), and its LambdaPi translation (bottom) generated by Definition 4 and Definition 5:

```
(declare-const U Type)
(declare-const x0 U)
(define @t1 () (= x0 x0))
(define @t2 () (not @t1))
(assume @p1 @t2)
(step @p2 (= @t1 true) :rule eq-refl :args (x0))
  ...
(step @p6 false :rule eq_resolve :premises (@p1 @p5))
```

```
require open cpc.Cpc;
constant symbol U : Set;
constant symbol x0 : τ U;
symbol {|@t1|} ≔ eo.app (eo.app = x0) x0;
symbol {|@t2|} ≔ eo.app not {|@t1|};
constant symbol {|@p1|} : eo.Proof {|@t2|};
symbol {|@p2|} ≔ eq-refl (x0);
assert ⊢ {|@p2|} : eo.Proof (eo.app (eo.app = {|@t1|}) true);
  ...
symbol {|@p6|} ≔ eq_resolve ({|@p1|}) ({|@p5|});
assert ⊢ {|@p6|} : eo.Proof false;
```

The preamble's U, x0 translate by case 1 and the define s by case 2 of Definition 4; the assumption @p1 becomes a constant symbol of type eo.Proof $[\![\varphi]\!]_{\mathsf{tm}}$ (case 1 of Definition 5); each step applies its rule to arguments then premises, with assert verifying the conclusion via type inference.

4 Implementation and Results

Our tool eo2lp[1] is an OCaml program (∼5,500 lines) that implements Sect. 3, with a Menhir-generated parser [29] and a back-end built against the LambdaPi OCaml API. A hand-written Prelude.lp module (∼335 lines) bootstraps the type embedding: it declares Set, τ, the function space $\leadsto$, the higher-order application symbol eo.app, Boolean logic, and arithmetic builtins as rewrite rules over LambdaPi's integers/rationals (e.g. eo::add (of_Z i) (of_Z j) $\hookrightarrow$ of_Z ($i + j$)). The prelude also declares the built-in heterogeneous list type eo.List : Set (the encoding of Eunoia's eo::List), together with its constructors eo.List::nil and eo.List::cons. These hold the (eo::var "x_i" T_i) entries produced by **elab** on binder applications (Sect. 2.3, item 2). Closed expressions reduce concretely, so CPC's $run_evaluate program—which recursively delegates to the eo::add, eo::mul, eo::and, eo::not, … builtins—normalises ground terms like (+ 2 3) to 5.

[1] https://github.com/deducteam/eo2lp.

4.1 CPC-MINI

The Cooperating Proof Calculus (CPC) is the Eunoia signature that formalizes cvc5's proof system. The full CPC comprises 35 core modules (~11,000 lines of Eunoia) plus 16 expert modules for additional theories (separation logic, bags, finite fields, floating points, transcendentals). To validate our approach on a manageable portion, we define *CPC-MINI*,[2] a fork of the upstream CPC included as a git submodule of `eo2lp`. It is a modified subset of 22 core modules (~5,000 lines) covering logic, integer arithmetic, arrays, sets, quantifiers, and uninterpreted functions—6 theory modules (57 constants), 8 rule modules (353 rules, 50 programs), and 7 program modules (38 programs, 36 macros), plus a root module `Cpc` that adds 6 further rules (e.g. `evaluate`, `trust`) for 359 rules in total.

CPC-MINI applies three classes of change to the upstream CPC. *(i) Theory pruning:* the expert modules and unsupported core theories (bitvectors, strings, datatypes, reals) are removed, since their primitives are not yet in our prelude. *(ii) Type-parameter tightening:* a few CPC declarations leave their numeric parameter type unconstrained so that the same rule applies at both `Int` and `Real`; we instantiate these to `Int` where required, which suffices for our integer-arithmetic benchmarks. *(iii) Bug fixes:* several upstream typos and mismatched type parameters are patched; we intend to contribute these upstream. For instance, the upstream `$mk_cong_rhs` program in `Uf.eo` typed its arguments with the codomain rather than the domain of its function parameter—a mismatch Ethos missed because it only typechecks program clauses at application time. All 22 modules pass `lambdapi check` with full subject-reduction verification; the entire CPC-MINI signature is translated in ~100 ms and type-checked in ~160 ms—this is one-off work, independent of the proofs to be verified later.

4.2 Proof Benchmarks

To evaluate the translation on proofs, we sampled up to 100 unsatisfiable problems from SMT-LIB for each of the 14 fragments covered by CPC-MINI and obtained Eunoia proof scripts from cvc5, yielding 1,036 proofs. Each proof is translated by `eo2lp` and the result is checked by `lambdapi check` with subject-reduction verification, under a 5-second timeout. Table 3 summarizes the results: 1,002 of 1,036 proofs (97%) are successfully translated and verified, with an average checking time of 0.47 s.

The seven equality and array fragments achieve a near-perfect pass rate (582 of 583), with the single failure being a timeout. The seven linear-arithmetic fragments pass 420 of 453 proofs (93%): QF_UFIDL, UFLIA, and LIA reach 98–100%; the remaining failures are 18 timeouts in QF_LIA and QF_IDL where large proofs exceed the 5-second limit, and 15 type-checking errors in QF_UFLIA caused by CPC rules whose type signatures mix `Real` and `Int`—most prominently `arith-int-geq-tighten`, which declares a `Real` parameter but is applied here in an integer-only context. Such mixed-arithmetic rules are excluded by

[2] https://github.com/ciaran-matthew-dunne/cpc-mini.

Table 3. Benchmark results on 1,036 cvc5 proofs across 14 SMT-LIB fragments, grouped by theory. Each proof is translated by `eo2lp` and the generated LambdaPi file is checked with subject-reduction verification under a 5 s timeout. Columns: number of proofs (**Tot.**), proofs passing (**Pass**), type-checking errors (**Chk.**), timeouts (**T/O**), average time for passing proofs (**Avg.**).

Fragment	Tot.	Pass	%	Chk.	T/O	Avg. (s)
Equality						
`QF_UF`	100	99	99	0	1	0.37
`UF`	100	100	100	0	0	0.51
Arrays						
`QF_AX`	72	72	100	0	0	0.50
`QF_ALIA`	33	33	100	0	0	0.86
`QF_AUFLIA`	100	100	100	0	0	0.33
`ALIA`	78	78	100	0	0	0.59
`AUFLIA`	100	100	100	0	0	0.40
Linear integer arithmetic						
`QF_IDL`	45	43	96	0	2	0.90
`QF_LIA`	56	42	75	0	14	0.32
`LIA`	100	99	99	0	1	0.44
`QF_UFIDL`	15	15	100	0	0	0.28
`QF_UFLIA`	95	80	84	15	0	0.41
`UFIDL`	42	41	98	1	0	0.49
`UFLIA`	100	100	100	0	0	0.45
Total	**1,036**	**1,002**	**97**	**16**	**18**	**0.47**

CPC-MINI's type-parameter tightening (change (ii) above); the failure is therefore a known *type coverage* gap at the `Real`/`Int` boundary, not a semantic mismatch with Ethos. Crucially, *zero* failures are caused by a semantic disagreement: every proof that Ethos accepts and we translate is accepted by LambdaPi up to coverage and time.

5 Conclusion and Future Work

We have presented an automatic translation from Eunoia to the $\lambda\Pi$-calculus modulo rewriting, unlike approaches that hand-write soundness lemmas per rule [16,28]. Translated rules are axioms, but their well-typedness and subject reduction are verified by LambdaPi; `eo2lp` translates all 22 modules of CPC-MINI and verifies 97% of 1,036 proof scripts. Relative to Ethos, our pipeline is slower (0.47 s vs. <0.1 s) and supports a subset of CPC, but adds two guarantees Ethos does not—rule-signature well-typedness and subject reduction of side-condition programs—the latter surfaced upstream CPC bugs. Future work includes extending CPC-MINI to the full CPC, proving CPC rules sound directly in $\lambda\Pi$ [26], and using the typed interpretation of Sect. 3 as a setting for the higher-order extensions proposed for SMT-LIB 3 [7,21].

Acknowledgements. Research reported in this document was supported by an Amazon Research Award, 2022, and by the CARMA associate team, whose funding for collaboration visits helped the progress of this work. The authors thank Haniel Barbosa, Hans-Jörg Schurr, Andrew Reynolds, and Yoni Zohar for discussions on the design of Eunoia and CPC, and on earlier iterations of this work. We also thank Frédéric Blanqui and Théo Winterhalter for their comments on the paper, and the rest of Deducteam for their support. This paper is dedicated to the memory of Gilles Dowek, who initiated this research project in particular and more generally the ecosystem of Dedukti.

Disclosure of Interests. The authors have no competing interests to declare that are relevant to the content of this article.

References

1. Armand, M., et al.: A modular integration of SAT/SMT solvers to Coq through proof witnesses. In: Jouannaud, J.-P., Shao, Z. (eds.) CPP 2011. LNCS, vol. 7086, pp. 135–150. Springer, Heidelberg (2011). https://doi.org/10.1007/978-3-642-25379-9_12
2. Assaf, A., Burel, G.: Translating HOL to Dedukti. In: Kaliszyk, C., Paskevich, A. (eds.) Fourth International Workshop on Proof eXchange for Theorem Proving. EPTCS, vol. 186, pp. 74–88 (2015). https://doi.org/10.4204/EPTCS.186.8
3. Assaf, A., et al.: Dedukti: a logical framework based on the calculus modulo theory (2023). arXiv: 2311.07185 [cs.LO]
4. Backes, J., et al.: Semantic-based automated reasoning for AWS access policies using SMT (2018). https://www.amazon.science/publications/semantic-based-automated-reasoning-for-aws-accesspolicies-using-smt
5. Barbosa, H., et al.: Language and proofs for higher-order SMT (work in progress). In: PxTP, vol. 262, pp. 15–22. EPTCS (2017). https://doi.org/10.4204/EPTCS.262.3
6. Barnett, M., Chang, B.-Y.E., DeLine, R., Jacobs, B., Leino, K.R.M.: Boogie: a modular reusable verifier for object-oriented programs. In: de Boer, F.S., Bonsangue, M.M., Graf, S., de Roever, W.-P. (eds.) FMCO 2005. LNCS, vol. 4111, pp. 364–387. Springer, Heidelberg (2006). https://doi.org/10.1007/11804192_17
7. Barrett, C., Fontaine, P., Tinelli, C.: SMT-LIB 3: bringing higher-order logic to smt
8. Barrett, C., Fontaine, P., Tinelli, C.: The SMT-LIB Standard: Version 2.6. Technical report. Department of Computer Science, The University of Iowa (2017). https://smt-lib.org/papers/smt-lib-referencev2.6-r2024-09-20.pdf
9. Barrett, C., et al.: Chapter 33: Satisfiability modulo theories. In: Frontiers in Artificial Intelligence and Applications, vol. 336, pp. 1267–1329 (2021). https://doi.org/10.3233/FAIA201017
10. Blanchette, J.C., Böhme, S., Paulson, L.C.: Extending sledgehammer with SMT solvers. J. Autom. Reason. **51**(1), 109–128 (2013). https://doi.org/10.1007/S10817-013-9278

11. Boespflug, M., Burel, G.: CoqInE: translating the calculus of inductive constructions into the Π calculus modulo. In: Pichardie, D., Weber, T. (eds.) Second International Workshop on Proof Exchange for Theorem Proving, vol. 878, pp. 44–50. CEUR Workshop Proceedings (2012). https://ceur-ws.org/Vol-878/paper3.pdf
12. Brown, C.E.: Notes on Semantics of and Proofs for SMT (2021). http://grid01.ciirc.cvut.cz/~chad/smtsempfs.pdf
13. Burel, G., Bury, G., Cauderlier, R., Delahaye, D., Halmagrand, P., Hermant, O.: First-order automated reasoning with theories: when deduction modulo theory meets practice. J. Autom. Reason. **64**(6), 1001–1050 (2019). https://doi.org/10.1007/s10817-019-09533-z
14. Bury, G.: Integrating rewriting, tableau and superposition into SMT. Ph.D. thesis. Université Sorbonne Paris Cité (2019). https://theses.hal.science/tel-02612985
15. Champion, A., Mebsout, A., Sticksel, C., Tinelli, C.: The KIND 2 model checker. In: Chaudhuri, S., Farzan, A. (eds.) CAV 2016. LNCS, vol. 9780, pp. 510–517. Springer, Cham (2016). https://doi.org/10.1007/978-3-319-41540-6_29
16. Coltellacci, A., Dowek, G., Merz, S.: Reconstruction of SMT proofs with Lambdapi. In: International Workshop on Satisfiability Modulo Theories, vol. 3725, pp. 13–23. CEUR Workshop Proceedings (2024). https://ceur-ws.org/Vol-3725/paper8.pdf
17. Coltellacci, A., Merz, S.: Checking linear integer arithmetic proofs in Lambdapi. In: FroCoS. LNCS, vol. 15979. Springer (2025). https://doi.org/10.1007/978-3-032-04167-8_20
18. Cousineau, D., Dowek, G.: Embedding pure type systems in the lambda-pi-calculus modulo. In: Della Rocca, S.R. (ed.) TLCA 2007. LNCS, vol. 4583, pp. 102–117. Springer, Heidelberg (2007). https://doi.org/10.1007/978-3-540-73228-0_9
19. Ethos User Manual. https://github.com/cvc5/ethos/blob/main/user_manual.md. Accessed 08 Dec 2024
20. Hondet, G., Blanqui, F.: The new rewriting engine of Dedukti. In: FSCD, vol. 167, p. 16 (2020). https://doi.org/10.4230/LIPIcs.FSCD.2020.35
21. The SMT-LIB Initiative: SMT-LIB Verion 3.0 - A Preliminary Proposal (2021). https://smt-lib.org/version3.shtml
22. isabelle_dedukti: Isabelle component exporting Isabelle proofs to Dedukti. https://github.com/Deducteam/isabelle_dedukti
23. Komel, A.P., Rawson, M., Suda, M.: Case study: verified vampire proofs in the LambdaPi-calculus modulo arXiv: 2503.15541 [cs.L0] (2025)
24. Kosmatov, N., Signoles, J.: Frama-C, a collaborative framework for C code verification: tutorial synopsis. In: Falcone, Y., Sánchez, C. (eds.) RV 2016. LNCS, vol. 10012, pp. 92–115. Springer, Cham (2016). https://doi.org/10.1007/978-3-319-46982-9_7
25. Krajono: A Matita to Dedukti translator. https://deducteam.gitlabpages.inria.fr/krajono/
26. Lachnitt H., et al.: IsaRare: automatic verification of SMT rewrites in Isabelle/HOL. In: TACAS. LNCS, vol. 14572, pp. 311–330. Springer (2024). https://doi.org/10.1007/978-3-031-57246-3_17
27. Mattarei, C., et al.: CoSA: integrated verification for agile hardware design. In: FMCAD. IEEE (2018). https://doi.org/10.23919/FMCAD.2018.8603014
28. Mohamed, A., et al.: Lean-SMT: an SMT tactic for discharging proof goals in lean. In: CAV. LNCS, vol. 15893, pp. 196–220. Springer (2025). https://doi.org/10.1007/978-3-031-98682-6_11
29. Pottier, F., Régis-Gianas, Y.: Menhir Reference Manual (2024). Version 20240715. http://gallium.inria.fr/~fpottier/menhir/

30. Riant, L.: Debugging support in atelier B. In: Masci, P., et al. (eds.) SEFM 2022 Collocated Workshops Revised Selected Papers, pp. 148–155. Springer (2023). https://doi.org/10.1007/978-3-031-26236-4_12
31. Rungta, N.: A billion SMT queries a day. In: Computer Aided Verification (CAV). LNCS. vol. 13371, pp. 3–18. Springer (2022). https://doi.org/10.1007/978-3-031-13185-1_1
32. Schurr, H.-J., et al.: Alethe: towards a generic SMT proof format (extended abstract). In: Electronic Proceedings in Theoretical Computer Science, vol. 336, pp. 49–54 (2021). https://doi.org/10.4204/EPTCS.336.6
33. Stump, A., et al.: SMT proof checking using a logical framework. Formal Methods Syst. Des. **42**(1), 91–118 (2013). https://doi.org/10.1007/S10703-012-0163-3
34. Sutcliffe, G., Blanqui, F., Burel, G.: Proof verification with GDV and LambdaPi - it's a matter of trust. In: Talbert, D.A., Biskri, I. (eds.) FLAIRS Florida Online Journals (2025). https://doi.org/10.32473/FLAIRS.38.1.138642
35. Vaishnav, R.: Lean4Less: eliminating definitional equalities from lean via an extensional-to-intensional translation. In: ICTAC 2025. LNCS. Springer (2025, accepted, to appear). https://rish987.github.io/files/lean4less.pdf

Open Access This chapter is licensed under the terms of the Creative Commons Attribution 4.0 International License (http://creativecommons.org/licenses/by/4.0/), which permits use, sharing, adaptation, distribution and reproduction in any medium or format, as long as you give appropriate credit to the original author(s) and the source, provide a link to the Creative Commons license and indicate if changes were made.

The images or other third party material in this chapter are included in the chapter's Creative Commons license, unless indicated otherwise in a credit line to the material. If material is not included in the chapter's Creative Commons license and your intended use is not permitted by statutory regulation or exceeds the permitted use, you will need to obtain permission directly from the copyright holder.

On Constructing Most General Solutions for Parametric Constraints

Viorica Sofronie-Stokkermans(✉)

University of Koblenz, Koblenz, Germany
sofronie@uni-koblenz.de

Abstract. Let $\mathcal{T}$ be a theory allowing a form of elimination of existential quantifiers (possibly for formulae in a certain class). We analyze possibilities of constructing (most general) solutions w.r.t. $\mathcal{T}$ for formulae of the form $\exists x_1 \dots \exists x_n \phi(x_1, \dots, x_n, y_1, \dots, y_m)$, where ϕ is a quantifier-free conjunction of literals in the signature of $\mathcal{T}$, and the free variables $y_1, \dots, y_m$ are regarded as parameters. We show that in the presence of function symbols which describe "if-then-else" constructions in certain models of $\mathcal{T}$, we can describe the most general solution of such formulae, thus generalizing results about the existence of most general unifiers in discriminator varieties. We illustrate the ideas on examples.

1 Introduction

Finding solutions for parametric constraints is important in many applications. While state of the art SMT-systems can generate models for satisfiable formulae, they usually do not distinguish between parameters (constants/function symbols) and existentially quantified symbols. In this paper we analyze possibilities of constructing parametric solutions and even most general solutions of parametric constraints w.r.t. logical theories $\mathcal{T}$ allowing some form of quantifier elimination. The constraints we consider are formulae of the form

$$\exists x_1, \dots, x_n \phi(x_1, \dots, x_n, y_1, \dots, y_m), \tag{1}$$

where ϕ is a conjunction of literals in the signature of $\mathcal{T}$. Our goals are two-fold:

(i) Find a necessary and sufficient condition on $y_1, \dots, y_m$, seen as parameters, under which $\exists x_1, \dots, x_n \phi(x_1, \dots, x_n, y_1, \dots, y_m)$ evaluates to true w.r.t. $\mathcal{T}$.
(ii) Analyze possibilities of obtaining most general solutions for problems of form (3), i.e. substitutions from which all solutions can be retrieved as instances.

We address (i) by showing that if $\mathcal{T}$ allows a form of quantifier elimination for a fragment to which the formula ϕ belongs, the quantifier free formula $\psi(y_1, \dots, y_m)$ equivalent to $\exists x_1, \dots, x_n \phi(x_1, \dots, x_n, y_1, \dots, y_m)$ w.r.t. $\mathcal{T}$ is such a necessary and sufficient condition. For (ii), we show that in the presence of suitable "if-then-else" constructions in certain models of $\mathcal{T}$ we can effectively describe the most general solution.

© The Author(s) 2026
A. Biere et al. (Eds.): IJCAR 2026, LNAI 16688, pp. 230–247, 2026.
https://doi.org/10.1007/978-3-032-32589-1_14

Our results are inspired by the study of unification in Boolean algebras [3, 4,9,11], in varieties generated by primal algebras [10] and, more generally, in discriminator varieties [5]. Consider the case of unification in Boolean algebras i.e. problems of the form $\exists x((t_a \wedge x) \vee (t_b \wedge \neg x) \approx 0)$, where t_a and t_b are terms containing other variables, which can be considered to be parametric.

It is known [4,9,11] that for every Boolean algebra B, if $a, b \in B$ then the equation $(a \wedge x) \vee (b \wedge \neg x) \approx 0$ has a solution x in B iff $a \wedge b = 0$, and in this case the set of solutions in B is the interval $S = [b, \neg a]$ of B. If $a \wedge b = 0$ then the set of solutions can also be described using the *reproductive solution*, $F : B \rightarrow B$ defined by $F(x) = (b \vee x) \wedge \neg a$, which has the properties:

(a) $F(x) \in S$ for every $x \in B$ (i.e. F is a parametric solution);
(b) For every $x \in S$ we have $F(x) = x$.

For problems of the form $\exists x_1 \dots, \exists x_n (f(x_1 \dots, x_n) \approx 0)$, where f is an n-ary Boolean function, the variables are eliminated successively and the reproductive solutions are reconstructed. If S is the set of all solutions in an algebra B, a reproductive solution is a map $F : B^n \rightarrow B^n$ with (a) $F(x) \in S$ for every $x \in B^n$ and (b) $F(x) = x$ for every $x \in S$. These ideas have been generalized in [10] to varieties generated by primal algebras and in [5] to discriminator varieties, i.e. classes of algebras generated by a subset K of algebras allowing a *switching term*, i.e. a term $s(x, y, u, v)$ with the property that for every algebra $\mathcal{A} \in K$, and all elements $a, b, c, d \in \mathcal{A}$ we have $s(a, b, c, d) = c$ if $a = b$ and $s(a, b, c, d) = d$ if $a \neq b$. Nipkow [10] investigated the links between reproductive solutions and most general unifiers for varieties generated by primal algebras, and Burris [5] proved that discriminator varieties have unitary unification and the most general unifiers can be expressed using the discriminator term (cf. Theorem 1 on page 5). However, these results consider only unification problems without parameters. In this paper we investigate the existence of most general solutions and reproductive solutions for more general parametric problems of the form (3).

While there are many examples of discriminator varieties relevant for computer science (cf. Example 1), the signature of many theories interesting in computer science is not purely equational (i.e. contains also other predicate symbols in addition to equality), and discriminator terms do not necessarily exist.

In this paper we identify examples of logical theories allowing "if-then-else" constructions on some of their models, which generalize the discriminator terms mentioned above. Having such operations is desirable in many cases: In the presence of parameters, solutions of equalities or inequalities in linear arithmetic are often described using case distinctions; also in applications we often consider functions defined using case distinctions. We identify situations in which (parametric) solutions of conjunctions of literals exist, and use these results for obtaining ways of describing most general solutions of such constraints, and to analyze possibilities of deciding if solutions depending only on a set of parameters exist. The main results can be summarized as follows:

- We extend the results on unification in discriminator varieties in [5] to a form of unification with constants.

- We prove that, in extensions of theories allowing quantifier elimination with "if-then-else" constructions, most general solutions of existential formulae can be described by terms.
- We give a criterion for deciding if for existential formulae with free variables $\overline{y}$ w.r.t. theories allowing quantifier elimination there are solutions which do not depend on a subset of the free variables in $\overline{y}$.
- We extend these results to a class of second-order quantifier elimination problems: We show how to find most general solutions of formulae with existentially quantified function symbols in such cases.

These results contribute to better understanding the links between satisfiability checking for parametric problems, symbol elimination, synthesis and unification with constants. Proof details and additional examples can be found in [13].

The Paper is Structured as Follows: In Sect. 2 we introduce the main notions needed in the paper (logical theories, algebra, unification, and in particular unification in discriminator varieties), and prove that the results on unification in discriminator varieties in [5] can be extended to a form of unification with constants. In Sect. 3 we show how most general solutions can be constructed for a class of parametric existential problems in classes of theories allowing quantifier elimination in the presence of "if-then-else"-operators. In Sect. 4 we show how these ideas can be extended to the analysis of certain second-order problems of the form $\exists f F_f(x_1, \dots, x_n)$, where F_f is a quantifier-free formula. In Sect. 5 we present the conclusions and plans for future work.

2 Preliminaries

We here introduce the main notions needed in the paper.

Notation: In what follows we will denote with (indexed versions of) $\overline{x}$ sequences of variables $x_1, \dots, x_n$, and will sometimes write $\exists \overline{x} \phi$ for $\exists x_1, \dots, x_n \phi$.

Logic and Logical Theories. We assume known standard definitions from first-order logic such as structures, models, entailment, satisfiability, unsatisfiability.

We consider signatures of the form $\Pi = (\Sigma, \mathsf{Pred})$, where Σ is a family of function symbols and Pred a family of predicate symbols. Let X be a set of variables. We assume known notions such as terms and formulae over Π with variables X. A Π-structure is a tuple $\mathcal{A} = (A, \{f_\mathcal{A}\}_{f \in \Sigma}, \{p_\mathcal{A}\}_{p \in \mathsf{Pred}})$, where A is a nonempty set (the universe of $\mathcal{A}$, denoted also $|\mathcal{A}|$) and for every $f \in \Sigma$ with arity n, $f_\mathcal{A} : A^n \rightarrow A$, and for every $p \in \mathsf{Pred}$ with arity m, $p_\mathcal{A} \subseteq A^m$. We assume known notions such as evaluation of a Σ-term t in a structure $\mathcal{A}$ w.r.t. a valuation $\beta : X \rightarrow \mathcal{A}$ (denoted $\mathcal{A}(\beta)(t)$) and the evaluation of a Π-formula ϕ in $\mathcal{A}$ w.r.t. β (notation $\mathcal{A}(\beta)(\phi)$). We say that $(\mathcal{A}, \beta) \models \phi$ if $\mathcal{A}(\beta)(\phi)$ is true. We denote "falsum" with $\perp$, so a formula ϕ is unsatisfiable iff $\phi \models \perp$.

In this paper, a theory $\mathcal{T}$ is described by a set of closed formulae (the axioms of the theory). If F and G are formulae we write $F \models G$ (resp. $F \models_{\mathcal{T}} G$) to express the fact that every model of F (resp. every model of F which is also a model of $\mathcal{T}$) is a model of G. The definitions can be extended in a natural way to the case when F is a set of formulae; in this case, $F \models_{\mathcal{T}} G$ if and only if $\mathcal{T} \cup F \models G$. $F \models \perp$ means that F is unsatisfiable; $F \models_{\mathcal{T}} \perp$ means that there is no model of $\mathcal{T}$ which is also a model of F. If there is a model of $\mathcal{T}$ which is also a model of F we say that F is $\mathcal{T}$-consistent. We say that F and G are equivalent (notation: $F \equiv G$) iff $F \models G$ and $G \models F$; F and G are equivalent w.r.t. $\mathcal{T}$ (notation: $F \equiv_{\mathcal{T}} G$) if $F \models_{\mathcal{T}} G$ and $G \models_{\mathcal{T}} F$.

A theory $\mathcal{T}$ with signature Π *allows quantifier elimination* if for every Π-formula ϕ there exists a quantifier-free Π-formula ϕ^* equivalent to ϕ w.r.t. $\mathcal{T}$.

Algebraic Structures. In the case in which $\mathsf{Pred} = \{\approx\}$ (i.e. the only predicate symbol is $\approx$ (equality)), the structures are called Σ-algebras. A class K of algebras satisfies an equation or implication γ (notation: $K \models \gamma$) if for every algebra $\mathcal{A} \in K$ we have $\mathcal{A} \models \gamma$. The equational theory of a class of structures is the set of universal atomic formulas that hold in all members of the class. For a class of algebras, this is simply the collection of all equations that hold in all members of the class. An equational class (or variety) is the class of all algebras in which a given set E of equations holds. We say that a variety $\mathcal{V}$ is generated by a subset $K \subseteq \mathcal{V}$ (notation: $\mathcal{V} = \mathcal{V}(K) = HSP(K)$) iff every algebra in $\mathcal{V}$ is homomorphic to a subalgebra of a product of algebras in K. For further definitions cf. [6].

Unification. We present some notions and results on unification. The problems discussed in this paper are related to unification with constants, so we restrict to this subclass of unification problems. For more general definitions cf. [1,2].

Let $\mathcal{V}$ be an equational theory axiomatized by a set E of equations, Σ its signature, and Δ a signature containing Σ such that $\Delta \backslash \Sigma$ is a set of new constant symbols. Let $\mathcal{S} : \{s_1 = t_1, \dots, s_k = t_k\}$ be a system of equations, where $s_i, t_i \in T_\Delta(Y)$, the set of terms over the signature Δ with variables in Y. Then $\mathcal{S}$ defines an *E-unification problem with free constants* in Δ. Unification with free constants is related to unification in which the terms contain free variables [1–3].

A unification problem $\mathcal{S}$ with free constants in Δ *has a solution* with respect to $\mathcal{V}$ if there is a substitution $\sigma : Y \to T_\Delta(Y)$ such that $\mathcal{V} \models \sigma(s_i) \approx \sigma(t_i)$ for every $1 \leq i \leq k$. If this is the case, σ is a solution (or a unifier) for $\mathcal{S}$. A substitution σ is more general w.r.t. $\mathcal{V}$ than a substitution σ' if there is a substitution δ such that $\mathcal{V} \models \sigma'(x) \approx \delta(\sigma(x))$ for every variable $x \in X$. A substitution σ is a most general solution (or a most general unifier) for $\mathcal{S}$ w.r.t. $\mathcal{V}$ if it is a solution for $\mathcal{S}$ w.r.t. $\mathcal{V}$ and is more general than any other solution for $\mathcal{S}$ w.r.t. $\mathcal{V}$. One can study decidability of unifiability, the existence of unifiers, and their classification according to generality. If every unification problem has a most general unifier w.r.t. $\mathcal{V}$, we say that $\mathcal{V}$ has unitary unification.

Unification in Discriminator Varieties. A term $t(x, y, z)$ is a discriminator term for an algebra $\mathcal{A}$ if for all $a, b, c \in |\mathcal{A}|$,

$$t(a, b, c) = \begin{cases} c & \text{if } a = b \\ a & \text{if } a \neq b. \end{cases}$$

A term $s(x, y, u, v)$ is a switching term for an algebra $\mathcal{A}$ if for all $a, b, c, d \in |\mathcal{A}|$

$$s(a, b, c, d) = \begin{cases} c & \text{if } a = b \\ d & \text{if } a \neq b. \end{cases}$$

From a discriminator term we can construct a switching term and vice-versa, by

$$s(x, y, u, v) = t(t(x, y, u), t(x, y, v), v) \quad \text{and} \quad t(x, y, z) = s(x, y, z, x).$$

A variety $\mathcal{V}$ of algebras is a discriminator variety if there is a class K of algebras which generates $\mathcal{V}$ such that there is a ternary term $t(x, y, z)$ which is a discriminator term for every member of K. If $\mathcal{V}$ is a discriminator variety then $t(x, y, z)$ is a discriminator term for precisely the simple algebras[1] in $\mathcal{V}$ (cf. [5]).

Example 1. *Some examples of discriminator varieties are: The variety of Boolean algebras; the variety of Boolean rings (generated by the ring $\mathbb{Z}_2$) – or more generally the variety generated by the ring $\mathbb{Z}_p$, for p a prime number; the variety of n-valued Post algebras; the variety of cylindric algebras of dimension n; the variety of relation algebras (cf. also [5]).*

Theorem 1. ([5]) *Let $\mathcal{V}$ be a discriminator variety with signature Σ, with switching term $s(x, y, u, v)$ on the simple algebras. Consider the unification problem $\exists x_1 \dots x_n(p(x_1, \dots, x_n) \approx q(x_1, \dots, x_n))$, where $x_1, \dots, x_n$ are variables in a set X. Assume that the unification problem has a solution, and let $t_1, \dots, t_n$ be terms in $T_\Sigma(X)$ such that $\mathcal{V} \models p(t_1, \dots, t_n) = q(t_1, \dots, t_n)$. Then the substitution $\sigma : \{x_1, \dots, x_n\} \to T_\Sigma(X)$ defined by:*

$$\sigma(x_i) = s(p, q, x_i, t_i) \text{ for } 1 \leq i \leq n,$$

is a most general unifier.

The proof given in [5] relies on the following facts: (i) Any discriminator variety $\mathcal{V}$ is generated by the class $\mathcal{V}_S$ of its simple algebras. (ii) For any discriminator variety $\mathcal{V}$, every algebra $\mathcal{A} \in \mathcal{V}$ and for every two terms $a, b \in |\mathcal{A}|$ we have $a = b$ iff $((a, b) \in \theta$ for every maximal congruence θ on $\mathcal{A})$.

Using the fact that in the presence of a discriminator term every conjunction of atoms can be equivalently rewritten (w.r.t. the class of nontrivial simple algebras of $\mathcal{V}$) as an equality between terms, it is concluded that discriminator varieties have unitary unification [5].

[1] A simple algebra is an algebra which has exactly two congruences, the total congruence and the identity.

We show that the proof of Theorem 1 given in [5] can be adapted to unification problems of the form

$$\exists x_1 \dots \exists x_n \,(p(x_1, \dots, x_n, \overline{y}) \approx q(x_1, \dots, x_n, \overline{y})) \tag{2}$$

in which the variables $\overline{y} = y_1, \dots, y_m$ are regarded as "parameters" (problems of type (2) can be regarded as unification with constants).

Theorem 2. *Let $\mathcal{V}$ be a discriminator variety with switching term $s(x, y, u, v)$ on its simple algebras. Consider the unification problem (2). Assume that it has a solution and let $t_1, \dots, t_n$ be terms such that*

$$\mathcal{V} \models \forall \overline{y}\,(p(t_1, \dots, t_n, \overline{y}) \approx q(t_1, \dots, t_n, \overline{y})).$$

Then the following hold (where $\overline{x}$ is $x_1, \dots, x_n$):

(i) The substitution defined by $\sigma(x_i) = s(p(\overline{x}, \overline{y}), q(\overline{x}, \overline{y}), x_i, t_i)$ for $1 \leq i \leq n$, and $\sigma(y) = y$ for every other variable, is a most general unifier.
(ii) For every algebra $\mathcal{A} \in \mathcal{V}$ and every $\beta : \{y_1, \dots, y_m\} \to \mathcal{A}$ let

$$S_{\mathcal{A},\beta} = \{\overline{a} \in |\mathcal{A}|^n \mid p(\overline{a}, \beta(y_1), \dots, \beta(y_m)) = q(\overline{a}, \beta(y_1), \dots, \beta(y_m))\},$$

and let $F : |\mathcal{A}|^n \to |\mathcal{A}|^n$ be defined for all $\overline{a} = (a_1, \dots, a_n) \in |\mathcal{A}|^n$ by:

$$F(a_1, \dots, a_n) = (\mathcal{A}(\beta^{\overline{a}})(\sigma(x_1)), \dots, \mathcal{A}(\beta^{\overline{a}})(\sigma(x_n))),$$

where $\beta^{\overline{a}}(y_i) = \beta(y_i)$ for all $1 \leq i \leq m$ and $\beta^{\overline{a}}(x_i) = a_i$ for all $1 \leq i \leq n$. Then (a) $F(|\mathcal{A}|^n) \subseteq S_{\mathcal{A},\beta}$, and (b) for every $(a_1, \dots, a_n) \in S_{\mathcal{A},\beta}$ we have $F(a_1, \dots, a_n) = (a_1, \dots, a_n)$; hence $F(|\mathcal{A}|^n) = S_{\mathcal{A},\beta}$.

Proof:. The proof can be found in [13]. □

Definition 1. *Let $\mathcal{V}$ be a variety. Consider the unification problem (2). Let X be a set of variables containing all variables occurring in the unification problem (2). Let $\mathcal{A} \in \mathcal{V}$, and $\beta : X \to \mathcal{A}$, and let $S_{\mathcal{A},\beta}$ be the set of solutions of (2) as defined in Theorem 2(ii). We say that a function $F : |\mathcal{A}|^n \to |\mathcal{A}|^n$ is a* reproductive solution *in $\mathcal{A}$ w.r.t. β if it has the property that (a) $F(|\mathcal{A}|^n) \subseteq S_{\mathcal{A},\beta}$ and (b) for every $\overline{a} \in S_{\mathcal{A},\beta}$ we have $F(\overline{a}) = \overline{a}$.*

This notion of reproductive solution generalizes the definitions of reproductive solution for Boolean algebras [11] and for primal algebras [10]. Theorem 2 shows how most general unifiers and reproductive solutions can be constructed for discriminator varieties.

3 If-Then-Else Operations

We would like to prove results similar to those established for discriminator varieties for other theories. We analyze problems of the form

$$\exists x_1 \dots x_n \phi(x_1, \dots, x_n, y_1, \dots, y_m), \tag{3}$$

where ϕ is a quantifier-free formula with free variables $x_1, \dots, x_n, y_1, \dots, y_m$ and analyze the existence of most general solutions w.r.t. a theory $\mathcal{T}$.
In general, discriminator terms do not exist, even for selected models of the theory $\mathcal{T}$. We will use "if-then-else"-operations which behave like the switching terms; usually such operations are easier to evaluate in certain models.

Example 2. *Let $\mathbb{R}[X_1, \dots, X_n]$ be the ring of polynomials in indeterminates $X_1, \dots, X_n$. Two polynomials are equal iff their coefficients are the same; a "switching operation" which tests the equality between polynomials (as formal objects) would be difficult to evaluate, because it would require a form of universal quantification. However, for all $a_1, \dots, a_n \in \mathbb{R}$ we can consider the maximal congruence on $\mathbb{R}[X_1, \dots, X_n]$ described by the ideal $(X_1 - a_1, \dots, X_n - a_n)$; the quotient ring $\mathbb{R}[X_1, \dots, X_n]/(X_1 - a_1, \dots, X_n - a_n)$ is simple (i.e. a simple algebra). Since the ideal $(X_1 - a_1, \dots, X_n - a_n)$ is the kernel of the evaluation map* ev *which maps every polynomial p into the value $p(a_1, \dots, a_n)$ and the equivalence class $[p]$ of a polynomial p in $\mathbb{R}[X_1, \dots, X_n]/(X_1 - a_1, \dots, X_n - a_n)$ can be identified with the value $p(a_1, \dots, a_n)$, there is a ring isomorphism:*

$$\mathbb{R}[X_1, \dots, X_n]/(X_1 - a_1, \dots, X_n - a_n) \simeq \mathbb{R}.$$

The $\mathsf{ite}_\approx$ *operation on $\mathbb{R}[X_1, \dots, X_n]/(X_1 - a_1, \dots, X_n - a_n)$ can be defined by:*

$$\mathsf{ite}_\approx(p(a_1, \dots, a_n), q(a_1, \dots, a_n), c, d) = \begin{cases} c & \text{if } p(a_1, \dots, a_n) = q(a_1, \dots, a_n) \\ d & \text{otherwise} \end{cases}$$

and can be regarded as an operation in (the simple ring) $\mathbb{R}$. ■

In addition, in many cases in the presence of parameters, we are not likely to find terms in the signature of the theory which are solutions for formulae of form (3).

Example 3. *Let $\mathcal{T} = LI(\mathbb{R})$, the theory of linear real arithmetic. Consider the problem $\exists x (x \geq x_1 \wedge x \geq x_2)$. Clearly, $LI(\mathbb{R}) \models \exists x (x \geq x_1 \wedge x \geq x_2)$, but one cannot find a term t built in the signature of linear real arithmetic such that*

$$LI(\mathbb{R}) \models t \geq x_1 \wedge t \geq x_2.$$

In the presence of if-then-else-*operations on $\mathbb{R}$, we can encode definitions by case distinctions as terms:*

$$t = \text{ if } x_1 \geq x_2 \text{ then } x_1 \text{ else } x_2 = \begin{cases} x_1 & \text{if } x_1 \geq x_2 \\ x_2 & \text{otherwise.} \end{cases}$$

■

Thus, if we can define "if-then-else" constructions on suitable models of the theories, we are likely to describe the solutions and the most general solutions for problems of the form (3) using terms over this extended signature.
Let $\mathcal{T}$ be a theory with signature $\Pi = (\Sigma, \mathsf{Pred})$, and $\mathcal{F}$ a subset of the quantifier-free Π-formulae. In what follows we consider the following assumptions:

(A1) There exists a model $\mathcal{A}$ of $\mathcal{T}$ with the property that for every quantifier-free formula $\phi(\overline{x}, \overline{y}) \in \mathcal{F}$ with free variables $\overline{x}, \overline{y}$ we have $\mathcal{T} \models \forall \overline{y} \exists \overline{x}\, \phi(\overline{x}, \overline{y})$ iff $\mathcal{A} \models \forall \overline{y} \exists \overline{x}\, \phi(\overline{x}, \overline{y})$.
(A2) $\mathcal{T}$ allows elimination of existential quantifiers for all formulae in $\mathcal{F}$ (i.e. for every $\phi(x, \overline{y}) \in \mathcal{F}$ there exists a quantifier-free formula $\psi(\overline{y}) \in \mathcal{F}$ such that $\exists x\, \phi(x, \overline{y}) \equiv_{\mathcal{T}} \psi(\overline{y})$).

Remark 1. *If (A1) holds, then for every m-ary predicate symbol $p \in \mathsf{Pred}$ we can define an ite_p function on $\mathcal{A}$ for all $a_1, \dots, a_m, a, b \in \mathcal{A}$ by:*

$$\mathsf{ite}_p(a_1, \dots, a_m, a, b) = \begin{cases} a & \text{if } p_{\mathcal{A}}(a_1, \dots, a_m) \text{ is true} \\ b & \text{if } p_{\mathcal{A}}(a_1, \dots, a_m) \text{ is false.} \end{cases}$$

The interpretation of $\mathsf{ite}_{\approx}(s_1, s_2, t_1, t_2)$ is the same as the semantics of a switching term. In (A1), $\mathcal{A}$ is usually chosen s.t. $p_{\mathcal{A}}(a_1, \dots, a_m)$ is easy to evaluate.

Example 4. *We give some examples of theories $\mathcal{T}$ and formula classes $\mathcal{F}$ which satisfy the assumptions above:*

Bool: *Let* Bool *be the theory of Boolean algebras, and $\mathcal{F}$ the class of all formulae in the signature of* Bool *of the form $\phi(\overline{x}) = p(\overline{x}) \approx q(\overline{x})$. It is known that* $\mathsf{Bool} \models \forall \overline{y} \exists \overline{x}\, (p(\overline{x}, \overline{y}) \approx q(\overline{x}, \overline{y}))$ *iff* $B_2 \models \forall \overline{y} \exists \overline{x}\, (p(\overline{x}, \overline{y}) \approx q(\overline{x}, \overline{y}))$, *where B_2 is the 2-element Boolean algebra (cf. e.g. [3]). The switching term satisfies the conditions of $\mathsf{ite}_{\approx}$. In addition,* Bool *allows quantifier elimination for formulae in $\mathcal{F}$: Indeed every equation of form $p(x, \overline{y}) \approx q(x, \overline{y})$ can be written in the form $(a \wedge x) \vee (b \wedge \neg x) \vee c \approx 0$, where a, b, c are terms containing the variables $\overline{y}$, and $\exists x((a \wedge x) \vee (b \wedge \neg x) \vee c \approx 0) \equiv_{\mathsf{Bool}} (a \wedge b) \vee c \approx 0 \in \mathcal{F}$.*
LI($\mathbb{R}$): *Let $\mathcal{A} = \mathbb{R}$, the model of $LI(\mathbb{R})$ having as support the set of real numbers and the usual interpretation for the function and predicate symbols and $\mathcal{F}$ be the class of all quantifier-free formulae in the signature of $LI(\mathbb{R})$. Then assumption (A1) holds, because for every quantifier-free formula ϕ: $LI(\mathbb{R}) \models \forall \overline{y} \exists \overline{x} \phi(\overline{x}, \overline{y})$ iff $\mathbb{R} \models \forall \overline{y} \exists \overline{y} \phi(\overline{x}, \overline{y})$. Since linear real arithmetic allows quantifier elimination, assumption (A2) holds as well. The operations $\mathsf{ite}_{\approx}, \mathsf{ite}_{\leq}$ on $\mathbb{R}$ are defined, for every $a, b, c, d \in \mathbb{R}$ by:*

$$\mathsf{ite}_{\approx}(a, b, c, d) := \begin{cases} c & \text{if } a = b \\ d & \text{if } a \neq b \end{cases} \qquad \mathsf{ite}_{\leq}(a, b, c, d) := \begin{cases} c & \text{if } a \leq b \\ d & \text{if } a > b. \end{cases}$$

Theory of real closed fields: *We can choose $\mathcal{A} = \mathbb{R}$, the field of real numbers and $\mathcal{F}$ the set of all formulae in the signature of real closed fields. Then assumption (A1) holds, and since the theory of real closed fields allows quantifier elimination assumption (A2) holds as well.* ■

Let $\mathcal{T}$ be a theory satisfying assumption (A1). Then for every m-ary predicate symbol p we can define a function $\mathsf{ite}_{\neg p}$ by $\mathsf{ite}_{\neg p}(\overline{x}, y, z) = \mathsf{ite}_p(\overline{x}, z, y)$.

For every conjunction of literals $\phi = p_1(\overline{x}_1) \wedge \cdots \wedge p_k(\overline{x}_k)$, where $p_i \in \{q_i, \neg q_i\}$, we can define a construction of the form if ϕ then y else z by:

$$\text{if } \bigwedge_{i=1}^{n} p_i(\overline{x}_i) \text{ then } y \text{ else } z := \mathsf{ite}_{p_1}(\overline{x}_1, \mathsf{ite}_{p_2}(\overline{x}_2, \dots, \mathsf{ite}_{p_k}(\overline{x}_k, y, z), \dots z), z).$$

Definition 2. *Let $\mathcal{T}$ be a theory with signature $\Pi = (\Sigma, \mathsf{Pred})$ satisfying assumption (A1), let $\Sigma_{\mathsf{ite}} = \{\mathsf{ite}_p \mid p \in \mathsf{Pred}\} \cup \{\mathsf{ite}_{\neg p} \mid p \in \mathsf{Pred}\}$, let $\Sigma' = \Sigma \cup \Sigma_{\mathsf{ite}}$ and $\Pi' = (\Sigma', \mathsf{Pred})$. Let $\mathcal{A}$ be the model in assumption (A1). The expansion $\mathcal{A}'$ of $\mathcal{A}$ with operations in Σ_{ite} is the* ite-expansion of $\mathcal{A}$; *the theory $\mathcal{T}'$ consisting of all consequences of $\mathcal{A}'$ (a theory with signature Σ') is the* ite-expansion of $\mathcal{T}$.

3.1 Solutions and Most General Solutions

A solution for a problem of the form (3) w.r.t. a theory $\mathcal{T}$ is a tuple of terms $t_1, \dots, t_n$ such that $\mathcal{T} \models \phi(t_1, \dots, t_n, \overline{y})$, or equivalently a substitution σ with $\sigma(x_i) = t_i$ for all $1 \leq i \leq n$ and $\sigma(y_i) = y_i$ for all $1 \leq i \leq m$ such that $\mathcal{T} \models \sigma(\phi)$. We now analyze the existence of most general solutions for problems of the form (3), i.e. solutions σ with the property that for every other solution μ there exists a substitution δ such that for every $x \in X$, $\mathcal{T} \models \mu(x) \approx \delta(\sigma(x))$.

Let $\mathcal{T}$ be a theory with signature Π and let $\mathcal{F}$ be a subset of the quantifier-free Π-formulae such that assumptions (A1) and (A2) hold. Let $\mathcal{T}', \Sigma', \Pi'$ and $\mathcal{A}'$ be as defined in Definition 2. We consider the following additional property:

(A3) For every $\phi(x_1, \dots, x_n, \overline{y}) \in \mathcal{F}$, if $\psi(\overline{y}) \equiv_{\mathcal{T}} \exists x_1 \dots \exists x_n \phi(x_1, \dots, x_n, \overline{y})$ is a quantifier-free formula which exists by assumption (A2), there exist Σ'-terms $t_1, \dots, t_n$ such that $\mathcal{T}' \models (\psi(\overline{y}) \rightarrow \phi(t_1, \dots, t_n, \overline{y}))$.

Example 5. *We present some examples:*

Bool: *The theory of Boolean algebras is a special case, since it has a switching term. We can therefore choose $\mathcal{T}' = \mathsf{Bool}$. Let $\phi(x, \overline{y}) = (a \wedge x) \vee (b \wedge \neg x) \approx 0$, where a and b are terms in the variables $\overline{y}$. We know that $\exists x((a \wedge x) \vee (b \wedge \neg x) \approx 0) \equiv_{\mathsf{Bool}} a \wedge b \approx 0$, and e.g. for the term $t = b$ we have: For every Boolean algebra B and every $\beta : X \rightarrow B$, if $(B, \beta) \models a \wedge b \approx 0$ then $(B, \beta) \models (a \wedge t) \vee (b \wedge \neg t) \approx 0$, so $\mathsf{Bool} \models (a \wedge b \approx 0 \rightarrow \phi(t, \overline{y}))$.*

LI($\mathbb{R}$): *Linear real arithmetic allows quantifier elimination. For this we can, for instance, use methods such as virtual substitution [8], which allows to compute a finite set T of testpoints such that:*

$$\exists x \phi(x, \overline{y}) \equiv \bigvee_{a \in T} \phi(a, \overline{y}).$$

T contains all terms $u_i(\overline{y})$ such that ϕ contains $x \approx u_i(\overline{y})$ or $x \geq u_i(\overline{y})$, and in addition (i) a term denoted with $-\infty$, (ii) terms of the form $u_i(\overline{y}) + \varepsilon$.

- *Instead of* $-\infty$ *we can choose the* Σ'*-expressible term* $t_m - 1$*, where* $t_m = \mathsf{min}(\{s_i(\overline{y}) \mid x \bowtie s_1(\overline{y})$ *occurs in* $\phi\})$ *(here* $\bowtie \in \{\leq, <, \geq, >, \approx, \not\approx\}$*).*
- *We can replace* ε *in the terms* $u_i(\overline{y}) + \varepsilon$ *with* $e/2$*, where* $e = \mathsf{min}(s_i - s_j \mid s_i \neq s_j, x \bowtie s_i, x \bowtie s_j$ *occur in* $\phi, \bowtie \in \{\leq, <, \geq, >, \approx, \not\approx\})$.

If $T = \{t_1, \ldots, t_k\}$*, a solution can be represented by the* Π'*-term:*

$\mathsf{if}\ \phi(t_1, \overline{y})\ \mathsf{then}\ t_1\ \mathsf{else}\ (\mathsf{if}\ \phi(t_2, \overline{y})\ \mathsf{then}\ t_2\ \mathsf{else}(\ldots(\mathsf{if}\ \phi(t_k, \overline{y})\ \mathsf{then}\ t_k\ \mathsf{else}\ c_f)\ldots))$

where c_f *is a special constant which stands for "no solution".*

Theory of real closed fields: *Finding testpoints* $t_1, \ldots, t_n$ *which can be used for obtaining solutions depends on the method for quantifier elimination used (e.g. cylindrical algebraic decomposition computes a decomposition of* $\mathbb{R}^n$ *into regions; the method needs to be adapted to generate suitable testpoints).* ■

In what follows we restrict, for the sake of simplicity (w.l.o.g.), to problems of form (3) for quantifier-free formulae $\phi(\overline{x}, \overline{y})$ which are *conjunctions of literals.* We show that under assumptions (A1), (A2) and (A3) the most general solutions for $\exists\overline{x}\phi(\overline{x}, \overline{y})$ (if solutions exist), can be described as substitutions over the signature $\Pi' = \Pi \cup \Sigma_{\mathsf{ite}}$, which can also be used to describe the reproductive solutions.

Theorem 3. *Let* $\mathcal{T}$ *be a theory satisfying assumptions (A1), (A2) and (A3), and* $\mathcal{T}'$ *be its* ite*-expansion (cf. Definition 2). Let* $\phi(x_1, \ldots, x_n, \overline{y})$ *be a conjunction of literals with free variables* $x_1, \ldots, x_n, \overline{y}$*, and* $\psi(\overline{y}) \equiv_{\mathcal{T}} \exists x_1 \ldots \exists x_n \phi(x_1, \ldots, x_n, \overline{y})$*. Let* $t_1, \ldots, t_n$ *be* Σ'*-terms such that* $\mathcal{T}' \models \psi(\overline{y}) \rightarrow \phi(t_1, \ldots t_n, \overline{y})$*. Let the substitution* σ *be defined by*

$$\sigma(x_i) := \mathsf{if}\ \phi(x_1, \ldots, x_n, \overline{y})\ \mathsf{then}\ x_i\ \mathsf{else}\ t_i,$$

and by $\sigma(y) = y$ *for the other variables.*

(i) The substitution σ *has the following properties:*
  (a) $\mathcal{T}' \models \psi(\overline{y}) \rightarrow \sigma(\phi)$*.*
  (b) For any other substitution μ *w.r.t.* Σ' *such that* $\mathcal{T}' \models \psi(\overline{y}) \rightarrow \mu(\phi)$ *we have* $\mathcal{T}' \models \psi(y) \rightarrow (\mu(\sigma(z)) \approx \mu(z))$ *for any variable* $z \in X$*.*

(ii) Let $\mathcal{A}$ *be as in assumption (A1),* $\mathcal{A}'$ *its* ite*-expansion, and* $\beta : X \rightarrow \mathcal{A}'$ *be such that* $(\mathcal{A}, \beta) \models \psi(\overline{y})$*. Let the set of solutions in* $\mathcal{A}$ *w.r.t.* β *be:*

$$S_{\mathcal{A},\beta} = \{(a_1, \ldots, a_n) \in |\mathcal{A}| \mid (\mathcal{A}, \beta^{\overline{a}}) \models \phi(x_1, \ldots, x_n, \overline{y})\},$$

where $\beta^{\overline{a}} = \beta[x_1 \mapsto a, \ldots, x_n \mapsto a_n]$*, and let*

$$F(a_1, \ldots, a_n) = (\mathcal{A}'(\beta^{\overline{a}})(\sigma(x_1)), \ldots, \mathcal{A}'(\beta^{\overline{a}})(\sigma(x_n))).$$

Then (a) $F(|\mathcal{A}|^n) \subseteq S_{\mathcal{A},\beta}$*, and (b) for every* $\overline{a} \in S_{\mathcal{A},\beta}$ *we have* $F(a_1, \ldots, a_n) = (a_1, \ldots, a_n)$*, hence* $F(|\mathcal{A}|^n) = S_{\mathcal{A},\beta}$*.*

Proof:. (i) (a) Let $\mathcal{A}$ be as in assumption (A1). Let $\mathcal{A}'$ its ite-expansion, and $\beta : X \rightarrow \mathcal{A}'$ such that $(\mathcal{A}', \beta) \models \psi(\overline{y})$. Then $(\mathcal{A}', \beta) \models \phi(t_1, \ldots, t_n, \overline{y})$ and:

$$\mathcal{A}'(\beta)(\sigma(\phi)) = \mathcal{A}'(\beta)(\phi(\sigma(x_1), \ldots, \sigma(x_n), \overline{y})) \\ = \begin{cases} \mathcal{A}'(\beta)(\phi(x_1, \ldots, x_n, \overline{y})) & \text{if } (\mathcal{A}', \beta) \models \phi(x_1, \ldots, x_n, \overline{y}) \\ \mathcal{A}'(\beta)(\phi(t_1, \ldots, t_n, \overline{y})) & \text{otherwise} \end{cases}$$

so $(\mathcal{A}', \beta) \models \sigma(\phi)$. Thus, $\mathcal{T}' \models \forall \overline{y}(\psi(\overline{y}) \rightarrow \sigma(\phi))$.

(i) (b) Let μ be a substitution w.r.t. Σ' with $\mathcal{T}' \models \forall \overline{y}(\psi \rightarrow \mu(\phi))$. Then for all $\beta : X \rightarrow \mathcal{A}'$ with $(\mathcal{A}', \beta) \models \psi(\overline{y})$ we have $(\mathcal{A}', \beta) \models \mu(\phi)$, and therefore:

$$\mathcal{A}'(\beta)(\mu(\sigma(x_i))) = \mathcal{A}'(\beta)(\mu(\mathsf{if}\ \phi\ \mathsf{then}\ x_i\ \mathsf{else}\ t_i)) \\ = \mathcal{A}'(\beta)(\ \mathsf{if}\ \mu(\phi)\ \mathsf{then}\ \mu(x_i)\ \mathsf{else}\ \mu(t_i)) = \mathcal{A}'(\beta)(\mu(x_i)).$$

So, for all $x \in X$: $\mathcal{A}' \models \psi(\overline{y}) \rightarrow \mu(\sigma(x)) \approx \mu(x)$, so $\mathcal{T}' \models \psi(\overline{y}) \rightarrow \mu(\sigma(x)) \approx \mu(x)$.

(ii) (a) Let $(a_1, \ldots, a_n) \in |\mathcal{A}|^n = |\mathcal{A}'|^n$. From the way σ is defined, we have:

$$\mathcal{A}'(\beta^{\overline{a}})(\sigma(x_i)) = \begin{cases} a_i & \text{if } (\mathcal{A}', \beta^{\overline{a}}) \models \phi(x_1, \ldots, x_n, \overline{y}) \\ \mathcal{A}'(\beta^{\overline{a}})(t_i) & \text{otherwise.} \end{cases}$$

Thus, if $(\mathcal{A}', \beta^{\overline{a}}) \models \phi(x_1, \ldots, x_n, \overline{y})$ then $F(a_1, \ldots, a_n) = (a_1, \ldots, a_n) \in S_{\mathcal{A},\beta}$, otherwise $F(a_1, \ldots, a_n) = (\mathcal{A}'(\beta^{\overline{a}})(t_1), \ldots, \mathcal{A}'(\beta^{\overline{a}})(t_n))$, which is also in $S_{\mathcal{A},\beta}$ because $\mathcal{T}' \models \psi(\overline{y}) \rightarrow \phi(t_1, \ldots, t_n, \overline{y})$ and $(\mathcal{A}', \beta) \models \psi(\overline{y})$.

(ii) (b) If $(a_1, \ldots, a_n) \in S_{\mathcal{A},\beta}$ then $(A, \beta^{\overline{a}}) \models \phi(x_1, \ldots, x_n, \overline{y})$, so $F(a_1, \ldots, a_n) = (\mathcal{A}'(\beta^a)(\sigma(x_1)), \ldots, \mathcal{A}'(\beta^a)(\sigma(x_n))) = (a_1, \ldots, a_n)$. □

Example: Linear arithmetic. The following result is an immediate consequence of Theorem 3. Note that the particular solution used in the most general solution can contain if-then-else operations.

Theorem 4. *Let $\mathcal{T} = LI(\mathbb{R})$ and $\phi(x, x_1, \ldots, x_n)$ be a quantifier-free formula in the signature Σ of $\mathcal{T}$. Assume that $\exists x \phi(x, x_1, \ldots, x_n) \equiv \bigvee_{t \in T} \phi(t, x_1, \ldots, x_n)$, where the set of testpoints $T = \{t_1, \ldots, t_m\}$ is a set of Σ' terms. For all $x_1, \ldots, x_n$, if $\bigvee_{t \in T} \phi(t, x_1, \ldots, x_n)$ holds, the most general solution can be expressed by:*

$$\sigma(x) = \mathsf{if}\ \phi(x, x_1, \ldots, x_n)\ \mathsf{then}\ x\ \mathsf{else}\ (\mathsf{if}\ \phi(t_1, x_1, \ldots, x_n)\ \mathsf{then}\ t_1\ \mathsf{else} \\ (\mathsf{if}\ \phi(t_2, x_1, \ldots, x_n)\ \mathsf{then}\ t_2\ \mathsf{else}(...(\mathsf{if}\ \phi(t_m, x_1, \ldots, x_n)\ \mathsf{then}\ t_m\ \mathsf{else}\ c_f)...)))$$

where c_f is a selected constant which stands for "no solution".

Example 6. *Let $\mathcal{T} = LI(\mathbb{R})$ and $\phi(x, x_1, x_2) = (x \geq x_1) \wedge (x \geq x_2)$. It is clear that $\exists x \phi(x, x_1, x_2)$ is true. To find a solution we proceed as follows: The set of testpoints is $T = \{-\infty, x_1, x_2\}$, and $\exists x \phi(x, x_1, x_2) \equiv \phi(x_1, x_1, x_2) \vee \phi(x_2, x_1, x_2)$. Therefore, a solution for $\exists x \phi(x, x_1, x_2)$ is the* if-then-else-*term:*

$$\begin{aligned} t &= \textsf{if } \phi(x_1, x_1, x_2) \textsf{ then } x_1 \textsf{ else } (\textsf{ if } \phi(x_2, x_1, x_2) \textsf{ then } x_2 \textsf{ else } x_1) \\ &= \textsf{if } (x_1 \geq x_1 \wedge x_1 \geq x_2) \textsf{ then } x_1 \textsf{ else } (\textsf{ if } (x_2 \geq x_1 \wedge x_2 \geq x_2) \textsf{ then } x_2 \textsf{ else } x_1) \\ &= \textsf{if } x_1 \geq x_2 \textsf{ then } x_1 \textsf{ else } x_2. \end{aligned}$$

The substitution σ with $\sigma(x) =$ if $\phi(x, x_1, x_2)$ then x else t*, $\sigma(x_1) = x_1$ and $\sigma(x_2) = x_2$ is the most general solution.* ■

Example 7. *Let $\phi(x, y, z) = (x + y + z \geq 3 \wedge y + 2z \leq 2)$. There is a value $x \in \mathbb{R}$ such that $\phi(x, y, z)$ holds iff $\exists x(x + y + z \geq 3 \wedge y + 2z \leq 2) \equiv y + 2z \leq 2$ holds.*
If $y + 2z \leq 2$, a solution for $\exists x \phi$ is $t = 3 - y - z$. The most general solution is:

$$\sigma(x) = \textsf{ if } x + y + z \geq 3 \wedge y + 2z \leq 2 \textsf{ then } x \textsf{ else } 3 - y - z.$$

This means: if $\beta(x) = a, \beta(y) = b, \beta(z) = c \in \mathbb{R}$ with $b + 2c \leq 2$ then we have:

$$(\mathbb{R}, \beta) \models y + 2z \leq 2 \quad \textit{and} \quad \mathbb{R}(\beta)(\sigma(x)) = \begin{cases} a & \textit{if } a + b + c \geq 3 \\ 3 - b - c & \textit{if } a + b + c < 3 \end{cases}$$ ■

Example: Boolean algebras. For $\mathcal{T} =$ Bool the results specialize (with the remarks on the choice of $\mathcal{T}' =$ Bool in Example 5) to Theorem 2.

3.2 Solutions Depending on Given Variables

Consider the problem $\exists x \phi(x, y_1, \dots, y_n)$. We analyze possibilities of deciding whether there exist solutions which do not depend on a given variable y_i, in situations in which the theory $\mathcal{T}$ *allows quantifier elimination.*

Theorem 5. *Let $\mathcal{T}$ be a theory allowing quantifier elimination, and $\phi(x, y_1, \dots, y_n)$ be a quantifier-free formula with variables $x, y_1, \dots, y_n$. Then we can decide whether there is a solution $x = t(y_{i_1}, \dots, y_{i_k})$ for $\exists x \phi(x, y_1, \dots, y_n)$ which only contains variables in a subset $\{y_{i_1}, \dots, y_{i_k}\} \subseteq \{y_1, \dots, y_n\}$.*

Proof:. Let
ψ be a quantifier-free formula with $\psi(y_1, \dots, y_n) \equiv \exists x \phi(x, y_1, \dots, y_n)$. If $\overline{y}$ is the sequence of variables in $\{y_1, \dots, y_n\} \backslash \{y_{i_1}, \dots, y_{i_k}\}$, let
$\xi(x', y_{i_1}, \dots, y_{i_k}) \equiv_{\mathcal{T}} \forall \overline{y}(\psi(y_1, \dots, y_n) \rightarrow \phi(x', y_1, \dots, y_n))$, where x' is a new variable. We prove that the following are equivalent:

(i) There exists a term t which only contains the variables $\{y_{i_1}, \dots, y_{i_k}\}$ such that $\mathcal{T} \models \forall \overline{y}(\psi(y_1, \dots, y_n) \rightarrow \phi(t, y_1, \dots, y_n))$.
(ii) There exists a term t which only contains the variables $\{y_{i_1}, \dots, y_{i_k}\}$ such that $\mathcal{T} \models \xi(t, y_{i_1}, \dots, y_{i_k})$.

(i) $\Rightarrow$ (ii): Let t be a term only containing the variables $\{y_{i_1}, \dots, y_{i_k}\}$ with $\mathcal{T} \models \forall \overline{y}(\psi(y_1, \dots, y_n) \rightarrow \phi(t, y_1, \dots, y_n))$. As $\xi(t, y_{i_1}, \dots, y_{i_k}) \equiv_{\mathcal{T}} \forall \overline{y}(\psi(y_1, \dots, y_n) \rightarrow \phi(t, y_1, \dots, y_n))$, we have $\mathcal{T} \models \xi(t, y_{i_1}, \dots, y_{i_k})$.

(ii) $\Rightarrow$ (i): Let t be a term only containing the variables $\{y_{i_1}, \dots, y_{i_k}\}$ with $\mathcal{T} \models \xi(t, y_{i_1}, \dots, y_{i_k})$. Then $\mathcal{T} \models \forall \overline{y}(\psi(y_1, \dots, y_n) \rightarrow \phi(t, y_1, \dots, y_n))$. □

Example 8. (Example 6 ctd.) *A most general solution for $\exists x(x \geq x_1 \wedge x \geq x_2)$ is the substitution which is the identity for all variables $y \neq x$ and with*

$$\sigma(x) = \text{if } x \geq x_1 \wedge x \geq x_2 \text{ then } x \text{ else } (\text{if } x_1 \geq x_2 \text{ then } x_1 \text{ else } (\text{if } x_2 \geq x_1 \text{ then } x_2 \text{ else } c_f))$$

We can test whether there is a solution which does not depend on x_1 as follows. Note that $\exists x(x \geq x_1 \wedge x \geq x_2) \equiv \top$, and $\forall x_1(\top \rightarrow x' \geq x_1 \wedge x' \geq x_2) \equiv \bot$, so there is no solution which does not depend on x_1. ■

Example 9. (Example 7 ctd.) *Let $\phi(x, y, z) = (x + y + z \geq 3 \wedge y + 2z \leq 2)$. There is a value $x \in \mathbb{R}$ such that $\phi(x, y, z)$ holds iff $\exists x \phi(x, y, z)$ holds. We know that $\exists x \phi(x, y, z) = \exists x(x + y + z \geq 3 \wedge y + 2z \leq 2) \equiv y + 2z \leq 2$. Assume that $y + 2z \leq 2$. To check if there is a solution $x = t(z)$ for ϕ which does not depend on y we proceed as follows: We use quantifier elimination and obtain:*

$$\begin{aligned} &\forall y(y + 2z \leq 2 \rightarrow x' + y + z \geq 3 \wedge y + 2z \leq 2) \\ &\equiv \neg[\exists y(y \leq 2 - 2z \wedge x' + y + z < 3)] \equiv \neg \top \equiv \bot \end{aligned}$$

so there is no solution for x which does not depend on y.

Consider now the formula $\phi(x, y, z) = (x + y + z \leq 3 \wedge y + 2z \leq 2)$. There exists a value $x \in \mathbb{R}$ such that $\phi(x, y, z)$ holds iff $\exists x \phi(x, y, z)$ holds. Also in this case we have $\exists x \phi(x, y, z) \equiv y + 2z \leq 2$. To check if there is a solution $x = t(z)$ for ϕ which does not depend on y (under the assumption that $y + 2z \leq 2$) we proceed as follows: We use quantifier elimination and obtain:

$$\begin{aligned} &\forall y(y + 2z \leq 2 \rightarrow x' + y + z \leq 3 \wedge y + 2z \leq 2) \\ &\quad \equiv \neg[\exists y(y \leq 2 - 2z \wedge x' + y + z > 3)] \equiv \neg(3 - x' - z < 2 - 2z) \equiv x' \leq z + 1. \end{aligned}$$

One can see for instance that – under the assumption that $y + 2z \leq 2$ – we have a solution depending only on z (e.g. $t = z + 1$ or $t = z$ are such solutions). ■

The theory of Boolean algebras does not allow in general quantifier elimination for formulae containing negative literals, so Theorem 5 cannot be applied. In [13] we present a situation in which the elimination of the universal quantifiers is possible, and Theorem 5 can be applied.

Algorithm 1. Algorithm for Function Elimination

Input: $\mathcal{T} := \mathcal{T}_0 \cup \mathsf{UIF}_\Sigma$ where $\mathcal{T}_0$ has signature Π_0 and $\Sigma = \Sigma_s \cup \Sigma_e$;
G, a finite set of flat $(\Pi_0 \cup \Sigma)$-clauses with variables $\overline{x}$;
Output: Quantifier-free Π_s-formula Γ with variables $\overline{x}$.

Step 1 Compute from G the set of Π_0-clauses $G_0 \cup \mathsf{Con}_0$ by introducing, in a bottom-up manner, new variables $x_t \in C$ for subterms $t=g(x_1, \dots, x_k)$ where $g \in \Sigma$, and storing the definitions $x_t \approx g(x_1, \dots, x_k)$ in a set Def, and:

$\mathsf{Con}_0 = \{\bigwedge_{i=1}^n x_i \approx y_i \rightarrow x \approx y \mid f(x_1, \dots, x_n) \approx x, f(y_1, \dots, y_n) \approx y \in \mathsf{Def}\}$

Step 2 Let $G_1 := G_0 \cup \mathsf{Con}_0$. Among the variables in G_1, identify
(i) the sets $\overline{x}_e$ and resp. $\overline{x}_s$ consisting of variables x_f introduced by a definition $x_f := f(x_1, \dots, x_k)$ with $f \in \Sigma_e$ resp. $f \in \Sigma_s$;
(ii) the remaining variables $\overline{x}$.
Consider the formula $\exists \overline{x}_e G_1(\overline{x}, \overline{x}_s, \overline{x}_e)$.

Step 3 Compute a quantifier-free formula $\Gamma_1(\overline{x}, \overline{x}_s)$ equivalent to $\exists \overline{x}_e G_1(\overline{x}, \overline{x}_s, \overline{x}_e)$ w.r.t. $\mathcal{T}_0$ using a method for quantifier elimination in $\mathcal{T}_0$.

Step 4 Let $\Gamma(\overline{x})$ be the formula obtained by replacing back in $\Gamma_1(\overline{x}, \overline{x}_s)$ the variables x_g in $\overline{x}_s$ introduced by definitions $x_g := g(x_1, \dots, x_k)$ with the terms $g(x_1, \dots, x_k)$.

4 Second-Order Quantifier Elimination

We now analyze how the idea introduced before can be extended to the analysis of second-order problems of the form

$$\exists f \, \phi(x_1, \dots, x_n),$$

where ϕ is a quantifier-free formula in the variables $x_1, \dots, x_n$ in a signature containing the function symbol f w.r.t. a theory $\mathcal{T}$.

We restrict to extensions $\mathcal{T} = \mathcal{T}_0 \cup \mathsf{UIF}_\Sigma$ of a theory $\mathcal{T}_0$ (with signature Π_0) with uninterpreted function symbols in a set Σ. The theory $\mathcal{T}_0 \cup \mathsf{UIF}_\Sigma$ does not in general allow quantifier elimination or second-order quantifier elimination. In [15], a method for eliminating function symbols with arity ≥ 1 was proposed for sets G of flat ground formulae w.r.t. a certain class of theory extensions (local theory extensions, cf. [14]). In Algorithm 1 we present a specialization of the method proposed in [15] to extensions with uninterpreted function symbols.

We identify a situation in which a most general solution w.r.t. $\mathcal{T} = \mathcal{T}_0 \cup \mathsf{UIF}_\Sigma$ can be found. We assume that $\mathcal{T}_0$ satisfies assumptions $(A1), (A2)$ and $(A3)$.

In what follows we assume, w.l.o.g., that $\phi = G$, where G is a conjunction of literals. Here we will only consider the case in which G is flat (i.e. the only arguments of function symbols with arity ≥ 1 are variables) and Algorithm 1 can be applied. The case in which G is not flat is discussed in [13].

Theorem 6. *Let $\mathcal{T} = \mathcal{T}_0 \cup \mathsf{UIF}_\Sigma$ be a theory with signature Π, where $\mathcal{T}_0$ allows quantifier elimination, and let G be a set of flat Π-clauses. Algorithm 1 applied to the case when $\Sigma_e = \{f\}$ and $\Sigma_s = \Sigma \backslash \{f\}$, returns a formula equivalent to $\exists f G$ w.r.t. $\mathcal{T}_0 \cup \mathsf{UIF}_\Sigma$.*

Proof:. The proof can be found in [13]. □

We make the following assumptions and use the following notation.

(A) $\mathcal{T} = \mathcal{T}_0 \cup \mathsf{UIF}_\Sigma$, where $\mathcal{T}_0$ is a theory with signature Π_0 satisfying assumptions (A1), (A2), (A3) with $\mathcal{F}$ being the set of all quantifier-free formulae.
(B) Let $\mathcal{A}$ as in assumption (A1), $\Sigma_0', \Pi_0' = (\Sigma_0', \mathsf{Pred})$, $\mathcal{A}'$, and $\mathcal{T}_0'$ as in Definition 2, and let $\Sigma' = \Sigma_0' \cup \Sigma$, and $\Pi' = (\Sigma', \mathsf{Pred})$. Let $\mathcal{T}'$ be the theory described by $\mathcal{M} = \{\mathcal{B} \mid \mathcal{B}$ is a Π'-structure with $\mathcal{B}_{|\Pi_0'} = \mathcal{A}'\}$, consisting of all Π-structures whose reduct to Π_0' is $\mathcal{A}'$.
(C) G is a conjunction of flat literals i.e. (with the notation used in Algorithm 1) $G_1 = G_0 \cup \mathsf{Con}_0 \in \mathcal{F}$, $\Sigma_e = \{f\}$ and $\Sigma_s = \Sigma \backslash \{f\}$. If $f_1(\overline{z})$ can be described by a Σ'-term we denote by $G[f \mapsto f_1]$ the formula obtained from G by replacing all occurrences $f(\overline{z})$ with the term $f_1(\overline{z})$.

Lemma 7. *Assume that $\mathcal{T}$, G and f satisfy conditions (A), (B), (C). Let σ be the most general solution w.r.t. $\mathcal{T}_0$ for the problem $\exists \overline{x}_e G_1(\overline{x}, \overline{x}_s, \overline{x}_e)$ obtained at the end of Step 2 of Algorithm 1, if Γ_1 holds. For every model $\mathcal{B}$ of $\mathcal{T}'$ in $\mathcal{M}$ and every valuation β with $(\mathcal{B}, \beta) \models \Gamma$ let $\mathcal{C}$ be obtained from $\mathcal{B}$ by interpreting all function symbols in Σ_s as in $\mathcal{B}$ and interpreting $f_\mathcal{C} = f_0$, where for all $a_1, \dots, a_m \in |\mathcal{A}| = |\mathcal{C}|$:*

$$f_0(a_1, \dots, a_m) := \begin{cases} \mathcal{B}(\beta)(\sigma(x_f)) & \text{if for all } i \text{ we have } a_i = \beta(x_{j_i}) \\ & \text{with } f(x_{j_1}, \dots, x_{j_m}) \approx x_f \in \mathsf{Def} \\ k_\mathcal{B} & \text{otherwise} \end{cases}$$

where k is a fixed constant in $\Pi_0 \cup \Sigma \cup C$. Then $(\mathcal{C}, \beta) \models G$.

Let $\overline{x}_e = x_1^f, \dots, x_k^f$, introduced by definitions $x_i^f = f(x_{j_1}^i, \dots, x_{j_m}^i)$, and $f_0(\overline{z}) = (\mathsf{if}\ f(\overline{z}) \approx x_1^f\ \mathsf{then}\ \sigma(x_1^f)\ \mathsf{else} \dots \mathsf{if}\ f(\overline{z}) \approx x_k^f\ \mathsf{then}\ \sigma(x_k^f)\ \mathsf{else}\ k)$. Then $(\mathcal{B}, \beta) \models G[f \mapsto f_0]$.

Proof:. Direct consequence of the proof of Theorem 6 and of assumptions (A1), (A2), (A3). The proof can be found in [13]. □

Theorem 8. *Assume that $\mathcal{T}$, G and f satisfy conditions (A), (B), (C). Let Γ be the formula returned by Algorithm 1 when used to eliminate f from G. Let f_0 be the particular solution in Lemma 7. Then $\tilde{\sigma}(f) = (\mathsf{if}\ G\ \mathsf{then}\ f\ \mathsf{else}\ f_0)$ is the most general solution for $\exists f G(\overline{x})$ under assumptions Γ, i.e.:*

(1) For every $\mathcal{B}$ model of $\mathcal{T}'$ in $\mathcal{M}$ and every $\beta : X \to \mathcal{B}$, if $(\mathcal{B}, \beta) \models \Gamma(\overline{x})$ then there is a model $\mathcal{C}$ of $\mathcal{T}'$ in $\mathcal{M}$ with $\mathcal{C}_{|\Pi_0 \cup \Sigma_s} = \mathcal{B}_{\Pi_0 \cup \Sigma_s}$, and

$$f_\mathcal{C}(a_1, \dots, a_n) = \begin{cases} f_\mathcal{B}(a_1, \dots, a_n) & \text{if } (\mathcal{B}, \beta) \models G \\ f_{0\mathcal{B}}(a_1, \dots, a_n) & \text{otherwise} \end{cases}$$

has the property that $(\mathcal{C}, \beta) \models G$, so $(\mathcal{B}, \beta) \models G[f \mapsto \tilde{\sigma}(f)]$.

(2) For every other solution $\mu(f)$ for which $\mathcal{T}' \models \Gamma \rightarrow G[f \mapsto \mu(f)]$ we have $\mathcal{T}' \models \Gamma \rightarrow \forall \overline{z}\, (\mu(\tilde{\sigma}(f))(\overline{z}) \approx \mu(f)(\overline{z}))$.

Proof:. The proof is given in [13]. □

Example 10. *Let $\mathcal{T} = LI(\mathbb{R}) \cup \mathsf{UIF}_{\{f,g\}}$ and $G = f(x_1) \approx g(x_2) \wedge f(x_1) \leq x_3 \wedge g(x_2) \geq x_4$. We can use Algorithm 1 to eliminate f as follows:*

Step 1: *With the definitions $\mathsf{Def} = \{x_f = f(x_1), x_g = g(x_2)\}$ we obtain $x_f \approx x_g \wedge x_f \leq x_3 \wedge x_g \geq x_4$.*
Step 2: *Only x_f needs to be eliminated. The test point is $T = \{x_g\}$.*
Step 3: *We obtain $\exists x_f(x_f \approx x_g \wedge x_f \leq x_3 \wedge x_g \geq x_4) \equiv x_g \leq x_3 \wedge x_g \geq x_4$.*
Step 4: *We replace back constants and obtain: $\Gamma = g(x_2) \leq x_3 \wedge g(x_2) \geq x_4$.*

Under the condition that $g(x_2) \leq x_3 \wedge g(x_2) \geq x_4$ a solution exists. It can be constructed as follows:

$$f_0(x) = \begin{cases} g(x_2) & \textit{if } x \approx x_1 \\ k & \textit{otherwise} \end{cases} = \mathsf{if}\ x \approx x_1\ \mathsf{then}\ g(x_2)\ \mathsf{else}\ k$$

Based on this, we can construct the most general solution:

$$\tilde{\sigma}(f)(x) = \mathsf{if}\ f(x_1) \approx g(x_2) \wedge f(x_1) \leq x_3 \wedge g(x_2) \geq x_4\ \mathsf{then}\ f(x)\ \mathsf{else}\ f_0(x).$$

■

5 Conclusion

We analyzed possibilities of constructing most general solutions of formulae of the form $\exists x_1, \ldots, \exists x_n \phi(x_1, \ldots, x_n, y_1, \ldots, y_m)$ w.r.t. certain theories $\mathcal{T}$ allowing quantifier elimination, where ϕ is a quantifier-free conjunction of literals in the signature of $\mathcal{T}$, and the free variables $y_1, \ldots, y_m$ are regarded as parameters. We proved that if we can extend the language with a type of "if-then-else" constructions, we can describe the most general solution of such formulae as terms. The idea generalizes results about the existence of most general unifiers in discriminator varieties. We then considered possibilities of generating most general solutions for certain problems related to second-order elimination in certain extensions of theories allowing quantifier elimination with free function symbols.

In future work we would like to extend the results to the situation in which the extension with if-then-else constructs $\mathcal{T}'$ is not described by one model only, but by a class of models, and to better understand the links between these results and results on unification for varieties generated by primal algebras, in discriminator varieties and beyond. We would also like to analyze the applicability of the results on generating most general solutions for second order existential constraints in the context of higher-order unification (cf. e.g. [7,12]).

Acknowledgments. We thank the reviewers for their helpful comments. The research reported here was funded by the Deutsche Forschungsgemeinschaft (DFG, German Research Foundation) – grant 465447331.

Disclosure of Interests. The author has no competing interests to declare.

References

1. Baader, F., Schulz, K.: Unification in the union of disjoint equational theories: combining decision procedures. J. Symbolic Comput. **21**, 211–243 (1996)
2. Baader, F., Snyder, W.: Unification theory. In: Robinson, J.A., Voronkov, A. (eds.) Handbook of Automated Reasoning, vol. 1, chap. 8, pp. 445–532. Elsevier (2001)
3. Baader, F.: On the complexity of boolean unification. Inf. Process. Lett. **67**(4), 215–220 (1998)
4. Boole, G.: A Mathematical Analysis of Logic. Blackwell (1847, Reprinted 1948)
5. Burris, S.: Discriminator varieties and symbolic computation. J. Symbolic Comput. **13**, 175–207 (1992)
6. Burris, S., Sankappanavar, H.: A Course in Universal Algebra. Springer, New York, NY(1981)
7. Dowek, G.: Higher-order unification and matching. In: Robinson, J.A., Voronkov, A. (eds.) Handbook of Automated Reasoning, vol. 2, pp. 1009–1062. Elsevier and MIT Press (2001)
8. Loos, R., Weispfenning, V.: Applying linear quantifier elimination. Comput. J. **36**(5), 450–462 (1993)
9. Löwenheim, L.: Über das Auflösungsproblem im logischen Klassenkalkül. Sitzungsber. Berl. Math. Gesell. **7**, 89–94 (1908)
10. Nipkow, T.: Unification in primal algebras, their powers and their varieties. J. ACM **37**(4), 742–776 (1990)
11. Rudeanu, S.: Boolean Functions and Equations. North-Holland, Amsterdam (1974)
12. Snyder, W., Gallier, J.H.: Higher-order unification revisited: complete sets of transformations. J. Symbolic Comput. **8**(1/2), 101–140 (1989)
13. Sofronie-Stokkermans, V.: On constructing most general solutions for parametric constraints (extended preprint). Extended version, available on ArXiv and under http://sofronie.home.uni-koblenz.de/papers/ijcar-2026-extended.pdf
14. Sofronie-Stokkermans, V.: Hierarchic reasoning in local theory extensions. In: Nieuwenhuis, R. (ed.) CADE 2005. LNCS (LNAI), vol. 3632, pp. 219–234. Springer, Heidelberg (2005). https://doi.org/10.1007/11532231_16
15. Sofronie-Stokkermans, V.: On symbol elimination and uniform interpolation in theory extensions. In: Barrett, C.W., Waldmann, U. (eds.) Automated Deduction - CADE 30 - 30th International Conference on Automated Deduction, Stuttgart, Germany, July 28–31, 2025, Proceedings. Lecture Notes in Computer Science, vol. 15943, pp. 35–55. Springer, Cham (2025). https://doi.org/10.1007/978-3-031-99984-0_3

Open Access This chapter is licensed under the terms of the Creative Commons Attribution 4.0 International License (http://creativecommons.org/licenses/by/4.0/), which permits use, sharing, adaptation, distribution and reproduction in any medium or format, as long as you give appropriate credit to the original author(s) and the source, provide a link to the Creative Commons license and indicate if changes were made.

The images or other third party material in this chapter are included in the chapter's Creative Commons license, unless indicated otherwise in a credit line to the material. If material is not included in the chapter's Creative Commons license and your intended use is not permitted by statutory regulation or exceeds the permitted use, you will need to obtain permission directly from the copyright holder.

Program Synthesis for Non-linear Real Arithmetic: Going Beyond Realizability

S. Akshay[1], Supratik Chakraborty[1], R. Govind[2,3(✉)], and Aniruddha R. Joshi[4]

[1] IIT Bombay, Mumbai, India
{akshayss,supratik}@cse.iitb.ac.in
[2] The Institute of Mathematical Sciences, Chennai, India
govind@imsc.res.in
[3] Homi Bhabha National Institute, Mumbai, India
[4] University of California at Berkeley, Berkeley, USA
aniruddhajoshi@berkeley.edu

Abstract. We study the problem of synthesizing programs from non-linear real arithmetic (NRA) specifications. Existing techniques, such as syntax-guided synthesis (SyGuS), fail to synthesize programs when the specification is *unrealizable.* We argue this is unsatisfactory in many situations, and aim to synthesize programs from arbitrary NRA specifications, such that for any input, the synthesized program either produces outputs satisfying the specification or reports non-existence of any such output. To avoid rounding errors inherent in floating-point arithmetic, we restrict our programs to work on rational inputs and outputs.

We first show that our variant of the synthesis problem is as hard as a long-standing open problem in number theory, and that synthesizing loop-free programs from arbitrary NRA specifications with rational inputs and outputs is impossible in general. Second, we present a sound and complete synthesis algorithm for the case where the specification involves a single output variable. We also show that for realizable specifications, a program generated by SyGuS for NRA (real inputs and outputs) serves as a solution to our problem, where inputs and outputs are rationals. Third, we provide a sound (but necessarily incomplete) synthesis algorithm for the general case of specifications. We have implemented our approach in a prototype tool called NQSynth that solves many benchmarks beyond the reach of state-of-the-art SyGuS tools, even when we render the specifications realizable.

1 Introduction

Automated program synthesis, or generating programs automatically from specifications, is arguably one of the holy grails of computer science. While the problem has a long and storied history [12,54], recent years have seen a surge of interest in synthesizing programs from logical specifications in specialized theories, viz. propositional logic, theory of bit-vectors, (non-)linear real/integer arithmetic, and the like [1,2,10,11,30,32,33,40,41,48,51]. One such theory, with

© The Author(s) 2026
A. Biere et al. (Eds.): IJCAR 2026, LNAI 16688, pp. 248–266, 2026.
https://doi.org/10.1007/978-3-032-32589-1_15

applications spanning multiple domains [19,26,29,35,39,57], is the quantifier-free theory of **N**on-linear **R**eal **A**rithmetic, also called NRA.

Over the last decade, **Syn**tax-**Gu**ided **S**ynthesis, or SyGuS, has emerged as a powerful paradigm for program synthesis from NRA (and other first-order theory) specifications [4–6,22]. At an abstract level, a SyGuS tool systematically searches through a space of candidate programs guided by a grammar, relying on logical checks to determine if a candidate program satisfies the given specification *for all possible* input values. In many practical applications, however, the natural specification is such that there are some input values for which no output values satisfy the specification. Such specifications are called *unrealizable* in the program synthesis literature. In such cases, the logical check referred to above must fail for every candidate program, preventing a SyGuS tool from synthesizing any program at all. This can be highly unsatisfactory for an end-user, who is left with no program simply because some (perhaps never-to-be-used) input values do not admit any correct outputs. From a practical point of view, it is often adequate to have a program that generates correct outputs whenever the inputs admit existence of outputs satisfying the specification, and faithfully reports the absence of correct outputs otherwise. Unfortunately, SyGuS tools fail to generate such programs for unrealizable specifications. In this paper, we propose a novel approach to address this problem, that works regardless of whether the specification is realizable, and solves problems beyond the capabilities of state-of-the-art SyGuS tools, even for realizable specifications. This effectively adds to the repertoire of techniques for program synthesis from NRA specifications.

To illustrate how unrealizability comes in the way of synthesizing programs using SyGuS tools, consider the specification $0.9 \leq x^2 + y^2 \leq 1$, where x is a real-valued input and y is a real-valued output. This specification is unrealizable (e.g. if $x = 2$, there is no real y that satisfies the specification) and state-of-the-art SyGuS tools like CVC5 [7] do not synthesize any program, and simply report this specification as unrealizable. Unfortunately, this may not be useful to the end-user, who wants a program to calculate a value of y satisfying the specification, whenever possible. A work-around would be to modify the specification and render it realizable before using a SyGuS tool. For example, the above specification could be modified to $(-1 \leq x \leq 1) \Rightarrow (0.9 \leq x^2 + y^2 \leq 1)$, where $-1 \leq x \leq 1$ is the *weakest pre-condition* on x that admits a real y satisfying $0.9 \leq x^2 + y^2 \leq 1$. Violation of the weakest pre-condition can indeed be used by the program to detect when no real output satisfying the specification exists. Unfortunately, finding the weakest pre-condition is equivalent to existentially projecting out output variables from the specification. This is technically involved and computationally expensive for NRA in general [42]. A primary goal of this paper is to develop techniques that can help users in such cases, without worrying about realizability or weakest pre-condition calculation.

An important point that deserves attention when discussing programs with real number arithmetic is the representation of real numbers. It is well known that arithmetic with fixed precision floating point representation of real numbers can incur significant rounding errors (see [25] for an excellent exposition on this topic). We discuss the challenge posed due to this problem in the full version [3]. For several applications (viz. scientific computing, high volume financial transactions etc.) such rounding errors are unacceptable, and we must use arbitrary precision floating point numbers or rationals, implemented in well-engineered libraries like GMP [50]. This comes at a price: software implementing arbitrary precision floating point or rational arithmetic are significantly slower than fixed-precision floating point arithmetic, implemented through dedicated hardware in modern processors. However, this tradeoff between accuracy and performance is inevitable in programs using real arithmetic. In our work, we wish to synthesize programs that have *zero rounding errors*. Since rationals strictly subsume arbitrary precision floating point numbers, we choose to synthesize programs from NRA specifications, *assuming rational inputs and outputs*. This yields a new variant of the program synthesis problem from NRA specifications, that is of independent interest. Interestingly, this also allows us to exploit properties of rational numbers to go beyond the capabilities of SyGuS tools for NRA specifications, as shown later in the paper.

The above discussion motivates the following problem definition. Let $\mathbb{Q}$ denote the set of rational numbers, and $\mathbf{X}$ and $\mathbf{Y}$ denote sequences of input and output variables respectively, with $|\mathbf{X}|$ and $|\mathbf{Y}|$ denoting their respective counts.

> Given an NRA specification $\varphi(\mathbf{X}, \mathbf{Y})$, generate a program Prog s.t.
>
> - All conditions and expressions in Prog are NRA formulas and terms
> - For every $\mathbf{A} \in \mathbb{Q}^{|\mathbf{X}|}$, Prog run with $\mathbf{A}$ as input terminates, and produces one of:
>   - $\bot$ (representing "no output") if $\forall \mathbf{Y} \in \mathbb{Q}^{|\mathbf{Y}|} : \neg\varphi(\mathbf{A}, \mathbf{Y})$ holds, or
>   - $\mathbf{B} \in \mathbb{Q}^{|\mathbf{Y}|}$ such that $\varphi(\mathbf{A}, \mathbf{B})$ holds

We allow Prog to have loops, conditional statements and assignment statements (a formal grammar appears in Sect. 2). We call the above problem *real program synthesis with rational inputs and outputs*, and use $\mathcal{RPS}_{\mathbb{Q}}$ to denote the class of all instances of this problem. Further, we denote by $\mathcal{RPS}$ the variant of the above problem where $\mathbb{Q}$ in the problem statement is replaced by $\mathbb{R}$ (set of reals).

The primary contributions of our paper can now be summarized as follows:

1. *Theoretical results* (Sect. 3)
   (a) We show that $\mathcal{RPS}_{\mathbb{Q}}$ and Hilbert's tenth problem over rationals (a long-standing open problem [20]) are inter-reducible.
   (b) We show the impossibility of solving $\mathcal{RPS}_{\mathbb{Q}}$ using loop-free programs.
2. *Algorithms* (Sect. 4)
   (a) We show that if $\varphi(\mathbf{X}, \mathbf{Y})$ is realizable over reals, any program synthesized by a SyGuS tool for NRA is also a solution to $\mathcal{RPS}_{\mathbb{Q}}$, but not vice versa.
   (b) We provide a sound and complete algorithm for $\mathcal{RPS}_{\mathbb{Q}}$ when $|\mathbf{Y}| = 1$.

(c) When $|\mathbf{Y}| > 1$, we provide a sound and (necessarily) incomplete procedure for $\mathcal{RPS}_{\mathbb{Q}}$. We can effectively detect when a solution generated by our algorithm solves the instance of $\mathcal{RPS}_{\mathbb{Q}}$ exactly.

3. *Implementation and experiments* (Sect. 5): We implement our algorithm in a prototype tool called NQSynth and use it to synthesize programs for a suite of NRA specifications. Our experiments show that NQSynth correctly synthesizes programs for several non-trivial specifications, many of which are unrealizable. Furthermore, our approach is significantly more performant than two competing approaches on many benchmarks.

Related Work. Program synthesis from NRA specifications with real (not rational) inputs and outputs is closely related to quantifier elimination in the existential theory of reals (ETR) [52], and to techniques for finding real roots of polynomials [8,31,36,56]. While existentially quantifying all outputs from a given specification yields the weakest pre-condition on inputs, for specifications with a single real output, polynomial root finding techniques can be used to find disjoint intervals for all admissible real values of the output. However, such root finding techniques do not distinguish between rational and irrational roots, and cannot guarantee zero rounding errors with floating-point implementations. There has been a long and illustrious line of work on quantifier elimination in ETR, starting with the seminal work of Tarski [52], followed by Collins' celebrated CAD algorithm [14,15], and several subsequent adaptations [10,17,38]. Similarly, finding real roots of polynomials is an intensely studied topic in algebraic geometry (see [8] for an excellent exposition). We leverage this rich line of work in our solution, while being cognizant of the high complexity of algorithms like CAD, and of the limitations of polynomial root finding techniques in the rational setting.

Earlier approaches to program synthesis from NRA specifications can be broadly classified as template-based approaches and syntax-guided approaches. The work of [23,24,49] present template-based techniques for synthesizing programs by filling holes in user-provided sketches or templates. Syntax-guided or SyGuS approaches [4–6,22] have also proven to be very effective with state-of-the-art competition-winning SyGuS tools, such as CVC5 [7] and DryadSynth [27], synthesizing non-trivial programs from a large class of specifications, but only if the specification is realizable. Our work neither fits the template-based synthesis paradigm, nor can it be viewed as an instance of SyGuS. Instead, it makes careful use of a handful of generic modules for reasoning about polynomials to synthesize programs from specifications that go beyond the capabilities of existing techniques.

There are also works that synthesize programs from restricted real/integer arithmetic specifications. For example, [33,34] discuss techniques to solve program synthesis for specifications that are combinations of *linear* constraints over rational/integer variables, and other SMT theories. Similarly, [2] considers specifications given as non-linear constraints over *bounded integers*. However, these techniques do not generalize easily to specifications in NRA in its full generality, and hence we don't compare against them.

2 Preliminaries and Problem Statement

Let $\mathbb{N}$, $\mathbb{Z}$, $\mathbb{Q}$, $\mathbb{R}$ denote the set of natural numbers, integers, rational numbers and real numbers, respectively. Let $\mathbf{X} = \{x_1, \dots x_m\}$ and $\mathbf{Y} = \{y_1, \dots y_n\}$ be disjoint sets of variables, representing program inputs and outputs respectively. A *relational specification*, or simply a *specification*, of a program is a first-order formula φ with free variables $\mathbf{V} = \mathbf{X} \cup \mathbf{Y}$. In this paper, we focus on specifications in the *quantifier-free theory of non-linear real arithmetic* (NRA), where variables are assumed to take values from $\mathbb{R}$.

Thus, our specifications are Boolean combinations of polynomial inequalities over real-valued input and output variables. However, for reasons related to rounding errors as explained in Sect. 1, we will restrict our discussion to rational input and output values. We use lower-case letters v, x, y, z, possibly with subscripts, to denote variables, while constants are represented by letters a, b. Sets of variables are denoted as $\mathbf{V} = \{v_1, \dots, v_k\}$, and similarly for $\mathbf{X}, \mathbf{Y}, \mathbf{Z}$. Likewise, sets of constants are denoted $\mathbf{A} = \{a_1, \dots, a_k\}$. A monomial over $\mathbf{V}$ is a (repeated) product of variables in $\mathbf{V}$, written as $v_1^{r_1} v_2^{r_2} \cdots v_k^{r_k}$, where $r_1, \dots r_k \in \mathbb{N} \cup \{0\}$. A polynomial is a rational weighted sum of monomials, i.e. $\sum_{j=1}^{t} a_j m_j$, where $a_j \in \mathbb{Q}$ and m_j is a monomial. Polynomials over $\mathbf{V}$ are represented as $p(\mathbf{V}), q(\mathbf{V}), r(\mathbf{V})$ etc. A polynomial inequality is a constraint of the form $p(\mathbf{V}) \bowtie 0$, where $\bowtie \ \in \{<, >, \leq, \geq\}$. Polynomial constraints over $\mathbf{V}$ are Boolean combinations of polynomial inequalities over $\mathbf{V}$, and are represented as $\varphi(\mathbf{V}), \psi(\mathbf{V})$ etc. For a constant a and $v \in \mathbf{V}$, we use $\varphi[v \mapsto a]$ to denote the constraint obtained by substituting a for v in φ. If $\mathbf{A}$ denotes the tuple of constants $(a_1, \dots a_k)$ and $\mathbf{V}$ denotes the tuple of variables $(v_1, \dots v_k)$, we use $\varphi[\mathbf{V} \mapsto \mathbf{A}]$ or simply $\varphi(\mathbf{A})$ to denote $\big(\cdots(\varphi[v_1 \mapsto a_1])\cdots\big)[v_k \mapsto a_k]$.

Problem Statement. Given an NRA specification $\varphi(\mathbf{X}, \mathbf{Y})$, our goal, as outlined in Sect. 1, is to synthesize a terminating program Prog that takes as input arbitrary rational values (say, $\mathbf{A} \in \mathbb{Q}^{|\mathbf{X}|}$), and either generates $\mathbf{B} \in \mathbb{Q}^{|\mathbf{Y}|}$ such that $\varphi(\mathbf{A}, \mathbf{B})$ holds, or reports that no such $\mathbf{B}$ exists in $\mathbb{Q}^{|\mathbf{Y}|}$. In the latter case, we allow our synthesized programs to return a special symbol $\perp$. A program satisfying this property is said to *realize* the NRA specification $\varphi(\mathbf{X}, \mathbf{Y})$. As we show shortly, synthesizing a program that realizes a specification in NRA is not possible in general, unless some long-standing problems in number-theory are resolved. Hence, we propose to develop a synthesis algorithm that is sound but incomplete in general. In other words, whenever the synthesized program returns $\mathbf{B} \in \mathbb{Q}^{|\mathbf{Y}|}$ for an input $\mathbf{A} \in \mathbb{Q}^{|\mathbf{X}|}$, then $\varphi(\mathbf{A}, \mathbf{B})$ indeed holds. However, there may exist some other $\mathbf{A} \in \mathbb{Q}^{|\mathbf{X}|}$ for which the synthesized program returns $\perp$ although $\exists \mathbf{Y}\ \varphi(\mathbf{A}, \mathbf{Y})$ holds. For some sub-classes of specifications, however, we can indeed obtain a sound and complete synthesis algorithm. Thus, for specifications in these sub-classes, the synthesized program returns $\perp$ for an input $\mathbf{A}$ iff $\forall \mathbf{Y}\ \neg\varphi(\mathbf{A}, \mathbf{Y})$ holds. The formal definition of the problem statement has already been given in the introduction.

Form of the Synthesized Program. To complete the description of the problem definition, we need to specify the form of programs that we wish to synthesize. For this, we give a simple context-free grammar $\mathcal{G}$ in Fig. 1 for imperative programs with variables that take rational values. Programs derived from this grammar use polynomial terms (including rational constants) in assignments (denoted PTerm) and polynomial constraints, i.e., Boolean combinations of polynomial inequalities in conditionals (denoted PCnstr). A program returns either a special symbol $\perp$ or a tuple of rational values of variables (denoted Var).

$$
\begin{aligned}
\mathsf{Prog} &::= \mathsf{AssignStmt} \mid \mathsf{CondStmt} \mid \mathsf{LoopStmt} \mid \\
&\quad\;\; \mathsf{RetStmt} \mid \mathsf{Prog}; \mathsf{Prog} \\
\mathsf{AssignStmt} &::= \mathsf{Var} \leftarrow \mathsf{PTerm} \\
\mathsf{CondStmt} &::= \textbf{if } (\mathsf{PCnstr}) \textbf{ then } \mathsf{Prog} \textbf{ else } \mathsf{Prog} \\
\mathsf{LoopStmt} &::= \textbf{while } (\mathsf{PCnstr}) \textbf{ do } \mathsf{Prog} \\
\mathsf{RetStmt} &::= \textbf{return } (\mathsf{VarTuple}) \mid \textbf{return } \perp \\
\mathsf{VarTuple} &::= \mathsf{Var} \mid \mathsf{VarTuple}, \mathsf{Var}
\end{aligned}
$$

Fig. 1. Grammar for programs

It is not hard to see that programs derived from this grammar are Turing powerful (e.g. counter-machines can be encoded). Let Prog be a program in the language of the grammar $\mathcal{G}$, and let $\mathbf{X}$ be a tuple of variables used in Prog. We use the notation $\mathsf{Prog}(\mathbf{X})$ to denote the fact that Prog does not assign to any variable in $\mathbf{X}$, and instead uses values of these variables as inputs. For $\mathbf{A} \in \mathbb{Q}^{|\mathbf{X}|}$, we also use $\mathsf{Prog}(\mathbf{A})$ to denote the result (return value) of running the program Prog with variables in $\mathbf{X}$ set to constants in $\mathbf{A}$. A special class of programs is obtained by disallowing the use of the non-terminal LoopStmt in the above grammar. Specifically, with this restriction, we can only derive *loop-free* programs. Hence, we call $\mathcal{G}$ with the above restriction as $\mathcal{G}^{lf}$ (for loop-free grammar).

Note that the above grammar, though simple, is quite expressive. For instance, number-theoretic algorithms often used in the context of rational numbers, such as real root isolation yielding rational bounds for real roots of polynomials [31], or application of rational root theorem [21] to a find rational root of a polynomial, can be expressed as programs derivable from our grammar. This can be easily checked from publicly available pseudo-code for these algorithms (see, e.g. [58] and [13]). We will make use this convenience later in the paper.

3 Hardness Results and Theoretical Characterizations

In this section, we state our theoretical characterization and hardness results. We start by recalling Hilbert's tenth problem [18] which asks, given a Diophantine equation (a polynomial equation with integer coefficients and a finite number of unknowns), whether we can decide if the equation has a solution over integers. This problem is famously undecidable by a sequence of results, which is collectively referred to as the MRDP theorem [18]. Over reals, on the other hand, this problem is decidable and an algorithm for it follows from Tarski's quantifier elimination [52]. However, over rationals, it turns out that this problem is still open. More precisely, *the Hilbert's tenth problem over rationals, denoted* $\mathcal{HTP}_{\mathbb{Q}}$, asks given a polynomial equation with integer or rational coefficients and a finite number of unknowns, whether we can decide if it has a solution over rationals. Despite significant effort in this direction [20], this question remains a long-standing open problem. It turns out that the problem defined in the previous section is as hard as $\mathcal{HTP}_{\mathbb{Q}}$. Note that while $\mathcal{HTP}_{\mathbb{Q}}$ is a decision problem, $\mathcal{RPS}_{\mathbb{Q}}$ is a synthesis problem; hence the statements are suitably framed.

Theorem 1. *1.* $\mathcal{RPS}_{\mathbb{Q}}$ *is at least as hard as* $\mathcal{HTP}_{\mathbb{Q}}$.
2. $\mathcal{HTP}_{\mathbb{Q}}$ *is at least as hard as* $\mathcal{RPS}_{\mathbb{Q}}$.

Proof. 1. From an instance of $\mathcal{HTP}_{\mathbb{Q}}$, i.e., a polynomial equation $\varphi(\mathbf{V})$, we build the specification $\varphi(\mathbf{X}, \mathbf{Y})$ with empty inputs $\mathbf{X} = \emptyset$ and output $\mathbf{Y} = \mathbf{V}$, an instance of $\mathcal{RPS}_{\mathbb{Q}}$. Now suppose we are able to synthesize a terminating program $\mathsf{Prog}(\mathbf{X})$ for this specification. Then on running Prog with no inputs (since $\mathbf{X} = \emptyset$), if it returns $\perp$, this implies $\varphi(\mathbf{V})$ has no solution. If, on the other hand, it returns $\mathbf{B} \in \mathbb{Q}^{|\mathbf{Y}|}$, then this is guaranteed to be a solution. Thus, Prog can be used to build a decision procedure for $\mathcal{HTP}_{\mathbb{Q}}$.
2. In the other direction, given an instance $\varphi(\mathbf{X}, \mathbf{Y})$ of $\mathcal{RPS}_{\mathbb{Q}}$, we show how to solve it using a decision procedure for $\mathcal{HTP}_{\mathbb{Q}}$ as a sub-routine. W.l.o.g. we assume φ to be in disjunctive normal form, i.e. of the form $\bigvee_{i=1}^{k} \psi_i(\mathbf{X}, \mathbf{Y})$, where ψ_i is a conjunction of polynomial inequalities (negation of a polynomial inequality is itself a polynomial inequality). We first observe that for each such ψ_i, we can obtain a single equi-satisfiable polynomial equation (details of this construction are in the long version at [3]) say $\psi_i''(\mathbf{X}, \mathbf{Y}, \mathbf{Z})$, such that $\psi_i(\mathbf{X}, \mathbf{Y}) \equiv \exists \mathbf{Z} \psi_i''(\mathbf{X}, \mathbf{Y}, \mathbf{Z})$ holds. Note that $\psi_i''(\mathbf{X}, \mathbf{Y}, \mathbf{Z})$ being a single polynomial equation is also an instance of $\mathcal{HTP}_{\mathbb{Q}}$. Now, for any input $\mathbf{A} \in \mathbb{Q}^{|\mathbf{X}|}$, if $\mathcal{HTP}_{\mathbb{Q}}$ on $\psi_i''(\mathbf{A}, \mathbf{Y}, \mathbf{Z})$ answers "No" for all $i \in \{1, \dots k\}$, then no $\mathbf{Y} \in \mathbb{Q}^{|\mathbf{Y}|}$ can satisfy $\varphi(\mathbf{A}, \mathbf{Y}) \equiv \bigvee_{i=1}^{k} \psi_i(\mathbf{A}, \mathbf{Y})$; hence a program realizing $\varphi(\mathbf{X}, \mathbf{Y})$ must return $\perp$. Otherwise, if $\mathcal{HTP}_{\mathbb{Q}}$ returns "Yes" for some $\psi_i''(\mathbf{A}, \mathbf{Y}, \mathbf{Z})$, then there exists $\mathbf{B} \in \mathbb{Q}^{|\mathbf{Y}|+|\mathbf{Z}|}$ s.t $\psi(\mathbf{A}, \mathbf{B})$ holds. Since this is a rational vector, we can now find it by enumeration, yielding a terminating program that realizes $\varphi(\mathbf{X}, \mathbf{Y})$.□

The above proof requires enumeration in the final step, and therefore does not guarantee that the synthesized program is loop-free, even if we had an $\mathcal{HTP}_{\mathbb{Q}}$ oracle. But could there be alternative ways of solving $\mathcal{RPS}_{\mathbb{Q}}$ using only loop-free programs? The answer turns out to be in the negative.

Theorem 2. $\mathcal{RPS}_{\mathbb{Q}}$ *cannot be solved using loop-free programs.*

The proof, given in [3], proceeds by showing that if $\mathcal{RPS}_{\mathbb{Q}}$ can be solved using loop-free programs, then this would imply that the theory of rational arithmetic admits quantifier elimination, and hence decidability. However, by a famous result of Robinson [47], we know that this is not the case.

4 Algorithmic Procedures for Solving $\mathcal{RPS}_{\mathbb{Q}}$

Given the hardness results above, a sound and complete algorithm for solving the $\mathcal{RPS}_{\mathbb{Q}}$ problem in its full generality is unlikely. This motivates us to (a) consider fragments of NRA for which we can design sound and complete synthesis algorithms, and (b) design sound but incomplete algorithms in general, that perform well in practice. We start with an interesting observation.

We show that every program derivable from grammar $\mathcal{G}$ (see Fig. 1) that realizes a specification $\varphi(\mathbf{X}, \mathbf{Y})$ over *reals*, also realizes $\varphi(\mathbf{X}, \mathbf{Y})$ over *rationals*. This immediately suggests the following result, whose proof is given in [3].

Theorem 3. *Let $\mathcal{L}$ be any fragment of NRA for which there is a sound and complete algorithm $\mathcal{A}_{\mathcal{L}}$ for solving $\mathcal{RPS}$, i.e. synthesis over reals using grammar $\mathcal{G}$. Then $\mathcal{A}_{\mathcal{L}}$ also solves $\mathcal{RPS}_{\mathbb{Q}}$, i.e. synthesis over rationals using $\mathcal{G}$, for fragment $\mathcal{L}$. Moreover, there exists a fragment of NRA for which there does not exist any sound and complete algorithm for solving $\mathcal{RPS}$, but for which there is a sound and complete algorithm for solving $\mathcal{RPS}_{\mathbb{Q}}$.*

A consequence of Theorem 3 is that whenever a SyGuS tool synthesizes a program $\mathsf{Prog}(\mathbf{X})$ for a (realizable) specification $\varphi(\mathbf{X}, \mathbf{Y})$ *over reals* using $\mathcal{G}$ or any fragment of it, we can effectively use $\mathsf{Prog}(\mathbf{X})$ as a solution for the $\mathcal{RPS}_{\mathbb{Q}}$ problem. If $\varphi(\mathbf{X}, \mathbf{Y})$ is not realizable, we can first compute the weakest precondition $\psi(\mathbf{X}) \equiv \exists \mathbf{Y}\, \varphi(\mathbf{X}, \mathbf{Y})$ using a quantifier elimination algorithm for reals. If a SyGuS tool can then synthesize a program realizing $\psi(\mathbf{X}) \rightarrow \varphi(\mathbf{X}, \mathbf{Y})$ *over reals*, then the same program with a check for satisfaction of $\psi(\mathbf{X})$ also serves as a solution for the $\mathcal{RPS}_{\mathbb{Q}}$ problem for $\varphi(\mathbf{X}, \mathbf{Y})$.

4.1 Complete Synthesis for Single-Output Specifications

We now propose a sound and complete synthesis procedure for solving $\mathcal{RPS}_{\mathbb{Q}}$ when the specification has only one output variable. Thus, the specification is a formula $\varphi(\mathbf{X}, y)$ in NRA, where y is the sole program output. At a high level, the synthesis procedure separates the reasoning into two cases: (i) finding solutions that satisfy the constraints with only strict inequalities, and (ii) finding solutions that arise only on the boundary of non-strict inequalities. These cases are handled using two classical results from number theory, namely *Real Root Isolation* (RRI) and the *Rational Root Theorem* (RRT), along with quantifier elimination from polynomial constraints using CAD or variant algorithms. For notational convenience, we refer to a generic quantifier elimination procedure using CAD as QEPCAD. Crucially, QEPCAD is used only while synthesizing the program; it is not invoked during execution of the synthesized program. We start with an overview of two key results we rely on.

Real Root Isolation. (RRI) [16,31,55] This refers to a family of algorithms that given a univariate polynomial, compute a collection of intervals with rational end-points on the real line, such that each interval contains exactly one real root of the polynomial (if any exist). The maximum size of an interval output by RRI, say $\varepsilon > 0$, can be user-specified. Using classical results on lower bounds of root separation [8,43], the value of ε can be chosen (or even iteratively reduced), so that the intervals for the real roots obtained from RRI are pairwise disjoint. Since the sign of a polynomial is invariant between its real roots, gaps between the disjoint intervals output by RRI give intervals of values where the polynomial's sign cannot change. Given a specification φ that is a conjunction of *strict inequalities*, the above discussion suggests the following procedure for computing values of y, given a value of $\mathbf{X}$, such that φ is satisfied. We first substitute the given value of $\mathbf{X}$ in every polynomial $p(\mathbf{X}, y)$ that appears in a constraint of the form $p(\mathbf{X}, y) \bowtie 0$ ($\bowtie \in \{<, >\}$) in $\varphi(\mathbf{X}, y)$. This effectively gives us a set of uni-variate polynomials in y. Next, we construct the product of all these uni-variate polynomials, and apply RRI with an appropriate value of ϵ to obtain the interval gaps where the product polynomial's sign is invariant. Clearly, none of the factor polynomials change sign in any of these intervals. By evaluating each factor polynomial at the mid-point of each such gap interval, we can find a rational value of y that satisfies $\varphi(\mathbf{X}, y)$, if one exists.

The above argument relies on the fact that the rationals are dense in $\mathbb{R}$. Specifically, after substituting a rational value for $\mathbf{X}$, if r_1 and r_2 are rationals such that every real y in $r_1 < y < r_2$ satisfies $\varphi(\mathbf{X}, y)$, then there exist rationals between r_1 and r_2 (for instance, $\frac{r_1+r_2}{2}$) that also satisfy $\varphi(\mathbf{X}, y)$. This immediately implies that if a rational value of $\mathbf{X}$ satisfies $\exists y\, \varphi(\mathbf{X}, y)$ over the reals, then the same value of $\mathbf{X}$ also satisfies $\exists y\, \varphi(\mathbf{X}, y)$ over rationals. We exploit this property in detecting when $\exists y\, \varphi(\mathbf{X}, y)$ has a solution over rationals.

Rational Root Theorem (RRT) [21]. The second result that we need is the rational root theorem, which can be formulated as follows.

Theorem 4 (Rational Root Theorem [21]). *Let $a_n x^n + a_{n-1} x^{n-1} + \cdots + a_1 x + a_0 = 0$ be a polynomial equation, where $a_0, \ldots a_n \in \mathbb{Z}$ and $a_0, a_n \neq 0$. Then every rational solution $x = \frac{u}{v}$ of the equation, where u and v are relatively prime, satisfies the conditions: (i) u is an integer factor of a_0, and (ii) v is an integer factor of a_n.*

An immediate consequence of Theorem 4 is that every rational solution of the polynomial equation lies in the set $\{\frac{u}{v} \mid u \in \mathsf{IntFactor}(a_0), v \in \mathsf{IntFactor}(a_n)\}$, where $\mathsf{IntFactor}(m)$ is the set of integer factors of $m \in \mathbb{N}$. As each natural number has finitely many divisors, the set of candidate rational solutions is finite.

We use these crucial observations to synthesize a program $\mathsf{Prog1OP}_\varphi(\mathbf{X})$ that realizes $\varphi(\mathbf{X}, y)$. Though the polynomials in our specification may use rational coefficients, an inequality involving such a polynomial can be converted to an equivalent inequality with only integer coefficients by multiplying both sides of the inequality by the least common multiple of all denominators of rational coefficients. Hence Theorem 4 applies to polynomial equations with rational coefficients as well, i.e., our specification class.

Recall that the formula $\varphi(\mathbf{X}, y)$ may contain both strict and non-strict polynomial inequalities. Let $\mathsf{NonStrict}(\varphi)$ denote the set of polynomial terms p that

Algorithm 1. Program realizing $\varphi(\mathbf{X}, y)$ with single output

Require: Formulas $\varphi(\mathbf{X}, y)$, $\widehat{\varphi}(\mathbf{X}, y)$ and $\psi(\mathbf{X})$ in NRA
  ▷ $\widehat{\varphi}$ (computed off-line) is obtained from φ converting every non-strict inequality to strict.
  ▷ $\psi(\mathbf{X})$ (computed off-line using QEPCAD) is equivalent to $\exists y\ \widehat{\varphi}(\mathbf{X}, y)$
1: **procedure** $\mathsf{Prog1OP}_{\varphi}(\mathbf{X})$
2:    **if** $\psi(\mathbf{X}) =$ `true` **then**
3:       $\Gamma_{\widehat{\varphi}} \leftarrow \mathsf{RationalSamplesNRA}(\widehat{\varphi}(\mathbf{X}, y))$ ▷ $\widehat{\varphi}(\mathbf{X}, y)$ is univariate in y, given $\mathbf{X}$
4:       **for all** a in $\Gamma_{\widehat{\varphi}}$ **do** ▷ Every $a \in \Gamma_{\widehat{\varphi}}$ is a rational number
5:          **if** $\widehat{\varphi}(\mathbf{X}, a) = \mathsf{true}$ **then return** a ▷ $\widehat{\varphi}(\mathbf{X}, a)$ implies $\varphi(\mathbf{X}, a)$
6:    **else**
7:       **for all** p in $\mathsf{NonStrict}(\varphi)$ **do**
8:          $\mathsf{Cand} \leftarrow \mathsf{CandRatRoot}(p = 0)$
9:          **for all** a in Cand **do**
10:             **if** $\varphi(\mathbf{X}, a)$ is `true` **then return** a
      return $\bot$

contain the output variable y and occur in non-strict inequalities of the form $p \geq 0$ or $p \leq 0$ in φ. From $\varphi(\mathbf{X}, y)$, we can always construct the formula $\widehat{\varphi}(\mathbf{X}, y)$ obtained by converting every non-strict inequality in $\mathsf{NonStrict}(\varphi)$ to a strict inequality. In other words, for every $p \in \mathsf{NonStrict}(\varphi)$, if $p \leq 0$ (resp. $p \geq 0$) is a polynomial inequality in φ, we replace all instances of this inequality in φ by $p < 0$ (resp. $p > 0$) to get $\widehat{\varphi}(\mathbf{X}, y)$. We use QEPCAD to obtain $\psi(\mathbf{X})$ by eliminating quantifiers from $\exists y\ \widehat{\varphi}(\mathbf{X}, y)$. The pseudocode of the program $\mathsf{Prog1OP}_{\varphi}(\mathbf{X})$ that realizes $\varphi(\mathbf{X}, y)$ in NRA is given in Algorithm 1.

This algorithm uses a function $\mathsf{CandRatRoot}(\cdot)$ that takes as argument a polynomial equation and returns a finite set of candidate rational roots of the equation, as described above. Further the algorithm uses function RationalSamplesNRA which, given a formula $\widehat{\varphi}$ on strict polynomial inequalities, returns a finite set of rational points, such that if there is any rational solution to $\widehat{\varphi}$, one of the returned points must satisfy it. This is implemented using the mid-points/end-points of gap-intervals computed by RRI [16,31,55]. There are two cases to consider.

- For a given value of $\mathbf{X}$, if $\psi(\mathbf{X})$ evaluates to `true`, we know that there is a real (and hence rational) value of y that satisfies $\widehat{\varphi}$ (with only strict inequalities). So, we first obtain the uni-variate constraint $\varphi'(y)$ by substituting the value of $\mathbf{X}$ in $\widehat{\varphi}(\mathbf{X}, y)$. Then we apply RRI on $\varphi'(y)$ to obtain rational points in the gap-intervals computed by RRI (see lines 2–3 of Algorithm 1). Next, we check if any of these points satisfies $\widehat{\varphi}$, and if so $\mathsf{Prog1OP}_{\varphi}$ outputs it.
- If $\psi(\mathbf{X})$ evaluates to `false` for the given value of $\mathbf{X}$, then we know that there is no rational value of y that satisfies $\widehat{\varphi}(\mathbf{X}, y)$. However, there may exist a rational value of y that satisfies $\varphi(\mathbf{X}, y)$ (that includes non-strict inequalities), although it doesn't satisfy $\widehat{\varphi}(\mathbf{X}, y)$. For this to be true, the corresponding values of $\mathbf{X}$ and y must necessarily satisfy $p = 0$ for at least one polynomial $p \in \mathsf{NonStrict}(\varphi)$. We can now apply Theorem 4 to each polynomial equation

$p = 0$, where $p \in \mathsf{NonStrict}(\varphi)$. Effectively, we enumerate the finite set of candidate rational solutions of $p = 0$, and check whether any of these satisfies $\varphi(\mathbf{X}, y)$. If so, the corresponding rational solution is output by $\mathsf{Prog1OP}_\varphi(\mathbf{X})$. Otherwise, $\mathsf{Prog1OP}_\varphi(\mathbf{X})$ outputs $\perp$.

From the above construction and reasoning, we conclude:

Theorem 5. *Given a specification $\varphi(\mathbf{X}, y)$ in NRA with a single output variable, the program $\mathsf{Prog1OP}_\varphi(\mathbf{X})$ realizes $\varphi(\mathbf{X}, y)$, thus solving $\mathcal{RPS}_\mathbb{Q}$.*

Example 6. We illustrate the two cases of Algorithm 1 on the specification $\varphi(x, y) \equiv 0.9 \leq x^2 + y^2 \leq 1$ from Sect. 1, with a detailed version available in [3]. Here, $\mathsf{NonStrict}(\varphi) = \{x^2 + y^2 - 0.9,\ x^2 + y^2 - 1\}$, and $\widehat{\varphi}$ is $x^2 + y^2 - 0.9 > 0 \wedge x^2 + y^2 - 1 < 0$. Eliminating y from $\widehat{\varphi}$ gives $\psi(x) \equiv x^2 < 1$. Thus, for inputs $x \in (-1, 1)$, Algorithm 1 invokes RationalSamplesNRA on the univariate strict constraint obtained by substituting the value of x, and returns a rational witness for y. For inputs where $\psi(x)$ is false, the algorithm instead examines the boundary equations induced by $\mathsf{NonStrict}(\varphi)$. For example, when $x = 1$ or $x = -1$, the equation $x^2 + y^2 - 1 = 0$ yields the rational solution $y = 0$. Thus the original formula is satisfiable even though the strict version of the formula is not, illustrating the role of the second part of the algorithm.

4.2 Synthesis for Full NRA

In this section, we present a sound but incomplete procedure that solves $\mathcal{RPS}_\mathbb{Q}$ for the general case. Given the hardness results in Sect. 3, we limit ourselves to providing a sound procedure that solves a large collections of benchmarks (including unrealizable specifications), as demonstrated by our experiments.

A naive way to solve the multiple output case would be to try to process it one output at a time by existentially quantifying the others. However, as explained earlier, existential quantification over rationals is at least as hard as $\mathcal{HTP}_\mathbb{Q}$, and hence we cannot hope for a practically efficient procedure. Instead, we propose an alternative approach that first considers a (rational) point that satisfies the given specification, and then uses this to decompose the synthesis problem to a collection of single output synthesis sub-problems. The sound and complete procedure for the one output case described in Sect. 4.1 is used to solve these sub-problems individually, and the solutions composed to incrementally synthesize the desired program. The process is repeated until the weakest precondition of the given specification is covered, or until the algorithm times out. The main difficulty of this approach is to maintain rationality (and correctness) of solutions, while ensuring progress at each iteration.

The pseudo-code for our technique is given in Algorithm 2, where snippets of the program being synthesized are represented in grey boxes. These are not executed during the run of the synthesis algorithm. We start by querying an NRA oracle for a satisfying assignment (or solution) for $\varphi(\mathbf{X}, \mathbf{Y})$. The function RSolve returns a rational satisfying assignment projected to the output variables, if there exists such a valuation; otherwise it returns $\perp$. Given the rational vector

Algorithm 2. Program for φ in NRA solving $\mathcal{RPS}_{\mathbb{Q}}$

Require: NRA specification $\varphi(\mathbf{X}, \mathbf{Y})$, where $\mathbf{Y} = \{y_1, \cdots, y_n\}$, and integer timeout.
1: **procedure** SynthNQA($\varphi, \mathbf{X}, \mathbf{Y}$)
2: count $\leftarrow 0$
3: $\sigma \leftarrow$ RSolve($\varphi, \mathbf{X}, \mathbf{Y}$) ▷ $\sigma = (\sigma_1, \ldots, \sigma_n) \in \mathbb{Q}^{|\mathbf{Y}|}$ or $\perp$
4: **while** $(\sigma \neq \perp) \wedge$ (count $\leq$ timeout) **do**
5: **for** i in $\{1, \cdots, |\mathbf{Y}|\}$ **do**
6: $\varphi_i(\mathbf{X}, y_i) \leftarrow \varphi(\mathbf{X}, \sigma_1, \ldots, \sigma_{i-1}, y_i, \sigma_{i+1}, \ldots \sigma_n)$
7: $\psi_i(\mathbf{X}) \leftarrow \exists y_i \varphi_i(\mathbf{X}, y_i)$ ▷ Quantifier elimination done using QEPCAD
8: Let $\mathsf{RProg}_i(\mathbf{X})$ be the program as follows:

RProg_i
$(y_1, \ldots, y_{i-1}, y_{i+1}, \ldots, y_n) \leftarrow (\sigma_1, \ldots \sigma_{i-1}, \sigma_{i+1}, \ldots, \sigma_n)$
$y_i \leftarrow \mathsf{Prog1OP}_{\varphi_i}$

9: $\varphi(\mathbf{X}, \mathbf{Y}) \leftarrow \varphi(\mathbf{X}, \mathbf{Y}) \wedge \neg\psi_1(\mathbf{X}) \wedge \neg\psi_2(\mathbf{X}) \wedge \ldots \wedge \neg\psi_n(\mathbf{X})$
10: $\sigma \leftarrow$ RSolve($\varphi, \mathbf{X}, \mathbf{Y}$)
11: count $\leftarrow$ count $+ 1$
12: **return** Prog defined as:

Prog
if $\psi_1(\mathbf{X})$ **then** $\mathsf{RProg}_1(\mathbf{X})$
else if $\psi_2(\mathbf{X})$ **then** $\mathsf{RProg}_2(\mathbf{X})$
...
else if $\psi_n(\mathbf{X})$ **then** $\mathsf{RProg}_n(\mathbf{X})$
else $\perp$

of values σ, for each y_i in $\mathbf{Y}$, we now consider the formula $\varphi_i(\mathbf{X}, y_i)$ obtained by fixing rational values for all output variables other than y_i. This specification is now a single output specification, and we use the procedure described in Sect. 4.1 to obtain the program $\mathsf{Prog1OP}_{\varphi_i}$. Then by substituting the values obtained from σ for all output variables other than y_i, we obtain $\mathsf{RProg}_i(\mathbf{X})$, where for the y_i^{th} output, we will use $\mathsf{Prog1OP}_{\varphi_i}$.

Let ψ_i be the weakest pre-condition (computed using QEPCAD) for the one output synthesis problem in the ith iteration. When we quit the for loop in line 5, we conjunct $\neg\psi_i$ with φ, effectively obtaining a new specification φ (in line 9) which has strictly fewer satisfying assignments, thus ensuring progress.

The while loop terminates by either a *time out*, i.e., if (count $\leq$ timeout) in line 4 is violated, or by running out of rational solutions to φ. At termination of the program, we return the program that has the form of a decision list, which results in a sound program. In addition, we can also provide a guarantee of partial completeness of the procedure. That is, if the procedure terminates before timing out, then we know that the there is no way to satisfy the specification while violating all the (partial) pre-conditions obtained so far. Hence, the program synthesized by the procedure realizes the post-condition.

In general, a query to the NRA solver in line 3 of Algorithm 2 may not return a vector of all rational values. If the ith component of the returned vector is not rational, we skip the ith iteration of the for loop in line 5. If no component of the returned vector is rational, we query the solver again until we get a rational solution. The following guarantee about our algorithm follows from the construction and discussion above.

Theorem 7. *Algorithm 2 accepts as input specification $\varphi(\mathbf{X}, \mathbf{Y})$ and terminates synthesizing a program such that (1) if* $\mathsf{Prog}(\mathbf{X})$ *returns* $\mathbf{B} \in \mathbb{Q}^{\mathbf{Y}}$, *then* $\varphi(\mathbf{X}, \mathbf{Y} \mapsto$

B) *holds, and (2) if the algorithm terminates before timeout, then* Prog($\mathbf{X}$) *solves* $\mathcal{RPS}_{\mathbb{Q}}$ *by realizing specification* $\varphi(\mathbf{X}, \mathbf{Y})$.

A detailed example (with multiple output variables), showing how repeated invocations of the single-output procedure synthesize values for several output variables, is included in the full version [3].

5 Implementation and Experiments

We have implemented Algorithm 2 in a prototype tool called NQSynth. Our tool outputs a Python implementation of the synthesized program, so that it is executable off-the-shelf. We use the SMT solver Z3 [45] for RSolve that finds satisfying assignments of polynomial constraints (steps 3, 10 of Algorithm 2), and the specific tool QEPCAD [17] in SageMath [53] – for quantifier elimination over reals (step 7 of the algorithm). The Python implementation of the synthesized program uses `sympy` modules for specific operations (viz. multiplication and constant substitution) on polynomials, and also for real-root isolation and for finding integer divisors when applying the Rational Root Theorem (see Sect. 4.1). Our tool, along with the benchmarks used in this paper, is available and can be downloaded from https://github.com/anirjoshi/NQSynth.

Since SyGuS tools don't synthesize programs for unrealizable specifications, we implemented an improvised SyGuS tool for purposes of comparison. This tool first invokes QEPCAD to compute a quantifier-free formula $\psi(\mathbf{X})$ equivalent to $\exists \mathbf{Y}\, \varphi(\mathbf{X}, \mathbf{Y})$ over reals. It then feeds $\psi(\mathbf{X}) \rightarrow \varphi(\mathbf{X}, \mathbf{Y})$ as a (realizable) specification over reals to a state-of-the-art SyGuS solver, viz. CVC5 [7]. We call this QEPCAD+CVC5. We also implemented a third tool ModEnum, inspired by a model-enumeration based quantifier elimination technique for linear real arithmetic, due to Monniaux [44]. This tool starts with $\varphi(\mathbf{X}, \mathbf{Y})$ and uses Z3 to find a real-valued model for φ. If all output variables are assigned rational values, ModEnum substitutes the values of all output variables in φ to obtain a pre-condition $\psi(\mathbf{X})$. We synthesize a program fragment (an `if-then` statement) that assigns the output variables values as in the model, whenever $\psi(\mathbf{X})$ holds. The specification is then refined to $\varphi(\mathbf{X}, \mathbf{Y}) \wedge \neg\psi(\mathbf{X})$ and the process repeated. The iterations continue until either the (refined) specification becomes unsatisfiable, or until timeout. We show the program synthesized by NQSynth for an example in the extended version at [3]. In our implementations, when Z3 is invoked to find a model of $\varphi(\mathbf{X}, \mathbf{Y})$ in `QF_NRA`, it may return a model with some output variables assigned irrational values. Both Algorithm 2 and ModEnum ignore these irrational values and block this model in the next invocation of Z3.

Benchmarks: We used two sets of benchmarks for our evaluation. The first set, henceforth called "NRA", are `QF_NRA` benchmarks in the SMT-LIB 2024 repository [46]. Since all inputs and outputs in $\mathcal{RPS}_{\mathbb{Q}}$ are assumed to be rational, we considered all variables in these benchmarks to have the rational type. We filtered out unsatisfiable benchmarks, and also benchmarks with terms in

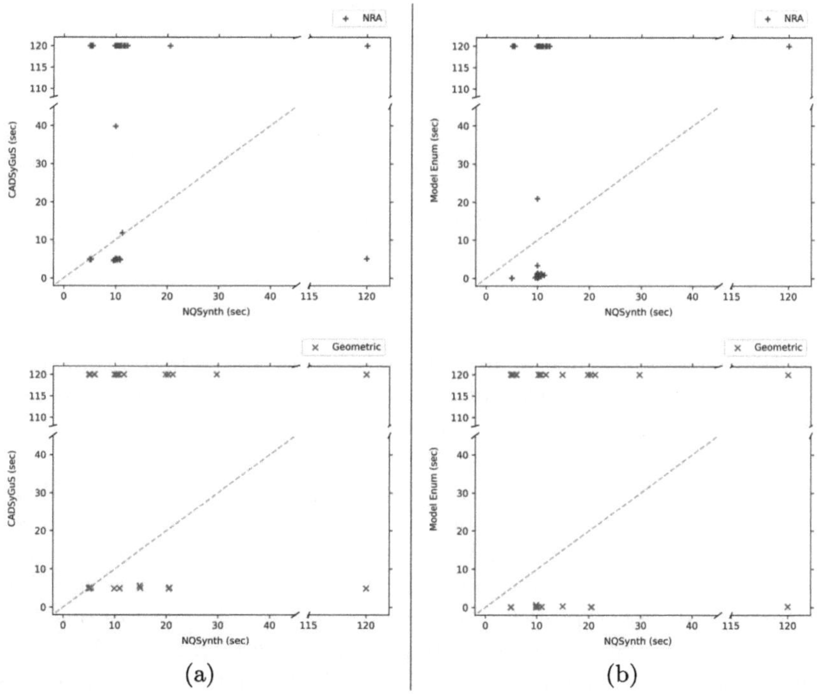

Fig. 2. Run-time scatter-plots of NQSynth with QEPCAD+CVC5, and ModEnum

mixed theories. During the course of experiments, we also noticed that QEPCAD encounters resource constraints for large inputs involving > 6 variables. Hence, we chose to evaluate our tool on 83 adapted benchmarks from the `meti-tarski/Arthan`, `meti-tarski/asin`, and `zankl` families in the SMT-LIB 2024 `QF_NRA` suite. Since `QF_NRA` benchmarks do not come with default listing of input/output variables, we partitioned the variables in each family to ensure that the resulting specifications (for synthesis) had non-linear constraints involving output variables. Specifically, for formulas in the `meti-tarski/Arthan` family (approximate trigonometric constraints), we used `skoSINS` and `skoCOSS` as output variables. For the `meti-tarski/asin` family, we used `skoSP` and `skoSM` as output variables, and for the `zankl` family, we used `b` as the output variable. The set of resulting 83 benchmarks is listed in the full version [3]. To make the benchmarks challenging, we also replaced each equality constraint with a more general relation (of which equality is a special case). Specifically, we introduced a new input variable δ, and replaced all (sub-)formulas of the form $term_1 = term_2$ by $(\delta \geq 0) \wedge (-\delta \leq term_1 - term_2 \leq \delta)$. Our second set of benchmarks, called "Geometric", consists of 51 Non-Linear Real Arithmetic (NRA) specifications motivated by problems in 2- and 3-dimensional geometry. These benchmarks model spatial relationships and bounding problems, such as intersecting circles, annular regions, and spheres with varying or fixed radii. The suite additionally

Table 1. Comparison of NQSynth, QEPCAD+CVC5, and ModEnum

Benchmark Set		NQSynth	QEPCAD + CVC5	ModEnum
NRA	Solved	59	26	23
Total: 83	Time (s)	(4.998, 9.096, 20.512)	(4.649, 6.560, 39.785)	(0.067, 3.529, 45.784)
	PAR2	75.864	166.856	174.472
Geometric	Solved	33	16	11
Total: 51	Time	(4.890, 10.436, 29.703)	(4.879, 5.030, 5.623)	(0.083, 0.205, 0.628)
	PAR2	91.459	166.284	188.280

also contains a broad range of non-linear behavior by including mixed-degree curves, parabolas, hyperbolas, and higher-power polynomial boundaries (ranging up to degree-100). While these benchmarks are easy to describe, synthesizing rational programs for them turns out to be difficult in most cases.

Evaluation Results: All our experiments were conducted on a MacBook Pro 2023 with Apple M2 Pro processor and 32 GB main memory. A timeout of 120 s was set for each technique. We say a technique *solves* a benchmark if it synthesizes a program that *realizes* the corresponding specification over rationals before timing out. When reporting time taken by a tool for a set of benchmarks, we report (minimum, average, maximum) triples. The PAR2 (Penalized Average Runtime 2) score is a widely used metric (smaller is better) that computes the average runtime by penalizing each timeout with twice the timeout value.

A comparison of the relative performance of NQSynth, QEPCAD+CVC5 and ModEnum on the two benchmark sets is given in Table 1. Scatter plots of the times taken on individual benchmarks are shown in Fig. 2a (NQSynth vs QEPCAD+SyGuS) and Fig. 2b (NQSynth vs ModEnum). There is only 1 NRA benchmark that NQSynth cannot solve in 120 s that QEPCAD+CVC5 solves in 5.07 s. On the other hand, there are 34 NRA benchmarks that QEPCAD+CVC5 can't solve in 120 s, but all of these are solved by NQSynth within 25 s. There is no NRA benchmark that NQSynth cannot solve but ModEnum can within 120 s.

Our results clearly show the effectiveness NQSynth over (QEPCAD+CVC5) and ModEnum. On further investigation, we found that quantifier elimination using QEPCAD in step 7 of Algorithm 2 was the sole reason for NQSynth timing out. In 8 out of 24 timeout cases in Set 1, it was the first quantifier elimination itself that timed out. In the remaining cases, the tool timed out during quantifier elimination while iterating in the outer `while` loop of Algorithm 2, having generated between 18 to 24 pre-conditions (whose disjunction was not yet the weakest pre-condition). In the case of Geometric benchmarks, out of 18 timeout cases for Algorithm 2, 3 timed out in the first quantifier elimination call. In the other 15 cases, the tool timed out after having generated between 2 and 25 pre-conditions, that did not yield the weakest pre-condition yet. Note that in all cases where at least one pre-condition was generated, Algorithm 2 outputs a sound program, even though it timed out. Interestingly, none of the invocations of Z3 resulted in any irrational model being generated. Hence, there were no "wasted" models, as per the check in line 8 of Algorithm 2. As one would expect, using more optimized commercial engines such as Maple[1] [9,37] and Mathematica [28] improves time performance, although in our experiments this did not significantly expand the class of benchmarks solved. Detailed total execution times for each benchmark across the three engines are reported in the extended version [3], along with further experimental details.

6 Conclusion

In this paper, we addressed rational program synthesis from polynomial specifications. We investigated theoretical aspects of the problem, loop-free conditions and links to quantifier elimination. We then developed algorithms for synthesis, sound and complete for subclasses and an NRA-oracle based sound algorithm in general. As future work, we would like to know when a particular polynomial specification has a loop-free program, if we can effectively synthesize it.

Acknowledgments. Aniruddha Joshi was partly supported by the DARPA Provably Correct Design of Adaptive Hybrid Neuro-Symbolic Cyber Physical Systems (ANSR) program award number FA8750-23-C-0080, and by Nissan and Toyota under the iCy-Phy Center.

References

1. Ábrahám, E., Davenport, J.H., England, M., Kremer, G.: Deciding the consistency of non-linear real arithmetic constraints with a conflict driven search using cylindrical algebraic coverings. J. Log. Algebraic Methods Program **119** (2021)
2. Akshay, S., Chakraborty, S., Goharshady, A.K., Govind, R., Motwani, H.J., Varanasi, S.T.: Automated synthesis of decision lists for polynomial specifications over integers. In: LPAR. EPiC Series in Computing vol. 100, pp. 484–502. EasyChair (2024)
3. Akshay, S., Chakraborty, S., Govind, R., Joshi, A.R.: Program synthesis for non-linear real arithmetic: Going beyond realizability (2026). https://arxiv.org/submit/7628173
4. Alur, R., Bodík, R., et al.: Syntax-guided synthesis. In: Dependable Software Systems Engineering, NATO Science for Peace and Security Series, D: Information and Communication Security, vol. 40, pp. 1–25. IOS Press (2015)
5. Alur, R., et al.: Syntax-guided synthesis. In: FMCAD. pp. 1–8 (2013)
6. Alur, R., Singh, R., Fisman, D., Solar-Lezama, A.: Search-based program synthesis. Commun. ACM **61**(12), 84–93 (2018)
7. Barbosa, H., et al.: cvc5: a versatile and industrial-strength SMT solver. In: TACAS 2022. LNCS, vol. 13243, pp. 415–442. Springer, Cham (2022). https://doi.org/10.1007/978-3-030-99524-9_24
8. Basu, S., Pollack, R., Roy, M.F.: Algorithms in Real Algebraic Geometry. Springer, Berlin, Heidelberg (2006)
9. Bernardin, L., et al.: Maple Programming Guide. Maplesoft, a division of Waterloo Maple Inc. (1996–2025)

[1] Computations performed by using Maple^{TM}, a trademark of Waterloo Maple Inc.

10. Brown, C.W.: Improved projection for cylindrical algebraic decomposition. J. Symb. Comput. **32**(5), 447–465 (2001)
11. Chen, C., Maza, M.M.: Quantifier elimination by cylindrical algebraic decomposition based on regular chains. J. Symb. Comput. **75**, 74–93 (2016)
12. Church, A.: Logic, arithmetic, and automata. In: Proceedings of the International Congress of Mathematicians, pp. 23–35 (1962)
13. Code with C: Mastering rational root theorem: A practical guide (2024). https://www.codewithc.com/mastering-rational-root-theorem-a-practical-guide/
14. Collins, G.E.: Quantifier elimination for real closed fields by cylindrical algebraic decompostion. In: Brakhage, H. (ed.) GI-Fachtagung 1975. LNCS, vol. 33, pp. 134–183. Springer, Heidelberg (1975). https://doi.org/10.1007/3-540-07407-4_17
15. Collins, G.E.: Quantifier elimination by cylindrical algebraic decomposition — twenty years of progress. In: Caviness, B.F., Johnson, J.R. (eds.) Quantifier Elimination and Cylindrical Algebraic Decomposition. Springer Vienna (1998). https://doi.org/10.1007/978-3-7091-9459-1_2
16. Collins, G.E., Akritas, A.G.: Polynomial real root isolation using descarte's rule of signs. In: SYMSACC, pp. 272–275. ACM (1976)
17. Collins, G.E., Hong, H.: Partial cylindrical algebraic decomposition for quantifier elimination. J. Symb. Comput. **12**(3), 299–328 (1991)
18. Davis, M., Matijasevic, Y., Robinson, J.: Hilbert's tenth problem. diophantine equations: positive aspects of a negative solution. In: Proceedings of Symposia in Pure Mathematics, vol. 28, pp. 323–378 (1976)
19. Dorato, P., Yang, W., Abdallah, C.T.: Robust multi-objective feedback design by quantifier elimination. J. Symb. Comput. **24**(2), 153–159 (1997)
20. Eisenträeger, K., Miller, R., Park, J., Shlapentokh, A.: As easy as $\mathbb{Q}$: Hilbert's tenth problem for subrings of the rationals and number fields. Trans. Am. Math. Soc. **369**(11), 8291–8315 (2017)
21. Field, J.V.: The historical roots of elementary mathematics. lucas n. h. bunt, phillip s. jones, jack d. bedient. Isis **69**(2), 274–274 (1978). https://doi.org/10.1086/352020
22. Fisman, D., Singh, R., Solar-Lezama, A.: Special issue on syntax-guided synthesis preface. Formal Methods Syst. Des. **58**(3), 469–470 (2021)
23. Goharshady, A.K., Hitarth, S., Mohammadi, F., Motwani, H.J.: Template-based program synthesis using stellensätze. CoRR abs/ arXiv:2209.03602 (2022)
24. Goharshady, A.K., Hitarth, S., Mohammadi, F., Motwani, H.J.: Algebro-geometric algorithms for template-based synthesis of polynomial programs. Proc. ACM Program. Lang. **7**(OOPSLA1), 727–756 (2023)
25. Goldberg, D.: What every computer scientist should know about floating-point arithmetic. ACM Comput. Surv. **23**(1), 5–48 (1991). https://doi.org/10.1145/103162.103163
26. Hong, H., Liska, R., Steinberg, S.L.: Testing stability by quantifier elimination. J. Symb. Comput. **24**(2), 161–187 (1997)
27. Huang, K., Qiu, X., Tian, Q., Wang, Y.: Reconciling enumerative and symbolic search in syntax-guided synthesis. CoRR abs/ arXiv:1802.04428 (2018)
28. Inc., W.R.: Mathematica, Version 14.3., champaign, IL (2025). https://www.wolfram.com/mathematica
29. Jirstrand, M.: Nonlinear control system design by quantifier elimination. J. Symb. Comput. **24**(2), 137–152 (1997)
30. Jovanovic, D., de Moura, L.M.: Solving non-linear arithmetic. In: IJCAR, pp. 339–354 (2012)

31. Kobel, A., Rouillier, F., Sagraloff, M.: Computing real roots of real polynomials ... and now for real! In: ISSAC, pp. 303–310. ACM (2016)
32. Kremer, G., Ábrahám, E.: Fully incremental cylindrical algebraic decomposition. J. Symb. Comput. **100**, 11–37 (2020)
33. Kuncak, V., Mayer, M., Piskac, R., Suter, P.: Complete functional synthesis. In: PLDI, pp. 316–329. ACM (2010)
34. Kuncak, V., Mayer, M., Piskac, R., Suter, P.: Functional synthesis for linear arithmetic and sets. Softw. Tools Technol. Transfer **14**(1), 1–22 (2012). https://doi.org/10.1007/s10009-011-0217-7
35. Lafferriere, G., Pappas, G.J., Yovine, S.: Symbolic reachability computation for families of linear vector fields. J. Symb. Comput. **32**(3), 231–253 (2001)
36. Lazard, S.: Real root isolation: a survey. Theoret. Comput. Sc. **410**(20), 1839–1850 (2009). https://doi.org/10.1016/j.tcs.2009.04.039
37. Maplesoft, a division of Waterloo Maple Inc.: Maple User Manual. Waterloo Maple Inc. (1996–2025)
38. McCallum, S.: Solving polynomial strict inequalities using cylindrical algebraic decomposition. Comput. J. **36**(5), 432–438 (1993)
39. McCallum, S.: Partial solution of a path finding problem using the cad method. In: Electronic Proceedings of the IMACS ACA (1995)
40. McCallum, S.: On projection in cad-based quantifier elimination with equational constraint. In: ISSAC, pp. 145–149. ACM (1999)
41. McCallum, S.: On propagation of equational constraints in cad-based quantifier elimination. In: ISSAC, pp. 223–231. ACM (2001)
42. McCullum, J., Tiwari, P.: Lower bounds for cylindrical algebraic decomposition and applications to quantifier elimination. Theoret. Comput. Sc. **507**, 38–56 (2013). https://doi.org/10.1016/j.tcs.2013.05.035, https://doi.org/10.1016/j.tcs.2013.05.035
43. Mignotte, M.: Some useful bounds. In: Buchberger, B., Collins, G.E., Loos, R. (eds.) Computer Algebra. Computing Supplementum, vol 4. Springer, Vienna (1982). https://doi.org/10.1007/978-3-7091-3406-1_16
44. Monniaux, D.: Quantifier elimination by lazy model enumeration. In: Touili, T., Cook, B., Jackson, P. (eds.) CAV 2010. LNCS, vol. 6174, pp. 585–599. Springer, Heidelberg (2010). https://doi.org/10.1007/978-3-642-14295-6_51
45. de Moura, L., Bjørner, N.: Z3: an efficient SMT solver. In: Ramakrishnan, C.R., Rehof, J. (eds.) TACAS 2008. LNCS, vol. 4963, pp. 337–340. Springer, Heidelberg (2008). https://doi.org/10.1007/978-3-540-78800-3_24
46. Preiner, M., Schurr, H.J., Barrett, C., Fontaine, P., Niemetz, A., Tinelli, C.: Smt-lib release 2024 (incremental benchmarks) (May 2024). https://doi.org/10.5281/zenodo.11186591
47. Robinson, J.: The undecidability of algebraic rings and fields. Proc. Am. Math. Soc. **10**(6), 950–957 (1959)
48. Sadeghimanesh, A., England, M.: An SMT solver for non-linear real arithmetic inside maple. ACM Commun. Comput. Algebra **56**(2), 76–79 (2022)
49. Solar-Lezama, A., Rabbah, R.M., Bodík, R., Ebcioglu, K.: Programming by sketching for bit-streaming programs. In: Proceedings of the ACM SIGPLAN 2005 Conference on Programming Language Design and Implementation, Chicago, IL, USA, 12-15 June 2005, pp. 281–294 (2005)
50. Stewart, T., Dupont, E.: The gnu multiple precision arithmetic library (gmp) (2000). https://gmplib.org/ Accessed 01 Feb 2025
51. Strzebonski, A.W.: Solving systems of strict polynomial inequalities. J. Symb. Comput. **29**(3), 471–480 (2000)

52. Tarski, A.: A Decision Method for Elementary Algebra and Geometry: Prepared for Publication with the Assistance of J.C.C. McKinsey. RAND Corporation, Santa Monica, CA (1951)
53. The Sage Developers: SageMath, the Sage Mathematics Software System (Version 10.2) (2023). https://www.sagemath.org
54. Turing, A.M.: On computable numbers, with an application to the entscheidungsproblem. Proc. Lond. Math. Soc. **42**(2), 230–265 (1936). https://doi.org/10.1112/plms/s2-42.1.230
55. Uspensky, J.V.: Theory of Equations. McGraw-Hill (1948)
56. Vincent, R.: The roots of polynomials with real coefficients. Math. Comput. **27**(123), 359–369 (1973). https://doi.org/10.1090/S0025-5718-1973-0337792-1
57. Weispfenning, V.: Semilinear motion planning in REDLOG. Appl. Algebra Eng. Commun. Comput. **12**(6), 455–475 (2001)
58. Wikipedia: Real-root isolation — Wikipedia, the free encyclopedia (2023). https://en.wikipedia.org/wiki/Real-root_isolation

Open Access This chapter is licensed under the terms of the Creative Commons Attribution 4.0 International License (http://creativecommons.org/licenses/by/4.0/), which permits use, sharing, adaptation, distribution and reproduction in any medium or format, as long as you give appropriate credit to the original author(s) and the source, provide a link to the Creative Commons license and indicate if changes were made.

The images or other third party material in this chapter are included in the chapter's Creative Commons license, unless indicated otherwise in a credit line to the material. If material is not included in the chapter's Creative Commons license and your intended use is not permitted by statutory regulation or exceeds the permitted use, you will need to obtain permission directly from the copyright holder.

Checking Regular Expressions in Cvc5 Proofs

Ofec Israel[1], Yoni Zohar[1(✉)], Andrew Reynolds[2], S. Hitarth[3], Bruno Dutertre[4], Clark Barrett[5], and Cesare Tinelli[2]

[1] Bar-Ilan University, Ramat Gan, Israel
yoni.zohar@biu.ac.il
[2] The University of Iowa, Iowa City, IA, USA
[3] Max Planck Institute for Software Systems, Saarbrücken, Germany
[4] Amazon Web Services, Santa Clara, CA, USA
[5] Stanford University, Stanford, CA, USA

Abstract. cvc5 is a state-of-the-art proof-producing SMT solver, capable of solving formulas over a myriad of theories, including Unicode strings. Matching regular expressions against concrete strings is done numerous times during the solving process, and forms a bottleneck in proof-checking for unsatisfiable formulas. We describe three approaches for checking regular expressions in the Eunoia proof-checking framework, and evaluate them on proofs produced by cvc5.

1 Introduction

This work is part of a research program to efficiently check unsatisfiability proofs produced by Satisfiability Modulo Theories (SMT) solvers [4]. We focus on the cvc5 [2] SMT solver and the Eunoia [10] proof framework. We implement checking procedures for a common reasoning step in the SMT-LIBtheory of strings: matching regular expressions. These are implemented as *side conditions*: Eunoiaprograms that are defined in proof rules executed during proof checking.

Solving string constraints involves matching many concrete strings and regular expressions, to the point that verifying these matching steps becomes a bottleneck in proof checking. Implementing standard algorithms for regular expression checking as side conditions in Eunoiais challenging, because Eunoiaoffers limited support for standard data structures and control flow commands.

We have implemented three approaches. The first and simplest is based on backtracking. However, this basic approach does not perform well in many cases. The second follows Thompson's construction, and the third adopts Brzozowski's derivatives [5]. Our experiments show that the derivatives-based approach performs best and is therefore now the default in cvc5's main branch.

Section 2 presents necessary background. Section 3 to 5 survey the three approaches. We evaluate them in Sect. 6,[1] and conclude in Sect. 7.

B. Dutertre—This work does not relate to the author's position at Amazon.
[1] An accompanying artifact is available at https://doi.org/10.5281/zenodo.18524263.

© The Author(s) 2026
A. Biere et al. (Eds.): IJCAR 2026, LNAI 16688, pp. 267–275, 2026.
https://doi.org/10.1007/978-3-032-32589-1_16

Table 1. Fragment of SMT-LIB strings.

Op.	Sort	SMT-LIB
none	$\mathcal{R}$	`re.none`
to_re	$\mathcal{S} \to \mathcal{R}$	`str.to_re`
comp	$\mathcal{R} \to \mathcal{R}$	`re.comp`
star	$\mathcal{R} \to \mathcal{R}$	`re.*`
rcon	$\mathcal{R} \times \mathcal{R} \to \mathcal{R}$	`re.++`
union	$\mathcal{R} \times \mathcal{R} \to \mathcal{R}$	`re.union`
inter	$\mathcal{R} \times \mathcal{R} \to \mathcal{R}$	`re.inter`

Table 2. Builtins in Eunoia.

Op.	Eunoia	Desc.
lconcat	eo::list_concat	List concat
find	eo::list_find	List find
diff	eo::list_diff	List diff
sconcat	eo::concat	Str concat
extract	eo::extract	Substr
len	eo::len	Str Length
eq	eo::is_eq	Equality

Related Work. The collection of proof rules for checking cvc5 proofs is described in [9]. Recent work [12] provides a solver whose calculus is verified in Lean. We focus on independent *proof-checking* for unsatisfiability results.

2 Preliminaries

Table 1 shows a sub-signature of the theory of strings [3], focusing on regular expressions (regexes). The sorts of strings and regular languages are $\mathcal{S}$ and $\mathcal{R}$, respectively. Operators *none*and *to_re*represent the empty language and string literals (w.l.o.g., of length 1), respectively, while ϵ denotes the empty string. Other constructors include *comp* (complementation), *star* (Kleene closure), *rcon* (concatenation), *union* (union), and *inter* (intersection). The signature includes all string literals, denoted with double quotes. We often use standard regex notation, e.g., writing a^*b instead of $rcon(star(to\_re(''a'')), to\_re(''b''))$. The implementation supports additional SMT-LIB operators (e.g. character ranges).

Eunoiais a logical framework for proofs, equipped with the Ethos proof checker [8,10], which supports dagification of terms and memoization of programs. Variadic terms are called *lists*. Internally, lists are LISP-style expressions. Eunoiaincludes a minimal standard library for lists and strings, which implements common operations natively for efficiency, such as the ones listed in Table 2. Eunoiaallows defining *side conditions* in the form of functional programs. The most direct rule that relies on regex matching is `str-in-re-eval`, which matches a string against a regex. Other rules include, e.g., `re-inter-inclusion` and `str-replace-re-eval`, that use matching for complex regex queries.

A *nondeterministic finite automaton (NFA)* $(\mathcal{Q}, \Sigma, \Delta, q_s, q_a)$ consists of finite sets $\mathcal{Q}$ and Σ of states and letters, with $\epsilon \notin \Sigma$, $\Delta : \mathcal{Q} \times (\Sigma \cup \{\epsilon\}) \to \mathcal{P}(\mathcal{Q})$, the *transition function*, and $q_s, q_a \in \mathcal{Q}$, the *start* and *accepting* states. The ϵ-*closure* of q is the set of states reachable from q by ϵ-transitions.

3 Backtracking-Based Approach

Backtracking works by analyzing the regular expression and applying sub-queries recursively. Pseudocode for this approach is given in Algorithm 1. Function BtRec takes a string s, index n, and two regular expressions r_1 and r_2. It

Algorithm 1. Backtracking algorithm for regex matching.

1: **function** BTREC(s, n, r_1, r_2)
2:     **if** $r_2 \neq$ *null* **then**
3:         $s_1 \leftarrow$ *extract*$(s, 0, n-1)$; $s_2 \leftarrow$ *extract*$(s, n, len(s)-1)$
4:         **if** BTREC($s_1, 0, r_1,$ *null*) $\wedge$ BTREC($s_2, 0, r_2,$ *null*) **then return true**
5:         **else if** $n = len(s)$ **then return false**
6:         **else return** BTREC($s, n+1, r_1, r_2$)
7:     **match** r_1 **with**
8:         **case** *to_re*(s')**: return** $s' = s$
9:         **case** *none***: return false**
10:         **case** *union*(r_a, r_b)**: return** BTREC($s, 0, r_a,$ *null*) $\vee$ BTREC($s, 0, r_b,$ *null*)
11:         **case** *inter*(r_a, r_b)**: return** BTREC($s, 0, r_a,$ *null*) $\wedge$ BTREC($s, 0, r_b,$ *null*)
12:         **case** *comp*(r_a)**: return** $\neg$BTREC($s, 0, r_a,$ *null*)
13:         **case** *rcon*(r_a, r_b)**: return** BTREC($s, 0, r_a, r_b$)
14:         **case** *star*(r_a)**:**
15:             **if** $s = \epsilon$ **then return true**
16:             **else return** BTREC($s, 1, r_a, r_1$)

```
(program $bt_rec (...)
  :signature (String Int RegLan RegLan) Bool
  (
   (($bt_rec s 0 (str.to_re s1) @re.null) (eo::is_eq s s1))
   (($bt_rec s 0 (re.++ r1 rr) @re.null) ($bt_rec s 0 r1 rr))
   ...
  )
)
```

Fig. 1. Eunoia code for BTREC.

determines whether s conforms to the pattern defined by regex r_1 followed immediately by regex r_2. Parameter n specifies the minimum size of the prefix of s that must be consumed by r_1. We use *null* as an internal marker for invalid regexes. When first calling BTREC, n is passed as 0 and r_2 as *null*. Some cases require considering every partition of the string (lines 3–6). If a match fails in the recursion, the algorithm backtracks, causing an exponential growth in execution time. We show a snippet from the Eunoiacode of BTREC in Figure 1.

Algorithm 2. Function BNR for constructing automata from regexes.

function BNR$(r, q_s, q_a, \delta, \sigma)$
    match r **with**
        case *none*: **return** δ
        case *to_re*(c): **return** $cons((q_s, c, q_a), \delta)$
        case $rcon(r_1, r_2)$:
            $q_{mid} \leftarrow sconcat(\sigma, "m")$
            $\delta_1 \leftarrow$ BNR$(r_1, q_s, q_{mid}, \delta, sconcat(\sigma, "l"))$
            return BNR$(r_2, q_{mid}, q_a, \delta_1, sconcat(\sigma, "r"))$
        case $union(r_1, r_2)$:
            $\delta_1 \leftarrow$ BNR$(r_1, q_s, q_a, \delta, sconcat(\sigma, "l"))$
            return BNR$(r_2, q_s, q_a, \delta_1, sconcat(\sigma, "r"))$
        case $star(r_1)$:
            $q_{hub} \leftarrow sconcat(\sigma, "h")$
            $\delta_{loop} \leftarrow lconcat(\delta, [(q_s, \epsilon, q_{hub}), (q_{hub}, \epsilon, q_a)])$
            return BNR$(r_1, q_{hub}, q_{hub}, \delta_{loop}, sconcat(\sigma, "l"))$

Example 1. Consider the execution of BtRec$("aab", 0, a^*b, null)$ to determine whether "aab" matches regex a^*b. Since $r_2 = null$, we skip the conditional. Then, we recurse on line 13, calling BtRec$("aab", 0, a^*, b)$. In the recursive call, $r_2 \neq null$, and so we enter the conditional. There, we consider all splits of $"aab"$ into two strings. When $i = 2$, the match succeeds.

4 NFA-Based Approach

The second approach is based on Thompson's construction of NFAs [11]. It requires the *construction* of an automaton and then the *simulation* of the automaton on the input string. We only use this approach on regexes that exclude *comp* and *inter*, as these operators require expensive transformations. For regexes including these operators, we fall back to backtracking.

Eunoiacannot naturally represent NFAs as directed graphs, due to its strict bottom-up evaluation that does not support cycles. Instead, we represent an NFA as a list of transitions of the form (q, α, q'), where q and q' are states and α is a character or ϵ. The states are represented by string identifiers. To ensure uniqueness, we use a *path-based* identifier scheme. Each recursive call carries a string that encodes its position.

The construction is described in Algorithm 2. Function BNR takes a regular expression r without *comp* and *inter*, and computes an equivalent NFA. For that, it takes additional arguments: (string identifiers for) start and accept states (q_s and q_a, respectively), a list δ of transitions, and a path context σ. It is called with a start state $"s"$, accepting state $"a"$, an empty transition list, and an empty path context. The result is a transition list that represents an NFA.

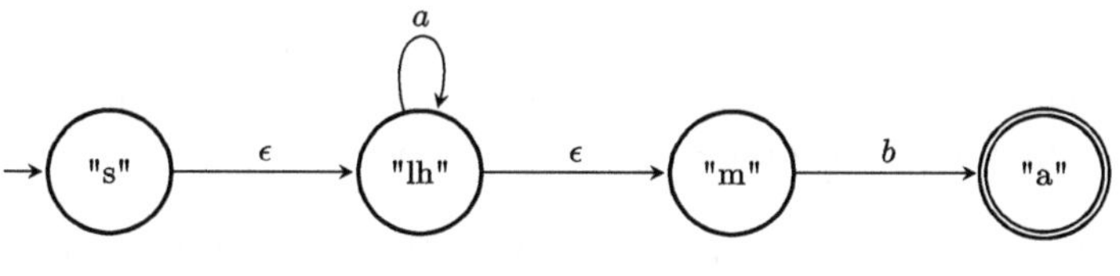

Fig. 2. The NFA for a^*b from the transition list generated by BNR.

Example 2. Running BNR (Algorithm 2) on regular expression $r = a^*b$ with $q_s :='' s''$, $q_a :='' a''$, $\delta := []$, and $\sigma :='' ''$, we identify expression a^*b as a concatenation and generate a unique intermediate identifier based on the current path σ: $q_{mid} = sconcat(\sigma, ''m'') ='' m''$. The problem is then split into two recursive calls. Eventually, we obtain four transitions: $(''s'', \epsilon, '' lh'')$, $(''lh'', '' a'', '' lh'')$, $(''lh'', \epsilon, '' m'')$, and $(''m'', '' b'', '' a'')$. A graphical representation is in Fig. 2.

After construction, we simulate the NFA on the input string. For each letter, we identify the list of reachable states by scanning the transition list, which can be costly. The algorithm updates the reachable states while scanning the input, and accepts if the final set contains the accepting state.

Example 3. Simulating the NFA of Example 2 with string $s ='' aab''$, the ϵ-closure of the initial state $''s''$ consists of $''s''$, $''lh''$, and $''m''$. The first character to match is "a". States $''s''$ and $''m''$ yield no transitions for "a". State $''lh''$ transitions to $''lh''$, so $''lh''$ is added as a reachable state. The algorithm continues until letter "b" is consumed, at which point q_a belongs to the reachable states.

4.1 Optimizations

To avoid quadratic simulation, we represent the automaton hierarchically, each letter points to a nested transition list. Due to term dagification in Ethos, this tree-shaped structure is stored as a DAG. Simulation shifts from global scanning to walking a decision tree. Since the underlying representation is acyclic, we implement cycles using an execution stack. The marks *LoopEntry* and *LoopExit* serve as control instructions that do not consume input and are used to simulate NFA loops. For a Kleene-star expression, the construction places a *LoopEntry* before the body and a matching *LoopExit* after it. When execution reaches a *LoopEntry*, it pushes a reference to this entry point onto the stack and proceeds into the loop body. When execution reaches the corresponding *LoopExit*, it pops this reference and branches nondeterministically.

Example 4. The optimized construction for a^*b results in the following hierarchical representation, which is illustrated in Fig. 3. Notice that the top level only contains two mappings, one for *LoopEntry* and one for b.

$$[(LoopEntry, [(a, [(LoopExit, [(b, [\text{ACCEPT}])])])]), (b, [\text{ACCEPT}])]$$

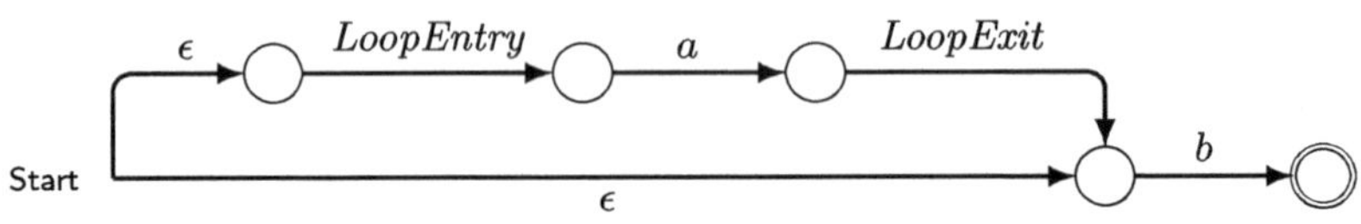

Fig. 3. Hierarchical representation for the optimized NFA construction of a^*b.

5 Derivatives-Based Approach

Our last approach is based on Brzozowski derivatives [5], as outlined in Algorithm 3. It uses function NLBL, which checks if a regex accepts ϵ. Function DER computes the regex remaining after matching a character, which is called a *derivative*. For $\emptyset$ and ϵ, this is *none*. For single characters, the derivative is ϵ if the current character matches. Boolean operators and *star* are handled recursively. The derivative of a concatenation r_1r_2 splits according to whether r_1 accepts ϵ. The string is accepted if the final derivative accepts ϵ.

Example 5. For string "*aab*" and regex a^*b, Algorithm 3 computes the derivative for "a", transforming a^*b to $\emptyset \cup (\epsilon \cdot a^*) \cdot b$, as a^* accepts ϵ. After the derivative for 'b' is computed, the string is accepted because the final expression is nullable. Notice that the final derivative is quite involved, even for this simple case, namely:

$$\emptyset \cup (\emptyset \cup (\epsilon \cup ((((\emptyset \cdot a^*) \cup (\emptyset \cdot a^*)) \cup (\emptyset \cdot a^*)) \cdot b)))$$

Algorithm 3. Function DER for computing derivatives.

function DER(c, r)
  match r **with**
    case *none*, *to_re*(ϵ): **return** *none*
    case *to_re*(c_0): **if** $c_0 = c$ **return** *to_re*(ϵ) **else return** *none*
    case *union*(r_1, r_2): **return** *union*(DER(c, r_1), DER(c, r_2))
    case *inter*(r_1, r_2): **return** *inter*(DER(c, r_1), DER(c, r_2))
    case *comp*(r_1): **return** *comp*(DER(c, r_1))
    case *star*(r_1): **return** *rcon*(DER(c, r_1), *star*(r_1))
    case *rcon*(r_1, r_2):
      if NLBL(r_1) **then return** *union*(DER(c, r_2), *rcon*(DER(c, r_1), r_2))
      else return *rcon*(DER(c, r_1), r_2)

5.1 Optimizations

The naive implementation frequently involves redundant expressions (e.g., $\emptyset \cup r$, $r \cup r$, or $\epsilon \cdot r$), leading to an unnecessary growth in the size of the regular expression. To mitigate this, we enforce the algebraic simplification rules from [5,6] during the construction of the derivative, which flatten and normalize applications of *union*, *inter*and *rcon*, while also eliminating unnecessary occurrences of ϵ and *none*. Crucially, we keep terms normalized during construction, relying on this invariant and Eunoia's native list operators (e.g., *lconcat*and *diff*).

Example 6. With the simplification, the partial derivative for "a" remains a^*b, without any ϵ or *none*. The final derivative is simply ϵ, which is trivially nullable, and significantly shorter than the equivalent derivative computed in Example 5.

6 Evaluation

We use a cluster of 23 machines with Intel Xeon Gold 6348 CPUs. Proofs are generated with cvc5 1.3.2 using limits of 60 s and 8GB, and are checked separately with Ethos 0.2.2 using the same limits. There are 103,405 benchmarks in logics QF_S, QF_SLIA, and QF_SNIA of the 2024 release of the SMT-LIB benchmark library [7]. Within the given resources, cvc5 is able to determine that 38,765 are unsatisfiable. 3,118 unsatisfiability proofs apply rule `str-in-re-eval`. These proofs comprise our **Organic** benchmark set. The second set consists of 35,627 **Synthetic** proofs, obtained by logging a sequence of calls to the regex matching rule, applied to all regex checks performed during solving. These are not unsat proofs, but sequences of calls to rule `str-in-re-eval`.

Our configurations are listed on the left of Table 3, which summarizes the results. In **LB** the regex matching rule accepts each application immediately. It provides a **lower bound** for checking time. For the other configurations, we list the relevant section and the number of lines of code (LOC). **NFA**$^+$ has fewer LOCs than **NFA** because it does not need to maintain unique string identifiers.

The number of proofs commonly checked by all approaches is in parentheses. Total run-times (T) and memory usage (M) are given for the set of commonly checked proofs. Number of checked proofs (# S) is also given. On **Organic**, **DER**$^+$ is nearly optimal, taking just 8 s more than **LB**. The results also show that the optimizations of the NFA and derivatives approaches are crucial.

On **Synthetic**, **BT** checks slightly more proofs than the optimized approaches. These proofs originate from the sub-family `redos_attack_detection` of QF_SLIA and share a similar pattern with extremely long strings. On these, the default search order of **BT** guides it to an early termination of the loop in Algorithm 1, avoiding an exhaustive search. Thus, **BT** remains a viable alternative with performance complementary to the others on such benchmarks.

When considering commonly checked proofs, the results are similar to set **Organic**. Configurations **NFA** and **NFA**$^+$ fall back to **BT** on ~5% of the checks. Finally, we remark that configuration **BT** is sensitive to the order in which the splits into two strings are considered in Algorithm 1. For example, when we reverse the order of the splits, its performance significantly degrades.

Table 3. Summary of configurations and results.

Config	Sec.	LOC	**Organic** (3,106 common)			**Synthetic** (34,050 common)		
			# S	T (s)	M (GB)	# S	T (s)	M (GB)
LB	–	–	3117	351	34	35620	1580	308
BT	3	40	3114	386	37	**35593**	3111	363
NFA	4	128	3112	517	42	35359	10214	743
NFA$^+$	4.1	91	**3117**	361	**34**	35580	2119	329
DER	5	46	3111	589	47	34204	12928	718
DER$^+$	5.1	66	**3117**	**359**	**34**	35556	**1743**	**314**

7 Conclusion

We have implemented and evaluated several approaches for checking regular expression membership in the Ethos checker for cvc5 proofs. The primary obstacle was reconciling efficiency with the strict architectural constraints of Eunoia. Future work includes further optimizing the derivatives and NFA approaches, and implementing similar support in Carcara [1].

Acknowledgments. This research was supported in part by the Stanford Center for Automated Reasoning, Defense Advanced Research Projects Agency (DARPA) contract FA875024-2-1001, Israel Science Foundation (ISF) grant number 209/25, Binational Science Foundation (BSF) grant number 2024049, and a gift from Amazon Web Services.

References

1. Andreotti, B., Lachnitt, H., Barbosa, H.: "Carcara: an efficient proof checker and elaborator for SMT proofs in the Alethe format. In: TACAS (1), vol. 13993. LNCS. Springer, pp. 367–386 (2023)
2. Barbosa, H., et al.: CVC5: a versatile and industrial-strength SMT solver. Presented at the (2022). https://doi.org/10.1007/978-3-030-99524-9_24
3. Barrett, C., Fontaine, P., Tinelli, C.: The Satisfiability Modulo Theories Library (SMT-LIB). www.SMT-LIB.org (2016)
4. Barrett, C., et al.: "Satisfiability modulo theories". In: Handbook of Satisfiability, Second Edition. Vol. 336. Frontiers in Artificial Intelligence and Applications. IOS Press. Chap. 33, pp. 825–885 (2021)
5. Brzozowski, J.A.: "Derivatives of regular expressions". J. ACM **11**(4), 481–494 (1964)
6. Owens, S., Reppy, J.H., Turon, A.: "Regular-expression derivatives re-examined". In: J. Funct. Program. **19**(2), 173–190 (2009)
7. Preiner, M.: SMT-LIB release 2024 (non-incremental benchmarks) (2024)

8. Reynolds, A., et al.: "Ethos: a fast proof checker for the eunoia logical framework". In: Automated Reasoning - 13th International Joint Conference, IJCAR 2026. Ed. by Armin Biere, Carsten Lutz, and Sara Negri. Lecture Notes in Computer Science. Springer (2026)
9. Reynolds, A., et al.: "The cooperating proof calculus: comprehensive proofs for an SMT solver". In: CAV. LNCS. To appear. Springer (2026)
10. The Ethos Manual. https://github.com/cvc5/ethos/blob/main/usermanual.md (2025)
11. Thompson, K.: "Regular expression search algorithm". Commun. ACM **11**(6), 419–422 (1968)
12. Varatalu, I.E., et al.: "Regex decision procedures in extended RE#". In: CAV. Springer, pp. 106–129 (2025)

Open Access This chapter is licensed under the terms of the Creative Commons Attribution 4.0 International License (http://creativecommons.org/licenses/by/4.0/), which permits use, sharing, adaptation, distribution and reproduction in any medium or format, as long as you give appropriate credit to the original author(s) and the source, provide a link to the Creative Commons license and indicate if changes were made.

The images or other third party material in this chapter are included in the chapter's Creative Commons license, unless indicated otherwise in a credit line to the material. If material is not included in the chapter's Creative Commons license and your intended use is not permitted by statutory regulation or exceeds the permitted use, you will need to obtain permission directly from the copyright holder.

Hardware Model Checking Certification with Certifaiger and Cerbtora

Nils Froleyks[1(✉)] and Emily Yu[2]

[1] KU Leuven, Leuven, Belgium
nfroleyks@gmail.com
[2] Leiden University, Leiden, The Netherlands

Abstract. Certificates are machine-checkable witnesses that help increase confidence in verification results by providing independently verifiable evidence beyond a simple yes/no answer. In this short paper, we present two certificate checkers for hardware model checking, Certifaiger and Cerbtora, which target bit-level and word-level verification of hardware designs, respectively. Certifaiger has been adopted in recent editions of the Hardware Model Checking Competition, but not described in the literature before. Cerbtora extends the same theoretical framework to the word level, in which certificates are expressed in the same modeling language as the design under test and are validated using efficient automated reasoning engines. We describe the architecture and main components of both tools and evaluate them on competition benchmarks.

1 Introduction

Certification has gained increasing attention in automated reasoning and formal verification as a way to provide an additional layer of trust in the correctness of safety-critical systems beyond a simple yes/no answer. The concept of certification spans several areas, such as Boolean satisfiability (SAT) solving [15,17], satisfiability modulo theories (SMT) [16,21], and software verification [2]. In hardware model checking, certification has also advanced recently. In particular, the bit-level track of the Hardware Model Checking Competition (HWMCC) now requires participating tools to generate certificates, with encouraging results [14]. In this setting, the certificates take the form of *witness circuits* produced at the end of the verification process. The certificate format is designed to accommodate a wide range of model checking techniques [13,25–27]. Validating a witness circuit is lightweight and efficient, reducing to a small number of SAT checks.

So far, most effort has focused on certifying safety properties in bit-level model checking (i.e., reasoning over Boolean variables). In contrast, certification support for *word-level* verification (i.e., reasoning over machine words and instructions) remains largely unexplored. Word-level methods model hardware systems at a higher level of abstraction, capturing arithmetic and datapath components such as adders and multipliers rather than individual wires and primitive gates, and are essential for scalable hardware verification [3,10]. A key goal of

© The Author(s) 2026
A. Biere et al. (Eds.): IJCAR 2026, LNAI 16688, pp. 276–285, 2026.
https://doi.org/10.1007/978-3-032-32589-1_17

the HWMCC is to make word-level certification mandatory, thereby promoting the development of certifying word-level model checkers; achieving this requires a dedicated word-level certificate checker. At present, the ecosystem of certifying word-level model checkers is still emerging, and there is no publicly available implementation that produces certificates. To exercise the end-to-end workflow, in this short paper, we generate word-level certificates using a prototype certifying k-induction engine, one of the essential model checking techniques. By providing a common validation backend, our checker aims to lower the barrier for tool developers and help catalyze broader community adoption, mirroring the progress achieved at the bit level.

We present Certifaiger and Cerbtora (*tora* means "tiger" in Japanese), two certificate checkers that implement a common framework [13, 25–27] for validating witness circuits at the bit level and word level, respectively. Certifaiger (available at https://github.com/Froleyks/certifaiger) has been used in the Hardware Model Checking Competition since 2024 [14], but has not previously been described in the literature. Cerbtora (available at https://github.com/Froleyks/cerbtora) is a new C++ tool that uses the SMT solver Bitwuzla [18] as its backend. Both tools are integrated into a complete certification workflow (cf. Section 3) and are released under the MIT license on GitHub.

2 Model Checking Certificates

In this section, we briefly describe the certificate format. Our certificate checkers accept two circuits as input: (i) the model circuit M under verification and (ii) a witness circuit M' that certifies correctness, produced by a model checker. A circuit $M = (I, L, R, F, P, C)$ has inputs I, latches L, reset and transition functions R, F, safety property P, and constraint C; it is safe if every state reachable from a C-respecting reset through C-respecting transitions satisfies P. We use the following symbolic formulas over input and latch variables: for any $S \subseteq L$, $R\{S\}$ denotes the reset condition for the latches in S (each latch equals its reset value), and $F_{0,1}\{S\}$ is the one-step transition relation for S, using time-stamped copies of I and L. For any formula φ over $I \cup L$, φ_t denotes its time-shifted copy (replace each latch $l \in L$ by l_t and each input $i \in I$ by i_t). Reset functions R are *stratified* [27] if their latch-dependency graph is acyclic.

Definition 1. (Witness circuit). *Given a circuit M, the circuit M', with $M = (I, L, R, F, P, C)$, $M' = (I', L', R', F', P', C')$, and $K = L \cap L'$, is a witness circuit if R' is stratified and the following conditions hold:*

Reset	$R\{K\} \wedge C \Rightarrow R'\{K\} \wedge C'$ *An initial state in the model implies an initial state in the witness.*
Transition	$F_{0,1}\{K\} \wedge C_0 \wedge C_1 \wedge C'_0 \Rightarrow F'_{0,1}\{K\} \wedge C'_1$ *A transition in the model implies a transition in the witness.*
Property	$(C \wedge C') \Rightarrow (P' \Rightarrow P)$ *A violation in the model implies a violation in the witness.*
Base	$R'\{L'\} \wedge C' \Rightarrow P'$ *The witness property holds in all initial states.*
Step	$P'_0 \wedge F'_{0,1}\{L'\} \wedge C'_0 \wedge C'_1 \Rightarrow P'_1$ *The witness property is inductive.*

model.aag
```
aag 10 0 3 1 7
2 3
4 13
6 19
20
8 4 3
10 5 2
12 11 9
14 4 2
16 6 4
18 17 15
20 16 14
```

witness.aag
```
aag 9 1 2 1 6
2
4 13
6 19
16
8 4 3
10 5 2
12 11 9
14 4 2
16 6 4
18 17 15
i0 = 2
l0 = 4
l1 = 6
c
MAPPING 2
2 2
4 4
6 6
```

model.btor2
```
1 sort bitvec 1
2 sort bitvec 3
3 constd 2 0
4 constd 2 1
5 constd 2 -3
6 constd 2 4
7 constd 2 5
8 constd 2 7
9 state 2
10 init 2 9 3
11 eq 1 9 6
12 eq 1 9 7
13 eq 1 9 8
14 or 1 11 12
15 or 1 13 14
16 ite 2 15 5 4
17 add 2 9 16
18 next 2 9 17
19 bad 13
```

witness.btor2
```
1 sort bitvec 1
2 sort bitvec 3
3 constd 2 0
4 constd 2 1
5 constd 2 -3
6 constd 2 4
7 constd 2 5
8 constd 2 7
9 state 2
10 init 2 9 3
11 eq 1 9 6
12 eq 1 9 7
13 eq 1 9 8
14 or 1 11 12
15 or 1 13 14
16 ite 2 15 5 4
17 add 2 9 16
18 next 2 9 17
19 constd 2 6
20 eq 1 9 19
21 or 1 13 20
22 bad 21
```

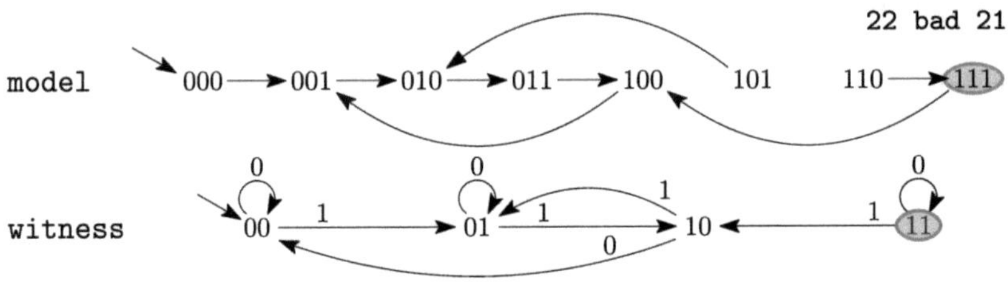

Fig. 1. A binary counter that increments by 1 or subtracts 3. The model contains three latches to encode values from 0 to 7, and no inputs. Its state space is depicted with the bad state 111 marked (the safety property enforces that the bad state is not reachable). The state space of the bit-level witness circuit with one input and two latches is shown at the bottom. We describe the model in both AIGER (`model.aag`) and Btor2 (`model.btor2`). Additionally, two witnesses, one in AIGER (`witness.aag`) and one in Btor2 (`witness.btor2`), are presented. The AIGER witness requires an explicit mapping (cf. Section 3) to the inputs and latches in the model. In this example, the mapping is (redundantly) specified in the symbol table and in the comment section.

The five conditions *Reset*, *Transition*, *Property*, *Base*, *Step* are encoded as SAT formulas whose validity certifies the correctness of the model checking result. Additionally, the witness circuit must be *stratified*. This is checked explicitly in Certifaiger, while at the word level it is syntactically enforced by the BTOR2 format [19]. A soundness proof of Def. 1 is provided in [14]. Fig. 1 illustrates the same model and witness circuits in both bit-level and word-level formats.

3 Certifaiger and Cerbtora

Certifaiger is a C++ application that takes as input a model and its witness in the AIGER [7] format and generates five CNF files, each corresponding to the negation of one check in Def. 1. These CNF files are solved by a SAT solver (Kissat [12] or CaDiCaL [4]). Our tool uses the AIGER library parser [8], constructs two copies of each circuit, encodes $R_0, C_0, C_1, \ldots$, and builds one output per check. The pipeline then applies cone-of-influence reduction and a Tseitin transformation [24] via `aigsplit` and `aigtocnf` to obtain the five SAT formulas. If all checks are proved unsatisfiable, the witness is successfully validated.

Cerbtora follows a similar workflow and is also implemented in C++. At the word level, models are given in the Btor2 [19] format; Cerbtora uses the Btor2Tools parser [9] and generates the five checks as combinational Btor2 files. These files are then passed to the SMT solver Bitwuzla [18]. If all five checks are unsatisfiable, the witness is validated and the model property is established.

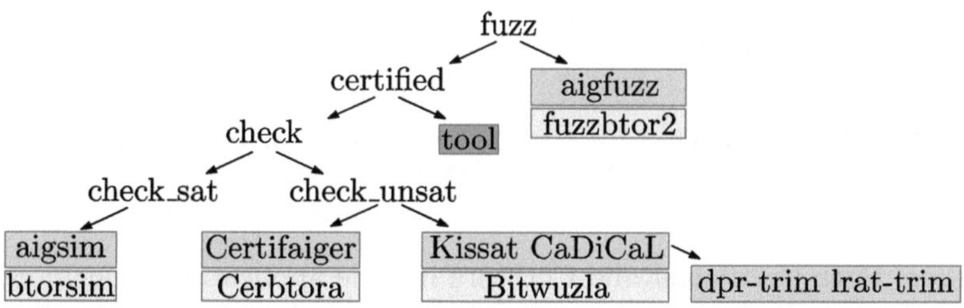

Fig. 2. Simulators, SAT/SMT solvers, SAT proof checkers, and fuzzers included.

Mapping. In Definition 1, the sets of inputs I and latches L of the model and the witness circuit have some intersection to connect them. In principle, we could rely on naming literals identically in both circuits; however, that causes gaps in literal numbering, which is incompatible with the binary format of AIGER [7]. We therefore allow the user to explicitly specify a literal *mapping*. The witness can define such a mapping in multiple ways, in decreasing order of precedence:

1. A comment `MAPPING <n>` followed by n lines of the form `<witness literal> <model literal>`;
2. symbol-table entries [7] of the form `=<model literal>`;
3. if no mapping is given, Certifaiger assumes a mapping between the first n inputs and first m latches in the model and witness, respectively.

Table 1. Comparison of formula generation and SAT solver configurations.

	Verified	PAR10[sec]	Max[sec]
Kissat			
Certifaiger (parallel + unsat bias)	1059	180.77	3577.93
parallel	1056	276.35	3155.87
split	1056	277.18	2935.26
merged	1022	1530.25	2469.53
CaDiCaL			
CaDiCaL	1057	189.15	1957.92
Kissat Features			
no-sweep	1052	412.88	3529.78
no-congruence	1027	1374.67	3484.84
no-congruence-no-sweep	992	2515.47	3321.83
UNSAT Proofs			
CaDiCaL + LRAT	1053	320.44	1097.20
Kissat + DRAT	974	3298.02	3528.02

Integration. Both Certifaiger and Cerbtora include applications that integrate a number of external tools. These applications and tools are automatically downloaded and built with the `-DTOOL` option. Fig. 2 gives an overview.

check `<model>` `<witness>` identifies whether the `witness` describes a simulation trace (SAT) or a witness circuit (UNSAT) and checks its correctness with the appropriate tool: `aigsim` [8] or `btorsim` [9] to simulate a trace, and Certifaiger or Cerbtora to generate five formulas, which are checked for unsatisfiability. If Certifaiger is configured with `-DPROOF`, proofs of unsatisfiability are produced by the SAT solver and checked using `dpr-trim` [23] or `lrat-trim` [20].

certified `<tool>` `<model>` wraps the model checker provided by the user to generate and check a produced simulation trace or witness circuit. The tool must follow the HWMCC interface: `<tool>` `<model>` `<witness.sat>` `<witness.unsat>` where the latter are paths for the violation trace and witness circuits respectively.

fuzz `<tool>` repeatedly uses `aigfuzz` (or `fuzzbtor2`) to generate random input circuits, runs the provided model checker, and verifies the resulting certificates. The AIGER version additionally integrates the delta debugger `aigdd` [28], used to automatically shrink failure-inducing inputs. If the provided tool supports the `--range` option, which lists all integer options as `<name>` `<default>` `<min>` `<max>`, option fuzzing [29] and delta debugging are performed.

Base of Trust. Certifaiger can reduce the number of trusted components by checking UNSAT proofs. At the word level, Bitwuzla does not support proofs, and while CVC5 [1] can generate Alethe proofs [22], QF_BV is only partially covered, so the SMT solver remains in the trusted computing base. A pragmatic route to stronger assurance is to bit-blast each QF_BV check to CNF and validate LRAT proofs, together with proofs of the bit-blasting step. Alternatively, one can use a verified translation, such as `bv_decide` in Lean or CoqQFBV.

4 Evaluation

Table 2. Comparison of bit-level and word-level certificate checks (in seconds), and inductive depth (k). The last row presents results over all 47 benchmarks.

	k		Reset	Transition	Base	Step	Property	Total
Problem-11	8	bit	0.01	1.30	0.63	180.81	0.62	183.38
		word	0.20	0.43	0.39	103.23	0.40	**104.66**
A19-p16	21	bit	0.02	0.18	0.29	310.07	0.23	310.80
		word	0.33	0.70	0.86	23.33	2.93	**28.15**
VexRiscv-p20-1	22	bit	0.01	0.05	0.13	143.51	0.10	**143.80**
		word	0.18	0.34	0.38	610.68	1.85	613.43
Dijkstra-1	34	bit	0.01	0.43	1.05	304.19	7.31	313.00
		word	0.06	0.11	0.13	203.45	15.55	**219.30**
ZipCPU-p10	97	bit	0.01	0.02	0.15	227.78	0.10	228.06
		word	0.32	0.72	1.03	22.29	2.96	**27.33**
ByteAdd-1	260	bit	0.01	0.02	0.41	655.08	0.28	655.81
		word	0.34	0.68	0.90	44.88	6.03	**52.83**
All (47)		bit	**1.37**	77.23	**4.44**	2009.81	**10.34**	2103.19
		word	15.54	**41.72**	20.43	**1488.18**	50.61	**1616.48**

In this section, we empirically evaluate our certificate checkers. We use an HPC cluster with Intel Xeon Platinum 8360Y CPUs at 2.4 GHz, 14 GB of memory and one hour of wall time per certificate validation. For the bit-level experiments, we use the 1062 valid witness circuits produced during the HWMCC'24 [14]. Word-level certification is not yet required by the HWMCC, so we developed our own prototype k-induction engine to produce certificates for the same benchmark set. We expect the number of certifying word-level model checkers to grow substantially after the release of Cerbtora.

Table 1 presents several configurations of Certifaiger with different SAT backends. PAR10 presents the average runtime, where each timeout is counted as 10 h. Across all configurations, we observe that formula generation time is negligible (mean 6 ms) compared to SAT solving. The configuration *split* validates Definition 1 via five sequential SAT checks. *merged* combines them into a single SAT instance, while *parallel* runs five instances of Kissat in parallel. *Certifaiger*,

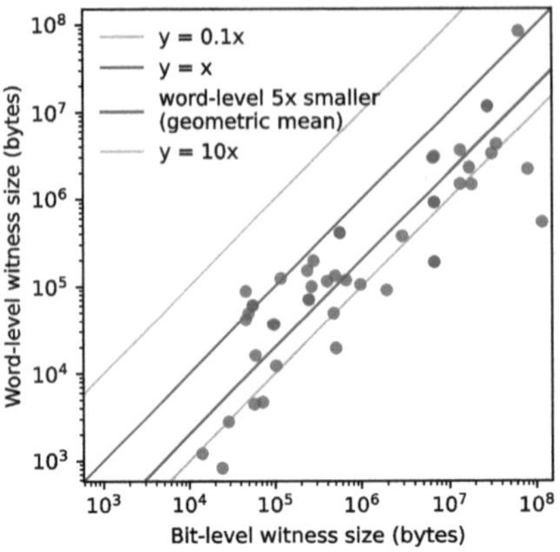

Fig. 3. Btor2 vs AIGER witnesses.

Table 3. Split vs multi-property. Times are measured in minutes. Merged compares verification time for merged circuits with redundancy (plain) to the result of structural hashing (hash).

Verified		**Split [m]**		**Merged [m]**		
Model Checker	n	total	mean	plain	hash	S
ric3	52	334	6.4	**4.1**	4.2	82
ncip-minicraig	26	134	5.0	4.7	**4.0**	34
ncip-cadicraig	26	158	5.9	**5.2**	5.4	30
ncip-portfolio	26	167	6.4	5.2	**4.0**	41
supercar	21	110	4.9	**5.4**	9.9	20

additionally configures the SAT solver to bias the search towards UNSAT. This configuration is used as the basis for the rest of the experiments (and the development of Cerbtora). Although CaDiCaL verified two fewer certificates, it was approximately 60% faster than Kissat on the remaining instances. Clausal congruence closure [5] and clausal equivalence sweeping [6] are both essential for witness circuit validation due to their ability to efficiently establish equivalences between the model and the witness. If we do not want to trust the SAT solver, Certifaiger can be configured to produce and check proofs of unsatisfiability for each SAT check. This is done using `dpr-trim` for Kissat's DRAT proofs and `lrat-trim` for CaDiCaL's LRAT proofs.

Certifaiger can handle multiple properties by considering their conjunction. To evaluate the performance implications of this, we implemented `aigmerge`, a tool that merges (witness) circuits by taking the union of inputs and latches, and concatenating their combinational structure. Table 3 considers the benchmark `cv32e40x` from YosysHQ. It originally featured 768 properties, of which 86 were used in HWMCC'24. The table presents the number of properties verified by each model checker, the *total* time to validate all, and the *mean* time, and compares these with the single *merged* witness circuit that verifies all properties at once. We also removed redundancy using structural *hashing* in ABC [11]. While structural hashing is ineffective, the speedup S, which compares the total time for individual checks to the best merged check, shows vast gains in efficiency when witnesses are merged prior to checking.

Word-Level Reasoning. Even though bit-blasting is a common approach to word-level model checking, for model checkers that operate directly on the word level, bit-level certification is not sufficient, and it leaves the bit-blasting process itself uncertified. In fact, during the development of Cerbtora and our prototype k-induction model checker, fuzzing immediately revealed bugs in `btor2aiger`, the bit blaster in the Btor2Tools library. Figure 3 compares certificate sizes obtained by bit-blasting the models for the 47 benchmarks solved by k-induction against certificates generated directly at the word level. This shows that the word-level certificates are five times more compact in the geometric mean.

Table 2 reports certificate checking times for both word-level and bit-blasted approaches. We display all benchmarks where the inductive depth k exceeds 3. *Step* is typically the most expensive check. In general, we observe certificate checking to be slightly more efficient at the word level.

5 Conclusion

We presented Certifaiger, a certificate checker for bit-level model checking, and its word-level friend Cerbtora. As ongoing work, we are extending both tools to support liveness properties. For a fully trusted certification pipeline, we are implementing our certification approach in a theorem proving environment, including verified bit blasting and on-the-fly verification of LRAT proofs.

Acknowledgments. Partially funded by the European Union project (ERC, CertiFOX, 101122653). Views and opinions expressed are however those of the author(s) only and do not necessarily reflect those of the European Union or the European Research Council. Neither the European Union nor the granting authority can be held responsible for them. Further funded by a gift from Intel Corporation.

Data Availability Statement. All experiments presented in this paper can be reproduced: https://doi.org/10.5281/zenodo.18629636

Disclosure of Interests. The authors have no competing interests to declare that are relevant to the content of this article.

References

1. Barbosa, H., et al.: cvc5: a versatile and industrial-strength SMT solver. In: TACAS 2022. LNCS, vol. 13243, pp. 415–442. Springer, Cham (2022). https://doi.org/10.1007/978-3-030-99524-9_24
2. Beyer, D., Dangl, M., Dietsch, D., Heizmann, M.: Correctness witnesses: exchanging verification results between verifiers. In: SIGSOFT FSE, pp. 326–337. ACM (2016). https://doi.org/10.1145/2950290.2950351
3. Biere, A.: Tutorial on world-level model checking. In: FMCAD, p. 1. IEEE (2020). https://doi.org/10.34727/2020/isbn.978-3-85448-042-6_3
4. Biere, A., Faller, T., Fazekas, K., Fleury, M., Froleyks, N., Pollitt, F.: CaDiCaL 2.0. n: Gurfinkel, A., Ganesh, V. (eds.) CAV 2024. LNCS, vol. 14681. Springer, Cham (2024). https://doi.org/10.1007/978-3-031-65627-9_7
5. Biere, A., Fazekas, K., Fleury, M., Froleyks, N.: Clausal congruence closure. In: Chakraborty, S., Jiang, J.R. (eds.) 27th International Conference on Theory and Applications of Satisfiability Testing, SAT 2024, 21-24 August 2024, Pune, India. LIPIcs, vol. 305, pp. 6:1–6:25. Schloss Dagstuhl - Leibniz-Zentrum für Informatik (2024). https://doi.org/10.4230/LIPICS.SAT.2024.6

6. Biere, A., Fazekas, K., Fleury, M., Froleyks, N.: Clausal equivalence sweeping. In: Narodytska, N., Rümmer, P. (eds.) Formal Methods in Computer-Aided Design, FMCAD 2024, Prague, Czech Republic, 15-18 October 2024. pp. 1–6. IEEE (2024). https://doi.org/10.34727/2024/ISBN.978-3-85448-065-5_29
7. Biere, A., Heljanko, K., Wieringa, S.: AIGER 1.9 and beyond. Tech. Rep. 11/2, Institute for Formal Models and Verification, Johannes Kepler University (2011). https://doi.org/10.35011/fmvtr.2011-2
8. Biere, A., Herbstritt, M., Berre, D.L., Wieringa, S., Niemetz, A.: Aiger: and-inverter graph (aig) format and tools (2006). https://github.com/arminbiere/aiger
9. Biere, A., Niemetz, A., Preiner, M.: Btor2tools: Btor2 utilities and libraries (2016). https://github.com/hwmcc/btor2tools
10. Bjesse, P.: A practical approach to word level model checking of industrial netlists. In: International Conference on Computer Aided Verification, pp. 446–458. Springer (2008). https://doi.org/10.1007/978-3-540-70545-1_43
11. Brayton, R., Mishchenko, A.: ABC: An Academic Industrial-Strength Verification Tool. In: Touili, T., Cook, B., Jackson, P. (eds.) CAV 2010. LNCS, vol. 6174, pp. 24–40. Springer, Heidelberg (2010). https://doi.org/10.1007/978-3-642-14295-6_5
12. Fleury, A., Heisinger, M.: Cadical, kissat, paracooba, plingeling and treengeling entering the sat competition 2020. Sat Competition **2020**, 50 (2020)
13. Froleyks, N., Yu, E., Biere, A., Heljanko, K.: Certifying phase abstraction. In: Benzmüller, C., Heule, M.J.H., Schmidt, R.A. (eds.) IJCAR 2024. LNCS, vol. 14739. Springer, Cham.(2024). https://doi.org/10.1007/978-3-031-63498-7_17
14. Froleyks, N., Yu, E., Preiner, M., Biere, A., Heljanko, K.: Introducing certificates to the hardware model checking competition. In: Piskac, R., Rakamaric, Z. (eds.) CAV 2025, LNCS, vol. 15931, pp. 281–295. Springer (2025). https://doi.org/10.1007/978-3-031-98668-0_14
15. Heule, M.J.H.: Proofs of unsatisfiability. In: Biere, A., Heule, M., van Maaren, H., Walsh, T. (eds.) Handbook of Satisfiability - Second Edition, Frontiers in Artificial Intelligence and Applications, vol. 336, pp. 635–668. IOS Press (2021). https://doi.org/10.3233/FAIA200998
16. Hoenicke, J., Schindler, T.: A simple proof format for smt. In: SMT, pp, pp. 54–70. (2022)
17. Lammich, P.: Fast and verified unsat certificate checking. In: International Joint Conference on Automated Reasoning, pp. 439–457. Springer (2024). https://doi.org/10.1007/978-3-031-63498-7_26
18. Niemetz, A., Preiner, M.: Bitwuzla. In: Enea, C., Lal, A. (eds.) CAV 2023. LNCS, vol. 13965, pp. 3–17. Springer (2023). https://doi.org/10.1007/978-3-031-37703-7_1
19. Niemetz, A., Preiner, M., Wolf, C., Biere, A.: BTOR2 , BtorMC and Boolector 3.0. In: Chockler, H., Weissenbacher, G. (eds.) CAV 2018. LNCS, vol. 10981, pp. 587–595. Springer, Cham (2018). https://doi.org/10.1007/978-3-319-96145-3_32
20. Pollitt, F., Fleury, M., Biere, A.: Faster LRAT checking than solving with CaDiCaL. In: Mahajan, M., Slivovsky, F. (eds.) 26th International Conference on Theory and Applications of Satisfiability Testing (SAT 2023). Leibniz International Proceedings in Informatics (LIPIcs), vol. 271, pp. 21:1–21:12. Schloss Dagstuhl – Leibniz-Zentrum für Informatik, Dagstuhl, Germany (2023). https://doi.org/10.4230/LIPIcs.SAT.2023.21
21. Schurr, H.J., Fleury, M., Barbosa, H., Fontaine, P.: Alethe: towards a generic smt proof format. arXiv preprint arXiv:2107.02354 (2021)

22. Schurr, H., Fleury, M., Barbosa, H., Fontaine, P.: Alethe: towards a generic SMT proof format (extended abstract). In: Keller, C., Fleury, M. (eds.) Proceedings Seventh Workshop on Proof eXchange for Theorem Proving, PxTP 2021, Pittsburg, PA, USA, 11 July 2021. EPTCS, vol. 336, pp. 49–54 (2021). https://doi.org/10.4204/EPTCS.336.6
23. Tan, Y.K., Heule, M.J.H., Myreen, M.O.: cake_lpr: verified propagation redundancy checking in CakeML. In: TACAS 2021. LNCS, vol. 12652, pp. 223–241. Springer, Cham (2021). https://doi.org/10.1007/978-3-030-72013-1_12
24. Tseitin, G.S.: On the complexity of derivation in propositional calculus. Stud. Math. Mathematical Logic **2**, 115–125 (1968)
25. Yu, E., Biere, A., Heljanko, K.: Progress in certifying hardware model checking results. In: Silva, A., Leino, K.R.M. (eds.) CAV 2021. LNCS, vol. 12760, pp. 363–386. Springer (2021). https://doi.org/10.1007/978-3-030-81688-9_17
26. Yu, E., Froleyks, N., Biere, A., Heljanko, K.: Stratified certification for k-Induction. In: Griggio, A., Rungta, N. (eds.) 22nd Formal Methods in Computer-Aided Design, FMCAD 2022, Trento, Italy, 17-21 October 2022, pp. 59–64. IEEE (2022). https://doi.org/10.34727/2022/ISBN.978-3-85448-053-2_11
27. Yu, E., Froleyks, N., Biere, A., Heljanko, K.: Towards compositional hardware model checking certification. In: Nadel, A., Rozier, K.Y. (eds.) Formal Methods in Computer-Aided Design, FMCAD 2023, Ames, IA, USA, 24-27 October 2023, pp. 1–11. IEEE (2023). https://doi.org/10.34727/2023/ISBN.978-3-85448-060-0_12
28. Zeller, A., Hildebrandt, R.: Simplifying and isolating failure-inducing input. IEEE Trans. Software Eng. **28**(2), 183–200 (2002). https://doi.org/10.1109/32.988498
29. Zhang, Z., Klees, G., Wang, E., Hicks, M., Wei, S.: Fuzzing configurations of program options. ACM Trans. Softw. Eng. Methodol. **32**(2), 53:1–53:21 (2023). https://doi.org/10.1145/3580597

Open Access This chapter is licensed under the terms of the Creative Commons Attribution 4.0 International License (http://creativecommons.org/licenses/by/4.0/), which permits use, sharing, adaptation, distribution and reproduction in any medium or format, as long as you give appropriate credit to the original author(s) and the source, provide a link to the Creative Commons license and indicate if changes were made.

The images or other third party material in this chapter are included in the chapter's Creative Commons license, unless indicated otherwise in a credit line to the material. If material is not included in the chapter's Creative Commons license and your intended use is not permitted by statutory regulation or exceeds the permitted use, you will need to obtain permission directly from the copyright holder.

Beyond Eager Encodings: A Theory-Agnostic Approach to Theory-Lemma Enumeration in SMT

Emanuele Civini[1], Gabriele Masina[1(✉)], Giuseppe Spallitta[2], and Roberto Sebastiani[1]

[1] DISI, University of Trento, Trento, Italy
{gabriele.masina,roberto.sebastiani}@unitn.it
[2] Rice University, Houston, TX, USA
gs81@rice.edu

Abstract. Lifting Boolean-reasoning techniques to the SMT level most often requires producing theory lemmas that rule out theory-inconsistent truth assignments. With standard SMT solving, it is common to "lazily" generate such lemmas on demand during the search; with some harder SMT-level tasks —such as unsat-core extraction, MaxSMT, $\mathcal{T}$-OBDD or $\mathcal{T}$-SDD compilation— it may be beneficial or even necessary to "eagerly" pre-compute all the needed theory lemmas upfront. Whereas in principle "classic" eager SMT encodings could do the job, they are specific for very few and easy theories, they do not comply with theory combination, and may produce lots of unnecessary lemma

In this paper, we present theory-agnostic methods for enumerating complete sets of theory lemmas tailored to a given formula. Starting from AllSMT as a baseline approach, we propose improved lemma-enumeration techniques, including divide&conquer, projected enumeration, and theory-driven partitioning, which are highly parallelizable and which may drastically improve scalability. An experimental evaluation demonstrates that these techniques significantly enhance efficiency and enable the method to scale to substantially more complex instances.

Keywords: SMT · Theory-lemma enumeration · Knowledge Compilation

1 Introduction

Context. Lifting Boolean-reasoning techniques to the SMT level most often requires producing $\mathcal{T}$-valid clauses (theory lemmas or $\mathcal{T}$-lemmas) that rule out truth assignments that propositionally satisfy the formula but are $\mathcal{T}$-inconsistent. (E.g., given $\varphi \stackrel{\text{def}}{=} (x = 0) \vee (x = 1)$, the $\mathcal{T}$-lemma $\neg(x = 0) \vee \neg(x = 1)$ rules out the $\mathcal{T}$-inconsistent truth assignment $(x = 0) \wedge (x = 1)$.) These lemmas prevent the Boolean engine from (re)visiting $\mathcal{T}$-inconsistent regions of the search space.

© The Author(s) 2026
A. Biere et al. (Eds.): IJCAR 2026, LNAI 16688, pp. 286–304, 2026.
https://doi.org/10.1007/978-3-032-32589-1_18

With standard SMT solving, $\mathcal{T}$-lemmas are commonly generated "lazily" on demand during the search [1], each time to rule out some $\mathcal{T}$-inconsistent truth assignment, generated by a SAT solver, propositionally satisfying the input formula.

With some harder SMT tasks, such as (minimal) unsat-core extraction [3,12], MaxSMT [5,9], $\mathcal{T}$-OBDD or $\mathcal{T}$-SDD compilation [17], it may be beneficial or even necessary to "eagerly" pre-compute upfront *a whole set of* $\mathcal{T}$*-lemmas* ruling out all the $\mathcal{T}$-inconsistent truth assignments propositionally satisfying the formula.

Unfortunately, with the exception of our own work in [17] (see below), in the literature, there seems to be no theory-agnostic way to achieve this task. Notice that, whereas in principle "classic" eager SMT encodings (e.g. [20,21,23], see below) could do the job, they are specific for very few and easy theories ($\mathcal{EUF}$,$\mathcal{DL}$,$\mathcal{LRA}$), they do not comply with theory combination, and may produce lots of unnecessary lemmas.

Contributions. In this paper, we address this problem explicitly, and we present efficient and theory-agnostic methods for enumerating complete sets of $\mathcal{T}$-lemmas ruling out all $\mathcal{T}$-inconsistent truth assignments propositionally satisfying a formula. Starting from our AllSMT-based technique in [17] as a baseline, we introduce three orthogonal improvements that drastically enhance scalability. First, we show how to use partial-assignment enumeration to decompose the Boolean search space into independent residual subproblems, enabling a divide-and-conquer strategy that can be parallelized. Second, we prove that projecting the enumeration on the $\mathcal{T}$-atoms still yields a complete set of $\mathcal{T}$-lemmas, reducing the dimension of the search. Third, we show that when the $\mathcal{T}$-atoms of φ can be partitioned into symbol-disjoint components, $\mathcal{T}$-lemmas can be enumerated independently within each component. These improvements are theory agnostic and can be combined into a single framework.

An experimental evaluation on all the problems in [17] and on temporal planning problems [22] demonstrates that these techniques drastically enhance efficiency, enabling the scaling to substantially more complex instances.

Related Work. With SMT via eager encodings (e.g. [20,21,23]), an input $\mathcal{T}$-formula φ is encoded into SAT by (i) enumerating a complete set of $\mathcal{T}$-lemmas ruling out all possible $\mathcal{T}$-unsatisfiable truth assignment on $Atoms(\varphi)$, (ii) conjoining them to φ and (iii) producing the Boolean abstraction of the result.

For SMT solving, these techniques ultimately proved to be much less efficient than the lazy approach [1].[1]

With the "lemma-lifting" approaches for (minimal) unsat-core extraction [3,12] and for MaxSMT [5,9] respectively, an SMT solver is invoked on

[1] In the SMT literature, the expression "eager encoding" is also used to denote another and quite successful approach to SMT solving for finite-domain theories, like bit-vectors, floating-point arithmetic or arithmetic over bounded integers, which encodes domain variables via sequences of Boolean atoms, and encodes functions and predicates into Boolean functions accordingly. We emphasize that this is *not* what we refer to here.

$\mathcal{T}$-inconsistent formulas to produce the $\mathcal{T}$-lemmas necessary for detecting their $\mathcal{T}$-inconsistency; these $\mathcal{T}$-lemmas are then conjoined to the formulas, whose Boolean abstractions are then fed to a Boolean unsat-core extractors or to a MaxSAT solver, respectively.

Most relevantly, in [17] we have presented a novel theory-agnostic technique to leverage to SMT level canonical Decision Diagrams (DD), e.g. OBDDs [2] and SDDs [7]. Importantly, unlike previous approaches, these decision diagrams are provably $\mathcal{T}$-*canonical*, i.e., $\mathcal{T}$-equivalent formulas are encoded into the same DD. The technique works by enumerating upfront a whole collection of $\mathcal{T}$-lemmas ruling out all the $\mathcal{T}$-inconsistent truth assignments propositionally satisfying the formula, conjoining them to the formula and producing the decision diagrams out of it. Unfortunately, the $\mathcal{T}$-lemma enumeration technique adopted there, which was based on total-assignment AllSMT, turned out to be the main bottleneck of the whole process.

Motivations and Goals. In Knowledge Compilation (KC) (see [8]), a propositional theory is compiled off-line into a target language, which is then used on-line to answer a large number of queries in polytime. The key motivation behind KC is to push as much of the computational overhead into the offline compiling phase, which is amortized over all online queries.

The main goal of this work is to play as an enabling technique for our approach to lift current KC methods to the SMT setting. A first step was presented in [17] for OBDDs and SDDs, and we recently generalized it to d-DNNFs in [15], in such a way to preserve the polynomial cost of the queries from the Boolean case (see [15]). The need for an eager $\mathcal{T}$-lemma enumeration upfront is motivated in [15,17].

Content of the Paper. In Sect. 2 we introduce the necessary background on SMT and AllSMT enumeration, which is the basis of our methods. In Sect. 3 we first recall the baseline method for $\mathcal{T}$-lemma enumeration from [17] (Sect. 3.1), and then present three novel theory-agnostic techniques for enumerating $\mathcal{T}$-lemmas, including divide-and-conquer (Sect. 3.2), projected enumeration (Sect. 3.3), and theory-driven partitioning (Sect. 3.4). In Sect. 4 we experimentally evaluate our techniques on a broad set of SMT problems, showing a dramatic improvement in efficiency and scalability wrt. the baseline. Finally, in Sect. 5, we summarize our contributions and discuss future research directions.

2 Background

Notation and Terminology. We assume the reader is familiar with the basic syntax, semantics, and results of propositional and first-order logics. We adopt the following terminology and notation.

A propositional formula is either a Boolean constant ($\top$ or $\bot$ representing "true" and "false", respectively), a Boolean atom, or a formula built from propositional connectives ($\neg, \wedge, \vee, \rightarrow, \leftrightarrow$) over propositional formulas. Propositional satisfiability (SAT) is the problem of deciding the satisfiability of propositional formulas. Satisfiability Modulo Theories (SMT) extends SAT to the context of first-order formulas modulo some background theory $\mathcal{T}$, which provides an intended interpretation for constant, function, and predicate symbols [1]. We restrict to quantifier-free formulas. A $\mathcal{T}$-formula is a combination of theory-specific atoms ($\mathcal{T}$-atoms) and Boolean atoms ($\mathbb{B}$-atoms) via Boolean connectives ("atoms" denotes $\mathcal{T}$- and $\mathbb{B}$-atoms indifferently). For instance, the theory of linear real arithmetic ($\mathcal{LRA}$) provides the standard interpretations of arithmetic operators ($+$, $-$, $\cdot$) and relations ($=$, $\leq$, $<$, $>$) over the reals. $\mathcal{LRA}$-atoms are linear (in)equalities over rational variables. An example of $\mathcal{LRA}$-formula is $((x-y \leq 3) \vee (x = z))$, where x, y, z are $\mathcal{LRA}$-variables, and $(x-y \leq 3), (x = z)$ are $\mathcal{LRA}$-atoms. Other theories of interest include equalities ($\mathcal{E}$), equalities with uninterpreted functions ($\mathcal{EUF}$), bit-vectors ($\mathcal{BV}$), arrays ($\mathcal{AR}$), and combinations thereof.

$\mathcal{T2B}$ is a bijective function ("theory to Boolean"), called *Boolean abstraction*, which maps Boolean atoms into themselves, $\mathcal{T}$-atoms into fresh Boolean atoms, and is homomorphic wrt. Boolean connectives and set inclusion. The function $\mathcal{B2T}$ ("Boolean to theory"), called *refinement*, is the inverse of $\mathcal{T2B}$. (For instance $\mathcal{T2B}(\{((x-y \leq 3) \vee (x = z))\}) = \{(A_1 \vee A_2)\}$, A_1 and A_2 being fresh Boolean variables, and $\mathcal{B2T}(\{\neg A_1, A_2\}) = \{\neg(x-y \leq 3), (x = z)\}$.)

The symbol $\boldsymbol{\alpha} \overset{\text{def}}{=} \{\alpha_i\}_i$, possibly with subscripts or superscripts, denotes a set of atoms. We represent truth assignments as conjunctions of literals. We denote by $2^{\boldsymbol{\alpha}}$ the set of all total truth assignments on $\boldsymbol{\alpha}$. The symbols φ, ψ denote $\mathcal{T}$-formulas, and μ, η, ρ denote conjunctions of literals. If $\mathcal{T2B}(\eta) \models \mathcal{T2B}(\varphi)$, then we say that η *propositionally (or* $\mathbb{B}$- *)satisfies* φ, written $\eta \models_{\mathbb{B}} \varphi$. (Notice that if $\eta \models_{\mathbb{B}} \varphi$ then $\eta \models_{\mathcal{T}} \varphi$, but not vice versa.) The notion of propositional/$\mathbb{B}$-satisfiability, entailment and validity follow straightforwardly. When both $\varphi \models_{\mathbb{B}} \psi$ and $\psi \models_{\mathbb{B}} \varphi$, we say that φ and ψ are *propositionally* /$\mathbb{B}$- *equivalent*, written "$\varphi \equiv_{\mathbb{B}} \psi$". When both $\varphi \models_{\mathcal{T}} \psi$ and $\psi \models_{\mathcal{T}} \varphi$, we say that φ and ψ are $\mathcal{T}$-*equivalent*, written "$\varphi \equiv_{\mathcal{T}} \psi$". (Notice that if $\eta \equiv_{\mathbb{B}} \varphi$ then $\eta \equiv_{\mathcal{T}} \varphi$, but not vice versa.) We call a $\mathcal{T}$-*lemma* any $\mathcal{T}$-valid clause.

Basic Definitions. We recall some definitions from [17].

We denote by $\varphi[\boldsymbol{\alpha}]$ the fact that $\boldsymbol{\alpha}$ is a superset of the set of atoms occurring in φ whose truth assignments we are interested in. The fact that it is a superset is sometimes necessary for comparing formulas with different sets of atoms: $\varphi[\boldsymbol{\alpha}]$ and $\varphi'[\boldsymbol{\alpha}']$ can be compared only if they are both considered as formulas on $\boldsymbol{\alpha} \cup \boldsymbol{\alpha}'$. (E.g., in order to check that the propositional formulas $(A_1 \vee A_2) \wedge (A_1 \vee \neg A_2)$ and $(A_1 \vee A_3) \wedge (A_1 \vee \neg A_3)$ are equivalent, we need considering them as formulas on $\{A_1, A_2, A_3\}$.)

Given a set of atoms $\boldsymbol{\alpha}$ and a $\mathcal{T}$-formula $\varphi[\boldsymbol{\alpha}]$, we denote by $H_{\boldsymbol{\alpha}}(\varphi) \overset{\text{def}}{=} \{\eta_i[\boldsymbol{\alpha}]\}_i$ and $P_{\boldsymbol{\alpha}}(\varphi) \overset{\text{def}}{=} \{\rho_j[\boldsymbol{\alpha}]\}_j$ respectively[2] the set of all $\mathcal{T}$-*consistent* and that of all $\mathcal{T}$-*inconsistent* total truth assignments on the set of atoms $\boldsymbol{\alpha}$ which $\mathbb{B}$-satisfy φ,

[2] Capital versions of the Greek letters η and ρ, respectively.

i.e., s.t.

$$\varphi[\boldsymbol{\alpha}] \equiv_{\mathbb{B}} \bigvee_{\eta_i[\boldsymbol{\alpha}] \in H_{\boldsymbol{\alpha}}(\varphi)} \eta_i[\boldsymbol{\alpha}] \vee \bigvee_{\rho_j[\boldsymbol{\alpha}] \in P_{\boldsymbol{\alpha}}(\varphi)} \rho_j[\boldsymbol{\alpha}]. \tag{1}$$

Given two $\mathcal{T}$-formulas $\varphi[\boldsymbol{\alpha}]$ and $\varphi'[\boldsymbol{\alpha}]$, we have that:

(a) $H_{\boldsymbol{\alpha}}(\varphi)$, $P_{\boldsymbol{\alpha}}(\varphi)$, $H_{\boldsymbol{\alpha}}(\neg\varphi)$, $P_{\boldsymbol{\alpha}}(\neg\varphi)$ are pairwise disjoint;
(b) $H_{\boldsymbol{\alpha}}(\varphi) \cup P_{\boldsymbol{\alpha}}(\varphi) \cup H_{\boldsymbol{\alpha}}(\neg\varphi) \cup P_{\boldsymbol{\alpha}}(\neg\varphi) = 2^{\boldsymbol{\alpha}}$;
(c) $\varphi[\boldsymbol{\alpha}] \equiv_{\mathbb{B}} \varphi'[\boldsymbol{\alpha}]$ if and only if $H_{\boldsymbol{\alpha}}(\varphi) = H_{\boldsymbol{\alpha}}(\varphi')$ and $P_{\boldsymbol{\alpha}}(\varphi) = P_{\boldsymbol{\alpha}}(\varphi')$;
(d) $\varphi[\boldsymbol{\alpha}] \equiv_{\mathcal{T}} \varphi'[\boldsymbol{\alpha}]$ if and only if $H_{\boldsymbol{\alpha}}(\varphi) = H_{\boldsymbol{\alpha}}(\varphi')$.

Example 1. Let $\boldsymbol{\alpha} = \{\alpha_1, \alpha_2\} \stackrel{\text{def}}{=} \{(x \leq 0), (x = 1)\}$. Consider $\varphi_1[\boldsymbol{\alpha}] \stackrel{\text{def}}{=} (x \leq 0) \vee (x = 1)$ and $\varphi_2[\boldsymbol{\alpha}] \stackrel{\text{def}}{=} \neg(x \leq 0) \leftrightarrow (x = 1)$. We have that $\varphi_1[\boldsymbol{\alpha}] \not\equiv_{\mathbb{B}} \varphi_2[\boldsymbol{\alpha}]$ and $\varphi_1[\boldsymbol{\alpha}] \equiv_{\mathcal{T}} \varphi_2[\boldsymbol{\alpha}]$. Then $H_{\boldsymbol{\alpha}}(\varphi_1[\boldsymbol{\alpha}]) = H_{\boldsymbol{\alpha}}(\varphi_2[\boldsymbol{\alpha}]) = \{\eta_1, \eta_2\} = \{(x \leq 0) \wedge \neg(x = 1), \neg(x \leq 0) \wedge (x = 1)\}$, $P_{\boldsymbol{\alpha}}(\varphi_1[\boldsymbol{\alpha}]) = \{(x \leq 0) \wedge (x = 1)\}$ and $P_{\boldsymbol{\alpha}}(\varphi_2[\boldsymbol{\alpha}]) = \emptyset$.

Definition 1. *We say that a set $\{C_1[\boldsymbol{\alpha}], \ldots, C_K[\boldsymbol{\alpha}]\}$ of clauses* ***rules out*** *a given set $\{\rho_1[\boldsymbol{\alpha}], \ldots, \rho_M[\boldsymbol{\alpha}]\}$ of total truth assignments if and only if, for every $\rho_j[\boldsymbol{\alpha}]$ in the set, there exists a $C_l[\boldsymbol{\alpha}]$ s.t. $\rho_j[\boldsymbol{\alpha}] \models_{\mathbb{B}} \neg C_l[\boldsymbol{\alpha}]$, that is, if and only if*

$$\bigvee_{j=1}^{M} \rho_j[\boldsymbol{\alpha}] \wedge \bigwedge_{l=1}^{K} C_l[\boldsymbol{\alpha}] \equiv_{\mathbb{B}} \bot.$$

Given $\boldsymbol{\alpha}$ and some $\mathcal{T}$-formula $\varphi[\boldsymbol{\alpha}]$, we denote as $Cl_{\boldsymbol{\alpha}}(\varphi)$ any function which returns a set of $\mathcal{T}$-lemmas $\{C_1[\boldsymbol{\alpha}], \ldots, C_K[\boldsymbol{\alpha}]\}$ which rules out $P_{\boldsymbol{\alpha}}(\varphi)$.

AllSMT and Projected AllSMT. Given a $\mathcal{T}$-formula $\varphi[\boldsymbol{\alpha}]$, AllSMT is the problem of enumerating a set of $\mathcal{T}$-satisfiable truth assignments covering all $\eta[\boldsymbol{\alpha}] \in H_{\boldsymbol{\alpha}}(\varphi)$ [14]. We call *total AllSMT* the task of enumerating all $\mathcal{T}$-satisfiable *total* truth assignments $\eta[\boldsymbol{\alpha}] \in H_{\boldsymbol{\alpha}}(\varphi)$. We call *partial AllSMT* the task of enumerating a set of $\mathcal{T}$-satisfiable *partial* truth assignments $\mu[\boldsymbol{\alpha}]$ such that $\mu[\boldsymbol{\alpha}] \models_{\mathbb{B}} \varphi$ and every $\eta[\boldsymbol{\alpha}] \in H_{\boldsymbol{\alpha}}(\varphi)$ is an extension of some $\mu[\boldsymbol{\alpha}]$.

Sometimes, we are interested in enumerating only the truth assignments on a subset $\boldsymbol{\alpha}' \subseteq \boldsymbol{\alpha}$ of "relevant" atoms, which we call *projection atoms*. Let $\boldsymbol{\alpha}'' \stackrel{\text{def}}{=} \boldsymbol{\alpha} \setminus \boldsymbol{\alpha}'$. Following [14], we call *projected total* [resp. *partial*] *AllSMT* the task of enumerating a set of $\mathcal{T}$-satisfiable *total* [resp. *partial*] truth assignments on $\boldsymbol{\alpha}'$, $\mu'[\boldsymbol{\alpha}']$, such that:

(i) for every $\mu'[\boldsymbol{\alpha}']$ there exists a total truth assignment $\eta''[\boldsymbol{\alpha}'']$ on $\boldsymbol{\alpha}''$ s.t. $\mu[\boldsymbol{\alpha}] \stackrel{\text{def}}{=} \mu'[\boldsymbol{\alpha}'] \wedge \eta''[\boldsymbol{\alpha}'']$ is such that $\mu[\boldsymbol{\alpha}] \models_{\mathbb{B}} \varphi$ and $\mu[\boldsymbol{\alpha}]$ is $\mathcal{T}$-satisfiable;
(ii) every $\eta[\boldsymbol{\alpha}] \in H_{\boldsymbol{\alpha}}(\varphi)$ is an extension of some $\mu'[\boldsymbol{\alpha}']$.

Note that if $\boldsymbol{\alpha}' = \boldsymbol{\alpha}$, the projected versions coincide with the non-projected ones.

Algorithm 1 describes a procedure for computing projected partial AllSMT, implemented, e.g., in MathSAT [4]; the procedure can be easily adapted to

Algorithm 1. ProjectedAllSMT($\varphi[\boldsymbol{\alpha}]$, $\boldsymbol{\alpha}'$)

input: $\varphi[\boldsymbol{\alpha}]$: a $\mathcal{T}$-formula, $\boldsymbol{\alpha}'$: set of atoms to project on, s.t. $\boldsymbol{\alpha}' \subseteq \boldsymbol{\alpha}$
output: $M_{\boldsymbol{\alpha}'}$: set of partial assignments $\mu'[\boldsymbol{\alpha}']$ for projected partial AllSMT
$Cl_{\boldsymbol{\alpha}}$: set of $\mathcal{T}$-lemmas learned during the enumeration

1: $M_{\boldsymbol{\alpha}'} \leftarrow \emptyset$
2: **while** SMT.Solve($\varphi[\boldsymbol{\alpha}]$) = SAT **do**
3: $\quad \eta[\boldsymbol{\alpha}] \leftarrow$ SMT.GetAssignment() ▷ find a $\mathcal{T}$-sat truth assignment on $\boldsymbol{\alpha}$ for φ
4: $\quad \mu[\boldsymbol{\alpha}] \leftarrow$ Minimize($\eta[\boldsymbol{\alpha}], \boldsymbol{\alpha}', \varphi[\boldsymbol{\alpha}]$) ▷ minimize $\eta[\boldsymbol{\alpha}]$ wrt. $\boldsymbol{\alpha}'$
5: $\quad \mu'[\boldsymbol{\alpha}'] \leftarrow$ Project($\mu[\boldsymbol{\alpha}], \boldsymbol{\alpha}'$) ▷ keep literals on $\boldsymbol{\alpha}'$ only
6: $\quad M_{\boldsymbol{\alpha}'} \leftarrow M_{\boldsymbol{\alpha}'} \cup \{\mu'[\boldsymbol{\alpha}']\}$
7: $\quad \varphi \leftarrow \varphi \wedge \neg\mu'[\boldsymbol{\alpha}']$ ▷ block $\mu'[\boldsymbol{\alpha}']$
8: **end while**
9: $Cl_{\boldsymbol{\alpha}} \leftarrow$ SMT.GetLemmas() ▷ get the learned $\mathcal{T}$-lemmas
10: **return** $M_{\boldsymbol{\alpha}'}, Cl_{\boldsymbol{\alpha}}$

compute the other versions of AllSMT, as we detail in the following. In particular, we denote by ProjectedAllSMT$_{\text{total}}$ the version of Algorithm 1 for projected total AllSMT, and by ProjectedAllSMT$_{\text{partial}}$ the version for projected partial AllSMT.

The algorithm is based on the blocking-clause approach, which iteratively checks for the satisfiability of $\varphi[\boldsymbol{\alpha}]$ conjoined with the negation of the previously found truth assignments, until it becomes unsatisfiable (lines 2-8).

In each iteration, it first finds a $\mathcal{T}$-satisfiable total truth assignment $\eta[\boldsymbol{\alpha}]$ on all the atoms $\boldsymbol{\alpha}$, which propositionally satisfies $\varphi[\boldsymbol{\alpha}]$ (line 3). This guarantees that all its sub-assignments are also $\mathcal{T}$-satisfiable.

The assignment is then minimized, by removing literals over $\boldsymbol{\alpha}'$ from $\eta[\boldsymbol{\alpha}] \stackrel{\text{def}}{=} \eta'[\boldsymbol{\alpha}'] \wedge \eta''[\boldsymbol{\alpha}'']$, to find a partial assignment $\mu[\boldsymbol{\alpha}] \stackrel{\text{def}}{=} \mu'[\boldsymbol{\alpha}'] \wedge \eta''[\boldsymbol{\alpha}''] \subseteq \eta[\boldsymbol{\alpha}]$ which still satisfies $\varphi[\boldsymbol{\alpha}]$ (line 4). For total (projected) AllSMT, this step is omitted and $\mu[\boldsymbol{\alpha}] = \eta[\boldsymbol{\alpha}]$. Then, the assignment is projected on $\boldsymbol{\alpha}'$ (line 5), obtaining $\mu'[\boldsymbol{\alpha}']$ satisfying Item 2. If $\boldsymbol{\alpha}' = \boldsymbol{\alpha}$, then $\mu'[\boldsymbol{\alpha}'] = \mu[\boldsymbol{\alpha}]$, and projected AllSMT reduces to AllSMT.

The projected assignment $\mu'[\boldsymbol{\alpha}']$ is then added to the set $M_{\boldsymbol{\alpha}'}$ (line 6), and it is blocked by conjoining the *blocking clause* $\neg\mu'[\boldsymbol{\alpha}']$ to $\varphi[\boldsymbol{\alpha}]$ (line 7). (In actual implementations, $\neg\mu'[\boldsymbol{\alpha}']$ may be fed to the conflict-analysis mechanism of the SAT solver, and the output conflict clause be used as blocking clause [14]; in Algorithm 1 we omit this step to simplify the narration.) The loop terminates when $\varphi[\boldsymbol{\alpha}]$ becomes unsatisfiable, which guarantees Item 2.

Finally, we return both the set of enumerated assignments $M_{\boldsymbol{\alpha}'}$, and also the set of $\mathcal{T}$-lemmas $Cl_{\boldsymbol{\alpha}}$ (line 9) learned by the SMT solver during the enumeration, i.e., during all the calls to SMT.Solve (line 2), since we will use this algorithm as a subroutine for enumerating $\mathcal{T}$-lemmas in Sect. 3.

We remark that $\mathcal{T}$-lemmas are typically much smaller than the blocking clauses negating partial or total assignments, as the former negate conflicting cores of $\mathcal{T}$-atoms; also, a $\mathcal{T}$-satisfiable partial assignment only implies that *one* of its total extension is $\mathcal{T}$-satisfiable, whereas a $\mathcal{T}$-unsatisfiable one implies that *all* its total extensions are $\mathcal{T}$-unsatisfiable. Thus, whereas a $\mathcal{T}$-lemma usually rules out a large amount of elements of $P_{\boldsymbol{\alpha}}(\varphi)$, a blocking clause rules out only one or relatively few elements of $H_{\boldsymbol{\alpha}}(\varphi)$. Thus, unless $H_{\boldsymbol{\alpha}}(\varphi)$ is drastically smaller than $P_{\boldsymbol{\alpha}}(\varphi)$, typically in AllSMT most of the search effort is devoted to rule out the assignments in $H_{\boldsymbol{\alpha}}(\varphi)$.

We also remark that *partial* AllSMT may be dramatically faster than total AllSMT, since a single $\mathcal{T}$-satisfiable partial assignment represents up to 2^k total ones, where k is the number of unassigned atoms. For the same reason, *projected* AllSMT may be dramatically faster than non-projected AllSMT, as a single $\mathcal{T}$-satisfiable assignment on $\boldsymbol{\alpha}'$ represents up to 2^k $\mathcal{T}$-satisfiable assignments on $\boldsymbol{\alpha}$.

As a final note, we also remark that the results presented in the rest of the paper also hold for projected AllSMT algorithms not based on blocking clauses, e.g., [19]. For simplicity, we carry out the discussion taking Algorithm 1 as a reference.

3 $\mathcal{T}$-Lemma Enumeration Techniques

We present four theory-agnostic methods for enumerating a set $Cl_{\boldsymbol{\alpha}}(\varphi)$ of $\mathcal{T}$-lemmas to rule out $P_{\boldsymbol{\alpha}}(\varphi)$ (see Definition 1). In Sect. 3.1 we describe the method used in [17], which we will use as a baseline. The method is simple to implement, but relies on basic, total AllSMT enumeration, which is often intractable on real-world instances due to the combinatorial explosion of total assignments. To address this issue, we introduce three orthogonal improvements that drastically enhance scalability. First, in Sect. 3.2 we describe a divide-and-conquer strategy that can be naturally parallelized. Second, in Sect. 3.3 we prove that projecting the enumeration onto the $\mathcal{T}$-atoms guarantees finding a complete set of $\mathcal{T}$-lemmas, thereby enabling more efficient enumeration. Finally, in Sect. 3.4 we prove that when the atoms of φ can be partitioned into disjoint sets, $\mathcal{T}$-lemmas can be enumerated for each partition separately. This results in a dramatic improvement in the efficiency of enumeration. Notably, these three improvements are orthogonal and can be combined. Due to space constraints, all the proofs have been moved to the extended version [6].

3.1 Enumerating $\mathcal{T}$-Lemmas via AllSMT

The baseline approach for $\mathcal{T}$-lemma enumeration, first presented in [17], is outlined in Algorithm 2 and consists of performing a call to *total, non-projected AllSMT* on $\varphi[\boldsymbol{\alpha}]$, using the procedure in Algorithm 1 with $\boldsymbol{\alpha}' \stackrel{\text{def}}{=} \boldsymbol{\alpha}$ and no minimization. (In Algorithm 2 we also consider the case with $\boldsymbol{\alpha}' \subset \boldsymbol{\alpha}$ because it will be used in Sect. 3.3 and Sect. 3.4.)

The $\mathcal{T}$-lemmas learned by the SMT solver during such enumeration rule out all $\mathcal{T}$-inconsistent truth assignments in $P_{\boldsymbol{\alpha}}(\varphi)$. In fact, the algorithm terminates when $\varphi \wedge \bigwedge_{\eta_i \in H_{\boldsymbol{\alpha}}(\varphi)} \neg\eta_i$ is found to be $\mathcal{T}$-unsatisfiable, that is, when the solver has found a set of $\mathcal{T}$-lemmas $Cl_{\boldsymbol{\alpha}}$ s.t. $\varphi \wedge \bigwedge_{\eta_i \in H_{\boldsymbol{\alpha}}(\varphi)} \neg\eta_i \wedge \bigwedge_{C \in Cl_{\boldsymbol{\alpha}}} C \equiv_{\mathbb{B}} \bot$.

Algorithm 2. LemmaEnumeratorAllSMT($\varphi[\boldsymbol{\alpha}], \boldsymbol{\alpha}'$)

input: $\varphi[\boldsymbol{\alpha}]$: a $\mathcal{T}$-formula, $\boldsymbol{\alpha}'$: a set of atoms to project on (default: $\boldsymbol{\alpha}$)
output: $Cl_{\boldsymbol{\alpha}}$: a set of $\mathcal{T}$-lemmas

$\_, Cl_{\boldsymbol{\alpha}} \leftarrow \mathsf{ProjectedAllSMT}_{\mathsf{total}}(\varphi[\boldsymbol{\alpha}], \boldsymbol{\alpha}')$ ▷ Keep only lemmas
return $Cl_{\boldsymbol{\alpha}}$

By construction, this guarantees that $Cl_{\boldsymbol{\alpha}}$ rules out all $\mathcal{T}$-unsatisfiable truth assignments in $P_{\boldsymbol{\alpha}}(\varphi)$ [17].

It is important to note that we must enumerate *total* truth assignments. Indeed, enumerating *partial* truth assignments may produce a set of $\mathcal{T}$-lemmas that does not rule out $P_{\boldsymbol{\alpha}}(\varphi)$ completely. This is because the definition of partial AllSMT (see Sect. 2) only requires that, for each partial assignment, all its total extensions *propositionally* satisfy φ, but only one extension needs to be $\mathcal{T}$-consistent. The following example illustrates why this can lead to missing $\mathcal{T}$-lemmas.

Example 2. Let $\varphi[\boldsymbol{\alpha}] \stackrel{\text{def}}{=} (x = 0) \vee (x = 1)$ with $\boldsymbol{\alpha} \stackrel{\text{def}}{=} \{(x = 0), (x = 1)\}$. Consider a partial AllSMT disjoint enumeration as performed by Algorithm 1 with $\boldsymbol{\alpha}' = \boldsymbol{\alpha}$ and minimization enabled. A possible run may proceed as follows.

The SMT solver sets $\neg(x = 0)$, so that unit propagation forces $(x = 1)$. The resulting total assignment $\eta[\boldsymbol{\alpha}] \stackrel{\text{def}}{=} \neg(x = 0) \wedge (x = 1)$ is $\mathcal{T}$-consistent (line 3). Minimization then drops $\neg(x = 0)$ and returns the partial assignment $\mu_1[\boldsymbol{\alpha}] \stackrel{\text{def}}{=} (x = 1)$ (line 4). Notice that no $\mathcal{T}$-conflict is exposed, and no $\mathcal{T}$-lemma is generated. The enumerator blocks the returned cube by adding $\neg(x = 1)$ (line 7). On the next iteration, $\neg(x = 1)$ is enforced, and unit propagation forces $(x = 0)$. The resulting total assignment $\eta_2[\boldsymbol{\alpha}] \stackrel{\text{def}}{=} (x = 0) \wedge \neg(x = 1)$ is again $\mathcal{T}$-consistent (line 3). Minimization (line 4) cannot reduce $\eta_2[\boldsymbol{\alpha}]$ because of the blocking clause $\neg(x = 1)$, and $\eta_2[\boldsymbol{\alpha}]$ is then blocked by adding $\neg(x = 0) \vee (x = 1)$ (line 7), terminating the search.

Along this run, no $\mathcal{T}$-conflict is encountered, hence no $\mathcal{T}$-lemma is generated. This is because the SMT solver never explored the $\mathcal{T}$-inconsistent total assignment $(x = 0) \wedge (x = 1)$ which belongs to $P_{\boldsymbol{\alpha}}(\varphi)$, and no $\mathcal{T}$-lemma is generated to rule it out.

This example shows that naive partial AllSMT enumeration *does not* reliably compute $Cl_{\boldsymbol{\alpha}}(\varphi)$. Enumerating total assignments, however, is typically infeasible on real-world instances due to prohibitive computational time and memory blow-ups. In fact, modern enumeration research emphasizes the importance of producing short assignments to scan the search space more efficiently (see e.g., [10,16,19]). These observations motivate the need for methods that produce $Cl_{\boldsymbol{\alpha}}(\varphi)$ without exhaustive enumeration, while still leveraging compact partial assignments.

Remark 1. For the case $\boldsymbol{\alpha}' \subset \boldsymbol{\alpha}$, the algorithm, in general, does not find a complete set of $\mathcal{T}$-lemmas ruling out $P_{\boldsymbol{\alpha}}(\varphi)$. In Sect. 3.3 and Sect. 3.4, however,

Algorithm 3. LemmaEnumeratorD&C($\varphi[\boldsymbol{\alpha}], \boldsymbol{\alpha}'$)

input: $\varphi[\boldsymbol{\alpha}]$: a $\mathcal{T}$-formula, $\boldsymbol{\alpha}'$: a set of atoms to project on (default: $\boldsymbol{\alpha}$)
s **output:** $Cl_{\boldsymbol{\alpha}}$: a set of $\mathcal{T}$-lemmas
1: $M_{\boldsymbol{\alpha}'p}, Cl_{\boldsymbol{\alpha}p} \leftarrow \text{ProjectedAllSMT}_{\text{partial}}(\varphi[\boldsymbol{\alpha}], \boldsymbol{\alpha}')$
2: $Cl_{\boldsymbol{\alpha}} \leftarrow Cl_{\boldsymbol{\alpha}p}$
3: **for all** $\mu \in M_{\boldsymbol{\alpha}'p}$ **do** ▷ Parallel loop
4: $\quad$ $\_, Cl_{\boldsymbol{\alpha}t} \leftarrow \text{ProjectedAllSMT}_{\text{total}}((\varphi \wedge \mu \wedge \bigwedge_{C \in Cl_{\boldsymbol{\alpha}p}} C)[\boldsymbol{\alpha}], \boldsymbol{\alpha}')$
5: $\quad$ $Cl_{\boldsymbol{\alpha}} \leftarrow Cl_{\boldsymbol{\alpha}} \cup Cl_{\boldsymbol{\alpha}t}$
6: **end for**
7: **return** $Cl_{\boldsymbol{\alpha}}$

we will show some special cases for $\boldsymbol{\alpha}'$ where the projected version is used without affecting completeness.

3.2 Divide and Conquer (and Parallelize)

Although partial enumeration alone is not sufficient to find a set of $\mathcal{T}$-lemmas that rules out $P_{\boldsymbol{\alpha}}(\varphi)$, it provides a useful decomposition of the Boolean search space into a family of residual, $\mathcal{T}$-satisfiable subproblems. This decomposition is inspired by the cube-and-conquer approach in SAT [13], recently used also for model counting [24].

To exploit this decomposition, we propose a divide-and-conquer approach to enumerate $\mathcal{T}$-lemmas, outlined in Algorithm 3. We consider first the case where $\boldsymbol{\alpha}' = \boldsymbol{\alpha}$.

First, the algorithm performs a *partial* AllSMT enumeration on $\varphi[\boldsymbol{\alpha}]$, obtaining a set of partial truth assignments $M_{\boldsymbol{\alpha}p} = \{\mu_1[\boldsymbol{\alpha}], \ldots, \mu_k[\boldsymbol{\alpha}]\}$, and also a set of $\mathcal{T}$-lemmas $Cl_{\boldsymbol{\alpha}p}$ learned during the enumeration (line 1).

Then, for each $\mu_i[\boldsymbol{\alpha}] \in M_{\boldsymbol{\alpha}p}$ (lines 3–6), the algorithm performs a *total* AllSMT enumeration on $\varphi \wedge \mu_i[\boldsymbol{\alpha}]$, conjoining also the previously learned $\mathcal{T}$-lemmas $Cl_{\boldsymbol{\alpha}p}$, to prevent the SMT solver from rediscovering them in the residual subproblems (line 4). After each iteration, we save the lemmas learned by total AllSMT. Overall, rather than paying for one large total AllSMT run on $\varphi[\boldsymbol{\alpha}]$, we pay for one cheaper decomposition step and for many smaller total AllSMT runs on restricted residual formulas, whose overall cost is typically lower than one monolithic total enumeration on $\varphi[\boldsymbol{\alpha}]$.

Moreover, the residual enumeration tasks (line 4) can be executed in parallel on multi-core machines, e.g., by assigning each μ_i to a process and finally merging the $\mathcal{T}$-lemmas produced by the processes. In our architecture, processes execute in isolation, and distinct processes may independently discover identical or redundant lemmas. In practice, in Sect. 4 we show empirically that the number of lemmas found is comparable to that of the AllSMT baseline.

The correctness of this approach follows from the fact that overall, in the different iterations, all the total truth assignments are explored, thus for each $\rho[\boldsymbol{\alpha}] \in P_{\boldsymbol{\alpha}}(\varphi)$, a $\mathcal{T}$-lemma is eventually generated that rules it out.

Algorithm 4. LemmaEnumeratorWithProjection($\varphi[\boldsymbol{\alpha}]$, LemmaEnumerator)

input: $\varphi[\boldsymbol{\alpha}]$: a $\mathcal{T}$-formula, LemmaEnumerator: a $\mathcal{T}$-lemma enumerator
output: $Cl_{\boldsymbol{\alpha}}$: a set of $\mathcal{T}$-lemmas

1: $\boldsymbol{\alpha}_{\mathcal{T}} \leftarrow$ GetTheoryAtoms($\boldsymbol{\alpha}$) ▷ Extract theory atoms from $\boldsymbol{\alpha}$
2: $Cl_{\boldsymbol{\alpha}} \leftarrow$ LemmaEnumerator($\varphi[\boldsymbol{\alpha}], \boldsymbol{\alpha}_{\mathcal{T}}$)
3: **return** $Cl_{\boldsymbol{\alpha}}$

We remark that, while our algorithm guarantees that the $\mu_i[\boldsymbol{\alpha}]$ are disjoint, $\mathcal{T}$-satisfiable, and propositionally satisfy $\varphi[\boldsymbol{\alpha}]$, the latter fact is not a strict requirement for the correctness of the approach. Indeed, this is only one of the possible decompositions of the search space, and any family of partial assignments that covers all propositional assignments of φ would suffice. This opens up the possibility of designing alternative heuristics to decompose the search space.

For the case $\boldsymbol{\alpha}' \subset \boldsymbol{\alpha}$, Remark 1 applies for Algorithm 3 as well.

3.3 Projection on Theory-Atoms

Enumerating all total truth assignments, even when parallelized, is often infeasible on real-world instances. In this section, we spotlight that this is often unnecessary to find a complete set of $\mathcal{T}$-lemmas, starting from the following observation.

Truth assignments explored during an AllSMT enumeration, whether via the classic or the divide-and-conquer approach, consist of two components: an assignment to $\mathcal{T}$-atoms and an assignment to $\mathbb{B}$-atoms. We note that the $\mathcal{T}$-inconsistency of a truth assignment is determined exclusively by its projection onto the $\mathcal{T}$-atoms. Consequently, a standard AllSMT procedure may inefficiently enumerate multiple truth assignments that share an identical $\mathcal{T}$-consistent projection but differ in their Boolean assignments. This redundancy is computationally wasteful, as variations in the Boolean assignment do not generate new $\mathcal{T}$-lemmas.

We can address this inefficiency by performing an AllSMT enumeration *projected on the $\mathcal{T}$-atoms of φ*. The correctness of this approach follows from the following theorem (proof in [6]).

Theorem 1. *Let $\varphi[\boldsymbol{\alpha}]$ be a $\mathcal{T}$-formula. Let $\boldsymbol{\alpha}_{\mathbb{B}}$ and $\boldsymbol{\alpha}_{\mathcal{T}}$ be the sets of Boolean and theory atoms in $\boldsymbol{\alpha}$, respectively.*

Let $BC_{\boldsymbol{\alpha}_{\mathcal{T}}}(\varphi) \stackrel{\text{def}}{=} \{\neg\eta_{\mathcal{T}}[\boldsymbol{\alpha}_{\mathcal{T}}] \text{ s.t. } \eta_{\mathcal{T}}[\boldsymbol{\alpha}_{\mathcal{T}}] \wedge \eta_{\mathbb{B}}[\boldsymbol{\alpha}_{\mathcal{T}}] \in H_{\boldsymbol{\alpha}}(\varphi)\}$, and let $Cl_{\boldsymbol{\alpha}}$ be a set of $\mathcal{T}$-lemmas s.t. $BC_{\boldsymbol{\alpha}_{\mathcal{T}}}(\varphi) \cup Cl_{\boldsymbol{\alpha}}$ rules out $P_{\boldsymbol{\alpha}}(\varphi)$.

Then $Cl_{\boldsymbol{\alpha}}$ rules out $P_{\boldsymbol{\alpha}}(\varphi)$.

This leads to the enumeration procedure outlined in Algorithm 4. This procedure invokes an AllSMT-based $\mathcal{T}$-lemma enumerator (e.g., the one in Algorithm 2 or Algorithm 3), projecting the enumeration onto $\mathcal{T}$-atoms only. If the lemma enumerator is based on Algorithm 1, which terminates when

Algorithm 5. LemmaEnumeratorWithPartitioning($\varphi[\boldsymbol{\alpha}]$, LemmaEnumerator)

```
input: φ[α]: a T-formula, LemmaEnumerator: a T-lemma enumerator
output: Cl_α: a set of T-lemmas
Cl_α ← ∅
{α_1, ..., α_n} ← PartitionAtoms(α)        ▷ Partition atoms as in Property 1
for all i ∈ [1..n] do
    Cl_αi ← LemmaEnumerator((φ ∧ ⋀_{C∈Cl_α} C)[α], α_i)
    Cl_α ← Cl_α ∪ Cl_αi
end for
return Cl_α
```

$\varphi \wedge \bigwedge_i \neg\eta_{\mathcal{T}i}[\boldsymbol{\alpha}_{\mathcal{T}}] \wedge \bigwedge_{C \in Cl_{\boldsymbol{\alpha}}} C \equiv_{\mathbb{B}} \bot$, it follows from Theorem 1 that the returned set $Cl_{\boldsymbol{\alpha}}$ of $\mathcal{T}$-lemmas rules out $P_{\boldsymbol{\alpha}}(\varphi)$.

Remark 2. Note that the projected assignments can be *exponentially fewer* than the assignments on the full set of atoms. Also, the blocking clauses added by Algorithm 1 (line 7) are much shorter, as they only contain $\mathcal{T}$-atoms. This can lead to a drastic reduction in both enumeration time and memory usage.

3.4 Theory-Driven Partitioning

We now present a further improvement for $\mathcal{T}$-lemmas enumeration, for the case where the set of atoms of $\varphi[\boldsymbol{\alpha}]$ can be partitioned into two or more disjoint sets wrt. variables and uninterpreted symbols. We first recall the following property, which characterizes the partitioning of atoms that we will use in the following results.

Property 1. Let $\boldsymbol{\alpha} \stackrel{\text{def}}{=} \boldsymbol{\alpha}_1 \cup \boldsymbol{\alpha}_2$ be a set of atoms s.t. no atom in $\boldsymbol{\alpha}_1$ shares variables or uninterpreted symbols with any atom in $\boldsymbol{\alpha}_2$. Then, for any truth assignment $\eta[\boldsymbol{\alpha}] \stackrel{\text{def}}{=} \eta_1[\boldsymbol{\alpha}_1] \wedge \eta_2[\boldsymbol{\alpha}_2]$, $\eta[\boldsymbol{\alpha}]$ is $\mathcal{T}$-satisfiable iff both $\eta_1[\boldsymbol{\alpha}_1]$ and $\eta_2[\boldsymbol{\alpha}_2]$ are $\mathcal{T}$-satisfiable.

Consequently, if the set of atoms of φ can be partitioned according to the conditions of Property 1, then in order to rule out a $\mathcal{T}$-inconsistent truth assignment $\rho[\boldsymbol{\alpha}] \stackrel{\text{def}}{=} \rho_1[\boldsymbol{\alpha}_1] \wedge \rho_2[\boldsymbol{\alpha}_2] \in P_{\boldsymbol{\alpha}}(\varphi)$, a $\mathcal{T}$-lemma must rule out $\rho_1[\boldsymbol{\alpha}_1]$ or $\rho_2[\boldsymbol{\alpha}_2]$.

This suggests a decomposition strategy: an AllSMT enumeration projected on $\boldsymbol{\alpha}_1$ will find a set of $\mathcal{T}$-lemmas that rule out all $\rho[\boldsymbol{\alpha}] \in P_{\boldsymbol{\alpha}}(\varphi)$ such that $\rho_1[\boldsymbol{\alpha}_1]$ is $\mathcal{T}$-inconsistent. Dually, an AllSMT enumeration projected on $\boldsymbol{\alpha}_2$, will find a set of $\mathcal{T}$-lemmas that rule out all $\rho[\boldsymbol{\alpha}] \in P_{\boldsymbol{\alpha}}(\varphi)$ such that $\rho_2[\boldsymbol{\alpha}_2]$ is $\mathcal{T}$-inconsistent. Thus, the enumeration of $\mathcal{T}$-lemmas can be decomposed into two separate enumerations.

This intuition is formalized in the following theorem (proof in [6]).

Theorem 2. *Let $\varphi[\boldsymbol{\alpha}]$ be a $\mathcal{T}$-formula, s.t. $\boldsymbol{\alpha} \stackrel{\text{def}}{=} \boldsymbol{\alpha}_1 \cup \boldsymbol{\alpha}_2$ and no atom in $\boldsymbol{\alpha}_1$ shares variables or uninterpreted symbols with any atom in $\boldsymbol{\alpha}_2$.*

Let $BC_{\alpha_1}(\varphi) \stackrel{\text{def}}{=} \{\neg\eta_1[\alpha_1] \text{ s.t. } \eta_1[\alpha_1] \wedge \eta_2[\boldsymbol{\alpha}_2] \in H_{\boldsymbol{\alpha}}(\varphi)\}$*, and let* $Cl_{\boldsymbol{\alpha}}$ *be a set of* $\mathcal{T}$*-lemmas s.t.* $BC_{\alpha_1}(\varphi) \cup Cl_{\boldsymbol{\alpha}}$ *rules out* $P_{\boldsymbol{\alpha}}(\varphi)$*.*

Let $\varphi'[\boldsymbol{\alpha}] \stackrel{\text{def}}{=} \varphi \wedge \bigwedge_{C \in Cl_{\boldsymbol{\alpha}}} C$*.*

Let $BC_{\boldsymbol{\alpha}_2}(\varphi') \stackrel{\text{def}}{=} \{\neg\eta_2[\boldsymbol{\alpha}_2] \text{ s.t. } \eta_1[\alpha_1] \wedge \eta_2[\boldsymbol{\alpha}_2] \in H_{\boldsymbol{\alpha}}(\varphi')\}$*, and let* $Cl'_{\boldsymbol{\alpha}}$ *be a set of* $\mathcal{T}$*-lemmas s.t.* $BC_{\boldsymbol{\alpha}_2}(\varphi') \cup Cl'_{\boldsymbol{\alpha}}$ *rules out* $P_{\boldsymbol{\alpha}}(\varphi')$*.*

Then $Cl_{\boldsymbol{\alpha}} \cup Cl'_{\boldsymbol{\alpha}}$ *rules out* $P_{\boldsymbol{\alpha}}(\varphi)$*.*

Note that this result can be easily generalized to the case where the set of atoms can be partitioned into more than two sets. Indeed, if $\boldsymbol{\alpha}_2$ can be further partitioned, we can apply the same reasoning recursively to it.

This result naturally leads to the enumeration strategy in Algorithm 5. The algorithm first partitions the set of atoms of $\varphi[\boldsymbol{\alpha}]$ as in Property 1, obtaining $\{\boldsymbol{\alpha}_1, \ldots, \boldsymbol{\alpha}_n\}$ (line 2). This step can be performed efficiently, e.g., using a union-find data structure to compute the connected components of the graph of atoms, where two atoms are directly connected if they share a variable or an uninterpreted symbol. Note that, in principle, every $\mathbb{B}$-atom can be considered as belonging to a separate, singleton partition. In practice, we assume that all the $\mathbb{B}$-atoms belong to the same partition, and can be handled via projection as discussed in Sect. 3.3.

Then, for each partition $\boldsymbol{\alpha}_i$, the algorithm performs an AllSMT-based $\mathcal{T}$-lemma enumeration projected on $\boldsymbol{\alpha}_i$ (line 4), and accumulates the enumerated $\mathcal{T}$-lemmas in $Cl_{\boldsymbol{\alpha}}$ (line 4). Note that, as in Theorem 2, we conjoin the returned $\mathcal{T}$-lemmas to the input formula in each enumeration, so as to rule out $\mathcal{T}$-inconsistent assignments that have already been ruled out by previous enumerations. Finally, we return the accumulated set $Cl_{\boldsymbol{\alpha}}$ of $\mathcal{T}$-lemmas (line 7), which, by Theorem 2, rules out $P_{\boldsymbol{\alpha}}(\varphi)$.

Similar considerations as in Remark 2 apply in this case. Indeed, if $n > 1$ then the improvement could be dramatic, as we decompose a single total enumeration step into n projected enumerations on *subsets* of atoms.

4 Experimental Evaluation

We evaluate the performance of the $\mathcal{T}$-lemma enumeration techniques of Sect. 3 in terms of *time* required to enumerate $\mathcal{T}$-lemmas. We also analyze the *number* of enumerated $\mathcal{T}$-lemmas, and their median *size*. We consider the following enumerators:

- Baseline, i.e., standard AllSMT as in [17] (Algorithm 2, Sect. 3.1);
- D&C, i.e., divide-and-conquer AllSMT (Algorithm 3, Sect. 3.2);
- D&C+Proj., i.e., D&C plus projection on $\mathcal{T}$-atoms (Algorithm 4, Sect. 3.3);
- D&C+Proj.+Part., i.e., D&C+Proj. plus partitioning (Algorithm 5, Sect. 3.4).

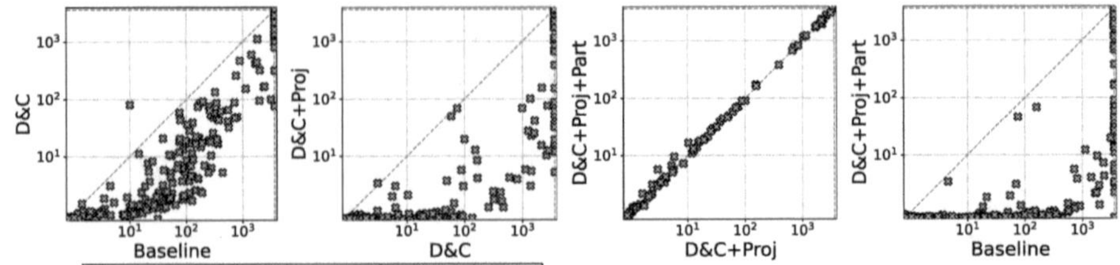

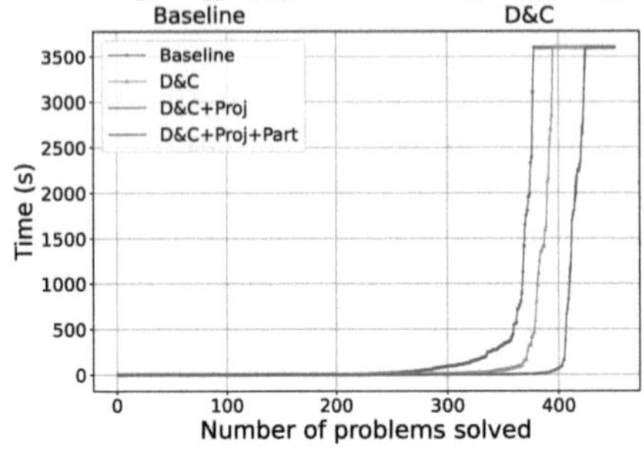

Strategy	Timeouts	Total
Baseline	73	450
D&C	56	450
D&C+Proj.	26	450
D&C+Proj.+Part.	27	450

Fig. 1. T-lemma enumeration time with different methods on problems from [17]. (Notice that in the cactus plot the green and red lines are almost indistinguishable.)

Reproducibility. All the experiments have been executed on three equivalent machines with an Intel(R) Xeon(R) Gold 6238R @ 2.20 GHz CPU and 128 GB of RAM. Divide-and-conquer-based enumerators use 45 cores for parallelization. For each instance, we set a timeout of 3600 s. We use PySMT [11] to manipulate SMT formulas and interface with solvers, and MathSAT5 [4] as AllSMT solver, as it implements the enumeration procedure described in Algorithm 1. For finding short partial assignments for non-CNF formulas we use the technique in [16]. The code for the algorithms[3] and for reproducing the experiments[4] are publicly available.

Benchmarks. We considered two sets of benchmarks. The first set consists of all the 450 SMT($\mathcal{LRA}$) synthetic instances from [17]. These problems were generated randomly by nesting Boolean operators up to a fixed depth varying from 4 to 8, involving 10 Boolean variables and 10 real variables.

The second set consists of 90 SMT($\mathcal{LRA}$) instances encoding temporal planning problems from the industrial-inspired "Painter" domain [22]. For each problem, we generated the SMT encoding for action applications up to a fixed horizon $h \in \{3, 4, 5\}$ using the Tempest tool.[5] The encoding is described in [18]; since [18] focuses on optimal temporal planning, in our encoding the optimization component and the abstract step are discarded. We also removed the goal constraints to increase the number of solutions and make the problems more challenging for $\mathcal{T}$-lemma enumeration.

[3] https://github.com/ecivini/tlemmas-enumeration.
[4] https://github.com/ecivini/tlemmas-enumeration-testbench.
[5] https://github.com/fbk-pso/tempest.

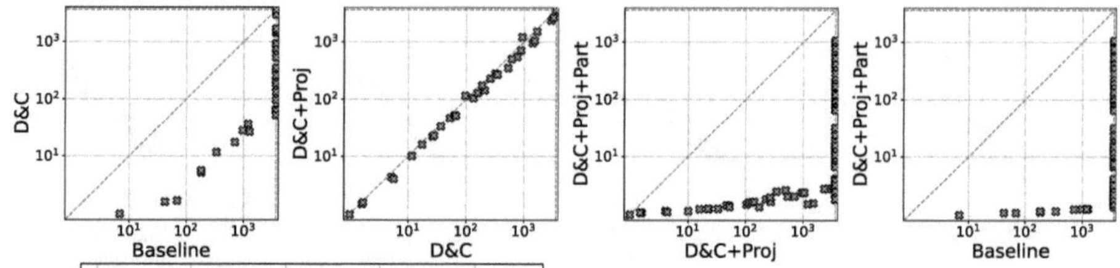

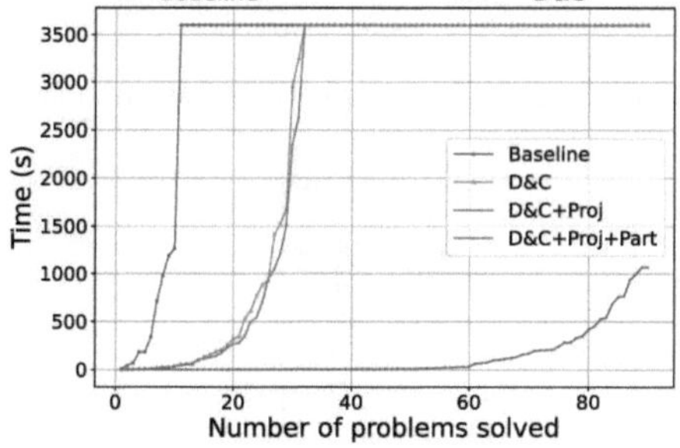

Strategy	**Timeouts**	**Total**
Baseline	80	90
D&C	59	90
D&C+Proj.	59	90
D&C+Proj.+Part.	0	90

Fig. 2. T-lemma enumeration time with different methods on planning problems.

Results on Enumeration Time. Figures 1 and 2 present the results for enumeration time on the synthetic and temporal planning benchmarks, respectively. Each figure is organized as follows: the top row shows scatter plots comparing the strategies pairwise. (Notice the logarithmic scale of the axes!) We focus on incremental improvements, i.e., Baseline vs. D&C, D&C vs. D&C+Proj., and D&C+Proj. vs. D&C+Proj.+Part.. The rightmost plot shows the overall speed-up (Baseline vs. D&C+Proj.+Part.). The bottom row contains a cactus plot comparing all strategies together, and a table summarizing the number of instances and timeouts.

In the problems from [17] (Fig. 1), we notice that the D&C significantly improves wrt. the baseline by up to 2 orders of magnitude, solving 17 more problems within the timeout. The improvement is even more pronounced when we add projection, which allows for solving 30 more problems and drastically reduces the enumeration time for problems already solved by D&C. Notably, the introduction of partitioning does not yield any improvement. This is because only 92 of 450 problems have at least two partitions. The hardest of these problems was solved by D&C+Proj. in less than 1 s; thus, partitioning has no room for improvement. Overall, the scatter plot in Fig. 1 (top right) is remarkable, showing a dramatic reduction in the time required by our best configuration wrt. the baseline.

On temporal planning problems (Fig. 2), we can see a similar trend, with some differences. While D&C is much faster than the baseline, solving 21 more problems within the timeout, the addition of projection does not yield any improvement. This is likely due to the fact that in planning problems, the assignment on $\mathcal{T}$-atoms is a deterministic consequence of the assignment on $\mathbb{B}$-atoms, so that projecting does not reduce the number of $\mathcal{T}$-satisfiable truth assignments

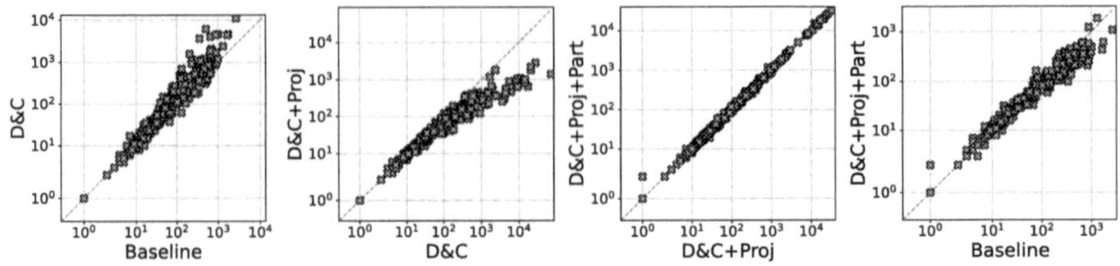

Fig. 3. Number of $\mathcal{T}$-lemmas found by different strategies on problems from [17].

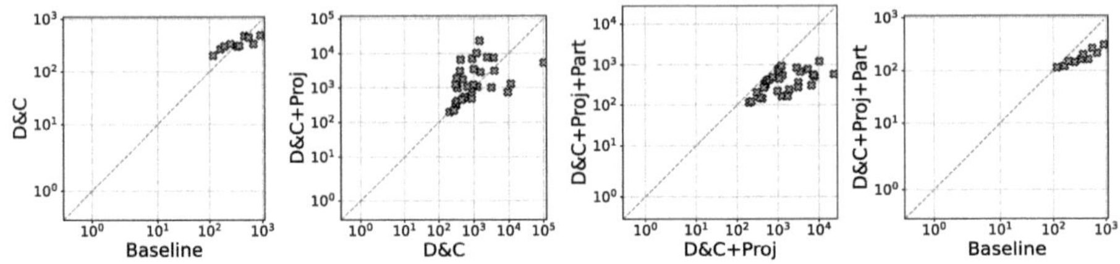

Fig. 4. Number of $\mathcal{T}$-lemmas found by different strategies on planning problems.

explored by the solver. On the other hand, partitioning is extremely effective here, dramatically reducing the enumeration time. In these problems, we have five $\mathcal{T}$-atoms partitions: atoms encoding time constraints, atoms with constraints on the values of the fluents, and three partitions with constraints on the parameters of three different actions. By reasoning separately on these partitions, we achieve a speedup of several orders of magnitude, solving problems up to horizon 5 that were before intractable.

Results on the number of enumerated $\mathcal{T}$-lemmas. We now analyze the number of $\mathcal{T}$-lemmas enumerated by the different strategies. Figures 3 and 4 show scatter plots for the synthetic and temporal planning benchmarks, respectively. As for the time plots, also here we present pairwise comparisons of incremental improvements. We remark that we only show points for problems solved by both the compared strategies, so that plots in Fig. 4 only have a limited number of points.

Overall, there is no big difference in the number of $\mathcal{T}$-lemmas enumerated by different strategies. We can, however, observe some trends.

First, D&C tends to enumerate more $\mathcal{T}$-lemmas than Baseline. This is expected as we said in Sect. 3.2, since the parallel enumeration can discover redundant $\mathcal{T}$-lemmas.

Second, both projection and partitioning help in reducing the number of enumerated $\mathcal{T}$-lemmas. This fact can have multiple explanations.

One is that early pruning to the $\mathcal{T}$-solver [1] may cause the SMT solver to enumerate $\mathcal{T}$-lemmas that rule out also $\mathcal{T}$-unsatisfiable assignments that do not propositionally satisfy the formula. By narrowing the search space, both projection and partitioning help mitigate this undesired behavior.

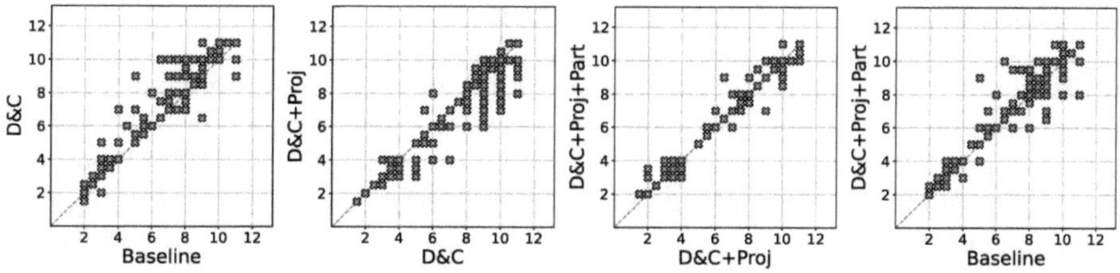

Fig. 5. Median $\mathcal{T}$-lemma size for different strategies on problems from [17].

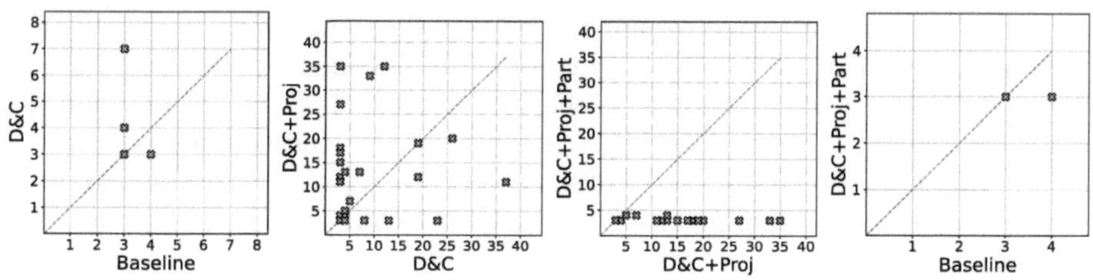

Fig. 6. Median $\mathcal{T}$-lemma size for different strategies on planning problems.

Additionally, for the divide-and-conquer strategy without projection, two parallel processes can find two $\mathcal{T}$-inconsistent assignments sharing the same $\mathcal{T}$-literals and different $\mathbb{B}$-literals, inevitably generating two redundant $\mathcal{T}$-lemmas. With projection, instead, the partial assignments fed to different processes differ only on $\mathcal{T}$-literals, thereby mitigating this issue.

Lastly, partitioning can help enumerate smaller $\mathcal{T}$-lemmas (see next), which have stronger pruning power, thus reducing the number of enumerated $\mathcal{T}$-lemmas.

Results on the Size of $\mathcal{T}$- lemmas. As a further insight, we analyze the median size (i.e., the number of literals) of the $\mathcal{T}$-lemmas enumerated by the different strategies. The results are shown in Figs. 5 and 6 for synthetic and planning problems, respectively. Since we only show points for problems solved by both the compared strategies, so that plots in Fig. 6 only have a limited number of points.

We observe that different techniques do not consistently improve or worsen the size of $\mathcal{T}$-lemmas, with a notable exception for partitioning, which, on planning problems, allows for finding much smaller $\mathcal{T}$-lemmas. We conjecture that this may be due to the fact that, with projected enumeration, the literal selection heuristics of the SMT solver may prefer selecting projection atoms first. Hence, early-pruning calls [1] to the $\mathcal{T}$-solver are more likely to cut $\mathcal{T}$-inconsistent branches involving only projection atoms. This hinders the generation of bigger $\mathcal{T}$-lemmas with atoms from different partitions, which are intrinsically redundant by Property 1.

5 Conclusions and Future Work

In this paper, we presented theory-agnostic techniques for enumerating a set of theory lemmas ruling out all theory-inconsistent truth assignments for a given SMT formula. Starting from a baseline method based on total AllSMT enumeration proposed in [17], we proposed three orthogonal, composable, techniques to enhance efficiency.

We experimentally evaluated our techniques on SMT problems from [17], and on a new set of SMT formulas encoding temporal planning problems [22]. Our techniques drastically improve the efficiency of lemma enumeration wrt. the baseline, allowing us to scale to much more complex instances.

This work is planned to play a crucial role in our ongoing research in *knowledge compilation modulo theories*, which we introduced in [17] for decision diagrams and in [15] for general d-DNNFs. Since in [17] the enumeration of theory lemmas was the major bottleneck in the compilation process, our novel lemma-enumeration techniques pave the way for scaling to complex, real-world instances.

Acknowledgements. We thank Alberto Griggio for his assistance with the MATHSAT usage. We thank Alessandro Valentini and Andrea Micheli for their assistance with TEMPEST for generating the temporal planning benchmarks. RS was supported in part by the TANGO project funded by the EU Horizon Europe research and innovation program under GA No 101120763, funded by the European Union. Views and opinions expressed are, however, those of the author(s) only and do not necessarily reflect those of the European Union, the European Health and Digital Executive Agency (HaDEA) or The European Research Council. Neither the European Union nor the granting authority can be held responsible for them.

Disclosure of Interests. The authors have no competing interests to declare that are relevant to the content of this article.

References

1. Barrett, C., Sebastiani, R., Seshia, S.A., Tinelli, C.: Satisfiability modulo theories. In: Handbook of Satisfiability, FAIA, vol. 336, , 2 edn., pp. 1267–1329. IOS Press(2021). https://doi.org/10.3233/FAIA201017
2. Bryant, R.E.: Graph-based algorithms for boolean function manipulation. IEEE Trans Comput **C-35**(8), 677–691 (1986). https://doi.org/10.1109/TC.1986.1676819
3. Cimatti, A., Griggio, A., Sebastiani, R.: Computing small unsatisfiable cores in satisfiability modulo theories. J. Artif. Intell. Res. **40**, 701–728 (2011). https://doi.org/10.1613/jair.3196
4. Cimatti, A., Griggio, A., Schaafsma, B.J., Sebastiani, R.: The MathSAT5 SMT solver. In: Piterman, N., Smolka, S.A. (eds.) TACAS 2013. LNCS, vol. 7795, pp. 93–107. Springer, Heidelberg (2013). https://doi.org/10.1007/978-3-642-36742-7_7
5. Cimatti, A., Griggio, A., Schaafsma, B.J., Sebastiani, R.: A modular approach to MaxSAT modulo theories. In: Järvisalo, M., Van Gelder, A. (eds.) SAT 2013. LNCS, vol. 7962, pp. 150–165. Springer, Heidelberg (2013). https://doi.org/10.1007/978-3-642-39071-5_12

6. Civini, E., Masina, G., Spallitta, G., Sebastiani, R.: Beyond Eager Encodings: A Theory-Agnostic Approach to Theory-Lemma Enumeration in SMT (2026).https://doi.org/10.48550/arXiv.2602.14634, (Extended version.)
7. Darwiche, A.: SDD: a new canonical representation of propositional knowledge bases. In: IJCAI 2011, vol. 2, pp. 819–826. AAAI Press (2011). https://doi.org/10.5591/978-1-57735-516-8/IJCAI11-143
8. Darwiche, A., Marquis, P.: A knowledge compilation map. J. Artif. Intell. Res. **17**(1), 229–264 (2002). https://doi.org/10.1613/jair.989
9. Fazekas, K., Bacchus, F., Biere, A.: Implicit hitting set algorithms for maximum satisfiability modulo theories. In: Galmiche, D., Schulz, S., Sebastiani, R. (eds.) IJCAR 2018. LNCS (LNAI), vol. 10900, pp. 134–151. Springer, Cham (2018). https://doi.org/10.1007/978-3-319-94205-6_10
10. Fried, D., Nadel, A., Sebastiani, R., Shalmon, Y.: Entailing generalization boosts enumeration. In: SAT 2024. LIPIcs, vol. 305, pp. 13:1–13:14. LZI (2024).https://doi.org/10.4230/LIPIcs.SAT.2024.13
11. Gario, M., Micheli, A.: PySMT: a solver-agnostic library for fast prototyping of SMT-based algorithms. In: SMT Workshop 2015 (2015). https://github.com/pysmt/pysmt
12. Guthmann, O., Strichman, O., Trostanetski, A.: Minimal unsatisfiable core extraction for SMT. In: FMCAD 2016, pp. 57–64 (2016). https://doi.org/10.1109/FMCAD.2016.7886661
13. Heule, M.J.H., Kullmann, O., Wieringa, S., Biere, A.: Cube and conquer: guiding CDCL SAT solvers by lookaheads. In: Eder, K., Lourenço, J., Shehory, O. (eds.) HVC 2011. LNCS, vol. 7261, pp. 50–65. Springer, Heidelberg (2012). https://doi.org/10.1007/978-3-642-34188-5_8
14. Lahiri, S.K., Nieuwenhuis, R., Oliveras, A.: SMT techniques for fast predicate abstraction. In: Ball, T., Jones, R.B. (eds.) CAV 2006. LNCS, vol. 4144, pp. 424–437. Springer, Heidelberg (2006). https://doi.org/10.1007/11817963_39
15. Masina, G., Civini, E., Michelutti, M., Spallitta, G., Sebastiani, R.: d-DNNF modulo theories: a general framework for polytime SMT queries. In: SAT 2026 (2026), extended version available as arXiv preprint. https://arxiv.org/abs/2603.09975
16. Masina, G., Spallitta, G., Sebastiani, R.: On CNF conversion for SAT and SMT enumeration. J. Artif. Intell. Res. **83** (2025). https://doi.org/10.1613/jair.1.16870
17. Michelutti, M., Masina, G., Spallitta, G., Sebastiani, R.: Canonical decision diagrams modulo theories. In: ECAI 2024, FAIA, vol. 392, pp. 4319–4327. IOS Press (2024). https://doi.org/10.3233/FAIA241007
18. Panjkovic, S., Micheli, A.: Expressive optimal temporal planning via optimization modulo theory. In: AAAI 2023 **37**(10), 12095–12102 (2023). https://doi.org/10.1609/aaai.v37i10.26426
19. Spallitta, G., Sebastiani, R., Biere, A.: Disjoint projected enumeration for SAT and SMT without blocking clauses. Artif. Intell. **345**, 104346 (2025). https://doi.org/10.1016/j.artint.2025.104346
20. Strichman, O.: On solving presburger and linear arithmetic with SAT. In: Aagaard, M.D., O'Leary, J.W. (eds.) FMCAD 2002. LNCS, vol. 2517, pp. 160–170. Springer, Heidelberg (2002). https://doi.org/10.1007/3-540-36126-X_10
21. Strichman, O., Seshia, S.A., Bryant, R.E.: Deciding separation formulas with SAT. In: Brinksma, E., Larsen, K.G. (eds.) CAV 2002. LNCS, vol. 2404, pp. 209–222. Springer, Heidelberg (2002). https://doi.org/10.1007/3-540-45657-0_16
22. Valentini, A., Micheli, A., Cimatti, A.: Temporal planning with intermediate conditions and effects. In: AAAI, vol. 34, pp. 9975–9982 (2020).https://doi.org/10.1609/aaai.v34i06.6553

23. Velev, M.N., Bryant, R.E.: Effective use of Boolean satisfiability procedures in the formal verification of superscalar and VLIW, pp. 226–231 (2001). https://doi.org/10.1145/378239.378469
24. Xu, Z., Yin, M., Lagniez, J.M.: An embarrassingly parallel model counter. In: KR, vol. 22, pp. 670–681 (2025). https://doi.org/10.24963/kr.2025/65

Open Access This chapter is licensed under the terms of the Creative Commons Attribution 4.0 International License (http://creativecommons.org/licenses/by/4.0/), which permits use, sharing, adaptation, distribution and reproduction in any medium or format, as long as you give appropriate credit to the original author(s) and the source, provide a link to the Creative Commons license and indicate if changes were made.

The images or other third party material in this chapter are included in the chapter's Creative Commons license, unless indicated otherwise in a credit line to the material. If material is not included in the chapter's Creative Commons license and your intended use is not permitted by statutory regulation or exceeds the permitted use, you will need to obtain permission directly from the copyright holder.

Ethos: A Fast Proof Checker for the Eunoia Logical Framework

Andrew Reynolds[1(✉)], Hans-Jörg Schurr[1,3,4], Mallku Soldevila[5], Haniel Barbosa[5], Clark Barrett[2], and Cesare Tinelli[1]

[1] The University of Iowa, Iowa City, USA
andrew-reynolds@uiowa.edu
[2] Stanford University, Stanford, USA
[3] KU Leuven, Leuven, Belgium
[4] Vrije Universiteit Brussel, Brussels, Belgium
[5] Universidade Federal de Minas Gerais, Belo Horizonte, Brazil

Abstract. SMT solvers are used in many safety-critical applications. To provide evidence of the correctness of their answers, some SMT solvers generate externally checkable proof certificates. We present a high-performance checker for SMT proof certificates called *Ethos*. In contrast with other dedicated SMT proof checkers, Ethos does not implement a fixed proof calculus. Instead, it allows users to specify their own calculus in the declarative language Eunoia, which extends the familiar SMT-LIB syntax to make that easy and convenient. We give a short overview of Eunoia and then focus on Ethos itself. We describe multiple optimization and implementation details which make Ethos fast and practical. We also evaluate Ethos on proofs generated by cvc5, showing that the flexibility of Ethos allows us to efficiently check fine-grained proofs, containing no proof holes, over all SMT-LIB logics without floating point arithmetic.

Keywords: SMT · proof checking · logical frameworks

1 Introduction

Satisfiability Modulo Theories (SMT) solvers reason about logical problems expressed in terms of a wide variety of theories (arithmetic, bit-vectors, strings, and so on). They are used as back ends for software verification tools as well as a variety of other safety-critical applications (e.g., [7]). A key concern for these applications is that SMT solvers are large and complex systems. As such, they are at risk of containing bugs that affect their correctness.

A pragmatic but rigorous approach for addressing this concern is for an SMT solver to produce a *proof certificate*, or just *proof* for short, for each its answers. This is typically a textual artifact, expressing a formal proof of the answer's correctness, which can be checked by an external tool, a *proof checker* [1, 17]. A proof accepted by a proof checker is a strong piece of evidence that the

© The Author(s) 2026
A. Biere et al. (Eds.): IJCAR 2026, LNAI 16688, pp. 305–314, 2026.
https://doi.org/10.1007/978-3-032-32589-1_19

solver's answer is correct. The reason is that, since proof checking is in general considerably simpler than proof finding, which is ultimately what SMT solvers do, even a proof checker that is not formally verified can strengthen the user's trust in the SMT solver's answer. This approach requires the definition of a format for SMT proofs, which is a serious challenge as different SMT solvers, or even different theory solvers within the same SMT solver, may use vastly different proof systems, or *calculi*, due to differences in the theories they support and in the preprocessing and reasoning methods they implement.

In this paper, we present *Ethos*, a generic proof checker for SMT. Instead of implementing a fixed calculus, Ethos supports the *Eunoia* logical framework, which is designed to make specifying proof systems and proofs in them simple and convenient for SMT developers. Eunoia's syntax extends that of Version 2.7 of the SMT-LIB standard [5] with commands for (*i*) defining theory *signatures*, i.e., the collection of types, constants, and proof rules that constitute a proof calculus, and (*ii*) expressing proofs themselves. Given a Eunoia file that provides both a signature and a proof, Ethos checks that the proof correctly applies the rules in the signature. It can also verify that the assumptions used in a proof in fact correspond to the assertions in a specific SMT-LIB problem, thus ensuring that the proof is not just a correct proof but a proof of the correct theorem.

While Ethos is not formally verified, it significantly reduces the trusted code base. For example, the source code of the cvc5 SMT solver [3] consists of over 300K lines of C++, while Ethos is less than 10K lines of C++. The signature for cvc5 proofs is expressed in 6,397 lines of Eunoia code. Strong runtime performance was a main goal when implementing Ethos, with the aim of reducing the cost, and thus incentivizing the use, of proof checking. To this end, Ethos implements multiple optimization techniques, which we discuss below.

Related Work. The main inspiration for Ethos comes from two related systems. The first is Alethe [15], a proof format and calculus for SMT supported by the Carcara checker [1]. In contrast to Eunoia, Alethe defines a fixed calculus, described in English in a reference document [4]. The SMT solver SMTInterpol [10] uses a custom proof format similar to Alethe. The second inspiration is LFSC, also a logical framework, and its proof checker [17]. In contrast to Eunoia, its syntax does not resemble SMT-LIB and rappresents proofs as terms. Based on our experience, SMT developers find it unintuitive and difficult to use, which may have hindered its wide adoption.

Both LFSC and Eunoia are inspired by other logical frameworks, starting with Edinburgh LF [8]. Among them, Dedukti [2] stands out as explicitly designed for proof exchange. Multiple calculi for SMT solvers and other automated reasoners have been modeled in Dedukti [6]. RARE is a domain specific language for declaring proofs based on rewriting [11]. Eunoia is partially inspired by it and can be seen as a generalization of its functionality to arbitrary proof rules.

Beyond those mentioned so far, there a number of additional approaches for defining proof formats. DRAT [19] is a unified proof format for propositional logic that enables SAT solvers to easily generate proofs for most state-of-the-art solving techniques in a manner that can be efficiently checked. As a result, most contemporary SAT solvers support DRAT. Unfortunately, due to the heterogeneous nature of SMT solving, it seems doubtful that a format with a fixed proof calculus could provide similar standardization benefits for SMT. The eDRAT format [9] uses DRAT together with unjustified theory lemmas, which must be checked separately. It does not support proofs for preprocessing.

The TPTP world [18] provides a proof format for automated theorem provers (ATPs). However, it does not prescribe a way to define proof rules, and theorem provers choose their own. A notable consequence of this design choice is that, since TPTP proofs rules can be quite high level, a trusted ATP, as opposed to a simpler checker, is needed to prove individual rule applications correct.

2 Eunoia

In this section, we provide an overview of Eunoia through an example containing a signature and a proof in that signature. The Ethos user manual [13] contains a a complete introduction to Eunoia.

Types and Constants. A Eunoia signature starts with a declaration of relevant types and constants (in the HOL sense), as shown in the following. The constants `Bool`, `true`, `false`, and `->` are not declared because they are built-in.

theory.eo
```
1 (declare-const Int Type) (declare-consts <numeral> Int)
2 (declare-const not (-> Bool Bool))
3 (declare-const and (-> Bool Bool Bool) :right-assoc-nil true)
4 (declare-parameterized-const = ((A Type :implicit)) (-> A A Bool))
5 (declare-const BitVec (-> Int Type))
6 (declare-parameterized-const concat ((m Int :implicit) (n Int :implicit))
7   (-> (BitVec n) (BitVec m) (BitVec (eo::add m n))))
```

Eunoia contains several built-in syntactic categories. It is up to the user though to give them a type. In the example above, the `declare-consts` command (line 1) tells Ethos that every (signed) numeral (`0`, `1`, `-1`, ...) has type `Int`. This makes it possible to change the type of numerals depending on the SMT-LIB logic of interest. For example, in the `QF_LIA` logic, numerals have type `Int`, while in `QF_LRA` they have type `Real`. The defined symbols do not carry any semantic information, beyond their type. They are simply constructors of the term language on which the proof rules operate.

The `:right-assoc-nil` annotation (line 3) for the constant `and` is an extension of SMT-LIB's `:right-assoc` annotation. It indicates that `and` can be used as a variadic operator with `true` as a neutral (or *nil*) element.[1] Like `:right-assoc`, it allows applications of the operator to more than two arguments as syntactic sugar for a nested application. However, it also allows applications of the form `(and a)`, treated as a shorthand for `(and a true)`. This implies that `(and a b c)` is parsed as `(and a (and b (and c true)))` and not `(and a (and b c))`, as would be the case with the `:right-assoc` annotation. One

[1] Eunoia also supports the specular annotations `:left-assoc` and `:left-assoc-nil`.

motivation for `:right-assoc-nil` is that, in contrast with the `:right-assoc` annotation, it distinguishes between terms like `(and a b c)` and `(and a (and b c))`, as the latter is parsed as `(and a (and (and b (and c true)) true))`. As we will see, Eunoia has additional features to facilitate working with such operators.

In Eunoia, it is also possible to define dependent types and parametric constants. In the example above, we first declare the usual polymorphic equality constant with an implicit type argument `A`. Afterwards, we declare a size-indexed type for bit-vectors and the bit-vector concatenation constant. The return type of `concat` (line 6) is defined by a computation performed by the built-in operator `eo::add` for adding two numbers. Eunoia has a large library of such operators. Some, like `eo::add`, are primitive operators that implement fundamental functionality; others are defined as Eunoia programs built from primitive operators.

Proof Rules. After declaring the *theory signature* we can declare a *proof signature*. That consists of proof rules and associated helper programs which can be used to implement side conditions. A file inclusion command allows us to isolate the theory signature in its own file. Proof rules follow the theory signature.

rules.eo

```
1 (include "theory.eo")
2 (declare-rule contra ((F Bool)) :premises (F (not F)) :conclusion false)
3 (program pick ((F Bool) (Fs Bool :list) (n Int)) :signature (Bool Int) Bool
4   (((pick          F 0)    F)
5    ((pick (and F Fs) n)    (pick Fs (eo::add n -1)))))
6 (declare-rule andE ((Fs Bool) (i Int))
7   :premises (Fs) :args (i) :conclusion (pick Fs i))
```

Every `declare-rule` command takes a rule name (e.g., `contra`, `andE` in lines 2 , 6) and lists parameters used in the declaration. The `:premises` attribute lists patterns for the rule's premises. To check a proof step using rule `contra`, the proof checker applies pattern matching to two previously derived formulas to find a matching substitution for the parameter `F`. This substitution is then applied to the conclusion, which in general is also a pattern, although not in this case. Rule `andE` illustrates the use of computations in proofs. The rule implements the elimination of variadic applications of `and` using a recursive program, `pick` (lines 3 –5), that returns the n-th argument of a conjunctive formula.

Like rules, programs have a name and a list of *local* parameters that serve as pattern variables. They also have a type signature that declares the argument types (`Bool` and `Int` for `pick`) and the return type (`Bool`). As in many functional programming languages, a program is defined by a list of cases that are considered in order. Abstractly, each case is a pair (p, b), where p lists a term pattern for each program input and b is the case's body. Each local parameter in b must appear at least once in p (non-linear patterns are supported). A program application is evaluated by a Eunoia checker by matching the application's arguments against each pattern list. When this succeeds, it applies the matching substitution to the body, evaluates it, and returns the resulting term. If no case matches, the checker raises an error and rejects the entire proof.

The example also demonstrates another feature of Eunoia's handling of variadic operators: the `:list` annotation. If an operator is annotated with `:list`, its last argument is not handled as syntactic sugar. Without it, the pattern `(and F Fs)` would be parsed as to `(and F (and Fs true))` which, however, would match only with binary conjunctions—of the form `(and t1 t2)`.

Proofs. We can construct a proof with the rules seen so far. With the `reference` command a proof can be linked to an SMT-LIB problem (e.g., `problem.smt2`) to check that all declared constants and assumptions appear in the problem.

```
(reference "problem.smt2") (include "rules.eo")
(declare-const F Bool)
(assume a1 (and F (not F)))
(step s1 (F) :rule andE :premises (a1) :args (0))
(step s2 (not F) :rule andE :premises (a1) :args (1))
(step s3 (false) :rule contra :premises (s1 s2))
```

The proof above has three derivation steps. The `assume` command introduces the assumption `(and F (not F))` and names it `a1`. The next two commands apply rule `andE` to `a1`, deriving formulas `F` and `(not F)`, respectively. The final command concludes `false` from the formulas derived by the previous two steps. The second argument of `step` is its expected conclusion and is optional. If provided, as in this case, it is matched during proof checking against the actual (computed) conclusion, generating an error in case of a mismatch. This is useful for debugging.

3 Proof Checking With Ethos

In this section, we sketch a few details on the implementation of Ethos. We first focus on a description of the general process used by Ethos to check proofs, and then discuss some low-level aspects.

Proof Checking Model. Ethos is designed to be, first and foremost, a *fast* proof checker. This means that it omits some checks that might be *convenient* for the signature programmer but are not *essential*, i.e., their absence cannot lead to Ethos accepting invalid proofs. For example, Ethos does not fully check the types of programs when they are defined. Instead, it checks the monomorphic types of the ground terms that are generated when checking a proof.

For Ethos, checking a proof amounts to evaluating a proof term. Every rule is in fact a program with only one case. For example, the `contra` rule from above is internally translated to the following program.

```
(declare-const Proof Type)
(declare-const pf (-> Bool Proof))
(program contra ((T Bool)) :signature (Proof Proof) Proof
  ((contra (pf T) (pf (not T))) (pf false)))
```

The earlier proof corresponds roughly to the term `(contra (andE A 0) (andE A 1))`, where `A` is the assumption `(and F (not F))`. This term is considered a correct proof if Ethos can evaluate it to `(pf false)` without error. Note that we use the symbols `Proof` and `pf` here for illustration purposes; they are not built-in in Eunoia.

Ethos implements a function $\texttt{eval}(t, \sigma)$, where t is a Eunoia term and σ is a grounding substitution over the parameters of t. It evaluates t bottom up, replacing each parameter x in it with $\sigma(x)$. When `eval` encounters a term $(c\ u_1\ \cdots\ u_n)$, where c is a program with cases $[(p_1, b_1), \cdots, (p_m, b_m)]$, it invokes a helper $\texttt{match}(p_i, u_1\ \cdots\ u_n)$ on each pattern p_i of c in order. If this function succeeds, it returns a substitution σ', and Ethos evaluates $\texttt{eval}(b_i, \sigma')$.

To ensure the conclusion of proof steps are not mistyped, Ethos can compute the type of parameter-free terms. This task is easier than general type checking because for the theories considered by Eunoia, all literals and constants have monomorphic types. Hence, computing types of applications amounts to pattern matching between the domain types and the monomorphic argument types. This approach has the benefit of being easy to implement, and optimize, at the expense of somewhat reduced statically checked guarantees.

Implementation. Ethos is written in C++, and currently has fewer than 10,000 lines of code. Terms are stored using a data structure with hash-consing (each unique AST is allocated exactly once) and reference counting on expressions. Number-like SMT-LIB literals (numerals, rationals, bit-vector constants) are stored in the AST using GMP arbitrary precision datatypes. Most built-in Eunoia operators on these literals translate directly to GMP functions. Ethos also implements the SMT-LIB policy for Unicode strings.

To accelerate proof checking, Ethos caches evaluation results. As mentioned, the evaluator takes as arguments a term to evaluate and a substitution, or *context*, mapping its free parameters to ground terms. The evaluator is implemented as a directed-acyclic graph traversal over terms. Since the evaluation primitives in Eunoia are stateless, Ethos can cache intermediate results in this process. This means that the result of invoking a side condition on a particular set of arguments is only computed once. However, this caching is not global, meaning that invoking the same computation on two independent proof steps will result in computing the result again. Ethos also evaluates parameter-free terms in rule and program bodies during parsing.

Since term construction is often the bottleneck, the core evaluation primitives on lists are optimized at a low level to minimize the number of terms that must be reallocated. For example, `eo::list_erase_all`, which removes all occurrences of a particular element from a list, will reuse the tail of the list after the last occurrence of the element. To ensure the correctness of the optimized implementation, we cross-check these optimizations against a simpler reference implementation of the list operators as ordinary Eunoia programs. The Ethos regression set contains tests that ensure that the built-in evaluation matches the results of these reference implementations.

Finally, Ethos can be extended with plugins. These are modules that register callbacks with the main loop of Ethos. The callbacks notify the plugin when an event occurs, e.g., when a proof step is parsed. The plugin system can be used to implement custom external proof checkers, or converters to other proof formats.

Table 1. Evaluation on benchmark sets (1) and (2).Proofs are either fully checked (**Verified**), or have holes (**Holey**). For each case, the table shows the sum of the time in seconds to **Generate** a proof and to **Check** it. The last three columns count failures: no proof was generated, checking timed out, some other checking error occurred.

	Verified	Gen.	Check	Holey	Gen.	Check	no Gen.	TO	Other
Alethe	19,502	90,908 s	13,869 s	867	7,172 s	1,192 s	23	26	522
LFSC	454	36 s	42 s	19,275	81,459 s	223,989 s	23	126	1,062
CPC	20,813	85,868 s	93,157 s	0	0 s	0 s	23	43	61
LFSC	705	36 s	221,911	136,482	229,300 s	221,911 s	468	460	2,133
CPC	138,912	657,911 s	219,267	0	0 s	0 s	473	617	247

4 Evaluation

The cvc5 solver supports three proof checking pipelines. It can produce proofs in the Alethe format which can be checked by Carcara. It can produce proofs in a calculus modeled in LFSC and checkable by the LFSC checker. Finally, it can produce proofs in its native calculus, called CPC, which is modeled in Eunoia and can be checked by Ethos. However, the support for cvc5 features differs significantly in these three pipelines. The Alethe proof format only supports uninterpreted functions, linear arithmetic, and quantifiers, and the LFSC calculus omits rules for many steps performed by cvc5. In those cases, the LFSC proof contains a step marked as `trust`. The Eunoia-based pipeline is the most complete. If cvc5 is run in *safe* mode, intended for users that require high assurance, the generated CPC proofs contains no *holes* (unjustified steps). An important factor in making this possible was the ease of writing proof rules in Eunoia.

To provide a perspective on the performance of Ethos, we compare the different proof production and checking pipelines of cvc5, and show that the Ethos pipeline is competitive with the other two, while also supporting more features (Table 1). We used all non-incremental SMT-LIB benchmarks [12] without floating-points that do not have status `sat` or have an `inferredStatus` of `sat` in the SMT-LIB catalog [14,16]. To get a collection of benchmarks cvc5 could solve, we ran it for 60 s in *safe mode* with proof generation off.[2] This gave us a set of 161,188 benchmarks. We split this benchmarks set in two: (1) benchmarks in logics supported by Alethe, and (2) the rest. Set (1) contains 20,940 benchmarks. We then ran cvc5 for 600 s on these sets with proofs turned on, and afterwards each checker on the generated proofs for another 600 s. For Eunoia and Alethe, we used fine-grained proof rules for term rewriting steps, which are not supported by LFSC. This is the main reason for the large number of proof holes in LFSC proofs. Support for such rewrite rules is also experimental in Alethe. On commonly solved problems, Ethos is 6.25 times slower than Carcara.

[2] We used machines with Intel Xeon E5-2620 v4 CPUs an an 8 GiB memory limit.

As we gain experience using Ethos in practice, we expect to find more opportunities to improve its performance and usability. We also plan to focus on the support infrastructure around Ethos to make Eunoia easier to use. This includes the development of a standardized unit testing framework for Eunoia signatures, a documentation generator for proof rules, and a language server. One of our goals is to make Eunoia and Ethos robust and flexible enough to be a useful proof checking infrastructure for other SMT solvers and automated theorem provers.

Acknowledgments. We thank the anonymous reviewers for their feedback on this paper. This work was supported in part by the Stanford Center for Automated Reasoning, a gift from Amazon Web Services, the Defense Advanced Research Projects Agency (DARPA) under contract FA8750-24-2-1001, the European Union (ERC, CertiFOX, 101122653), and Fonds Wetenschappelijk Onderzoek—Vlaanderen (project G070521N). Any opinions, findings, and conclusions or recommendations expressed here are those of the authors and do not necessarily reflect the views of DARPA, the European Union or the European Research Council. Neither the European Union nor the granting authority can be held responsible for them.

Disclosure of Interests. The authors have no competing interests to declare that are relevant to the content of this article.

References

1. Andreotti, B., Lachnitt, H., Barbosa, H.: Carcara: An efficient proof checker and elaborator for SMT proofs in the alethe format. In: Sankaranarayanan, S., Sharygina, N. (eds.) Tools and Algorithms for Construction and Analysis of Systems (TACAS), Part I. Lecture Notes in Computer Science, vol. 13993, pp. 367–386. Springer (2023). https://doi.org/10.1007/978-3-031-30823-9_19
2. Assaf, A., et al.: DEDUKTI: a logical framework based on the λΠ-calculus modulo theory. CoRR **abs/2311.07185** (2023). https://doi.org/10.48550/ARXIV.2311.07185
3. Barbosa, H., et al.: CVC5: a versatile and industrial-strength SMT solver. In: Fisman, D., Rosu, G. (eds.) TACAS 2022. LNCS, vol. 13243, pp. 415–442. Springer (2022). https://doi.org/10.1007/978-3-030-99524-9_24
4. Barbosa, H., Fleury, M., Fontaine, P., Schurr, H.J.: The Alethe proof format: an evolving specification and reference (2026). https://verit.gitlabpages.uliege.be/alethe/specification.pdf
5. Barrett, C., Fontaine, P., Tinelli, C.: The satisfiability modulo theories library (SMT-LIB) (2016). https://www.smt-lib.org
6. Blanqui, F.: Translating libraries of definitions and theorems between proof systems (invited talk). In: Bertot, Y., Kutsia, T., Norrish, M. (eds.) 15th International Conference on Interactive Theorem Proving, ITP 2024, Tbilisi, Georgia, 9–14 September 2024. LIPIcs, vol. 309, pp. 2:1–2:1. Schloss Dagstuhl - Leibniz-Zentrum für Informatik (2024). https://doi.org/10.4230/LIPIcs.ITP.2024.2
7. Bouchet, M., et al.: Block public access: trust safety verification of access control policies. In: Devanbu, P., Cohen, M.B., Zimmermann, T. (eds.) ESEC/FSE '20: 28th ACM Joint European Software Engineering Conference and Symposium on the Foundations of Software Engineering, Virtual Event, USA, 8–13 November 2020, pp. 281–291. ACM (2020). https://doi.org/10.1145/3368089.3409728

8. Harper, R., Honsell, F., Plotkin, G.D.: A framework for defining logics. J. ACM **40**(1), 143–184 (1993). https://doi.org/10.1145/138027.138060
9. Hitarth, S., Codel, C.R., Lachnitt, H., Dutertre, B.: Extending DRAT to SMT. In: Narodytska, N., Rümmer, P. (eds.) Formal Methods in Computer-Aided Design, FMCAD 2024, Prague, Czech Republic, 15–18 October 2024, pp. 1–11. IEEE (2024). https://doi.org/10.34727/2024/ISBN.978-3-85448-065-5_8
10. Hoenicke, J., Schindler, T.: A simple proof format for SMT. In: Déharbe, D., Hyvärinen, A.E.J. (eds.) Proceedings of the 20th Internal Workshop on Satisfiability Modulo Theories co-located with the 11th International Joint Conference on Automated Reasoning (IJCAR 2022) part of the 8th Federated Logic Conference (FLoC 2022), Haifa, Israel, 11–12 August 2022. CEUR Workshop Proceedings, vol. 3185, pp. 54–70. CEUR-WS.org (2022). https://ceur-ws.org/Vol-3185/paper9527.pdf
11. Nötzli, A., et al.: Reconstructing fine-grained proofs of rewrites using a domain-specific language. In: Griggio, A., Rungta, N. (eds.) 22nd Formal Methods in Computer-Aided Design, FMCAD 2022, Trento, Italy, 17–21 October 2022, pp. 65–74. IEEE (2022). https://doi.org/10.34727/2022/ISBN.978-3-85448-053-2_12
12. Preiner, M., Schurr, H.J., Barrett, C., Fontaine, P., Niemetz, A., Tinelli, C.: SMT-LIB release 2025 (non-incremental benchmarks) (2025). https://doi.org/10.5281/zenodo.16740866
13. Reynolds, A., Schurr, H.J., Soldevila, M., Tinelli, C.: The ethos user manual (2026). https://github.com/cvc5/ethos/blob/main/user_manual.md
14. Schurr, H., et al.: Exploring the SMT-LIB benchmark library. In: Junges, S., Katz, G. (eds.) Tools and Algorithms for the Construction and Analysis of Systems - 32nd International Conference, TACAS 2026, Held as Part of the International Joint Conferences on Theory and Practice of Software, ETAPS 2026, Turin, Italy, 11–16 April 2026, Proceedings, Part I, pp. 150–169. Lecture Notes in Computer Science, Springer (2026). https://doi.org/10.1007/978-3-032-22752-2_8
15. Schurr, H., Fleury, M., Barbosa, H., Fontaine, P.: Alethe: towards a generic SMT proof format (extended abstract). In: Keller, C., Fleury, M. (eds.) Proceedings Seventh Workshop on Proof eXchange for Theorem Proving, PxTP 2021, Pittsburg, PA, USA, 11 July 2021. EPTCS, vol. 336, pp. 49–54 (2021). https://doi.org/10.4204/EPTCS.336.6
16. Schurr, H.J., Preiner, M., Niemetz, A., Barrett, C., Fontaine, P., Tinelli, C.: SMT-LIB catalog 2025 (2025). https://doi.org/10.5281/zenodo.16290040
17. Stump, A., Oe, D., Reynolds, A., Hadarean, L., Tinelli, C.: SMT proof checking using a logical framework. Formal Meth. Syst. Des. **42**(1), 91–118 (2013). https://doi.org/10.1007/S10703-012-0163-3
18. Sutcliffe, G.: Stepping stones in the TPTP world. In: Benzmüller, C., Heule, M.J.H., Schmidt, R.A. (eds.) Automated Reasoning - 12th International Joint Conference, IJCAR 2024, Nancy, France, 3–6 July 2024, Proceedings, Part I. Lecture Notes in Computer Science, vol. 14739, pp. 30–50. Springer (2024). https://doi.org/10.1007/978-3-031-63498-7_3
19. Wetzler, N., Heule, M.J.H., Hunt, W.A.: DRAT-trim: efficient checking and trimming using expressive clausal proofs. In: Sinz, C., Egly, U. (eds.) SAT 2014. LNCS, vol. 8561, pp. 422–429. Springer, Cham (2014). https://doi.org/10.1007/978-3-319-09284-3_31

Open Access This chapter is licensed under the terms of the Creative Commons Attribution 4.0 International License (http://creativecommons.org/licenses/by/4.0/), which permits use, sharing, adaptation, distribution and reproduction in any medium or format, as long as you give appropriate credit to the original author(s) and the source, provide a link to the Creative Commons license and indicate if changes were made.

The images or other third party material in this chapter are included in the chapter's Creative Commons license, unless indicated otherwise in a credit line to the material. If material is not included in the chapter's Creative Commons license and your intended use is not permitted by statutory regulation or exceeds the permitted use, you will need to obtain permission directly from the copyright holder.

Intuitionistic, Modal, and Temporal Logics

Finite Model Finding in First-Order Modal Logics

Happy Khairunnisa Sariyanto[1(✉)], Alexander Steen[1], and Geoff Sutcliffe[2]

[1] University of Greifswald, Greifswald, Germany
happy.sariyanto@stud.uni-greifswald.de, alexander.steen@uni-greifswald.de
[2] University of Miami, Miami, USA
geoff@cs.miami.edu

Abstract. Modal logics extend classical first-order logic with the modalities of necessity ($\Box$) and possibility ($\Diamond$). A model of a set of modal logic formulae can be represented by a Kripke structure. This paper describes a method and implementation for finding finite Kripke models for formulae in first-order modal logics. The approach relies on translating the modal logic formulae to classical logic formulae, using an SMT solver to generate a finite model of the classical logic formulae, then translating the classical model to a finite Kripke model. This process has been implemented in the new model finding system MoMo which produces TPTP-compliant Kripke model representations. An evaluation on the modal logic problems in the TPTP problem library confirms the practicality of this approach. Up to the authors' knowledge, MoMo is the first model finder for first-order modal logics.

Keywords: Quantified modal logic · Model finding · TPTP

1 Introduction

Non-classical logics are used in many applications of Automated Theorem Proving (ATP) [40], including artificial intelligence (e.g., knowledge representation [22], planning [29], multi-agent systems [12]), philosophy (e.g., formal ethics [5], metaphysics [6]), natural language semantics (e.g., generalized quantifiers [4], modalities [26]), and computer science (e.g., software and hardware verification [11]). Methods and tools for automated reasoning in non-classical logics have received less attention than for classical logics, in particular for quantified non-classical logics.[1] Particularly noteworthy within non-classical logics is the family of quantified modal logics, having numerous applications in the areas mentioned above.

This work addresses model finding in first-order modal logics. Model finding is the task of finding an interpretation that satisfies a given set of formulae Φ –

[1] There do exist methods and systems for a number of specific non-classical logics, e.g., for propositional modal logics [32], description logics [13], linear logics [24], and intuitionistic logics [34].

© The Author(s) 2026
A. Biere et al. (Eds.): IJCAR 2026, LNAI 16688, pp. 317–335, 2026.
https://doi.org/10.1007/978-3-032-32589-1_20

the *model* of Φ. Applications of model finding include counter-example generation in interactive theorem provers like Isabelle/HOL [9], verification [16], defect detection [15], and, prospectively, elaboration in explainable hybrid AI systems. For classical logics the Tarskian form of an interpretation [55] is standard, while in modal logics Kripke structures [27] are most common. In finite model finding for modal logics, only models with a finite number of worlds containing finite Tarskian interpretations are considered.

The TPTP World [49] is the well established infrastructure that supports research, development, and deployment of ATP systems. The TPTP World includes the TPTP problem library [49], the TSTP solution library [48], standards for writing ATP problems and reporting ATP solutions [47,53], tools and services for processing ATP problems and solutions [48]. The web page of the TPTP World provides access to all components.[2] The TPTP World supports a range of classical logics, and since release v9.0.0 has also supported non-classical logics. In particular, the TPTP World supports modal logics [17], using its first-order NXF and higher-order NHF languages [41]. The TPTP format for interpretations [43,54] can express Tarskian interpretations for classical logics and Kripke interpretations for modal logics.

This work describes a method and implementation for finding finite Kripke models for formulae in first-order modal logics. The approach relies on translating the modal logic formulae to classical logic formulae, using a Satisfiability Modulo Theory (SMT) solver [35] to generate a finite model of the classical logic formulae, then translating the classical model to a finite Kripke model in TPTP format. The method is implemented in the new MoMo system. Up to the authors' knowledge there do not exist any other model finding systems for quantified modal logics to this date, in particular none that output models in the TPTP interpretation format. This is of high interest, however, as TPTP format interpretations can be further processed and utilized by various tools in the TPTP World, e.g., checking the correctness of models using the `AGMV` model verifier [43].

In the remainder of this section relevant related work is presented and discussed. In Sect. 2, an overview of quantified modal logics and the TPTP infrastructure, as relevant to this work, is given. Section 3 presents the reduction of modal logic formulae to classical logic, the translation of the classical SMT models to Kripke models, and the correctness results of the approach. The implementation is described in Sect. 4, and evaluated in Sect. 5. Finally, Sect. 6 concludes and sketches future work.

Related Work. There exist several model finding systems for classical logics. They can roughly be separated into (a) systems that implement specialized search routines, and (b) systems that translate into another logic (e.g., propositional logic) and use another system (e.g., a SAT solver) to find a model. A prominent example of the first kind is the SEM [58] system for quantifier-free typed first-order logic. Examples of the second kind include MACE [30] and Paradox [14]

[2] www.tptp.org.

for first-order logic, KodKod [56] for relational first-order logic, FEST [16] for typed first-order logic, and Refute [57] and Nitpick [9] for higher-order logic. For propositional and quantified modal logics, there are systems that establish the *existence* of models for propositional modal logics. For instance, K$_S$P [32], natively implements a resolution-based calculus for modal logic $\mathbf{K}_n$ for which model generation is in development. As [28] implies, tableaux-based provers, like InKreSAT [25] and Spartacus [23] (for hybrid logic), are technically able to generate models due to the constructive solving process yet do not always output complete models or need extensive modifications to support model generation. LoTREC 2.0 [21] supports model generation for some predefined modal and description logics, and allows the user to define their own logic. In contrast to this work, neither support quantified logics natively, nor do they support the TPTP languages.

2 Preliminaries

2.1 First-Order Modal Logics

The language of first-order (mono-)modal logics (FOMLs) is that of first-order classical logic extended with the modalities of necessity ($\Box$) and possibility ($\Diamond$). Given a signature Σ of predicate and function symbols, the set of FOML terms over Σ is defined as usual. FOML formulae over Σ are then given by:

$$\begin{aligned}\varphi, \psi ::= p(t_1, \ldots, t_n) \mid t_1 = t_2 \mid \neg\varphi \mid \varphi \wedge \psi \mid \varphi \vee \psi \mid \varphi \rightarrow \psi \mid \varphi \leftrightarrow \psi \mid \\ \forall x.\, \varphi \mid \exists x.\, \varphi \mid \Box\varphi \mid \Diamond\varphi\end{aligned}$$

where t_i is a FOML term, $p \in \Sigma$ is a predicate symbol of arity n and x is a variable. As usual, $t_1 \neq t_2$ is syntactic sugar for $\neg(t_1 = t_2)$.

Given a signature Σ, a Kripke structure is a tuple $M = (W, R, \mathcal{D}, \mathcal{I})$, where W is a non-empty set of worlds, $R \subseteq W \times W$ is the accessibility relation between worlds, $\mathcal{D} = \{D_w\}_{w \in W}$ is a collection of non-empty domains, one for each world, and $\mathcal{I} = \{I_w\}_{w \in W}$ is a collection of interpretation functions, one for each world, that interpret the symbols Σ in world $w \in W$. An interpretation function I_w assigns the denotation of a symbol in the following way: $I_w(p) \in D^n$ if p is an n-ary predicate symbol, and $I_w(f) : D^n \rightarrow D$ if f is an n-ary function symbol, where $D = \bigcup_{w \in W} D_w$ is the *frame domain* of M [17]. The notion of validity of a FOML formula φ with respect to a Kripke structure M and a world $w \in W$, denoted $M, w \models \varphi$, is defined as usual. A formula φ is satisfiable iff there exists a Kripke structure $M = (W, R, \mathcal{D}, \mathcal{I})$ and a world $w \in W$ such that $M, w \models \varphi$. A formula φ is valid iff $M, w \models \varphi$ for all Kripke structures M and all worlds $w \in W$. If $M, w \models \varphi$ only for all $w \in W$ in M, then φ is true in M, which is denoted $M \models \varphi$. Following [17], a formula φ is a consequence of a set of global assumptions G and a set of local assumptions L, denoted $G \models L \Rightarrow \varphi$, iff, for every Kripke structure M with $M \models g$ for each $g \in G$, it holds that if $M, w \models \ell$ for all $\ell \in L$ then $M, w \models \varphi$.

Additional conditions can be imposed to select only a certain class of Kripke structures, hence refining the notions of satisfiability and validity:

1. **Frame conditions:** The Kripke structures defined above yield the modal logic **K**. By imposing restrictions on the accessibility relation R stronger modal logics are formed [36], e.g., modal logic **D** is the modal logic where R is a serial relation, i.e., $\forall w.\exists u.wRu$ for all worlds $w, u \in W$. See [19] for various modal logics' frame conditions.
2. **Domain conditions:** The Kripke structures defined above have *varying domains*, as they permit different domains D_w in each world $w \in W$. *Constant domains* have $D_w = D_v$ for all worlds $w, v \in W$. *Cumulative domains* and *decreasing domains* require (anti-)monotony of the domains along worlds connected by the accessibility relation R [10].
3. **Rigidity conditions:** The Kripke structures defined above have *flexible* constant and function symbols, as they can be interpreted differently in each world. *Rigid* symbols have the same interpretation in every world $w \in W$ [10].
4. **Locality conditions:** The Kripke structures defined above have *global terms*, i.e., constant and function symbols are interpreted as elements of the global frame domain. *Local terms* interpret constant and function symbols as elements of the domain of the local world where the term is being interpreted, i.e., $I_w(.) \in D_w$ [20].

A *modal logic specification* L provides a representation of a specific modal logic, i.e., which choices have been made for the conditions above. Formally, it is a tuple $L = (\mathfrak{F}, \mathfrak{D}, \mathfrak{R}, \mathfrak{L})$, where $\mathfrak{F}$ is a set of modal axiom schemes that correspond to the aforementioned restrictions on R, $\mathfrak{D}$ is a domain condition (constant, varying, cumulative or decreasing), $\mathfrak{R}$ is a rigidity condition (rigid or flexible), and $\mathfrak{L}$ is a locality condition (global or local). A Kripke structure M that satisfies the conditions of L is also called a Kripke L-structure. Notions of satisfiability, validity, and consequence wrt. a given class of Kripke L-structures are defined analogously. For details see, e.g., [7,19,20].

As FOML is an extension of FOL it is also not decidable (in contrast to many propositional modal logics).

The presented implementation of the method in Sect. 4 is restricted to a fragment of first-order mono-modal logics. While all domain conditions $\mathfrak{D}$ and locality conditions $\mathfrak{L}$ can be handled, there are restrictions on $\mathfrak{R}$ and $\mathfrak{F}$. Only `rigid` constant and function symbols are supported. Possible elements of $\mathfrak{F}$ are given in Table 1. Thus, common modal logic systems as presented in the modal cube (e.g., **K**, **D**, **S4** or **S5**) can be handled. For example, to specify the **K**-modal logic system, $\mathfrak{F} = \{(K)\}$.

2.2 The TPTP World Infrastructure for Modal Logics

The TPTP language [50] is one of the keys to the success of the TPTP World. It is used for writing both problems and solutions, which enables convenient communication between ATP systems and tools. Problems and solutions are built from *annotated formulae* of the form ...

language(name, role, formula, source, useful_info).

Table 1. Possible modal axiom schemes in $\mathfrak{F}$

name	axiom scheme	frame condition
(K)	$\Box(\varphi \rightarrow \psi) \rightarrow (\Box\varphi \rightarrow \Box\psi)$	-
(T)	$\Box\varphi \rightarrow \varphi$	$\forall w.wRw$
(B)	$\varphi \rightarrow \Box\Diamond\varphi$	$\forall w.\forall u.(wRu \rightarrow uRw)$
(D)	$\Box\varphi \rightarrow \Diamond\varphi$	$\forall w.\exists u.wRu$
(4)	$\Box\varphi \rightarrow \Box\Box\varphi$	$\forall w.\forall u.\forall v.((wRu \wedge uRv) \rightarrow wRv)$
(5)	$\Diamond\varphi \rightarrow \Box\Diamond\varphi$	$\forall w.\forall u.\forall v.((wRu \wedge wRv) \rightarrow uRv)$
(C4)	$\Box\Box\varphi \rightarrow \Box\varphi$	$\forall w.\forall v.(wRv \rightarrow \exists u.(wRu \wedge uRv))$
(CD)	$\Diamond\varphi \rightarrow \Box\varphi$	$\forall w.\forall u.\forall v.((wRu \wedge wRv) \rightarrow (u = v))$

The *language* of interest in the context of the paper is `tff` (typed first-order form), which is used for formulae in both classical and non-classical logics based on a typed first-order language (such as FOML). The *role*, e.g., `axiom`, `lemma`, `conjecture`, defines the use of the formula. In a *formula*, terms and atoms follow Prolog conventions – functions and predicates start with a lowercase letter or are `'single quoted'`, and variables start with an uppercase letter. The language also supports interpreted symbols, e.g., the truth constants `$true` and `$false`. The logical connectives in the TPTP language are `!`, `?`, `~`, `|`, `&`, `=>`, `<=`, `<=>`, and `<~>` Equality and inequality are expressed as the infix operators `=` and `!=`. The *source* and *useful_ info* are optional.

The TPTP language supports non-classical logics using its first-order NXF language and higher-order NHF language. These are respectively based on the classical typed extended first-order TXF language [52] and the typed higher-order THF language [51]. In this work only NXF is used. All constructs of the underlying TXF language are available in NXF. Figure 1 shows a modal logic problem in NXF. The modal necessity and possibility operators, $\Box$ and $\Diamond$, are represented as `{$necessary}` and `{$possible}`, and are explicitly applied using the `@` operator (a purely syntactic construct). In the context of modal logic, the *roles* `hypothesis` and `axiom` denote local and global assumptions, respectively. Modal logic specifications $L = (\mathfrak{F}, \mathfrak{D}, \mathfrak{R}, \mathfrak{L})$ are represented in annotated formulae with the role `logic`, where $\mathfrak{F}$, $\mathfrak{D}$, $\mathfrak{R}$, and $\mathfrak{L}$ are designated by the TPTP keywords `$modalities`, `$domains`, `$designation` and `$terms`, respectively.

The TPTP format for interpretations [43,54] can express both Tarskian and Kripke interpretations. Figure 2 shows parts of a Tarskian interpretation for the first-order aspects of Fig. 1 (omitting the problem type declarations from Fig. 1). Note how function and predicate symbols are interpreted by applying them directly to domain elements, *à la* [18, §5.3.4], rather than introducing a new interpreting function for each symbol. The direct application requires using type-promotion bijections to keep formulae well-typed, e.g., `d2child` in Fig. 2.

A TPTP format Kripke interpretation provides information about the worlds and their mutual (in)accessibility, and a Tarskian interpretation for each world. Figure 3 shows parts of a Kripke model for the formulae in Fig. 1 (omitting

```
%------------------------------------------------------------------------
tff(semantics,logic,
    $modal ==
      [ $domains == $constant,
        $designation == $rigid,
        $terms == $local,
        $modalities == $modal_system_K ] ).

tff(child_type,type,    child: $tType ).
tff(adult_type,type,    adult: $tType ).
tff(agatha_decl,type,   agatha: adult ).
tff(charly_decl,type,   charly: child ).
tff(quiet_decl,type,    quiet: child > $o ).
tff(sleepy_decl,type,   sleepy: adult > $o ).
tff(peaceful_decl,type, peaceful: child > $o ).
tff(serves_decl,type,   serves: adult > child ).
tff(rains_decl,type,    rains: $o ).

tff(a1,axiom,
    ! [C: child] : ~ ( ~quiet(C) & ? [A: adult] : sleepy(A) ) ).

tff(a2,axiom,
    ( ( rains & ? [C: child] : quiet(C) )
   => ! [C: child] : ~peaceful(C) ) ).

tff(a3,axiom,
    ( peaceful(charly) | ( ~quiet(charly) & quiet(serves(agatha)) ) ) ).

tff(a4,axiom,
    ~quiet(charly) => ! [C: child] : ~quiet(C) ).

tff(a5,axiom,
    {$necessary} @ ( peaceful(charly) => rains ) ).
%------------------------------------------------------------------------
```

Fig. 1. A modal logic problem in the TPTP NXF language.

the problem type declarations from Fig. 1 and the Tarskian type declarations from Fig. 2). The Kripke model shown was generated by MoMo using its option to specify the number of worlds. Four new defined symbols are introduced for Kripke interpretations: the type `$world` to declare the worlds, the predicate `$accessible_world` to specify the accessibility relation, the constant `$local_world` to specify the local world (if any) in which a conjecture is to be proved, and the predicate `$in_world` to specify the Tarskian interpretation in each world.

3 Model Search

MoMo follows a translational approach for finite model finding in first-order modal logic: A modal logic problem is translated into classical logic by a shallow embedding, and represented in SMT format [3]. An SMT solver is used to

```
%------------------------------------------------------------------------
tff(child_d_decl,type, child_d: $tType).
tff(adult_d_decl,type, adult_d: $tType).
tff(child_1_decl,type, child_1: child_d).
tff(adult_1_decl,type, adult_1: adult_d).
tff(d2child_decl,type, d2child: child_d > child).
tff(d2adult_decl,type, d2adult: adult_d > adult).

tff(people_domains,interpretation-domains,
    ( ! [C: child] : ? [CD: child_d] : ( C = d2child(CD) )
    & ! [CD: child_d] : ( CD = child_1 )
    & ! [CD1: child_d,CD2: child_d] :
        ( d2child(CD1) = d2child(CD2) => CD1 = CD2 )
    & ! [A: adult] : ? [AD: adult_d] : ( A = d2adult(AD) )
    & ! [AD: adult_d] : ( AD = adult_1 )
    & ! [AD1: adult_d,AD2: adult_d] :
        ( d2adult(AD1) = d2adult(AD2) => AD1 = AD2 ) ) ).

tff(people_mappings,interpretation-mappings,
    ( charly = d2child(child_1)
    & agatha = d2adult(adult_1)
    & serves(d2adult(adult_1)) = d2child(child_1)
    & ~ quiet(d2child(child_1))
    & ~ sleepy(d2adult(adult_1))
    & peaceful(d2child(child_1))
    & rains ) ).
%------------------------------------------------------------------------
```

Fig. 2. The Tarskian interpretation for the worlds of Fig. 1.

find a model, and subsequently the model is translated to the TPTP Kripke interpretation format. Details of each step are presented next.

3.1 Shallow Embedding of FOML to FOL

A shallow embedding is the translation of the semantics of terms and formulae of the source logic (here: FOML) to terms and formulae of the target logic (here: classical many-sorted FOL) [42]. Embedding machinery presented here is adapted from [33].

The embedding is given by the function $\Psi = (\Psi_F^L, \Psi_S^L, \Psi_I)$, where Ψ_F^L translates FOML formulae wrt. a given modal logic specification L, Ψ_S^L generates auxiliary formulae that encode restrictions of the modal logic specification L, and Ψ_I translates interpretations. The latter is relevant in Sect. 3.2 and further defined there. The former introduces the FOL sort W' for possible worlds and the FOL predicate R of type $W' \times W' \to o$ for the accessibility relation between worlds, where o is assumed to be the (pseudo-) type of formulae. Furthermore, let ι denote a type of individuals, introduced to mirror the (untyped) terms of FOML.

For each FOML predicate symbol p of arity n, a new FOL predicate symbol p' of type $W \times \iota \times \cdots \times \iota \to o$ (arity $n+1$) is introduced. The translation of a

```
%------------------------------------------------------------------------------
tff(w1_decl,type,w1:     $world).
tff(w2_decl,type,w2:     $world).
tff(w3_decl,type,w3:     $world).

tff(people_worlds,interpretation-worlds,
    ( ! [W: $world] : ( W = w1 | W = w2 | W = w3 )
    & $distinct(w1,w2,w3)
    & $local_world = w1
    & $accessible_world(w1,w1) & $accessible_world(w2,w2)
    & $accessible_world(w1,w2) & $accessible_world(w2,w3)
    & $accessible_world(w3,w1)
    & ~ $accessible_world(w1,w3) & ~ $accessible_world(w2,w1)
    & ~ $accessible_world(w3,w2) & ~ $accessible_world(w3,w3) ) ).

%----All worlds have the same Tarskian interpretation.
tff(people_ds,interpretation-domains,
    ! [W: $world] :
      $in_world(W,
        ( ! [C: child] :
        ...
           => AD1 = AD2 ) )) ).

tff(people_mappings,interpretation-mappings,
    ! [W: $world] :
      $in_world(W,
        ( charly = d2adult(child_1)
        ...
        & rains )) ).
%------------------------------------------------------------------------------
```

Fig. 3. A Kripke model for the formulae in Fig. 1.

given FOML formula ϕ with respect to a world $w_0 \in W$, denoted $\Psi_F^L(\phi, w_0)$, is defined as follows:

- $\Psi_F^L(p(t_1, ..., t_n), w_0) = p'(w_0', t_1', ..., t_n')$,
- $\Psi_F^L(\neg\phi, w_0) = \neg\Psi_F^L(\phi, w_0)$
- $\Psi_F^L(\phi \wedge \psi, w_0) = \Psi_F^L(\phi, w_0) \wedge \Psi_F^L(\psi, w_0)$
- $\Psi_F^L(\Box\phi, w_0) = \forall(u' : W').(R(w_0', u') \rightarrow \Psi_F^L(\phi, u))$
- $\Psi_F^L(\Diamond\phi, w_0) = \exists(u' : W').(R(w_0', u') \wedge \Psi_F^L(\phi, u))$

where w_0' a fresh atom of type W' corresponding to world w_o. Similar cases for the other connectives are omitted. This shallow embedding corresponds to the *standard translation* of modal logic, and is adapted to first-order quantified variants as follows:

Depending on the domain conditions specified by L, quantification is translated as follows.

- $(\Psi_F^L(\forall x.\phi, w_0) = \begin{cases} \forall x : \iota. \Psi_F^L(\phi, w_0), & \text{if } \mathfrak{D} = \text{constant} \\ \forall x : \iota. \left(\text{EXISTS}'(x, w_0') \rightarrow \Psi_F^L(\phi, w_0)\right), & \text{otherwise} \end{cases}$

- $(\Psi_F^L(\exists x.\phi, w_0) = \begin{cases} \exists x : \iota . \Psi_F^L(\phi, w_0), & \text{if } \mathfrak{D} = \mathsf{constant} \\ \exists x : \iota . \left(\text{EXISTS}'(x, w_0') \land \Psi_F^L(\phi, w_0)\right), & \text{otherwise} \end{cases}$

where $\text{EXISTS}' : \iota \times W'$ a FOL predicate representing whether a specific object exists in the given world (i.e., simulating varying domains in FOL).

If L specifies rigid symbols, then for each FOML function symbol f of arity n, a FOML function symbol f' of type $\iota^n \to \iota$ is introduced (constants are assumed to be function symbols of arity 0). If symbols are flexible, f' is of type $W \times \iota \times \cdots \times \iota \to o$ (arity $n+1$), similar to predicate symbols. For the translation of terms, Ψ_F^L is then extended to terms as follows:

- $\Psi_F^L(x, w_0) = x$
- $\Psi_F^L(f(t_1, ...t_n), w_0) = \begin{cases} f'(t_1', ..., t_n') & \text{if } \mathfrak{R} = \mathsf{rigid} \\ f'(w_0', t_1', ..., t_n') & \text{if } \mathfrak{R} = \mathsf{flexible} \end{cases}$

where the t_i' are the recursively translated subterms t_i, respectively.

Finally, Ψ_S^L is the smallest set of formulae such that ...

F.1 $\forall w\colon W'.R(w, w)$, if $\mathfrak{F}$ contains the (T) axiom scheme,
F.2 $\forall w\colon W'.\exists v\colon W'.\, R(w, v)$, if $\mathfrak{F}$ contains the (D) axiom scheme,
F.3 $\forall w\colon W'.\forall v\colon W'.\, R(w, v) \to R(v, w)$, if $\mathfrak{F}$ contains the (B) axiom scheme,

⋮

F.n ... *analogously for the other modal axiom schemes* ...
D.1 $\forall w\colon W'.\forall v\colon W'.\forall x\colon \iota.\, (\text{EXISTS}'(x, w) \land R(w, v)) \to \text{EXISTS}'(x, v)$, if $\mathfrak{D} = \mathsf{cumulative}$,
D.2 $\forall w\colon W'.\forall v\colon W'.\forall x\colon \iota.\, (\text{EXISTS}'(x, w) \land R(v, w)) \to \text{EXISTS}'(x, v)$, if $\mathfrak{D} = \mathsf{decreasing}$,
D.3 $\forall w\colon W'.\exists x\colon \iota.\, \text{EXISTS}'(x, w)$, if $\mathfrak{D} \neq \mathsf{constant}$,
L.1 $\forall w\colon W'.\forall v_1\colon \iota.\, \ldots \forall v_n\colon \iota.\, (\text{EXISTS}'(v_1, w) \to ... \to \text{EXISTS}'(v_n, w) \to \text{EXISTS}'(f^*, w))$, if $\mathfrak{L} = \mathsf{local}$, where $f^* = f'(v_1, ..., v_n)$ if $\mathfrak{R} = \mathsf{rigid}$ and $f^* = f'(w, v_1, ..., v_n)$ if $\mathfrak{R} = \mathsf{flexible}$.

Intuitively, the first group of formulae (the **F.i**) restricts the accessibility relation according to the conditions corresponding to the respective modal axiom schemes. The second group of formulae (the **D.i**) enforces the EXISTS' predicate to be monotone (resp. anti-monotone) wrt. the accessibility relation, and that quantification domains are non-empty. The last group (**L.1**) asserts the existence of the interpretation of terms in each world, if term interpretation is local.

Lemma 1 (Correctness of translation [42]). *Let L be a logic specification of some modal logic, let Φ be a set of FOML formulae. It holds that Φ is satisfiable by some Kripke L-structure M if and only if $\Psi_S^L \cup \{\Psi_F^L(\phi, w_0) \mid \phi \in \Phi\}$ is satisfiable in FOL.*

The so-called local world w_0 in which formulae are evaluated is a world from where all other worlds are accessible with a finite amount of steps. It is enough to only view Kripke structures in which such a world exists since satisfiability of closed formulae only depends on accessible worlds of this nature [8].

The embedding process is implemented in the *Logic Embedding Tool* (LET) [44] that outputs TPTP format formulae. These formulae are directly translated to SMT format, with any conjecture being negated. The SMT formulae are submitted to an SMT solver. If the formulae are satisfiable, i.e., if there is a conjecture it is not a theorem of the axioms, or if there is no conjecture the axioms are satisfiable, the SMT solver outputs a Tarskian model in SMT format (modulo resource limits).

3.2 Reconstruction of SMT-LIB Models

Continuing from Sect. 3.1, Ψ_I defines a sound and complete bidirectional mapping for the translation of models. Ψ_I^{-1} translates a FOL model to a corresponding Kripke model. The domain for the FOL sort W' is translated to the set of possible worlds W in the Kripke model. The accessibility relation R is defined via the interpretation of the special FOL-predicate R' with $w_1 R w_2$ iff $R'(w_1, w_2)$ is interpreted as true. Interpretations of FOML functions are rigid, as given in the interpretation of their corresponding FOL functions. FOML predicates P are interpreted in world w according to the interpretation of their corresponding FOL predicate P for which the first argument is w' – the corresponding domain element in W' for the possible world w.

The resulting Kripke model is output in the TPTP format for Kripke interpretations. The exact structure in which Kripke models are given follows the example in Fig. 3. The TPTP Kripke model starts with the logic specification and the declaration of the problem's symbols. The definition of the FOML domains and the set of possible worlds are translated from the abstract representation of the corresponding FOL-domains in the SMT model. Each abstract FOL domain element corresponds to a possible world of type `$world`, or a FOML domain element. Definitions of `$accessible_world` and the interpretation of FOML constants, functions and predicates are translated from the interpretation of the corresponding symbols in the SMT model. In both formats, this is given via formulae. Thus, relevant parts of the SMT formulae can be translated to TPTP formulae.

3.3 Correctness

The correctness of the overall method is based on the correctness of the individual steps. Due to the correspondence of the TPTP and SMT languages the translation of the problem in the TPTP language to the SMT language is correct. Due to empirical evidence of mature SMT solvers, the output of the SMT solver is assumed to be correct. This includes the generated FOL models. The translation to a Kripke model follows Ψ_I^{-1}, and the notation complies with TPTP's Kripke interpretation format. Thus, the Kripke model is correct by construction as well. Therefore, the following theorem holds:

Theorem 1 (Correctness). *Let L be some modal logic specification and Φ be some set of FOML formulae. If M' is a FOL model for $\Psi_F^L(\Phi)$, then $\Psi_I^{-1}(M')$ is a Kripke L-structure satisfying Φ.*

Pragmatically, the correctness of a Kripke model can be verified by evaluating the modelled formule wrt the model. This approach has been used in this work, as explained in Sect. 4.2.

4 The *MoMo* Model Finder

4.1 System Architecture

The process described in Sect. 3 has been implemented in the MoMo model finder. The overall system architecture is shown in Fig. 4. The key subsystems of MoMo are colored dark gray (the logic embedding and SMT solver), purple items represent intermediate representations, and the orange ellipses are translation procedures. The process is as follows:

1. MoMo reads the modal logic problem in TPTP NXF and hands it to the non-classical-to-classical logic embedding tool.
2. The translation yields a classical FOL problem in TPTP TXF format.
3. The FOL problem in TPTP format is translated to SMT format.
4. The SMT problem is handed to the SMT solver to find a model.
5. (a) If no model is found, MoMo terminates with a failure message.
   (b) If a model is found, the model in SMT format is translated to the corresponding representation in TPTP format. MoMo returns the model in TPTP format.

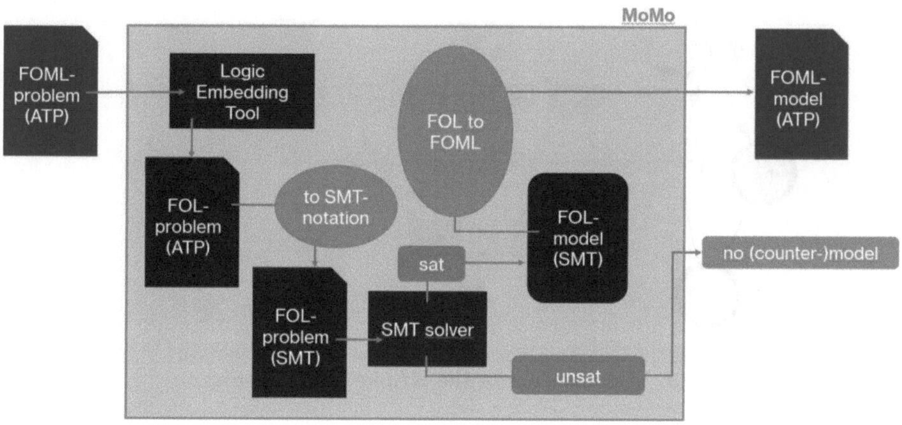

Fig. 4. MoMo's system architecture. Arrows indicate data flow.

MoMo accepts first-order mono-modal logic problems in the TPTP NXF language, and produces results in the TPTP non-classical interpretation format. Currently, for translating modal logic problems into classical logic the logic embedding tool v1.8.8 [39] is used, and cvc5 v1.2.1 [2] is used as the SMT solver. Of course any SMT solver can be used. MoMo v0.1.0 is available via Zenodo [37].

4.2 Implementation Details

MoMo is written in Python (version 3.13.2). This is motivated, among other reasons, by the fact that cvc5 offers a flexible and comfortable Python API that can be used to implement SMT checking subroutines in larger contexts. Here, version 1.2.1 of cvc5's Base Python API is used. Unfortunately, the logic embedding tool does not offer such an API. Instead, it is invoked directly from within MoMo via the standard `os.system` library.

The translation process between TPTP and SMT-LIB was implemented from scratch. However, at the current state, some translation details are specifically tailored to the inputs and outputs of LET and cvc5. This is mainly an engineering backlog, which will be addressed in future versions.

To enrich and support the development of the modal logical infrastructure of the TPTP, MoMo translates SMT-LIB models back to Kripke-models in the TPTP interpretation format. This allows tools from the TPTP World infrastructure to be used for assessment of generated models. The **AGMV** model verifier can be used to verify generated Kripke models. The IIV interpretation viewer [31] can be used to visualize Kripke interpretations presented in the TPTP format. The left hand side of Fig. 5 shows IIV's visualization of the worlds of a model for the problem in Fig. 2. The user can interact with the image by hovering over a world to highlight its accessible worlds. Clicking on a world displays the Tarskian interpretation in that world, shown in the right hand side of Fig. 5.

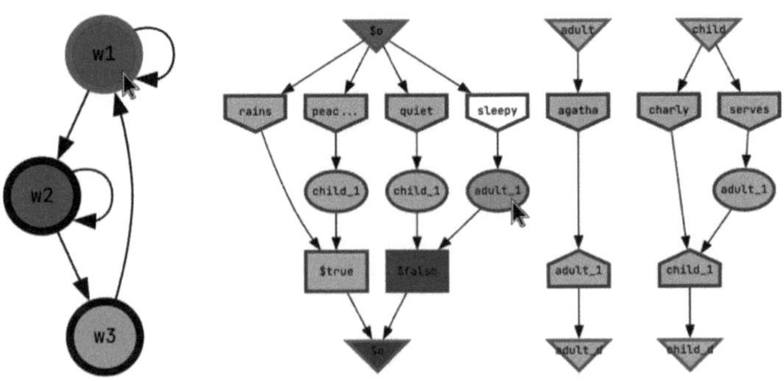

Fig. 5. Visualization of the Kripke model in Fig. 3.

By default MoMo uses a wall clock timeout of 300 s; this can be overridden by the user using command-line options. As the Python API of cvc5 does not offer any functionality to limit the wall clock time usage, a wrapper function is employed that externally controls the time limit for executing the SMT solver. MoMo's optional parameter `-w` n allows specifying a fixed number of worlds n for generated models. When specified, additional formulae restricting the cardinality of the set of worlds W to n are included in the submission of formulae to the SMT solver.

5 Evaluation

5.1 Experimental Setup

For the evaluation the forthcoming TPTP problem library[3] v9.3.0 was used as the benchmark problem source. It contains 204 propositional and first-order modal logic problems in NXF syntax. The following steps were conducted to prepare the benchmark files:

1. 60 of the `SYO886` problems were rejected because they are semantic duplicates: All variants of `SYO886` do not contain any function symbols, hence their semantics is identical regardless of whether the constants are rigid or flexible, and whether local or global terms are assumed. Only the variants with rigid designation and global terms were retained.
2. Due to the restriction to *mono*-modal problems, the multi-modal TPTP problem `SYN000_7` lies out of scope of MoMo. However, since the problem uses only one modal operator index, it is de-facto mono-modal. For the evaluation it was reformulated as a mono-modal problem.[4]
3. The remaining problems were used as-is.

This gave a set of 144 problems, of which 8 contain only axioms (no conjecture) and are satisfiable, 58 contain a conjecture and are countersatisfiable, and the remainder are either unsatisfiable or theorems, i.e., do not have a (counter-)model. Thus there were 66 problems for which a model might be found. Of the 66 problems, 28 are propositional and 38 are first-order. The problems use modal logic **K**, **D**, **T**, **S4**, or **S5**, dominated by 33 problems in **K** and 22 problems in **S4**. Testing was also done on the 78 problems for which there is no (counter-)model, as a pragmatic test of soundness – no models were found. The set of benchmark problems is available at Zenodo [38].

MoMo was run with a wall clock time limit of 300 s on a x64-based machine with a 12th Gen Intel(R) Core(TM) i7-1255U 2600 MHz CPU and 8 GB of physical memory, running Microsoft Windows 11 Home version 10.02.26100.

5.2 Results

The evaluation results are summarized in Table 2, and the times taken are summarized in Table 3. MoMo found a model for 60 of the 66 (counter-)satisfiable problems. Of the 60 models, 23 are for propositional problems and 37 for first-order problems. All the models have maximally two worlds.

[3] www.tptp.org/TPTP.

[4] Every expression `$necessary(#agent)` and `$possible(#agent)` in the problem was changed to `$necessary` resp. `$possible`.

Table 2. Numbers of models found

	K	D	T	S4	S5	ALL
problems	33	2	6	22	3	66
– propositional	8	0	0	20	0	28
– first-order	25	2	6	2	3	38
models	29	2	6	21	2	60
– propositional	4	0	0	19	0	23
– first-order	25	2	6	2	2	37
1 world	11	0	0	14	1	26
2 worlds	18	2	6	7	1	34

Table 3. Runtimes for models found, in seconds

	K	D	T	S4	S5	PRP	FOF	ALL
average	1.46	1.05	1.37	8.49	0.97	8.60	1.41	3.99
median	1.28	1.05	1.20	1.72	1.01	1.80	1.28	1.31
std dev	3.56	0.11	0.68	23.61	0.13	23.58	0.61	14.75
min	0.79	0.95	0.84	1.02	0.80	0.81	0.79	0.79
max	30.20	1.16	2.82	113.18	1.11	113.18	3.46	113.18

Table 3 shows the average, median, standard deviation, minimum, and maximum run times, excluding timeouts. Overall, the average and the median of the runtime are considerably different with the average being higher than the median. As the standard deviation is quite high, the expected runtime for a problem would be closer to the median rather than the average. High run times like the maximum of the observed runtime of 113.18 s do not occur often.

All models found by MoMo in this evaluation were checked for syntax errors via the `TPTP4X` utility [46], with no errors found. The models were also given to the `AGMV` model verifier [41], and roughly half of the models were verified; for the other models `AGMV` timed out. Both `TPTP4X` and `AGMV` were used via the SystemOnTPTP interface of the TPTP World [45].

Note that MoMo is capable of finding models with more than two worlds. The reason only such models were found is due to the model finding approach of cvc5 that tries to find minimal models, and the fact that these simple problems coincidentally can be satisfied with such models.

The chosen system of modalities seems to have a major influence on the behaviour of cvc5's finite model finding. Problems for which models were expected but not found use modal logic **K**, or **S4**. Four of them are propositional problems in modal logic **K**. The translations of modal logic problems in **S4** seemed to produce harder problems for cvc5. During the embedding, modal axioms are translated as additional axioms in the classical problem, reflecting the corresponding condition on the frame of the FOML model that is to be found.

With the modal axiom scheme of **S4** it is plausible that the models require more worlds, making it harder to find a model. In the specific case of the TPTP benchmark set, many propositional modal logic problems stem from the LWB benchmark suite [1]. Formulae often have highly nested modal logic connectives. Models for such problems tend to require many worlds, and the models are thus often harder to find than for structurally simpler problems.

6 Conclusion

This paper has described a method and implementation for finding finite Kripke models for a wide range of first-order modal logics. The approach relies on translating the modal logic formulae to classical logic formulae, using an SMT solver to generate a finite model of the classical logic formulae, then translating the classical model to a finite Kripke model. This process has been implemented in the new model finding system MoMo which produces TPTP-compliant Kripke model representations. The evaluation on the modal logic problems in the TPTP problem library confirms the practicality of this approach for various modalities in the modal cube, constant and varying domains, local and global terms, and (only) rigid functions. Presented results also showcase (dis-)advantages of the current composition. Up to the authors' knowledge, MoMo is the first model finder for first-order modal logics.

Further Work. Optimising the employment of classical model finding methods is one avenue of further research. Studying classical model finding methods can help to identify suitable methods for handling the structure of embedded FOML-formulae. This includes comparing several classical model finders and potentially different option settings for them, including the currently employed SMT solver. To combine different strengths, multiple model finders can be employed instead of only one. This can also extend the scope of model finding from finite to possibly infinite models, by using model finders capable of this, e.g., FEST [16].

Another avenue of improvement is the translation process. Possibly, further processing steps before invoking the (classical) model finding tool could improve performance. Investigating alternative shallow embeddings could lead to computationally more efficient embedded formulae. Besides the relational embedding approach, a functional approach as presented in [33], could be used.

Supported modal logics can be further extended regarding rigidity conditions and multi-modality.

Acknowledgement. Esteban Morales, for the development of IIV.

Disclosure of Interests. The authors have no competing interests to declare that are relevant to the content of this article.

References

1. Balsiger, P., Heuerding, A., Schwendimann, S.: Logics workbench 1.0. In: de Swart, H. (ed.) TABLEAUX 1998. LNCS (LNAI), vol. 1397, pp. 35–35. Springer, Heidelberg (1998). https://doi.org/10.1007/3-540-69778-0_8
2. Barbosa, H., et al.: cvc5: a versatile and industrial-strength SMT solver. In: TACAS 2022. LNCS, vol. 13243, pp. 415–442. Springer, Cham (2022). https://doi.org/10.1007/978-3-030-99524-9_24
3. Barrett, C., Stump, A., Tinelli, C.: The SMT-LIB standard: version 2.0. In: Gupta, A., Kroening, D. (eds.) Proceedings of the 8th International Workshop on Satisfiability Modulo Theories (2010)
4. Benthem, J.: Towards a computational semantics. In: Gärdenfors, P. (ed.) Generalized Quantifiers. SLP, vol. 31, pp. 31–71. Springer, Dordrecht (1987). https://doi.org/10.1007/978-94-009-3381-1_2
5. Benzmüller, C., Parent, X., van der Torre, L.: Designing normative theories for ethical and legal reasoning: logikey framework, methodology, and tool support. Artifi. Intell. **287**, Article 103348 (2020)
6. Benzmüller, C., Woltzenlogel Paleo, B.: The Inconsistency in Gödel's ontological argument: a success story for AI in metaphysics. In: Kambhampati, S. (ed.) Proceedings of the 25th International Joint Conference on Artificial Intelligence, pp. 936–942. AAAI Press (2016)
7. Blackburn, P., van Benthem, J., Wolther, F.: Handbook of Modal Logic. No. 3 in Studies in Logic and Practical Reasoning. Elsevier Science (2006)
8. Blackburn, P., de Rijke, M., Venema, Y.: Modal Logic. Cambridge University Press (2001)
9. Blanchette, J.C., Nipkow, T.: Nitpick: a counterexample generator for higher-order logic based on a relational model finder. In: Kaufmann, M., Paulson, L.C. (eds.) ITP 2010. LNCS, vol. 6172, pp. 131–146. Springer, Heidelberg (2010). https://doi.org/10.1007/978-3-642-14052-5_11
10. Braüner, T., Ghilardi, S.: First-Order Modal Logic. In: Blackburn, P., van Benthem, J., Wolter, F. (eds.) Handbook of Modal Logic, pp. 549–620. Elsevier B.V. (2007)
11. Bryant, R.: A methodology for hardware verification based on logic simulation. J. Associat. Comput. Mach. **38**(2), 299–328 (1991)
12. Cachin, C., Lehnherr, D., Studer, T.: Modal and justification logics for multi-agent systems (invited talk). In: Herzig, A., Luo, J., Pardo, P. (eds.) CLAR 2023. LNCS, vol. 14156. Springer, Cham (2023). https://doi.org/10.1007/978-3-031-40875-5_1
13. del Cerro, L.F., Fauthoux, D., Gasquet, O., Herzig, A., Longin, D., Massacci, F.: Lotrec: the generic tableau prover for modal and description logics. In: Goré, R., Leitsch, A., Nipkow, T. (eds.) IJCAR 2001. LNCS, vol. 2083, pp. 453–458. Springer, Heidelberg (2001). https://doi.org/10.1007/3-540-45744-5_38
14. Claessen, K., Sörensson, N.: New Techniques that Improve MACE-style Finite Model Finding. In: Baumgartner, P., Fermueller, C. (eds.) Proceedings of the CADE-19 Workshop: Model Computation - Principles, Algorithms, Applications (2003)
15. Diedrich, A., Maier, A., Niggemann, O.: Model-based diagnosis of hybrid systems using satisfiability modulo theory. In: Nalon, C., Steen, A., Suda, M. (eds.) Proceedings of the 33rd AAAI Conference on Artificial Intelligence, vol. 33, pp. 1452–1459 (2019).https://doi.org/10.1609/aaai.v33i01.33011452

16. Elad, N., Padon, O., Shoham, S.: An infinite needle in a finite haystack: finding infinite counter-models in deductive verification. In: Dreyer, D. (ed.) Proceedings of the ACM on Programming Languages, vol. 8, pp. 970–1000. ACM Press (2024)
17. Fitting, M., Mendelsohn, R.: First-Order Modal Logic. No. 480 in Synthese Library. Springer-Verlag (2023)
18. Gallier, J.: Logic for Computer Science - Foundations of Automatic Theorem Proving. Dover Publications (2015)
19. Garson, J.: Modal Logic. In: Zalta, E. (ed.) Stanford Encyclopedia of Philosophy (2018)
20. Garson, J.W.: Quantification in modal logic. In: Gabbay, D., Guenthner, F. (eds.) Handbook of Philosophical Logic, vol. 2, pp. 249–307 (1984)
21. Gasquet, O., Herzig, A., Longin, D., Sahade, M.: Lotrec: logical tableaux research engineering companion. In: Beckert, B. (ed.) Automated Reasoning with Analytic Tableaux and Related Methods, pp. 318–322. Springer, Berlin Heidelberg, Berlin, Heidelberg (2005). https://doi.org/10.1007/11554554_25
22. Giordano, L., Gliozzi, V., Olivetti, N., Pozzato, G., Schwind, C.: Non-classical Logics for Knowledge Representation and Reasoning. Intelligenza Artificiale **5**(1), 127–131 (2011)
23. Götzmann, D., Kaminski, M., Smolka, G.: Spartacus: a tableau prover for hybrid logic. In: Bolander, T., Braüner, T. (eds.) M4M-6. ENTCS, vol. 262, pp. 127–139. Elsevier (May 2010)
24. S., J., Tamura, N.: lolliCoP — a linear logic implementation of a lean connection-method theorem prover for first-order classical logic. In: Goré, R., Leitsch, A., Nipkow, T. (eds.) IJCAR 2001. LNCS, vol. 2083, pp. 670–684. Springer, Heidelberg (2001). https://doi.org/10.1007/3-540-45744-5_55
25. Kaminski, M., Tebbi, T.: Inkresat: modal reasoning via incremental reduction to sat. In: Bonacina, M.P. (ed.) Automated Deduction - CADE-24:24th International Conference on Automated Deduction, pp. 436–442. Springer, Berlin, Heidelberg (2013). https://doi.org/10.1007/978-3-642-38574-2_31
26. Kratzer, A.: What "must" and "can" Must and Can Mean. Linguist. Philos. **1**, 337–355 (1977)
27. Kripke, S.: Semantical Considerations on Modal Logic. Acta Philosophica Fennica **16**, 83–94 (1963)
28. Lagniez, J.M., Le Berre, D., de Lima, T., Montmirail, V.: On checking kripke models for modal logic K. In: Proceedings of the 5th Workshop on Practical Aspects of Automated Reasoning co-located with International Joint Conference on Automated Reasoning (IJCAR 2016), Coimbra, Portugal, July 2nd, 2016. Coimbra, Portugal (Jul 2016). https://univ-cotedazur.hal.science/hal-02271413
29. Liberman, A., Achen, A., Rendsvig, R.: Dynamic term-modal logics for first-order epistemic planning. Artif. Intell. **286** (2020). https://doi.org/10.1016/j.artint.2020.103305
30. McCune, W.: A Davis-Putnam Program and its Application to Finite First-Order Model Search: Quasigroup Existence Problems. Tech. Rep. ANL/MCS-TM-194, Argonne National Laboratory, Argonne, USA (1994)
31. McKeown, J., Sutcliffe, G.: Reinforcement learning for guiding the E theorem prover. In: Ae Chun, A., Franklin, M. (eds.) Proceedings of the 36th International FLAIRS Conference (2023). https://doi.org/10.32473/flairs.36.133334
32. Nalon, C., Hustadt, U., Dixon, C.: KSP: architecture, refinements, strategies and experiments. J. Autom. Reason. **64**(3), 461–484 (2020)
33. Ohlbach, H.: Semantics based translation methods for modal logics. J. Log. Comput. **1**(5), 691–746 (1991)

34. Otten, J.: The nanoCoP 2.0 connection provers for classical, intuitionistic and modal logics. In: Das, A., Negri, S. (eds.) TABLEAUX 2021. LNCS (LNAI), vol. 12842, pp. 236–249. Springer, Cham (2021). https://doi.org/10.1007/978-3-030-86059-2_14
35. Reynolds, A., Tinelli, C., Goel, A., Krstić, S.: Finite model finding in SMT. In: Sharygina, N., Veith, H. (eds.) CAV 2013. LNCS, vol. 8044, pp. 640–655. Springer, Heidelberg (2013). https://doi.org/10.1007/978-3-642-39799-8_42
36. Sahlqvist, H.: Completeness and correspondence in the first and second order semantics for modal logic. In: Kanger, S. (ed.) Proceedings of the 3rd Scandinavian Logic Symposium, pp. 110–143. No. 82 in Studies in Logic and the Foundations of Mathematics. Elsevier (1975)
37. Sariyanto, H.: MoMo: Finite Model Finder For First-order Modal Logics v0.1.0 (2025). https://doi.org/10.5281/zenodo.17375151
38. Sariyanto, H., Steen, A., Sutcliffe, G.: Benchmark Data Set for the Evaluation of MoMo v0.1.0 (2026). https://doi.org/10.5281/zenodo.18608518
39. Steen, A.: logic-embedding v1.8.8 (2025). https://doi.org/10.5281/zenodo.15755328
40. Steen, A., Benzmüller, C.: What are non-classical logics and why do we need them? an extended interview with Dov Gabbay and Leon van der Torre. Künstl. Intell. (2024). https://doi.org/10.1007/s13218-023-00824-7
41. Steen, A., Sutcliffe, G.: TPTP world infrastructure for non-classical logics. In: Nalon, C., Steen, A., Suda, M. (eds.) Proceedings of the 9th Workshop on Practical Aspects of Automated Reasoning, pp. 74–90. No. 3717 in CEUR Workshop Proceedings (2024)
42. Steen, A., Sutcliffe, G., Benzmüller, C.: Solving quantified modal logic problems by translation to classical logics. J. Log. Comput. (2025). https://doi.org/10.1093/logcom/exaf006
43. Steen, A., Sutcliffe, G., Fontaine, P., McKeown, J.: Representation, verification, and visualization of tarskian interpretations for typed first-order logic. In: Piskac, R., Voronkov, A. (eds.) Proceedings of 24th International Conference on Logic for Programming Artificial Intelligence and Reasoning, pp. 369–385. No. 94 in EPiC Series in Computing, EasyChair Publications (2023)
44. Steen, A.: An extensible logic embedding tool for lightweight non-classical reasoning (short paper). In: Konev, B., Schon, C., Steen, A. (eds.) Proceedings of the 8th Workshop on Practical Aspects of Automated Reasoning. p. Online. No. 3201 in CEUR Workshop Proceedings (2022)
45. Sutcliffe, G.: System description: SystemOnTPTP. In: McAllester, D. (ed.) CADE 2000. LNCS (LNAI), vol. 1831, pp. 406–410. Springer, Heidelberg (2000). https://doi.org/10.1007/10721959_31
46. Sutcliffe, G.: TPTP, TSTP, CASC, etc. In: Diekert, V., Volkov, M.V., Voronkov, A. (eds.) CSR 2007. LNCS, vol. 4649, pp. 6–22. Springer, Heidelberg (2007). https://doi.org/10.1007/978-3-540-74510-5_4
47. Sutcliffe, G.: The SZS ontologies for automated reasoning software. In: Sutcliffe, G., Rudnicki, P., Schmidt, R., Konev, B., Schulz, S. (eds.) Proceedings of the LPAR Workshops: Knowledge Exchange: Automated Provers and Proof Assistants, and the 7th International Workshop on the Implementation of Logics, pp. 38–49. No. 418 in CEUR Workshop Proceedings (2008)
48. Sutcliffe, G.: The TPTP world – infrastructure for automated reasoning. In: Clarke, E.M., Voronkov, A. (eds.) LPAR 2010. LNCS (LNAI), vol. 6355, pp. 1–12. Springer, Heidelberg (2010). https://doi.org/10.1007/978-3-642-17511-4_1

49. Sutcliffe, G.: The TPTP Problem Library and Associated Infrastructure. From CNF to TH0., TPTP v6.4.0. J. Autom. Reason. **59**(4), 483–502 (2017). https://doi.org/10.1007/s10817-017-9407-7
50. Sutcliffe, G.: The logic languages of the TPTP world. Logic J. IGPL **31**(6), 1153–1169 (2023)
51. Sutcliffe, G., Benzmüller, C.: Automated reasoning in higher-order logic using the TPTP THF infrastructure. J. Formalized Reasoning **3**(1), 1–27 (2010)
52. Sutcliffe, G., Kotelnikov, E.: TFX: the TPTP extended typed first-order form. In: Konev, B., Urban, J., Schulz, S. (eds.) Proceedings of the 6th Workshop on Practical Aspects of Automated Reasoning, pp. 72–87. No. 2162 in CEUR Workshop Proceedings (2018)
53. Sutcliffe, G., Schulz, S., Claessen, K., Van Gelder, A.: Using the TPTP language for writing derivations and finite interpretations. In: Furbach, U., Shankar, N. (eds.) IJCAR 2006. LNCS (LNAI), vol. 4130, pp. 67–81. Springer, Heidelberg (2006). https://doi.org/10.1007/11814771_7
54. Sutcliffe, G., Steen, A., Fontaine, P.: The New TPTP Format for Interpretations. arXiv:2406.06108 (2024)
55. Tarski, A., Vaught, R.: Arithmetical extensions of relational systems. Compos. Math. **13**, 81–102 (1956)
56. Torlak, E., Jackson, D.: Kodkod: a relational model finder. In: Grumberg, O., Huth, M. (eds.) TACAS 2007. LNCS, vol. 4424, pp. 632–647. Springer, Heidelberg (2007). https://doi.org/10.1007/978-3-540-71209-1_49
57. Weber, T.: SAT-based Finite Model Generation for Higher-Order Logic, Ph.D. thesis, Technische Universitüat München, Munich, Germany (2008)
58. Zhang, J., Zhang, H.: SEM: a system for enumerating models. In: Mellish, C. (ed.) Proceedings of the 14th International Joint Conference on Artificial Intelligence, pp. 298–303. Morgan Kaufmann (1995)

Open Access This chapter is licensed under the terms of the Creative Commons Attribution 4.0 International License (http://creativecommons.org/licenses/by/4.0/), which permits use, sharing, adaptation, distribution and reproduction in any medium or format, as long as you give appropriate credit to the original author(s) and the source, provide a link to the Creative Commons license and indicate if changes were made.

The images or other third party material in this chapter are included in the chapter's Creative Commons license, unless indicated otherwise in a credit line to the material. If material is not included in the chapter's Creative Commons license and your intended use is not permitted by statutory regulation or exceeds the permitted use, you will need to obtain permission directly from the copyright holder.

Pitts and Intuitionistic Multi-Succedent: Uniform Interpolation for KM

Hugo Férée[1] and Ian Shillito[2,3](✉)

[1] Université Paris Cité, CNRS, IRIF, 75013 Paris, France
[2] University of Birmingham, Birmingham, UK
ian.shillito@outlook.fr
[3] University of Melbourne, Melbourne, Australia

Abstract. Pitts' proof-theoretic technique for uniform interpolation, which generates uniform interpolants from terminating sequent calculi, has only been applied to logics on an intuitionistic basis through single-succedent sequent calculi. We adapt the technique to the intuitionistic multi-succedent setting by focusing on the intuitionistic modal logic KM. To do this, we design a novel multi-succedent sequent calculus for this logic which terminates, eliminates cut, and provides a decidability argument. Then, we adapt Pitts' technique to our calculus to construct uniform interpolants for KM, while highlighting the hurdles we overcame. Finally, by (re)proving the algebraisability of KM, we deduce the coherence of the class of KM-algebras. All our results are fully mechanised in the Rocq proof assistant, ensuring correctness and enabling effective computation of interpolants.

Keywords: uniform interpolation · formal verification · proof theory · intuitionistic modal logic

1 Introduction

Uniform interpolation is a mighty form of interpolation, ensuring for any formula φ and variable p the existence of *left* and *right uniform interpolants*, respectively denoted $\forall p\varphi$ and $\exists p\varphi$. Intuitively, $\forall p\varphi$ is the strongest formula without p that implies φ, and $\exists p\varphi$ the weakest p-free formula that is implied by φ. Technically, these interpolants satisfy the following, where ψ is a p-free formula:

$$\vdash \forall p\varphi \to \varphi \qquad \frac{\vdash \psi \to \varphi}{\vdash \psi \to \forall p\varphi} \qquad \vdash \varphi \to \exists p\varphi \qquad \frac{\vdash \varphi \to \psi}{\vdash \exists p\varphi \to \psi}$$

Uniform interpolants are propositional formulas, but their notation is suggestive: they provide an interpretation of propositional quantifiers inside the logic.

Because of its strength, uniform interpolation is a notoriously difficult property to prove. Still, a variety of proof techniques are presented in the literature: model-theoretic [55], universal-algebraic [27,34,41], and proof-theoretic [49]. The

© The Author(s) 2026
A. Biere et al. (Eds.): IJCAR 2026, LNAI 16688, pp. 336–356, 2026.
https://doi.org/10.1007/978-3-032-32589-1_21

latter kind of technique, developed in 1992 for intuitionistic logic IPC by Pitts, requires a *terminating* sequent calculus: a calculus whose naive backward proof search, i.e. the process of repetitively applying backward rules of the calculus in no specific order, necessarily comes to a halt. The proof search tree of a sequent in a terminating calculus is *finite*, and hence becomes data from which uniform interpolants are computed via mutual recursion.

In his proof, Pitts used the *single-succedent* terminating calculus G4iP for IPC, which was invented several times through the decades by Vorob'ev [56], Dyckhoff [19] and Hudelmaier [38]. By exploiting the existence of such calculi, which extend G4iP through Iemhoff's methodology [40], Pitts' original technique was recently applied to a variety of intuitionistic modal logics [28,39], including the intuitionistic provability logic iSL [21] for which a single-succedent terminating calculus G4iSLt was defined [51]. In parallel, Bílková ported the technique to *multi*-succedent calculi for *classical* modal logics K, T and provability logic GL [2]. The shift to a classical basis allowed for technical simplifications, e.g. the recursive definition stops being mutual: it focuses on the left uniform interpolant without needing the right one. Following her footsteps, van der Giessen, Jalali and Kuznets extended her approach to additional classical modal logics using multi-succedent but richer, i.e. nested or labelled, sequents [31–33]. As it stands, the applicability of Pitts' technique to *multi*-succedent calculi for logics on an *intuitionistic* basis remains unclear.

By scanning the literature, one easily finds logics with an intuitionistic basis requiring multi-succedent calculi. Most famous is the Gödel-Dummett logic LC [17], an intermediate logic extending IPC with the linearity axiom $(\varphi \to \psi) \vee (\psi \to \varphi)$. This logic is given a crucially multi-succedent terminating calculus in Dyckhoff's work [18]. While uniform interpolation is known for LC, as it is locally finite and has Craig interpolation [26,46], it could at least serve as a good example for methodological purposes. Of yet better interest is the intuitionistic modal logic KM [47], which extends iSL [29] (and hence iK [5] and IPC) with the *Kuznetsov-Muravitsky* axiom $\Box\varphi \to (\psi \vee (\psi \to \varphi))$. This logic possesses several multi-succedent calculi [8,11], and lacks a (dis)proof for uniform interpolation [42]. From a mathematical viewpoint, the interest in KM lies in its deep ties to GL and IPC: its lattice of extensions is isomorphic to the lattice of extensions of GL, and its extension with any non-modal axiom is conservative over the extension of IPC with the same axiom. Additionally, KM received some attention in computer science [8] in light of its connection to Nakano's "later" modality [48], capturing the notion of *guarded recursion* [9]. Given its proximity to iSL and the recent application of Pitts' technique to the latter logic [21], KM presents itself as a natural candidate for an investigation on the applicability of this technique to a combination of multi-succedent sequents and intuitionism.

Unfortunately, existing calculi for KM are not adequate for this investigation: the first sequent calculi for KM given by Darjania [11] clearly do not terminate, while Clouston and Goré's calculus [8, Section 4] has complex rules and uses an alternative syntax for KM. So, we provide in Sect. 3 a novel multi-succedent terminating calculus for KM. Our calculus G4KM can be obtained from G4iSLt in two steps: first, port G4iSLt to a multi-succedent setting, making it an extension of the terminating multi-succedent calculus G4iP′ for IPC [20, Section 7]; second, modify the implication right rule, following (Kripke) semantic intuitions, to capture the characteristic axiom of KM. We show that naive backward proof search in G4KM terminates, which, together with cut elimination, provides a decidability procedure for KM. Our syntactic proof of cut elimination uses the termination measure as induction measure, a now standard methodology for provability logics [35,36,51], but requires a non-trivial refactoring of Dyckhoff and Negri's argument for the admissibility of contraction [20].

To obtain uniform interpolation for KM using G4KM, it remains to adapt Pitts' technique to multi-succedent sequents. This step mainly consists of a careful rephrasing of the uniform interpolation property for *sequents* from single- to multi-succedent. This boils down to restricting enough the properties pertaining to the left uniform interpolant $\forall p\varphi$ to avoid the capture of the *constant domain* propositional quantifier, satisfying the axiom $\forall p(\varphi(p) \vee \psi) \to (\forall\varphi(p) \vee \psi)$ when ψ is p-free. With this subtlety in mind, we use the adapted technique to prove uniform interpolation for KM in Sect. 4. We expect this adaptation to be reusable at least for LC and KM_{lin} [8], the combination of KM and LC.

We directly put our novel result to work in Sect. 5 and infer from it the *coherence* of a class of algebras corresponding to KM, a consequence of uniform interpolation, the algebraisability of KM [47], and a bridge theorem [41] from abstract algebraic logic [23].

Our work fits in the fast-growing literature on the mechanisation of proof theory [7,12,13,43], modal logic [1,14,15,24,35,45,57], intuitionistic modal logic [37,53] and its proof theory [3,4,21,36,51]. Indeed, all our results - spanning axiomatic calculus, Kripke and algebraic semantics, algebraisability, sequent calculus, decidability, admissibility of cut, uniform interpolation - are formalised in the interactive theorem prover Rocq [52]: https://github.com/ianshil/KM. On top of ensuring the correctness of these results, the mechanisation allows for the extraction of executable programs, e.g. for effectively computing interpolants. Throughout this paper, definitions and results are accompanied by a clickable symbol leading to an online-readable version of their Rocq implementations and proofs.

2 Preliminaries

We introduce the syntax, axiomatic system, and Kripke semantics of KM.

2.1 Syntax

Let $\mathsf{Prop} = \{p, q, r \dots\}$ be a countably infinite set of propositional variables on which equality is decidable. Modal formulas ( ) are defined as below:

$$\varphi ::= p \in \mathsf{Prop} \mid \bot \mid \varphi \wedge \varphi \mid \varphi \vee \varphi \mid \varphi \to \varphi \mid \Box\varphi$$

$$\begin{array}{ll} \text{K} & \Box(\varphi \to \psi) \to (\Box\varphi \to \Box\psi) \\ \text{SL} & (\Box\varphi \to \varphi) \to \varphi \\ \text{KM} & \Box\varphi \to (\psi \vee (\psi \to \varphi)) \end{array} \qquad \frac{\Gamma \vdash \varphi}{\Gamma \vdash \Box\varphi}\ (\text{Nec})$$

$$\frac{\varphi \text{ is an instance of an axiom}}{\Gamma \vdash \varphi}\ (\text{Ax}) \qquad \frac{\varphi \in \Gamma}{\Gamma \vdash \varphi}\ (\text{El}) \qquad \frac{\Gamma \vdash \varphi \quad \Gamma \vdash \varphi \to \psi}{\Gamma \vdash \psi}\ (\text{MP})$$

Fig. 1. Generalised Hilbert calculus KMH for KM.

We use the greek letters $\varphi, \psi, \chi, \delta, \ldots$ for formulas and $\Gamma, \Delta, \Sigma, \Pi \ldots$ for finite multisets of formulas. We say that φ is a *boxed formula* if $\Box$ is its main connective. We write $\mathrm{Vars}(\varphi)$ to denote the set of all propositional variables occurring as subformulas in the formula φ, and define $\mathrm{Vars}(\Gamma) := \{q \in \mathsf{Prop} \mid q \in \mathrm{Vars}(\varphi) \text{ for some } \varphi \in \Gamma\}$. The *disjoint sum* of Γ and Δ will be denoted by Γ, Δ. Single formulas φ will also often be coerced implicitly to the multiset singleton $\{\varphi\}$. For a multiset Γ, we define the multiset $\Box\Gamma := \{\Box\varphi : \varphi \in \Gamma\}$. By $\Box^{-1}\Gamma$ we mean the multiset $\{\gamma \in \Gamma \mid \gamma \text{ is not a boxed formula}\} \cup \{\gamma \mid \Box\gamma \in \Gamma\}$. We write $\bigvee \Gamma$ for the disjunction of all the elements in Γ, where Γ is a finite multiset.

2.2 Axiomatic System

We introduce an axiomatic system manipulating *consecutions*, i.e. expressions of the form $\Gamma \vdash \varphi$ where Γ is a *set* of formulas.

The generalised Hilbert calculus KMH for KM extends the one for intuitionistic logic IPC with the modal axioms and rules displayed in Fig. 1. It notably extends the intuitionistic modal logic iSL [51], itself an extension of iGL [30], with the Kuznetsov-Muravitsky axiom $\Box\varphi \to (\psi \vee (\psi \to \varphi))$, and therefore proves some notable axioms:

$$(4)\ \Box\varphi \to \Box\Box\varphi \qquad (\text{GL})\ \Box(\Box\varphi \to \varphi) \to \Box\varphi \qquad (\text{CP})\ \varphi \to \Box\varphi$$

The strength of the Completeness Principle (CP) allows us to replace the (Nec) rule with its variant where the premise is $\emptyset \vdash \varphi$, and obtain an equivalent logic. We write $\Gamma \vdash_{\mathsf{KMH}} \varphi$ if $\Gamma \vdash \varphi$ is provable in KMH.

2.3 Kripke Semantics

We now present the Kripke semantics for KM [47] which we use to provide intuitions for the rules of our sequent calculus.

The Kripke semantics of KM restricts the one for iSL on the class of models: the class of models for KM is strictly contained in the one for iSL. The models for KM are defined below, where $\mathcal{P}(W) := \{U \mid U \subseteq W\}$.

Definition 1. *A model $\mathcal{M}$ is a tuple $(W, \leq, R, I)$ satisfying the following: $(W, \leq)$ is a preordered set; R is equal to the irreflexive part of $\leq$, noted $<$,* *i.e.* $R = <$*; R is converse well-founded; and* $I : \mathsf{Prop} \to \mathcal{P}(W)$ *is a* persistent *interpretation function such that*

$$\forall v, w \in W. \forall p \in \mathsf{Prop}. (w \leq v \quad \to \quad w \in I(p) \quad \to \quad v \in I(p))$$

Although the models of iSL require that $R \subseteq <$, a stricter condition is imposed for KM by enforcing the equality between R and $<$, thereby making R and $\leq$ interdefinable. In other words, whenever we travel along the modal relation we know that we effectively perform a jump to a *strict* intuitionistic successor.

Definition 2 (). *Given a model* $\mathcal{M} = (W, \leq, R, I)$*, we define the forcing relation* $\mathcal{M}, w \Vdash \varphi$ *between a world* $w \in W$ *and a formula* φ *as follows:*

$$\begin{array}{lcl}
\mathcal{M}, w \Vdash p & := & w \in I(p) \\
\mathcal{M}, w \Vdash \bot & := & \textit{Never} \\
\mathcal{M}, w \Vdash \varphi \wedge \psi & := & \mathcal{M}, w \Vdash \varphi \textit{ and } \mathcal{M}, w \Vdash \psi \\
\mathcal{M}, w \Vdash \varphi \vee \psi & := & \mathcal{M}, w \Vdash \varphi \textit{ or } \mathcal{M}, w \Vdash \psi \\
\mathcal{M}, w \Vdash \varphi \to \psi & := & \textit{for all } v \geq w,\ \mathcal{M}, v \Vdash \varphi \textit{ implies } \mathcal{M}, v \Vdash \psi \\
\mathcal{M}, w \Vdash \Box\varphi & := & \textit{for all } v,\ wRv \textit{ implies } \mathcal{M}, v \Vdash \varphi
\end{array}$$

We abbreviate the negation of $\mathcal{M}, w \Vdash \varphi$ *by* $\mathcal{M}, w \nVdash \varphi$*, and write* $\mathcal{M}, w \Vdash \Gamma$ *for* $\forall \varphi \in \Gamma. \mathcal{M}, w \Vdash \varphi$*. We define the local consequence () as follows:*

$$\Gamma \models \varphi \qquad \textit{iff} \qquad \forall \mathcal{M}. \forall w. (\mathcal{M}, w \Vdash \Gamma \quad \textit{implies} \quad \mathcal{M}, w \Vdash \varphi)$$

As expected, the Kripke semantics for intuitionistic logic, i.e. *persistence*, is preserved in our semantics for KM.

Lemma 1 (Persistence). *For any model* $\mathcal{M} = (W, \leq, R, I)$*, formula* φ *and points* $w, v \in W$*, if* $w \leq v$ *and* $\mathcal{M}, w \Vdash \varphi$ *then* $\mathcal{M}, v \Vdash \varphi$*.*

Observation 1. *A striking feature of this semantics is the ability it gives the language to distinguish reflexive intuitionistic jumps and jumps to strict intuitionistic successors, an impossible feat in* IPC *or even in* iSL*. Indeed, by jumping to a strict successor* v *of* w *all boxed formulas forced in it become* unboxed *in* v*, while this unboxing is not generally performed by jumping to* w *itself. Joined with persistence, this observation gives that* $\mathcal{M}, w \Vdash \Gamma$ *and* $w < v$ *entail* $\mathcal{M}, v \Vdash \Box^{-1}\Gamma$*.*

While this semantics will be handy to explain the rules of our calculus, it is not tightly corresponding to the logic: KM and the local consequence coincide on theorems ($\emptyset \models \varphi$ if and only if $\emptyset \vdash_{\mathsf{KMH}} \varphi$), but KM is not *strongly complete* w.r.t. the semantics. Indeed, we have $\Gamma \nvdash_{\mathsf{KMH}} p_0$ while $\Gamma \models p_0$, where Γ is the infinite set $\{\Box p_{n+1} \to p_n \mid n \in \mathbb{N}\}$.[1] As for most provability logics, this failure of strong completeness boils down to the tendency converse well-founded frames have to make the local consequence non-compact, as is known for GL and iGL [54, Section 3.3]. But for the case of KM (and iSL), the argument does not hold using the usual infinite set $\{\Diamond p_0\} \cup \{\Box(p_n \to \Diamond p_{n+1}) \mid n \in \mathbb{N}\}$.

[1] We thank Mojtaba Mojtahedi for designing, and sharing with us, this set.

3 A G4 Calculus for KM

In this section we introduce our *multi-succedent* sequent calculus for KM and prove several major results for it: termination of naive backward proof search, cut elimination, and equivalence with KMH.

$$\frac{}{\Gamma, \bot \Rightarrow \Delta}\,(\bot\mathrm{L}) \qquad \frac{}{\Gamma, p \Rightarrow p, \Delta}\,(\mathrm{IdP}) \qquad \frac{\Gamma, \varphi, \psi \Rightarrow \Delta}{\Gamma, \varphi \wedge \psi \Rightarrow \Delta}\,(\wedge L)$$

$$\frac{\Gamma \Rightarrow \varphi, \Delta \quad \Gamma \Rightarrow \psi, \Delta}{\Gamma \Rightarrow \varphi \wedge \psi, \Delta}\,(\wedge R) \qquad \frac{\Gamma, \varphi \Rightarrow \Delta \quad \Gamma, \psi \Rightarrow \Delta}{\Gamma, \varphi \vee \psi \Rightarrow \Delta}\,(\vee L) \qquad \frac{\Gamma \Rightarrow \varphi, \psi, \Delta}{\Gamma \Rightarrow \varphi \vee \psi, \Delta}\,(\vee\mathrm{R})$$

$$\frac{\Gamma, \varphi \to (\psi \to \chi) \Rightarrow \Delta}{\Gamma, (\varphi \wedge \psi) \to \chi \Rightarrow \Delta}\,(\wedge\to\mathrm{L}) \qquad \frac{\Gamma, \varphi \to \chi, \psi \to \chi \Rightarrow \Delta}{\Gamma, (\varphi \vee \psi) \to \chi \Rightarrow \Delta}\,(\vee\to\mathrm{L}) \qquad \frac{\Gamma, p, \varphi \Rightarrow \Delta}{\Gamma, p, p \to \varphi \Rightarrow \Delta}\,(p\to\mathrm{L})$$

$$\frac{\Box^{-1}\Gamma, \Box\varphi \Rightarrow \varphi}{\Gamma \Rightarrow \Box\varphi, \Delta}\,(\Box\mathrm{R}) \qquad \frac{\Box^{-1}\Gamma, \Box\varphi, \psi \Rightarrow \varphi \quad \Gamma, \psi \Rightarrow \Delta}{\Gamma, \Box\varphi \to \psi \Rightarrow \Delta}\,(\Box\to\mathrm{L})$$

$$\frac{\Gamma, \varphi \Rightarrow \psi, \Delta \quad \Box^{-1}\Gamma, \varphi \Rightarrow \psi}{\Gamma \Rightarrow \varphi \to \psi, \Delta}\,(\to\mathrm{R})$$

$$\frac{\Gamma, \chi \to \psi, \varphi \Rightarrow \Delta, \chi \quad \Box^{-1}\Gamma, \chi \to \psi, \varphi \Rightarrow \chi \quad \Gamma, \psi \Rightarrow \Delta}{\Gamma, (\varphi \to \chi) \to \psi \Rightarrow \Delta}\,(\to\to\mathrm{L})$$

Fig. 2. The sequent calculus G4KM ( ).

As is standard in structural proof theory, sequents are expressions of the shape $\Gamma \Rightarrow \Delta$ where the *antecedent* Γ and the *succedent* Δ are multisets of formulas. We present the calculus G4KM in Fig. 2.

The modal rules of G4KM are straightforwardly adapted from G4iSLt [51] to the multi-succedent context, and most non-modal rules are directly taken from G4iP′. See in particular [51, Section 2.4] for an explanation of the rule $(\Box\to\mathrm{L})$. Still, two essential - and interdependent - features of our calculus need commenting: the presence of multisets on the right-hand side of sequents, and the surprising shape of the implication right rule. Both are targeted at proving the axiom KM and hence the sequent $\Box p \Rightarrow q \vee (q \to p)$.

Without a rule for disjunction on the right preserving both disjuncts we cannot prove this sequent: this calls for multi-succedent sequents, giving the rule $(\vee\mathrm{R})$ of our calculus. Such sequents can be used for IPC, as first shown by Maehara [44], and popularised by Dragalin [16]. Furthermore, this approach can be ported to the terminating calculus G4iP to obtain a multi-succedent terminating calculus G4iP′ for IPC [20, Section 7]. This calculus has been used as basis for intuitionistic modal logics (with diamond) [10], an example we follow for our calculus by straightforwardly adapting G4iSLt's modal rules [51] to multi-succedent sequents, and providing modifications to the rules $(\to\text{R})$ and $(\to\!\!\to\text{L})$.

The multi-succedent $(\vee\text{R})$ reduces $\Box p \Rightarrow q \vee (q \to p)$ to $\Box p \Rightarrow q, q \to p$, but the implication right rule of G4iP′ presented below does not help prove the latter sequent, as it forces us to delete q on the right.

$$\frac{\Gamma, \varphi \Rightarrow \psi}{\Gamma \Rightarrow \Delta, \varphi \to \psi}$$

The upward deletion of Δ in this rule, notably preventing the provability of the excluded middle $\varphi \vee \neg\varphi$, is semantically justified as the rule, read upwards, corresponds to a jump to an *arbitrary* intuitionistic successor. We could hope for a more detailed semantic analysis in the rule, by distinguishing *reflexive* and *strict-successor* jumps. The rule below attempts at doing just this.

$$\frac{\Gamma, \varphi \Rightarrow \Delta, \psi \quad \Gamma, \varphi \Rightarrow \psi}{\Gamma \Rightarrow \Delta, \varphi \to \psi}$$

Unfortunately, this is pointless: this last rule is equivalent to the previous one, as the left premise is provable from the right one via weakening. This issue is nothing but an expression of the well-known inability of intuitionistic logic to syntactically distinguish reflexive from strict-successor jumps.

In KM, the story is different: by the semantic Observation 1, we can syntactically distinguish the two. Our rule $(\to\text{R})$ leverages this insight.

$$\frac{\Gamma, \varphi \Rightarrow \Delta, \psi \quad \Box^{-1}\Gamma, \varphi \Rightarrow \psi}{\Gamma \Rightarrow \Delta, \varphi \to \psi}\ (\to\text{R})$$

The reflexive jump corresponds to the left premise, as we preserved Δ, and the strict-successor jump corresponds to the right premise, as we obtained $\Box^{-1}\Gamma$ and deleted Δ. With the rule $(\to\text{R})$, we can finally prove our sequent.

$$\frac{\dfrac{}{\Box p, q \Rightarrow q, p}\ (\text{IdP}) \quad \dfrac{}{p, q \Rightarrow p}\ (\text{IdP})}{\Box p \Rightarrow q, q \to p}\ (\to\text{R})$$

The modifications made to $(\to\text{R})$ forced us to change the rule $(\to\!\!\to\text{L})$ accordingly: the two leftmost premises of $(\to\!\!\to\text{L})$ are inspired from the premises of $(\to\text{R})$.

We contrast our new calculus with the existing ones for KM. Darjania's multi-succedent calculi [11] follow a similar intuition to ours (see also [50]), splitting the implication right into two rules. Contrarily to ours, they are not targeted at termination as evidenced by the explicit structural rules it contains for the one, and the repetition of principal formulas in premises for the other. Therefore, these calculi do not fit our bill: proving uniform interpolation à la Pitts. Clouston and Goré's calculus [8, Section 4] for KM terminates, but their approach is different: instead of using the expressivity of the modality to create the case distinction in our rule $(\to\text{R})$, they split the implication *connective* into a reflexive $\to$ and a strict successor $\twoheadrightarrow$ version. The complexity of their rules and the semantic nature of their cut-free completeness proof, via countermodel construction, pushed us to favour our calculus, for which we could provide a syntactic proof of *cut elimination.*

We can now show that naive backward proof search terminates in G4KM. This is easily obtained by finding a well-founded ordering on sequents decreasing on each instance of a rule from conclusion to premise. For this, we reuse the adaptation to iSL of Dyckhoff's notion of weight of a formula [19], and simply adapt the ordering induced by it from G4iSLt [51] to multi-succedent sequents.

Definition 3 ( ). *The weight $w(\varphi)$ of a formula is the sum of its size and of its number of conjunctions. In other words, every symbol in a formula accounts for* 1 *in the weight, except for conjunctions which account for* 2.

Definition 4 (Ordering on sequents). *The ordering on sequents denoted by $(\Gamma \Rightarrow \Delta) \prec (\Gamma' \Rightarrow \Delta')$ is defined as the Dershowitz–Manna multiset-ordering between (Γ, Δ, Δ) and $(\Gamma', \Delta', \Delta')$ induced by the well-founded ordering on formulas induced by Definition 3.*

Concretely, formulas from a multiset can repeatedly be replaced by finitely-many strictly smaller formulas in order to obtain a smaller multiset. Such an ordering is well-known to be well-founded since the ordering on formulas is. In the following, we implicitly use this ordering when performing a well-founded induction on a sequent.

It is easy to see that this ordering decreases between the conclusion and each premise of each rule from Fig. 2 as a formula from the conclusion is either preserved in the premises, or replaced with several, strictly smaller formulas.

Proposition 1. *For any instance of a* G4KM*-rule with premises $s_1, \ldots, s_n$ and conclusion s, we have $s_i \prec s$ for any $1 \leq i \leq n$.*

Proof. An interesting case is the ($\wedge\!\rightarrow$L)-rule: it requires that $w(\varphi \rightarrow (\psi \rightarrow \chi)) < w((\varphi \wedge \psi) \rightarrow \chi)$, which holds as a conjunction adds 2 to the weight of a formula. Another one is the rule ($\Box$R) which may not delete any formula from the sequent if Δ is empty, but moves $\Box\varphi$ to the left-hand-side of the sequent while keeping a copy of φ on the right. This is taken into account in the ordering by counting twice multisets on the right, so that $(\{\Box\varphi\} \Rightarrow \{\varphi\}) \prec (\emptyset \Rightarrow \{\Box\varphi\})$. ■

Remark 1. The multiset-ordering may be too strong of a tool here, as each formula is only replaced by at most three smaller ones, not arbitrarily many. Then if we define the weight of a sequent $\Gamma \Rightarrow \Delta$ as $\Sigma\{3^{w(\varphi)} | \varphi \in \Gamma, \Delta, \Delta\}$, where $w(\varphi)$ is the weight of a formula defined as above, we obtain a well-founded ordering that is strictly contained in $\prec$, still compatible with G4KM and that gives an explicit upper-bound for the depth of a proof tree.

However, the more general ordering $\prec$ (or at least the ordering above with a higher constant than 3) still is useful when proving admissibility results for G4KM, or when defining and proving uniform interpolation.

Now, as the applicability of each rule is decidable and only finitely many rules can be applied on a given sequent, the well-foundedness of the ordering ensures the decidability of provability in G4KM.

Proposition 2 (Decidability). *Provability in* G4KM *is decidable.*

We are now required to prove several admissibility lemmas for G4KM. Cut, in particular, will ensure that the calculus is complete for KM.

Before focusing on cut we have to prove the admissibility of contraction, which has to be abandoned as a rule in G4KM to ensure termination, as done in G4iP and G4iSLt. In the following, we highlight differences between our calculus G4KM and those inspired by Dyckhoff and Negri [20] mentioned earlier.

First, let us observe the invertibility of the new rules.

Proposition 3 *The following rules are admissible:*

$$\frac{\Gamma \Rightarrow \varphi \vee \psi, \Delta}{\Gamma \Rightarrow \varphi, \psi, \Delta}\ (\vee R^{-1}) \qquad \frac{\Gamma \Rightarrow \varphi \to \psi, \Delta}{\Gamma, \varphi \Rightarrow \psi, \Delta}\ (\to R^{-1})$$

In other words, $(\vee\text{R})$ is invertible thanks to multi-succedent sequents, and $(\to\text{R})$ is here only partially invertible, in contrast with G4iP where it is fully invertible.

The proofs of admissibility of contraction on the left for G4iP and G4iSLt both follow the same pattern: prove the admissibility of left implication $(\to\text{L})$, then the partial invertibility of $(\to\to\text{L})$ up to contraction, i.e. $(\to\to\text{L}_{dup})$, before finally focusing on contraction on the left. When turning to the multi-succedent calculus G4iP′ for IPC, Dyckhoff and Negri lightly adapt the proof: they first need to prove the admissibility of contraction on the right (contrR) and then follow the pattern described above, though they prove a strengthened lemma for left-implication. Unfortunately, we cannot replicate here this succession because of a circularity caused by the dependency of the admissibility of (contrR) on the admissibility of contraction on the left. The root of this dependency lies in the rule $(\to\text{R})$ for KM: when proving the admissibility of (contrR) on $\Gamma \Rightarrow \varphi \to \psi, \varphi \to \psi, \Delta$ with $\varphi \to \psi$ principal in the last rule applied, the duplicate is not simply weakened from premises to conclusion, as in G4iP, but comes from the left premise $\Gamma, \varphi \Rightarrow \psi, \varphi \to \psi, \Delta$. To deal with this duplicate in the premise, we apply Proposition 3 to get $\Gamma, \varphi, \varphi \Rightarrow \psi, \psi, \Delta$, and then need to contract on both left and right. So, contraction on the right requires contraction on the left, but also is at the start of a succession of lemmas leading to contraction on the left. We solve this circular dependency by proving all these lemmas in a single mutual induction, using the well-founded ordering on sequents from Definition 4.

Proposition 4 ( ). *The following rules are admissible.*

$$\frac{\Gamma \Rightarrow \psi, \psi, \Delta}{\Gamma \Rightarrow \psi, \Delta}\ (contrR) \qquad \frac{\Gamma, \psi, \psi \Rightarrow \Delta}{\Gamma, \psi \Rightarrow \Delta}\ (contrL)$$

$$\frac{\Gamma \Rightarrow \varphi, \Delta \quad \Gamma, \psi \Rightarrow \Delta}{\Gamma, \varphi \to \psi \Rightarrow \Delta}\ (\to L) \qquad \frac{\Gamma, (\varphi \to \psi) \to \chi \Rightarrow \Delta}{\Gamma, \varphi, (\psi \to \chi), (\psi \to \chi) \Rightarrow \Delta}\ (\to\to L_{dup})$$

Proof. The four statements are proved simultaneously by well-founded induction on the conclusion of each rule, followed by a case analysis on the proof of the rightmost assumption. Here, we only sketch the cases that significantly differ from Dyckhoff and Negri's proofs and highlight the circular dependency between these properties. Crucially, we start by by proving (→L), as it is used at the same level in the case of $(\to\to\mathrm{L}_{dup})$.

- (→L) When the last rule is (→→L), we use the induction hypothesis for (→L), (contrL) and $(\to\to\mathrm{L}_{dup})$.
- (contrR) The main case is for the (→R)-rule with $\psi = \psi_1 \to \psi_2$ as principal formula. The sequent $\Gamma \Rightarrow \Delta, \psi_1 \to \psi_2$ is then proved by applying successively (→R), left contraction on ψ_1, right contraction on ψ_2 and partial invertibility of (→R) (Proposition 3).
- $(\to\to\mathrm{L}_{dup})$ The main case is when the premise is proved by using the (→→L) rule on the principal formula. Immediately applying the rule (→L) we just obtained (not the induction hypothesis!) leaves us with deriving the sequents $\Gamma, \varphi, (\psi \to \chi) \Rightarrow \Delta$ which we have by assumption ; and $\Gamma, \varphi, (\psi \to \chi), \chi \Rightarrow \Delta$, which we have by weakening on the left.
- (contrL) The critical case is (→→L), which uses the induction hypothesis for $(\to\to\mathrm{L}_{dup})$.

■

With contraction under our belt, we proceed to prove the admissibility of cut by local proof transformations, giving us cut elimination. We follow the argument developed for terminating calculi for provability logics [35,36,51], which uses the inductive principle extracted from the well-founded ordering on sequents.

We prove the admissibility of the following additive variant of the cut rule. The multiplicative variant easily follows via weakening.

Proposition 5 ( ). *The additive cut rule is admissible:*

$$\frac{\Gamma \Rightarrow \Delta, \varphi \qquad \Gamma, \varphi \Rightarrow \Delta}{\Gamma \Rightarrow \Delta}\ (\mathit{Cut})$$

Proof. By induction first on the weight of the cut formula, then by well-founded induction on the sequent $\Gamma \Rightarrow \Delta$ as for G4iSLt [51]. ■

The results accumulated so far allow us to show that our calculus G4KM captures exactly the logic KM.

Theorem 1 (,). *If $\Gamma, \Delta, \{\varphi\}$ is a multiset of formulas, then we have*

$$\vdash \Gamma \Rightarrow \Delta \ \rightsquigarrow\ \Gamma \vdash_{\mathsf{KMH}} \bigvee \Delta \qquad \text{and} \qquad \Gamma \vdash_{\mathsf{KMH}} \varphi \ \rightsquigarrow\ \vdash \Gamma \Rightarrow \varphi$$

Proof. For the implication on the left, we reason by induction on the proof of $\vdash \Gamma \Rightarrow \Delta$. Most rules of G4KM are trivially simulated in KMH, with the exception of (→R) and (→→L). We focus on the former, as the latter is treated using a similar argument. We assume that we have proofs of $\Box^{-1}\Gamma, \varphi \vdash \psi$ and $\Gamma, \varphi \vdash \psi \vee \bigvee \Delta$, and prove $\Gamma \vdash (\varphi \to \psi) \vee \bigvee \Delta$. The pivot of the proof is the obtaining of $\Gamma \vdash_{\mathsf{KMH}} \varphi \vee (\varphi \to \psi)$ from $\Box^{-1}\Gamma, \varphi \vdash_{\mathsf{KMH}} \psi$. We first use the monotonicity of KMH ( ) and the deduction theorem ( ) to obtain $\Box^{-1}\Gamma, \Box(\varphi \to \psi) \vdash \varphi \to \psi$. Then, we can use a lemma simulating the sequent ($\Box$R) ( ) giving us $\Gamma \vdash \Box(\varphi \to \psi)$. As $\Box(\varphi \to \psi) \to (\varphi \vee (\varphi \to (\varphi \to \psi))$ is an instance of the axiom KM, we get $\Gamma \vdash \varphi \vee (\varphi \to (\varphi \to \psi))$, hence $\Gamma \vdash \varphi \vee (\varphi \to \psi)$. A reasoning by cases ( ) and the use of $\Gamma, \varphi \vdash_{\mathsf{KMH}} \psi \vee \bigvee \Delta$ gives us $\Gamma \vdash (\varphi \to \psi) \vee \bigvee \Delta$.

Now, for the right direction assume $\Gamma \vdash_{\mathsf{KMH}} \varphi$. We reason by induction on the proof, essentially proving that the sequent calculus simulates the axiomatic step, crucially using the admissibility of cut in the MP case. ∎

Remark 2. Two universes co-exist in Rocq: the impredicative universe `Prop` and the predicative universe `Type`. Proving a statement in `Type` requires constructing a concrete proof term, which can later be inspected to build other terms. However, a proof of a statement in `Prop` only guarantees that the property holds, without granting the ability to inspect the proof. As we defined KMH in `Prop` and G4KM in `Type`, the second part of our proof above is illegal in Rocq: the sheer existence of an axiomatic proof cannot directly be used to build a concrete sequent proof. However, the decidability of G4KM comes to the rescue by allowing us to produce a proof from the knowledge of the existence of one.

4 Uniform Interpolation for KM à la Pitts

We recall the definition of the uniform interpolation property for a logic.

Definition 5. *A logic* L *has the* uniform interpolation property *if, for every* L*-formula* φ *and variable* p*, there exist* L*-formulas, denoted by* $\forall p\varphi$ *and* $\exists p\varphi$*, satisfying the following three properties:*

1. p-freeness: $\mathit{Vars}(\exists p\varphi) \subseteq \mathit{Vars}(\varphi) \setminus \{p\}$ *and* $\mathit{Vars}(\forall p\varphi) \subseteq \mathit{Vars}(\varphi) \setminus \{p\}$,
2. implication: $\vdash_{\mathsf{L}} \varphi \to \exists p\varphi$ *and* $\vdash_{\mathsf{L}} \forall p\varphi \to \varphi$*, and*
3. uniformity: *for each formula* ψ *with* $p \notin \mathit{Vars}(\psi)$*:*

$$\vdash_{\mathsf{L}} \varphi \to \psi \quad \textit{implies} \quad \vdash_{\mathsf{L}} \exists p\varphi \to \psi,$$
$$\vdash_{\mathsf{L}} \psi \to \varphi \quad \textit{implies} \quad \vdash_{\mathsf{L}} \psi \to \forall p\varphi.$$

As suggested by the notation, this property is related to the interpretability in the propositional language of existential and universal propositional quantifiers.

As we are going to prove this property for KM via its sequent calculus, we first need to generalise its definition to sequent calculi.

Definition 6. *A set of provable sequents, denoted* $\vdash$*, has the* uniform interpolation property *if, for any sequent* $\Gamma \Rightarrow \Delta$ *and variable* p*, there exist formulas* $\mathsf{E}_p(\Gamma)$ *and* $\mathsf{A}_p(\Gamma \Rightarrow \Delta)$ *such that the following three properties hold:*

1. p-freeness: *(a)* $Vars(\mathsf{E}_p(\Gamma)) \subseteq Vars(\Gamma) \setminus \{p\}$
   (b) $Vars(\mathsf{A}_p(\Gamma \Rightarrow \Delta)) \subseteq Vars(\Gamma, \Delta) \setminus \{p\}$,
2. implication: *(a)* $\vdash \Gamma \Rightarrow \mathsf{E}_p(\Gamma)$ *and (b)* $\vdash \Gamma, \mathsf{A}_p(\Gamma \Rightarrow \Delta) \Rightarrow \Delta$, *and*
3. uniformity : *for any multisets* Π *and* Σ *such that* $p \notin Vars(\Pi, \Sigma)$:

   (a) if $p \notin Vars(\Sigma)$ *and* $\vdash \Pi, \Gamma \Rightarrow \Sigma$ *then* $\vdash \Pi, \mathsf{E}_p(\Gamma) \Rightarrow \Sigma$
   (b) if $\vdash \Pi, \Gamma \Rightarrow \Delta$ *then* $\vdash \Pi, \mathsf{E}_p(\Gamma) \Rightarrow \mathsf{A}_p(\Gamma \Rightarrow \Delta)$.

We say that a sequent calculus S *has* uniform interpolation *if* $\vdash_{\mathsf{S}}$ *has the uniform interpolation property.*

Proposition 6. *If* G4KM *has the uniform interpolation property (Definition 6), then the logic* KM *has the uniform interpolation property (Definition 5).*

Proof. Choose $\exists p\varphi := \mathsf{E}_p(\{\varphi\})$ and $\forall p\varphi := \mathsf{A}_p(\emptyset \Rightarrow \{\varphi\})$ and notice that $\mathsf{E}_p\emptyset$ is a tautology. ■

Remark 3. The generalisation of the uniform interpolation property from formulas to sequents is not straightforward, especially for multi-succedents sequents. Indeed one could be tempted to formulate the sub-property 3.(b) as:

$$\text{if } \vdash \Pi, \Gamma \Rightarrow \Delta, \Sigma \text{ then } \vdash \Pi, \mathsf{E}_p(\Gamma) \Rightarrow \mathsf{A}_p(\Gamma \Rightarrow \Delta), \Sigma.$$

However, this is *a priori* a strictly stronger statement as it would entail the interpretability of a universal propositional quantifier satisfying the constant domain axiom [25]:

$$\forall p.(\varphi(p) \vee \psi) \to (\forall p.\varphi(p) \vee \psi)$$

for any p-free formula ψ. This axiom is provable in second-order classical logic, but not in the intuitionistic counterpart. While the left uniform interpolants of IPC provide an interpretation of this universal quantifier [2], our work seems to only establish the interpretation of a weaker, more standard universal quantifier. However, we see no theoretical contradiction (yet) in the possibility of interpreting stronger versions of this quantifier in KM.

We follow the structure of Pitts' original construction and its adaptation [22] by defining both interpolants of sequents via mutual induction on the well-founded ordering on sequents.

Definition 7. *We define* $\mathsf{E_p}(\Gamma) := \bigwedge \mathcal{E}_\mathsf{p}(\Gamma)$ *and* $\mathsf{A_p}(\Gamma \Rightarrow \Delta) := \bigvee \mathcal{A}_\mathsf{p}(\Gamma \Rightarrow \Delta)$ *where* $\mathcal{E}_\mathsf{p}(\Gamma)$ *and* $\mathcal{A}_\mathsf{p}(\Gamma \Rightarrow \Delta)$ *are sets of formulas defined by the table in Fig. 3.*

[2] In fact, in IPC they provide an interpretation of the stronger universal quantifier which fully distributes over disjunctions [49, Example 10].

	Γ matches	$\mathcal{E}_p(\Gamma)$ contains
$(\mathsf{E_p}0)^*$	$\Gamma', \bot$	$\bot$
$(\mathsf{E_p}1)^*$	Γ', q	$\mathsf{E}_p(\Gamma') \wedge q$
$(\mathsf{E_p}2)^*$	$\Gamma', \psi_1 \wedge \psi_2$	$\mathsf{E}_p(\Gamma', \psi_1, \psi_2)$
$(\mathsf{E_p}3)^*$	$\Gamma', \psi_1 \vee \psi_2$	$\mathsf{E}_p(\Gamma', \psi_1) \vee \mathsf{E}_p(\Gamma', \psi_2)$
$(\mathsf{E_p}4)$	$\Gamma', (q \to \psi)$	$q \to \mathsf{E}_p(\Gamma', \psi)$
$(\mathsf{E_p}5)^*$	$\Gamma', r, (r \to \psi)$	$\mathsf{E}_p(\Gamma', r, \psi)$
$(\mathsf{E_p}6)^*$	$\Gamma', (\delta_1 \wedge \delta_2) \to \delta_3$	$\mathsf{E}_p(\Gamma', \delta_1 \to (\delta_2 \to \delta_3))$
$(\mathsf{E_p}7)^*$	$\Gamma', (\delta_1 \vee \delta_2) \to \delta_3$	$\mathsf{E}_p(\Gamma', \delta_1 \to \delta_3, \delta_2 \to \delta_3))$
$(\mathsf{E_p}8)$	$\Gamma', (\delta_1 \to \delta_2) \to \delta_3$	$\Box[\mathsf{E}_p(\Box^{-1}\Gamma', (\delta_2 \to \delta_3), \delta_1) \to \mathsf{A}_p(\Box^{-1}\Gamma', (\delta_2 \to \delta_3), \delta_1 \Rightarrow \delta_2)] \to (\mathsf{E}_p(\Gamma', \delta_3) \vee \mathsf{E}_p(\Gamma', \delta_1 \to \delta_3, \delta_1))$
$(\mathsf{E_p}9)$	$\Gamma', \Box\psi$	$\Box\mathsf{E}_p(\Box^{-1}\Gamma')$
$(\mathsf{E_p}10)$	$\Gamma', \Box\delta_1 \to \delta_2$	$\Box[\mathsf{E}_p(\Box^{-1}\Gamma', \Box\delta_1, \delta_2) \to \mathsf{A}_p(\Box^{-1}\Gamma', \Box\delta_1, \delta_2 \Rightarrow \delta_1)] \to \mathsf{E}_p(\Gamma', \delta_2)$

	$\Gamma \Rightarrow \Delta$ matches	$\mathcal{A}_p(\Gamma \Rightarrow \Delta)$ contains
$(\mathsf{A_p}1)^*$	$\Gamma', q \Rightarrow \Delta$	$\mathsf{A}_p(\Gamma' \Rightarrow \Delta)$
$(\mathsf{A_p}2)^*$	$\Gamma', \psi_1 \wedge \psi_2 \Rightarrow \Delta$	$\mathsf{A}_p(\Gamma', \psi_1, \psi_2 \Rightarrow \Delta)$
$(\mathsf{A_p}3)^*$	$\Gamma', \psi_1 \vee \psi_2 \Rightarrow \Delta$	$[\mathsf{E}_p(\Gamma', \psi_1) \to \mathsf{A}_p(\Gamma', \psi_1 \Rightarrow \Delta)] \wedge [\mathsf{E}_p(\Gamma', \psi_2) \to \mathsf{A}_p(\Gamma', \psi_2 \Rightarrow \Delta)]$
$(\mathsf{A_p}4)$	$\Gamma', (q \to \psi) \Rightarrow \Delta$	$q \wedge \mathsf{A}_p(\Gamma', \psi \Rightarrow \Delta)$
$(\mathsf{A_p}5)^*$	$\Gamma', r, (r \to \psi) \Rightarrow \Delta$	$\mathsf{A}_p(\Gamma', r, \psi \Rightarrow \Delta)$
$(\mathsf{A_p}6)^*$	$\Gamma', (\delta_1 \wedge \delta_2) \to \delta_3 \Rightarrow \Delta$	$\mathsf{A}_p(\Gamma', \delta_1 \to (\delta_2 \to \delta_3) \Rightarrow \Delta)$
$(\mathsf{A_p}7)^*$	$\Gamma', (\delta_1 \vee \delta_2) \to \delta_3 \Rightarrow \Delta$	$\mathsf{A}_p(\Gamma', \delta_1 \to \delta_3, \delta_2 \to \delta_3 \Rightarrow \Delta)$
$(\mathsf{A_p}8)$	$\Gamma', (\delta_1 \to \delta_2) \to \delta_3 \Rightarrow \Delta$	$[\mathsf{E}_p(\Gamma', (\delta_2 \to \delta_3), \delta_1) \to \mathsf{A}_p(\Gamma', (\delta_2 \to \delta_3), \delta_1 \Rightarrow \Delta)] \wedge \Box[\mathsf{E}_p(\Box^{-1}\Gamma', (\delta_2 \to \delta_3), \delta_1) \to \mathsf{A}_p(\Box^{-1}\Gamma', (\delta_2 \to \delta_3), \delta_1 \Rightarrow \delta_2)] \wedge \mathsf{E}_p(\Gamma', \delta_3) \to \mathsf{A}_p(\Gamma', \delta_3 \Rightarrow \Delta)$
$(\mathsf{A_p}9)$	$\Gamma \Rightarrow \Delta, q$	q
$(\mathsf{A_p}10)^*$	$\Gamma, p \Rightarrow \Delta, p$	$\top$
$(\mathsf{A_p}11)^*$	$\Gamma \Rightarrow \Delta, \varphi_1 \wedge \varphi_2$	$\mathsf{A}_p(\Gamma \Rightarrow \Delta, \varphi_1) \wedge \mathsf{A}_p(\Gamma \Rightarrow \Delta, \varphi_2)$
$(\mathsf{A_p}12)^*$	$\Gamma \Rightarrow \Delta, \varphi_1 \vee \varphi_2$	$\mathsf{A}_p(\Gamma \Rightarrow \Delta, \varphi_1, \varphi_2)$
$(\mathsf{A_p}13)$	$\Gamma \Rightarrow \Delta, \varphi_1 \to \varphi_2$	$\Box[\mathsf{E}_p(\Box^{-1}\Gamma', \varphi_1) \to \mathsf{A}_p(\Box^{-1}\Gamma', \varphi_1 \Rightarrow \varphi_2)] \wedge [\mathsf{E}_p(\Gamma, \varphi_1) \to \mathsf{A}_p(\Gamma, \varphi_1 \Rightarrow \Delta, \varphi_2)]$
$(\mathsf{A_p}14)$	$\Gamma \Rightarrow \Delta, \Box\varphi$	$\Box[\mathsf{E}_p(\Box^{-1}\Gamma', \Box\varphi) \to \mathsf{A}_p(\Box^{-1}\Gamma', \Box\varphi \Rightarrow \varphi)]$
$(\mathsf{A_p}15)$	$\Gamma', \Box\delta_1 \to \delta_2 \Rightarrow \Delta$	$\Box[\mathsf{E}_p(\Box^{-1}\Gamma', \Box\delta_1, \delta_2) \to \mathsf{A}_p(\Box^{-1}\Gamma', \Box\delta_1, \delta_2 \Rightarrow \delta_1)] \wedge \mathsf{A}_p(\Gamma', \delta_2 \Rightarrow \Delta)$

Fig. 3. Clauses to define $\mathsf{E}_p(\Gamma)$ and $\mathsf{A}_p(\Gamma \Rightarrow \Delta)$. In all clauses, $q \neq p$.

Remark 4. While we show in Theorem 2 that Definition 7 indeed defines uniform interpolants for G4KM, syntactically smaller formulas may also work. For instance, when Γ (resp. $\Gamma \Rightarrow \Delta$) matches a line of the form $(\mathsf{E_p}n)^*$ (resp. $(\mathsf{A_p}n)^*$) in the table, then $\mathsf{E_p}(\Gamma)$ (resp. $\mathsf{A_p}(\Gamma \Rightarrow \Delta)$) can be *defined* as the right-hand side of that line. Indeed, such lines correspond to invertible rules in G4KM.

The (very!) astute reader may have noticed an oddity in $(\mathsf{A_p}8)$ of the definition of the interpolant: in the first line, the recursive $\mathsf{A_p}$ call is on $\Gamma', (\delta_2 \to \delta_3), \delta_1 \Rightarrow \Delta$, and not on the premise $\Gamma', (\delta_2 \to \delta_3), \delta_1 \Rightarrow \delta_2, \Delta$ of the rule $(\to\to\text{L})$. This disappearance of δ_2 on the right-hand side of this sequent in $(\mathsf{A_p}8)$ is motivated by the case of the $(\to\to\text{L})$-rule in the proof of uniformity: if it appeared in the recursive call, then the proof for this case would not go through. The source of this problem is the fact that $(\to\to\text{L})$ is the only left rule with a premise whose right-hand side mixes formulas from the conclusion's left- and right-hand sides. The following alternative to $(\twoheadrightarrow\text{L})$ does not suffer from this issue.

$$\frac{\Gamma, \chi \to \psi, \varphi \Rightarrow \Delta \qquad \Box^{-1}\Gamma, \chi \to \psi, \varphi \Rightarrow \chi \qquad \Gamma, \psi \Rightarrow \Delta}{\Gamma, (\varphi \to \chi) \to \psi \Rightarrow \Delta}\ (\twoheadrightarrow\text{L2})$$

Implicitly, this is the rule we use in $(\mathsf{A_p}8)$. Why is it safe to do so? Well, though we do not need to formally prove it, $(\twoheadrightarrow\text{L})$ and $(\twoheadrightarrow\text{L2})$ seem equivalent: the latter is easily proved admissible from the former and weakening on the right, while the former is admissible from the latter in presence of cut.[3]

A property of $(\twoheadrightarrow\text{L2})$ we crucially use in the proof of uniformity is its invertibility with respect to its left premise. Note that through weakening it entails the same result for $(\twoheadrightarrow\text{L})$.

Proposition 7. *The following rule is admissible in* G4KM.

$$\frac{\Gamma, (\varphi \to \psi) \to \chi \Rightarrow \Delta}{\Gamma, \varphi, (\psi \to \chi) \Rightarrow \Delta}\ (\twoheadrightarrow L^{-1})$$

A notable consequence of this result, reinforcing our trust in the choice for $(\mathsf{A_p}8)$, is that any sequent with a proof ending with $(\twoheadrightarrow\text{L})$ can also be proved by immediately applying $(\twoheadrightarrow\text{L2})$.

Theorem 2 ( ). KM *has the uniform interpolation property.*

Proof. It suffices to show that Definition 7 provides us with uniform interpolants for G4KM, i.e. prove the three properties of Definition 6. The *p-freeness* property ( ) is easily checked and the proof of *implication* ( ) does not differ much from the literature. The main new difficulty is the proof of *uniformity* ( ), which goes by well-founded induction, in particular in the case (b) of $(\twoheadrightarrow\text{L})$: we are given a p-free Π and a proof π of $\Pi, \Gamma \Rightarrow \Delta$ whose last rule applied is $(\twoheadrightarrow\text{L})$ with principal formula $(\varphi \to \psi) \to \chi$, which can either belong to Π or Γ.

If $(\varphi \to \psi) \to \chi \in \Pi$ then π has the following shape.

$$\frac{\overset{\pi_1}{\Pi', \psi \to \chi, \varphi, \Gamma \Rightarrow \Delta, \psi} \quad \overset{\pi_2}{\Box^{-1}\Pi', \psi \to \chi, \varphi, \Box^{-1}\Gamma \Rightarrow \psi} \quad \overset{\pi_3}{\Pi', \chi, \Gamma \Rightarrow \Delta}}{\Pi', (\varphi \to \psi) \to \chi, \Gamma \Rightarrow \Delta}\ (\twoheadrightarrow\text{L})$$

We now need to prove the sequent $\Pi', (\varphi \to \psi) \to \chi, \mathsf{E}_p(\Gamma) \Rightarrow \mathsf{A}_p(\Gamma \Rightarrow \Delta)$. For brevity, denote $\mathsf{E}_p(\Gamma)$ by E_p^0 and $\mathsf{A}_p(\Gamma \Rightarrow \Delta)$ by A_p^0.

$$\frac{\Pi', \psi \to \chi, \varphi, \mathsf{E}_p^0 \Rightarrow \mathsf{A}_p^0, \psi \quad \Box^{-1}\Pi', \psi \to \chi, \varphi, \Box^{-1}\mathsf{E}_p^0 \Rightarrow \psi \quad \Pi', \chi, \mathsf{E}_p^0 \Rightarrow \mathsf{A}_p^0}{\Pi', (\varphi \to \psi) \to \chi, \mathsf{E}_p^0 \Rightarrow \mathsf{A}_p^0}\ (\twoheadrightarrow\text{L})$$

The middle premise is obtained by noticing that $\mathsf{E}_p(\Gamma)$ implies $\Box\mathsf{E}_p(\Box^{-1}\Gamma)$ using rule $(\mathsf{E_p}9)$ and then applying (IH) on π_2. The rightmost premise is a direct application of (IH) on π_3. The leftmost premise however, cannot be

[3] Whether cut is admissible in the system with $(\twoheadrightarrow\text{L2})$ instead of $(\twoheadrightarrow\text{L})$ is unclear: a straightforward adaptation of the argument for G4KM does not seem to work.

derived from (IH) on π_1. Indeed, case (a) is not applicable as Δ is not necessarily p-free; and case (b) only proves $\Pi', \psi \to \chi, \varphi, \mathsf{E}_p(\Gamma) \Rightarrow \mathsf{A}_p(\Gamma \Rightarrow \Delta, \psi)$. This is where Proposition 7 crucially plays a role: from π, we can obtain a proof π_1' of $\Pi', \psi \to \chi, \varphi, \Gamma \Rightarrow \Delta$. This allows the first premise to be proved by weakening ψ on the right and applying the induction hypothesis (IH) on π_1', whose end sequent is smaller than that of π.

If $(\varphi \to \psi) \to \chi \in \Gamma$ then π has the following shape.

$$\dfrac{\overset{\pi_1}{\Pi, \Gamma', \psi \to \chi, \varphi \Rightarrow \Delta, \psi} \quad \overset{\pi_2}{\Box^{-1}\Pi, \Box^{-1}\Gamma', \psi \to \chi, \varphi \Rightarrow \psi} \quad \overset{\pi_3}{\Pi, \Gamma', \chi \Rightarrow \Delta}}{\Pi, \Gamma, (\varphi \to \psi) \to \chi \Rightarrow \Delta}\ (\to\to\mathrm{L})$$

Again, Proposition 7 entails that there is a proof π_1' of $\Pi, \Gamma', \psi \to \chi, \varphi \Rightarrow \Delta$. We now need to prove the sequent $\Pi, \mathsf{E}_p(\Gamma', (\varphi \to \psi) \to \chi \Rightarrow \Delta) \Rightarrow \mathsf{A}_p(\Gamma', (\varphi \to \psi) \to \chi \Rightarrow \Delta)$. After weakening on the left, we notice an instance of ($\mathsf{A_p}8$) on the right, producing three formulas which easily follow using $(\to\mathrm{R})$ and $(\Box\mathrm{R})$ and the induction hypothesis on π_1', π_2 and π_3:

$$(1) \vdash \Pi, \mathsf{E}_p(\Gamma', \psi \to \chi, \varphi \Rightarrow \Delta) \Rightarrow \mathsf{A}_p(\Gamma', \psi \to \chi, \varphi \Rightarrow \Delta)$$
$$(2) \vdash \Box^{-1}\Pi, \mathsf{E}_p(\Box^{-1}\Gamma', \psi \to \chi, \varphi \Rightarrow \psi) \Rightarrow \mathsf{A}_p(\Box^{-1}\Gamma', \psi \to \chi, \varphi \Rightarrow \psi)$$
$$(3) \vdash \Pi, \mathsf{E}_p(\Gamma', \chi \Rightarrow \Delta) \Rightarrow \mathsf{A}_p(\Gamma', \chi \Rightarrow \Delta).$$

■

5 Algebraic Consequence of Uniform Interpolation

Uniform interpolation for KM has a direct consequence on the class of algebras corresponding to this logic: *coherence.*

Definition 8 ( ). *A KM-algebra is a Heyting algebra* $(A, \bot, \wedge, \vee, \to)$ *together with a unary operator* $\Box : A \to A$ *satisfying*

$\Box\top = \top \quad \Box a \wedge \Box b = \Box(a \wedge b) \quad a \leq \Box a \quad \Box a \to a = a \quad \Box a \leq b \vee (b \to a)$

where $\top := \bot \to \bot$ *and* $a \leq b$ *is notation for* $a = a \wedge b$*. We denote the class of KM-algebras by* KMAlg.

Formulas are evaluated over KM-algebras via the notion of interpretation.

Definition 9 ( ). *Let* A *be a KM-algebra. A* valuation *on* A *is a function* $v : \mathsf{Prop} \to A$*. Given a valuation* v *over* A *and a formula* φ*, we recursively define the* interpretation $\hat{v}(\varphi)$ of φ in A via v *as follows, where* $\star \in \{\wedge, \vee, \to\}$*:*

$$\hat{v}(p) := v(p) \qquad \hat{v}(\bot) := \bot \qquad \hat{v}(\varphi_1 \star \varphi_2) := \hat{v}(\psi) \star \hat{v}(\chi) \qquad \hat{v}(\Box\psi) := \Box\hat{v}(\psi)$$

We define the algebraic entailment as follows:

$$\Gamma \models_{\mathcal{A}} \varphi \qquad \textit{iff} \qquad \forall A \in \mathsf{KMAlg}.\, \forall v.\ [\forall \gamma \in \Gamma.\ \hat{v}(\gamma) = \top] \Rightarrow \hat{v}(\varphi) = \top$$

In contrast to the Kripke case, we have that KM coincides with its algebraic semantics [47, Proposition 3.7]: $\Gamma \vdash_{\mathsf{KMH}} \varphi$ if and only if $\Gamma \models_{\mathcal{A}} \varphi$ ( ). In fact, this coincidence is extremely strong: KM is *finitely algebraisable* over KM-algebras (, , ,) in the sense of abstract algebraic logic [23], with $\{x = \top\}$ as defining equations and $\{x \leftrightarrow y\}$ as equivalence formulas.

A so-called *bridge theorem* [23, Section 3.6] leverages algebraisability to inform us that if KM satisfies uniform interpolation, then KMAlg satisfies the property of coherence [34,41]: any finitely generated subalgebra of a finitely presented member of KMAlg is finitely presented. Consequently, Theorem 2 and the algebraisability of KM give us the coherence of KMAlg, a novel result.

Corollary 1. *The class* KMAlg *of KM-algebras is coherent.*

6 Conclusion

Our novel multi-succedent calculus G4KM helped us establish uniform interpolation for KM via a porting of Pitts' technique to the multi-succedent setting. Some difficulties had to be overcome on the way: the semantically inspired modifications made to the rule $(\to\text{R})$, and the generalisation of the definition of uniform interpolation to multi-succedent sequents in an intuitionistic setting which avoids capturing the constant-domain universal quantifier. We also drew a direct algebraic consequence of uniform interpolation by showing that coherence holds of the class of KM-algebras. To ensure the highest level of trust in our results, we mechanised them all in the proof assistant Rocq.

In future work, we intend to leverage the insights gained in this paper, both in the design of G4KM and in the adaptation of Pitts' technique, to show uniform interpolation for relevant logics: the Gödel-Dummett logic LC and the combination of KM and LC, called KM_{lin}. While uniform interpolation is only open for the latter and not the former [27,46], applying the adaptation of Pitts' technique to LC can still be of interest: the size or production time of interpolants [6] may be smaller using the technique employed here than with the usual procedure exploiting the locally finiteness and Craig interpolation of LC.

Acknowledgments. The authors would like to thank Rosalie Iemhoff for her encouragements in pursuing this project, Mojtaba Mojtahedi for his counterexample of strong completeness for KM, Rodrigo Nicolau Almeida for bringing this logic (back) to our attention, Sam van Gool for his clarifications on the proof of uniform interpolation for LC, and Rajeev Goré for helpful comments on a late version of our draft. The second author has been supported by (1) a UKRI Future Leaders Fellowship, 'Structure vs Invariants in Proofs', project reference MR/S035540/1, and (2) the Renaissance Philanthropy grant DEEPER.

Reference

1. D'Abrera, C., Dawson, J., Goré, R.: A formally verified cut-elimination procedure for linear nested sequents for tense logic. In: Das, A., Negri, S. (eds.) TABLEAUX 2021. LNCS (LNAI), vol. 12842, pp. 281–298. Springer, Cham (2021). https://doi.org/10.1007/978-3-030-86059-2_17
2. Bílková, M.: Uniform interpolation and propositional quantifiers in modal logics. Studia Logica **85**(1), 1–31 (2007). http://www.jstor.org/stable/40210757
3. Bilotta, A., Maggesi, M., Perini Brogi, C.: A modular proof of semantic completeness for normal systems beyond the modal cube, formalised in HOLMS. In: Moscardelli, L., Scozzari, F. (eds.) Proceedings of the 26th Italian Conference on Theoretical Computer Science, Pescara, Italy, 10–12 September 2025. CEUR Workshop Proceedings, vol. 4039, pp. 154–162. CEUR-WS.org (2025). https://ceur-ws.org/Vol-4039/paper10.pdf
4. Bilotta, A., Maggesi, M., Perini Brogi, C., Quartini, L.: Growing holms, a HOL light library for modal systems. In: Porello, D., Vinci, C., Zavatteri, M. (eds.) Short Paper Proceedings of the 6th International Workshop on Artificial Intelligence and Formal Verification, Logic, Automata, and Synthesis, OVERLAY 2024, Bolzano, Italy, 28–29 November 2024. CEUR Workshop Proceedings, vol. 3904, pp. 41–48. CEUR-WS.org (2024). https://ceur-ws.org/Vol-3904/paper5.pdf
5. Božić, M., Došen, K.: Models for normal intuitionistic modal logics. Stud. Logica. **43**, 217–245 (1984). https://doi.org/10.1007/BF02429840
6. CateTen Cate, B., Kuijer, L., Wolter, F.: The Size of Interpolants in Modal Logics (2025). https://arxiv.org/abs/2511.04577
7. Chapman, P.: Tools and techniques for formalising structural proof theory. St Andrews, Ph.D. thesis (2010)
8. Clouston, R., Goré, R.: Sequent calculus in the topos of trees. In: Pitts, A. (ed.) FoSSaCS 2015. LNCS, vol. 9034, pp. 133–147. Springer, Heidelberg (2015). https://doi.org/10.1007/978-3-662-46678-0_9
9. Coquand, T.: Infinite objects in type theory. In: Barendregt, H., Nipkow, T. (eds.) TYPES 1993. LNCS, vol. 806, pp. 62–78. Springer, Heidelberg (1994). https://doi.org/10.1007/3-540-58085-9_72
10. Dalmonte, T., Grellois, C., Olivetti, N.: Terminating calculi and countermodels for constructive modal logics. In: Das, A., Negri, S. (eds.) TABLEAUX 2021. LNCS (LNAI), vol. 12842, pp. 391–408. Springer, Cham (2021). https://doi.org/10.1007/978-3-030-86059-2_23
11. Darjania, G.K.: A sequential variant of modal system I^{Δ}. Metalogical Studies (1984). in Russian
12. Dawson, J.E., Clouston, R., Goré, R., Tiu, A.: From display calculi to deep nested sequent calculi: formalised for full intuitionistic linear logic. In: Diaz, J., Lanese, I., Sangiorgi, D. (eds.) TCS 2014. LNCS, vol. 8705, pp. 250–264. Springer, Heidelberg (2014). https://doi.org/10.1007/978-3-662-44602-7_20
13. Dawson, J.E., Goré, R.: Generic methods for formalising sequent calculi applied to provability logic. In: Fermüller, C.G., Voronkov, A. (eds.) LPAR 2010. LNCS, vol. 6397, pp. 263–277. Springer, Heidelberg (2010). https://doi.org/10.1007/978-3-642-16242-8_19
14. Doczkal, C.: A machine-checked constructive metatheory of computation tree logic. Ph.D. thesis, Saarland University (2016). http://scidok.sulb.uni-saarland.de/volltexte/2016/6451/

15. Doczkal, C., Bard, J.: Completeness and decidability of converse PDL in the constructive type theory of coq. In: Andronick, J., Felty, A.P. (eds.) Proceedings of the 7th ACM SIGPLAN International Conference on Certified Programs and Proofs, CPP 2018, Los Angeles, CA, USA, 8–9 January 2018, pp. 42–52. ACM (2018https://doi.org/10.1145/3167088
16. Dragalin, A.G.: Mathematical Intuitionism. Introduction to Proof Theory (Russian). Nauka, Moscow (1979). (Translation in Translations of mathematical monographs, vol. 67. American Mathematical Society, 1988)
17. Dummett, M.: A propositional calculus with denumerable matrix. J. Symb. Logic **24**(2), 97–106 (1959). http://www.jstor.org/stable/2964753
18. Dyckhoff, R.: A deterministic terminating sequent calculus for Gödel-Dummett logic. Logic J. IGPL **7**(3), 319–326 (1999). https://doi.org/10.1093/jigpal/7.3.319
19. Dyckhoff, R.: Contraction-free sequent calculi for intuitionistic logic. J. Symb. Log. **57**(3), 795–807 (1992). https://doi.org/10.2307/2275431
20. Dyckhoff, R., Negri, S.: Admissibility of structural rules for contraction-free systems of intuitionistic logic. J. Symb. Logic **65**(4), 1499–1518 (2000). https://doi.org/10.2307/2695061
21. Férée, H., Giessenvan der Giessen, I., Goolvan Gool, S., Shillito, I.: Mechanised uniform interpolation for modal logics K, GL, and iSL. In: Benzmüller, C., Heule, M., Schmidt, R. (eds.) Automated Reasoning. Lecture Notes in Computer Science, vol. 2, pp. 43–60. Springer, Heidelberg (2024).https://doi.org/10.1007/978-3-031-63501-4_3
22. Férée, H., van Gool, S.: Formalizing and computing propositional quantifiers. In: Proceedings of the 12th ACM SIGPLAN International Conference on Certified Programs and Proofs, CPP 2023, pp. 148–158. Association for Computing Machinery (2023). https://doi.org/10.1145/3573105.3575668
23. Font, J.M.: Abstract Algebraic Logic - An Introductory Textbook, Studies in Logic, vol. 60. College Publications, London (2016)
24. From, A.H.: Formalized soundness and completeness of epistemic and public announcement logic. J. Logic Comput. **35**(6) (2025). https://doi.org/10.1093/LOGCOM/EXAE054
25. Gabbay, D.M.: Second Order Propositional Calculus, pp. 159–169. Springer, Heidelberg (1981). https://doi.org/10.1007/978-94-017-2977-2_10
26. Ghilardi, S., Zawadowski, M.: Sheaves, Games, and Model Completions, A Categorical Approach to Nonclassical Propositional Logics, vol. 14. Springer, Dordrecht (2002). https://doi.org/10.1007/978-94-015-9936-8
27. Ghilardi, S., Zawadowski, M.: Model completions and r-Heyting categories. Ann. Pure Appl. Logic **88**(1), 27–46 (1997). https://doi.org/10.1016/S0168-0072(97)00012-2
28. GiessenVan der Giessen, I.: Uniform Interpolation and Admissible Rules. Proof-theoretic investigations into (intuitionistic) modal logics. Ph.D. thesis, Utrecht University (2022). https://dspace.library.uu.nl/bitstream/handle/1874/423244/proefschrift%20-%206343c2623d6ab.pdf
29. GiessenVan der Giessen, I., Iemhoff, R.: Proof theory for intuitionistic strong Löb logic. Accepted for publication in Special Volume of the Workshop Proofs! held in Paris in 2017 (2020). https://doi.org/10.48550/arXiv.2011.10383. preprint arXiv:2011.10383v2

30. GiessenVan der Giessen, I., Iemhoff, R.: Sequent calculi for intuitionistic Gödel-Löb logic. Notre Dame J. Formal Logic **62**(2) (2021). https://doi.org/10.1215/00294527-2021-0011
31. van der Giessen, I., Jalali, R., Kuznets, R.: Uniform interpolation via nested sequents. In: Silva, A., Wassermann, R., de Queiroz, R. (eds.) WoLLIC 2021. LNCS, vol. 13038, pp. 337–354. Springer, Cham (2021). https://doi.org/10.1007/978-3-030-88853-4_21
32. GiessenVan der Giessen, I., Jalali, R., Kuznets, R.: Extensions of K5: proof theory and uniform lyndon interpolation. In: Ramanayake, R., Urban, J. (eds.) Automated Reasoning with Analytic Tableaux and Related Methods, TABLEAUX, pp. 263–282. Springer, Cham (2023)https://doi.org/10.1007/978-3-031-43513-3_15
33. GiessenVan der Giessen, I., Jalali, R., Kuznets, R.: Uniform interpolation via nested sequents and hypersequents. J. Logic Comput. **35**(6) (2025). https://doi.org/10.1093/LOGCOM/EXAE053
34. GoolVan Gool, S., Metcalfe, G., Tsinakis, C.: Uniform interpolation and compact congruences. Ann. Pure Appl. Logic **168**(10), 1927–1948 (2017). https://doi.org/10.1016/j.apal.2017.05.001
35. Goré, R., Ramanayake, R., Shillito, I.: Cut-elimination for provability logic by terminating proof-search: formalised and deconstructed using coq. In: Das, A., Negri, S. (eds.) TABLEAUX 2021. LNCS (LNAI), vol. 12842, pp. 299–313. Springer, Cham (2021). https://doi.org/10.1007/978-3-030-86059-2_18
36. Goré, R., Shillito, I.: Direct elimination of additive-cuts in GL4ip: verified and extracted. In: Fernández-Duque, D., Palmigiano, A., Pinchinat, S. (eds.) Advances in Modal Logic, AiML, pp. 429–449. College Publications (2022). http://www.aiml.net/volumes/volume14/26-Gore-Shillito.pdf
37. Hagemeier, C., Kirst, D.: Constructive and mechanised meta-theory of IEL and similar modal logics. J. Log. Comput. **32**(8), 1585–1610 (2022). https://doi.org/10.1093/LOGCOM/EXAC068
38. Hudelmaier, J.: An O(n log n)-space decision procedure for intuitionistic propositional logic. J. Logic Comput. **3**(1), 63–75 (1993). https://doi.org/10.1093/logcom/3.1.63
39. Iemhoff, R.: Uniform interpolation and sequent calculi in modal logic. Arch. Math. Logic **58**(1–2), 155–181 (2019)
40. Iemhoff, R.: The G4i analogue of a G3i sequent calculus. Stud. Logica. **110**(6), 1493–1506 (2022). https://doi.org/10.1007/s11225-022-10008-3
41. Kowalski, T., Metcalfe, G.: Uniform interpolation and coherence. Ann. Pure Appl. Logic **170**(7), 825–841 (2019). https://doi.org/10.1016/j.apal.2019.02.004
42. Kurahashi, T.: Interpolation properties for several logics. https://www2.kobe-u.ac.jp/~tk/jp/notes/ULIP.html. Accessed 06 Jan 2026
43. Larchey-Wendling, D.: Constructive decision via redundancy-free proof-search. J. Autom. Reason. **64**(7), 1197–1219 (2020). https://doi.org/10.1007/s10817-020-09555-y
44. Maehara, S.: Eine darstellung der intuitionistischen logik in der klassischen. Nagoya Math. J. **7**, 45–64 (1954). https://doi.org/10.1017/S0027763000018055
45. Maggesi, M., Perini Brogi, C.: Mechanising Gödel-Löb provability logic in HOL light. J. Autom. Reason. **67**(3), 29 (2023). https://doi.org/10.1007/S10817-023-09677-Z

46. Maksimova, L.L.: Craig's theorem in superintuitionistic logics and almagamable varieties of pseudo-boolean algebras. Algebra Logic **16**, 427–455 (1977). https://doi.org/10.1007/BF01670006
47. Muravitsky, A.: Logic KM: a biography. In: Bezhanishvili, G. (ed.) Leo Esakia on Duality in Modal and Intuitionistic Logics, pp. 155–185. Springer, Dordrecht (2014). https://doi.org/10.1007/978-94-017-8860-1_7
48. Nakano, H.: A modality for recursion. In: Proceedings Fifteenth Annual IEEE Symposium on Logic in Computer Science (Cat. No.99CB36332), pp. 255–266 (2000). https://doi.org/10.1109/LICS.2000.855774
49. Pitts, A.M.: On an interpretation of second order quantification in first order intuitionistic propositional logic. J. Symb. Log. **57**(1), 33–52 (1992). https://doi.org/10.2307/2275175
50. Savateev, Y., Shamkanov, D.: Non-well-founded proofs for the grzegorczyk modal logic. Rev. Symb. Logic **14**(1), 22–50 (2021)
51. Shillito, I., van der Giessen, I., Goré, R., Iemhoff, R.: A new calculus for intuitionistic strong löb logic: strong termination and cut-elimination, formalised. In: Ramanayake, R., Urban, J. (eds.) Automated Reasoning with Analytic Tableaux and Related Methods - 32nd International Conference, TABLEAUX. Lecture Notes in Computer Science, vol. 14278, pp. 73–93. Springer, Heidelberg (2023). https://doi.org/10.1007/978-3-031-43513-3_5
52. The Rocq Development Team: The rocq prover (2025). https://doi.org/10.5281/zenodo.15149629
53. Valliappan, N.: Lax modal lambda calculi. In: Guerrini, S., König, B. (eds.) 34th EACSL Annual Conference on Computer Science Logic. CSL. LIPIcs. Schloss Dagstuhl - Leibniz-Zentrum für Informatik (2026)
54. Verbrugge, R.L.: The Stanford Encyclopedia of Philosophy. Presented at the (2024) Summer 2024 edn
55. Visser, A.: Uniform interpolation and layered bisimulation. In: Hájek, P. (ed.) Gödel '96 Proceedings, Lecture Notes in Logic, vol. 6, pp. 139–164. Springer, Cham (1996). http://projecteuclid.org/download/pdf_1/euclid.lnl/1235417019
56. Vorob'ev, N.N.: A new algorithm of derivability in a constructive calculus of statements. Trudy Matematicheskogo Instituta imeni V. A. Steklova **52**, 193–225 (1958). (Translation in American Mathematical Society Translations, series 2, volume 94, 1970)
57. Wu, M., Goré, R.: Verified decision procedures for modal logics. In: Harrison, J., O'Leary, J., Tolmach, A. (eds.) 10th International Conference on Interactive Theorem Proving, ITP. LIPIcs, vol. 141, pp. 31:1–31:19. Schloss Dagstuhl - Leibniz-Zentrum für Informatik (2019). https://doi.org/10.4230/LIPICS.ITP.2019.31

Open Access This chapter is licensed under the terms of the Creative Commons Attribution 4.0 International License (http://creativecommons.org/licenses/by/4.0/), which permits use, sharing, adaptation, distribution and reproduction in any medium or format, as long as you give appropriate credit to the original author(s) and the source, provide a link to the Creative Commons license and indicate if changes were made.

The images or other third party material in this chapter are included in the chapter's Creative Commons license, unless indicated otherwise in a credit line to the material. If material is not included in the chapter's Creative Commons license and your intended use is not permitted by statutory regulation or exceeds the permitted use, you will need to obtain permission directly from the copyright holder.

Uniform Interpolation with Constructive Diamond

Iris van der Giessen[1] and Ian Shillito[2,3(✉)]

[1] University of Amsterdam, Amsterdam, The Netherlands
i.vandergiessen@uva.nl
[2] University of Birmingham, Birmingham, UK
[3] University of Melbourne, Melbourne, Australia
ian.shillito@unimelb.edu.au

Abstract. Uniform interpolation is a strong form of interpolation providing an interpretation of propositional quantifiers within a propositional logic. Pitts' seminal work establishes this property for intuitionistic propositional logic relying on a sequent calculus in which naïve backward proof-search terminates. This constructive approach has been adapted to a wide range of logics, including intuitionistic modal logics. Surprisingly, no intuitionistic modal logic with independent box and diamond has yet been shown to satisfy uniform interpolation. We fill in this gap by proving the uniform interpolation property for Constructive K (CK) and Wijesekera's K (WK). We build on Pitts' technique by exploiting existing terminating calculi for CK and WK, which we prove to eliminate cut, and formalise all our results in the proof assistant Rocq. Together, our results constitute the first positive uniform interpolation results for intuitionistic modal logics with diamond.

Keywords: Uniform Interpolation · Proof Theory · Intuitionistic Modal Logic · Rocq

1 Introduction

Intuitionistic modal logics form a rich class of logics that formalise modal reasoning over an intuitionistic propositional base. They pop up in different forms and applications and are sensitive to many design choices. When considering intuitionistic modal logics with both $\Box$ and $\Diamond$, a common feature is that $\Box$ and $\Diamond$ are not interdefinable (this in contrast to classical modal logics). One traditionally identifies two main streams to define such logics: *Intuitionistic modal logic* and *Constructive modal logic*. Intuitionistic modal logics were early investigated by, e.g., Fischer Servi [29,30], Plotkin and Stirling [44], and Ewald [25] and are motivated by their algebraic connection to classical bi-modal logics [29,54–56] and their interpretation via the standard translation into first-order intuitionistic logic [48]. The base system in this setting is Intuitionistic K, here denoted IK, as a counterpart to classical modal logic K. Constructive modal logics are mostly

© The Author(s) 2026
A. Biere et al. (Eds.): IJCAR 2026, LNAI 16688, pp. 357–376, 2026.
https://doi.org/10.1007/978-3-032-32589-1_22

motivated by computational applications. Constructive K, here denoted CK, and its modal extensions are motivated by their Curry-Howard interpretation in type theory and their categorical semantics [5,10,11,39]. A closely related constructive modal logic is Wijesekera's system introduced to model reasoning in dynamic systems [52]. We denote its propositional part by WK.[1] Recently, new approaches have been proposed to define intuitionistic versions of classical K [8,9]. In this paper we concentrate on the well-studied constructive modal logics CK and WK.

The research on these two logics is extensive and revealed some surprises in recent years. Axiomatically, the two logics form extensions of intuitionistic propositional logic IL with the following modal rule and (subset) of modal axioms below. These axioms follow classically from the usual normality axiom $K_\Box$, but are independent in an intuitionistic setting. We define $\mathsf{CK} = \mathsf{IL} + \{K_\Box, K_\Diamond\}$ and $\mathsf{WK} = \mathsf{CK} + \{N\}$, and note that $\mathsf{CK} \subset \mathsf{WK}$.

$$\frac{\emptyset \vdash \varphi}{\Gamma \vdash \Box\varphi}\ (\mathrm{Nec}) \qquad \begin{array}{ll} K_\Box & \Box(\varphi \to \psi) \to (\Box\varphi \to \Box\psi) \\ K_\Diamond & \Box(\varphi \to \psi) \to (\Diamond\varphi \to \Diamond\psi) \\ N & \neg\Diamond\bot \end{array}$$

For semantic characterisations of the logics one can consult [34]. Recent studies [19–21,34] surprisingly resolved a common misbelief that the $\Diamond$-free fragments of Constructive and Intuitionistic modal logics coincide: those for CK and WK coincide with the $\Box$-only logic iK, but the one for IK is strictly stronger.

We are interested in the interpolation properties for CK and WK. Interpolation properties form a central theme in logic due to their good mathematical properties and widespread applications in computer science (see [16] for a recent overview on foundations, methods and applications of interpolation). *Craig interpolation* states that if φ entails ψ, there is a formula θ in the common vocabulary of φ and ψ such that φ entails θ and θ entails ψ. The formula θ is called the *interpolant* and explains the reason why φ entails ψ. *Uniform interpolation* is stronger, as the interpolant only depends on φ and uniformly works for any ψ in a specified vocabulary. This property makes it possible to provide an interpretation of propositional quantifiers within the propositional base [43].

Proof-theoretic methods are ideal for establishing metalogical results such as interpolation. Indeed, the Craig interpolation property has been established for WK in Wijesekera's original paper using a sequent calculus [52]. In [18], terminating sequent calculi for CK and WK were designed, but the uniform interpolation question was left open. Even though other systems are designed for CK and WK including a sequent system, a natural deduction system [10], a nested sequent calculus [7] and a focused 2-sequent calculus [42] for CK, and a tableaux calculus for the richer version CCDL of WK [53], neither Craig interpolation for CK nor uniform interpolation for CK or WK has been investigated. Most surprising, to the best of our knowledge, no other interpolation result is known

[1] Wijesekera's full system could be viewed as a more general intuitionistic modal logic than the Constructive Concurrent Dynamic Logic CCDL from [53]. Some authors also denote WK as CCDL (e.g., in [18]), although, originally, CCDL was introduced over a richer syntax including program constructors.

for *any* Constructive or Intuitionistic modal logic with independent □ and ◇ [40], also not via semantic means, except for one. We came to know via personal communication with N. Bezhanishvili that the intuitionistic modal logic MIPC [12,13,45], which can be viewed as an S5-extension of IK, does not have the Craig interpolation property.

In this paper we focus on constructive methods towards uniform interpolation. The seminal work of Pitts provides a proof-theoretic proof of uniform interpolation for IL using a strongly terminating sequent calculus. It is now a fruitful technique for proving uniform interpolation among many types of modal logic: classical modal logics [14,15,26], intuitionistic modal logics [26,38], modal substructural logics and linear logics [4,6], and non-normal modal and conditional logics [2]. However, these studies only treat mono-modal logics (with □), but do not cover intuitionistic modal logics with independent □ and ◇.

Our Contributions. We positively answer the uniform interpolation question for CK and WK. This question is specifically posed by Dalmonte, Grellois and Olivetti in [18] in which they designed strongly terminating sequent calculi for CK and WK. Our work can be seen as a follow-up in which we (1) provide single-succedent variants of these calculi and provide termination and cut-elimination proofs, (2) provide a *constructive* proof of uniform interpolation à la Pitts for CK and WK, and (3) contribute to The Rocq Prover [49] library for logics between CK and IK [34] by formalising all our results. All results described in this paper are accompanied by a clickable symbol “ ” leading to their formalisation.

Our work establishes the first positive uniform interpolation result among intuitionistic modal logics with independent □ and ◇. Since uniform interpolation is stronger than Craig interpolation, we immediately obtain the Craig interpolation property for CK and WK as well. The constructive approach in Rocq provides us with a uniform interpolation calculator for WK and CK already available for some classical and intuitionistic modal logics [26,27].

2 Preliminaries

In this section we fix the syntax and axiomatic calculi for CK and WK as presented in de Groot, Shillito and Clouston's work [34]. For the mechanisation of most of the elements of this section, we refer to their paper.

Using a countably infinite set of propositional variables $\mathsf{Prop} = \{p, q, r, \dots\}$, we define the language $\mathcal{L}$ via the following grammar in BNF notation ( ):

$$\varphi ::= p \in \mathsf{Prop} \mid \bot \mid \varphi \wedge \varphi \mid \varphi \vee \varphi \mid \varphi \rightarrow \varphi \mid \Box\varphi \mid \Diamond\varphi$$

We abbreviate $\neg\varphi := \varphi \rightarrow \bot$ and $\top := \neg\bot$. We use Greek lowercase letters, e.g. φ, ψ, χ and δ, to denote formulas, and Greek uppercase letters, e.g. $\Gamma, \Delta, \Phi, \Psi$, for multisets of formulas. For such a multiset Γ we define the two multisets $\Box\Gamma := \{\Box\varphi \mid \varphi \in \Gamma\}$ and $\Box^{-1}\Gamma := \{\varphi \mid \Box\varphi \in \Gamma\}$ and similarly for $\Diamond\Gamma$ and $\Diamond^{-1}\Gamma$. We also write $\Gamma \uplus \Delta$ for the *disjoint union* of multisets Γ and Δ. If Γ

Axioms

A_1 $\varphi \to (\psi \to \varphi)$
A_2 $(\varphi \to (\psi \to \chi)) \to (\varphi \to \psi) \to (\varphi \to \chi)$
A_3 $\varphi \to (\varphi \vee \psi)$
A_4 $\psi \to (\varphi \vee \psi)$
A_5 $(\varphi \to \chi) \to (\psi \to \chi) \to ((\varphi \vee \psi) \to \chi)$
A_6 $(\varphi \wedge \psi) \to \varphi$
A_7 $(\varphi \wedge \psi) \to \psi$
A_8 $(\varphi \to \psi) \to (\varphi \to \chi) \to (\varphi \to (\psi \wedge \chi))$
A_9 $\bot \to \varphi$
$K_\Box$ $\Box(\varphi \to \psi) \to (\Box\varphi \to \Box\psi)$
$K_\Diamond$ $\Box(\varphi \to \psi) \to (\Diamond\varphi \to \Diamond\psi)$
N $\neg\Diamond\bot$

Rules of Inference

$$\frac{\varphi \text{ is an instance of an axiom}}{\Gamma \vdash \varphi}\ (\mathrm{Ax}) \qquad \frac{\varphi \in \Gamma}{\Gamma \vdash \varphi}\ (\mathrm{El})$$

$$\frac{\emptyset \vdash \varphi}{\Gamma \vdash \Box\varphi}\ (\mathrm{Nec}) \qquad \frac{\Gamma \vdash \varphi \quad \Gamma \vdash \varphi \to \psi}{\Gamma \vdash \psi}\ (\mathrm{MP})$$

Fig. 1. Generalised Hilbert calculi CKH ( ) and WKH ( ).

is finite, $\bigvee \Gamma$ denotes the disjunction of all formulas in Γ and $\bigwedge \Gamma$ denotes the conjunction of all formulas in Γ, with the convention that $\bigvee \emptyset = \bot$ and $\bigwedge \emptyset = \top$.

To finish with the syntax, we define a notion which we use to show termination of backward proof-search in our sequent calculi.

Definition 1 ( ). *The weight $w(\varphi)$ of a formula is defined as follows.*

$$\begin{aligned} w(\bot) = w(p) &= 1 \\ w(\psi \vee \chi) = w(\psi \to \chi) &= w(\psi) + w(\chi) + 1 \\ w(\psi \wedge \chi) &= w(\psi) + w(\chi) + 2 \\ w(\Box\psi) = w(\Diamond\psi) &= w(\psi) + 1 \end{aligned}$$

We provide generalised Hilbert calculi for CK and WK, i.e. axiomatic calculi manipulating *consecutions* of the shape $\Gamma \vdash \varphi$ where Γ is a *set* of formulas. The calculus CKH for CK extends the one for intuitionistic logic IL, with its axioms and rules, with the necessitation rule (Nec) and axioms $K_\Box$ and $K_\Diamond$. The calculus WKH for WK is nothing but the calculus CKH augmented with the axiom N. All the axioms and rules just mentioned are presented in Fig. 1. We write $\Gamma \vdash_{\mathsf{H}} \varphi$ if $\Gamma \vdash \varphi$ is provable in H, for $\mathsf{H} \in \{\mathsf{CKH}, \mathsf{WKH}\}$.

3 Sequent Calculi for CK and WK

In this section we introduce the sequent calculi G4CK ( ) and G4WK ( ) for CK and WK, respectively. Sequents in these calculi, which are presented in Fig. 2, are expressions of the shape $\Gamma \Rightarrow \Delta$ where the *antecedent* Γ and the *succedent* Δ are both finite multisets of formulas. Note that Γ, φ and Γ, Π stand for $\Gamma \uplus \{\varphi\}$ and $\Gamma \uplus \Pi$, respectively. While antecedents are unconstrained multisets in both calculi, succedents need to have a cardinality of *exactly one* (i.e. $|\Delta| = 1$) in G4CK, and of *at most one* (i.e. $|\Delta| \leq 1$) in G4WK. This technically makes G4CK a *single-succedent* calculus, and G4WK a calculus with either *empty* or *singleton*

$$\frac{}{\Gamma, \bot \Rightarrow \Delta}\ (\bot\mathrm{L}) \qquad \frac{}{\Gamma, p \Rightarrow p}\ (\mathrm{IdP}) \qquad \frac{\Gamma, \varphi, \psi \Rightarrow \Delta}{\Gamma, \varphi \wedge \psi \Rightarrow \Delta}\ (\wedge\mathrm{L}) \qquad \frac{\Gamma \Rightarrow \varphi \quad \Gamma \Rightarrow \psi}{\Gamma \Rightarrow \varphi \wedge \psi}\ (\wedge\mathrm{R})$$

$$\frac{\Gamma, \varphi \Rightarrow \Delta \quad \Gamma, \psi \Rightarrow \Delta}{\Gamma, \varphi \vee \psi \Rightarrow \Delta}\ (\vee\mathrm{L}) \qquad \frac{\Gamma \Rightarrow \varphi_i}{\Gamma \Rightarrow \varphi_1 \vee \varphi_2}\ (\vee R_i)(i{\in}\{1,2\}) \qquad \frac{\Gamma, \varphi \Rightarrow \psi}{\Gamma \Rightarrow \varphi \to \psi}\ (\to\mathrm{R})$$

$$\frac{\Gamma, \varphi \to (\psi \to \chi) \Rightarrow \Delta}{\Gamma, (\varphi \wedge \psi) \to \chi \Rightarrow \Delta}\ (\wedge{\to}\mathrm{L}) \qquad \frac{\Gamma, \varphi \to \chi, \psi \to \chi \Rightarrow \Delta}{\Gamma, (\varphi \vee \psi) \to \chi \Rightarrow \Delta}\ (\vee{\to}\mathrm{L})$$

$$\frac{\Gamma, p, \varphi \Rightarrow \Delta}{\Gamma, p, p \to \varphi \Rightarrow \Delta}\ (p\ {\to}\mathrm{L}) \qquad \frac{\Gamma, \psi \to \chi \Rightarrow \varphi \to \psi \quad \Gamma, \chi \Rightarrow \Delta}{\Gamma, (\varphi \to \psi) \to \chi \Rightarrow \Delta}\ ({\to}{\to}\mathrm{L})$$

$$\frac{\Box^{-1}\Gamma \Rightarrow \varphi}{\Gamma \Rightarrow \Box\varphi}\ (\Box\mathrm{R}) \qquad \frac{\Box^{-1}\Gamma \Rightarrow \varphi \quad \Gamma, \psi \Rightarrow \Delta}{\Gamma, \Box\varphi \to \psi \Rightarrow \Delta}\ (\Box{\to}\mathrm{L})$$

$$\frac{\Box^{-1}\Gamma, \gamma \Rightarrow \varphi \quad \Gamma, \Diamond\gamma, \psi \Rightarrow \Delta}{\Gamma, \Diamond\gamma, \Diamond\varphi \to \psi \Rightarrow \Delta}\ (\Diamond{\to}\mathrm{L})$$

$$\frac{\Box^{-1}\Gamma, \varphi \Rightarrow \psi}{\Gamma, \Diamond\varphi \Rightarrow \Diamond\psi}\ (\Diamond\mathrm{L}) \qquad \frac{\Box^{-1}\Gamma, \varphi \Rightarrow \Diamond^{-1}\Delta}{\Gamma, \Diamond\varphi \Rightarrow \Delta}\ (\Diamond\mathrm{L'})$$

Fig. 2. The sequent calculi G4CK and G4WK. In the former succedents Δ are singletons of the shape $\{\delta\}$, while in the latter succedents are either singletons or the empty set. The rule ($\Diamond$L) (resp. ($\Diamond$L')) belongs to G4CK (resp. G4WK) exclusively.

succedents.[2] For simplicity, we call both calculi single-succedent. Beyond their succedents, these calculi differ on their rule for diamond on the left: the rule ($\Diamond$L) of G4CK is replaced by the rule ($\Diamond$L') in G4WK. Note that $\Diamond^{-1}\Delta$ is non-empty only if $\Delta = \{\Diamond\delta\}$. As shown below, ($\Diamond$L') is crucial to prove N.

$$\dfrac{\dfrac{\dfrac{}{\bot \Rightarrow}\ (\bot\mathrm{L})}{\Diamond\bot \Rightarrow \bot}\ (\Diamond\mathrm{L'})}{\Rightarrow \Diamond\bot \to \bot}\ (\to\mathrm{R})$$

We write $\vdash_{\mathsf{S}} \Gamma \Rightarrow \Delta$ when $\Gamma \Rightarrow \Delta$ is provable in S, with $\mathsf{S} \in \{\mathsf{G4CK}, \mathsf{G4WK}\}$.

G4CK and G4WK are connected to multiple calculi in the literature. First, they extend with rules for modalities the strongly terminating calculus G4ip for IL, which has been invented many times [23,35,51]. Second, they are extensions of Iemhoff's single-succedent calculus for iK [37] with rules for $\Diamond$. Third, our

[2] In Rocq, instead of using multisets restricted by a cardinality of at most 1, which is cumbersome, we used the `option` type ( ).

This type takes another type as argument, in our case the type of formulas, and has two constructor: `None`, simulating $\emptyset$, and `Some(`φ`)`, simulating $\{\varphi\}$.

calculi are single-succedent versions of Dalmonte, Grellois and Olivetti's multi-succedent calculi for CK and WK (which they call CCDL) [18]. As suggested by these last authors, the adaptation of their calculi to a single-succedent setting is straightforward. The only noteworthy element in this transformation is the use of the single rule (◇L') in G4WK for the treatment of ◇ on the left, in contrast with their counterpart multi-succedent calculus which has two.

3.1 Termination, Cut Admissibility and Equivalence

In this section we prove of both our calculi that they strongly terminate, eliminate cut, and are equivalent to their corresponding axiomatic system.

First, we prove that G4CK and G4WK *strongly terminate*. We say that a calculus strongly terminates if the process of naive backward proof-search, i.e. freely and iteratively applying rules backward on a sequent, necessarily comes to a halt. To show strong termination, it is sufficient to provide a well-founded ordering on sequents which decreases upwards in any application of any rule of our calculi. To define such an order we exploit the Dershowitz-Manna order on finite multisets [22]: a finite multiset A of elements of type T is smaller than another finite multiset B of T-elements if A is obtained from B by replacing T-elements from B by finitely many T-elements which are strictly smaller according to a well-founded order over T.

Definition 2 (Sequent ordering ,). *We define the well-founded order $\prec_f$ on formulas using their weight: $\varphi \prec_f \psi$ whenever $w(\varphi) < w(\psi)$. We generate the well-founded Dershowitz-Manna order on multisets $\prec_m$ using $\prec_f$. Finally, we write $\Gamma \Rightarrow \Delta \prec \Pi \Rightarrow \Sigma$ whenever $\Gamma \uplus \Delta \prec_m \Pi \uplus \Sigma$.*

Note that a G4WK sequent $\Gamma \Rightarrow$ with an empty succedent is compared in the order over sequents via the multiset $\Gamma \uplus \emptyset = \Gamma$. A quick inspection of the rules of our calculi shows that any premise of a rule is smaller in $\prec$ than its conclusion.

Proposition 1. *The calculi* G4CK *and* G4WK *strongly terminate.*

This directly establishes the decidability of provability in G4CK and G4WK.

Proposition 2 (,). *Provability in* G4CK *and* G4WK *is decidable.*

In Theorem 2, at the end of this section, we prove that our calculi capture CK and WK, respectively. In this light, the proposition above constitutes a *constructive and mechanised* proof of decidability for these logics. Such proofs for the two logics were already given by Dalmonte et al. [18], constructively but not mechanised, and for CK in particular by Mendler and de Paiva [41], though neither constructive nor mechanised.

Second, we aim at proving cut elimination for both calculi, building on proofs of cut admissibility via local proof transformations. To get there, we need to follow a path, first established by Dyckhoff and Negri [24], paved by a succession of technical lemmas, and leading to the admissibility of contraction. We omit the majority of these intermediate lemmas, referring to our mechanisation and Dyckhoff and Negri's work [24], except for the admissibility of some useful rules.

Lemma 1 (, , , , ,). *The following rules are admissible in* G4CK *and* G4WK.

$$\frac{\Gamma \Rightarrow \Delta}{\Gamma, \Pi \Rightarrow \Delta}\ (wk) \qquad \frac{}{\Gamma, \varphi \Rightarrow \varphi}\ (Id) \qquad \frac{\Gamma \Rightarrow \varphi \quad \psi, \Gamma \Rightarrow \Delta}{\Gamma, \varphi \to \psi \Rightarrow \Delta}\ (\to L)$$

Next, we state the admissibility of contraction.

Proposition 3 (,). *The contraction rule is admissible in* G4CK *and* G4WK.

$$\frac{\Gamma, \psi, \psi \Rightarrow \Delta}{\Gamma, \psi \Rightarrow \Delta}\ (cntr)$$

We leverage contraction to prove the admissibility of the cut rule. Our proof goes by primary induction on the weight of the cut formula and secondary (well-founded) induction on $\prec$, a standard method for terminating calculi [32,33,46,47].

Theorem 1 (,). *The additive cut rule is admissible in* G4CK *and* G4WK.

$$\frac{\Gamma \Rightarrow \varphi \quad \varphi, \Gamma \Rightarrow \Delta}{\Gamma \Rightarrow \Delta}\ (cut)$$

As this theorem is proved syntactically via local proof transformations, it entails that both calculi *eliminate* cut: any proof in the calculus augmented with the cut rule can be transformed into a proof without instances of cut.

Third, and finally, we show that G4CK and G4WK capture exactly the logics CK and WK. For this, we exploit both the decidability of the sequent calculi and the admissibility of cut.

Theorem 2 (, , ,). *The following equivalences hold.*

$$\begin{array}{lcl} \vdash_{\mathsf{G4CK}} \Gamma \Rightarrow \Delta & \textit{if and only if} & \Gamma \vdash_{\mathsf{CK}} \Delta \\ \vdash_{\mathsf{G4WK}} \Gamma \Rightarrow \Delta & \textit{if and only if} & \Gamma \vdash_{\mathsf{WK}} \Delta \end{array}$$

Proof We focus on G4WK, as the equivalence for G4CK is treated similarly. Note that we abused notation: Δ in $\Gamma \vdash_{\mathsf{WK}} \Delta$ denotes the *formula* φ if the succedent $\Delta = \{\varphi\}$, and $\bot$ if $\Delta = \emptyset$.

For the left to right direction it suffices to show all rules of G4WK are admissible in WK.

For the right to left direction, the pen-and-paper proof boils down to showing all axioms provable and all rules of the axiomatic system admissible in G4WK. The admissibility of cut crucially helps in the case of (MP). In the mechanisation, we encounter the following obstacle. We are trying to prove that $\vdash_{\mathsf{G4WK}} \Gamma \Rightarrow \Delta$, a statement we mechanised in Rocq in the type `Type`, which requires the construction of an *explicit* proof. As an assumption we have $\Gamma \vdash_{\mathsf{WK}} \Delta$, a statement in the type `Prop`, which promises the opaque *existence* of a proof without giving an explicit one. We are then in a dead end: we cannot build an explicit proof for $\vdash_{\mathsf{G4WK}} \Gamma \Rightarrow \Delta$ by relying on the opaque one of $\Gamma \vdash_{\mathsf{WK}} \Delta$. To circumvent this difficulty we exploit the decidability of G4WK: if the decision procedure outputs $\vdash_{\mathsf{G4WK}} \Gamma \Rightarrow \Delta$ then we are done, else we show that the output $\nvdash_{\mathsf{G4WK}} \Gamma \Rightarrow \Delta$ and our assumption $\Gamma \vdash_{\mathsf{WK}} \Delta$ leads to a contradiction (which does not require the construction of an explicit proof). ■

4 Uniform Interpolation

We start this section by introducing general definitions and facts about uniform interpolation.

Definition 3. *A modal logic L over the language $\mathcal{L}$ has the* uniform interpolation property *if, for every $\mathcal{L}$-formula φ and variable p, there exist $\mathcal{L}$-formulas, denoted by $\forall p\varphi$ and $\exists p\varphi$, satisfying the following three properties:*

1. p-freeness: $Vars(\exists p\varphi) \subseteq Vars(\varphi) \setminus \{p\}$ *and* $Vars(\forall p\varphi) \subseteq Vars(\varphi) \setminus \{p\}$,
2. implication: $\vdash_L \varphi \to \exists p\varphi$ *and* $\vdash_L \forall p\varphi \to \varphi$, *and*
3. uniformity: *for each formula ψ with $p \notin Vars(\psi)$:*

$$\vdash_L \varphi \to \psi\& \textit{ implies } \vdash_L \exists p\varphi \to \psi,$$
$$\vdash_L \psi \to \varphi\& \textit{ implies } \vdash_L \psi \to \forall p\varphi.$$

Formula $\exists p\varphi$ is called the uniform post-interpolant *of φ w.r.t. p and $\forall p\varphi$ the* uniform pre-interpolant *of φ w.r.t. p.*

The notation of $\exists p\varphi$ and $\forall p\varphi$ is suggestive: the formulas do not really contain quantifiers, but they are defined over the modal language $\mathcal{L}$. This notation is justified by Pitts' result stating that uniform interpolants provide *an interpretation* for propositional quantifiers of second order intuitionistic logic into the propositional language [43].

Remark 1. It is interesting to mention that both in classical and intuitionistic based (modal) logics, the formulas $\forall p(\varphi \to \psi)$ and $\exists p(\varphi) \to \forall p(\varphi \to \psi)$ are equivalent. This was shown in [26, Lemma 1] for modal logics based on $\Box$. Since the proof only relies on intuitionistic propositional reasoning, the same result holds in the intuitionistic modal setting with $\Box$ and $\Diamond$. So in case uniform interpolants exist for CK (which we will show in this paper), we have $\vdash_{\mathsf{CK}} \forall p(\varphi \to \psi)$ if and only if $\vdash_{\mathsf{CK}} \exists p(\varphi) \to \forall p(\varphi \to \psi)$. The analogous result holds for WK.

Remark 2. In a classical setting, $\forall p\varphi$ and $\exists p\varphi$ are dual to each other, but that is not true when working in an intuitionistic logic like CK. However, note that it is possible to define formulas of the form $\exists p\varphi$ in terms of $\forall$ and $\to$ as follows using an extra propositional variable q not free in φ:

$$\exists p\varphi := \forall q(\forall p(\varphi \to q) \to q).$$

This is a folklore result when the quantifiers denote the quantifiers in second order intuitionistic propositional logic (see [43]). Here we write the quantifiers to denote uniform interpolants for which the equivalence also holds ([31], Remark 2.2.7). This means that from a method constructing all formulas of the form $\forall p\varphi$, one gets a definition of $\exists p\varphi$. However, the known proof-theoretic method [43] for IL constructs $\forall p\varphi$ and $\exists p\varphi$ via a mutual recursion.

We provide a proof-theoretic construction to prove the uniform interpolation property. In light of Remark 2 we use a sequent-style definition of uniform interpolation in which pre- and post-uniform interpolants are constructed simultaneously.

Definition 4. *A set of provable single-succedent sequents, denoted $\vdash$, has the* uniform interpolation property *if, for any single-succedent sequent $\Gamma \Rightarrow \Delta$ and variable p, there exist modal formulas $\mathsf{E}_p(\Gamma)$ and $\mathsf{A}_p(\Gamma \Rightarrow \Delta)$ such that the following three properties hold:*

1. p-freeness:
   (a) $Vars(\mathsf{E}_p(\Gamma)) \subseteq Vars(\Gamma) \setminus \{p\}$, *and*
   (b) $Vars(\mathsf{A}_p(\Gamma \Rightarrow \Delta)) \subseteq Vars(\Gamma, \Delta) \setminus \{p\}$;
2. implication:
   (a) $\vdash \Gamma \Rightarrow \mathsf{E}_p(\Gamma)$, *and*
   (b) $\vdash \Gamma, \mathsf{A}_p(\Gamma \Rightarrow \Delta) \Rightarrow \Delta$;
3. uniformity: *for any finite multiset of formulas Π such that $p \notin Vars(\Pi)$, if it holds that $\vdash \Pi, \Gamma \Rightarrow \Delta$, then it also holds that:*
   (a) $\vdash \Pi, \mathsf{E}_p(\Gamma) \Rightarrow \Delta$ *if* $p \notin Vars(\Delta)$, *and*
   (b) $\vdash \Pi, \mathsf{E}_p(\Gamma) \Rightarrow \mathsf{A}_p(\Gamma \Rightarrow \Delta)$.

We say that a sequent calculus S *has the* uniform interpolation property *if* $\vdash_{\mathsf{S}}$ *has the uniform interpolation property.*

Note that in the above definition, we have $|\Delta| = 1$ for G4CK and $|\Delta| \leq 1$ for G4WK. In the latter case, Definition 4 is equivalent to the uniform interpolant properties from [38]. We have the following well-known fact.

Lemma 2. *Suppose sequent calculus* S *is sound and complete with respect to logic L. If* S *has the uniform interpolation property, then L has the uniform interpolation property.*

Proof. The proof is well-known and can be found in [14,43]. The essence is to define $\exists p\varphi := \mathsf{E}_p(\varphi)$ and $\forall p\varphi := \mathsf{A}_p(\Rightarrow \varphi)$. ■

4.1 Uniform Interpolation for CK

To prove the uniform interpolation property for CK, we use the sequent calculus G4CK to construct $\mathsf{E}_p(\Gamma)$ and $\mathsf{A}_p(s)$ for any multiset Γ and any sequent s. Our construction adapts the one for iK [38] by adding extra cases for the $\Diamond$.

Definition 5. *We define sets $\mathcal{E}_\mathsf{p}(\Gamma)$ and $\mathcal{A}_\mathsf{p}(s)$ based on a mutual recursion on the ordering $\prec$ according to the rows in Fig. 3. We define:*

$$\mathsf{E}_p(\Gamma) := \bigwedge \mathcal{E}_\mathsf{p}(\Gamma) \text{ and } \mathsf{A}_p(s) := \bigvee \mathcal{A}_\mathsf{p}(s).$$

Theorem 3. *The algorithm defining $\mathsf{E}_p(\Gamma)$ and $\mathsf{A}_p(\Gamma \Rightarrow \varphi)$ is terminating.*

Proof. $\mathsf{E}_p(\Gamma)$ and $\mathsf{A}_p(\Gamma \Rightarrow \varphi)$ are defined by mutual induction on the ordering $\prec$ where for $\mathsf{A}_p(\Gamma \Rightarrow \varphi)$ we look at the multiset Γ, φ. Each recursive call in Fig. 3 reduces in that ordering. Moreover, for each multiset Γ there are finitely many matches of rows ($\mathsf{E}_p^{\mathsf{CK}}0$)-($\mathsf{E}_p^{\mathsf{CK}}13$), and similarly so for sequent $\Gamma \Rightarrow \varphi$ and rows ($\mathsf{A}_p^{\mathsf{CK}}1'$)-($\mathsf{A}_p^{\mathsf{CK}}19$). This means that $\mathcal{A}_\mathsf{p}(\Gamma \Rightarrow \varphi)$ and $\mathcal{E}_\mathsf{p}(\Gamma)$ are finite sets of formulas. So, the constructions of $\mathsf{E}_p(\Gamma)$ and $\mathsf{A}_p(\Gamma \Rightarrow \varphi)$ are terminating. ∎

Let us explain the construction of Fig. 3. Rows ($\mathsf{E}_p^{\mathsf{CK}}0$), ($\mathsf{E}_p^{\mathsf{CK}}1'$), ($\mathsf{E}_p^{\mathsf{CK}}4'$) and ($\mathsf{A}_p^{\mathsf{CK}}1'$), ($\mathsf{A}_p^{\mathsf{CK}}4'$), ($\mathsf{A}_p^{\mathsf{CK}}9$) take care of boolean constants and variables other than p, which can be smartly taken out of the recursive call since these are atomic p-free formulas. Rows ($\mathsf{E}_p^{\mathsf{CK}}1''$), ($\mathsf{E}_p^{\mathsf{CK}}4''$) and rows ($\mathsf{A}_p^{\mathsf{CK}}1''$), ($\mathsf{A}_p^{\mathsf{CK}}4''$) are not necessary for the construction, as $\bot$ is a neutral element for $\mathsf{E}_p(\cdot)$ and $\top$ is a neutral element for $\mathsf{A}_p(\cdot)$, but are required in Rocq to ensure the functionality of $\mathsf{E}_p(\cdot)$ and $\mathsf{A}_p(\cdot)$ by making them defined on all inputs.

Rows ($\mathsf{E}_p^{\mathsf{CK}}2$), ($\mathsf{E}_p^{\mathsf{CK}}3$), ($\mathsf{E}_p^{\mathsf{CK}}5'$)-($\mathsf{E}_p^{\mathsf{CK}}8'$), ($\mathsf{E}_p^{\mathsf{CK}}10$), ($\mathsf{E}_p^{\mathsf{CK}}12$) and ($\mathsf{A}_p^{\mathsf{CK}}2$), ($\mathsf{A}_p^{\mathsf{CK}}3$), ($\mathsf{A}_p^{\mathsf{CK}}5'$)-($\mathsf{A}_p^{\mathsf{CK}}8'$), ($\mathsf{A}_p^{\mathsf{CK}}11$)-($\mathsf{A}_p^{\mathsf{CK}}17$) correspond to what we call a *full* application of a calculus rule where the middle column presents the conclusion of the rule and the right column uses the premise of that rule in the recursive call.

Rows ($\mathsf{E}_p^{\mathsf{CK}}9$), ($\mathsf{E}_p^{\mathsf{CK}}11$), ($\mathsf{E}_p^{\mathsf{CK}}13$), ($\mathsf{A}_p^{\mathsf{CK}}18$) and ($\mathsf{A}_p^{\mathsf{CK}}19$) correspond to what we call *partial* applications of a rule from the calculus. When considering the *uniformity* property of uniform interpolation in Definition 4, a rule application might be possible due to extra formulas in the p-free context Π outside the reach of the interpolant construction meaning that these rows in the table *partially* match the form of rule from the calculus. For example, row ($\mathsf{E}_p^{\mathsf{CK}}11$) is used in case there is a formula $\Diamond\delta_1' \to \delta_2'$ in the hidden p-free context that would together with $\Diamond\delta \in \Gamma$ make an application of the rule ($\Diamond\!\to$L) possible. Row ($\mathsf{E}_p^{\mathsf{CK}}9$) is used for partial applications of ($\Box$R) and ($\Diamond$L).

We will use the following simple facts.

Lemma 3.

1. *Let Γ be a multiset such that $\mathcal{E}_\mathsf{p}(\Gamma) \neq \emptyset$. For any $\chi \in \mathcal{E}_\mathsf{p}(\Gamma)$, multiset Π and formula φ, if $\vdash_{\mathsf{G4CK}} \Pi, \chi \Rightarrow \varphi$, then $\vdash_{\mathsf{G4CK}} \Pi, \mathsf{E}_p(\Gamma) \Rightarrow \varphi$.*

	Γ matches	$\mathcal{E}_p(\Gamma)$ contains
$(\mathsf{E}_p^{\mathsf{CK}}0)$	$\Gamma', \bot$	$\bot$
$(\mathsf{E}_p^{\mathsf{CK}}1')$	Γ', q	q
$(\mathsf{E}_p^{\mathsf{CK}}1'')$	Γ', p	$\top$
$(\mathsf{E}_p^{\mathsf{CK}}2)$	$\Gamma', \psi_1 \wedge \psi_2$	$\mathsf{E}_p(\Gamma', \psi_1, \psi_2)$
$(\mathsf{E}_p^{\mathsf{CK}}3)$	$\Gamma', \psi_1 \vee \psi_2$	$\mathsf{E}_p(\Gamma', \psi_1) \vee \mathsf{E}_p(\Gamma', \psi_2)$
$(\mathsf{E}_p^{\mathsf{CK}}4')$	$\Gamma', q \to \psi$ with $q \notin \Gamma'$	$q \to \mathsf{E}_p(\Gamma', \psi)$
$(\mathsf{E}_p^{\mathsf{CK}}4'')$	$\Gamma', p \to \psi$ with $p \notin \Gamma'$	$\top$
$(\mathsf{E}_p^{\mathsf{CK}}5')$	$\Gamma', r, r \to \psi$	$\mathsf{E}_p(\Gamma', r, \psi)$
$(\mathsf{E}_p^{\mathsf{CK}}6)$	$\Gamma', (\delta_1 \wedge \delta_2) \to \delta_3$	$\mathsf{E}_p(\Gamma', \delta_1 \to (\delta_2 \to \delta_3))$
$(\mathsf{E}_p^{\mathsf{CK}}7)$	$\Gamma', (\delta_1 \vee \delta_2) \to \delta_3$	$\mathsf{E}_p(\Gamma', \delta_1 \to \delta_3, \delta_2 \to \delta_3)$
$(\mathsf{E}_p^{\mathsf{CK}}8')$	$\Gamma', (\delta_1 \to \delta_2) \to \delta_3$	$[\mathsf{E}_p(\Gamma', \delta_2 \to \delta_3, \delta_1) \to \mathsf{A}_p(\Gamma', \delta_2 \to \delta_3, \delta_1 \Rightarrow \delta_2)]$ $\to \mathsf{E}_p(\Gamma', \delta_3)$
$(\mathsf{E}_p^{\mathsf{CK}}9)$	$\Gamma \neq \emptyset$	$\Box \mathsf{E}_p(\Box^{-1}\Gamma)$
$(\mathsf{E}_p^{\mathsf{CK}}10)$	$\Gamma', \Box\delta_1 \to \delta_2$	$\Box[\mathsf{E}_p(\Box^{-1}\Gamma') \to \mathsf{A}_p(\Box^{-1}\Gamma' \Rightarrow \delta_1)] \to \mathsf{E}_p(\Gamma', \delta_2)$
$(\mathsf{E}_p^{\mathsf{CK}}11)$	$\Gamma', \Diamond\delta$	$\Diamond \mathsf{E}_p(\Box^{-1}\Gamma', \delta)$
$(\mathsf{E}_p^{\mathsf{CK}}12)$	$\Gamma', \Diamond\delta_3, \Diamond\delta_1 \to \delta_2$	$\Box[\mathsf{E}_p(\Box^{-1}\Gamma', \delta_3) \to \mathsf{A}_p(\Box^{-1}\Gamma', \delta_3 \Rightarrow \delta_1)]$ $\to \mathsf{E}_p(\Gamma', \Diamond\delta_3, \delta_2)$
$(\mathsf{E}_p^{\mathsf{CK}}13)$	$\Gamma', \Diamond\delta_1 \to \delta_2$	$\Diamond[\mathsf{E}_p(\Box^{-1}\Gamma') \to \mathsf{A}_p(\Box^{-1}\Gamma' \Rightarrow \delta_1)] \to \mathsf{E}_p(\Gamma', \delta_2)$

	s matches	$\mathcal{A}_p(s)$ contains
$(\mathsf{A}_p^{\mathsf{CK}}1')$	$\Gamma, q \Rightarrow \varphi$	$\bot$
$(\mathsf{A}_p^{\mathsf{CK}}1'')$	$\Gamma, p \Rightarrow \varphi$ with $\varphi \neq p$	$\bot$
$(\mathsf{A}_p^{\mathsf{CK}}2)$	$\Gamma, \psi_1 \wedge \psi_2 \Rightarrow \varphi$	$\mathsf{A}_p(\Gamma, \psi_1, \psi_2 \Rightarrow \varphi)$
$(\mathsf{A}_p^{\mathsf{CK}}3)$	$\Gamma, \psi_1 \vee \psi_2 \Rightarrow \varphi$	$[\mathsf{E}_p(\Gamma, \psi_1) \to \mathsf{A}_p(\Gamma, \psi_1 \Rightarrow \varphi)] \wedge$ $[\mathsf{E}_p(\Gamma, \psi_2) \to \mathsf{A}_p(\Gamma, \psi_2 \Rightarrow \varphi)]$
$(\mathsf{A}_p^{\mathsf{CK}}4')$	$\Gamma, q \to \psi \Rightarrow \varphi$ with $q \notin \Gamma$	$q \wedge \mathsf{A}_p(\Gamma, \psi \Rightarrow \varphi)$
$(\mathsf{A}_p^{\mathsf{CK}}4'')$	$\Gamma, p \to \psi \Rightarrow \varphi$ with $p \notin \Gamma$	$\bot$
$(\mathsf{A}_p^{\mathsf{CK}}5')$	$\Gamma, r, r \to \psi \Rightarrow \varphi$	$\mathsf{A}_p(\Gamma, r, \psi \Rightarrow \varphi)$
$(\mathsf{A}_p^{\mathsf{CK}}6)$	$\Gamma, (\delta_1 \wedge \delta_2) \to \delta_3 \Rightarrow \varphi$	$\mathsf{A}_p(\Gamma, \delta_1 \to (\delta_2 \to \delta_3) \Rightarrow \varphi)$
$(\mathsf{A}_p^{\mathsf{CK}}7)$	$\Gamma, (\delta_1 \vee \delta_2) \to \delta_3 \Rightarrow \varphi$	$\mathsf{A}_p(\Gamma, \delta_1 \to \delta_3, \delta_2 \to \delta_3 \Rightarrow \varphi)$
$(\mathsf{A}_p^{\mathsf{CK}}8')$	$\Gamma, (\delta_1 \to \delta_2) \to \delta_3 \Rightarrow \varphi$	$[\mathsf{E}_p(\Gamma, \delta_2 \to \delta_3, \delta_1) \to \mathsf{A}_p(\Gamma, \delta_2 \to \delta_3, \delta_1 \Rightarrow \delta_2)]$ $\wedge\ \mathsf{A}_p(\Gamma, \delta_3 \Rightarrow \varphi)$
$(\mathsf{A}_p^{\mathsf{CK}}9)$	$\Gamma \Rightarrow q$	q
$(\mathsf{A}_p^{\mathsf{CK}}10)$	$\Gamma, p \Rightarrow p$	$\top$
$(\mathsf{A}_p^{\mathsf{CK}}11)$	$\Gamma \Rightarrow \varphi_1 \wedge \varphi_2$	$\mathsf{A}_p(\Gamma \Rightarrow \varphi_1) \wedge \mathsf{A}_p(\Gamma \Rightarrow \varphi_2)$
$(\mathsf{A}_p^{\mathsf{CK}}12)$	$\Gamma \Rightarrow \varphi_1 \vee \varphi_2$	$\mathsf{A}_p(\Gamma \Rightarrow \varphi_1) \vee \mathsf{A}_p(\Gamma \Rightarrow \varphi_2)$
$(\mathsf{A}_p^{\mathsf{CK}}13)$	$\Gamma \Rightarrow \varphi_1 \to \varphi_2$	$\mathsf{E}_p(\Gamma, \varphi_1) \to \mathsf{A}_p(\Gamma, \varphi_1 \Rightarrow \varphi_2)$
$(\mathsf{A}_p^{\mathsf{CK}}14)$	$\Gamma \Rightarrow \Box\delta$	$\Box(\mathsf{E}_p(\Box^{-1}\Gamma) \to \mathsf{A}_p(\Box^{-1}\Gamma \Rightarrow \delta))$
$(\mathsf{A}_p^{\mathsf{CK}}15)$	$\Gamma, \Box\delta_1 \to \delta_2 \Rightarrow \varphi$	$\Box[\mathsf{E}_p(\Box^{-1}\Gamma) \to \mathsf{A}_p(\Box^{-1}\Gamma \Rightarrow \delta_1)] \wedge \mathsf{A}_p(\Gamma, \delta_2 \Rightarrow \varphi)$
$(\mathsf{A}_p^{\mathsf{CK}}16)$	$\Gamma, \Diamond\delta_1 \Rightarrow \Diamond\delta_2$	$\Box(\mathsf{E}_p(\Box^{-1}\Gamma, \delta_1) \to \mathsf{A}_p(\Box^{-1}\Gamma, \delta_1 \Rightarrow \delta_2))$
$(\mathsf{A}_p^{\mathsf{CK}}17)$	$\Gamma, \Diamond\delta_3, \Diamond\delta_1 \to \delta_2 \Rightarrow \varphi$	$\Box[\mathsf{E}_p(\Box^{-1}\Gamma, \delta_3) \to \mathsf{A}_p(\Box^{-1}\Gamma, \delta_3 \Rightarrow \delta_1)]$ $\wedge \mathsf{A}_p(\Gamma, \Diamond\delta_3, \delta_2 \Rightarrow \varphi)$
$(\mathsf{A}_p^{\mathsf{CK}}18)$	$\Gamma \Rightarrow \Diamond\delta$	$\Diamond(\mathsf{E}_p(\Box^{-1}\Gamma) \to \mathsf{A}_p(\Box^{-1}\Gamma \Rightarrow \delta))$
$(\mathsf{A}_p^{\mathsf{CK}}19)$	$\Gamma, \Diamond\delta_1 \to \delta_2 \Rightarrow \varphi$	$\Diamond[\mathsf{E}_p(\Box^{-1}\Gamma) \to \mathsf{A}_p(\Box^{-1}\Gamma \Rightarrow \delta_1)] \wedge \mathsf{A}_p(\Gamma, \delta_2 \Rightarrow \varphi)$

Fig. 3. Constructions of $\mathsf{E}_p(\Gamma)$ and $\mathsf{A}_p(\Gamma \Rightarrow \varphi)$ for G4CK where in all clauses $q \neq p$. The constructions are divided into three parts: rows for propositional logic IL that are a slight modification from [43] (indicated here with $'$ or $''$), rows that cover the box modality as in [38] for box-only logic iK, and rows that cover the diamond.

2. *Let $\Gamma \Rightarrow \varphi$ be a sequent such that $\mathcal{A}_\mathsf{p}(\Gamma \Rightarrow \varphi) \neq \emptyset$. For any $\chi \in \mathcal{A}_\mathsf{p}(\Gamma \Rightarrow \varphi)$ and multiset Π, if $\vdash_{\mathsf{G4CK}} \Pi \Rightarrow \chi$, then $\vdash_{\mathsf{G4CK}} \Pi \Rightarrow \mathsf{A}_p(\Gamma \Rightarrow \varphi)$.* (, , ,)

Proof. (1) follows from the fact that $\mathsf{E}_p(\Gamma) = \bigwedge \mathcal{E}_\mathsf{p}(\Gamma)$. So multiple applications of weakening and ($\wedge$L) applied to $\Pi, \chi \Rightarrow \varphi$ gives a proof for $\Pi, \mathsf{E}_p(\Gamma) \Rightarrow \varphi$. For (2), observe that $\mathsf{A}_p(\Gamma \Rightarrow \varphi) = \bigvee \mathcal{A}_\mathsf{p}(\Gamma \Rightarrow \varphi)$, so multiple applications of ($\vee$R$_1$) and ($\vee$R$_2$) applied to $\Pi \Rightarrow \chi$ provide a proof for $\Pi \Rightarrow \mathsf{A}_p(\Gamma \Rightarrow \varphi)$. ■

Lemma 4 ( ). *If $\vdash_{\mathsf{G4CK}} \Pi, \Box \mathsf{E}_p(\Box^{-1}\Gamma) \Rightarrow \varphi$, then $\vdash_{\mathsf{G4CK}} \Pi, \mathsf{E}_p(\Gamma) \Rightarrow \varphi$.*

Proof If $\Gamma = \emptyset$, then $\Box^{-1}\Gamma = \emptyset$ and so $\Box \mathsf{E}_p(\Box^{-1}\Gamma) = \Box\top = \top$. In that case $\vdash_{\mathsf{G4CK}} \Pi, \top \Rightarrow \varphi$, and so $\vdash_{\mathsf{G4CK}} \Pi, \mathsf{E}_p(\Gamma) \Rightarrow \varphi$ by weakening. If $\Gamma \neq \emptyset$ we know by ($\mathsf{E}_p^{\mathsf{CK}}$9) that $\Box \mathsf{E}_p(\Box^{-1}\Gamma) \in \mathcal{E}_\mathsf{p}(\Gamma)$. So by Lemma 3 we conclude that $\vdash_{\mathsf{G4CK}} \Pi, \mathsf{E}_p(\Gamma) \Rightarrow \varphi$. ■

We now present the main theorem of this section. Due to space restrictions we highlight some of the important steps of the proof below.

Theorem 4. *Sequent calculus* G4CK *has the uniform interpolation property.*

Proof. We take the construction of $\mathsf{A}_p(\cdot)$ and $\mathsf{E}_p(\cdot)$ from Definition 5. We have to show all properties from Definition 4. The *p-freeness* property follows easily by examining the construction of $\mathsf{A}_p(\cdot)$ and $\mathsf{E}_p(\cdot)$ ( ).

The *implication* properties (2a) and (2b) are simultaneously proved by the multiset ordering $\prec$ on Γ, φ, i.e., we prove (2a) $\vdash_{\mathsf{G4CK}} \Gamma \Rightarrow \mathsf{E}_p(\Gamma)$, and (2b) $\vdash_{\mathsf{G4CK}} \Gamma, \mathsf{A}_p(\Gamma \Rightarrow \varphi) \Rightarrow \varphi$. The implementation ( ) is an elegant extension of the existing implementation for IL [27]. For (2a), we have $\mathsf{E}_p(\Gamma) := \bigwedge \mathcal{E}_\mathsf{p}(\Gamma)$ given in Fig. 3, so it is sufficient to prove every conjunct in $\mathcal{E}_\mathsf{p}(\Gamma)$. Let us here treat two cases for $\Diamond$.

Case ($\mathsf{E}_p^{\mathsf{CK}}$9):
In this case $\Gamma \neq \emptyset$, which means that $\Box^{-1}\Gamma \prec \Gamma$, so the induction hypothesis (IH) applies:

$$\dfrac{\overset{\text{(IH)}}{\Box^{-1}\Gamma \Rightarrow \mathsf{E}_p(\Box^{-1}\Gamma)}}{\Gamma \Rightarrow \Box \mathsf{E}_p(\Box^{-1}\Gamma)}\ (\Box\text{R})$$

Case ($\mathsf{E}_p^{\mathsf{CK}}$13):
Let us write $\chi := \mathsf{E}_p(\Box^{-1}\Gamma') \to \mathsf{A}_p(\Box^{-1}\Gamma' \Rightarrow \delta_1)$. We have the following derivation in which we use the rules ($\to$L) and (wk) shown admissible in Lemma 1.

$$\dfrac{\dfrac{\dfrac{\overset{\text{(IH)}}{\Box^{-1}\Gamma' \Rightarrow \mathsf{E}_p(\Box^{-1}\Gamma')} \quad \overset{\text{(IH)}}{\Box^{-1}\Gamma', \mathsf{A}_p(\Box^{-1}\Gamma' \Rightarrow \delta_1) \Rightarrow \delta_1}}{\Box^{-1}\Gamma', \chi \Rightarrow \delta_1}\ (\to\text{L}) \qquad \dfrac{\overset{\text{(IH)}}{\Gamma', \delta_2 \Rightarrow \mathsf{E}_p(\Gamma', \delta_2)}}{\Gamma', \delta_2, \Diamond\chi \Rightarrow \mathsf{E}_p(\Gamma', \delta_2)}\ (\text{wk})}{\Gamma', \Diamond\delta_1 \to \delta_2, \Diamond\chi \Rightarrow \mathsf{E}_p(\Gamma', \delta_2)}\ (\Diamond\!\to\!\text{L})}{\Gamma', \Diamond\delta_1 \to \delta_2 \Rightarrow \Diamond\chi \to \mathsf{E}_p(\Gamma', \delta_2)}\ (\to\text{R})$$

For (2b) we prove that $\vdash_{\mathsf{G4CK}} \Gamma, \mathsf{A}_p(\Gamma \Rightarrow \varphi) \Rightarrow \varphi$. We have $\mathsf{A}_p(\Gamma \Rightarrow \varphi) := \bigvee \mathcal{A}_\mathsf{p}(\Gamma \Rightarrow \varphi)$ given in Fig. 3, so it is sufficient to prove every disjunct in $\mathsf{A}_p(\Gamma \Rightarrow \varphi)$ placed on the left of the sequent. As an example, we treat the following case.

Case ($\mathsf{A}_p^{\mathsf{CK}}19$):
Let us write $\chi := \mathsf{E}_p(\Box^{-1}\Gamma') \to \mathsf{A}_p(\Box^{-1}\Gamma' \Rightarrow \delta_1)$. Note that in the following derivation, $\Box^{-1}\mathsf{A}_p(\Gamma', \delta_2 \Rightarrow \varphi)$ represents a formula when $\mathsf{A}_p(\Gamma', \delta_2 \Rightarrow \varphi)$ is a boxed formula and $\emptyset$ when $\mathsf{A}_p(\Gamma', \delta_2 \Rightarrow \varphi)$ is not a boxed formula. In both cases, our weakening rule from Lemma 1 works.

$$\dfrac{\dfrac{\dfrac{\dfrac{\overset{\text{(IH)}}{\Box^{-1}\Gamma' \Rightarrow \mathsf{E}_p(\Box^{-1}\Gamma')} \qquad \overset{\text{(IH)}}{\Box^{-1}\Gamma', \mathsf{A}_p(\Box^{-1}\Gamma' \Rightarrow \delta_1) \Rightarrow \delta_1}}{\Box^{-1}\Gamma', \chi \Rightarrow \delta_1}\,(\to\text{L})}{\Box^{-1}\Gamma', \chi, \Box^{-1}\mathsf{A}_p(\Gamma', \delta_2 \Rightarrow \varphi) \Rightarrow \delta_1}\,(\text{wk}) \qquad \dfrac{\overset{\text{(IH)}}{\Gamma', \delta_2, \mathsf{A}_p(\Gamma', \delta_2 \Rightarrow \varphi) \Rightarrow \varphi}}{\Gamma', \delta_2, \Diamond\chi, \mathsf{A}_p(\Gamma', \delta_2 \Rightarrow \varphi) \Rightarrow \varphi}\,(\text{wk})}{\dfrac{\Gamma', \Diamond\delta_1 \to \delta_2, \Diamond\chi, \mathsf{A}_p(\Gamma', \delta_2 \Rightarrow \varphi) \Rightarrow \varphi}{\Gamma', \Diamond\delta_1 \to \delta_2, \Diamond\chi \wedge \mathsf{A}_p(\Gamma', \delta_2 \Rightarrow \varphi) \Rightarrow \varphi}\,(\wedge\text{L})}\,(\Diamond{\to}\text{L})$$

Now we turn to the *uniformity* property of uniform interpolation ( ). Let Π be a finite multiset such that $p \notin \mathrm{Vars}(\Pi)$ and suppose $\vdash_{\mathsf{G4CK}} \Pi, \Gamma \Rightarrow \varphi$ by proof π. By induction on $\Pi, \Gamma \Rightarrow \varphi$ via $\prec$ we simultaneously prove that (3a) $\vdash \Pi, \mathsf{E}_p(\Gamma) \Rightarrow \varphi$ if $p \notin \mathrm{Vars}(\varphi)$ and (3b) $\vdash_{\mathsf{G4CK}} \Pi, \mathsf{E}_p(\Gamma) \Rightarrow \mathsf{A}_p(\Gamma \Rightarrow \varphi)$. In the sequel we use primes to denote that a formula is p-free, so for (3a) we write $\varphi = \varphi'$. We look at the last rule applied in proof π. Here we only discuss the rule ($\Diamond$L).

Case ($\Diamond$L):
Subcase: The principal formula is in p-free Π, i.e., $\Pi = \Pi_0, \Diamond\delta_1'$.

(a) The conclusion of the rule is of the form $\Pi_0, \Diamond\delta_1', \Gamma \Rightarrow \Diamond\varphi_0'$ with p-free formula φ_0'. By induction we have $\vdash_{\mathsf{G4CK}} \Box^{-1}\Pi_0, \delta_1', \mathsf{E}_p(\Box^{-1}\Gamma) \Rightarrow \varphi_0'$. We obtain the desired result with the following derivation:

$$\dfrac{\dfrac{\overset{\text{(IH)}}{\Box^{-1}\Pi_0, \delta_1', \mathsf{E}_p(\Box^{-1}\Gamma) \Rightarrow \varphi_0'}}{\Pi_0, \Diamond\delta_1', \Box\mathsf{E}_p(\Box^{-1}\Gamma) \Rightarrow \Diamond\varphi_0'}\,(\Diamond\text{L})}{\Pi_0, \Diamond\delta_1', \mathsf{E}_p(\Gamma) \Rightarrow \Diamond\varphi_0'}\,\text{Lemma 4}$$

(b) The conclusion of the rule is of the form $\Pi_0, \Diamond\delta_1', \Gamma \Rightarrow \Diamond\varphi$. By induction, we get $\vdash_{\mathsf{G4CK}} \Box^{-1}\Pi_0, \delta_1', \mathsf{E}_p(\Box^{-1}\Gamma) \Rightarrow \mathsf{A}_p(\Box^{-1}\Gamma \Rightarrow \varphi)$. We have the following:

$$\dfrac{\dfrac{\dfrac{\dfrac{\overset{\text{(IH)}}{\Box^{-1}\Pi_0, \delta_1', \mathsf{E}_p(\Box^{-1}\Gamma) \Rightarrow \mathsf{A}_p(\Box^{-1}\Gamma \Rightarrow \varphi)}}{\Box^{-1}\Pi_0, \delta_1' \Rightarrow \mathsf{E}_p(\Box^{-1}\Gamma) \to \mathsf{A}_p(\Box^{-1}\Gamma \Rightarrow \varphi)}\,(\to\text{R})}{\Pi_0, \Diamond\delta_1' \Rightarrow \Diamond[\mathsf{E}_p(\Box^{-1}\Gamma) \to \mathsf{A}_p(\Box^{-1}\Gamma \Rightarrow \varphi)]}\,(\Diamond\text{L})}{\Pi_0, \Diamond\delta_1', \mathsf{E}_p(\Gamma) \Rightarrow \Diamond[\mathsf{E}_p(\Box^{-1}\Gamma) \to \mathsf{A}_p(\Box^{-1}\Gamma \Rightarrow \varphi)]}\,(\text{wk})}{\Pi_0, \Diamond\delta_1', \mathsf{E}_p(\Gamma) \Rightarrow \mathsf{A}_p(\Gamma \Rightarrow \Diamond\varphi)}\,(\mathsf{A}_p^{\mathsf{CK}}18),\ \text{Lemma 3}$$

Subcase: The principal formula is in Γ, i.e., $\Gamma = \Gamma_0, \Diamond\delta_1$.

(a) This case proceeds in a similar way as the previous subcase (a), where now, instead of Lemma 4 we use Lemma 3 with ($\mathsf{E}_p^{\mathsf{CK}}$11).
(b) This case proceeds in a similar way as the previous subcase (b), where, instead of ($\mathsf{A}_p^{\mathsf{CK}}$18) we use ($\mathsf{A}_p^{\mathsf{CK}}$16) and rule ($\Box$R) instead of ($\Diamond$L).

We have checked the properties of p-freeness, implication, and uniformity for sequent calculus G4CK, concluding that G4CK has uniform interpolation. ∎

Corollary 1 ( ). *Logic* CK *has the uniform interpolation property.*

4.2 Uniform Interpolation for WK

The construction of uniform interpolants for WK only requires two modifications compared to the construction of uniform interpolants for CK in Fig. 3, because the two calculi G4CK and G4WK only differ in two aspects. First, since sequents $\Gamma \Rightarrow \Delta$ in G4WK obey $|\Delta| \leq 1$ instead of $|\Delta| = 1$, we should read any row in Fig. 3 that matches a sequent s with φ in the succedent, as having Δ in the succedent with $|\Delta| \leq 1$. So we replace all occurrences of φ (without a subscript) in Fig. 3 with Δ. To be precise, this applies to rows ($\mathsf{A}_p^{\mathsf{CK}}1'$)-($\mathsf{A}_p^{\mathsf{CK}}8'$), ($\mathsf{A}_p^{\mathsf{CK}}$15), ($\mathsf{A}_p^{\mathsf{CK}}$17), and ($\mathsf{A}_p^{\mathsf{CK}}$19).

Second, the main difference between the calculi G4CK and G4WK lies in the left rule for $\Diamond$ which in G4WK has the form:

$$\frac{\Box^{-1}\Gamma, \varphi \Rightarrow \Diamond^{-1}\Delta}{\Gamma, \Diamond\varphi \Rightarrow \Delta}\ (\Diamond\text{L'})$$

That is why we modify row ($\mathsf{A}_p^{\mathsf{CK}}$16) from Fig. 3 to the following row ( ):

($\mathsf{A}_p^{\mathsf{WK}}$16)	$\Gamma, \Diamond\delta \Rightarrow \Delta$	$\Box(\mathsf{E}_p(\Box^{-1}\Gamma, \delta) \to \mathsf{A}_p(\Box^{-1}\Gamma, \delta \Rightarrow \Diamond^{-1}\Delta))$

Now, $\mathsf{E}_p(\Gamma)$ and $\mathsf{A}_p(s)$ with respect to G4WK are defined as in Definition 5 with the modified table as described above. The analogues of Theorem 3 and Lemmas 3 and 4 hold for G4WK by the same proofs.

Theorem 5. *Sequent calculus* G4WK *has the uniform interpolation property.*

Proof. (, ,) Compared to the proof of uniform interpolation for G4CK (Theorem 4), a few modifications are needed, mostly in those places where ($\mathsf{A}_p^{\mathsf{CK}}$16) plays a role. The proof of the *implication* property (2a) does not change, and for (2b) the case for ($\mathsf{A}_p^{\mathsf{WK}}$16) works via the same proof as for ($\mathsf{A}_p^{\mathsf{CK}}$16) in Theorem 4, where we replace each occurrence of $\Diamond\delta_2$ by Δ and each δ_2 by $\Diamond^{-1}\Delta$. For the *uniformity* property, we check the case for ($\Diamond$L') which comes with two subcases. They show similarities to the proof for ($\Diamond$L) of Theorem 4:
Case ($\Diamond$L'):
Subcase: The principal formula is in the p-free context Π, i.e., $\Pi = \Pi_0, \Diamond\delta'$.

(a) The conclusion of the rule is of the form $\Pi_0, \Diamond\delta', \Gamma \Rightarrow \Delta'$ where Δ' is p-free. By induction we have $\vdash_{\mathsf{G4WK}} \Box^{-1}\Pi_0, \delta', \mathsf{E}_p(\Box^{-1}\Gamma) \Rightarrow \Diamond^{-1}\Delta'$. We have:

$$\dfrac{\dfrac{\overset{(\text{IH})}{\Box^{-1}\Pi_0, \delta', \mathsf{E}_p(\Box^{-1}\Gamma) \Rightarrow \Diamond^{-1}\Delta'}}{\Pi_0, \Diamond\delta', \Box\mathsf{E}_p(\Box^{-1}\Gamma) \Rightarrow \Delta'}\ (\Diamond\text{L'})}{\Pi_0, \Diamond\delta', \mathsf{E}_p(\Gamma) \Rightarrow \Delta'}\ \text{Lemma 4}$$

(b) The conclusion of the rule is of the form $\Pi_0, \Diamond\delta', \Gamma \Rightarrow \Delta$. We now consider two possibilities: $\Delta = \{\Diamond\psi\}$ for some ψ or not. If not, then $\Diamond^{-1}\Delta = \emptyset$ and $\mathsf{A}_p(\Gamma \Rightarrow \Delta)$ is not a $\Diamond$-formula by inspection of its construction. This means that we can reason as follows:

$$\dfrac{\dfrac{\overset{(\text{IH})}{\Box^{-1}\Pi_0, \delta', \mathsf{E}_p(\Box^{-1}\Gamma) \Rightarrow}}{\Pi_0, \Diamond\delta', \Box\mathsf{E}_p(\Box^{-1}\Gamma) \Rightarrow \mathsf{A}_p(\Gamma \Rightarrow \Delta)}\ (\Diamond\text{L'})}{\Pi_0, \Diamond\delta', \mathsf{E}_p(\Gamma) \Rightarrow \mathsf{A}_p(\Gamma \Rightarrow \Delta)}\ \text{Lemma 4}$$

If $\Delta = \{\Diamond\psi\}$, then the same derivation applies as case (b) for ($\Diamond$L) in the proof of Theorem 4.

Subcase: The principal formula is in Γ, i.e., $\Gamma = \Gamma_0, \Diamond\delta_1$. This subcase is analogous to the previous subcase where instead of Lemma 4 we use Lemma 3 with ($\mathsf{E}_p^{\mathsf{WK}}11$) and instead of using ($\mathsf{A}_p^{\mathsf{WK}}18$) we apply ($\mathsf{A}_p^{\mathsf{WK}}16$). ■

Corollary 2 ( ). *Logic* WK *has the uniform interpolation property.*

5 Conclusion

We have established the uniform interpolation property for constructive modal logics CK and WK, the first positive result of this kind among intuitionistic modal logics with independent $\Box$ and $\Diamond$. Our proof is *constructive* where we extend Pitts' proof technique to constructive $\Diamond$ by exploiting terminating sequent calculi for CK and WK. Our results have been formalised in Rocq which could contribute to the uniform interpolation calculator available in [26,27].

Our construction aims at showing that uniform interpolants *can* be constructed. Our approach is based on Pitts' naive construction, which can be simplified and optimised, as shown for the case of IL in [28]. Such simplifications, optimisations and hence more efficient algorithms, would be welcome in modal logics. A recent overview on complexity bounds on (uniform) interpolants in classical modal logics is provided in [17].

Another interesting direction for future research is to study the definability of so-called *bisimulation quantifiers*. These are interpreted over relational semantics and closely linked to uniform interpolants [1,50]. It would be interesting to see whether these are also definable in the birelational models of intuitionistic modal logics. Birelational semantics have been developed for CK [41] and WK [52] and a general study of such semantics is provided and formalised in Rocq in [34].

Finally, Pitts' technique received attention in the recent field of *universal proof theory* in which the uniform interpolation is linked to nicely behaved proof systems by inspecting the form of inference rules. So-called negative results have been established in the realm of intermediate logics stating that many of such logics cannot have a *semi-analytic* sequent calculus [38]. Modal logics are also treated in this context [3,4,36], but the negative results are in our opinion quite restrictive in the modal setting because only a few $\Box$-only rules are treated and a general format of 'modal rule' is not provided. We hope to provide a first step to widen the scope of universal proof theory by studying both $\Box$ and $\Diamond$.

Acknowledgments. The first author acknowledges the support by the Dutch Research Council (NWO) under the project *Finding Interpolants: Proofs in Action* with file number VI.Veni.232.369 of the research programme Veni. The second author has been supported by (1) a UKRI Future Leaders Fellowship, 'Structure vs Invariants in Proofs', project reference MR/S035540/1, and (2) the Renaissance Philanthropy grant DEEPER.

References

1. D'Agostino, G.: Uniform interpolation, bisimulation quantifiers, and fixed points. In: ten Cate, B.D., Zeevat, H.W. (eds.) TbiLLC 2005. LNCS (LNAI), vol. 4363, pp. 96–116. Springer, Heidelberg (2007). https://doi.org/10.1007/978-3-540-75144-1_8
2. Akbar Tabatabai, A., Iemhoff, R., Jalali, R.: Uniform Lyndon interpolation for basic non-normal modal and conditional logics. J. Logic Comput. **35**(6), exae057 (2024). https://doi.org/10.1093/logcom/exae057
3. Akbar Tabatabai, A., Jalali, R.: Universal proof theory: semi-analytic rules and Craig interpolation. Ann. Pure Appl. Logic **176**(1), 103509 (2025). https://doi.org/10.1016/j.apal.2024.103509
4. Akbar Tabatabai, A., Jalali, R.: Universal proof theory: semi-analytic rules and uniform interpolation (2025). https://arxiv.org/abs/1808.06258
5. Alechina, N., Mendler, M., de Paiva, V., Ritter, E.: Categorical and kripke semantics for constructive S4 modal logic. In: Fribourg, L. (ed.) CSL 2001. LNCS, vol. 2142, pp. 292–307. Springer, Heidelberg (2001). https://doi.org/10.1007/3-540-44802-0_21
6. Alizadeh, M., Derakhshan, F., Ono, H.: Uniform interpolation in substructural logics. Rev. Symb. Logic **7**(3), 455–483 (2014). https://doi.org/10.1017/S175502031400015X
7. Arisaka, R., Das, A., Straßburger, L.: On nested sequents for constructive modal logics. Log. Methods Comput. Sci. **11**(3) (2015). https://doi.org/10.2168/LMCS-11(3:7)2015
8. Balbiani, P., Gao, H., Gencer, Ç., Olivetti, N.: A natural intuitionistic modal logic: axiomatization and bi-nested calculus. In: Murano, A., Silva, A. (eds.) 32nd EACSL Annual Conference on Computer Science Logic (CSL 2024). Leibniz International Proceedings in Informatics (LIPIcs), vol. 288, pp. 13:1–13:21. Schloss Dagstuhl – Leibniz-Zentrum für Informatik, Dagstuhl, Germany (2024). https://doi.org/10.4230/LIPIcs.CSL.2024.13

9. Balbiani, P., Gao, H., Gencer, Ç., Olivetti, N.: Local intuitionistic modal logics and their calculi. In: Benzmüller, C., Heule, M.J., Schmidt, R.A. (eds.) Automated Reasoning, pp. 78–96. Springer, Cham (2024)
10. Bellin, G., de Paiva, V., Ritter, E.: Extended Curry-Howard correspondence for a basic constructive modal logic. In: Methods for Modalities 2 (M4M-2) (2001)
11. Bierman, G.M., de Paiva, V.: On an intuitionistic modal logic. Stud. Logica **65**(3), 383–416 (2000). https://doi.org/10.1023/A:1005291931660
12. Bull, R.A.: A modal extension of intuitionistic logic. Notre Dame J. Formal Logic **6**(2), 142–146 (1965). https://doi.org/10.1305/ndjfl/1093958154
13. Bull, R.A.: MIPC as the formalisation of an intuitionistic concept of modality. J. Symb. Logic **31**(4), 609–616 (1966). https://doi.org/10.2307/2269696
14. BBílková, M.: Interpolation in Modal Logics. Ph.D. thesis, Univerzita Karlova, Prague (2006)
15. Bílková, M.: Uniform interpolation in provability logics (2022). https://arxiv.org/pdf/2211.02591.pdf
16. Ten Cate, B., Jung, J.C., Koopmann, P., Wernhard, C., Wolter, F. (eds.): Theory and Applications of Craig Interpolation. Ubiquity Press (To appear in spring 2026)
17. Ten Cate, B., Kuijer, L., Wolter, F.: The size of interpolants in modal logics (2025). https://arxiv.org/abs/2511.04577
18. Dalmonte, T., Grellois, C., Olivetti, N.: Terminating calculi and countermodels for constructive modal logics. In: Das, A., Negri, S. (eds.) Automated Reasoning with Analytic Tableaux and Related Methods, pp. 391–408. Springer, Cham (2021)
19. Das, A., Groot, J., Shillito, I.: Diamond-free parts of intuitionistic modal logics (2025). https://prooftheory.blog/2025/10/03/diamond-free-parts-of-intuitionistic-modal-logics/, post on The Proof Theory Blog. Accessed 13 Feb 2026
20. Das, A., Marin, S.: Brouwer meets Kripke: constructivising modal logic (2022). https://prooftheory.blog/2022/08/19/brouwer-meets-kripke-constructivising-modal-logic/, post on The Proof Theory Blog. Accessed 13 Feb 2026
21. Das, A., Marin, S.: On intuitionistic diamonds (and lack thereof). In: Ramanayake, R., Urban, J. (eds.) Proceedings TABLEAUX 2023, pp. 283–301 (2023). https://doi.org/10.1007/978-3-031-43513-3_16
22. Dershowitz, N., Manna, Z.: Proving termination with multiset orderings. Commun. ACM **22**(8), 465–476 (1979). https://doi.org/10.1145/359138.359142
23. Dyckhoff, R.: Contraction-free sequent calculi for intuitionistic logic. J. Symb. Logic **57**(3), 795–807 (1992). https://doi.org/10.2307/2275431
24. Dyckhoff, R., Negri, S.: Admissibility of structural rules for contraction-free systems of intuitionistic logic. J. Symb. Logic **65**(4), 1499–1518 (2000). https://doi.org/10.2307/2695061
25. Ewald, W.B.: Intuitionistic tense and modal logic. J. Symb. Logic **51**(1), 166–179 (1986). https://doi.org/10.2307/2273953
26. Férée, H., van der Giessen, I., van Gool, S., Shillito, I.: Mechanised uniform interpolation for modal logics K, GL, and iSL. In: Benzmüller, C., Heule, M., Schmidt, R. (eds.) Automated Reasoning. Lecture Notes in Computer Science, vol. 2, pp. 43–60. Springer (2024). https://doi.org/10.1007/978-3-031-63501-4_3
27. Férée, H., van Gool, S.: Formalizing and computing propositional quantifiers. In: Proceedings of the 12th ACM SIGPLAN International Conference on Certified Programs and Proofs, CPP 2023, pp. 148–158. Association for Computing Machinery (2023). https://doi.org/10.1145/3573105.3575668

28. Férée, H., van Gool, S., Iglesias Vázquez, Y.: Formulas rewritten and normalized computationally, and intuitionistically simplified. In: 36es Journées Francophones des Langages Applicatifs (JFLA 2025), Roiffé, France (2025). https://hal.science/hal-04859429
29. Fischer Servi, G.: On modal logic with an intuitionistic base. Stud. Logica **36**, 141–149 (1977). https://doi.org/10.1007/bf02121259
30. Fischer Servi, G.: Axiomatizations for some intuitionistic modal logics. Rendiconti del Seminario Matematico dell' Universita Politecnica di Torino **42**, 179–194 (1984)
31. Van der Giessen, I.: Uniform Interpolation and Admissible Rules. Proof-theoretic investigations into (intuitionistic) modal logics. Ph.D. thesis, Utrecht University (2022). https://dspace.library.uu.nl/bitstream/handle/1874/423244/proefschrift%20-%206343c2623d6ab.pdf
32. Goré, R., Ramanayake, R., Shillito, I.: Cut-elimination for provability logic by terminating proof-search: formalised and deconstructed using coq. In: Das, A., Negri, S. (eds.) TABLEAUX 2021. LNCS (LNAI), vol. 12842, pp. 299–313. Springer, Cham (2021). https://doi.org/10.1007/978-3-030-86059-2_18
33. Goré, R., Shillito, I.: Direct elimination of additive-cuts in GL4ip: verified and extracted. In: Fernández-Duque, D., Palmigiano, A., Pinchinat, S. (eds.) Advances in Modal Logic, AiML 2022, Rennes, France, 22–25 August 2022, pp. 429–449. College Publications (2022). http://www.aiml.net/volumes/volume14/26-Gore-Shillito.pdf
34. De Groot, J., Shillito, I., Clouston, R.: Semantical analysis of intuitionistic modal logics between CK and IK. In: 2025 40th Annual ACM/IEEE Symposium on Logic in Computer Science (LICS), pp. 169–182 (2025). https://doi.org/10.1109/LICS65433.2025.00020
35. Hudelmaier, J.: An O(n log n)-space decision procedure for intuitionistic propositional logic. J. Logic Comput. **3**(1), 63–75 (1993). https://doi.org/10.1093/logcom/3.1.63
36. Iemhoff, R.: Uniform interpolation and sequent calculi in modal logic. Arch. Math. Logic **58**(1–2), 155–181 (2019)
37. Iemhoff, R.: Terminating sequent calculi for two intuitionistic modal logics. J. Logic Comput. **28**(7), 1701–1712 (2018). https://doi.org/10.1093/logcom/exy026
38. Iemhoff, R.: Uniform interpolation and the existence of sequent calculi. Ann. Pure Appl. Logic **170**(11), 102711 (2019). https://doi.org/10.1016/j.apal.2019.05.008
39. Kavvos, G.A.: The many worlds of modal λ-calculi: I. Curry-Howard for necessity, possibility and time. CoRR abs/1605.08106 (2016). http://arxiv.org/abs/1605.08106
40. Kurahashi, T.: Interpolation properties for several logics. https://www2.kobe-u.ac.jp/~tk/jp/notes/ULIP.html. Accessed 13 Feb 2026
41. Mendler, M., de Paiva, V.: Constructive CK for contexts. In: Proceedings CRR 2005 (2005)
42. Mendler, M., Scheele, S.: Cut-free Gentzen calculus for multimodal CK. Inf. Comput. **209**(12), 1465–1490 (2011). https://doi.org/10.1016/j.ic.2011.10.003, intuitionistic Modal Logic and Applications (IMLA 2008)
43. Pitts, A.M.: On an interpretation of second order quantification in first order intuitionistic propositional logic. J. Symb. Log. **57**(1), 33–52 (1992). https://doi.org/10.2307/2275175
44. Plotkin, G., Stirling, C.: A framework for intuitionistic modal logics: extended abstract. In: Proceedings of the 1986 Conference on Theoretical Aspects of Reasoning about Knowledge, TARK 1986, pp. 399–406. Morgan Kaufmann Publishers Inc., San Francisco, CA, USA (1986)

45. Prior, A.N.: Time and Modality. John Locke Lectures. Clarendon Press (1957)
46. Shillito, I.: New Foundations for the Proof Theory of Bi-Intuitionistic and Provability Logics Mechanized in Coq. Ph.D. thesis, Australian National University, Canberra (2023). http://www.proquest.com/docview/2812065824?pq-origsite=gscholar&fromopenview=true
47. Shillito, I., van der Giessen, I., Goré, R., Iemhoff, R.: A new calculus for intuitionistic strong Löb logic: strong termination and cut-elimination, formalised. In: Ramanayake, R., Urban, J. (eds.) Automated Reasoning with Analytic Tableaux and Related Methods, TABLEAUX 2023, pp. 73–93. Springer, Cham (2023). https://doi.org/10.1007/978-3-031-43513-3_5
48. Simpson, A.K.: The proof theory and semantics of intuitionistic modal logic. Ph.D. thesis, University of Edinburgh (1994)
49. The Rocq Development Team: The Rocq Prover (2025). https://doi.org/10.5281/zenodo.15149629
50. Visser, A.: Uniform interpolation and layered bisimulation. In: Hájek, P. (ed.) Gödel 1996 Proceedings. Lecture Notes in Logic, vol. 6, pp. 139–164. Springer (1996). http://projecteuclid.org/download/pdf_1/euclid.lnl/1235417019
51. Vorob'ev, N.N.: A new algorithm of derivability in a constructive calculus of statements. Trudy Matematicheskogo Instituta imeni V. A. Steklova **52**, 193–225 (1958), (Translation in American Mathematical Society Translations, series 2, volume 94, 1970)
52. Wijesekera, D.: Constructive modal logics I. Ann. Pure Appl. Logic **50**(3), 271–301 (1990). https://doi.org/10.1016/0168-0072(90)90059-B
53. Wijesekera, D., Nerode, A.: Tableaux for constructive concurrent dynamic logic. Ann. Pure Appl. Logic **135**(1), 1–72 (2005). https://doi.org/10.1016/j.apal.2004.12.001
54. Wolter, F., Zakharyaschev, M.: On the relation between intuitionistic and classical modal logics. Algebra Logic **36**, 73–92 (1997). https://doi.org/10.1007/BF02672476
55. Wolter, F., Zakharyaschev, M.: Intuitionistic modal logic. In: Cantini, A., Casari, E., Minari, P. (eds.) Logic and Foundations of Mathematics: Selected Contributed Papers of the Tenth International Congress of Logic, Methodology and Philosophy of Science, Florence, August 1995, pp. 227–238. Springer, Dordrecht (1999). https://doi.org/10.1007/978-94-017-2109-7_17
56. Wolter, F., Zakharyaschev, M.: Intuitionistic modal logics as fragments of classical bimodal logics. Logic Work Stud. Fuzziness Soft Comput. **24**, 168–186 (1999)

Open Access This chapter is licensed under the terms of the Creative Commons Attribution 4.0 International License (http://creativecommons.org/licenses/by/4.0/), which permits use, sharing, adaptation, distribution and reproduction in any medium or format, as long as you give appropriate credit to the original author(s) and the source, provide a link to the Creative Commons license and indicate if changes were made.

The images or other third party material in this chapter are included in the chapter's Creative Commons license, unless indicated otherwise in a credit line to the material. If material is not included in the chapter's Creative Commons license and your intended use is not permitted by statutory regulation or exceeds the permitted use, you will need to obtain permission directly from the copyright holder.

A Complete Proof System for HyperLTL

Naijun Zhan[1,2(✉)], Wen Tang[3], and Dimitar Guelev[4]

[1] School of Computer Science and Key Laboratory of High Confidence Software Technologies of Ministry of Education, Peking University, Beijing, China
njzhan@pku.edu.cn
[2] Zhongguancun Laboratory, Beijing, China
[3] Department of Philosophy, Peking University, Beijing, China
[4] Institute of Mathematics and Informatics, Bulgarian Academy of Sciences, Sofia, Bulgaria

Abstract. HyperLTL extends Linear Temporal Logic (LTL) with explicit trace variables and quantification over traces, allowing formulas to relate multiple executions within a single specification. Consequently, HyperLTL has become an important specification formalism for hyperproperties, i.e., properties of *sets* of traces rather than individual traces. However, the satisfiability of HyperLTL is undecidable, so fully automatic reasoning cannot, in general, replace deductive methods to establish validity. Furthermore, HyperLTL restricts trace quantification to the outermost scope of formulas. In this paper, we study HyperLTL*, a generalization that removes this restriction by allowing trace quantifiers to occur under temporal operators. We present a Gentzen-style sequent calculus for HyperLTL* and establish completeness by means of suitable infinitary rules. We then derive sound finitary principles that are amenable to interactive theorem proving and can serve as a foundation for mechanized reasoning. We illustrate the use of the calculus on representative HyperLTL-style specifications that are difficult to discharge by existing automatic procedures. Finally, we analyze the expressiveness of HyperLTL* and discuss how the calculus can be combined with first-order reasoning infrastructure.

Keywords: HyperLTL · proof system · interactive theorem proving · first-order logic · satisfiability

1 Introduction

Hyperproperties [19] generalize the notion of trace properties [2] from sets of traces (paths) to sets of sets of traces. Requirements on computing systems that are hyperproperties but not trace properties include information flow security policies such as noninterference [36], observational determinism [50], sensitivity and robustness requirements in cyber-physical systems [49], and consistency conditions such as linearizability in concurrent data structures [13], and so on.

Formulas in classical temporal logics, such as Linear Temporal Logic (LTL) [44], Computation Tree Logics (CTL and CTL*) [17,26], and μ-calculus [41],

© The Author(s) 2026
A. Biere et al. (Eds.): IJCAR 2026, LNAI 16688, pp. 377–395, 2026.
https://doi.org/10.1007/978-3-032-32589-1_23

characterize sets of traces or sets of Kripke models. However, expressing specific properties of sets of traces, such as epistemic properties, typically requires the addition of dedicated modalities to these logics. HyperLTL [18], due to Clarkson *et al.*, extends LTL by introducing trace variables and quantification over the trace domain. This mechanism makes it possible to express relational specifications by correlating the valuations of propositions across multiple traces. Hence, HyperLTL provides a powerful framework for expressing properties over sets of traces. Automatic verification techniques have been developed for HyperLTL, including model- and satisfiability-checking algorithms [27–29,33]. With these techniques, HyperLTL has become a predominant specification logic for hyperproperties and has been successfully applied to fundamental security policies, distributed protocols and coding theories [28,30].

The model-checking complexity of HyperLTL formulas over finite Kripke structures is non-elementary [18]; moreover, neither satisfiability [27] nor synthesis [29] is decidable for the full logic. This inherent complexity makes deductive methods particularly relevant: they provide a complementary reasoning mode when algorithmic procedures diverge or do not apply. In this paper, we consider HyperLTL*, which extends HyperLTL by removing the restriction on quantifiers not to appear in the scope of temporal operators. We propose a complete proof system for HyperLTL*, obtained by extending a Gentzen-style calculus with ω- and Coω-rules. This yields a proof-theoretic basis for interactive theorem proving for HyperLTL*, complementing automated verification techniques and enabling the formal derivation of specifications that remain beyond the reach of fully automatic methods.

Our proof system is presented in the Gentzen style, building upon the one for LTL [35] while incorporating modified temporal rules and extra trace quantifier rules. Additionally, more powerful induction rules, the ω-rule and Coω-rule, are required. This necessity arises because HyperLTL lacks the finite model property [34], rendering the finiteness-of-premise assumption in LTL's proof system [35] inadequate. Consequently, an induction axiom similar to that of LTL [35] is insufficient to guarantee the existence of witnesses for trace quantifiers. Indeed, it is well established that no finitary proof system for a non-compact logic can achieve strong completeness [45]. We provide rigorous proofs for both the soundness and the completeness of our proof system.

Furthermore, we show that HyperLTL* is more expressive than HyperLTL but still strictly subsumed by the first-order logic $FO[<, E]$. To showcase the utility of our proof system, we illustrate its application to formulas with multiple quantifier alternations, which are hard to handle by automatic techniques.

1.1 Related Work

We briefly review prior work on (i) specification formalisms for hyperproperties and (ii) reasoning and verification techniques for such formalisms.

Hyperlogics. Alur *et al.* observed that *opacity* is not expressible in the μ-calculus [4], despite the fact that the μ-calculus subsumes LTL, CTL*, dynamic logic, and related modal formalisms. This illustrates a general phenomenon: many security and consistency requirements are not properties of a single execution, but rather constrain *sets* of executions (hyperproperties). To capture such requirements, a variety of hyperlogics has been developed, can be briefly summarized as follows:

1. *Encoding via model restrictions.* Structural assumptions on the model (e.g., symmetry) can make certain hyperproperties definable in standard logics; examples include observational determinism [6,39] and noninterference [7].
2. *Adding dedicated modalities.* Examples include path-equivalence modalities in branching-time logics [3], the hide modality H in SecLTL [24], and epistemic modalities [5].
3. *First-order and first-order inspired formalisms.* Monadic first-order logic with the equal-level predicate is studied in [34], and alternative quantifier disciplines are investigated in [8].
4. *Explicit trace/path quantification.* This line includes QLTL [47], HyperPDL-Δ [37], HyperATL* [10], HyperCTL* [18], and so on. In which HyperLTL is a prominent instance.

Further perspectives include team semantics for temporal logics [42,48]. Beyond the synchronous finite-state setting, the high complexity of reasoning about asynchronous systems has motivated dedicated logics [9,14,38]; similarly, quantitative and probabilistic variants have been considered [1,25,33]. A preliminary comparison of these formalisms in terms of expressiveness and algorithmic problems is given in [21].

From a proof-theoretic viewpoint, strong completeness for non-compact logics is typically obtained via infinitary inference principles; examples include intuitionistic temporal logic [15] and higher-order duration calculus [51,52]. However, these systems are Hilbert-style and do not target trace-quantifying temporal hyperlogics; to the best of our knowledge, a strongly complete Gentzen-style calculus in this setting has not previously been developed.

Verification of Hyperproperties. Inspired by the success of classical modal and temporal logics, most of the existing work on hyperlogics focus on automatic verification techniques such as model- and satisfiability-checking, synthesis, and monitoring. Model- and satisfiability-checking tools for HyperLTL were presented in [22,33] and [27,28,30], respectively. Synthesis tools were presented in [29]. Runtime monitoring tools of HyperLTL were reported in [31,32]. Recently, repairing programs w.r.t. HyperLTL was investigated in [11].

In general, the computational complexity of HyperLTL exceeds that of classical temporal logics [27]. It is well known that LTL model checking is PSPACE-COMPLETE [46]. In contrast, HyperLTL model checking over finite Kripke structures is nonelementary [33], and its satisfiability is not semi-decidable [34]. As a consequence, HyperLTL admits no finitary proof system that is strongly complete. The largest known decidable fragment of HyperLTL consists of formulas with quantifier prefix of the form $\exists^*\forall^*$ [21]; important information-flow policies such as general noninterference (GNI) and state opacity lie outside this fragment. This motivates interactive and semi-automated reasoning, for which a proof system is a prerequisite. To the best of our knowledge, the only proof system available in the literature [20] handles only a fragment of HyperLTL and does not establish full proof-theoretic metatheory such as (strong) completeness. More recently, a set of co-induction proof rules for a fragment of HyperLTL of the type $\forall^*\exists^*\Box\psi$ is reported in [23], where ψ is an LTL formula. This motivates us to investigate this issue in this paper.

Organization. The rest of this paper is organized as follows: Sect. 2 defines the syntax and semantics of HyperLTL*, Sect. 3 presents a proof system in Gentzen style for HyperLTL*, while Sect. 4 proves the completeness of the proof system, Sect. 5 discusses the expressiveness of HyperLTL*, Sect. 6 presents a case study, and finally Sect. 7 draws a conclusion and discusses future work.

2 Syntax and Semantics of HyperLTL*

In this section, we define HyperLTL* by lifting the HyperLTL restriction that trace quantifiers cannot occur within the scope of temporal operators. The logic HyperLTL* has the same syntax as HyperCTL* [18]. However, HyperCTL* is interpreted over Kripke structures, HyperLTL* is interpreted over trace sets, as in HyperLTL.

Definition 1. *A HyperLTL* vocabulary consists of a countable set of trace variables* $\mathbb{T}$, *and a countable set of propositional letters* $\mathbb{P}$. *The syntax of HyperLTL* formulas is defined by the following BNF:*

$$\varphi ::= \top \mid a_\pi \mid \exists\pi\varphi \mid \neg\varphi \mid \varphi\wedge\varphi \mid \bigcirc\varphi \mid \varphi\,\mathcal{U}\varphi$$

where $a \in \mathbb{P}$ *and* $\pi \in \mathbb{T}$.

In Definition 1, $\bigcirc$ reads *next* and $\mathcal{U}$ reads *until*, as in LTL. The propositional constant $\bot$, the Boolean connectives $\vee$ and $\rightarrow$, the universal quantifier $\forall$, and the temporal operators $\mathcal{R}$, $\Diamond$, $\Box$, and $\mathcal{W}$ are treated as standard abbreviations: $\varphi\mathcal{R}\psi \hat{=} \neg(\neg\varphi\mathcal{U}\neg\psi)$, $\Diamond\varphi \hat{=} \top\mathcal{U}\varphi$, $\Box\varphi \hat{=} \neg\Diamond\neg\varphi$, $\varphi\mathcal{W}\psi \hat{=} \Box\varphi \vee (\varphi\mathcal{U}\psi)$.

Let $\Sigma \hat{=} 2^{\mathbb{P}}$. A model $\mathcal{M}$ is a pair (T, Π) consisting of a set of traces $T \subseteq \Sigma^\omega$ and a partial *trace assignment* $\Pi : \mathbb{T} \rightarrow T$.

Definition 2. *Given a HyperLTL* formula* φ, *a model* $\mathcal{M} \hat{=} (T, \Pi)$, *and a reference position* $i < \omega$, *the satisfaction of* φ *in* $\mathcal{M}$ *at position* i, *denoted by* $\mathcal{M}, i \models \varphi$, *is defined inductively as follows:*

$$\begin{array}{lll}
\mathcal{M}, i \models \top & & \\
\mathcal{M}, i \models a_\pi & \textit{iff} & a \in \Pi(\pi)[i] \\
\mathcal{M}, i \models \neg\varphi & \textit{iff} & \mathcal{M}, i \not\models \varphi \\
\mathcal{M}, i \models \varphi\vee\psi & \textit{iff} & \mathcal{M}, i \models \varphi \textit{ or } \mathcal{M}, i \models \psi \\
\mathcal{M}, i \models \bigcirc\varphi & \textit{iff} & \mathcal{M}, i+1 \models \varphi \\
\mathcal{M}, i \models \varphi\mathcal{U}\psi & \textit{iff} & \exists j \geq 0. \mathcal{M}, i+j \models \psi \textit{ and } \forall k < j. \mathcal{M}, i+k \models \varphi \\
\mathcal{M}, i \models \exists\pi\varphi & \textit{iff} & \textit{there exists } t \in T \textit{ such that } \mathcal{M}[\pi \mapsto t], i \models \varphi
\end{array}$$

where $\mathcal{M}[\pi \mapsto t] \hat{=} (T, \Pi[\pi \mapsto t])$ *denotes the model obtained from* $\mathcal{M}$ *by updating* Π *to map* π *to* t. *The empty assignment is written* $\Pi_\emptyset$. *Given a sentence* φ, *we write* $T, i \models \varphi$ *for* $(T, \Pi_\emptyset), i \models \varphi$. *Given a set of formulas* Γ *and a formula* φ, *we write* $\Gamma \models \varphi$ *if, for all* $i \in \mathbb{N}$ *and all models* $\mathcal{M}$, $\mathcal{M}, i \models \gamma$ *for all* $\gamma \in \Gamma$ *implies* $\mathcal{M}, i \models \varphi$.

The sets $\mathrm{FV}(\varphi)$ and $\mathrm{BV}(\varphi)$ of trace variables which have free and bound occurrences in formula φ, respectively, are defined as usual.

The following coincidence lemma is straightforward.

Lemma 1. *If* $\Pi_1|_{\mathrm{FV}(\varphi)} = \Pi_2|_{\mathrm{FV}(\varphi)}$, *then* $(T, \Pi_1), i \models \varphi$ *iff* $(T, \Pi_2), i \models \varphi$.

In what follows, $\varphi[\pi'/\pi]$ denotes the substitution of π by π' for all free occurrences of π in φ.

Lemma 2. *If* $\pi' \notin \mathrm{BV}(\varphi)$, *then* $\mathcal{M}, i \models \varphi[\pi'/\pi]$ *is equivalent to* $\mathcal{M}[\pi \mapsto \Pi(\pi')], i \models \varphi$ *for all* $\mathcal{M}$ *and all* $i < \omega$.

3 A Sequent Calculus $\mathcal{L}_{H\omega}$ for HyperLTL*

A sequent is a pair of (possibly infinite) sets of HyperLTL* formulas, written $\Gamma \vdash \Delta$. We call $\Gamma \vdash \Delta$ *valid* if, for every model $\mathcal{M}$ and every $i \in \mathbb{N}$, $\mathcal{M}, i \models \Gamma$ implies that there exists $\varphi \in \Delta$ such that $\mathcal{M}, i \models \varphi$. In what follows, we write "Γ, Δ" for $\Gamma \cup \Delta$, "Γ, φ" for $\Gamma \cup \{\varphi\}$, and $\bigcirc^{-1} \Gamma$ for $\{\gamma \mid \bigcirc \gamma \in \Gamma\}$.

We present a Gentzen-style proof system for HyperLTL*, denoted by $\mathcal{L}_{H\omega}$, in Table 1. The system $\mathcal{L}_{H\omega}$ consists of four groups of inference rules, respectively for Boolean connectives, temporal operators, trace quantifiers, and general structures. The rules for connectives $\neg$ and $\wedge$ are standard, the same as in first-order logic. The rules for temporal operators $\bigcirc$, $\Diamond$, and $\mathcal{U}$ (and their combinations) are essentially the same as in LTL, except that we use infinitary rules (ω and Coω) in place of the induction axiom $\Box(\varphi \to \bigcirc \varphi) \to (\varphi \to \Box \varphi)$. We will explain why later. The rules for trace quantifiers are new, but follow standard proof-theoretic patterns. The structural rules are essentially the same as in LTL, but we omit the generalization rule $\frac{\vdash \varphi}{\vdash \Box \varphi}$. The role of its infinitary sequent counterpart $\frac{\Gamma \vdash \varphi}{\{\Box \gamma \mid \gamma \in \Gamma\} \vdash \Box \varphi}$ is largely assumed by the derived rule $G\Box$ (see below).

3.1 Why ω-Rule

It is well-known that LTL has the small (lasso) model property [40], thus it is reasonable to assume a premise set Δ to be finite. Without this assumption, LTL cannot have a finite complete proof system [15]. A notable counterexample is $\Gamma = \{\bigcirc^k p \mid k \in \mathbb{N}\} \cup \{\Diamond \neg p\}$. Clearly, Γ is infinite and not satisfiable, and for any LTL formula φ, we have $\Gamma \models \varphi$ and $\Gamma \models \neg \varphi$. If LTL has a finite complete proof system without the assumption, it follows $\Gamma \vdash \varphi$ and $\Gamma \vdash \neg \varphi$,

Table 1. Proof System $\mathcal{L}_{H\omega}$

Boolean rules:

$$(L\neg)\ \frac{\Gamma \vdash \varphi}{\Gamma, \neg\varphi \vdash \chi} \quad (R\neg)\ \frac{\Gamma, \varphi \vdash \bot}{\Gamma \vdash \neg\varphi} \quad (L\wedge)\ \frac{\Gamma, \varphi, \psi \vdash \chi}{\Gamma, \varphi \wedge \psi \vdash \chi} \quad (R\wedge)\ \frac{\Gamma \vdash \varphi \quad \Gamma \vdash \psi}{\Gamma \vdash \varphi \wedge \psi}$$

Temporal rules:

$$(R\bigcirc)\ \frac{\bigcirc^{-1}\Gamma \vdash \varphi}{\Gamma \vdash \bigcirc\varphi} \quad (R\neg\bigcirc)\ \frac{\Gamma \vdash \bigcirc\neg\varphi}{\Gamma \vdash \neg\bigcirc\varphi} \quad (L\neg\bigcirc)\ \frac{\Gamma, \bigcirc\neg\varphi \vdash \chi}{\Gamma, \neg\bigcirc\varphi \vdash \chi}$$

$$(\Diamond\bigcirc)\ \frac{\Gamma \vdash \bigcirc\Diamond\varphi}{\Gamma \vdash \Diamond\bigcirc\varphi} \quad (\omega)\ \frac{}{\{\bigcirc^k \varphi \mid k \in \mathbb{N}\} \vdash \Box\varphi} \quad (\mathrm{Co}\omega)\ \frac{}{\Diamond\varphi \vdash \bigcirc^k \varphi, \exists k \in \mathbb{N}}$$

$$(\Diamond\mathcal{U})\ \frac{\Gamma \vdash \varphi\mathcal{U}\psi}{\Gamma \vdash \Diamond\psi} \quad (L\mathcal{U})\ \frac{\Gamma, \psi \vdash \chi \ \Gamma, \varphi, \neg\psi, \bigcirc(\varphi\mathcal{U}\psi) \vdash \chi}{\Gamma, \varphi\mathcal{U}\psi \vdash \chi} \quad (R\mathcal{U})\ \frac{\Gamma, \neg\varphi \vdash \psi \ \Gamma, \varphi, \neg\bigcirc(\varphi\mathcal{U}\psi) \vdash \psi}{\Gamma \vdash \varphi\mathcal{U}\psi}$$

Quantifier rules:

$$(R\exists)\ \frac{\Gamma \vdash \varphi[\pi'/\pi]}{\Gamma \vdash \exists\pi\varphi} \quad (L\exists)\ \frac{\Gamma, \psi[\pi'/\pi] \vdash \varphi}{\Gamma, \exists\pi\psi \vdash \varphi} \quad \pi' \notin \mathrm{FV}(\Gamma \cup \{\exists\pi\psi, \varphi\})$$

$$(R\bigcirc\exists)\ \frac{\Gamma \vdash \bigcirc\exists\pi\varphi}{\Gamma \vdash \exists\pi\bigcirc\varphi} \quad (L\bigcirc\exists)\ \frac{\Gamma, \bigcirc\exists\pi\varphi \vdash \chi}{\Gamma, \exists\pi\bigcirc\varphi \vdash \chi}$$

Structural rules:

$$(\mathrm{As})\ \frac{}{\Gamma, \varphi \vdash \varphi} \quad (\mathrm{Wk})\ \frac{\Gamma \vdash \chi}{\Gamma, \Delta \vdash \chi} \quad (\mathrm{Cd})\ \frac{\Gamma, \neg\varphi \vdash \bot}{\Gamma \vdash \varphi} \quad (\bigcirc\bot)\ \frac{\Gamma \vdash \bigcirc\bot}{\Gamma \vdash \chi} \quad (\mathrm{Cut})\ \frac{\Gamma \vdash \psi \ \Gamma, \psi \vdash \varphi}{\Gamma \vdash \varphi}$$

which is a contradiction. On the other hand, [34] proved that HyperLTL, let alone HyperLTL*, have no established form of small model property. Hence, the proof system $\mathcal{L}_{H\omega}$ has to have two infinitary rules (ω) and (Coω), that relate $\bigcirc$ to $\Box$ (dually $\Diamond$) with infinitely many premises (conclusions). Fortunately, these infinitely many premises can sometimes, if not often, be obtained by induction, which could be proved automatically in interactive theorem provers, like Rocq.

3.2 Proofs and Derivability in $\mathcal{L}_{H\omega}$

A proof P in a proof system with infinitary rules such as $\mathcal{L}_{H\omega}$ is a tree P of height $H(P)$, possibly with infinite width, labeled with sequents, defined as follows:

- any instance of an axiom, that is, a proof rule without premises, is a proof, with $H(P) = 1$;
- if P_is are proofs of all the premises of some instance of a proof rule, where $i \in I$ and I may be finite or infinite, then the tree P is with the conclusion of the rule instance as root, and P_is as immediate descendants, with $H(P) = \sup_{i \in I}(H(P_i) + 1)$.

Sequent $\Gamma \vdash \varphi$ is derivable in $\mathcal{L}_{H\omega}$, written $\Gamma \vdash_{\mathcal{L}_{H\omega}} \varphi$, if it is the label of the root of a proof.

3.3 Soundness of $\mathcal{L}_{H\omega}$

Theorem 1 (Soundness). *For any sequent $\Gamma \vdash \varphi$, $\Gamma \vdash_{\mathcal{L}_{H\omega}} \varphi$ implies $\Gamma \models \varphi$.*

Proof. This is done by induction on $H(P)$. We only provide proofs for $(R\exists)$ and $(L\exists)$, the remaining cases are straightforward.

- $(R\exists)$: Suppose $\Gamma \vdash \varphi[\pi'/\pi]$. The induction hypothesis implies $\Gamma \models \varphi[\pi'/\pi]$. This means that for any $\mathcal{M}, i$ as given in Definition 2, $\mathcal{M}, i \models \Gamma$ implies $\mathcal{M}, i \models \varphi[\pi'/\pi]$. By Lemma 2, $\mathcal{M}, i \models \varphi[\pi'/\pi]$ means that $\mathcal{M}[\pi \mapsto \Pi(\pi')], i \models \varphi[\pi'/\pi]$, i.e., $\mathcal{M}, i \models \exists\pi\varphi$ according to Definition 2.
- $(L\exists)$: Suppose $\Gamma, \psi[\pi'/\pi] \vdash \varphi$ with π' being not free in $\Gamma, \exists\pi\psi, \varphi$. Thus, it follows $\Gamma, \psi[\pi'/\pi] \models \varphi$ by the induction hypothesis. That is, for any $\mathcal{M}, i$, $\mathcal{M}, i \models \Gamma$ and $\mathcal{M}, i \models \psi[\pi'/\pi]$ implies $\mathcal{M}, i \models \varphi$. As π' is not free in $\Gamma, \exists\pi\psi, \varphi$, according to Definition 2, $\mathcal{M}, i \models \psi[\pi'/\pi]$ iff $\mathcal{M}, i \models \exists\pi\psi$. Whence, for any $\mathcal{M}, i$, $\mathcal{M}, i \models \Gamma$ and $\mathcal{M}, i \models \exists\pi\psi$ implies $\mathcal{M}, i \models \varphi$, i.e., $\Gamma, \exists\pi\psi \models \varphi$. □

4 Completeness of $\mathcal{L}_{H\omega}$

We establish the completeness of $\mathcal{L}_{H\omega}$ by the following steps: first showing that, for any set of formulas Δ, if Δ is consistent w.r.t. $\mathcal{L}_{H\omega}$, that is $\Delta \nvdash_{\mathcal{L}_{H\omega}} \bot$, then a maximal $\Delta' \supseteq \Delta$ exists such that $\Delta' \nvdash_{\mathcal{L}_{H\omega}} \bot$ too; then showing how such a Δ' can be used to build a model to refute $\Delta \models \bot$; finally, by contraposition, this implies that $\Delta \vdash_{\mathcal{L}_{H\omega}} \varphi$ which is immediately derivable with $\Delta, \neg\varphi \vdash_{\mathcal{L}_{H\omega}} \bot$, follows from $\Delta \models \varphi$, by virtue of its equivalence with $\Delta, \neg\varphi \models \bot$.

4.1 The Conservativeness of HyperLTL* over LTL

To cut down the parts of the proof which essentially pertain to LTL, we establish and use the fact that $\mathcal{L}_{H\omega}$ extends theoremhood as known for LTL in a conservative way.

Proposition 1. *Every substitution instance of a valid propositional LTL formula is a theorem in $\mathcal{L}_{H\omega}$.*

This means that, e.g., $\vdash_{\mathcal{L}_{H\omega}} \bigcirc\exists\pi\Diamond a_\pi \vee \bigcirc\neg\exists\pi\Diamond a_\pi$ follows from the validity of $\bigcirc q \vee \bigcirc\neg q$ in LTL, regardless of the fact that the position of q in the latter formula is taken by $\exists\pi\Diamond a_\pi$, which is HyperLTL*-specific.

Proof. Induction on the construction of LTL Hilbert-style proofs (cf. e.g., [43]) of the translation

$$t(\alpha[\exists\pi_1\chi_1/q_{\exists\pi_1\chi_1}, \ldots, \exists\pi_N\chi_N/q_{\exists\pi_N\chi_N}, a^1_{\rho_1}/a^1_{\rho_1}, \ldots, a^M_{\rho_M}/a^M_{\rho_M}]) \hat{=} \alpha$$

of the given LTL substitution instance of LTL formula α which maps every quantified HyperLTL formula $\exists\pi\chi$ or subscripted atomic proposition a_ρ to distinct fresh propositional variables $q_{\exists\pi\chi}$ and (the eponymous) a_ρ, respectively. □

4.2 The Deduction Theorem and Some Derived Rules in $\mathcal{L}_{H\omega}$

Proposition 2 (Deduction Theorem). *For any set of formulas Γ and formula φ, $\Gamma, \varphi \vdash \theta$ iff $\Gamma \vdash \varphi \rightarrow \theta$.*

Proof. $\Rightarrow$: $\Gamma, \varphi \vdash \theta$ implies $\Gamma, \varphi, \neg\theta \vdash \bot$ by (L$\neg$). It follows $\Gamma, \varphi \wedge \neg\theta \vdash \bot$ by (L$\wedge$). Hence, it derives $\Gamma \vdash \neg(\varphi \wedge \neg\theta)$ by (R$\neg$), that is $\Gamma \vdash \varphi \rightarrow \theta$.
$\Leftarrow$: Clearly, $\Gamma \vdash \varphi \rightarrow \theta$ implies $\Gamma \vdash \neg(\varphi \wedge \neg\theta)$, which gives $\Gamma, \varphi \wedge \neg\theta \vdash \bot$ by (L$\neg$). Moreover, we have $\Gamma, \varphi, \neg\theta \vdash \varphi \wedge \neg\theta$ by (As) and $(R\wedge)_2$. It follows that $\Gamma, \varphi, \neg\theta \vdash \bot$ by (Cut). Hence $\Gamma, \varphi \vdash \theta$ by $(R\neg)$. □

Now the rule shown in Table 2 can be easily derived in $\mathcal{L}_{H\omega}$:

Table 2. Some Derived Rules

$(\neg\bigcirc)^k$	$\dfrac{\Delta \vdash \neg\bigcirc^k\varphi}{\Delta \vdash \bigcirc^k\neg\varphi}, k \in \mathbb{N}$	$(L\forall)$	$\dfrac{\Delta, \psi[\pi'/\pi] \vdash \chi}{\Delta, \forall\pi\psi \vdash \chi}$
$(\Diamond\bigcirc)^k$	$\dfrac{\Delta \vdash \bigcirc^k\Diamond\varphi}{\Delta \vdash \Diamond\bigcirc^k\varphi}, k \in \mathbb{N}$	$(R\forall)$	$\dfrac{\Delta \vdash \varphi[\pi'/\pi], \pi' \notin \mathrm{FV}(\Delta \cup \{\forall\pi\varphi\})}{\Delta \vdash \forall\pi\varphi}$
$(L\Box)$	$\dfrac{\Delta, \varphi, \bigcirc\Box\varphi \vdash \chi}{\Delta, \Box\varphi \vdash \chi}$	$(R\Box)$	$\dfrac{\Delta \vdash \varphi \quad \Delta, \bigcirc(\top\mathcal{U}\neg\varphi) \vdash \neg\varphi}{\Delta \vdash \Box\varphi}$
$(G\Box)$	$\dfrac{\Delta \vdash \Box(\neg\varphi \vee \bigcirc\varphi)}{\Delta, \varphi \vdash \Box\varphi}$	$(L\vee)$	$\dfrac{\Delta, \varphi \vdash \chi, \quad \Delta, \psi \vdash \chi}{\Delta, \varphi \vee \psi \vdash \chi}$
$(R\vee_1)$	$\dfrac{\Delta \vdash \varphi}{\Delta \vdash \varphi \vee \psi}$	$(R\vee_2)$	$\dfrac{\Delta \vdash \psi}{\Delta \vdash \varphi \vee \psi}$

Proof. $R\forall$ and $L\forall$ can be proved by the following proof fragments respectively, for instance:

$$\dfrac{\dfrac{\dfrac{\Delta, \psi[\pi'/\pi] \vdash \chi}{\Delta, \neg\chi \vdash \neg\psi[\pi'/\pi]}\, L\neg, R\neg}{\Delta, \neg\chi \vdash \exists\pi\neg\psi}\, R\exists}{\Delta, \neg\exists\pi\neg\psi \vdash \chi}\, L\neg, R\neg \qquad \dfrac{\dfrac{\dfrac{\Delta \vdash \psi[\pi'/\pi]}{\Delta, \neg\psi[\pi'/\pi] \vdash \bot}\, L\neg}{\Delta, \exists\pi\neg\psi \vdash \bot}\, L\exists}{\Delta \vdash \neg\exists\pi\neg\psi}\, R\neg$$

The other rules can be obtained as single applications of Proposition 1, possibly Proposition 2, and *MP*, using the theoremhood in LTL of the following formulas, given in the order of appearance of the related rules: $\neg\bigcirc^k\varphi \rightarrow \bigcirc^k\neg\varphi$, $\bigcirc^k\Diamond\varphi \rightarrow \Diamond\bigcirc^k\varphi$, $(\varphi \wedge \bigcirc\Box\varphi \rightarrow \chi) \leftrightarrow (\Box\varphi \rightarrow \chi)$, $\varphi \rightarrow (\Box(\varphi \rightarrow \bigcirc\varphi) \rightarrow \Box\varphi)$, $\varphi \rightarrow ((\varphi \rightarrow \neg\bigcirc\Diamond\neg\varphi) \rightarrow \Box\varphi)$, $(\varphi \rightarrow \chi) \rightarrow ((\psi \rightarrow \chi) \rightarrow (\varphi \vee \psi \rightarrow \chi))$, and $\varphi \rightarrow \varphi \vee \psi$. □

4.3 A Canonical Model

Definition 3. *A set of formulas Δ is called* consistent, *if $\Delta \nvdash_{\mathcal{L}_{H\omega}} \bot$. Δ is called* a maximal consistent set, *if there does not exist $\Delta' \supsetneq \Delta$ that satisfies $\Delta' \nvdash \bot$.*

In the sequel we often omit the $_{\mathcal{L}_{H\omega}}$ in $\vdash_{\mathcal{L}_{H\omega}}$ to improve readability.

Lemma 3. *Let Δ be a maximal consistent set and φ, ψ be formulas. Then*

(i) $\varphi \notin \Delta$ *iff* $\neg\varphi \in \Delta$, *and* $\Delta \vdash \varphi$ *implies* $\varphi \in \Delta$;
(ii) $\varphi \wedge \psi \in \Delta$ *iff* $\varphi \in \Delta$ *and* $\psi \in \Delta$;
(iii) $\varphi \mathcal{U} \psi \in \Delta$ *iff* $\psi \in \Delta$, *or* $\neg\psi, \varphi, \bigcirc(\varphi \mathcal{U} \psi) \in \Delta$;
(iv) $\neg \bigcirc \varphi \in \Delta$ *iff* $\bigcirc \neg\varphi \in \Delta$;
(v) $\exists\pi \bigcirc \varphi \in \Delta$ *iff* $\bigcirc \exists\pi\varphi \in \Delta$.

Given the consistency of Δ, the first statement of (i) is indeed equivalent to the maximality of Δ.

Proof. The proofs of (i) and (ii) are as in classical propositional logic. We skip the easy directions in the proofs of (iii), (iv) and (v) below too:

(iii) ($\Rightarrow$) Assume $\varphi \mathcal{U} \psi \in \Delta$, $\psi \notin \Delta$ and $\chi \notin \Delta$, for some $\chi \in \{\neg\psi, \varphi, \bigcirc(\varphi \mathcal{U} \psi)\}$.

- $\chi = \neg\psi$: From (i), we have $\neg\psi \in \Delta$ and $\neg\neg\psi \in \Delta$, obviously contradicts to the consistency of Δ.
- $\chi = \varphi$: Also, by (i), we have $\neg\varphi \in \Delta$. Obviously, $\neg\psi, \neg\varphi, \psi \vdash \bot$, and $\neg\psi, \neg\varphi, \varphi, \bigcirc(\varphi \mathcal{U} \psi) \vdash \bot$. Hence, $\neg\psi, \neg\varphi, \varphi \mathcal{U} \psi \vdash \bot$ by $(L\mathcal{U})$, which gives $\neg\varphi, \neg\psi \vdash \neg(\varphi \mathcal{U} \psi)$ by $(R\neg)$. This concludes that $\Delta \vdash \neg(\varphi \mathcal{U} \psi)$, that contradicts to the consistency of Δ.
- $\chi = \bigcirc(\varphi \mathcal{U} \psi)$: Likewise, by (i), we have $\neg \bigcirc(\varphi \mathcal{U} \psi) \in \Delta$. Obviously, $\neg\psi, \neg \bigcirc(\varphi \mathcal{U} \psi), \psi \vdash \bot$, and $\neg\psi, \neg \bigcirc(\varphi \mathcal{U} \psi), \varphi, \bigcirc(\varphi \mathcal{U} \psi) \vdash \bot$. Hence, $\neg\psi, \neg \bigcirc(\varphi \mathcal{U} \psi), \varphi \mathcal{U} \psi \vdash \bot$ by $(L\mathcal{U})$, which gives $\neg\varphi, \neg \bigcirc(\varphi \mathcal{U} \psi) \vdash \neg(\varphi \mathcal{U} \psi)$ by $(R\neg)$. This concludes that $\Delta \vdash \neg(\varphi \mathcal{U} \psi)$ by (Wk), which contradicts the consistency of Δ.

(iv) ($\Rightarrow$): $\bigcirc \neg\varphi \in \Delta$ implies $\Delta \vdash \bigcirc \neg\varphi$ by (As), which implies $\Delta \vdash \neg \bigcirc \varphi$ by $(R\neg \bigcirc)$. Hence, it follows $\neg \bigcirc \varphi \in \Delta$ by (i).
($\Leftarrow$): $\bigcirc \neg\varphi \notin \Delta$ implies $\Delta, \bigcirc \neg\varphi \vdash \bot$ by (i), which implies $\Delta, \neg \bigcirc \varphi \vdash \bot$ by $(L\neg \bigcirc)$. Thus, it follows $\neg \bigcirc \varphi \notin \Delta$ by (i).
(v) Similar to the proof of (iv). □

Lemma 4. *If Δ is a maximal consistent set then so is $\bigcirc^{-1} \Delta$.*

Proof. Any hypothetical proof of $\bigcirc^{-1} \Delta \vdash_{\mathcal{L}_{H\omega}} \bot$ can be used to obtain a proof of $\Delta \vdash_{\mathcal{L}_{H\omega}} \bigcirc \bot$ by means of $(R\bigcirc)$, and $(\bigcirc\bot)$ allows deriving $\Delta \vdash_{\mathcal{L}_{H\omega}} \bot$ from that, which gives rise to a contradiction. Maximality is established by observing that the equivalence between $\bigcirc \varphi \in \Delta$ and $\neg \bigcirc \varphi \notin \Delta$ implies the equivalence between $\varphi \in \bigcirc^{-1} \Delta$ and $\neg\varphi \notin \bigcirc^{-1} \Delta$. □

Definition 4. *Let Δ be a set of formulas.*

- *Δ has the $\exists$-property iff for any $\exists\pi\varphi \in \Delta$, there exists a trace variable π' such that $\varphi[\pi'/\pi] \in \Delta$.*
- *Δ has the $\mathcal{U}$-property iff for any $\varphi \mathcal{U} \psi \in \Delta$, there exists a $k \in \mathbb{N}$ such that $\bigcirc^k \psi \in \Delta$.*
- *Δ has the strengthened $\mathcal{U}$-property iff for any $\bigcirc^j(\varphi \mathcal{U} \psi) \in \Delta$, there exists an $n \geq j$ such that $\bigcirc^n \psi \in \Delta$.*

Lemma 5. *If a maximal consistent set Δ has the $\exists$-property, then so does $\bigcirc^{-1}\Delta$.*

Proof. For any $\exists\pi\varphi \in \bigcirc^{-1}\Delta$, by the definition of $\bigcirc^{-1}\Delta$, we have $\bigcirc\exists\pi\varphi \in \Delta$. By Lemma 3, we have $\exists\pi\bigcirc\varphi \in \Delta$. Since Δ has the $\exists$-property, $\bigcirc\varphi[\pi'/\pi] \in \Delta$ for some π', and thus $\varphi[\pi'/\pi] \in \bigcirc^{-1}\Delta$. □

Let $\mathbb{T}' \hat{=} \mathbb{T} \cup \{\pi_k : k < \omega\}$, where $\{\pi_k : k < \omega\}$ is a countable set of fresh trace variables.

Definition 5. *Given a set Γ of HyperLTL* formulas over $\mathbb{T}'$, $Cn(\Gamma) \hat{=} \{\varphi \mid \Gamma \vdash \varphi\}$, and $\Gamma + \varphi \hat{=} \{\theta \mid \varphi \to \theta \in Cn(\Gamma)\}$.*

Using this notation, Proposition 2 can be written as $\Gamma + \varphi = Cn(\Gamma \cup \{\varphi\})$.

Lemma 6 (Lindenbaum Lemma). *For any set of formulas Δ in the given vocabulary $\mathbb{T} \cup \mathbb{P}$, if $\Delta \nvdash \bot$, then there exists a maximal consistent set $\Delta_{max} \supset \Delta$ of formulas in $\mathbb{T}' \cup \mathbb{P}$ with the $\exists$-property and the strengthened $\mathcal{U}$-property.*

Proof. As argued in [28] for HyperLTL, the set of HyperLTL* formulas on the vocabulary $\mathbb{T}' \cup \mathbb{P}$ is recursively enumerable, which are assumed to be enumerated by $\varphi_0, \varphi_1, \ldots$. Let $\Delta' = Cn(\Delta)$. Clearly, Δ' is also consistent. In addition, let $\kappa_1, \kappa_2 : \mathbb{N} \mapsto \mathbb{N}$ be the respective left and right functions of a pair function $\kappa : \mathbb{N} \times \mathbb{N} \mapsto \mathbb{N}$. So, for any $k_1, k_2 < \omega$, there is a $k < \omega$ such that $k = \kappa(k_1, k_2)$, $k_1 = \kappa_1(k)$ and $k_2 = \kappa_2(k)$. In what follows, we construct a sequence of consistent sets $\Delta_0, \Delta_1, \ldots, \Delta_n, \ldots$, with $\Delta_0 \subseteq \Delta_1 \subseteq \cdots \subseteq \Delta_n \subseteq \cdots$.

Let $\Delta_0 = \Delta'$, and suppose that we have Δ_k with $k_1 = \kappa_1(k)$ and $k_2 = \kappa_2(k)$, now we construct Δ_{k+1} as follows: $\Delta_{k+1} = \Delta_k$ if $\Delta_k, \varphi_{k_1} \vdash \bot$, otherwise

- $\Delta_{k+1} \hat{=} \Delta_k \cup \{\varphi_{k_1}, \bigcirc^m \psi\}$ for some $m \in \mathbb{N}$ such that $\Delta \cup \{\varphi_{k_1}, \bigcirc^m \psi\} \nvdash \bot$, if $\varphi_{k_1} = \varphi \mathcal{U} \psi$.
- $\Delta_{k+1} \hat{=} \Delta_k \cup \{\varphi_{k_1}, \bigcirc^j \bigcirc^m \psi\}$ for some $m \in \mathbb{N}$ such that $\Delta \cup \{\varphi_{k_1}, \bigcirc^j \bigcirc^m \psi\} \nvdash \bot$, if $\varphi_{k_1} = \bigcirc^j(\varphi \mathcal{U} \psi)$, $j \in \mathbb{N}^+$.
- $\Delta_{k+1} \hat{=} \Delta_k \cup \{\varphi_{k_1}, \bigcirc^m \neg\psi\}$ for some $m \in \mathbb{N}$ such that $\Delta \cup \{\varphi_{k_1}, \bigcirc^m \neg\psi\} \nvdash \bot$, if $\varphi_{k_1} = \neg\Box\psi$.
- $\Delta_{k+1} \hat{=} \Delta_k \cup \{\varphi_{k_1}, \psi[\pi_m/\pi]\}$, where m is the least number such that the fresh variable π_m does not occur in Δ_k, nor in φ_{k_1}, if $\varphi_{k_1} = \exists\pi\psi$;
- $\Delta_{k+1} \hat{=} \Delta_k \cup \{\varphi_{k_1}\}$, otherwise.

We show that Δ_k is consistent for all $k \in \mathbb{N}$ by induction on k. The base case follows immediately from $\Delta_0 = \Delta'$. Suppose Δ_k is consistent, now the inductive step is proved as follows:

- if $\Delta_k \cup \{\varphi_{k_1}\} \vdash \bot$, so $\Delta_{k+1} = \Delta_k$. The consistency is obtained by the hypothesis. Now, suppose $\Delta_k \cup \{\varphi_{k_1}\} \nvdash \bot$, consider the following cases:
  - $\varphi_{k_1} = \varphi \mathcal{U} \psi$: First we show that the desired m always exists. Suppose that for any $m \in \mathbb{N}$, $\Delta, \varphi_{k_1}, \bigcirc^m \psi \vdash \bot$. By $(R\neg)$ we have $\Delta_k, \varphi \mathcal{U} \psi \vdash \neg\bigcirc^m \psi$ for all $m \in \mathbb{N}$. By $(R\neg\bigcirc)$, we have $\Delta_k, \varphi \mathcal{U} \psi \vdash \bigcirc^m \neg\psi$ for all $m \in \mathbb{N}$. Then by (ω) and (Cut), we have $\Delta_k, \varphi \mathcal{U} \psi \vdash \Box\neg\psi$, that is, $\Delta_k, \varphi \mathcal{U} \psi \vdash \neg\Diamond\psi$ by duality. In addition, we have $\Delta_k, \varphi \mathcal{U} \psi \vdash \Diamond\psi$ by $(\Diamond\mathcal{U})$, which contradicts the consistency of $\Delta_k \cup \{\varphi_{k_1}\}$. Hence, there exists always some m such that $\Delta_k \cup \{\varphi_{k_1}, \bigcirc^m \psi\} \nvdash \bot$, i.e. Δ_{k+1} is consistent.

- $\varphi_{k_1} = \bigcirc^j(\varphi\mathcal{U}\psi)$: Similarly, suppose that for any $m \in \mathbb{N}$, $\Delta_k \cup \{\varphi_{k_1}, \bigcirc^j \bigcirc^m \psi\} \vdash \bot$. Then we have $\Delta_k, \bigcirc^j(\varphi\mathcal{U}\psi) \vdash \neg \bigcirc^j \bigcirc^m \psi$ for all $m \in \mathbb{N}$. By $(R\bigcirc\neg)$, it follows that $\Delta_k, \bigcirc^j(\varphi\mathcal{U}\psi) \vdash \bigcirc^m \neg \bigcirc^j \psi$, $\forall m \in \mathbb{N}$. By (ω), we have $\Delta_k, \bigcirc^j(\varphi\mathcal{U}\psi) \vdash \neg\Diamond \bigcirc^j \psi$. On the other hand, by $(\Diamond\mathcal{U})$, it follows that $\varphi\mathcal{U}\psi \vdash \Diamond\psi$. So, by $(R\bigcirc)$, $\bigcirc^j(\varphi\mathcal{U}\psi) \vdash \bigcirc^j \Diamond\psi$. By $(\Diamond\bigcirc)$ and (Wk), it follows $\Delta_k, \bigcirc^j(\varphi\mathcal{U}\psi) \vdash \Diamond \bigcirc^j \psi$, which is a contradiction.
- $\varphi_{k_1} = \neg\Box\psi$: Suppose that there is no such $m \in \mathbb{N}$, that is, for any $m \in \mathbb{N}$, we have $\Delta_k, \varphi_{k_1}, \bigcirc^m \neg\psi \vdash \bot$. Hence, for any $m \in \mathbb{N}$, $\Delta_k, \varphi_{k_1} \vdash \neg \bigcirc^m \neg\psi$ by (R$\neg$), which further implies $\Delta_k, \varphi_{k_1} \vdash \bigcirc^m \psi$ by $(\neg\bigcirc)^k$. Thus, $\Delta_k, \varphi_{k_1} \vdash \Box\psi$ follows by $(\bigcirc\mathbb{N})$ and (Cut). So, it can be concluded that $\Delta_k, \varphi_{k_1} \vdash \bot$ by (As) and duality, which contradicts consistency.
- $\varphi_{k_1} = \exists\pi\psi$: Suppose $\Delta \cup \{\exists\pi\psi, \psi[\pi'/\pi]\} \vdash \bot$, so $\Delta_k, \exists\pi\psi, \psi[\pi'/\pi] \vdash \bot$. Since π' is not free in $\Delta_k, \exists\pi\psi$ and ψ (because Δ uses only finitely many of the new variables), by $(L\exists)$ we have $\Delta_k, \exists\pi\psi, \exists\pi\psi \vdash \bot$, which is a contradiction.
- The last case is straightforward.

Now, let $\Delta_{\max} \hat{=} \bigcup_{i\in\mathbb{N}} \Delta_i$. Clearly, $\Delta_{\max}$ has the $\exists$-property and the strengthened $\mathcal{U}$-property. So, in what follows, we only need to prove $\Delta_{\max}$ is the maximal consistent set with $\Delta \subseteq \Delta_{\max}$.

Suppose $\Delta_{\max} \vdash \bot$. Then we need to consider the following two cases: 1) there exists a k such that $\cup_{j=0}^k \Delta_j \subseteq \Delta_{\max}$ and $\cup_{j=0}^k \Delta_j \vdash \bot$. That means that Δ_k is inconsistent with the above construction, which is a contradiction. 2) $\Delta_{\max}$ contains $\neg\Box\varphi$, and for any $k \in \mathbb{N}$, there is $i_k \in \mathbb{N}$ with $\Delta_{i_k} \vdash \bigcirc^k \varphi$. Thus, by the Cut rule, we have $\Delta_{\max} \vdash \Box\varphi$. On the other hand, by (Coω), it follows that $\Delta_{\max} \vdash \bigcirc^{k^*} \neg\varphi$ for some $k^* \in \mathbb{N}$. This implies that there exists $i_{k^*} \in \mathbb{N}$ such that $\bigcirc^{k^*} \neg\varphi \in \Delta_{i_{k^*}}$ due to the maximality of $\Delta_{\max}$. Meanwhile, by assumption, $\bigcirc^{k^*} \varphi \in \Delta_{i_{k'}}$. Let $i_{k''} = \max\{i_{k^*}, i_{k'}\}$. By $(\neg\bigcirc)^k$, it follows that $\Delta_{i_{k''}}$ is inconsistent, which is a contradiction.

Suppose that there exists a consistent Δ^* with $\Delta_{\max} \subseteq \Delta^*$ and $\psi \in \Delta^* \backslash \Delta_{\max}$ for some ψ, which is a formula HyperLTL* over the vocabulary $\mathbb{T}' \cup \mathbb{P}$. So, there is k with $\psi = \varphi_k$. Clearly, $\psi \notin \Delta_{k+1}$, so $\Delta_{k+1} + \psi$ is inconsistent. On the other hand, $\Delta_{k+1} + \psi \subseteq \Delta^*$, which contradicts the consistency of Δ^*. □

Let $\bigcirc^{-j} \Gamma \hat{=} \{\delta \mid \underbrace{\bigcirc \ldots \bigcirc}_{j \text{ times}} \gamma \in \Gamma\}$.

Lemma 7. *If Δ is maximal consistent and has the strengthened $\mathcal{U}$-property, then so is $\bigcirc^{-j} \Delta$ for all $j \in \mathbb{N}$.*

Proof. By Definition 3, $\bigcirc^j(\varphi\mathcal{U}\psi) \in \Delta$ for all $\varphi\mathcal{U}\psi \in \bigcirc^{-j} \Delta$). By the strengthened $\mathcal{U}$-property, there exists a $n \geq j$ such that $\bigcirc^n \psi \in \Delta$. We can reformulate $\bigcirc^n \psi$ as $\bigcirc^j \bigcirc^k \psi$ with $n = j + k$ and $k \geq 0$, thus $\bigcirc^k \psi \in \bigcirc^{-1} \Delta$, which indicates the strengthened $\mathcal{U}$-property. □

Given a maximal consistent set Δ with the $\exists$-property and the strengthened $\mathcal{U}$-property, consider the canonical trajectory $\langle \bigcirc^{-i} \Delta \rangle_{i\in\mathbb{N}}$. Obviously, this infinite sequence consists of maximal consistent sets with the $\exists$-property and the reinforced $\mathcal{U}$-property by Definition 3 and Lemmas 4, 5 and 7. For every $\pi \in \mathbb{T}'$, we define $t_\pi(i) \mathrel{\hat{=}} \{a \mid a_\pi \in \bigcirc^{-i} \Delta\}$, for $i \in \mathbb{N}$. Consider the model $\mathcal{M}^c_\Delta = (T^c_\Delta, \Pi^c_\Delta)$ where $T^c_\Delta \mathrel{\hat{=}} \{t_\pi \mid \pi \in \mathbb{T}'\}$ and $\Pi^c_\Delta(\pi) \mathrel{\hat{=}} t_\pi$, $\pi \in \mathbb{T}'$. Models built in the way employed for $\mathcal{M}^c_\Delta$ are called canonical. The following lemma establishes the equivalence between $\varphi \in \bigcirc^{-i} \Delta$ and $\mathcal{M}^c_\Delta, i \models \varphi$, which implies that $\mathcal{M}^c_\Delta$ is a model for Δ.

Lemma 8 (Truth Lemma). *For any φ and $i \in \mathbb{N}$, $\mathcal{M}^c_\Delta, i \models \varphi$ iff $\varphi \in \bigcirc^{-i} \Delta$.*

Proof. Structural induction on φ.

- $\varphi = a_\pi$: By Definition 2, $\mathcal{M}^c_\Delta, i \models a_\pi$ iff $a \in \Pi^c_\Delta(\pi)[i]$; iff $a \in \{a \mid a_\pi \in \bigcirc^{-i} \Delta\}$; iff $a_\pi \in \bigcirc^{-i} \Delta$.
- $\varphi = \neg\psi$: This case follows from Lemma 3 (i), i.e., $\mathcal{M}^c_\Delta, i \models \neg\psi$ iff $\mathcal{M}^c_\Delta, i \not\models \psi$, iff $\psi \notin \bigcirc^{-i} \Delta$, iff $\neg\psi \in \bigcirc^{-i} \Delta$.
- $\varphi = \psi \wedge \chi$: Like the previous case, according to Lemma 3 (ii), $\psi \wedge \chi \in \bigcirc^{-i} \Delta$ iff $\psi, \chi \in \bigcirc^{-i} \Delta$.
- $\varphi = \bigcirc\psi$: Lemma 3 (iv) implies that $\mathcal{M}^c_\Delta, i \models \bigcirc\psi$ iff $\mathcal{M}^c_\Delta, i+1 \models \psi$, iff $\psi \in \bigcirc^{-(i+1)} \Delta$, iff $\bigcirc\psi \in \bigcirc^{-i} \Delta$.
- $\varphi = \psi\mathcal{U}\chi$: The forward direction follows immediately from the induction hypothesis. For the backward direction, let $\psi\mathcal{U}\chi \in \bigcirc^{-i} \Delta$. Since $\bigcirc^{-i} \Delta$ has the reinforced $\mathcal{U}$-property by Lemma 7, there exists a minimum $k \in \mathbb{N}$ such that $\bigcirc^k \chi \in \bigcirc^{-i} \Delta$. Thus, $\chi \in \bigcirc^{-(i+k)} \Delta$. Consider the following two cases:
  - $\chi \notin \bigcirc^{-(i+j)} \Delta$ for all $j < k$. Lemma 3 (iii) implies $\psi, \bigcirc(\psi\mathcal{U}\chi) \in \bigcirc^{-(i+j)} \Delta$. The induction hypothesis implies $\mathcal{M}, i+k \models \chi, \mathcal{M}, i+j \models \psi$ for all $j < k$. This implies $\mathcal{M}^c_\Delta, i \models \psi\mathcal{U}\chi$;
  - $\chi \in \bigcirc^{-(i+j')} \Delta$ for some $j' < k$. This case admits a similar proof.
- $\varphi = \exists\pi\psi$: $\mathcal{M}^c_\Delta, i \models \exists\pi\psi$ iff there exists a $t \in T^c_\Delta$ s.t. $T^c_\Delta, \Pi^c_\Delta[\pi \mapsto t], i \models \psi$ by Definition 2; iff there exists a $\pi' \in \mathbb{T}'$ s.t. $\mathcal{M}^c_\Delta[\pi \mapsto \Pi^c_\Delta(\pi')], i \models \psi$, as Π^c_Δ is a bijection from $\mathbb{T}'$ to T^c_Δ; iff there exists a $\pi' \in \mathbb{T}'$ s.t. $\mathcal{M}^c_\Delta, i \models \psi[\pi'/\pi]$ by Lemma 2; iff there exists a $\pi' \in \mathbb{T}'$ s.t. $\psi[\pi'/\pi] \in \bigcirc^{-i} \Delta$ by the induction hypothesis; iff $\exists\pi\psi \in \Delta$ according to the $\exists$-property and $(R\exists)$. □

Theorem 2 (Completeness of HyperLTL*). *For any Δ and φ, $\Delta \models \varphi$ implies $\Delta \vdash \varphi$.*

Proof. Suppose $\Delta \not\vdash \varphi$, so $\Delta \cup \{\neg\varphi\}$ is consistent. Hence, $\mathcal{M}^c_{\Delta\cup\{\neg\varphi\}}, 0 \models \psi$ for all $\psi \in \Delta \cup \{\neg\varphi\}$ by Lemma 8, which contradicts to $\Delta \models \varphi$. □

5 Expressiveness of HyperLTL*

HyperLTL can be viewed as a proper subset of HyperLTL* in which trace quantifiers do not occur in the scope of $\bigcirc$ or $\mathcal{U}$. Consequently, every HyperLTL* formula in prenex normal form is a HyperLTL formula. The following theorem shows that allowing trace quantifiers under temporal operators strictly increases expressiveness.

Theorem 3 ([34]). *There is no HyperLTL formula, that can be equivalent to HyperLTL* formula* $\Diamond\forall\pi\neg p_\pi$.

HyperLTL* is still subsumed by the predicate-logic theory $FO[<, E]$ from [34].

Definition 6. *The syntax of* $FO[<, E]$ *is defined by the following BNF:*

$$\varphi ::= P_a(x) \mid E(x, y) \mid x = y \mid x < y \mid \neg\varphi \mid \varphi \wedge \varphi \mid \exists x.\varphi \mid \forall x.\varphi$$

where P_a *is a unary predicate, corresponding to the proposition letter* a *in HyperLTL*, and* x, y *represents the positions of the trace, interpreted as natural numbers. Given a trace set* T, *we let* $\underline{T} \hat{=} (T \times \mathbb{N}, <^{\underline{T}}, E^{\underline{T}}, P_a^{\underline{T}})$, *where the non-logical symbols of* $FO[<, E]$ *are interpreted in* $\underline{T}$, *where* $<^{\underline{T}} \hat{=} \{(t, n), (t, n') \mid t \in T, n < n'\}$, $E^{\underline{T}} \hat{=} \{(t, n), (t', n) \mid t, t' \in T\}$, $P_a^{\underline{T}} \hat{=} \{(t, n) \mid a \in t[n]\}$.

Next, we define a satisfaction-preserving translation f from HyperLTL* to $FO[<, E]$. Each trace variable π in φ is associated with an individual variable x_π. The translation $f(\varphi)$ is a formula of $FO[<, E]$ with the individual variables x_π and z as its free variables, where $\pi \in \mathrm{FV}(\varphi)$. The variable z is called the time variable of $f(\varphi)$, standing for the reference position.

Definition 7. *The translation function* f *is inductively defined as follows:*

- $f(a_\pi) \hat{=} \exists y. y \geq x_\pi \wedge E(z, y) \wedge P_a(y)$, *where* z *is the time-variable for* $f(a_\pi)$;
- $f(\neg\varphi) \hat{=} \neg f(\varphi)$;
- $f(\varphi_1 \wedge \varphi_2) \hat{=} f(\varphi_1) \wedge f(\varphi_2)$;
- $f(\bigcirc\varphi) \hat{=} \exists z_1. Succ(z, z_1) \wedge f(\varphi)[z_1/z]$, *where* $Succ(z, z_1)$ *stands for* $z < z_1 \wedge \forall z_2. z < z_2 \rightarrow z_1 \leq z_2$;
- $f(\varphi_1 \mathcal{U} \varphi_2) \hat{=} \exists z_2. z \leq z_2 \wedge f(\varphi_2)[z_2/z] \wedge \forall z_1. z \leq z_1 < z_2 \rightarrow f(\varphi_1)[z_1/z]$;
- $f(\exists\pi\varphi) = \exists x_\pi. f(\varphi)$.

The following theorem shows that $FO[<, E]$ subsumes HyperLTL*.

Theorem 4. *Let* φ *be a HyperLTL* formula and let* T *be a set of traces. Let* $\underline{T}$ *be the corresponding* $FO[<, E]$*-structure. Let the trace assignment* Π *and the* $FO[<, E]$ *variable assignment* β *satisfy the equivalence*

$$\Pi(\pi) = t \text{ iff } \beta(x_\pi) = (t, i) \text{ for } \pi \in \mathrm{FV}(\varphi), \text{ and } \beta(z) = (\lambda, i),$$

where λ *in* T *is a dummy value. Then* $(T, \Pi), i \models \varphi$ *iff* $(\underline{T}, \beta) \models f(\varphi)$

Proof. Structural induction on φ. □

Moreover, according to the proof of Theorem 8 in [34], clearly the property discussed there is not expressible in HyperLTL* either, so $FO[<, E]$ is strictly more expressive than HyperLTL*.

6 Case Study

We present a revised example of EDAS from [12] and prove that an EDAS model adapted from [11] satisfies the refined noninterference property from [12].

EDAS is a paper-submission system: each execution assigns a submission either `acc` (accepted) or `rej` (rejected) and decides the session to which it is assigned. If the session has not been decided, the system displays "yet to decide", which is represented by a Boolean variable *ses*.

We now provide a simple model of EDAS following the repaired program in [11] in Fig. 1, which can be represented as the HyperLTL formula in Table 3. φ_1 says that any trace whenever passing through the initial state will enter either the accepted state or the rejected state in the next step; φ_2 says that any trace whenever passing through the accepted state cannot enter the rejected state in the next step; symmetrically, φ_3 says that any trace whenever passing through the rejected state cannot enter the accepted state in the next step; φ_4 says that any trace should start from the initial state l_0.

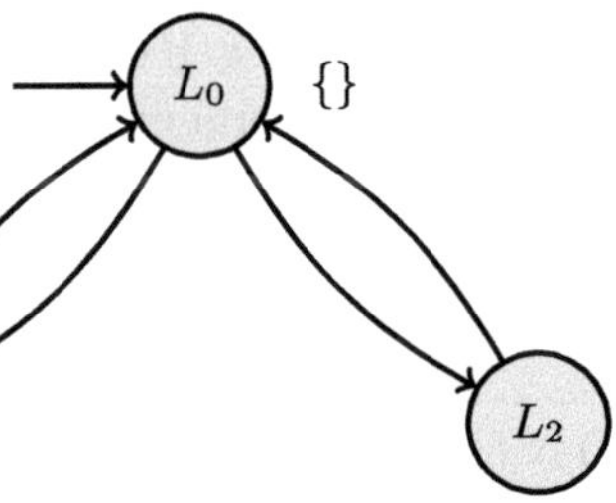

Fig. 1. EDAS: A simple paper submission system

Table 3. HyperLTL formula encoding the EDAS model

$$\begin{aligned}
\varphi_1 =& \forall\pi\Box(\neg\mathtt{acc}_\pi \wedge \neg\mathtt{rej}_\pi \wedge \neg ses_\pi \rightarrow \\
& \bigcirc(\mathtt{acc}_\pi \wedge \neg\mathtt{rej}_\pi \wedge ses_\pi) \vee \bigcirc(\neg\mathtt{acc}_\pi \wedge \mathtt{rej}_\pi \wedge ses_\pi)) \\
\varphi_2 =& \forall\pi\Box(\mathtt{acc}_\pi \wedge \neg\mathtt{rej}_\pi \wedge ses_\pi \rightarrow \bigcirc(\neg\mathtt{acc}_\pi \wedge \neg\mathtt{rej}_\pi \wedge \neg ses_\pi)) \\
\varphi_3 =& \forall\pi\Box(\neg\mathtt{acc}_\pi \wedge \mathtt{rej}_\pi \wedge ses_\pi \rightarrow \bigcirc(\neg\mathtt{acc}_\pi \wedge \neg\mathtt{rej}_\pi \wedge \neg ses_\pi)) \\
\varphi_4 =& \forall\pi(\neg acc_\pi \wedge \neg rej_\pi \wedge \neg ses_\pi)
\end{aligned}$$

We are interested in the refined noninterference property given in [12], represented by the following HyperLTL formula

$$\varphi_{ref} \mathrel{\hat{=}} \forall\pi_1\exists\pi_2\forall\pi_3\exists\pi_4\ \mathrm{obj}(\pi_1,\pi_2) \wedge \Box(dec_{\pi_4} = dec_{\pi_2}) \wedge \Box(ses_{\pi_4} \leftrightarrow ses_{\pi_3})$$

where $\text{obj}(\pi_1, \pi_2)$ stands for $(\Diamond \texttt{acc}_{\pi_1} \rightarrow \Diamond \texttt{acc}_{\pi_2}) \wedge (\Diamond \texttt{rej}_{\pi_1} \rightarrow \Diamond \texttt{rej}_{\pi_2})$, and $dec_{\pi_1} = dec_{\pi_2}$ for $(\texttt{acc}_{\pi_1} \leftrightarrow \texttt{acc}_{\pi_2}) \wedge (\texttt{rej}_{\pi_1} \leftrightarrow \texttt{rej}_{\pi_2})$. Clearly, $\text{obj}(\pi_1, \pi_2)$ says executions π_1 and π_2 make the same decision at last, while $dec_{\pi_1} = dec_{\pi_2}$ says executions π_1 and π_2 share the same decision at the reference position. φ_{ref} (with three quantifier alternations) expresses a refined noninterference with the modification that the universally quantified trace π_1 is replaced by an existentially quantified trace π_2 that satisfies the same objectives.

Now we need to prove the model satisfies the property, i.e., $\Delta \vdash \varphi_{ref}$, where $\Delta = \{\varphi_1, \varphi_2, \varphi_3, \varphi_4\}$. Obviously, the satisfiability and validity of the above formula falls into the undecidable fragment of HyperLTL [27], as the number of quantifier alternations in φ_{ref} is three.

For simplicity, we use ψ_1, ψ_2, ψ_3 and ψ_4 to denote the trace quantifier free part of $\varphi_1, \varphi_2, \varphi_3$ and φ_4 in Table 3, respectively.

Now consider the following quantifier-free sequent first.

$$\bigcup_{j \in [1,2]} \{\psi_i[\pi'_j/\pi] \mid i \in [1,4]\} \vdash \quad \text{obj}(\pi'_1, \pi'_1) \wedge \Box(dec_{\pi'_1} = dec_{\pi'_1}) \wedge \Box(ses_{\pi'_1} \leftrightarrow ses_{\pi'_2})$$

We abbreviate the antecedent of the sequent as Δ' and the succedent as φ'. The quantifier-free part of HyperLTL is exactly the same as LTL (taking each combination of propositional letter and trace variable as a unique propositional letter). Therefore, we can use a state-of-the-art automatic tool for LTL such as NuSMV [16] to prove the quantifier-free sequent by checking whether $\bigwedge \Delta' \rightarrow \varphi'$ is valid. We use the symbolic model checker NuSMV for the task. The reader may refer to repository[1] for the NuSMV code. Now, we focus on proving the quantifier-related part of the sequent as follows:

(1) $\psi_i[\pi'_1/\pi], \psi_i[\pi'_2/\pi], i \in [1,4] \vdash \text{obj}(\pi'_1, \pi'_1) \wedge \Box(dec_{\pi'_1} = dec_{\pi'_1}) \wedge \Box(ses_{\pi'_1} \leftrightarrow ses_{\pi'_2})$
(2) $\forall \pi \psi_1, \forall \pi \psi_2, \forall \pi \psi_3, \forall \pi \psi_4 \vdash \text{obj}(\pi'_1, \pi'_1) \wedge \Box(dec_{\pi'_1} = dec_{\pi'_1}) \wedge \Box(ses_{\pi'_1} \leftrightarrow ses_{\pi'_2})$
by (1) and $(\forall L)$ and Boolean rules
(3) $\Delta \vdash \exists \pi_4 \, \text{obj}(\pi'_1, \pi'_1) \wedge \Box(dec_{\pi_4} = dec_{\pi'_1}) \wedge \Box(ses_{\pi_4} \leftrightarrow ses_{\pi'_2})$ by (2) and $(R\exists)$
(4) $\Delta \vdash \forall \pi_3 \exists \pi_4 \, \text{obj}(\pi'_1, \pi'_1) \wedge \Box(dec_{\pi_4} = dec_{\pi'_1}) \wedge \Box(ses_{\pi_4} \leftrightarrow ses_{\pi_3})$ by (3) and $(R\forall)$
(5) $\Delta \vdash \exists \pi_2 \forall \pi_3 \exists \pi_4 \, \text{obj}(\pi'_1, \pi_2) \wedge \Box(dec_{\pi_4} = dec_{\pi_2}) \wedge \Box(ses_{\pi_4} \leftrightarrow ses_{\pi_3})$
by (4) and $(R\exists)$
(6) $\Delta \vdash \forall \pi_1 \exists \pi_2 \forall \pi_3 \exists \pi_4 \, \text{obj}(\pi_1, \pi_2) \wedge \Box(dec_{\pi_4} = dec_{\pi_2}) \wedge \Box(ses_{\pi_4} \leftrightarrow ses_{\pi_3})$
by (5) and $(R\forall)$

7 Conclusion and Future Work

In this paper, we present a proof system $\mathcal{L}_{H\omega}$ for HyperLTL*. Our main contribution is the completeness of $\mathcal{L}_{H\omega}$ over trace models. Existing research on hyperlogics has mainly focused on semantic considerations, whereas this paper develops a deductive treatment. The proof system provides a basis for formalizing HyperLTL-style reasoning in proof assistants and thereby facilitates the

[1] https://zenodo.org/records/14885502.

verification of hyperproperties that cannot be handled by fully automatic techniques.

For future work, it deserves to investigate formalization and implementation of the proof system in proof assistants such as Rocq and Isabelle/HOL

Acknowledgments. The authors thank anonymous reviewers for their valuable comments and helpful suggestions. This work is partially funded by the National Key R&D Program under grant No. 2022YFA1005101 and 2022YFA1005102, the NSFC under grant No. 62192732, W2511064 and 62502475, and the CAS Project for Young Scientists in Basic Research under grant No. YSBR-040.

References

1. Ábrahám, E., Bartocci, E., Bonakdarpour, B., Dobe, O.: Probabilistic hyperproperties with nondeterminism. In: Hung, D.V., Sokolsky, O. (eds.) ATVA 2020. LNCS, vol. 12302, pp. 518–534. Springer, Cham (2020). https://doi.org/10.1007/978-3-030-59152-6_29
2. Alpern, B., Schneider, F.B.: Defining liveness. Inf. Process. Lett. **21**(4), 181–185 (1985)
3. Alur, R., Černý, P., Chaudhuri, S.: Model checking on trees with path equivalences. In: Grumberg, O., Huth, M. (eds.) TACAS 2007. LNCS, vol. 4424, pp. 664–678. Springer, Heidelberg (2007). https://doi.org/10.1007/978-3-540-71209-1_51
4. Alur, R., Černý, P., Zdancewic, S.: Preserving secrecy under refinement. In: Bugliesi, M., Preneel, B., Sassone, V., Wegener, I. (eds.) ICALP 2006. LNCS, vol. 4052, pp. 107–118. Springer, Heidelberg (2006). https://doi.org/10.1007/11787006_10
5. Balliu, M., Dam, M., Guernic, G.L.: Epistemic temporal logic for information flow security. In: PLAS 2011, p. 6. ACM (2011)
6. Barthe, G., Crespo, J.M., Kunz, C.: Beyond 2-safety: asymmetric product programs for relational program verification. In: Artemov, S., Nerode, A. (eds.) LFCS 2013. LNCS, vol. 7734, pp. 29–43. Springer, Heidelberg (2013). https://doi.org/10.1007/978-3-642-35722-0_3
7. Barthe, G., D'Argenio, P.R., Rezk, T.: Secure information flow by self-composition. In: CSFW-17 2004, pp. 100–114. IEEE Computer Society (2004)
8. Bartocci, E., Ferrère, T., Henzinger, T.A., Nickovic, D., da Costa, A.O.: Flavors of sequential information flow. In: Finkbeiner, B., Wies, T. (eds.) VMCAI 2022. LNCS, vol. 13182, pp. 1–19. Springer, Cham (2022). https://doi.org/10.1007/978-3-030-94583-1_1
9. Baumeister, J., Coenen, N., Bonakdarpour, B., Finkbeiner, B., Sánchez, C.: A temporal logic for asynchronous hyperproperties. In: Silva, A., Leino, K.R.M. (eds.) CAV 2021. LNCS, vol. 12759, pp. 694–717. Springer, Cham (2021). https://doi.org/10.1007/978-3-030-81685-8_33
10. Beutner, R., Finkbeiner, B.: A temporal logic for strategic hyperproperties. In: CONCUR 2021. LIPIcs, vol. 203, pp. 24:1–24:19 (2021)
11. Beutner, R., Hsu, T., Bonakdarpour, B., Finkbeiner, B.: Syntax-guided automated program repair for hyperproperties. In: Gurfinkel, A., Ganesh, V. (eds.) CAV 2024. LNCS, vol. 14683, pp. 3–26. Springer (2024). https://doi.org/10.1007/978-3-031-65633-0_1

12. Bonakdarpour, B., Finkbeiner, B.: The complexity of monitoring hyperproperties. In: 2018 IEEE 31st Computer Security Foundations Symposium (CSF), July 2018. IEEE (2018)
13. Bonakdarpour, B., Sanchez, C., Schneider, G.: Monitoring hyperproperties by combining static analysis and runtime verification. In: Margaria, T., Steffen, B. (eds.) ISoLA 2018. LNCS, vol. 11245, pp. 8–27. Springer, Cham (2018). https://doi.org/10.1007/978-3-030-03421-4_2
14. Bozzelli, L., Peron, A., Sánchez, C.: Asynchronous extensions of HyperLTL. In: LICS 2021. pp. 1–13. IEEE (2021)
15. Chopoghloo, S., Moniri, M.: A strongly complete axiomatization of intuitionistic temporal logic. J. Logic Comput. **31**(7), 1640–1659 (2021)
16. Cimatti, A.: NuSMV 2: an OpenSource tool for symbolic model checking. In: Brinksma, E., Larsen, K.G. (eds.) CAV 2002. LNCS, vol. 2404, pp. 359–364. Springer, Heidelberg (2002). https://doi.org/10.1007/3-540-45657-0_29
17. Clarke, E.M., Emerson, E.A.: Design and synthesis of synchronization skeletons using branching time temporal logic. In: Kozen, D. (ed.) Logic of Programs 1981. LNCS, vol. 131, pp. 52–71. Springer, Heidelberg (1982). https://doi.org/10.1007/BFb0025774
18. Clarkson, M.R., Finkbeiner, B., Koleini, M., Micinski, K.K., Rabe, M.N., Sánchez, C.: Temporal logics for hyperproperties. In: Abadi, M., Kremer, S. (eds.) POST 2014. LNCS, vol. 8414, pp. 265–284. Springer, Heidelberg (2014). https://doi.org/10.1007/978-3-642-54792-8_15
19. Clarkson, M.R., Schneider, F.B.: Hyperproperties. J. Comput. Secur. **18**(6), 1157–1210 (2010)
20. Coenen, N.: A proof system for HyperLTL. Bachelor's Thesis. University of Saarland (2016)
21. Coenen, N., Finkbeiner, B., Hahn, C., Hofmann, J.: The hierarchy of hyperlogics. In: LICS 2019, pp. 1–13. IEEE (2019)
22. Coenen, N., Finkbeiner, B., Sánchez, C., Tentrup, L.: Verifying hyperliveness. In: Dillig, I., Tasiran, S. (eds.) CAV 2019. LNCS, vol. 11561, pp. 121–139. Springer, Cham (2019). https://doi.org/10.1007/978-3-030-25540-4_7
23. Correnson, A., Finkbeiner, B.: Coinductive proofs for temporal hyperliveness. Proc. ACM Program. Lang. **9**(POPL), 1568–1595 (2025)
24. Dimitrova, R., Finkbeiner, B., Kovács, M., Rabe, M.N., Seidl, H.: Model checking information flow in reactive systems. In: Kuncak, V., Rybalchenko, A. (eds.) VMCAI 2012. LNCS, vol. 7148, pp. 169–185. Springer, Heidelberg (2012). https://doi.org/10.1007/978-3-642-27940-9_12
25. Dimitrova, R., Finkbeiner, B., Torfah, H.: Probabilistic hyperproperties of Markov decision processes. In: Hung, D.V., Sokolsky, O. (eds.) ATVA 2020. LNCS, vol. 12302, pp. 484–500. Springer, Cham (2020). https://doi.org/10.1007/978-3-030-59152-6_27
26. Emerson, E.A., Halpern, J.Y.: "Sometimes" and "not never" revisited: on branching versus linear time temporal logic. J. ACM **33**(1), 151–178 (1986)
27. Finkbeiner, B., Hahn, C.: Deciding hyperproperties. In: CONCUR 2016. LIPIcs, vol. 59, pp. 13:1–13:14 (2016)
28. Finkbeiner, B., Hahn, C., Hans, T.: MGHyper: checking satisfiability of HyperLTL formulas beyond the $\exists^*\forall^*$ fragment. In: Lahiri, S.K., Wang, C. (eds.) ATVA 2018. LNCS, vol. 11138, pp. 521–527. Springer, Cham (2018). https://doi.org/10.1007/978-3-030-01090-4_31

29. Finkbeiner, B., Hahn, C., Lukert, P., Stenger, M., Tentrup, L.: Synthesizing reactive systems from hyperproperties. In: Chockler, H., Weissenbacher, G. (eds.) CAV 2018. LNCS, vol. 10981, pp. 289–306. Springer, Cham (2018). https://doi.org/10.1007/978-3-319-96145-3_16
30. Finkbeiner, B., Hahn, C., Stenger, M.: EAHyper: satisfiability, implication, and equivalence checking of hyperproperties. In: Majumdar, R., Kunčak, V. (eds.) CAV 2017. LNCS, vol. 10427, pp. 564–570. Springer, Cham (2017). https://doi.org/10.1007/978-3-319-63390-9_29
31. Finkbeiner, B., Hahn, C., Stenger, M., Tentrup, L.: Monitoring hyperproperties. Formal Meth. Syst. Des. **54**(3), 336–363 (2019). https://doi.org/10.1007/s10703-019-00334-z
32. Finkbeiner, B., Hahn, C., Stenger, M., Tentrup, L.: RVHyper: a runtime verification tool for temporal hyperproperties. In: Beyer, D., Huisman, M. (eds.) TACAS 2018. LNCS, vol. 10806, pp. 194–200. Springer, Cham (2018). https://doi.org/10.1007/978-3-319-89963-3_11
33. Finkbeiner, B., Hahn, C., Torfah, H.: Model checking quantitative hyperproperties. In: Chockler, H., Weissenbacher, G. (eds.) CAV 2018. LNCS, vol. 10981, pp. 144–163. Springer, Cham (2018). https://doi.org/10.1007/978-3-319-96145-3_8
34. Finkbeiner, B., Zimmermann, M.: The first-order logic of hyperproperties. In: STACS 2017. LIPIcs, vol. 66, pp. 30:1–30:14 (2017)
35. Gaintzarain, J., Hermo, M., Lucio, P., Navarro, M., Orejas, F.: A cut-free and invariant-free sequent calculus for PLTL. In: Duparc, J., Henzinger, T.A. (eds.) CSL 2007. LNCS, vol. 4646, pp. 481–495. Springer, Heidelberg (2007). https://doi.org/10.1007/978-3-540-74915-8_36
36. Goguen, J.A., Meseguer, J.: Security policies and security models. In: 1982 IEEE Symposium on Security and Privacy, Oakland, CA, USA, 26–28 April 1982. pp. 11–20. IEEE Computer Society (1982)
37. Gutsfeld, J.O., Müller-Olm, M., Ohrem, C.: Propositional dynamic logic for hyperproperties. In: CONCUR 2020. LIPIcs, vol. 171, pp. 50:1–50:22 (2020)
38. Gutsfeld, J.O., Müller-Olm, M., Ohrem, C.: Automata and fixpoints for asynchronous hyperproperties. Proc. ACM Program. Lang. **5**(POPL), 1–29 (2021)
39. Huisman, M., Worah, P., Sunesen, K.: A temporal logic characterisation of observational determinism. In: CSFW-19 2006, p. 3. IEEE Computer Society (2006)
40. Kesten, Y., Pnueli, A.: A complete proof systems for QPTL. In: LICS 1995, pp. 2–12. IEEE Computer Society (1995)
41. Kozen, D.: Results on the propositional μ-Calculus. Theor. Comput. Sci. **27**, 333–354 (1983)
42. Krebs, A., Meier, A., Virtema, J., Zimmermann, M.: Team semantics for the specification and verification of hyperproperties. In: MFCS 2018. LIPIcs, vol. 117, pp. 10:1–10:16 (2018)
43. Lichtenstein, O., Pnueli, A.: Propositional temporal logics: decidability and completeness. Logic J. IGPL **8**(1), 55–85 (2000)
44. Pnueli, A.: The temporal logic of programs. In: FOCS 1977, pp. 46–57. IEEE Computer Society (1977)
45. Segerberg, K.: A model existence theorem in infinitary propositional modal logic. J. Philos. Logic **23**(4), 337–367 (1994)
46. Sistla, A.P., Clarke, E.M.: The complexity of propositional linear temporal logics. J. ACM **32**(3), 733–749 (1985)
47. Sistla, A.P., Vardi, M.Y., Wolper, P.: The complementation problem for Büchi automata with applications to temporal logic. Theor. Comput. Sci. **49**, 217–237 (1987)

48. Virtema, J., Hofmann, J., Finkbeiner, B., Kontinen, J., Yang, F.: Linear-time temporal logic with team semantics: expressivity and complexity. In: FSTTCS 2021. LIPIcs, vol. 213, pp. 52:1–52:17 (2021)
49. Wang, Y., Zarei, M., Bonakdarpour, B., Pajic, M.: Statistical verification of hyperproperties for cyber-physical systems. ACM Trans. Embed. Comput. Syst. **18**(5s), 92:1–92:23 (2019)
50. Zdancewic, S., Myers, A.C.: Observational determinism for concurrent program security. In: 16th IEEE Computer Security Foundations Workshop (CSFW-16 2003), 30 June–2 July 2003, Pacific Grove, CA, USA, p. 29. IEEE Computer Society (2003)
51. Zhan, N.: Completeness of higher-order duration calculus. In: Clote, P.G., Schwichtenberg, H. (eds.) CSL 2000. LNCS, vol. 1862, pp. 442–456. Springer, Heidelberg (2000). https://doi.org/10.1007/3-540-44622-2_30
52. Zhou, C., Guelev, D.P., Zhan, N.: A higher-order duration calculus. In: Millennial Perspectives in Computer Science, pp. 407–416 (1999)

Open Access This chapter is licensed under the terms of the Creative Commons Attribution 4.0 International License (http://creativecommons.org/licenses/by/4.0/), which permits use, sharing, adaptation, distribution and reproduction in any medium or format, as long as you give appropriate credit to the original author(s) and the source, provide a link to the Creative Commons license and indicate if changes were made.

The images or other third party material in this chapter are included in the chapter's Creative Commons license, unless indicated otherwise in a credit line to the material. If material is not included in the chapter's Creative Commons license and your intended use is not permitted by statutory regulation or exceeds the permitted use, you will need to obtain permission directly from the copyright holder.

Learning Computation Tree Logic with Neural Networks

Benjamin Bordais[1,2,3], Daniel Neider[2,3], and Mustafa Yalçıner[2,3(✉)]

[1] Université Libre de Bruxelles, Brussels, Belgium
benjamin.bordais@ulb.be
[2] TU Dortmund University, Dortmund, Germany
daniel.neider@tu-dortmund.de
[3] Center for Trustworthy Data Science and Security, University Alliance Ruhr, Dortmund, Germany
mustafa.yalciner@tu-dortmund.de

Abstract. Automatically identifying temporal properties from observations of a system's behavior provides valuable insight into that system's inner workings. Temporal properties are often expressed in temporal logics, such as Computation Tree Logic (CTL). Existing approaches to learning CTL specifications from observations rely on constraint-solving by encoding the search for formulas into a satisfiability problem that perfectly separates observations that the system can (positive) or cannot (negative) perform. While adequate in noise-free settings, these methods often struggle with noisy data, such as incomplete executions or mislabeled traces, and scale poorly to large inputs. To overcome these limitations, we propose a neural approach for learning CTL specifications from positive- and negative-labeled observations represented as transition systems. Our method employs a neural network in which neurons encode the presence of CTL operators at specific positions. After training, a deterministic extraction procedure converts network weights into interpretable CTL formulas. In contrast to satisfiability-based learning approaches, our framework efficiently produces high-quality specifications even under noisy data conditions. It supports arbitrary CTL formulas up to a user-defined size budget and consistently yields accurate results within short computation times, demonstrating that neural architectures can provide a fast and noise-tolerant method for inferring temporal properties.

Keywords: Temporal Logic · Specification Mining · Neural Networks

1 Introduction

Temporal logics play a central role in automated reasoning about reactive, concurrent, and autonomous systems [18]. In particular, temporal specifications provide a compact and human-readable way of describing admissible system behaviors and are widely used in various fields, such as formal verification [9], runtime monitoring [13], and synthesis [19].

© The Author(s) 2026
A. Biere et al. (Eds.): IJCAR 2026, LNAI 16688, pp. 396–413, 2026.
https://doi.org/10.1007/978-3-032-32589-1_24

In practice, however, temporal specifications may not be readily available. Instead, one may observe a system through sensors, logs, or black-box interactions [23]. Automatically inferring a temporal specification from such observations is, therefore, an appealing task that supports system understanding [14] and anomaly detection. A common formulation of this problem considers a set of *positive* and *negative* observations, where positive examples correspond to behaviors that can occur, while negative examples cannot occur [5,17,20,22]. The goal is then to synthesize a temporal formula separating the two sets. Among the most prominent formalisms for temporal formulae is *Computation Tree Logic* (CTL), which is particularly well suited for systems with branching behavior, such as concurrent- and reactive systems [11].

Existing approaches to learning CTL specifications from labeled observations are based on constraint solving [5,20]. These methods encode the search for a separating formula into a satisfiability problem, by defining constraints that enforce consistency with all labeled samples. While recent learners following this paradigm have demonstrated success for moderately sized instances, they inherit two fundamental limitations. First, as these learners are designed to solve an NP-complete problem [6], their runtime often grows with the size of the formula space, or the number of observations, limiting scalability. Second, they are only designed to solve an exact separation problem and thus could be unable to handle noise; even a small number of mislabeled observations, which in practice could occur with faulty sensors, may render the constraints inconsistent, forcing the solver into expensive searches and potential timeouts.

To overcome these limitations, we propose the first neural approach for learning CTL specifications from system observations. In contrast to constraint-based learners, neural methods are inherently robust to noise and can exploit gradient-based optimization to search for formulae efficiently. The input to our learner is a set of Kripke structures, i.e., transition systems with state labels for atomic propositions and a binary label per structure indicating whether its behavior is admissible. The goal is to synthesize a CTL formula that maximizes classification accuracy over this dataset. Our method employs a neural network whose weights encode the presence of CTL operators at specific positions in the formula. During training, the weights are guided towards a formula that best classifies the observations. After training, we apply a deterministic extraction procedure that converts the learned network weights into a ranked set of CTL formulas, from which the formula with the highest accuracy is selected.

We evaluate our approach on the benchmark dataset introduced by Bordais et al. [5] and compare it against two state-of-the-art CTL learners [5,20]. Our results show that the proposed neural learner consistently produces accurate CTL specifications in short computation times. Moreover, under label noise, constraint-based learners become largely impractical due to excessive timeout rates, while our method remains reliable and continues to return accurate formulas. These findings demonstrate that neural architectures can provide a fast and noise-tolerant alternative for inferring branching-time temporal properties, while still yielding interpretable symbolic specifications.

2 Related Work

Closely related are works on learning *Linear Temporal Logic (LTL)* specifications from traces. LTL logic is an instantiation of CTL logic that has no branching properties. The problem of learning LTL formulae has been extensively studied from both *machine learning* and *formal methods* perspectives, with approaches capable of inferring arbitrary LTL specifications even in the presence of noise [7, 12,15,17,22]. Of particular interest to us are the last two papers [17,22] that employ methods similar to ours to learn LTL formulas with neural networks. In contrast, methods for learning Computation Tree Logic (CTL) provide no support for noisy data [5,20].

Other works have investigated the passive learning of CTL formulae; that is, the problem described above in which two fixed sets of positive and negative instances are given as input. In particular, Bordais et al. [6] studied the computational complexity of the passive learning problem for LTL, CTL, and ATL (Alternating-time Temporal Logic) formulae, establishing several NP-completeness results. By contrast to passive learning, in an *active learning* setting, a learner may query an oracle to gather more information, typically with two types of queries: membership queries (is a new instance positive or negative?) and equivalence queries (is this model equivalent to the one to learn?). The active learning setting has mostly been studied for learning automata, most notably with Angluin's infamous L* algorithm [2], although the study of automata active learning continues to this day [21]. For a broad overview of ML applications in the domain of automated reasoning we refer to a recent survey paper [4].

3 Background

Kripke Structures. The observations from which we learn temporal properties are state-labeled graphs, called Kripke structures [11]. Formally, given a non-empty set of propositions P, a Kripke structure $\mathcal{K}$ over P is a tuple $\mathcal{K} = (S, R, L, s_{\mathsf{init}})$, where S is a non-empty finite set of states, $R \subseteq S \times S$ is a total transition relation (every state has at least one successor), $L\colon S \to 2^P$ maps each state to the set of atomic propositions that hold in that state, and $s_{\mathsf{init}} \in S$ is the initial state. We let S^ω denote the set of infinite sequences $\pi = \pi_1 \cdot \pi_2 \cdots$, with each $\pi_i \in S$. For all states $s \in S$ and $n \in \mathbb{N}$, we let $\mathsf{Paths}(s) := \{\pi \in S^\omega \mid \pi_1 = s, \forall i \in \mathbb{N} : (\pi_i, \pi_{i+1}) \in R\} \subseteq S^\omega$ be the set of infinite feasible paths starting from s.

Example 1. A Kripke structure $\mathcal{K} = (S, R, L, s_{\mathsf{init}})$ on the set of propositions $P = \{p, q\}$ is represented in Fig. 1, with $S = \{s_0, s_1, s_2, s_3\}$, $R = \{(s_0, s_1), (s_0, s_2), (s_1, s_0), (s_1, s_2), (s_2, s_3), (s_3, s_1), (s_3, s_3)\}$, $L(s_0) = \{p\}$, $L(s_1) = \{q\}$, $L(s_2) = \{p, q\}$, $L(s_3) = \emptyset$ and $s_{\mathsf{init}} = s_0$. In that structure, we have e.g. $s_2 \cdot s_3^\omega \in \mathsf{Paths}(s_2)$.

Computation Tree Logic. Computation Tree Logic formulae [8] express branching temporal properties by quantifying (existentially or universally) over

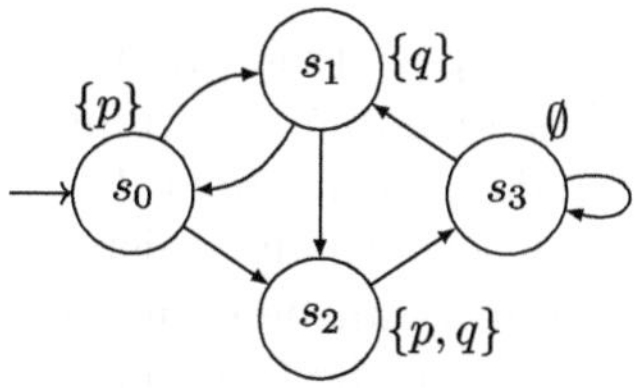

Fig. 1. Kripke structure.

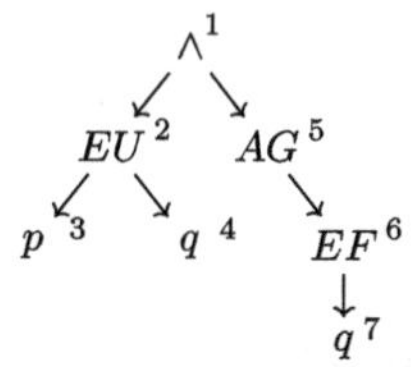

Fig. 2. CTL syntax-tree representation.

paths that satisfy a temporal property. With CTL formulae, we are able to formalize properties such as "on all possible executions, every request is eventually followed by a response". More formally, given a non-empty finite set of atomic propositions P, CTL formulae are built from atomic propositions in P, standard Boolean operators ($\neg$, $\wedge$,$\vee$), path quantifiers A (universal) and E (existential), combined with temporal operators next (X), eventually (F), globally (G), and until (U). The CTL syntax is given by the grammar below, where $p \in P$ and $C \in \{A, E\}$:

$$\varphi ::= p \mid \neg\varphi \mid \varphi_1 \wedge \varphi_2 \mid \varphi_1 \vee \varphi_2 \mid CX\,\varphi \mid CF\,\varphi \mid CG\,\varphi \mid C[\varphi_1 U\,\varphi_2]$$

Representation of CTL Formulae. Each CTL formula φ is represented by its syntax tree $T(\varphi)$, whose leafs are atomic propositions and whose internal nodes are logical or temporal operators connecting their subformulae. The size of a formula is simply the number of nodes and leafs in this tree. A preorder traversal from the root produces an ordered list of elements that forms the prefix form $pre(\varphi)$, where each operator appears directly before the subformula it applies to.

Example 2. Consider the CTL formula $\varphi = E(p\;U\;q) \wedge (AG\;EF\;q)$. The syntax tree $T(\varphi)$ of this formula φ is represented in Fig. 2. The ordering in which the nodes of the tree are listed with a depth-first-search from the root is depicted near each node. The prefix form of the formula φ is thus equal to: $pre(\varphi) = \wedge\;(EU\;p\;q)\;(AG\;EF\;q)$.

Semantics of CTL. CTL formulae are interpreted over the states of Kripke structures. Formally, for a Kripke structure $\mathcal{K} = (S, R, L, s_{\mathsf{init}})$, the satisfaction relation $\models$ between a state $s \in S$ and a CTL formula is defined inductively:

$s \models p$	**iff** $p \in L(s)$
$s \models \neg\varphi$	**iff** $s \not\models \varphi$
$s \models \varphi_1 \wedge \varphi_2$	**iff** $s \models \varphi_1$ and $s \models \varphi_2$
$s \models \varphi_1 \vee \varphi_2$	**iff** $s \models \varphi_1$ or $s \models \varphi_2$
$s \models C\,X\,\varphi$	**iff** $\mathcal{Q}_C(s, s') \in R:\; s' \models \varphi$
$s \models C\,G\,\varphi$	**iff** $\mathcal{Q}_C\;\pi \in \mathsf{Path}(s):\; \forall k \in \mathbb{N},\; \pi_k \models \varphi$
$s \models C[\varphi_1 U \varphi_2]$	**iff** $\mathcal{Q}_C\;\pi \in \mathsf{Path}(s):\; \exists k \in \mathbb{N},\; \pi_k \models \varphi_2$ and $\forall j < k:\; \pi_j \models \varphi_1$

with $C \in \{A, E\}$ and $\mathcal{Q}_A = \forall$ and $\mathcal{Q}_E = \exists$. The Kripke structure $\mathcal{K}$ satisfies a CTL formula φ, denoted $\mathcal{K} \models \varphi$, if $s_{\mathsf{init}} \models \varphi$. For example, a formula $EX\varphi$ expresses that a successor state satisfies the formula φ; a formula $E(\varphi_1 U \varphi_2)$ expresses the existence of a path whose visited states eventually satisfy φ_2 and until then satisfy φ_1. Note that the eventually operator can be expressed with the until operator, since the formula $CF\varphi$ is equivalent to the formula $C[\top U \varphi]$.

Model Checking. Our neural network and both constraint-solving based approaches [5,20] compute satisfaction of a Kripke structure very similarly to how model checkers do. It can be decided in polynomial time if a Kripke structure satisfies a CTL formula [1]. The classical CTL model checking algorithm iteratively computes the set of states of the Kripke structure satisfying each sub-formula, following a bottom-up procedure (which thus starts with the atomic propositions). This algorithm is based on the idea that the set of states $SAT(\varphi)$ satisfied by a formula φ can be computed inductively from the set of states satisfying its direct sub-formula(e). For more details, we refer to standard literature [8,10].

Problem Definition. Given a set Π^+ of positive Kripke structures and a set Π^- of negative ones, we aim to find a CTL formula φ that maximizes the classification accuracy over the entire dataset $\Pi = \Pi^+ \cup \Pi^-$:

$$\mathrm{acc}(\varphi, \Pi) = \frac{|\{K \in \Pi^+ \mid K \models \varphi\}| + |\{K \in \Pi^- \mid K \not\models \varphi\}|}{|\Pi|}$$

The case where we aim to synthesize a formula φ achieving perfect accuracy, $\mathrm{acc}(\varphi, \Pi) = 1$, has been investigated in previous constraint-solving works [5,20]. These approaches employ constraint-solving techniques because the associated decision problem, determining whether there exists a CTL formula with perfect accuracy and size at most L (encoded in unary), has been proven to be NP-complete [6].

4 A Neural Approach to Learning CTL Formulae

This section details our approach to learning CTL formulae from positive and negative examples, which we illustrate in Fig. 3. At a high level, the weights of our neural network can encode all CTL formulae up to a configurable size budget L. We describe the structure of these weight matrices in Sect. 4.1. Before training, the weights are initialized with zeros and therefore do not yet represent any formula. As training progresses, our neural learner computes the satisfaction relation between the currently represented formula and each labeled training sample using a set of differentiable functions introduced in Sect. 4.2. When the predicted satisfaction diverges from the true label of a Kripke structure in the dataset, the resulting error is backpropagated through the network, adjusting its weights toward an encoding that yields a formula more consistent with the true label. Importantly, while the weight matrices can theoretically encode all CTL formulae within the given size budget L, gradient updates during training are

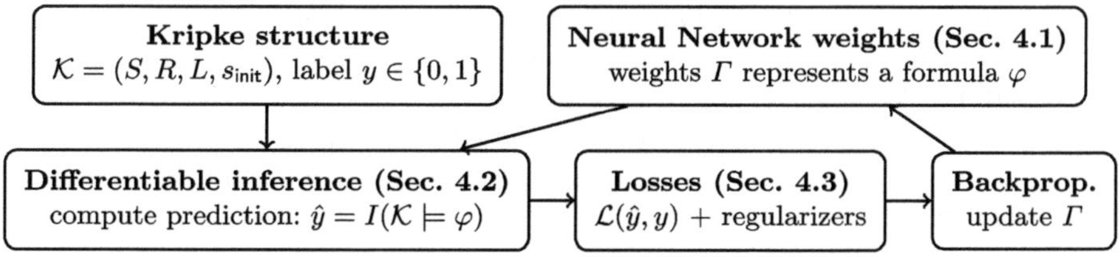

Fig. 3. The weights Γ encode a candidate CTL formula φ. Inference evaluates whether $\mathcal{K} \models \varphi$ holds ($I(\cdot)$ denotes the indicator function). Backpropagation adjusts Γ to better align predictions with true labels, gradually refining the encoded formula.

unconstrained and may yield arbitrary real-valued assignments. These raw values do not necessarily correspond to valid choices in a CTL formula. To address this issue, we introduce normalization and regularization terms in Sect. 4.3 that guide training toward encodings that faithfully represent well-formed CTL formulae. How we proceed in the next sections shares many similarities with what was done in [17,22] for learning LTL formulae, though there is a significant difference in how we compute the inference: here, we use a min/max-based semantics, whereas in [17,22], a sum-based semantics is used. We investigate the impact of this architectural difference in the ablation studies.

4.1 Parameter Encoding

We first introduce the trainable parameters of our neural network.

Definition 1. *Let P be a set of atomic propositions and let $L \in \mathbb{N}$ be a bound on the size of a prospective CTL formula. The parameter set of the neural CTL model of size L is:*

$$\Gamma = \left\{ (\Gamma_{right})_{i,k} \in [0,1] \;\middle|\; 1 \leq i \leq L-2,\ i+2 \leq k \leq L \right\}$$
$$\cup \left\{ (\Gamma_o)_i \in [0,1] \mid o \in \mathsf{Op},\ 1 \leq i \leq L \right\}.$$

for $\mathsf{Op} := \{p, none, \neg, \wedge, \vee, EX, AX, EF, AF, EG, AG, EU, AU \mid p \in P\}$.

Intuitively, these parameters have the following meaning: the operator-selector components $(\Gamma_o)_i$ indicate whether node i in the formula's syntax tree is the operator o. The special selector $(\Gamma_{\text{none}})_i$, which may only occur as a sequence at the end of a formula, encodes a null node, allowing smaller trees (and thus smaller formulae) to be embedded into a larger fixed L encoding. The only child of a unary operator, and the left child of a binary operator at node i are always assumed to be rooted at node $i+1$; the components $(\Gamma_{\text{right}})_{i,k}$ select the right child index k of node i (which is only relevant if there is a binary operator at node i). Together, the parameter set Γ is sufficient for representing any CTL formula of size up to L.

Example 3 (well-formed encoding). To encode the CTL formula $\varphi = E(p\ U\ q) \wedge (AG\ EF\ q)$ whose syntax tree is shown in Fig. 2, we could use an assignment $e\colon \Gamma \to [0,1]$. We write $(\Gamma_o)^e_j$ to denote the value assigned by e to parameter Γ_o at position j. The assignment is defined by: $(\Gamma_{\text{right}})^e_{1,5} = 1$, $(\Gamma_\wedge)^e_1 = 1$, $(\Gamma_{EU})^e_2 = 1$, $(\Gamma_p)^e_3 = 1$, $(\Gamma_q)^e_4 = 1$, $(\Gamma_{AG})^e_5 = 1$, $(\Gamma_{EF})^e_6 = 1$, and $(\Gamma_q)^e_7 = 1$; all other parameters are set to 0 by e.

Example 4 (ill-formed encoding). Although every CTL formula admits an encoding in the parameter space of Γ, the converse is not true: most assignments to Γ do not yield a syntactically well-formed formula. Consider an assignment $e\colon \Gamma \to [0,1]$ with $(\Gamma_\wedge)^e_1 = 1$, $(\Gamma_\vee)^e_2 = 1$, $(\Gamma_p)^e_3 = 1$, $(\Gamma_q)^e_4 = 1$, $(\Gamma_r)^e_5 = 1$, $(\Gamma_{\text{right}})^e_{1,4} = 1$, $(\Gamma_{\text{right}})^e_{2,4} = 1$, and all other parameters set to zero. This encoding is ill-formed because both $\wedge$ and $\vee$ assign their right child to the same node q, which violates the requirement that each node has a unique parent. A simple fix is to set $(\Gamma_{\text{right}})^e_{1,5} = 1$ and $(\Gamma_{\text{right}})^e_{1,4} = 0$. The resulting encoding is well-formed and corresponds to $(p \vee q) \wedge r$.

4.2 Inference

Next, we present how we compute the CTL semantics in our neural network. More precisely, we present a differentiable function that computes the satisfaction of a prospective CTL formula by different states of Kripke structures. Given a Kripke structure $\mathcal{K} = (S, R, L, s_{\mathsf{init}})$ and a parameter assignment e, for each state $s \in S$ the model computes a satisfaction vector $x^e_s \in [0,1]^L$, where $(x^e_s)_j$ indicates whether the state s satisfies the CTL formula rooted at node j corresponding to assignment e. We first define intermediary variables $(y^e_s)^o$ parameterized by operators $o \in \mathsf{Op}$, the vector x^e is then defined as a clipped sum of the variables $(y^e)^o$ for all operators $o \in \mathsf{Op}$.

Atomic Propositions. For $p \in P$ and $1 \leq j \leq L$, we compute satisfaction using the indicator function $I : \{\top, \bot\} \to \{0,1\}$ via $(y^e_s)^p_j := I(p \in L(s)) \cdot (\Gamma_p)^e_j$.

Unary Operators. We then continue with unary operators. Recall that the left child of a unary operator at position j is assumed to be at position $j+1$.

Negation. We start with the propositional unary operator. For all states $s \in S$ and nodes $1 \leq j \leq L$, we let:

$$(y^e_s)^{\neg}_j := (\Gamma_\neg)^e_j \cdot (1 - (x^e_s)_{j+1})$$

Next Operator. We continue with the unary temporal operator next. For all states $s \in S$ and nodes $1 \leq j \leq L$, we let:

$$(y^e_s)^{EX}_j := (\Gamma_{\text{EX}})^e_j \cdot \max_{(s,t)\in R} (x_t)^e_{j+1} \quad \text{and} \quad (y^e_s)^{AX}_j := (\Gamma_{\text{AX}})^e_j \cdot \min_{(s,t)\in R} (x_t)^e_{j+1}$$

Eventually Operator. For the operator F, we define $(y_s^e)_j^F$ analogously to $(y_s^e)_j^U$, which will be introduced below for the *until* operator. This definition follows directly from the equivalence stating that, for any CTL formula φ, the formula $CF\varphi$ is logically equivalent to $C[\top U\varphi]$ for $C \in \{A, E\}$.

Globally Operator. Let us now turn to the operator G and the definition of $(y_s^e)_j^G$. This case is trickier than the previous ones since computing the corresponding set of satisfied states requires a fixed-point computation. Our encoding mimics this iterative computation indexed by $n = 0, 1, \ldots, N$, where $N = |S|$ is the number of states of the Kripke structure. We start with the initialization step for each state $s \in S$:

$$(y^e_{s,(0)})_j^{E\,G} := (x_s)^e_{j+1} \quad \text{and} \quad (y^e_{s,(0)})_j^{A\,G} := (x_s)^e_{j+1}$$

We then iterate over $0 \leq n \leq N-1$ by expansion laws:

$$(y^e_{s,(n+1)})_j^{E\,G} := \min\Big\{(y^e_{s,(n)})_j^{E\,G},\ \max_{(s,t)\in R}(y^e_{t,(n)})_j^{E\,G}\Big\}$$

$$(y^e_{s,(n+1)})_j^{A\,G} := \min\Big\{(y^e_{s,(n)})_j^{A\,G},\ \min_{(s,t)\in R}(y^e_{t,(n)})_j^{A\,G}\Big\}$$

The case of AG is similar to EG, except that the innermost max is replaced by a min: We then weight them with the respective score of the the globally operator:

$$(y_s^e)_j^{EG} := (\Gamma_{EG})_j^e \cdot (y^e_{s,(N)})_j^{E\,G} \quad \text{and} \quad (y_s^e)_j^{AG} := (\Gamma_{AG})_j^e \cdot (y^e_{s,(N)})_j^{A\,G}$$

Binary Operators As an intermediate step for computing the satisfaction relation of binary operators, we first handle the right child selection. Specifically, for each state $s \in S$ and node $1 \leq j \leq L$ we measure the satisfaction of the right child of node j's sub-formula by state s:

$$r_j^e(s) = \sum_{k=j+2}^{L} (\Gamma_{\text{right}})^e_{j,k} \cdot (x_s)^e_k$$

Conjunction and Disjunction. For all states $s \in S$ and nodes $1 \leq j \leq L$, we let:

$$(y_s^e)_j^{\wedge} := (\Gamma_\wedge)_j^e \cdot \min\{(x_s^e)_{j+1},\, r_j^e(s)\} \text{ and } (y_s^e)_j^{\vee} := (\Gamma_\vee)_j^e \cdot \max\{(x_s^e)_{j+1},\, r_j^e(s)\}$$

Until. Let us now consider the until operator. This case is similar to the case of the G operator.

We initialize, for each state $s \in S$:

$$(y^e_{s,(0)})_j^{E\,U} := r_j^e(s) \quad \text{and} \quad (y^e_{s,(0)})_j^{A\,U} := r_j^e(s)$$

We then iterate over $0 \leq n \leq N-1$.

$$(y^e_{s,(n+1)})_j^{E\,U} := \max\Big\{\,(y^e_{s,(n)})_j^{E\,U},\ \min\Big\{(x_s^e)_{j+1},\ \max_{(s,t)\in R}(y^e_{t,(n)})_j^{E\,U}\Big\}\Big\}$$

$$(y^e_{s,(n+1)})_j^{A\,U} := \max\Big\{\,(y^e_{s,(n)})_j^{A\,U},\ \min\Big\{(x_s^e)_{j+1},\ \min_{(s,t)\in R}(y^e_{t,(n)})_j^{A\,U}\Big\}\Big\}$$

The two operators differ only in the innermost aggregator.

Finally, we apply the score of the operator in the learned parameter:

$$(y_s^e)_j^{EU} := (\Gamma_{EU})_j^e \cdot (y_{s,(N)}^e)_j^{E\,U} \quad \text{and} \quad (y_s^e)_j^{AU} := (\Gamma_{AU})_j^e \cdot (y_{s,(N)}^e)_j^{A\,U}$$

Full Value. We can finally put everything together and obtain the vector x as follows. For all states $s \in S$ and $1 \leq j \leq L$:

$$(x_s^e)_j = \sigma\Big(\sum_{p \in P} (y_s^e)_j^p + (y_s^e)_j^{\neg} + (y_s^e)_j^{\wedge} + (y_s^e)_j^{\vee} + \sum_{C \in \{A,E\}} (y_s^e)_j^{CX} + (y_s^e)_j^{CF} + (y_s^e)_j^{CG} + (y_s^e)_j^{CU} \Big)$$

where $\sigma(a) := \min(1, \max(0, a)) \in [0, 1]$ applies clipping to $a \in \mathbb{R}$.

4.3 Faithfulness

During training, the values of Γ evolve as real-valued assignments. Since these raw values are unconstrained, they do not directly represent valid symbolic choices in a CTL formula. To obtain faithful encodings, we employ two techniques. First, we employ a local normalization step after each gradient update. Secondly, we define regularization terms that guide the gradient updates towards a faithful representation during training. While a strictly binary and perfectly faithful representation of a formula cannot be guaranteed after training, the techniques presented here reduce structural inconsistencies and ill-formed representations.

Normalization. Our normalization step ensures that for every node position i, the weights associated with possible operators at that node sum to one, and likewise for all potential right-child indices of i. In other words, each local group of parameters forms a probability-like distribution over discrete options, while remaining differentiable for gradient-based optimization. More precisely, given a parameter assignment e, we update the weights in Γ as follows:

$$\forall i + 2 \leq k \leq L: \; (\Gamma_{\text{right}})_{i,k}^e \;\leftarrow\; \frac{exp^{(\Gamma_{\text{right}})_{i,k}}}{\eta_{\text{right},i}} \text{ with } \eta_{\text{right},i} \;=\; \sum_{k=i+2}^{L} exp^{(\Gamma_{\text{right}})_{i,k}}$$

Similarly, for all $o \in \mathsf{Op}$ we normalize the weights as follows:

$$(\Gamma_o)_i^e \;\leftarrow\; \frac{exp^{(\Gamma_o)_i}}{\eta_{\text{op},i}} \text{ with } \eta_{\text{op},i} \;=\; \sum_{o' \in \mathsf{Op}} exp^{(\Gamma_{o'})_i}$$

Main Objective and Regularization. Regularization terms are additional loss functions that are minimized during training alongside a main objective. Our main objective is the correct classification of the input Kripke structures in Π, and our regularization terms are designed to push the neural network's weights towards a faithful representation of a CTL formula. We first explain our main objective. For each $K \in \Pi$, we let $\text{lab}(K) := 1$ if $K \in \Pi_+$, and $\text{lab}(K) := 0$ if $K \in \Pi_-$; we also use x_K to denote element $(x_s)_1$ of the vector x, for the initial state s of the Kripke structure K. Then, the main objective is to minimize the classification error:

$$\zeta_1 = \sum_{K \in \Pi} (x_K - \text{lab}(K))^2$$

Next, we present our regularization terms. We use squared losses when the objective requires an *exact match* to the target value, as in the main classification objective above. The $\max(0, x)$ formulation is used instead to enforce *inequality constraints*. For example, none-nodes must remain continuous: once a position is set to "none", all subsequent positions must also be "none" to preserve syntactic consistency. Thus, we minimize the loss:

$$\zeta_2 = \sum_{i=1}^{L-1} \max\left(0, (\Gamma_{\text{none}})_i - (\Gamma_{\text{none}})_{i+1}\right)$$

We also enforce that every child node has exactly one parent node:

$$\zeta_3 = \sum_{i=2}^{L} \left(\sum_{j=1}^{i-2} (\Gamma_{\text{right}})_{j,i} + \sum_{op \in \mathsf{Op}'} (\Gamma_{op})_{i-1} - 1 \right)^2$$

where $\mathsf{Op}' = \{\text{none}, \neg, \wedge, \vee, \text{EX}, \text{AX}, \text{EF}, \text{AF}, \text{EG}, \text{AG}, \text{EU}, \text{AU}\}$

Example 5 (Example for high ζ_3-loss). Consider the ill-formed assignment e from Example 4, where q has two parent nodes: $e\colon \Gamma \to [0,1]$ with $(\Gamma_\wedge)_1^e = 1$, $(\Gamma_\vee)_2^e = 1$, $(\Gamma_p)_3^e = 1$, $(\Gamma_q)_4^e = 1$, $(\Gamma_r)_5^e = 1$, $(\Gamma_{\text{right}})_{1,4}^e = 1$, $(\Gamma_{\text{right}})_{2,4}^e = 1$. For $i = 3$, the inner sum is 0, indicating no loss since p has exactly one parent $(\Gamma_\vee)_2^e$. For $i = 4$, the inner sum is 1, incurring loss because q has two parents $(\Gamma_{\text{right}})_{1,4}^e$ and $(\Gamma_{\text{right}})_{2,4}^e$. For $i = 5$, the inner sum is $(-1)^2 = 1$, again incurring loss since r has no parent. Thus, the total loss is 2. This loss gives an incentive to assignments for each node to have exactly one parent.

Finally, we ensure that the binary operators are nested faithfully:

$$\zeta_4 = \sum_{i=1}^{L-2} \sum_{j=i+2}^{L} \sum_{t=i+1}^{j-1} \sum_{t'=j+1}^{L} \max\left(0, (\Gamma_{\text{right}})_{i,j} + (\Gamma_{\text{right}})_{t,t'} - 1\right)$$

All four terms $\zeta_1, \zeta_2, \zeta_3, \zeta_4$ are minimized during training.

Example 6 (Example for high ζ_4-loss). Consider an ill-formed assignment e where the right child of a $\vee$-node is incorrectly placed within the right subtree of its parent: $e\colon \Gamma \to [0,1]$ with $(\Gamma_\wedge)_1^e = 1$, $(\Gamma_\vee)_2^e = 1$, $(\Gamma_p)_3^e = 1$, $(\Gamma_q)_4^e = 1$, $(\Gamma_\neg)_5^e = 1$, $(\Gamma_r)_6^e = 1$, $(\Gamma_{\text{right}})_{1,5}^e = 1$, $(\Gamma_{\text{right}})_{2,6}^e = 1$. The ζ_4-loss is non-zero because for $i = 1$, $j = 5$, $t = 2$, and $t' = 6$, the inner term evaluates to $\max(0, (\Gamma_{\text{right}})_{1,5}^e + (\Gamma_{\text{right}})_{2,6}^e - 1) = \max(0, 1 + 1 - 1) = 1$, penalizing the conflicting right-child assignments.

Algorithm 1. Extracting CTL Formula

Require: CTL encoding Γ of size L, beam width ω, data set Π
$\Gamma_{\text{right}}, \Gamma_{\text{o}} \leftarrow$ extracted from Γ, where $\text{o} \in \mathsf{Op}$
$i \leftarrow L$
while $i \geq 1$ **do**
  $f_i \leftarrow \emptyset$
  for $p \in P$ **do**
    $f_i \leftarrow f_i \cup \{(p, (\Gamma_p)_i)\}$
  end for
  for $(\varphi_k, s_k) \in f_{i+1}$ **do**
    $f_i \leftarrow f_i \cup \{((\neg, \varphi_k), (\Gamma_\neg)_i \cdot s_k)\}$
    $f_i \leftarrow f_i \cup \{((AX, \varphi_k), (\Gamma_{AX})_i \cdot s_k), ((EX, \varphi_k), (\Gamma_{EX})_i \cdot s_k)\}$
    $f_i \leftarrow f_i \cup \{((AF, \varphi_k), (\Gamma_{AF})_i \cdot s_k), ((EF, \varphi_k), (\Gamma_{EF})_i \cdot s_k)\}$
    $f_i \leftarrow f_i \cup \{((AG, \varphi_k), (\Gamma_{AG})_i \cdot s_k), ((EG, \varphi_k), (\Gamma_{EG})_i \cdot s_k)\}$
  end for
  for $j = i + 2$ to L **do**
    for $((\varphi_l, s_l), (\varphi_r, s_r)) \in f_{i+1} \times f_j$ **do**
      $f_i \leftarrow f_i \cup \{((\wedge, \varphi_l, \varphi_r), (\Gamma_\wedge)_i \cdot (\Gamma_{\text{right}})_{i,r} \cdot s_l \cdot s_r)\}$
      $f_i \leftarrow f_i \cup \{((\vee, \varphi_l, \varphi_r), (\Gamma_\vee)_i \cdot (\Gamma_{\text{right}})_{i,r} \cdot s_l \cdot s_r)\}$
      $f_i \leftarrow f_i \cup \{((AU, \varphi_l, \varphi_r), (\Gamma_{AU})_i \cdot (\Gamma_{\text{right}})_{i,r} \cdot s_l \cdot s_r)\}$
      $f_i \leftarrow f_i \cup \{((EU, \varphi_l, \varphi_r), (\Gamma_{EU})_i \cdot (\Gamma_{\text{right}})_{i,r} \cdot s_l \cdot s_r)\}$
    end for
  end for
  Sort $f_i = \{(\varphi_j, s_j)\}$ according to s_j, keep top ω elements and remove the others
  $i \leftarrow i - 1$
end while
$\varphi \leftarrow$ best formula obtained from f_1 according to the classification accuracy on Π
return φ

Formula Extraction. To extract a CTL formula from an encoding Γ, we follow a procedure similar to [17,22]. The extraction is performed bottom-up: starting from atomic propositions, we iteratively construct larger subformulae by applying unary and binary CTL operators according to the encoding weights. Each generated subformula is assigned a score obtained by multiplying the corresponding operator's weight from Γ with the scores of its subformulae. At every position, we retain only the ω highest-scoring candidates, where ω is a beam-width hyperparameter, in order to keep the search space manageable. The final extracted formula is then chosen as the best candidate from the root position according to its classification accuracy on the training set. This procedure is described in Algorithm 1.

5 Experiments

Baselines. We compare our learner with two state-of-the-art (SOTA) CTL learners of Bordais et al. [5] and Pommellet et al. [20]. Both baselines rely on constraint solving; the former is implemented in Python, while the latter is implemented in C++. To the best of our knowledge, there are no other methods for learning CTL formulae.

Implementation.[1] Our learner is implemented in PyTorch and natively supports 12 operators, most of which occur in the benchmark dataset: $\neg, \wedge, \vee, \implies, AU, EU, AX, EX, AG, EG, AF, EF$. We use a size budget of 7, and after training, we run the formula extraction procedure with beam width $\omega = 100$. We discuss both hyperparameter choices in the ablation studies. For training, we use the AdamW optimizer [16] and train our neural network for 30 epochs with a learning rate of 0.1, which suffices for fast convergence across all settings. In addition to the encoding weights Γ, we train a learnable *sharpness* parameter that influences how decisive the network outputs are. Smaller values lead to softer (more continuous) truth values, which is beneficial for gradient-based optimization. On the other hand, larger values push outputs closer to 0 or 1, making the encoded formula more explicit over the course of the training process. The regularization terms $\zeta_2, \zeta_3, \zeta_4$ receive less importance than the main objective ζ_1 by reducing the regularization-losses by a factor 10 before the gradient-update. The batch size is set to 20, corresponding to the dataset size of the smallest experimental configuration. We implement two training strategies for our learner. The first strategy, referred to as "Neur", jointly optimizes the operators at all positions in a single training process. The second strategy, referred to as "Neur-it", uses an *it*erative heuristic designed to improve accuracy at the expense of runtime. Specifically Neur-it sequentially trains up to 12 learners, each with its first operator fixed to one of the 12 available operators. Learning for all remaining queued learners is terminated once any learner discovers a formula with 100% accuracy. If no such formula is found, the best formula is returned. This heuristic encourages exploration of a larger formula space and reduces the likelihood of convergence to local minima.

Dataset. We use the dataset provided by Bordais et al. [5], which consists of 84 experimental settings with varying CTL formulae, varying Kripke structure sizes, and varying numbers of training samples. Specifically, the dataset contains 7 CTL formulae taken from a standard textbook [3]. For each formula, there are 12 configurations: 6 configurations where each Kripke structure has at most 5 nodes, and 6 configurations where each Kripke structure has at most 15 nodes. Within each group, the number of training samples varies from 10 positive and 10 negative examples up to 60 positive and 60 negative examples. We use a timeout of 600 s for all experiments. We do not consider the dataset proposed by Pommellet et al. [20] due to its limited size and diversity, as it contains only two to ten training samples per formula. All experiments were conducted on a 13th Gen Intel® Core™ i7-1365U × 12.

Benchmark Results. We report the results on the benchmark dataset in Figs. 4a and 4b. The blue bars in Fig. 4a summarize the average classification accuracy of the returned formulae across all 84 experimental settings. Both constraint-based baselines achieve perfect 100% accuracy whenever they return a

[1] Source Code: https://github.com/YalcinerMustafa/CTLLearning-Sources.

solution, as expected, since these approaches explicitly search for a formula consistent with all training samples. In contrast, our neural learner (Neur) attains an average accuracy of $87.6 \pm 12\%$, while the iterative variant (Neur-it) improves this to $96.3 \pm 4\%$. The orange bars in Fig. 4a report the fraction of experimental settings in which a method failed to return any formula within the timeout limit. Here, both constraint-based approaches frequently time out, with Bordais et al. timing out in 53.6% of the cases and Pommellet et al. in 33.3%. In comparison, both neural approaches complete successfully in all settings, i.e., they never time out.

Finally, Fig. 4b compares runtimes, considering only those configurations where all approaches finished within the time limit. Note that this experiment is skewed in favor of the constraint based approaches, since all experimental setups that resulted in a timeout were removed. Despite this skew, our learners remain competitive. Specifically, Fig. 4b shows that Bordais et al. shows the highest runtime, with an average of 173 s. Neur-it requires 42 s on average, while Pommellet et al. averages 34 s. The fastest method is Neur, with an average runtime of 16.8 s and the lowest observed variance.

Key takeaway: Neural learners provide formulae with consistently high accuracy without any timeouts.

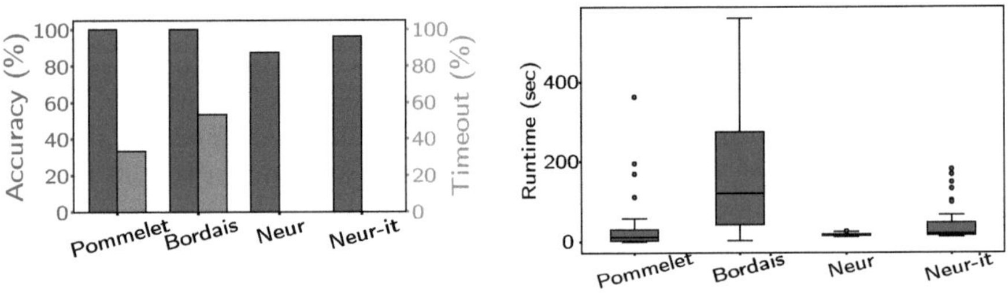

(a) Accuracy (b) Runtime

Fig. 4. Comparison on Benchmark

Noise. In many real-world settings, observations of a system may be corrupted by noise, e.g., due to faulty sensors. Such noise can affect the extracted Kripke structures, for instance by dropping existing edges, adding spurious edges, or assigning incorrect values to atomic propositions. In some cases, these perturbations are benign in the sense that the underlying system could still exhibit the observed behavior despite the sensing errors. In other cases, however, the corruption yields a Kripke structure that no longer faithfully represents the system, effectively inducing incorrect labels. That is, an observation may be labeled positive (negative) even though the underlying system cannot (can) exhibit the corresponding behavior. Since such label noise is particularly challenging for constraint-based learners, we explicitly evaluate robustness under mislabeled training data. To this end, we construct a noisy version of the benchmark dataset by randomly flipping the labels of 10% of the Kripke structures in each experimental configuration. We report the corresponding results next.

We run all baselines on this perturbed dataset and report the results in Fig. 5. As shown in Fig. 5, the performance of the neural methods decreases moderately: Neur drops from 87.6% $\pm$ 12% to 80.0% $\pm$ 10%, and Neur-it drops from 96.3% $\pm$ 4% to 86.8% $\pm$ 4%. Both constraint-based approaches can still occasionally return a formula that perfectly classifies the mislabeled instances, thus achieving 100% accuracy. However, Fig. 5 also highlights that constraint-based methods struggle substantially under noise, timing out in the vast majority of cases: 91.6% timeouts for Pommellet et al. and 97.6% for Bordais et al. In contrast, both neural learners again complete successfully in all settings, returning formulae with comparatively high classification accuracy.

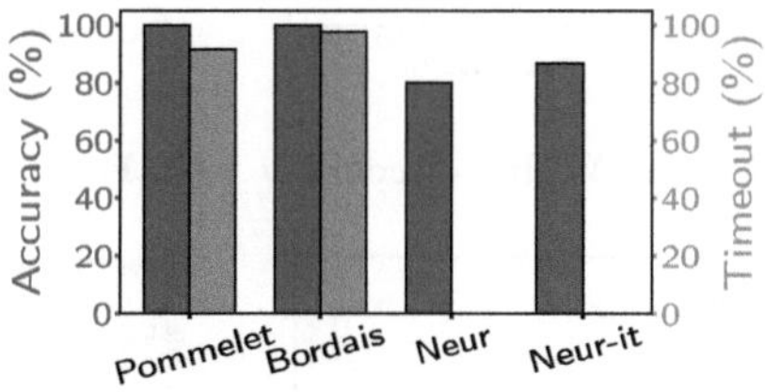

Fig. 5. Benchmark with Noise

Key Takeaway: Under label noise, neural learners remain reliable and avoid timeouts, whereas constraint-based baselines become largely impractical due to excessive timeout rates.

Ablation. The beam width ω is a parameter of Algorithm 1 that controls how many candidate formulae are retained during formula extraction from the neural network output. Following common practice in related work [17,22], we set the beam width to $\omega = 100$ in all experiments. To study the effect of this choice, we conduct an ablation in which we use the same learner described in the *Implementation* paragraph, but vary ω and measure the resulting accuracy and runtime. Figure 6a reports the average accuracy over the full benchmark dataset for different beam widths. The results show that while it is important to not just consider the *one* highest-scoring formula from the neural network, increasing ω beyond 20 yields only slight improvements in accuracy. Similar observations were also made in [22]. Figure 6d shows the corresponding runtime for formula extraction. As expected, the runtime increases with larger beam widths; nevertheless, for $\omega = 100$ the extraction time remains below 10 s. Overall, these results justify the use of $\omega = 100$ as the beam width, but also indicate that smaller values can further reduce runtime while only slightly affecting accuracy.

We fix the size budget for learned formulae to 7 and its impact is visualized in Figs. 6b and 6d. Specifically, Fig. 6b shows the average accuracy on the full benchmark dataset for various size budgets, and Fig. 6d shows the runtime impact. Interestingly, while runtime increases linearly with the size budget (Fig. 6d), performance does not even increase monotonically with larger size budgets (Figs. 6a) – a trend also observed in [22]. Still, a size budget of 7 yields the highest accuracy in our experiments and is therefore selected. Lastly, we show that our min-max based implementation is better suited for learning CTL

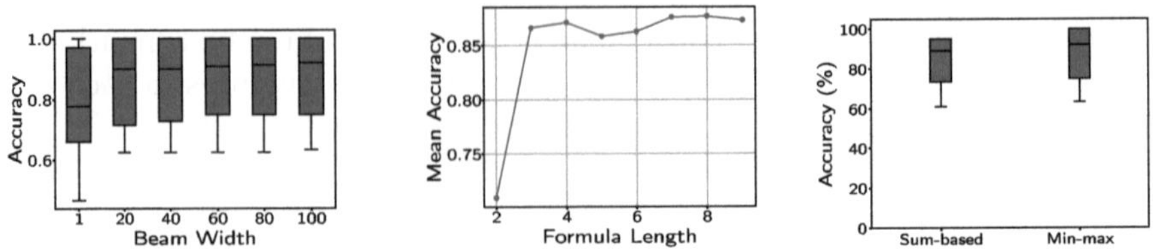

(a) Beam Width - Accuracy (b) Formula size - Accuracy (c) Impl. - Accuracy

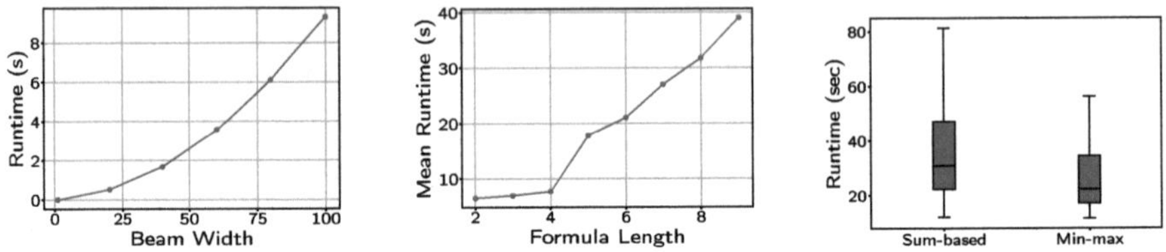

(d) Beam Width - Runtime (e) Formula size - Runtime (f) Impl. - Runtime

Fig. 6. Impact of beam width, size budget, and implementation type.

formulae than the implementation based on sum-rules used in [22] for learning LTL formulae. Specifically, we compare the accuracy over the whole benchmark dataset and the runtime of both implementations of our learner. Figures 6c and 6f show that the min-max based implementation has slightly higher accuracy and a lower runtime than its sum-based counterpart.

Key Takeaway. Our learner is largely insensitive to the hyperparameter choices, with accuracy saturating quickly beyond moderate values. Thus, smaller beam widths and size budgets can reduce runtime while maintaining nearly the same performance.

6 Conclusion and Future Work

We introduced the first neural approach for learning CTL specifications from labeled Kripke structures. In contrast to existing constraint-based learners, our method leverages gradient-based optimization to efficiently search the space of CTL formulae while remaining robust to noisy data. While employing gradient based optimization approaches to learning logical formulae is theoretically incomplete and is not guaranteed to find a good solution, our experimental evaluation on a standard benchmark demonstrates that the proposed learner returns CTL specifications with high accuracy, low runtime, and without timeouts, even in challenging settings where satisfiability-based approaches frequently fail.

For future work, it would be interesting to investigate how neural and satisfiability-based methods could be combined and applied to other logics such as ATL.

Acknowledgements. This work has been financially supported by Deutsche Forschungsgemeinschaft, DFG Project number 434592664.

References

1. Alur, R., Henzinger, T.A., Kupferman, O.: Alternating-time temporal logic. J. ACM **49**(5), 672–713 (2002). https://doi.org/10.1145/585265.585270
2. Angluin, D.: Learning regular sets from queries and counterexamples. Inf. Comput. **75**(2), 87–106 (1987). https://doi.org/10.1016/0890-5401(87)90052-6
3. Baier, C., Katoen, J.: Principles of Model Checking. MIT Press (2008)
4. Blaauwbroek, L., et al.: Learning guided automated reasoning: a brief survey. In: Capretta, V., Krebbers, R., Wiedijk, F. (eds.) Logics and Type Systems in Theory and Practice. LNCS, vol. 14560, pp. 54–83. Springer, Cham (2024). https://doi.org/10.1007/978-3-031-61716-4_4
5. Bordais, B., Neider, D., Roy, R.: Learning branching-time properties in CTL and ATL via constraint solving. In: Platzer, A., Rozier, K.Y., Pradella, M., Rossi, M. (eds.) FM 2024, Part I. LNCS, vol. 14933, pp. 304–323. Springer, Cham (2024). https://doi.org/10.1007/978-3-031-71162-6_16
6. Bordais, B., Neider, D., Roy, R.: The complexity of learning LTL, CTL and ATL formulas. In: Beyersdorff, O., Pilipczuk, M., Pimentel, E., Nguyen, K.T. (eds.) 42nd International Symposium on Theoretical Aspects of Computer Science, STACS 2025, Jena, Germany, 4–7 March 2025. LIPIcs, vol. 327, pp. 19:1–19:20. Schloss Dagstuhl - Leibniz-Zentrum für Informatik (2025). https://doi.org/10.4230/LIPICS.STACS.2025.19
7. Camacho, A., McIlraith, S.A.: Learning interpretable models expressed in linear temporal logic. In: Benton, J., Lipovetzky, N., Onaindia, E., Smith, D.E., Srivastava, S. (eds.) Proceedings of the Twenty-Ninth International Conference on Automated Planning and Scheduling, ICAPS 2019, Berkeley, CA, USA, 11–15 July 2019, pp. 621–630. AAAI Press (2019). https://ojs.aaai.org/index.php/ICAPS/article/view/3529
8. Clarke, E.M., Emerson, E.A.: Design and synthesis of synchronization skeletons using branching time temporal logic. In: Kozen, D. (ed.) Logic of Programs 1981. LNCS, vol. 131, pp. 52–71. Springer, Heidelberg (1982). https://doi.org/10.1007/BFb0025774
9. Clarke, E.M., Emerson, E.A., Sistla, A.P.: Automatic verification of finite-state concurrent systems using temporal logic specifications. ACM Trans. Program. Lang. Syst. **8**(2), 244–263 (1986). https://doi.org/10.1145/5397.5399
10. Clarke, E.M., Henzinger, T.A., Veith, H., Bloem, R.: Handbook of Model Checking, vol. 10. Springer, Cham (2018)
11. Emerson, E.A., Halpern, J.Y.: "Sometimes" and "not never" revisited: on branching versus linear time. In: Wright, J.R., Landweber, L., Demers, A.J., Teitelbaum, T. (eds.) Conference Record of the Tenth Annual ACM Symposium on Principles of Programming Languages, Austin, Texas, USA, January 1983, pp. 127–140. ACM Press (1983). https://doi.org/10.1145/567067.567081
12. Gaglione, J.-R., Neider, D., Roy, R., Topcu, U., Xu, Z.: Learning linear temporal properties from noisy data: a MaxSAT-based approach. In: Hou, Z., Ganesh, V. (eds.) ATVA 2021. LNCS, vol. 12971, pp. 74–90. Springer, Cham (2021). https://doi.org/10.1007/978-3-030-88885-5_6

13. Havelund, K., Reger, G., Roşu, G.: Runtime verification past experiences and future projections. In: Steffen, B., Woeginger, G. (eds.) Computing and Software Science. LNCS, vol. 10000, pp. 532–562. Springer, Cham (2019). https://doi.org/10.1007/978-3-319-91908-9_25
14. Kästner, L., Crook, B.: Explaining AI through mechanistic interpretability. Eur. J. Philos. Sci. **14**(4) (2024). https://epub.uni-bayreuth.de/id/eprint/8273/
15. Kim, J., Muise, C., Shah, A., Agarwal, S., Shah, J.: Bayesian inference of linear temporal logic specifications for contrastive explanations. In: Proceedings of the Twenty-Eighth International Joint Conference on Artificial Intelligence, IJCAI-19, pp. 5591–5598. International Joint Conferences on Artificial Intelligence Organization (2019). https://doi.org/10.24963/ijcai.2019/776
16. Loshchilov, I., Hutter, F.: Decoupled weight decay regularization. In: International Conference on Learning Representations (2017). https://api.semanticscholar.org/CorpusID:53592270
17. Luo, W., Liang, P., Du, J., Wan, H., Peng, B., Zhang, D.: Bridging LTLf inference to GNN inference for learning LTLf formulae. In: Proceedings of the AAAI Conference on Artificial Intelligence, vol. 36, no. 9, pp. 9849–9857 (2022). https://doi.org/10.1609/aaai.v36i9.21221
18. Manna, Z., Pnueli, A.: The Temporal Logic of Reactive and Concurrent Systems - Specification. Springer, Cham (1992). https://doi.org/10.1007/978-1-4612-0931-7
19. Neider, D.: Intelligent formal methods. Rheinland-Pfälzische Technische Universität Kaiserslautern-Landau (2022). https://kluedo.ub.rptu.de/frontdoor/index/index/docId/8178
20. Pommellet, A., Stan, D., Scatton, S.: SAT-based learning of computation tree logic. In: Benzmüller, C., Heule, M.J.H., Schmidt, R.A. (eds.) IJCAR 2024, Part I. LNCS, vol. 14739, pp. 366–385. Springer, Cham (2024). https://doi.org/10.1007/978-3-031-63498-7_22
21. Steffen, B., Howar, F., Isberner, M.: Active automata learning: From dfas to interface programs and beyond. In: Heinz, J., de la Higuera, C., Oates, T. (eds.) Proceedings of the Eleventh International Conference on Grammatical Inference, ICGI 2012, University of Maryland, College Park, USA, 5–8 September 2012. JMLR Proceedings, vol. 21, pp. 195–209. JMLR.org (2012). http://proceedings.mlr.press/v21/steffen12a.html
22. Wan, H., Liang, P., Du, J., Luo, W., Ye, R., Peng, B.: End-to-end learning of LTLf formulae by faithful LTLf encoding. In: Proceedings of the AAAI Conference on Artificial Intelligence, vol. 38, no. 8, pp. 9071–9079 (2024). https://doi.org/10.1609/aaai.v38i8.28757
23. Wasylkowski, A., Zeller, A.: Mining temporal specifications from object usage. Autom. Softw. Eng. **18**(3–4), 263–292 (2011). https://doi.org/10.1007/S10515-011-0084-1

Open Access This chapter is licensed under the terms of the Creative Commons Attribution 4.0 International License (http://creativecommons.org/licenses/by/4.0/), which permits use, sharing, adaptation, distribution and reproduction in any medium or format, as long as you give appropriate credit to the original author(s) and the source, provide a link to the Creative Commons license and indicate if changes were made.

The images or other third party material in this chapter are included in the chapter's Creative Commons license, unless indicated otherwise in a credit line to the material. If material is not included in the chapter's Creative Commons license and your intended use is not permitted by statutory regulation or exceeds the permitted use, you will need to obtain permission directly from the copyright holder.

Growing HOLMS: A Verified Automated Prover for Grzegorczyk Logic in HOL Light

Antonella Bilotta[1(✉)], Marco Maggesi[2], and Cosimo Perini Brogi[3]

[1] Scuola Normale Superiore di Pisa, Pisa, Italy
antonella.bilotta@sns.it
[2] University of Florence, Florence, Italy
marco.maggesi@unifi.it
[3] IMT School for Advanced Studies Lucca, Lucca, Italy
cosimo.perinibrogi@imtlucca.it

Abstract. This paper presents a certified theorem prover for Grzegorczyk logic (Grz) implemented in the general-purpose proof assistant HOL Light. Our prover builds on original HOL Light formalisations of modal adequacy for Grz with respect to finite partially ordered frames, and on the standard full and faithful translation of Grz into Gödel–Löb logic (GL). This formalised embedding allows us to extend the range of modal systems supported by the HOLMS library for automated modal reasoning, and constitutes a new methodology experimented in our framework, being the first logic added to the library through a modal translation.

The deductive engine performs an automated proof search in the labelled sequent calculus for GL. When the proof search on the translated formula succeeds, the system returns a HOL Light theorem certifying provability of the original Grz formula. When proof search terminates negatively, the system constructs a verified GL countermodel and thus certifies that the original formula is not provable in Grz.

Keywords: Automated Theorem Proving · Modal Reasoning · HOL Light · Grzegorczyk Logic · Gödel-Löb Logic · Modal Embedding · Logical Verification

1 Introduction

Recent formalisations of modal logic have progressed from verifying isolated systems to building comprehensive, modular tools.[1] The HOL Light Library for Modal Systems (HOLMS) [13,14,17] exemplifies this trend, providing a unified framework for reasoning about and within seven normal modal logics (K, T, B, K4, S4, S5, and GL) using the HOL Light proof assistant [54,55].

HOLMS employs a dual methodology: a *deep embedding* of axiomatic calculi and relational semantics to prove modal adequacy theorems, alongside a *shallow*

[1] See, e.g., [38–40,43,61].

© The Author(s) 2026
A. Biere et al. (Eds.): IJCAR 2026, LNAI 16688, pp. 414–435, 2026.
https://doi.org/10.1007/978-3-032-32589-1_25

embedding of labelled sequent calculi to facilitate automated reasoning. Consequently, the framework yields both verified theorems within the modal systems and certified countermodels upon proof search failure.

Our Contribution. We integrate HOLMS with a first significant example of certified modal translations. The intent is to extend the range of modal logic implemented in the library and experiment with applications of modal embeddings to modular automated reasoning in HOL Light. Here, we instantiate the methodology on Grzegorczyk logic (Grz) [46], a system bridging classical modal logic, intuitionistic mathematics, and topology [26].

Automated reasoning for Grz is traditionally hindered by its characteristic frame condition – specifically, the *weakly Noetherian* property (converse weak well-foundedness). Consequently, to implement a sequent calculus for Grz constructively typically demands non-trivial, ad hoc design choices to handle this condition, such as in [31] or in [73].

Rather than complicating the uniform architecture of HOLMS with such mechanisms, we circumvent the weak Noetherian condition entirely by formalising the Kuznetsov-Goldblatt-Boolos theorem [20,21]. In particular, we mechanise a full and faithful embedding of Grz into Gödel-Löb provability logic (GL) in two steps:

- implementing the standard *splitting translation* within HOL Light;
- reducing validity problems in Grz to corresponding validity problems in GL.

By doing so, we directly reuse HOLMS's existing verified decision procedure for GL [59] to decide Grz-theoremhood automatically.

More Technically. Consistent with HOLMS's architectural principles, we first provide a deep embedding of Grzegorczyk axiomatisation ($\mathbb{GRZ}$) as the extension of the minimal normal system $\mathbb{K}$ by the Grzegorczyk schema:

$$\Box(\Box(A \to \Box A) \to A) \to A.$$

We then prove that this axiomatisation is equivalent to $\mathbb{S}4\mathbb{GRZ}$ obtained by adding the same schema to the system $\mathbb{S}4$.

On the semantic side, we formalise the classes of RTWN (Reflexive, Transitive, Weakly Noetherian) frames and RATF (Reflexive, Antisymmetric, Transitive, Finite) frames. By proving the soundness and completeness of the axiomatic systems with respect to these classes, we integrate Grz into the library's existing semantic hierarchy alongside S4 and GL.

Whereas HOLMS typically relies on a shallow embedding of labelled sequents to drive automation, we adopt a translational approach for Grz to bypass the proof-theoretic complexities of its calculi. We implement the standard *splitting translation*, denoted `TRANSL` ↗ or $(\cdot)^+$, as a recursive function mapping modal formulas to modal formulas:

$$(\Box A)^+ := A^+ \wedge \Box(A^+)$$

This translation "internalises" reflexivity into the irreflexive framework of GL. We formally prove fullness and faithfulness of the embedding (`GRZ_TRANSL` ↗), establishing that $\mathbb{GRZ} \vdash A$ if and only if $\mathbb{GL} \vdash A^+$. This result allows us to repurpose the original, certified decision procedure for GL (`HOLMS_RULE` ↗), to decide validity in Grz.

A distinct advantage of the HOLMS automated reasoning is its capacity to produce certified countermodels for unprovable formulas in normal systems present in the codebase, including GL. Our approach preserves this constructive feature via a certified model transformation, executed in three steps:

1. When GL decision procedure refutes a translated formula A^+, the original tactic `HOLMS_BUILD_COUNTERMODEL` ↗ returns a finite, irreflexive, transitive countermodel for A^+;
2. We formally define a transformation, `R_PLUS` ↗, which computes the reflexive closure of such models.
3. We prove that this transformation maps finite GL-models for A^+ to finite Grz-models for A within the class RATF.

Thus, a failed proof search yields a concrete, verified Grz-countermodel for the original formula.

This automation of Grz-reasoning paves the way for extending the library's certification guarantees to intuitionistic validity via the Gödel-McKinsey-Tarski translation [41,60], which is an additional instance of the method of verified modal embeddings we advocate for.

Structure of the Paper. The remainder of this paper is organised as follows. Section 2 provides background on the HOLMS library, detailing its existing deep and shallow embeddings. Section 3 presents our formalisation of Grzegorczyk logic, including the axiomatic definitions and the proof of modal adequacy with respect to the standard frame classes. Section 4 details the formal verification of the Kuznetsov-Goldblatt-Boolos theorem, establishing the faithfulness of the splitting translation. In Sect. 5, we describe the decision procedure and the countermodel transformation R^+, by also presenting concrete examples of application; furthermore, we discuss aspects of the computational costs involved in the implementation of Grz-reasoning via modal embedding in GL. Section 6 concludes the main body of the paper with a summary and directions for future work, particularly regarding other modal companions.

A preprinted version of this work [15] includes two supplementary appendices to which we refer in the following. These detail the decision algorithm used in HOLMS, and the labelled sequent calculi underlying the procedure, respectively.

Source Code. The HOLMS codebase is freely available on GitHub ↗, with the version presented here permanently archived as release v2026-05-24 ↗. Additionally, the HOLMS project webpage [16] offers links to practical and theoretical documentation, concerning HOL Light and the framework.

The existing core library was extensively detailed in Appendix A of our previous work [14], while the updated code extends this repository with three additional Ocaml files:

- `grz.ml` ↗ contains the formalisation of Grz and the implementation of its decision procedure via modal translation described in Sects. 3–5;
- `translations.ml` ↗ defines and exemplifies the splitting translation, as described in Sect. 4;
- `grz_tests.ml` ↗ provides some tests of the decision procedure for Grz, alongside those discussed in Sect. 5.

In the following pages, hyperlinks – denoted by the symbol ↗ – point to code snippets relevant for the presentation.

2 Background on the Core Library

The HOLMS library provides a modular environment for formal reasoning about seven modal logics (K, T, K4, S4, B, S5, GL) within the HOL Light proof assistant. Its architecture is characterised by three interconnected presentations of modal logics: axiomatic calculi, relational semantics, and labelled sequents.

The library's principal innovation lies in its modularity, structured around Strachey's distinction between *parametric polymorphism* and *ad hoc polymorphism* [81]. This methodological choice clearly separates the verified infrastructure common to all systems from the bespoke components required for individual logics during proof development.

Parametric polymorphism denotes constructions where a single, uniform implementation serves all logic instances. In HOLMS, this encompasses the modal syntax, the deducibility relation, and the foundational lemmas underlying completeness proofs, such as the standard model construction and the truth lemma.

Conversely, *ad hoc polymorphism* describes bespoke implementations tailored to specific logics, with the appropriate variant selected at the meta-theoretical level. This category includes logic-specific accessibility relations (e.g., the irreflexive and transitive relation for GL), individual decision procedures, and the correspondence lemmas for distinct frame properties.

This section discusses the key aspects of the library; for a more detailed account, we refer the reader to [14].

2.1 Deep Embedding: Axiomatic and Semantic Presentations

The library employs a deep embedding for both the syntax and relational semantics of normal modal logics.

The modal language $\mathcal{L}$ is defined via an inductive type `:form` ↗. Deducibility is captured by a ternary relation $\mathcal{S}.\mathcal{H} \vdash A$ ↗, parameterised by a set of axiom schemas $\mathcal{S}$, which modularly extends the standard calculus $\mathbb{K}$ [33] into logics such as T, K4, S4, B, S5, and GL according to standard literature [18,19].[2]

[2] The notation `[S.{}|~ a]` denotes thus a term of HOL Light metalanguage representing a theorem of the object modal logic axiomatised by the schemas in $\mathcal{S}$.

Semantic validity is defined over Kripke frames $\langle W, R\rangle$ via a standard forcing relation $\Vdash$ (the formal predicate `holds` ↗) induced by an evaluation function $v : \mathtt{Atoms}_{\mathcal{L}} \times W \longrightarrow \{0,1\}$ [4]. Correspondence theory then maps these frames to specific logics.

While the notions of frames and characteristic classes are parametric, specific correspondence lemmas – such as `MODAL_TRANSNT` ↗ for GL – are ad hoc implementations tailored to the distinct relational properties of each system.

In the codebase, `CHAR S` ↗ denotes the class of frames satisfying the characteristic property of S, and `APPR S` ↗ denotes the class of finite frames in which any theorem of the axiomatic calculus defined by S is valid. The lemma `APPR_EQ_CHAR_FINITE` ↗ proves that the class of appropriate frames `APPR S` coincides with the characteristic class `CHAR S` restricted to finite frames.

The modular formalisation of modal adequacy (soundness and completeness) connects the seven axiomatic systems with their semantic presentations. Completeness is established via a principled modularisation of Boolos's strategy from [21], first mechanised in [58], decomposing the proof into:

- *Parametric components*, providing a uniform implementation applicable to all systems. These encompass construction of a `GEN_STANDARD_MODEL` ↗ from maximal consistent lists of formulas, proof of a `GEN_TRUTH_LEMMA` ↗, and identification of a generic counterworld via `GEN_COUNTERMODEL_ALT` ↗.
- *Ad hoc components*, necessitating logic-specific customisation. These include the definition of standard accessibility relations, as `GL_STANDARD_REL` ↗, the `ACCESSIBILITY_LEMMA` instances (e.g., `GL_ACCESSIBILITY_LEMMA` ↗), and theorems that verify that the constructed countermodel inhabits the correct characteristic frame class (e.g., `ITF_MAXIMAL_CONSISTENT` ↗) .

This dual approach aims to guarantee the meta-theory remains scalable: extending the library to a new logic primarily requires supplying the requisite ad hoc relational definitions while reusing the existing parametric infrastructure.

2.2 Shallow Embedding: Labelled Sequents and Automation

For automated reasoning across its seven supported systems, HOLMS employs a shallow embedding of G3-style labelled sequent calculi [77,85], optimised according to the methodology of [66–68]. Definitions of these calculi are collected in Appendix B of [15].

This embedding maps labelled sequents directly onto the HOL Light goal stack: formulas on the left-hand side of a sequent manifest as native hypotheses, while those on the right-hand side are encoded as subgoals in disjunctive form. In this architecture, a generic labelled sequent $\mathcal{R}, \Gamma \Rightarrow \Delta$ is encoded such that:

- The relational atoms in $\mathcal{R}$ and the forcing atoms in Γ serve as HOL Light assumptions;
- The succedent Δ is encoded as the disjunction of its constituent forcing atoms within the current HOL Light goal.

This shallow embedding strategy permits the direct reuse of the meta-logic's native deductive engine. Notably, classical propositional connectives require no bespoke encoding: they are handled directly by standard HOL Light tactics such as `IMP_TAC`, `CONJ_TAC`, and `DISJ_TAC`.

Modal rules, by contrast, are reconstructed at the meta-level by appealing to the forcing relation on relational frames.[3] Within this framework, each modal rule is implemented as a HOL Light tactic, even those capturing the semantic properties summarised in Table 3 of Appendix B from [15]. For instance, `BOX_RIGHT_THEN` ↗ tactic realises the $\Box$-rule in the consequent.[4]

The labelled sequent calculus we employ for reasoning about Grzegorczyk logic, via modal embedding to GL, is G3KGL. Its rules are summarised in Table 4 of Appendix B from [15], and we shallowly embedded them in HOL Light in previous work [59]. The automated decision procedure is then realised by `HOLMS_RULE` ↗ and the associated tactic `HOLMS_TAC` ↗. Such a realisation implements the the goal transitions shown in Fig. 1 of Appendix A from [15], which we rephrase as follows:

- **Starting Goal**: The user supplies a modal formula A, a set of hypotheses $\mathcal{G}$, and specifies one of seven modal logics $* \in \{$K, T, K4, S4, B, S5, GL$\}$. Each logic is characterised by a specific set $\mathcal{S}$ of axiom schemas.
- **Goal A:** The provability question is first translated into a semantic one: *is A valid within the class of Kripke frames characteristic of $\mathcal{S}$?* Our mechanised adequacy theorems justify this translation.
- **Goal B:** Using the shallow embedding and its internalisation of Kripke semantics, the problem is then recast as checking whether *A can be formally derived in the labelled calculus associated with $*$.*
- **Automated Proof Search:** We implement a root-first proof search for each calculus, which yields a decision procedure for $*$ [67]. The outcome branches as follows:
  - **Success branch:** When the search reaches initial sequents, `HOLMS_TAC` generates a shallowly embedded derivation of A which HOL Light certifies as a fully trusted proof of validity.
  - **Failure branch:** If the search fails, `HOLMS_BUILD_COUNTERMODEL` ↗ extracts a candidate countermodel from the HOL Light goal-stack.[5] Finally, `CERTIFY_COUNTERMODEL_TAC` ↗ calls HOL Light to verify that the candidate falsifies the input formula A at its root.

Currently, HOLMS provides decision procedures for four logics (K, T, B, and GL) – each halts by either proving validity or producing a certified finite countermodel – and semi-decision procedures for K4, S4, and S5.[6] In Appendix

[3] Refer to [68] for a detailed discussion of the method.

[4] Crucially, weakening, contraction, and cut rules are not introduced axiomatically but emerge naturally from HOL Light's underlying logical engine.

[5] This extraction mirrors the countermodel construction from failed proof searches well known in proof theory [67,72,82].

[6] For K4 and its extensions, the algorithm may terminate owing to a bound on the size of the generated countermodel, which prevents infinite loops caused by the

A of [15] we give a more detailed account of the design and functioning of the certified theorem-proving mechanism within HOLMS.

3 Grzegorczyk Logic, Formalised

We present the deep embedding of Grzegorczyk logic (Grz) in HOLMS, covering both its axiomatic derivability relation and its characteristic frame classes, following the methods of Sect. 2.1. The syntactic and semantic presentations are then bridged by formalising soundness and completeness for Grz, following the strategy developed in [21, § 12]. Observe that this is a different strategy from the modular one developed in [21, § 5] and implemented in the previous version of the HOLMS core library.

3.1 Axiomatic Systems for Grz

We introduce two distinct axiomatisations of Grz and formally prove their deductive equivalence. The core Grzegorczyk axiom schema, standardly denoted Grz, is

$$\Box(\Box(A \to \Box A) \to A) \to A.$$

In our code this is captured by the definition `GRZ_AX` ↗. The purely axiomatic calculus $\mathbb{GRZ}$ is then obtained by instantiating the general derivability predicate $\mathcal{S}.\mathcal{H} \vdash A$ ↗ with $\mathcal{S} := \{\mathsf{Grz}\}$, side-stepping at once the debate about the failure of necessitation [50].

Definition 1. *The predicate* $\mathit{Grz}.\mathcal{H} \vdash A$*, denoting derivability of a formula* A *from a set of hypotheses* $\mathcal{H}$ *in* $\mathbb{GRZ}$*, is inductively defined as follows:*

- *for each instance* A *of a schema of classical propositional logic,* $\mathit{Grz}.\mathcal{H} \vdash A$*;*
- *for each instance* A *of schema* $\mathsf{K} := \Box(B \to C) \to \Box B \to \Box C$*,* $\mathit{Grz}.\mathcal{H} \vdash A$*;*
- *for each instance* A *of schema* Grz*,* $\mathit{Grz}.\mathcal{H} \vdash A$*;*
- *for each* $A \in \mathcal{H}$*,* $\mathit{Grz}.\mathcal{H} \vdash A$*;*
- *if* $\mathit{Grz}.\mathcal{H} \vdash B \to A$ *and* $\mathit{Grz}.\mathcal{H} \vdash B$*, then* $\mathit{Grz}.\mathcal{H} \vdash A$*;*
- *if* $\mathit{Grz}.\varnothing \vdash A$*, then* $\mathit{Grz}.\mathcal{H} \vdash \Box A$ *for any set of formulas* $\mathcal{H}$*.*

Alternatively, Grz can be presented as an extension of the modal logic $\mathbb{S}4$. We define the calculus $\mathbb{S4GRZ}$ (`S4GRZ_AX` ↗) analogously to Definition 1, but with the axiom schemas supplemented by $\mathsf{4} := \Box A \to \Box\Box A$ (`FOUR_SCHEMA` ↗) and $\mathsf{T} := \Box A \to A$ (`T_SCHEMA` ↗); thus the axiomatic base consists of classical logic, K, T, $\mathsf{4}$, and Grz. Formalising the known equivalence between the two axiomatisations (`GRZ_EQ_S4GRZ` ↗) allows us to work interchangeably with whichever presentation is most convenient. Accordingly, we prove the adequacy theorem for $\mathbb{S4GRZ}$.

---

interaction between transitive closure and logical rules. However, the present tactic does not yet certify this bounded countermodel; established termination results [37] are planned for integration into future versions of the library.

3.2 Relational Frames for Grz

We now turn to the semantic characterisation of Grzegorczyk logic. A Kripke frame $\langle W, R\rangle$ validates Grz precisely when R is reflexive, transitive, and *weakly Noetherian*: the converse R^{-1} is well-founded in the sense that every non-empty subset of W contains an R-maximal element. To formalise this we introduce the definition of weakly well-founded relations `WWF` ↗. For a relation $\prec$,

$$\texttt{WWF}(\prec) \;:=\; \forall P \subseteq \mathrm{fld}(\prec).\, P \neq \emptyset \implies \exists x \in P.\, \forall y \in P.\, \neg(y \prec x \wedge y \neq x).$$

states that every non-empty subset of the field of $\prec$ contains a minimal element w.r.t. the strict version of $\prec$.[7] Equivalent formulations that facilitate different styles of reasoning are provided by `WWF_EQ` ↗, `WWF_IND` ↗, and `WWF_ALT` ↗.

A relation that is reflexive, transitive, and antisymmetric is a partial order; we capture this with `POSET_EQ` ↗. The key fact that any finite, non-empty partial order is weakly well-founded is established in `POSET_WWF` ↗, together with its set-theoretic counterpart `POSET_WWF_ALT` ↗.

With these foundations we define the specific frame classes relevant to Grz.

Definition 2 (`RTWN_DEF` ↗). *A frame $\langle W, R\rangle$ belongs to the class RTWN if R is reflexive, transitive, and the converse R^{-1} is weakly well-founded (`WWF`(R^{-1})).*

Definition 3 (`RATF_DEF` ↗). *A frame $\langle W, R\rangle$ belongs to the class RATF if R is reflexive, antisymmetric, transitive, and W is finite.*

By `POSET_WWF_ALT` ↗, each finite partial order satisfies the weakly Noetherian condition, so we can prove RATF $\subseteq$ RTWN (`RATF_SUBSET_RTWN` ↗).

3.3 Formal Proof of Adequacy

Following Boolos [21, § 12], we do not apply the general frame strategy of Sect. 2.1 to obtain adequacy for $\mathbb{GRZ}$. Instead, using the logical equivalence of $\mathbb{GRZ}$ and $\mathbb{S}4\mathbb{GRZ}$, we proceed in three steps:

1. RATF $\subseteq$ RTWN (`RATF_SUBSET_RTWN` ↗)
2. RTWN is sound for $\mathbb{S}4\mathbb{GRZ}$ (Lemma 1);
3. RATF is complete for $\mathbb{S}4\mathbb{GRZ}$ (Theorem 1).

Soundness. The core of the soundness argument is `MODAL_RTWN` ↗, which proves that the schema Grz is valid in every frame whose accessibility relation is reflexive, transitive, and weakly Noetherian.[8] Combined with the correspondence lemmas of T (reflexivity, `MODAL_REFL` ↗) and 4 (transitivity, `MODAL_TRANS` ↗), we obtain that the class RTWN validates all axioms of $\mathbb{S}4\mathbb{GRZ}$ (`RTWN_SUBSET_CHAR_S4GRZ` ↗). Instantiating the generic soundness theorem of the library then yields:

[7] Notice that $\mathrm{fld}(\prec) = W$ whenever the relation $\prec$ is reflexive; thus we can define `WWF`$(\prec)$ on subsets of W.

[8] The proof relies on the induction principle `WWF_IND` to exclude infinite, strictly ascending R-chains.

Lemma 1 (S4GRZ_RTWN_VALID ↗). *If S4GRZ.$\mathcal{H} \vdash A$ and every formula in $\mathcal{H}$ is valid on RTWN, then RTWN $\models A$.*

From this, soundness for RATF follows immediately (S4GRZ_RATF_VALID ↗). As a consistency check, S4GRZ_CONSISTENT ↗ is derived trivially.

Completeness. We prove completeness w.r.t. the finite frames in RATF.

Theorem 1 (S4GRZ_COMPLETENESS_THM ↗). *If* RATF $\models A$, *then S4GRZ.$\varnothing \vdash A$.*

Proof (Sketch). By contraposition, suppose A is not provable in $\mathbb{S4GRZ}$. The worlds of the countermodel we are aiming for are maximal consistent lists of formulas built from the subformulas of A together with their $\Box$-subformulas (S4GRZ_STANDARD_WORLDS_DEF ↗).

A Lindenbaum construction (GRZ_NONEMPTY_MAXIMAL_CONSISTENT ↗) produces such a list l containing $\neg A$. The accessibility relation S4GRZ_STANDARD_REL_DEF ↗ is obtained from a base relation Q_REL ↗ by enforcing antisymmetry ($l\ Q\ l' \wedge l'\ Q\ l \implies l = l'$); S4GRZ_STANDARD_REL_PROP ↗ proves it reflexive, antisymmetric, and transitive. Since the list of subformulas is finite, the frame is finite, hence belongs to RATF. The truth lemma (S4GRZ_TRUTH_LEMMA ↗) then yields $l \not\Vdash A$ as required.[9]

4 Certified Splitting Translation

The core formalised result in this section is that every theorem of $\mathbb{GRZ}$ can be fully and faithfully translated into a theorem of $\mathbb{GL}$. Since Grzegorczyk logic is complete for finite posets (RATF) and Gödel-Löb logic is complete for irreflexive, transitive and finite frames (ITF), the proof proceeds by formally converting the accessibility relations back and forth and implementing the standard splitting translation $(\cdot)^+$ of $\mathbb{GRZ}$-theorems into $\mathbb{GL}$-theorems.

4.1 Translation Function

Let us recall first the translation between formulas.

Definition 4 (Splitting translation, TRANSL ↗**).** *The function $(\cdot)^+$: $\mathtt{Form}_{\mathcal{L}} \to \mathtt{Form}_{\mathcal{L}}$ is defined by induction on the size of a formula:*

$$\begin{aligned}(\bot)^+ &= \bot,\\ (p)^+ &= p \text{ for any atom } p,\\ (\neg A)^+ &= \neg(A^+),\\ (A \circ B)^+ &= A^+ \circ B^+ \text{ for any binary operator } \circ,\\ (\Box A)^+ &= \Box(A^+) \wedge A^+.\end{aligned}$$

[9] By POSET_WWF_ALT, the countermodel we get from the Lindenbaum construction is indeed in RTWN, so that Boolos' proof could be even simplified, as noticed by a reviewer.

Notice that the effective, non-trivial translation happens for the modal clause: $(\Box A)^+$ coincides with $\boxdot(A^+)$, where $\boxdot B := \Box B \wedge B$ is the usual "box-and" modality.

This translation precisely bridges the semantic gap between the two logics. In $\mathbb{GRZ}$ (and $\mathbb{S4GRZ}$), the $\Box$ is reflexive: what is necessary is also actually true. In $\mathbb{GL}$, by contrast, $\Box$ represents formal provability and is strictly irreflexive – because of Gödel's incompleteness theorems [78,79]. Simulating a $\mathbb{GRZ}$ box-modality inside $\mathbb{GL}$ therefore requires explicitly asserting the actual truth of the formula together with its modal truth. The wider significance of this translation for the study of formal provability via Grz is discussed in [20,21].

4.2 Relational Transformers

To mediate between the frame classes ITF and RATF we define two operators that geometrically manipulate the accessibility relation R of a frame.

- R^+ is the reflexive closure operator (`R_PLUS_DEF` ↗):
  $R^+ := R \cup \{\langle x, x\rangle : x \in W\}$.
- R^- is the irreflexive core operator (`R_MIN_DEF` ↗):
  $R^- := R \setminus \{\langle x, x\rangle : x \in W\}$.

Basic sanity checks are immediate: if R is already irreflexive, R^- leaves it unchanged (`IRREFL_THEN_EQ` ↗); conversely, a reflexive relation can be exactly recovered by taking its irreflexive core and then adding back all reflexive arrows (`REFL_THEN_EQ` ↗).

4.3 Kuznetsov-Goldblatt-Boolos Theorem

We now establish the mathematical heart of the translation: the syntactic mapping $(\cdot)^+$ mirrors the geometric lifting $R \mapsto R^+$ in the sense that evaluating a translated formula A^+ on an ITF frame yields the same truth value as evaluating the original formula A on the reflexively closed version of that very frame.

Lemma 2 (`GRZ_TRANSL_LEMMA` ↗, `ITF_IMP_R_PLUS_RATF` ↗). *Let $\langle W, R, v\rangle$ be a model with $\langle W, R\rangle \in$ ITF. For any world $w \in W$ and formula $A \in$ `Form`$_{\mathcal{L}}$:*

i) $w \Vdash_{\langle W,R,v\rangle} A^+ \iff w \Vdash_{\langle W,R^+,v\rangle} A$;
ii) $\langle W, R^+, v\rangle \in$ RATF.

The next step links validity on RATF frames to provability in $\mathbb{GL}$: we prove that a formula A is valid on all finite reflexive posets if and only if A^+ is a theorem of $\mathbb{GL}$ (`RATF_TRANSL` ↗).[10] With this, we obtain the complete formalisation of the theorem by Kuznetsov, Goldblatt, and Boolos.

[10] The proof uses a two-way contrapositive argument, combining Lemma 2 with the existing soundness and completeness theorems for $\mathbb{GL}$ (`GL_ITF_VALID` ↗ and `GL_COMPLETENESS_THM` ↗).

Theorem 2 (Kuznetsov-Goldblatt-Boolos, GRZ_TRANSL ☑). *For every formula $A \in \mathtt{Form}_{\mathcal{L}}$,*

$$\mathsf{Grz}.\varnothing \vdash A \iff \mathsf{GL}.\varnothing \vdash A^+.$$

Proof (Sketch). Combine RATF_TRANSL with the adequacy theorem for $\mathbb{GRZ}$ (GRZ_ADEQ_THM ☑) to eliminate the semantic middleman from Lemma 2.

5 Grzegorczyk Logic, Automated

The theoretical results established in the preceding sections directly yield an automated decision procedure for Grzegorczyk logic. By leveraging the full and faithful embedding of Theorem 2, we reuse the existing verified solver for Gödel-Löb logic within HOLMS.

The pipeline underlying our novel HOL Light tactic, GZR_TAC ☑, integrates into the general HOLMS_TAC ☑ as follows, with each stage illustrated by examples:

1. We intercept a goal of the form $\mathsf{Grz}.\varnothing \vdash A$ and rewrite it into $\mathsf{GL}.\varnothing \vdash A^+$, in virtue of the formal proof of the core embedding theorem GRZ_TRANSL ☑;

   Example 1:

   Suppose that we wish to check whether Grz proves:
   $(\star)$ *contingent*$(a) \to \Diamond($*penultimate*$(a) \vee$ *penultimate*$(\neg a))$[a]
   where *contingent*$(a) := \Diamond a \wedge \Diamond(\neg a)$ and
   penultimate$(a) := a \wedge \Diamond(\neg a) \wedge \Box(\neg a \to \Box\neg a)$, so the formula is:
   $(\star)\ \Diamond a \wedge \Diamond\neg a \to \Diamond(a \wedge \Diamond\neg a \wedge \Box(\neg a \to \Box\neg a) \vee \neg a \wedge \Diamond\neg\neg a \wedge \Box(\neg\neg a \to \Box\neg\neg a))$

   [a] This corresponds to the axiom $\mathsf{Grz}^\star$ from [1].

   Example 2:

   Suppose that we wish to check if Grz proves the convergence axiom:

   $$(.2)\ \Diamond\Box a \to \Box\Diamond a$$

2. We traverse the abstract syntax tree of the formula, replacing every $\Box B$ with $\boxdot B$, mathematically computing the shape of the splitting translation of A;

   Example 1 (Continued):

   We convert $(\star)$ into its GL-equivalent, which we denote by $(\star)^+$:

   $$\begin{aligned}&\neg \boxdot \neg a \wedge \neg \boxdot \neg\neg a\\ &\quad \to \neg \boxdot \neg\Big(a \wedge \neg \boxdot \neg\neg a \wedge \Big(\boxdot(\neg a \to \boxdot\neg a)\\ &\qquad\qquad \vee\ (\neg a \wedge \neg \boxdot \neg\neg\neg a \wedge \boxdot(\neg\neg a \to \boxdot\neg\neg a))\Big)\Big)\end{aligned}$$

Example 2 (Continued):

We convert (.2) into its $\mathbb{GL}$-equivalent, which we denote by $(.2)^+$:

$$\neg \boxdot (\neg \boxdot (a)) \to \boxdot(\neg \boxdot (\neg a)).$$

3. We invoke `GL_TAC`, delegating proof search to the existing decision procedure for the shallow embedding of G3KGL;

Example 1 (Continued)

The proof search operates on the computed conjunctive normal form of $(\star)^+$ For brevity, we provide the following statistics about the resulting formula:

Metric	Formula Size	Number of Clauses	Clause Size (Max)	Clause Size (Min)
Value	4359	44	7	3

Example 2 (Continued)

The proof search operates on the computed conjunctive normal form of $(.2)^+$. For brevity, we provide the following statistics about the resulting formula:

Metric	Formula Size	Number of Clauses	Clause Size (Max)	Clause Size (Min)
Value	59	4	2	2

4. If proof search succeeds, the system returns a HOL Light theorem certifying the validity of A^+. Upon failure, `HOLMS_BUILD_COUNTERMODEL` generates a certified countermodel $\langle W, R, v\rangle$ for A^+ in $\mathbb{GL}$.

Example 1 (Continued)

The tactic succeeds for $(\star)^+$, completing the proof-search in 1.58 seconds, on mid-level personal computer.

Example 2 (Continued)

The tactic fails for $(.2)^+$, and the system returns the countermodel built at the end of the proof search, graphically rendered here as:

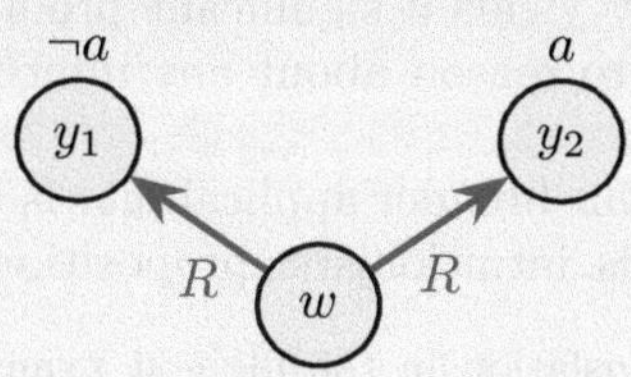

5. GRZ_CONV certifies the validity of the whole decision procedure by exploiting Kuznetsov-Goldblatt-Boolos Theorem (GRZ_TRANSL).

Example 1 (Completed)

The system returns a new HOL Light theorem stating that the original formula (1) is provable in Grz, that is:

```
|- [GRZ_AX . {}
    |~ Contingent(Atom "a") -->
          Diamond (Penultimate(Atom "a") \/
                     Penultimate(Not Atom "a"))]
```

Example 2 (Completed)

The $\mathbb{GL}$-countermodel is transformed into a Grz-countermodel via the transformer $(\cdot)^{-}$, and the schema (.2) is automatically model-checked against the resulting structure:

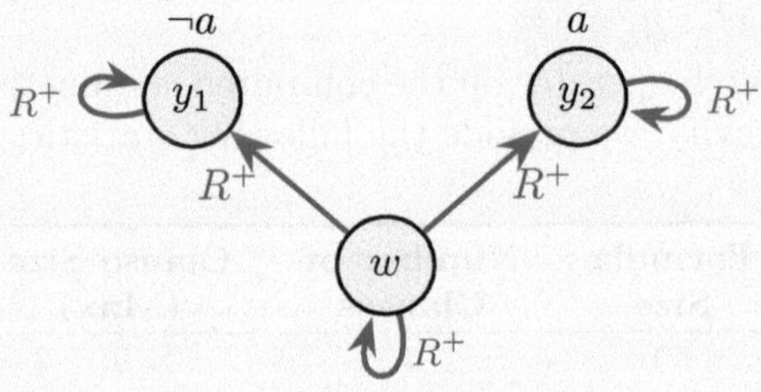

which is formally proven to be a countermodel by GRZ_CONV to $\Diamond\Box a \to \Box\Diamond a$.

5.1 Scalability, Complexity, and Practical Boundaries

The viability of leveraging translation-based frameworks in modal proof theory depends heavily on the trade-offs between conceptual modularity and computational efficiency.

The primary merit of our approach lies in its architectural extensibility: the splitting translation enables the re-use of the existing automated solver in HOLMS. This modularity yields a significant proof-theoretic dividend: it provides a uniform pipeline to reason about any intermediate logic or translation that embeds into Grz.

A prime exemplar of this broader applicability is the Gödel-McKinsey-Tarski translation, which embeds intuitionistic propositional logic (IPC) into Grz.[11]

[11] We implemented the translation in the file god_transl.ml of our library, without discussing its computational ramifications here.

Thus HOLMS inherits a native and verified pipeline from IPC to GL, suggesting that our method is not an isolated curiosity, but a theoretically scalable paradigm for executing cross-logic proof searches within a singular target back-end.

Despite these structural advantages, the naïve application of the splitting translation introduces a severe structural bottleneck regarding formula size. Because the translation duplicates subformulas, it suffers from severe spatial inefficiency. This subformula duplication induces exponential growth in the total size of the formula relative to its modal depth. Consider a worst-case syntactic benchmark consisting of n nested modalities, $B = \Box^n A$. Under the splitting map, the size of the translated formula behaves according to the recurrence relation $\text{size}((\Box^k A)^+) = \text{size}((\Box^{k-1} A)^+) + \text{size}(\Box(\Box^{k-1} A)^+) + 1$ yielding an asymptotic complexity strictly bounded by $\mathcal{O}(2^n)$. For deeply nested formulas, this exponential blow-up rapidly exhausts memory bandwidth and generates massive inputs for the underlying back-end.

The validity problem for Grz is well-established in the literature as PSPACE-complete; because GL shares this identical complexity class [84], the exponential blow-up induced by the translation artificially exacerbates the computational cost for the target GL prover.[12] This significantly impacts the scalability of the method during intense proof searches, such as those arising from the modal analysis of intuitionistic statements. Following the insightful remarks of a reviewer, in future work, we intend to explore the possibility of restoring the practical advantages of the shared PSPACE complexity class.

6 Conclusions

We have presented a methodology for exploring modal translations within the HOL Light Library for Modal Systems (HOLMS). We illustrated this approach through the splitting translation of Grzegorczyk logic (Grz), a central system in mathematical modal logic [26]. This demonstrates that a modular formalisation strategy effectively circumvents the proof-theoretic intricacies arising from non-trivial frame conditions, notably weak Noetherianity.

Our development comprises three components. First, we provided a deep embedding of the axiomatic systems for Grz, establishing soundness and completeness w.r.t. RTWN (reflexive, transitive, weakly Noetherian) and RATF (reflexive, antisymmetric, transitive, finite) frames. Second, we formalised the Kuznetsov–Goldblatt–Boolos theorem, reducing $\mathbb{GRZ}$-theoremhood checking to the existing, verified decision procedure for $\mathbb{GL}$. Finally, we mechanised the model transformation underlying the semantic proof of faithfulness, so that failed proof attempts yield certified RATF countermodels derived via the reflexive closure of the GL-countermodel generated by HOLMS tactic for Gödel-Löb logic.

[12] GL proof search can theoretically be executed using polynomial space relative to its input; solving a translated formula B should thus remain tractable, but the translation itself shifts the problem from $\text{poly}(|B|)$ to $\text{poly}(2^{|B|})$, effectively degrading the practical performance to EXPSPACE boundaries.

This extension consolidates HOLMS as a unified platform for modal metatheory and automated reasoning, establishing a foundation for further developments along different directions.

Future Work. The success of this first experiment with orthogonal extensions of HOLMS via modal embeddings invites us to plan optimisations (inspired by Tseitin transformations [83]) of the decision procedures in terms of performance and usability of the framework as the library grows. A promising complementary direction is the formalisation of a shallow embedding of Dyckhoff and Negri's non-harmonic labelled calculus G3Grz [31], which would provide a jump from exponential complexity to polynomial constraint on the proof search, and would also demonstrate HOLMS's capabilities in unifying disparate reasoning paradigms. We also aim to certify the Gödel–McKinsey–Tarski translation, reflecting the established connections between Grz and intuitionistic logic [26]. Further extensions include formalising Solovay's system GLS and interpretability logics from both semantic [61,79] and proof-theoretic perspectives [51,71]. Finally, building on recent work integrating modal reasoning into higher-order logic [6], we plan to investigate monadic Grz within our framework.

Related Work. Automated theorem proving for modal logics spans specialised Grz-specific systems and general modular frameworks. Dedicated tableau-based provers for Grz are presented in [74] and via the lean tableaux methodology [2,3]. Translational approaches into decidable first-order fragments [27] further enable the use of established FOL provers for Grz. A broader strategy embeds modal systems, including GL and Grz, into higher-order logic to exploit automation features of Isabelle and similar assistants [5,7–10,52,80]; related ideas for handling non-classical reasoning appear in the HOL Light tutorial [53, §20.4].

Within the Prolog ecosystem, decision procedures have been developed for classical and intuitionistic modal logics [38–40,69]. In proof assistants, substantial efforts include the NAMOR library in Agda [22,23], tableau-based automation in Lean [86], and extensive meta-theoretical developments in Isabelle [34–36] and Rocq [28–30,32,44,45,47–49,57,75,76].

Hybrid techniques such as CEGAR-Tableaux enhance satisfiability checking for normal modal logics [42,43], while systems like Goéland [24,25] provide concurrent tableau-based reasoning adaptable to modal settings.

Complementary foundational work clarifies the structural properties underpinning extensible modal decision procedures [56,62–65,70] and explores automated proofs of non-trivial proof-theoretic results [11,12].

We propose our work as a novel and coherent synthesis, in a fully computerised environment, of the mentioned work in: the intrinsic extensibility of decision procedures for modal systems; the mathematical generality provided by rigorous completeness proofs constructed through modular proof strategies; and the potential for further extensions of automated modal reasoning via translations and embeddings, fully formalised.

Acknowledgments. We gratefully acknowledge the constructive feedback provided by three anonymous reviewers on the initial submission.

This work was partially funded by the project SERICS – Security and Rights in the CyberSpace PE0000014, financed within PNRR, M4C2 I.1.3, funded by the European Union - NextGenerationEU (MUR Code: 2022CY2J5S, CUP: D67G22000340001); the Istituto Nazionale di Alta Matematica – INdAM group GNSAGA; the research project "Differential, Algebraic, Complex and Arithmetic Geometry (2025)"; The International Research Network "Logic and Interaction".

Disclosure of Interests. The authors have no competing interests to declare that are relevant to the content of this article.

Bibliography

1. Aleksander Wołoszyn, W.: Grzegorczyk logic unlocked. arXiv e-prints arXiv:2505.09836, May 2025. https://doi.org/10.48550/arXiv.2505.09836
2. Beckert, B., Goré, R.: Free-variable tableaux for propositional modal logics. Stud Logica **69**(1), 59–96 (2001). https://doi.org/10.1023/A:1013886427723
3. Beckert, B., Posegga, J.: leanTAP: lean Tableau-based deduction. J. Autom. Reason. **15**(3), 339–358 (1995). https://doi.org/10.1007/BF00881804
4. van Benthem, J., Blackburn, P.: Modal logic: a semantic perspective. In: Handbook of Modal Logic, vol. 3, pp. 1–84. Elsevier (2007)
5. Benzmueller, C., Paulson, L.C.: Multimodal and intuitionistic logics in simple type theory. Logic J. IGPL **18**(6), 881–892 (01 2010). https://doi.org/10.1093/jigpal/jzp080
6. Benzmüller, C.: Universal (meta-)logical reasoning: recent successes. Sci. Comput. Program. **172**, 48–62 (2019). https://doi.org/10.1016/J.SCICO.2018.10.008
7. Benzmüller, C.: Faithful logic embeddings in HOL - a recipe to have it all: deep and shallow, automated and interactive, heavy and light, proofs and counterexamples, meta and object level. CoRR abs/2502.19311 (2025). https://doi.org/10.48550/ARXIV.2502.19311
8. Benzmüller, C., Claus, M., Sultana, N.: Systematic verification of the modal logic cube in Isabelle/HOL. In: Kaliszyk, C., Paskevich, A. (eds.) Proceedings Fourth Workshop on Proof eXchange for Theorem Proving, PxTP 2015, Berlin, Germany, 2–3 August 2015. EPTCS, vol. 186, pp. 27–41 (2015). https://doi.org/10.4204/EPTCS.186.5
9. Benzmüller, C., Woltzenlogel Paleo, B.: Higher-order modal logics: automation and applications. In: Faber, W., Paschke, A. (eds.) Reasoning Web 2015. LNCS, vol. 9203, pp. 32–74. Springer, Cham (2015). https://doi.org/10.1007/978-3-319-21768-0_2
10. Benzmüller, C., Paulson, L.C.: Quantified multimodal logics in simple type theory. Logica Universalis **7**(1), 7–20 (2013). https://doi.org/10.1007/S11787-012-0052-Y
11. Bezhanishvili, N., Ghilardi, S.: Bounded proofs and step frames. In: Galmiche, D., Larchey-Wendling, D. (eds.) TABLEAUX 2013. LNCS (LNAI), vol. 8123, pp. 44–58. Springer, Heidelberg (2013). https://doi.org/10.1007/978-3-642-40537-2_6
12. Bezhanishvili, N., Ghilardi, S.: The bounded proof property via step algebras and step frames. Ann. Pure Appl. Log. **165**(12), 1832–1863 (2014). https://doi.org/10.1016/J.APAL.2014.07.005

13. Bilotta, A., Maggesi, M., Perini Brogi, C.: A modular proof of semantic completeness for normal systems beyond the modal cube, formalised in HOLMS. In: Moscardelli, L., Scozzari, F. (eds.) Proceedings of the 26th Italian Conference on Theoretical Computer Science, Pescara, Italy, 10–12 September 2025. CEUR Workshop Proceedings, vol. 4039, pp. 154–162. CEUR-WS.org (2025). https://ceur-ws.org/Vol-4039/paper10.pdf
14. Bilotta, A., Maggesi, M., Perini Brogi, C.: A modular framework for proof-search via formalised modal completeness in HOL light. In: Guerrini, S., König, B. (eds.) 34th EACSL Annual Conference on Computer Science Logic (CSL 2026). Leibniz International Proceedings in Informatics (LIPIcs), vol. 363, pp. 18:1–18:29. Schloss Dagstuhl – Leibniz-Zentrum für Informatik, Dagstuhl, Germany (2026). https://doi.org/10.4230/LIPIcs.CSL.2026.18. https://drops.dagstuhl.de/entities/document/10.4230/LIPIcs.CSL.2026.18
15. Bilotta, A., Maggesi, M., Perini Brogi, C.: Growing HOLMS: a verified automated prover for Grzegorczyk logic in HOL light (extended version) (2026). https://hdl.handle.net/20.500.11771/41542
16. Bilotta, A., Maggesi, M., Perini Brogi, C.: A HOL light library for modal systems (HOLMS) (2026). https://holms-lib.github.io/. Accessed May 2026
17. Bilotta, A., Maggesi, M., Perini Brogi, C., Quartini, L.: Growing HOLMS, a HOL light library for modal systems. In: Porello, D., Vinci, C., Zavatteri, M. (eds.) Short Paper Proceedings of the 6th International Workshop on Artificial Intelligence and Formal Verification, Logic, Automata, and Synthesis, OVERLAY 2024, Bolzano, Italy, 28–29 November 2024. CEUR Workshop Proceedings, vol. 3904, pp. 41–48. CEUR-WS.org (2024). https://ceur-ws.org/Vol-3904/paper5.pdf
18. Blackburn, P., van Benthem, J.F.A.K., Wolter, F. (eds.): Handbook of Modal Logic, Studies in Logic and Practical Reasoning, vol. 3. North-Holland (2007). https://www.sciencedirect.com/bookseries/studies-in-logic-and-practical-reasoning/vol/3/suppl/C
19. Blackburn, P., de Rijke, M., Venema, Y.: Modal Logic, Cambridge Tracts in Theoretical Computer Science, vol. 53. Cambridge University Press (2001). https://doi.org/10.1017/CBO9781107050884
20. Boolos, G.: Provability in arithmetic and a schema of Grzegorczyk. Fundamenta Mathematicae **106**(1), 41–45 (1980). http://eudml.org/doc/211104
21. Boolos, G.: The Logic of Provability. Cambridge University Press (1995)
22. Borsetto, R., Zorzi, M.: An agda implementation of the modal logic S4.2: first investigations. In: Moscardelli, L., Scozzari, F. (eds.) Proceedings of the 26th Italian Conference on Theoretical Computer Science, Pescara, Italy, 10–12 September 2025. CEUR Workshop Proceedings, vol. 4039, pp. 163–168. CEUR-WS.org (2025). https://ceur-ws.org/Vol-4039/paper17.pdf
23. Borsetto, R., Zorzi, M.: NAMOR: a new agda library for modal extended sequents. In: Short Paper Proceedings of the 7th International Workshop on Artificial Intelligence and Formal Verification, Logic, Automata, and Synthesis, OVERLAY 2025, Bologna, Italy, 26 October 2025 (2025). https://overlay.uniud.it/workshop/2025/papers/borsetto-zorzi.pdf
24. Cailler, J.: Designing an automated concurrent tableau-based theorem prover for first-order logic. (Conception d'un prouveur automatique de théorèmes concurrent basé sur la méthode des tableaux pour la logique du premier ordre). Ph.D. thesis, University of Montpellier, France (2023). https://tel.archives-ouvertes.fr/tel-04526940

25. Cailler, J., Rosain, J., Delahaye, D., Robillard, S., Bouziane, H.: Goéland: a concurrent tableau-based theorem prover (system description). In: Blanchette, J., Kovács, L., Pattinson, D. (eds.) Automated Reasoning - 11th International Joint Conference, IJCAR 2022, Haifa, Israel, 8–10 August 2022, Proceedings. LNCS, vol. 13385, pp. 359–368. Springer (2022). https://doi.org/10.1007/978-3-031-10769-6_22
26. Chagrov, A.V., Zakharyaschev, M.: Modal Logic, Oxford Logic Guides, vol. 35, Oxford University Press (1997)
27. Demri, S., Goré, R.: An O $((n{\cdot}\log n)^3)$-time transformation from Grz into decidable fragments of classical first-order logic. In: Caferra, R., Salzer, G. (eds.) Automated Deduction in Classical and Non-Classical Logics, Selected Papers. LNCS, vol. 1761, pp. 152–166. Springer (1998). https://doi.org/10.1007/3-540-46508-1_10
28. Doczkal, C., Bard, J.: Completeness and decidability of converse PDL in the constructive type theory of Coq. In: Proceedings of the 7th ACM SIGPLAN International Conference on Certified Programs and Proofs, CPP 2018, pp. 42–52. Association for Computing Machinery, New York, NY, USA (2018). https://doi.org/10.1145/3167088
29. Doczkal, C., Smolka, G.: Constructive formalization of hybrid logic with eventualities. In: Jouannaud, J.P., Shao, Z. (eds.) Certified Programs and Proofs, pp. 5–20. Springer, Heidelberg (2011)
30. Doczkal, C., Smolka, G.: Completeness and decidability results for CTL in constructive type theory. J. Autom. Reason. **56**(3), 343–365 (2016)
31. Dyckhoff, R., Negri, S.: A cut-free sequent system for Grzegorczyk logic, with an application to the Gödel-McKinsey-Tarski embedding. J. Log. Comput. **26**(1), 169–187 (2016). https://doi.org/10.1093/LOGCOM/EXT036
32. Férée, H., van der Giessen, I., van Gool, S., Shillito, I.: Mechanised uniform interpolation for modal logics K, GL, and iSL. In: Benzmüller, C., Heule, M.J.H., Schmidt, R.A. (eds.) Automated Reasoning - 12th International Joint Conference, IJCAR 2024, Nancy, France, 3–6 July 2024, Proceedings, Part II. LNCS, vol. 14740, pp. 43–60. Springer (2024). https://doi.org/10.1007/978-3-031-63501-4_3
33. Fitting, M.: Modal proof theory. In: Handbook of Modal Logic, pp. 85–138. Elsevier (2007)
34. From, A.H.: Formalized soundness and completeness of epistemic logic. In: Silva, A., Wassermann, R., de Queiroz, R. (eds.) WoLLIC 2021. LNCS, vol. 13038, pp. 1–15. Springer, Cham (2021). https://doi.org/10.1007/978-3-030-88853-4_1
35. From, A.H.: An Isabelle/HOL framework for synthetic completeness proofs. In: Proceedings of the 14th ACM SIGPLAN International Conference on Certified Programs and Proofs, CPP 2025, pp. 171–186. Association for Computing Machinery, New York, NY, USA (2025). https://doi.org/10.1145/3703595.3705882
36. From, A.H., Schlichtkrull, A.: Abstract, compositional consistency: Isabelle/HOL locales for completeness à la fitting. In: Forster, Y., Keller, C. (eds.) 16th International Conference on Interactive Theorem Proving, ITP 2025, Reykjavik, Iceland, 28 September–1 October 2025. LIPIcs, vol. 352, pp. 8:1–8:20. Schloss Dagstuhl - Leibniz-Zentrum für Informatik (2025). https://doi.org/10.4230/LIPICS.ITP.2025.8
37. Garg, D., Genovese, V., Negri, S.: Countermodels from sequent calculi in multimodal logics. In: Proceedings of the 27th Annual IEEE Symposium on Logic in Computer Science, LICS 2012, Dubrovnik, Croatia, 25–28 June 2012, pp. 315–324. IEEE Computer Society (2012). https://doi.org/10.1109/LICS.2012.42

38. Girlando, M., Lellmann, B., Olivetti, N., Pozzato, G.L., Vitalis, Q.: VINTE: an implementation of internal calculi for Lewis' logics of counterfactual reasoning. In: Schmidt, R.A., Nalon, C. (eds.) TABLEAUX 2017. LNCS (LNAI), vol. 10501, pp. 149–159. Springer, Cham (2017). https://doi.org/10.1007/978-3-319-66902-1_9
39. Girlando, M., Lellmann, B., Olivetti, N., Pesce, S., Pozzato, G.L.: Calculi, countermodel generation and theorem prover for strong logics of counterfactual reasoning. J. Log. Comput. (2022). https://doi.org/10.1093/logcom/exab084
40. Girlando, M., Straßburger, L.: MOIN: a nested sequent theorem prover for intuitionistic modal logics (system description). In: Peltier, N., Sofronie-Stokkermans, V. (eds.) IJCAR 2020. LNCS (LNAI), vol. 12167, pp. 398–407. Springer, Cham (2020). https://doi.org/10.1007/978-3-030-51054-1_25
41. Gödel, K.: Eine Interpretation des Intuitionistischen Aussagenkalküls. Ergebnisse eines Mathematischen Kolloquiums, **4**, 39–40 (1933). English translation, with an introductory note by A.S. Troelstra. Kurt Gödel, Collected Works **1**, 296–303 (1986)
42. Goré, R., Kelly, J.: Automated proof search in Gödel-Löb provability logic. In: Abstract, British Logic Colloquium (2007)
43. Goré, R., Kikkert, C.: CEGAR-tableaux: improved modal satisfiability via modal clause-learning and SAT. In: Das, A., Negri, S. (eds.) TABLEAUX 2021. LNCS (LNAI), vol. 12842, pp. 74–91. Springer, Cham (2021). https://doi.org/10.1007/978-3-030-86059-2_5
44. Goré, R., Ramanayake, R., Shillito, I.: Cut-elimination for provability logic by terminating proof-search: formalised and deconstructed using coq. In: Das, A., Negri, S. (eds.) Automated Reasoning with Analytic Tableaux and Related Methods, pp. 299–313. Springer International Publishing, Cham (2021)
45. de Groot, J., Shillito, I., Clouston, R.: Semantical analysis of intuitionistic modal logics between CK and IK. In: 40th Annual ACM/IEEE Symposium on Logic in Computer Science, LICS 2025, Singapore, 23–26 June 2025, pp. 169–182. IEEE (2025). https://doi.org/10.1109/LICS65433.2025.00020
46. Grzegorczyk, A.: Some relational systems and the associated topological spaces. Fundamenta Mathematicae **60**(3), 223–231 (1967). http://eudml.org/doc/213962
47. Hagemeier, C.: Formalizing intuitionistic epistemic logic in Coq. BSc thesis (2021)
48. Hagemeier, C., Kirst, D.: Constructive and mechanised meta-theory of IEL and similar modal logics. J. Log. Comput. **32**(8), 1585–1610 (2022). https://doi.org/10.1093/LOGCOM/EXAC068
49. Hagemeier, C., Kirst, D.: Constructive and mechanised meta-theory of intuitionistic epistemic logic. In: Artemov, S., Nerode, A. (eds.) LFCS 2022. LNCS, vol. 13137, pp. 90–111. Springer, Cham (2022). https://doi.org/10.1007/978-3-030-93100-1_7
50. Hakli, R., Negri, S.: Does the deduction theorem fail for modal logic? Synthese **187**(3), 849–867 (2012)
51. Hakoniemi, T.A., Joosten, J.J.: Labelled tableaux for interpretability logics. In: Liber Amicorum Alberti: A Tribute to Albert Visser (2016)
52. Hardt, M., Smolka, G.: Higher-order syntax and saturation algorithms for hybrid logic. In: Blackburn, P., Bolander, T., Braüner, T., de Paiva, V., Villadsen, J. (eds.) Proceedings of the International Workshop on Hybrid Logic, HyLo@FLoC 2006, Seattle, WA, USA, 11 August 2006. ENTCS, vol. 174, pp. 15–27. Elsevier (2006). https://doi.org/10.1016/J.ENTCS.2006.11.023
53. Harrison, J.: HOL Light tutorial (2017). http://www.cl.cam.ac.uk/~jrh13/hol-light/tutorial.pdf
54. Harrison, J.: The HOL Light system reference (2023). https://www.cl.cam.ac.uk/~jrh13/hol-light/reference.pdf

55. Harrison, J.: The HOL Light Theorem Prover (2025). https://hol-light.github.io/
56. Hustadt, U., Papacchini, F., Nalon, C., Dixon, C.: Model construction for modal clauses. In: International Joint Conference on Automated Reasoning, pp. 3–23. Springer (2024)
57. Kirst, D., Shillito, I.: Completeness of first-order bi-intuitionistic logic. In: Endrullis, J., Schmitz, S. (eds.) 33rd EACSL Annual Conference on Computer Science Logic, CSL 2025, 10–14 February 2025, Amsterdam, Netherlands. LIPIcs, vol. 326, pp. 40:1–40:19. Schloss Dagstuhl - Leibniz-Zentrum für Informatik (2025). https://doi.org/10.4230/LIPICS.CSL.2025.40
58. Maggesi, M., Perini Brogi, C.: A formal proof of modal completeness for provability logic. In: Cohen, L., Kaliszyk, C. (eds.) 12th International Conference on Interactive Theorem Proving (ITP 2021). Leibniz International Proceedings in Informatics (LIPIcs), vol. 193, pp. 26:1–26:18. Schloss Dagstuhl – Leibniz-Zentrum für Informatik, Dagstuhl, Germany (2021). https://doi.org/10.4230/LIPIcs.ITP.2021.26. https://drops.dagstuhl.de/opus/volltexte/2021/13921
59. Maggesi, M., Perini Brogi, C.: Mechanising Gödel-Löb provability logic in HOL light. J. Autom. Reason. **67**(3), 29 (2023). https://doi.org/10.1007/S10817-023-09677-Z
60. McKinsey, J.C.C., Tarski, A.: Some theorems about the sentential calculi of Lewis and Heyting. J. Symbolic Log. **13**(1), 1–15 (1948). http://www.jstor.org/stable/2268135
61. Mikec, L.: Satisfiability verifiers for certain modal logics concerned with provability (2026). https://luka.doublebuffer.net/o/il/. Accessed Feb 2026. https://github.com/luka-mikec/provability_sat
62. Nalon, C.: Efficient theorem-proving for modal logics. In: Ciabattoni, A., Gabelaia, D., Sedlár, I. (eds.) Advances in Modal Logic, AiML 2024, Prague, Czech Republic, 19–23 August 2024, pp. 13–16. College Publications (2024)
63. Nalon, C., Dixon, C., Hustadt, U.: Modal resolution: proofs, layers, and refinements. ACM Trans. Comput. Log. (TOCL) **20**(4), 1–38 (2019)
64. Nalon, C., Hustadt, U., Papacchini, F., Dixon, C.: Local reductions for the modal cube. In: International Joint Conference on Automated Reasoning. pp. 486–505. Springer International Publishing Cham (2022)
65. Nalon, C., Hustadt, U., Papacchini, F., Dixon, C.: Buy one get 14 free: evaluating local reductions for modal logic. In: Pientka, B., Tinelli, C. (eds.) Automated Deduction - CADE 29, pp. 382–400. Springer Nature Switzerland, Cham (2023)
66. Negri, S.: Proof analysis in modal logic. J. Philos. Log. **34**(5), 507–544 (2005)
67. Negri, S.: Proofs and countermodels in non-classical logics. Log. Univers. **8**(1), 25–60 (2014)
68. Negri, S., von Plato, J.: Proof Analysis: A Contribution to Hilbert's Last Problem. Cambridge University Press (2011)
69. Olivetti, N., Pozzato, G.L.: NESCOND: an implementation of nested sequent calculi for conditional logics. In: Demri, S., Kapur, D., Weidenbach, C. (eds.) IJCAR 2014. LNCS (LNAI), vol. 8562, pp. 511–518. Springer, Cham (2014). https://doi.org/10.1007/978-3-319-08587-6_39
70. Pattinson, D., Olivetti, N., Nalon, C.: Resolution calculi for non-normal modal logics. In: International Conference on Automated Reasoning with Analytic Tableaux and Related Methods, pp. 322–341. Springer (2023)
71. Perini Brogi, C., Negri, S., Olivetti, N.: Modular sequent calculi for interpretability logics. Rev. Symb. Log. **18**(3), 704–743 (2025). https://doi.org/10.1017/S1755020325100701

72. Poggiolesi, F.: The method of tree-hypersequents for modal propositional logic. In: Makinson, D., Malinowski, J., Wansing, H. (eds.) Towards Mathematical Philosophy. TL, vol. 28, pp. 31–51. Springer, Dordrecht (2009). https://doi.org/10.1007/978-1-4020-9084-4_3
73. Savateev, Y., Shamkanov, D.: Non-well-founded proofs for the Grzegorczyk modal logic. Rev. Symbolic Log. **14**(1), 22–50 (2021). https://doi.org/10.1017/S1755020319000510
74. Schoeber, N.: Automatic Tableau builder for Grzegorczyk logic. Bachelor's Thesis, Faculty of Science and Engineering, University of Groningen (2017)
75. Shillito, I., van der Giessen, I., Goré, R., Iemhoff, R.: A new calculus for intuitionistic strong Löb logic: strong termination and cut-elimination, formalised. In: Ramanayake, R., Urban, J. (eds.) Automated Reasoning with Analytic Tableaux and Related Methods - 32nd International Conference, TABLEAUX 2023, Prague, Czech Republic, 18–21 September 2023, Proceedings. LNCS, vol. 14278, pp. 73–93. Springer (2023). https://doi.org/10.1007/978-3-031-43513-3_5
76. Shillito, I., Kirst, D.: A mechanised and constructive reverse analysis of soundness and completeness of bi-intuitionistic logic. In: Timany, A., Traytel, D., Pientka, B., Blazy, S. (eds.) Proceedings of the 13th ACM SIGPLAN International Conference on Certified Programs and Proofs, CPP 2024, London, UK, 15–16 January 2024, pp. 218–229. ACM (2024). https://doi.org/10.1145/3636501.3636957
77. Simpson, A.K.: The Proof Theory and Semantics of Intuitionistic Modal Logic. Ph.D. thesis, University of Edinburgh. College of Science and Engineering. School of Informatics (1994)
78. Smorynski, C.: The incompleteness theorems. In: Barwise, J. (ed.) Handbook of Mathematical Logic, pp. 821–865. North-Holland (1977)
79. Solovay, R.M.: Provability interpretations of modal logic. Israel J. Math. **25**(3–4), 287–304 (1976)
80. Steen, A., Sutcliffe, G., Benzmüller, C.: Solving quantified modal logic problems by translation to classical logics. J. Log. Comput., exaf006 (2025)
81. Strachey, C.: Fundamental concepts in programming languages. Higher-Order Symbolic Comput. **13**, 11–49 (2000)
82. Troelstra, A.S., Schwichtenberg, H.: Basic Proof Theory, Cambridge Tracts in Theoretical Computer Science, 2nd edn., vol. 43. Cambridge University Press (2000)
83. Tseitin, G.S.: On the complexity of derivation in propositional calculus, pp. 466–483. Springer, Heidelberg (1983). https://doi.org/10.1007/978-3-642-81955-1_28
84. Verbrugge, R.L.: Provability logic. In: Zalta, E.N., Nodelman, U. (eds.) The Stanford Encyclopedia of Philosophy. Metaphysics Research Lab, Stanford University, Summer 2024 edn. (2024)
85. Viganò, L.: Labelled Non-Classical Logics. Springer Science & Business Media (2013)
86. Wu, M., Goré, R.: Verified decision procedures for modal logics. In: Harrison, J., O'Leary, J., Tolmach, A. (eds.) 10th International Conference on Interactive Theorem Proving (ITP 2019). Leibniz International Proceedings in Informatics (LIPIcs), vol. 141, pp. 31:1–31:19. Schloss Dagstuhl – Leibniz-Zentrum für Informatik, Dagstuhl, Germany (2019). https://doi.org/10.4230/LIPIcs.ITP.2019.31. https://drops.dagstuhl.de/entities/document/10.4230/LIPIcs.ITP.2019.31

Open Access This chapter is licensed under the terms of the Creative Commons Attribution 4.0 International License (http://creativecommons.org/licenses/by/4.0/), which permits use, sharing, adaptation, distribution and reproduction in any medium or format, as long as you give appropriate credit to the original author(s) and the source, provide a link to the Creative Commons license and indicate if changes were made.

The images or other third party material in this chapter are included in the chapter's Creative Commons license, unless indicated otherwise in a credit line to the material. If material is not included in the chapter's Creative Commons license and your intended use is not permitted by statutory regulation or exceeds the permitted use, you will need to obtain permission directly from the copyright holder.

Automatic Abstraction Refinement for Hyperproperties Verification

Malak Marrid[1], Shachar Itzhaky[1], Sharon Shoham[2], and Yakir Vizel[1](✉)

[1] The Technion, Haifa, Israel
yvizel@cs.technion.ac.il
[2] Tel Aviv University, Tel Aviv, Israel

Abstract. This paper proposes a novel automatic abstraction-refinement procedure for verifying hyperproperties. Hyperproperties specify the behavior of a system across multiple executions, and are an important extension of standard temporal properties. Our verification procedure is based on predicate abstraction and the recently introduced reduction of hyperproperty verification to satisfiability of Constrained Horn Clauses (CHCs). Moreover, it formalizes and uses CHC-based refinement for abstract counterexamples in the shape of directed acyclic graphs.

We implemented our new algorithm on top of the SMT solver Z3. Our experimental evaluation shows our automatic abstraction refinement procedure can solve a variety of hyperproperty verification problems, completely automatically. This is in contrast to other existing techniques that require a user-given abstraction.

1 Introduction

Verification of hyperproperties [11] is notorious for being computationally hard. Hyperproperties encode relations between multiple traces of a program (or programs), and extend standard temporal logic by allowing quantification (universal and existential) over traces. As a result, verifying hyperproperties requires a few ingredients that depend on one another: (i) finding *relational* inductive invariants; (ii) finding an *alignment* that determines how different traces are executed; and (iii) finding witness traces in case the hyperproperty includes existential trace quantifiers. The dependency between the different ingredients is what makes hyperproperty verification complex [6,23,31,34].

A well known approach for handling the complexity of verification is *abstraction-refinement* [10,21,27]. Abstraction provides a mechanism for removing parts of the concrete program and creating a smaller *abstract program* [4,17], by that reducing the complexity of verification. However, abstraction comes at the cost of precision and the abstract program may include spurious counterexamples even if the concrete program satisfies the property. In case a spurious

An extended version of this paper appears in [26].

© The Author(s) 2026
A. Biere et al. (Eds.): IJCAR 2026, LNAI 16688, pp. 436–454, 2026.
https://doi.org/10.1007/978-3-032-32589-1_26

counterexample is found, a *refinement* procedure is invoked. The goal of refinement is to eliminate that spurious counterexample, and create a refined, more precise abstract program. This process is iterated until either the property is proved, or a real counterexample is found.

In this paper we present a novel *automatic* abstraction-refinement algorithm for the verification of hyperproperties, based on a new formalization of abstraction-refinement in the context of non-linear Constrained Horn Clauses (CHCs) [7]. Our algorithm, `AbsHyHorn`, builds on our recently introduced reduction of hyperproperty verification to satisfiability of CHCs [23]. The reduction presented in [23] delegates the search for all three aforementioned hyperproperty verification ingredients to a CHC solver (instead of fixing some of them apriori). While this greatly improves the performance of hyperproperty verification, the resulting CHCs are *non-linear*, therefore posing a challenge even for state-of-the-art CHC solvers [8,22,25]. For that reason [23] relies on user-provided abstraction predicates, from which the solution to the CHCs is constructed. Notably, since all necessary ingredients reason about multiple traces, the predicates needed are often *relational*. In contrast to [23], `AbsHyHorn` automatically synthesizes the relevant predicates, requiring no input from the user.

As noted, `AbsHyHorn` uses *predicate abstraction* [4,9,16,17]. Given a set of predicates $\mathbb{P}$, it encodes the hyperproperty verification problem as a set of CHCs $\Pi_{\mathbb{P}}$, which is an abstraction of the concrete encoding Π. Both Π and $\Pi_{\mathbb{P}}$ consist of non-linear CHCs. If $\Pi_{\mathbb{P}}$ is satisfiable, then so is the concrete encoding Π, which means that the hyperproperty is verified. Otherwise, $\Pi_{\mathbb{P}}$ is unsatisfiable and an abstract counterexample is found. While counterexamples to linear CHCs (as in safety verification), have the form of a single trace, in the case of $\Pi_{\mathbb{P}}$, non-linearity of the CHCs entails that the proof of unsatisfiability and the counterexample it represents have the shape of a *directed acyclic graph* (DAG). For example, if the property is a k-safety hyperproperty, which states that a tuple of k traces never reaches a "bad configuration", then the counterexample "contains" k traces that violate the property for *every* possible interleaving of the k traces.

Upon detecting an abstract counterexample, `AbsHyHorn` invokes a refinement procedure that is likewise based on a CHC encoding. Using the DAG-shaped proof of unsatisfiability, a new set of *refinement* CHCs, Π_R, is created. Π_R is defined in terms of the *concrete* states, and can be understood as an unrolling of Π according to the counterexample. Importantly, unlike the original set of CHCs Π, which is recursive, Π_R is not recursive, and therefore easier to solve. If Π_R is unsatisfiable then a real counterexample is found, which means that the hyperproperty does not hold. Otherwise, if Π_R is satisfiable, then the counterexample is spurious. In this case, `AbsHyHorn` extracts new predicates from the solution of Π_R, adding them to $\mathbb{P}$. Although this method resembles refinement techniques based on tree/DAG interpolants [1,3,19,28,30], it avoids the need to explicitly expand the DAG into a tree or a sequence, and thus sidesteps the complexity introduced by such an expansion.

Lastly, once `AbsHyHorn` synthesizes the required predicates, it performs a *generalization* step with the goal of learning "better" predicates for refinement.

F_1
```
x = 1;
while (x < N) {
  y = 2 * x;
  while (y > 0) {
    x = 2 * x;
    y = y - 1;
  }
}
```

F_2
```
x = 1;
while (x < N) {
  y = x;
  while (y > 0) {
    x = 4 * x;
    y = y - 1;
  }
}
```

$$
\begin{aligned}
fact_M &:= (x^1 \neq x^2 \vee \neg \mathrm{valid}_M(\mathcal{V}^1, \mathcal{V}^2)) \rightarrow D_M(\mathcal{V}^1, \mathcal{V}^2) \\
rule_{\{1\}} &:= \bigwedge_M D_M(\mathcal{V}'^1, \mathcal{V}'^2) \wedge Tr^1(\mathcal{V}^1, \mathcal{V}'^1) \wedge \bigwedge_{v \in \mathcal{V}^2} v = v' \rightarrow D_{\{1\}}(\mathcal{V}^1, \mathcal{V}^2) \\
rule_{\{2\}} &:= \bigwedge_M D_M(\mathcal{V}'^1, \mathcal{V}'^2) \wedge Tr^2(\mathcal{V}^2, \mathcal{V}'^2) \wedge \bigwedge_{v \in \mathcal{V}^1} v = v' \cdots \rightarrow D_{\{2\}}(\mathcal{V}^1, \mathcal{V}^2) \\
rule_{\{1,2\}} &:= \bigwedge_M D_M(\mathcal{V}'^1, \mathcal{V}'^2) \wedge Tr^1(\mathcal{V}^1, \mathcal{V}'^1) \wedge Tr^2(\mathcal{V}^2, \mathcal{V}'^2) \rightarrow D_{\{1,2\}}(\mathcal{V}^1, \mathcal{V}^2) \\
query &:= \bigwedge_M D_M(\mathcal{V}'^1, \mathcal{V}'^2) \wedge x'^1 = 1 \wedge x'^2 = 1 \rightarrow \bot \\
&\text{where } M \in \{\{1\}, \{2\}, \{1,2\}\}
\end{aligned}
$$

Fig. 1. Two programs and the CHC encoding of a 2-safety property.

Our generalization heuristic is tailored towards hyperproperty verification since it focuses on generating relational predicates.

We implemented AbsHyHorn on top of Z3 [29], using Spacer [25] as a CHC solver and evaluated it on a set of benchmarks that includes hyper-safety (k-safety) and hyper-liveness properties ($\forall^*\exists^*$-OHyperLTL properties [6]). While previous approaches require user-provided predicates in order to solve these benchmarks, and the latest CHC-based tool from [23] cannot solve most of them when using the concrete programs, AbsHyHorn can solve all properties (but one) completely automatically, without any user-provided predicates.

To summarize, our contributions are as follows: (i) a novel *automatic* abstraction-refinement algorithm for verification of $\forall^*\exists^*$-OHyperLTL hyperproperties; (ii) a formalization of CHC-based refinement for DAG counterexamples; and (iii) a predicate generalization heuristic for generating relational predicates.

1.1 Motivating Example

Consider the two programs F_1 and F_2 in Fig. 1. A valid 2-safety property for these two programs states that at the beginning of the i-th iteration of the outer loop, the value of x in F_1 (x^1) equals the value of x in F_2 (x^2). This 2-safety property follows from the fact that $x^1 = x^2$ holds at the beginning of the inner loop, provided we consider only even iterations of F_1's inner loop. Such a proof requires a non-standard alignment.

When reducing this 2-safety problem to satisfiability of CHCs [23] using the concrete semantics (i.e. without abstraction), Z3 cannot solve it given a two hours timeout. We use this example throughout the paper to demonstrate a few of the key elements of our approach.

2 Preliminaries

Throughout this paper, we use the standard syntax and semantics of first-order logic (FOL). Since we only consider satisfiability modulo theories, we fix a background first-order theory $\mathcal{T}$ and denote its signature by Σ. We denote the set of Σ-formulas over a set of variables X as $\mathcal{F}(\Sigma, X)$, and the set of Σ-terms as $T_\Sigma(X)$. Given a Σ-formula η, we denote by $Vars(\eta)$ and $Atoms(\eta)$ the set of free variables and the set of atoms that appear in η, respectively. Lastly, given a substitution $\sigma : Vars(\eta) \to T_\Sigma(\emptyset)$ that maps variables to *closed terms*, we denote by $\eta[\sigma]$ the result of substituting every free variable v in η with $\sigma(v)$.

2.1 Constrained Horn Clauses

Let P^U be a set of fresh predicate symbols, called *uninterpreted predicates*, s.t. $\Sigma \cap P^U = \emptyset$. Constrained Horn Clauses (CHCs) are closed formulas over the signature $\Sigma \cup P^U$ of the form: $\forall X \cdot (\bigwedge_{i=1}^{n} P_i(X_i) \wedge \eta(X) \to H(X_H))$ where X is a set of variables; $\eta(X)$ is a quantifier-free Σ-formula with free variables X, and $P_i(X_i)$ is an application of an uninterpreted predicate $P_i \in P^U$ with $X_i \subseteq X$; The part $(\bigwedge_i P_i(X_i) \wedge \eta(X))$ is called the *body* of the CHC; $H(X_H)$ is called the *head* and is either $\bot$ or an application of an uninterpreted predicate from P^U with $X_H \subseteq X$. The universal quantification over X is often omitted for brevity. We say a CHC is linear if its body contains at most one application of a predicate from P^U. Otherwise, it is called non-linear. Moreover, a CHC is *normalized* if $X_H \cap (\bigcup_{i=1}^{n} X_i) = \emptyset$. In the sequel we only consider normalized CHCs.

CHC Satisfiability Modulo $\mathcal{T}$. Given a finite set of CHCs Π, the problem of deciding if Π is satisfiable (modulo $\mathcal{T}$) is called CHC-SAT. The set Π is satisfiable if it has a satisfying model M such that the projection of M onto Σ is a model of $\mathcal{T}$. CHC solvers, however, do not search for arbitrary satisfying models, and instead look for a *solution* in the form of a Σ-interpretation. A Σ-interpretation $\mathcal{I}$ for Π is a map that assigns to every uninterpreted predicate $P \in P^U$ a Σ-formula $\mathcal{I}(P)$ over variables Y_P. For $\pi \in \Pi$, we denote by $\mathcal{I}(\pi)$ the Σ-formula obtained through substitution of every uninterpreted predicate application $P_i(X_i)$ in π with its interpretation $\mathcal{I}(P_i)[Y_{P_i} \leftarrow X_i]$. A Σ-interpretation $\mathcal{I}$ is a *solution* of Π, denoted $\mathcal{I} \models_\mathcal{T} \Pi$, if $\mathcal{I}(\pi)$ is $\mathcal{T}$-valid for every $\pi \in \Pi$. If a set of CHCs has a solution then it is satisfiable (SAT). However, the converse may not hold due to the limited expressive power of first-order formulas.

A set of CHCs Π is unsatisfiable (UNSAT) iff $\bot$ is derivable from it using the following *Hyper-Resolution* inference rule:

$$\frac{\forall X \cdot \eta(X) \wedge P_1(X_1) \wedge \cdots \wedge P_n(X_n) \implies H(X_H), \qquad P_1(X_1)[\sigma], \ldots, P_n(X_n)[\sigma]}{H(X_H)[\sigma]}$$

where:

- $\forall X \cdot \eta(X) \wedge P_1(X_1) \wedge \cdots \wedge P_n(X_n) \implies H(X_H)$ is a CHC $\pi \in \Pi$.
- $\sigma : X \to T_\Sigma(\emptyset)$ is a substitution such that $\models_\mathcal{T} \eta(X)[\sigma]$.

We denote this inference rule as HYPERRES and use HYPERRES(π, σ) to indicate an application of the rule on a CHC $\pi \in \Pi$. We refer to $P_1(X_1)[\sigma], \ldots, P_n(X_n)[\sigma]$ as the *ground* premises of the rule.

If Π is UNSAT, the derivation of $\perp$ is represented by a *directed acyclic graph* (DAG), to which we refer as a *hyper-resolution proof* of unsatisfiability of Π. Throughout this section, given a DAG $G = (V, E)$ and a node $v \in V$, we denote by $in(v) = \{u \in V \mid (u, v) \in E\}$ the set of nodes on its incoming edges.

Definition 1. *Let Π be an unsatisfiable set of CHCs, where X is a set of variables used in Π. A* hyper-resolution proof *of unsatisfiability for Π is a finite* directed acyclic graph (DAG) $G_\Pi = (V, E, r, L_S, L_F)$ *where:*

- $V = V_T \uplus V_I$ *is a set of nodes, where V_T are terminal nodes with no incoming edges, and V_I is a set of internal nodes.*
- $E \subseteq V \times V$ *is a set of directed edges, such that $\forall v \in V_I \cdot |in(v) \cap V_T| = 1$; The unique terminal node leading to v is denoted by $in_T(v)$.*
- $r \in V_I$ *is the root (no outgoing edges).*
- $L_S : V_I \to T_\Sigma(\emptyset)^X$ *is a labeling function mapping V_I to substitutions.*
- $L_F : V \to \mathcal{F}(\Sigma, X)$ *is a labeling function mapping V to FOL formulas s.t.: (1) $L_F(r) = \perp$; (2) $\forall v \in V_T : L_F(v) \in \Pi$; and (3) $\forall v \in V_I$: $L_F(v)$ is the consequence of* HyperRes$(L_F(in_T(v)), L_S(v))$ *where $\{L_F(v') \mid v' \in in(v) \cap V_I\}$ are the ground premises of the rule.*

2.2 Hyperproperty Verification

Transition Systems. A transition system is a tuple $TS = (\mathcal{V}, \mathit{Init}, \mathit{Tr})$, where $\mathcal{V}$ is a vector of variables denoting state variables; *Init* is a formula over Σ with free variables in $\mathcal{V}$ representing the initial states, and *Tr* is a formula over Σ with free variables in $\mathcal{V} \cup \mathcal{V}'$, representing the transition relation ($\mathcal{V}'$ consists of the primed variants of $\mathcal{V}$). A state of TS is a valuation to $\mathcal{V}$. A trace of TS is an infinite sequence of states $t = s_0, s_1, \ldots$ such that for every $i \geq 0$ $(s_i, s_{i+1}) \models \mathit{Tr}$, where (s_i, s_{i+1}) should be understood as a valuation to $(\mathcal{V}, \mathcal{V}')$. For $i \in \mathbb{N}$, we define $TS^i = (\mathcal{V}^i, \mathit{Init}^i, \mathit{Tr}^i)$ as a copy of TS, where variables in $\mathcal{V}$ are substituted by $\mathcal{V}^i := \{v^i \mid v \in \mathcal{V}\}$.

Hyperproperties. We consider formulas in the $\forall^*\exists^*$ fragment of OHyperLTL [6]:

$$\varphi \triangleq \psi \to \forall \pi_1 : \xi_1, \ldots, \pi_\ell : \xi_\ell . \exists \pi_{\ell+1} : \xi_{\ell+1}, \ldots, \pi_k : \xi_k . \, G \, \phi,$$

where π_i are trace variables over the set of traces $\mathbb{T}$, ξ_i are Σ-formulas over $\mathcal{V}^i$ that define the observation points where traces synchronize, ψ is the precondition on the initial states of the k traces, and ϕ is the safety formula required to hold globally at all synchronization points. Both ψ and ϕ are Σ-formulas over $X := \mathcal{V}^1 \cup \ldots \cup \mathcal{V}^k$. When $\ell = k$, φ expresses a k-safety property; otherwise, it generalizes to $\forall^*\exists^*$ hyperproperties that capture relational liveness aspects.

$\forall^*\exists^*$-OHyperLTL formulas are interpreted over transition systems: φ holds in a transition system if from every k initial states that jointly satisfy the precondition ψ, and for every ℓ traces from the first ℓ states, there exist corresponding $k - \ell$ traces from the remaining $k - \ell$ states such that the composed states of all traces globally satisfy ϕ, when projected to their observation points.

Hyperproperty Verification as CHCs. Verifying hyperproperties is challenging since it requires the discovery of relational inductive invariants, which relate states of k execution traces. As a result, verification of such properties requires finding an *alignment* of any k traces, where the alignment determines how the different traces advance in tandem. In the case of hyperliveness properties (in the $\forall^*\exists^*$-OHyperLTL fragment), verification also requires witness traces (due to existential quantifiers) that match the universally quantified traces and the alignment.

In [23], we show how verification of $\forall^*\exists^*$-OHyperLTL properties can be reduced to CHC-SAT, which allows the witness traces, alignment of traces and relational inductive invariants to be constructed simultaneously. For simplicity of presentation, we present the key ideas for the universal fragment of $\forall^*\exists^*$-OHyperLTL (namely, k-safety properties). The interested reader is referred to [23] for the complete presentation.

Let $TS = (\mathcal{V}, \mathit{Init}, \mathit{Tr})$ be a transition system and φ a k-safety property. Deciding if $TS \models \varphi$ requires either finding a counterexample, which is a set of k traces that shows why φ does not hold, or finding an *alignment* and a *relational inductive invariant* that proves φ holds in TS. For the latter, it is natural to consider a composed transition system $\hat{TS} := TS^1 \times \ldots \times TS^k$. We refer to a state in $\hat{TS}$ as a composed state. A composed state is a valuation over $\mathcal{V}^1 \times \ldots \times \mathcal{V}^k$.

The CHC-SAT reduction in [23] captures the alignment by introducing an arbiter that, given the current composed state, selects a non-empty subset of traces $\emptyset \neq M \subseteq \{1, \ldots, k\}$ to advance. We refer to such M as a *schedule* and the set of all possible schedules is denoted as $\mathbb{M}_k = \mathcal{P}(\{1, \ldots, k\}) \setminus \{\emptyset\}$. In addition to being non-empty, a schedule M must also be *valid*: only traces that are not already at a synchronization point can advance in the current step, or if all traces are at a synchronization point – all advance together. We encode validity of a schedule M using the predicate $\mathit{valid}_M(X)$ (see [23] for details).

Following the notion of an arbiter and schedules, in order to encode the problem into CHCs, in [23] we define uninterpreted predicates that represent *doomed states*. A composed state $\hat{s}$ is *doomed* if for every schedule (alignment), $\hat{s}$ eventually reaches a bad state that violates the property φ. This results in the following set of CHCs:

Definition 2. *Let* $TS = (\mathcal{V}, \mathit{Init}, \mathit{Tr})$ *be a transition system and let* φ *be a* k*-safety hyperproperty with precondition* ψ*. Let* $\{D_M \mid M \in \mathbb{M}_k\}$ *be a set of uninterpreted predicates. We define the set of CHCs* $\Pi(TS, \varphi) := \{\mathit{fact}_M, \mathit{rule}_M, \mathit{query} \mid M \in \mathbb{M}_k\}$ *where*

$$\mathit{fact}_M := (\mathit{Bad}(X') \vee \neg \mathit{valid}_M(X')) \wedge X' = X \rightarrow D_M(X)$$
$$\mathit{rule}_M := \bigwedge_{M'} D_{M'}(X') \wedge \delta_M(X, X') \rightarrow D_M(X)$$
$$\mathit{query} := \bigwedge_{M} D_M(X) \wedge \bigwedge_{i} \mathit{Init}(\mathcal{V}^i) \wedge \psi(X) \rightarrow \bot$$

where $X = \bigcup_{i=1}^{k} \mathcal{V}^i$, $Bad(X) = \bigwedge_i \xi_i(\mathcal{V}^i) \wedge \neg\phi(X)$ *and* $\delta_M(X, X') = \bigwedge_{i\in M} Tr^i(\mathcal{V}^i, \mathcal{V}^{i\prime}) \wedge \bigwedge_{i\notin M}(\mathcal{V}^i = \mathcal{V}^{i\prime})$ *encodes transitions according to schedule* M.

For simplicity of presentation, the above definition considers k copies of the same transition system. Therefore, each Tr^i is the result of substituting $\mathcal{V}$ and $\mathcal{V}'$ in Tr with $\mathcal{V}^i$ and $\mathcal{V}'^i$, respectively. Note that the CHCs are normalized.

We use X' and X in $fact_M$ to ensure it is normalized. This is only done for simplicity of presentation in the following section. The *doomed* CHCs encoding presented above provides a sound and complete characterization of k-safety:

Theorem 1 **([23]).** *Let* $TS = (\mathcal{V}, Init, Tr)$ *be a transition system and let* φ *be a* k*-safety hyperproperty.* $TS \models \varphi$ *iff* $\Pi(TS, \varphi)$ *is satisfiable.*

Example 1. The CHCs encoding for the motivating example (Sect. 1.1) appears in Fig. 1. Note that $\mathcal{V}^i = \{x^i, y^i\}$ is the set of variables and Tr^i is the transition system for F_i, where $i \in \{1, 2\}$. The schedule is represented by M: if $M = \{1\}$ only F_1 executes, if $M = \{2\}$ only F_2 executes, and if $M = \{1, 2\}$ both F_1 and F_2 execute.

3 Automatic Predicate Abstraction Refinement for CHCs

We now describe an automatic abstraction refinement procedure for verification of $\forall^*\exists^*$-OHyperLTL. Throughout this section we fix a transition system TS, a $\forall^*\exists^*$-OHyperLTL property φ and their corresponding set of CHCs $\Pi(TS, \varphi)$. Our abstraction technique is based on *implicit predicate abstraction* [9].

Definition 3. *Let* $\pi \in \Pi(TS, \varphi)$ *be a normalized CHC of the following form* $\bigwedge_{i=1}^{n} P_i(X') \wedge \delta(X, X') \to H(X)$, *over a set of uninterpreted predicates* P^U. *Let* $\mathbb{P} = \{\rho_1, \dots, \rho_m\}$ *be a set of predicates, where* ρ_i *is a* Σ*-formula for* $1 \le i \le m$, $B = \{b_1, \dots, b_m\}$ *a set of fresh Boolean variables, and* B' *consists of the primed variants of* B. *Let* $\{\hat{P} \mid P \in P^U\}$ *be a set of uninterpreted predicates over* B. *The* abstraction *of* π *w.r.t.* $\mathbb{P}$ *and* B *is defined by the function* α *s.t.*

$$\alpha(\pi, \mathbb{P}) := \bigwedge_{i=1}^{n} \hat{P}_i(B') \wedge \bigwedge_{j=1}^{m} (b_j' \leftrightarrow \rho_j(X')) \wedge \bigwedge_{j=1}^{m} (b_j \leftrightarrow \rho_j(X)) \wedge \delta(X, X') \to \hat{H}(B)$$

Given a set of predicates $\mathbb{P}$, applying the abstraction to $\Pi(TS, \varphi)$ results in the set $\Pi_{\mathbb{P}}(TS, \varphi) := \alpha(\Pi(TS, \varphi), \mathbb{P}) = \{\alpha(\pi, \mathbb{P}) \mid \pi \in \Pi(TS, \varphi)\}$. Note that CHCs in $\Pi_{\mathbb{P}}(TS, \varphi)$ are over a new set of uninterpreted predicates ($\hat{P}(B)$ instead of $P(X)$). Moreover, the set of variables $X \cup X' \cup B \cup B'$ is bound by universal quantifiers in all CHCs. From this point on, we omit TS and φ and refer to $\Pi(TS, \varphi)$ and $\Pi_{\mathbb{P}}(TS, \varphi)$ as Π and $\Pi_{\mathbb{P}}$, respectively.

Procedure 1 `HyAbsRefine`$(TS, \varphi, \text{gen})$

1: $\Pi \leftarrow$ `DoomEncoding`(TS, φ)
2: $\mathbb{P} \leftarrow \emptyset$
3: **while** true **do**
4: $\quad \Pi_{\mathbb{P}} \leftarrow \alpha(\Pi, \mathbb{P})$
5: $\quad res \leftarrow \text{SOLVE}(\Pi_{\mathbb{P}})$
6: $\quad$ **if** $res = \text{sat}$ **then**
7: $\quad\quad$ **return** $TS \models \varphi$
8: $\quad$ **else if** $res = \text{unsat}$ **then**
9: $\quad\quad$ Get unsat proof $G = (V, E, r, L_F, L_S)$
10: $\quad\quad \Pi_R \leftarrow$ `CHCRefinement`(G)
11: $\quad\quad res \leftarrow$ `Solve`(Π_R)
12: $\quad\quad$ **if** $res = \text{unsat}$ **then**
13: $\quad\quad\quad$ **return** $TS \not\models \varphi$
14: $\quad\quad$ **else**
15: $\quad\quad\quad$ Get interpretation $\mathcal{I} \models \Pi_R$
16: $\quad\quad\quad P_I \leftarrow \emptyset$
17: $\quad\quad\quad$ **for all** $v \in V$ **do**
18: $\quad\quad\quad\quad P_I \leftarrow P_I \cup \text{Atoms}(\mathcal{I}(I_v))$
19: $\quad\quad\quad$ **end for**
20: $\quad\quad\quad$ **if** gen = true **then**
21: $\quad\quad\quad\quad P_I \leftarrow P_I \cup$ `GenPreds`$(G, \mathcal{I}, \mathbb{P}, P_I)$
22: $\quad\quad\quad$ **end if**
23: $\quad\quad\quad \mathbb{P} \leftarrow \mathbb{P} \cup P_I$
24: $\quad\quad$ **end if**
25: $\quad$ **end if**
26: **end while**

Procedure 2 `GenPreds`$(G, \mathcal{I}, \mathbb{P}, P_I)$

$P_g \leftarrow \emptyset$
for all $v \in V$ **do**
$\quad P_g \leftarrow P_g \cup$ `Generalize`$(\text{Atoms}(\mathcal{I}(I_v)))$
end for
if $P_g = \emptyset$ **then**
$\quad$ **return** $\emptyset$
end if
sort P_g into levels: $P_g^{(1)}, \ldots, P_g^{(m)}$
$C \leftarrow \emptyset$
for $i = 1 \rightarrow m$ **do**
$\quad C \leftarrow C \cup P_g^{(i)}$
$\quad \hat{\Pi}_R \leftarrow$ `AbsCHCRefine`$(G, \mathbb{P} \cup P_I \cup C)$
$\quad res \leftarrow \text{SOLVE}(\hat{\Pi}_R)$
$\quad$ Get interpretation $\mathcal{I}_R$
$\quad R \leftarrow \emptyset$
$\quad$ **for all** $v \in V$ **do**
$\quad\quad R \leftarrow R \cup \text{Atoms}(\mathcal{I}_R(I_v))$
$\quad$ **end for**
$\quad$ **if** $R \cap C \neq \emptyset$ **then**
$\quad\quad$ **return** $R \cap C$
$\quad$ **end if**
end for
return $\emptyset$

Example 2. Assume $\mathbb{P} = \{x^1 = x^2\}$ and $B = \{b_1\}$. Consider the second CHC $rule_{\{1\}}$ from Fig. 1. Then $\alpha(\pi_2, \mathbb{P})$ is of the form:

$$\bigwedge_M \hat{D}_M(b_1') \wedge (b_1' \leftrightarrow x'^1 = x'^2) \wedge (b_1 \leftrightarrow x^1 = x^2) \wedge Tr^1(\mathcal{V}^1, \mathcal{V}'^1) \wedge x^2 = x'^2 \wedge y^2 = y'^2 \rightarrow \hat{D}_{\{1\}}(b_1)$$

The above abstraction function is used in the abstraction-refinement procedure that appears in Procedure 1. It starts by first encoding the verification problem of a $\forall^*\exists^*$-OHyperLTL property φ w.r.t. a transition system TS using the method from [23] and initializes the set of predicates $\mathbb{P}$ to be empty (lines 1–2). At each iteration of the abstraction-refinement loop, the procedure first generates the abstract set of CHCs $\Pi_{\mathbb{P}}$ using the method described above (line 4). If $\Pi_{\mathbb{P}}$ is satisfiable then the procedure terminates, concluding $TS \models \varphi$ (line 7).

If $\Pi_{\mathbb{P}}$ is UNSAT, an abstract counterexample is found. Note that since the set of CHCs is non-linear, the counterexample is represented by a proof in the form of a DAG (see Definition 1). Therefore, in order to check if the counterexample is spurious, the proof G is used to create a new set of *non-recursive* CHCs for refinement Π_R (see Definition 4 below) (line 10). If Π_R is UNSAT, the counterexample is real and the procedure terminates (line 13). Otherwise, there exists a satisfying interpretation $\mathcal{I} \models \Pi_R$. The interpretation is used to compute predicates that are needed for refinement (lines 16-23). Namely, for each uninterpreted predicate I_v that appears in Π_R, the atoms of $\mathcal{I}(I_v)$ are added to a set of refinement predicates P_I. In case the parameter *gen* is set to true, the collected predicates in P_I are generalized further using `GenPreds` (Procedure 2). A new iteration then begins using the updated set of predicates.

In the remainder of this section we describe the translation of the hyper-resolution proof produced by the CHC solver into Π_R, and the generation of predicates for refinement, deferring the generalization of refinement predicates (lines 20–22) to Sect. 4.

3.1 Hyper-Resolution Proof to CHCs

Assume that $\Pi_{\mathbb{P}}$ is unsatisfiable and let $G = (V, E, r, L_S, L_F)$ be the corresponding hyper-resolution proof for $\Pi_{\mathbb{P}}$. Intuitively, one can view the proof G as an "unrolling" of $\Pi_{\mathbb{P}}$ up to some bound n. In the context of $\forall^*\exists^*$-OHyperLTL verification, the proof G represents a counterexample in the shape of a DAG.

Example 3. Consider our running example (Fig. 1). When $\mathbb{P} = \{x^1 = x^2\}$ the abstraction is too coarse and a spurious counterexample exists. A fragment of the proof, which represents the counterexample, appears in Fig. 2. The nodes u_1, u_2 and u_3 represent all possible choices for a schedule M after F_1 makes a step (represented by the nodes ℓ and v).

In order to check if G represents a real or spurious counterexample, we construct a new *non-recursive* set of CHCs Π_R, which mirrors the structure of G. Using the "unrolling" analogy again, G demonstrates how CHCs in $\Pi_{\mathbb{P}}$ derive $\bot$. However, since G is generated w.r.t. the abstract CHCs, we need to try constructing a similarly structured proof using the concrete CHCs from Π. This attempt is captured by Π_R.

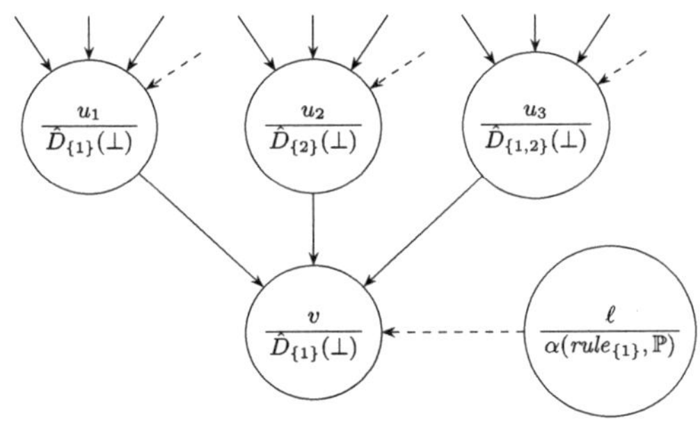

Fig. 2. A proof fragment.

We consider two abstraction-refinement paradigms: *counterexample guided abstraction-refinement* (CEGAR) [10], which aims to eliminate the counterexample represented by G; and *proof-based* abstraction (PBAR) [27], which aims to eliminate all counterexamples whose structure is similar to G. For each of these paradigms, the resulting Π_R has the same overall structure.

Definition 4 (Refinement CHCs). *Assume $\Pi_{\mathbb{P}}$ is* UNSAT *and let $G = (V, E, r, L_S, L_F)$ be the proof. Let $P^V = \{I_v \mid v \in V_I\}$ be a set of uninterpreted predicates over B. Let γ be a* constraining function *such that for all σ, in the case of* PBAR *$\gamma(X, B, \sigma) := \top$, otherwise, in the case of* CEGAR *$\gamma(X, B, \sigma) := \bigwedge_{j=1}^{m}((b_j[\sigma] \leftrightarrow \rho_j(X)))$. The* Refinement CHCs of G *is defined as $\Pi_R(G, \gamma) = \{\forall X, X' \cdot \pi_v \mid v \in V_I\}$ where:*

1. *(Fact) For a node $v \in V_I \setminus \{r\}$ s.t. $L_F(in_T(v)) = \eta(X) \wedge \bigwedge_{j=1}^{m}(b_j \leftrightarrow \rho_j(X)) \rightarrow \hat{H}(B)$ define $\pi_v := \gamma(X, B, L_S(v)) \wedge \eta(X) \rightarrow I_v(X)$*
2. *(Rule) For a node $v \in V_I \setminus \{r\}$ s.t.*

$$L_F(in_T(v)) = \bigwedge_{i=1}^{n} \hat{P}_i(B') \wedge \bigwedge_{j=1}^{m} ((b'_j \leftrightarrow \rho_j(X')) \wedge (b_j \leftrightarrow \rho_j(X))) \wedge \delta(X, X') \rightarrow \hat{H}(B)$$

$$define\ \pi_v := \bigwedge_{u \in in(v) \setminus \{in_T(v)\}} I_u(X') \wedge \gamma(X', B', L_S(v)) \wedge \gamma(X, B, L_S(v)) \wedge \delta(X, X') \rightarrow I_v(X)$$

3. *(Query) For the root r, s.t. $L_F(in_T(r)) = \bigwedge_{i=1}^{n} \hat{P}_i(B) \wedge \bigwedge_{j=1}^{m}(b_j \leftrightarrow \rho_j(X)) \wedge \eta(X) \rightarrow \bot$ define $\pi_r := \bigwedge_{u \in in(r) \setminus \{in_T(r)\}} I_u(X) \wedge \gamma(X, B, L_S(r)) \wedge \eta(X) \rightarrow \bot$*

Note that in the case of CEGAR, γ constrains the values X can take by using the values that the corresponding substitution (e.g. $L_S(v)$) assigns to the abstract Boolean variables in B.

Example 4. Consider the proof fragment that appears in Fig. 2. Then, the corresponding CHC that is added to Π_R has one of the following forms. In the case of PBAR

$$\bigwedge_{i=0}^{2} I_{u_i}(\mathcal{V}'^1, \mathcal{V}'^2) \wedge Tr^1(\mathcal{V}^1, \mathcal{V}'^1) \wedge x^2 = x'^2 \wedge y^2 = y'^2 \rightarrow I_v(\mathcal{V}^1, \mathcal{V}^2)$$

while in the case of CEGAR, since $\sigma(b_1) = \bot$ and $\sigma(b_1') = \bot$, then:

$$\bigwedge_{i=0}^{2} I_{u_i}(\mathcal{V}'^1, \mathcal{V}'^2) \wedge x'^1 \neq x'^2 \wedge x^1 \neq x^2 \wedge Tr^1(\mathcal{V}^1, \mathcal{V}'^1) \wedge x^2 = x'^2 \wedge y^2 = y'^2 \rightarrow I_v(\mathcal{V}^1, \mathcal{V}^2)$$

Our goal is to check if a proof, similar in structure to G, also exists for Π. Therefore, the CHCs in Π_R are defined according to G. Namely, every uninterpreted predicate I_v in Π_R and every CHC $\pi \in \Pi_R$ correspond to an internal node $v \in V_I$ and to a terminal node $v \in V_T$, respectively. Moreover, the abstraction is removed, and CHCs in Π_R refer to the concrete set of variables X and X'. Since Π_R mirrors the structure of G, which is a DAG, the resulting set of CHCs is non-recursive (i.e. has no cycles). As a result, if Π_R is also UNSAT, then a proof with a similar structure to G exists for Π. In the context of $\forall^*\exists^*$-OHyperLTL verification, this means a real counterexample exists.

Theorem 2. *Assume $\Pi_{\mathbb{P}}$ is* UNSAT *and let G be the corresponding hyper-resolution proof. If Π is* SAT *then $\Pi_R(G, \gamma)$ is* SAT *when γ is defined as above.*

3.2 Generating Predicates with Refinement CHCs

The computation of predicates for refinement appears in Procedure 1 (lines 16–23). First, predicates are extracted from the formulae associated with each uninterpreted predicate in Π_R and stored in the set P_I (lines 17–19). If the parameter *gen* is set to true (line 20), the generalization procedure `GenPreds` is called, possibly updating P_I. We discuss the generalization of predicates in the following section (Sect. 4). Lastly, P_I is added to the set of predicates $\mathbb{P}$ and refinement is complete (line 23).

When generalization is not applied, the refinement procedure in `HyAbsRefine` is, intuitively, similar to interpolation-based refinement [2,20,24,35]. More precisely, if a counterexample is proved to be spurious, the satisfying interpretation

$\mathcal{I}$ for Π_R "summarizes" the facts that prove why the counterexample is spurious and provides details about a possible refinement. Using the predicates that appear in $\mathcal{I}$ is sufficient to eliminate the spurious counterexample from the abstract model, and progress is achieved.

Theorem 3. *Assume $\Pi_{\mathbb{P}}$ is* UNSAT *and let G be the corresponding hyper-resolution proof. In addition, assume $\mathcal{I}$ is a satisfying interpretation for $\Pi_R(G,\gamma)$. Let $\mathbb{P}' = \mathbb{P} \cup \bigcup_{v\in V} Atoms(\mathcal{I}(I_v))$. If $\Pi_{\mathbb{P}'}$ is* UNSAT, *then for every possible hyper-resolution proof of unsatisfiability G' for $\Pi_{\mathbb{P}'}$ it holds that $G' \neq G$.*

It is important to note that Theorem 3 guarantees progress since it ensures that if a counterexample exists after refinement, the hyper-resolution proof must be different. Yet, there are subtle differences depending on the kind of refinement used. In the case of PBAR the structure of G and G', namely the graph itself, is different. However, in the case of CEGAR, G and G' may have a similar structure (same graph) but then for a given node v, the substitutions $L_S(v)$ and $L'_S(v)$ must not agree on some variable. This means that G and G' represent different ground refutations.

4 Generalizing Predicates for Refinement

In this section we present the procedure that generalizes predicates during the refinement stage. We start by presenting a general procedure, followed by a specific implementation used for verification of $\forall^*\exists^*$-OHyperLTL properties.

One known limitation of the refinement approach presented in the previous section is that the predicates used in $\mathcal{I}$ may be "too specific" (since they may refer to specific states). This limitation may result in iterative refinement steps that fail to converge. In order to overcome this limitation, we suggest a more general framework that aims to *generalize* the predicates extracted from $\mathcal{I}$.

4.1 Generalizing Predicates

We now provide a high-level description of our suggested generalization procedure. The algorithm `GenPreds` appears in Procedure 2. It starts by iterating over all nodes of G. For each node v it calls the function `generalize`, which processes the atoms that appear in $\mathcal{I}(I_v)$ (line 3). For example, if a given $\mathcal{I}(I_v)$ includes the atoms $x_1 = 0$ and $x_2 = 0$, the generalization procedure may produce the predicate $x_1 = x_2$. Note that this predicate is a generalization of the two predicates since $(x_1 = 0 \wedge x_2 = 0) \rightarrow x_1 = x_2$. Next, `GenPreds` sorts the resulting set P_g into priority buckets using a pre-defined priority metric.

In the last phase, `GenPreds` iterates over the priority buckets. At the i-th iteration, a set of *abstract* refinement CHCs $\hat{\Pi}_R$ is created using the set of predicates $\mathbb{P} \cup P_I \cup \bigcup_{j=1}^{i} P_g^j$ in similar fashion to the procedure that appears in the beginning of Sect. 3. Unlike the set of CHCs Π_R, the uninterpreted predicates that appear in $\hat{\Pi}_R$ are over the predicates used for abstraction. Hence, the solver is "forced" to generate a satisfying interpretation that only uses the supplied set of predicates. If the generated interpretation includes generalized predicates, `GenPreds` terminates and returns these generalized predicates. Otherwise, it returns the empty set.

It is important to note that since `AbsCHCRefinement` is given $\mathbb{P} \cup P_I \cup C$, there must be a satisfying interpretation and the set $\hat{\Pi}_R$ cannot be UNSAT. This is due to the fact that $\mathbb{P} \cup P_I$ is already guaranteed to be precise enough in order to rule out the given spurious counterexample.

The extra solving phase over the abstract set of CHCs is used to sift through the set of generalized predicates and identify those that are useful, using the pre-defined priorities to decide the order in which sifting occurs. The abstract CHCs used for refinement are defined as follows:

Definition 5 (Abstract Refinement CHCs). *Let Π_R be a set of refinement CHCs with respect to $\Pi_{\mathbb{P}}$, where $\mathbb{P} = \{\rho_1, \dots, \rho_m\}$. Let $\mathbb{Q} = \mathbb{P} \uplus \{\rho_{m+1}, \dots, \rho_q\}$ and $\hat{B} = B \uplus \{b_{m+1}, \dots, b_q\} (q > m)$ be a set of predicates and corresponding Boolean variables, respectively. The* abstract refinement CHCs *of Π_R w.r.t. $\mathbb{Q}$ is defined as $\hat{\Pi}_R := \alpha(\Pi_R, \mathbb{Q}) = \{\alpha(\pi, \mathbb{Q}) \mid \pi \in \Pi_R\}$.*

It is important to note that unlike Π_R, the set $\hat{\Pi}_R$ is in terms of the abstract Boolean variables $\hat{B}$. After solving the set of CHCs $\hat{\Pi}_R$, if the interpretation uses any of the generalized predicates that appear in C, we conclude these are useful for refinement. Moreover, since they are a generalization of the predicates in P_I, they are more likely to rule-out more spurious counterexamples and hence allow `HyAbsRefine` to converge faster.

4.2 Learning Generalized Predicates for Hyperproperty Verification

Recall that hyperproperties refer to multiple traces of a transition system. Therefore, the invariants, schedulers, and witnesses (for existential quantifiers) often refer to states of the composed transition system. As a result, when considering predicate abstraction, it is natural that expressing, for example, an invariant requires relational predicates. Namely, predicates that relate state variables of different copies of the transition system.

The heuristic we use in our implementation tries to generate predicates that express equality between variables from different copies of the transition system. Let Π_R be the set of CHCs used for refinement and let $\mathcal{I}$ be its satisfying interpretation. Our procedure analyzes the predicates in $Atoms(\mathcal{I}(I_v))$ and applies unification that generates possible generalized relational predicates.

Given the atoms $\rho_1 = (f_1 \ \mathsf{op}_1 \ g_1)$ and $\rho_2 = (f_2 \ \mathsf{op}_2 \ g_2)$, where $\mathsf{op}_i \in \{=, \leq, \geq, <, >\}$, the unification of these two atoms is defined as:

$$\textsc{Unify}(\rho_1, \rho_2) = \begin{cases} g_1 = g_2, & \text{if } \mathsf{op}_1 = \mathsf{op}_2 \text{ and } f_1 = f_2, Vars(g_i) \neq \emptyset, i \in \{1,2\} \\ f_1 = f_2, & \text{if } \mathsf{op}_1 = \mathsf{op}_2 \text{ and } g_1 = g_2, Vars(f_i) \neq \emptyset, i \in \{1,2\} \\ \bot, & \text{otherwise.} \end{cases}$$

In our implementation of Algorithm 2, the call to `Generalize` (line 3) iterates over pairs of predicates $\rho_1, \rho_2 \in Atoms(\mathcal{I}(I_v))$ and executes $\textsc{Unify}(\rho_1, \rho_2)$.

Prioritized Predicate Selection. Our heuristic uses two priority levels: (i) high-priority for predicates that relate variables from different copies of the program and are syntactically concise; and (ii) low-priority for predicates that only refer to a single copy of a program or are syntactically complex. For instance, generalized predicates that include only single trace variables such as $(x_1 = y_1)$, which could be the unification of $(x_1 = c), (y_1 = c)$ for some constant c, are less effective for refinement in practice than predicates that are "relational", e.g. $(x_1 = x_2/4)$ which could be the unification of $(x_1 = c'), (x_2/4 = c')$ for some constant c'.

5 Experimental Evaluation

We implemented our automatic abstraction-refinement algorithm in a tool called AbsHyHorn[1]. The new tool is built on top of the existing HyHorn tool, which implements the reduction of $\forall^*\exists^*$-OHyperLTL verification to CHC-SAT [23]. AbsHyHorn is implemented on top of Z3 (4.12.0) [29] through its Python API, using SPACER [18,25] as a CHC solver. AbsHyHorn takes as input a program in the form of a CFG and a $\forall^*\exists^*$-OHyperLTL property (following the format introduced in [6]). AbsHyHorn supports all first-order theories supported by SPACER. In our experiments, we used the theories of Linear Integer Arithmetic and Arrays.

The experimental evaluation compares two variants of AbsHyHorn, one that uses PBAR and another that uses CEGAR for refinement. Both these variants are compared against HyHorn, when applied to the concrete programs with no user-provided abstraction[2].

For the benchmark, we adopt all examples from [23], which include many k-safety and liveness hyperproperties (such as Generalized Non-Interference) from the $\forall^*\exists^*$-OHyperLTL fragment. In addition, two new benchmarks, which were not part of the original suite, are added—div monotone (monotonicity of integer division) for k-safety, and sum nondet for $\forall^*\exists^*$. In $\forall^*\exists^*$ benchmarks, when the transition relation has infinite branching as in the general case defined by [23], the restrictions were provided and encoded in the transition relation. All experiments were performed on a server that uses an AMD EPYC 74F3 CPU with 32GB of memory, with a timeout of 7200 s for each experiment.

Table 1 and Table 2 present the evaluation for k-safety and $\forall^*\exists^*$ hyperproperties, respectively. The time is reported in seconds. The columns with $\#P/\#I$ represent the number of predicates AbsHyHorn learns and the number of abstraction-refinement iterations it executes.

For k-safety benchmarks AbsHyHorn solves significantly more examples when compared to HyHorn. PBAR solves all of the benchmarks, except mult dist (a 3-safety property). When comparing PBAR against CEGAR, it is clear that PBAR

[1] https://github.com/TechnionFV/hyperprops_as_chcs.

[2] Other tools for verification of $\forall^*\exists^*$-OHyperLTL do not operate on the concrete program and require user-provided predicates. Hence, the comparison is only against HyHorn.

performs better. One observation regarding this difference is that when using CEGAR, `AbsHyHorn` learns predicates that are "too specific", eliminating only one counterexample at each iteration. In contrast, when using PBAR, most of the extracted predicates are relational (relating variables from different program traces). For the $\forall^*\exists^*$ benchmarks, `AbsHyHorn` with PBAR solves all the examples, while when using CEGAR it is outperformed by `HyHorn`. The main reason for this

Table 1. Results for k-safety benchmarks. "–" indicates timeout.

k-safety	Concrete	PBAR				CEGAR			
		w/o gen	#P/#I	w gen	#P/#I	w/o gen	#P/#I	w gen	#P/#I
double square NI ff	–	–	–	10.03	19/2	–	–	–	–
double square NI ff (simp)	–	–	–	6.62	20/3	–	–	–	–
half square NI	0.29	6.15	14/2	17.71	34/3	4.11	11/2	4.14	11/2
squares sum	4.11	30.44	27/6	15.98	27/5	21.60	18/6	37.06	25/6
squares sum (simp)	0.20	205.40	31/9	197.51	33/8	126.38	16/6	19.14	13/6
array insert	–	168.56	53/4	178.97	54/4	140.40	24/4	500.79	31/8
array insert (simp)	–	62.05	44/2	110.1	52/2	–	–	–	–
exp1x3	0.08	1.52	6/2	1.71	8/3	1.15	4/2	1.15	4/2
col item symm	0.48	11.82	53/1	16.25	59/1	12.71	59/1	22.46	70/1
fig 2 from [6]	–	–	–	16.08	27/6	–	–	–	–
fig 3 from [13]	0.12	5.79	18/3	6.12	19/3	17.66	15/6	7.01	13/3
counter det	–	2.09	9/2	1.71	9/2	1.80	8/2	2.14	8/2
mult equiv	–	–	–	234.22	56/7	–	–	–	–
mult equiv (simp)	–	–	–	33.94	25/4	–	–	–	–
array int mod	–	–	–	619.22	91/4	–	–	–	–
div monotone	–	0.51	4/1	0.52	4/1	0.61	6/1	1.07	7/1
mult dist	–	–	–	–	–	–	–	–	–

Table 2. Results for $\forall^*\exists^*$ benchmarks. "–" indicates timeout.

$\forall^*\exists^*$	Concrete	PBAR				CEGAR			
		w/o gen	#P/#I	w gen	#P/#I	w/o gen	#P/#I	w gen	#P/#I
counter negate	0.08	0.97	4/2	2.15	7/2	3.52	6/3	6.95	10/4
p1 simple	0.22	2.38	6/3	5.23	8/3	4.51	9/3	6.01	8/3
refine	0.12	1.09	3/1	1.07	3/1	1.63	3/1	1.61	3/1
refine 2	0.85	0.89	3/1	0.87	3/1	1.23	3/1	1.23	3/1
compiler opt 1	2.31	0.44	2/1	0.41	2/1	0.65	2/1	0.65	2/1
compiler opt 2	0.20	1.54	8/2	2.89	9/2	5.13	8/3	19.16	15/4
sum nondet	–	21.26	15/3	35.17	16/3	–	–	–	–
smaller	–	0.54	2/1	0.53	2/1	0.44	2/1	0.43	2/1
async gni	0.34	16.57	7/3	16.29	7/3	8.79	4/3	8.81	4/3
P1 (GNI)	0.18	2.14	4/1	5.47	4/1	2.32	4/1	4.04	5/1
P2 (GNI)	6.85	298.63	8/2	–	–	–	–	–	–
P3 (GNI)	0.15	3.52	5/1	9.88	7/1	3.76	5/1	6.91	6/1
P4 (GNI)	0.67	5.47	5/1	9.75	6/1	5.94	5/1	9.77	6/1
counter sum	0.15	14.85	16/3	37.10	17/3	–	–	53.91	13/5
counter diff	–	6.74	5/2	–	–	–	–	48.08	11/5

behavior is that most of these examples are very simple. Hence, in most cases, the abstraction-refinement loop only adds an overhead. This also explains why in this case, using the predicate generalization technique (Sect. 4) is not particularly helpful.

6 Related Work

There exists a large body of work on verification of hyperproperties [5,6,12,14, 15,23,31,33,34,36]. However, to the best of our knowledge, there is no previous work that performs automatic abstraction-refinement for a comprehensive fragment of hyperproperties, such as $\forall^*\exists^*$-OHyperLTL. Previous works either use a fixed, user-given abstraction, or implement abstraction-refinement for a user-given self-composed system [33] and limited to k-safety hyperproperties only.

The work that is closest to ours is [32], where the authors suggest an abstraction-refinement algorithm for k-safety properties. However, unlike our algorithm the work in [32] is based on [31], where the alignment is pre-determined and verification is executed on a self-composition of the program/system. As a result, if the alignment that was chosen to encode the self-composed system is incorrect, abstraction-refinement never terminates. Since our algorithm extends the more general CHC-based approach of [23], in the case of k-safety it searches for the alignment, relational invariant and the abstraction, simultaneously. Moreover, `HyAbsRefine` supports the entire $\forall^*\exists^*$-OHyperLTL fragment, and is not limited to k-safety only. The work in [36] also uses abstraction-refinement, but is limited only to information-flow properties, and like [31,32] operates on a fixed self-composed program.

For refinement, our algorithm formalizes and uses CHCs. It transforms a DAG hyper-resolution proof into non-recursive set of CHCs. Intuitively, this is similar to tree/DAG-interpolation refinement [1,3,19,28,30]. However, unlike the interpolation-based approaches, our CHC-based refinement does not require an explicit expansion of the DAG neither into a tree nor sequences. This fact avoids the complexity that such an expansion incurs. Moreover, if the underlying CHC solver is not based on interpolation (Spacer, like in our implementation), this expansion does not happen implicitly by the solver.

7 Conclusions and Future Work

We present `HyAbsRefine`, an automatic abstraction-refinement algorithm for verification of $\forall^*\exists^*$-OHyperLTL hyperproperties. Our refinement approach is based on a transformation of a DAG counterexample to a non-recursive, non-linear set of CHCs. When the refinement CHCs are solved, new predicates are derived from their satisfying interpretation. Our evaluation shows that $\forall^*\exists^*$-OHyperLTL is able to synthesize the relational predicates that are required in order to solve all benchmarks in our set, but one. We emphasize that `HyAbsRefine` achieves this without any user-given predicates.

As a future work, we intend to extend this algorithm to support transition systems with infinite branching, without requiring restrictions that are encoded into the transition relation apriori.

Acknowledgments. This research is partially funded by the Israel Science Foundation (ISF), grant no. 2875/21 and grant no. 2117/23. The research leading to these results has also received funding from the European Union's Horizon Europe research and innovation programme (ERC, StrongMC, 101231745), and from the European Research Council under the European Union's Horizon 2020 research and innovation programme (grant agreement No [759102-SVIS]).

Views and opinions expressed are, however, those of the author(s) only and do not necessarily reflect those of the European Union or the European Research Council Executive Agency. Neither the European Union nor the granting authority can be held responsible for them.

References

1. Albarghouthi, A.: Software verification with program-graph interpolation and abstraction. Ph.D. thesis, University of Toronto, Canada (2015). http://hdl.handle.net/1807/69199
2. Albarghouthi, A., Gurfinkel, A., Chechik, M.: Craig interpretation. In: Miné, A., Schmidt, D. (eds.) SAS 2012. LNCS, vol. 7460, pp. 300–316. Springer, Heidelberg (2012). https://doi.org/10.1007/978-3-642-33125-1_21
3. Asadi, S., Blicha, M., Hyvärinen, A., Fedyukovich, G., Sharygina, N.: Farkas-based tree interpolation. In: Pichardie, D., Sighireanu, M. (eds.) SAS 2020. LNCS, vol. 12389, pp. 357–379. Springer, Cham (2020). https://doi.org/10.1007/978-3-030-65474-0_16
4. Ball, T., Majumdar, R., Millstein, T.D., Rajamani, S.K.: Automatic predicate abstraction of C programs. In: Burke, M., Soffa, M.L. (eds.) Proceedings of the 2001 ACM SIGPLAN Conference on Programming Language Design and Implementation (PLDI), Snowbird, Utah, USA, 20–22 June 2001, pp. 203–213. ACM (2001)
5. Barthe, G., Gaboardi, M., Hsu, J.: Relational verification using product programs. J. ACM (JACM) **65**(1), 1–49 (2018)
6. Beutner, R., Finkbeiner, B.: Software verification of hyperproperties beyond k-safety. In: Shoham, S., Vizel, Y. (eds.) Computer Aided Verification - CAV 2022, Part I. LNCS, vol. 13371, pp. 341–362. Springer, Cham (2022). https://doi.org/10.1007/978-3-031-13185-1_17
7. Bjørner, N., Gurfinkel, A., McMillan, K., Rybalchenko, A.: Horn clause solvers for program verification. In: Beklemishev, L.D., Blass, A., Dershowitz, N., Finkbeiner, B., Schulte, W. (eds.) Fields of Logic and Computation II. LNCS, vol. 9300, pp. 24–51. Springer, Cham (2015). https://doi.org/10.1007/978-3-319-23534-9_2
8. Blicha, M., Britikov, K., Sharygina, N.: The golem horn solver. In: Enea, C., Lal, A. (eds.) Computer Aided Verification - CAV 2023, Part II. LNCS, vol. 13965, pp. 209–223. Springer, Cham (2023)
9. Cimatti, A., Griggio, A., Mover, S., Tonetta, S.: IC3 modulo theories via implicit predicate abstraction. CoRR abs/1310.6847 (2013). http://arxiv.org/abs/1310.6847

10. Clarke, E.M., Grumberg, O., Jha, S., Lu, Y., Veith, H.: Counterexample-guided abstraction refinement for symbolic model checking. J. ACM **50**(5), 752–794 (2003). https://doi.org/10.1145/876638.876643
11. Clarkson, M.R., Schneider, F.B.: Hyperproperties. J. Comput. Secur. **18**(6), 1157–1210 (2010). https://doi.org/10.3233/JCS-2009-0393
12. Cousot, P., Wang, J.: Calculational design of hyperlogics by abstract interpretation. Proc. ACM Program. Lang. **9**(POPL), 446–478 (2025). https://doi.org/10.1145/3704852
13. Farzan, A., Vandikas, A.: Automated hypersafety verification. In: Dillig, I., Tasiran, S. (eds.) CAV 2019. LNCS, vol. 11561, pp. 200–218. Springer, Cham (2019). https://doi.org/10.1007/978-3-030-25540-4_11
14. Finkbeiner, B.: Model checking algorithms for hyperproperties (invited paper). In: Henglein, F., Shoham, S., Vizel, Y. (eds.) VMCAI 2021. LNCS, vol. 12597, pp. 3–16. Springer, Cham (2021). https://doi.org/10.1007/978-3-030-67067-2_1
15. Finkbeiner, B., Hahn, C., Stenger, M.: Hyperproperty model checking. In: Computer Aided Verification (CAV), pp. 200–214. Springer (2015)
16. Flanagan, C., Qadeer, S.: Predicate abstraction for software verification. In: Launchbury, J., Mitchell, J.C. (eds.) Conference Record of POPL 2002: The 29th SIGPLAN-SIGACT Symposium on Principles of Programming Languages, Portland, OR, USA, 16–18 January 2002, pp. 191–202. ACM (2002). https://doi.org/10.1145/503272.503291
17. Graf, S., Saidi, H.: Construction of abstract state graphs with PVS. In: Grumberg, O. (ed.) CAV 1997. LNCS, vol. 1254, pp. 72–83. Springer, Heidelberg (1997). https://doi.org/10.1007/3-540-63166-6_10
18. Gurfinkel, A.: Program verification with constrained horn clauses (invited paper). In: Computer Aided Verification – 34th International Conference, CAV 2022, Haifa, Israel, 7–10 August 2022, Proceedings, Part I. Lecture Notes in Computer Science, vol. 13371, pp. 19–29. Springer (2022)
19. Heizmann, M., Hoenicke, J., Podelski, A.: Nested interpolants. In: Hermenegildo, M.V., Palsberg, J. (eds.) Proceedings of the 37th ACM SIGPLAN-SIGACT Symposium on Principles of Programming Languages, POPL 2010, Madrid, Spain, 17–23 January 2010, pp. 471–482. ACM (2010). https://doi.org/10.1145/1706299.1706353
20. Henzinger, T.A., Jhala, R., Majumdar, R., McMillan, K.L.: Abstractions from proofs. In: Jones, N.D., Leroy, X. (eds.) Proceedings of the 31st ACM SIGPLAN-SIGACT Symposium on Principles of Programming Languages, POPL 2004, Venice, Italy, 14–16 January 2004, pp. 232–244. ACM (2004). https://doi.org/10.1145/964001.964021
21. Henzinger, T.A., Jhala, R., Majumdar, R., Sutre, G.: Lazy abstraction. In: Launchbury, J., Mitchell, J.C. (eds.) Conference Record of POPL 2002: The 29th SIGPLAN-SIGACT Symposium on Principles of Programming Languages, Portland, OR, USA, 16–18 January 2002, pp. 58–70. ACM (2002)
22. Hojjat, H., Rümmer, P.: The ELDARICA horn solver. In: Bjørner, N.S., Gurfinkel, A. (eds.) 2018 Formal Methods in Computer Aided Design, FMCAD 2018, Austin, TX, USA, October 30 - November 2 2018, pp. 1–7. IEEE (2018)
23. Itzhaky, S., Shoham, S., Vizel, Y.: Hyperproperty verification as CHC satisfiability. In: Weirich, S. (ed.) Programming Languages and Systems - 33rd European Symposium on Programming, ESOP 2024, Held as Part of the European Joint Conferences on Theory and Practice of Software, ETAPS 2024, Luxembourg City, Luxembourg, 6–11 April 2024, Proceedings, Part II. Lecture Notes in Computer

Science, vol. 14577, pp. 212–241. Springer (2024). https://doi.org/10.1007/978-3-031-57267-8_9
24. Jhala, R., McMillan, K.L.: A practical and complete approach to predicate refinement. In: Hermanns, H., Palsberg, J. (eds.) TACAS 2006. LNCS, vol. 3920, pp. 459–473. Springer, Heidelberg (2006). https://doi.org/10.1007/11691372_33
25. Komuravelli, A., Gurfinkel, A., Chaki, S.: SMT-based model checking for recursive programs. In: Biere, A., Bloem, R. (eds.) Computer Aided Verification - 26th International Conference, CAV 2014, Held as Part of the Vienna Summer of Logic, VSL 2014, Vienna, Austria, 18–22 July 2014. Proceedings. Lecture Notes in Computer Science, vol. 8559, pp. 17–34. Springer (2014)
26. Malak, M., Itzhaky, S., Shoham, S., Vizel, Y.: Automatic abstraction refinement for hyperproperties verification (2026). https://doi.org/10.5281/zenodo.20022299
27. McMillan, K.L., Amla, N.: Automatic abstraction without counterexamples. In: Garavel, H., Hatcliff, J. (eds.) Tools and Algorithms for the Construction and Analysis of Systems, 9th International Conference, TACAS 2003, Held as Part of the Joint European Conferences on Theory and Practice of Software, ETAPS 2003, Warsaw, Poland, 7–11 April 2003, Proceedings. Lecture Notes in Computer Science, vol. 2619, pp. 2–17. Springer (2003)
28. McMillan, K.L., Rybalchenko, A.: Solving constrained horn clauses using interpolation (2013). https://api.semanticscholar.org/CorpusID:123198987
29. de Moura, L.M., Bjørner, N.: Z3: An efficient SMT solver. In: Tools and Algorithms for the Construction and Analysis of Systems, 14th International Conference, TACAS 2008, Held as Part of the Joint European Conferences on Theory and Practice of Software, ETAPS 2008, Budapest, Hungary, March 29–April 6, 2008. Proceedings. Lecture Notes in Computer Science, vol. 4963, pp. 337–340. Springer (2008)
30. Rümmer, P., Hojjat, H., Kuncak, V.: On recursion-free horn clauses and craig interpolation. Formal Methods Syst. Des. **47**(1), 1–25 (2015)
31. Shemer, R., Gurfinkel, A., Shoham, S., Vizel, Y.: Property directed self composition. CoRR abs/1905.07705 (2019). http://arxiv.org/abs/1905.07705
32. Shenoy, A., et al.: Automated property directed self composition. In: André, É., Sun, J. (eds.) Automated Technology for Verification and Analysis - 21st International Symposium, ATVA 2023, Singapore, 24–27 October 2023, Proceedings, Part II. Lecture Notes in Computer Science, vol. 14216, pp. 139–158. Springer (2023). https://doi.org/10.1007/978-3-031-45332-8_7
33. Terauchi, T., Aiken, A.: Secure information flow as a safety problem. In: Static Analysis, 12th International Symposium, SAS 2005, London, UK, 7–9 September 2005, Proceedings, pp. 352–367 (2005). https://doi.org/10.1007/11547662_24
34. Unno, H., Terauchi, T., Koskinen, E.: Constraint-based relational verification. In: Silva, A., Leino, K.R.M. (eds.) CAV 2021. LNCS, vol. 12759, pp. 742–766. Springer, Cham (2021). https://doi.org/10.1007/978-3-030-81685-8_35
35. Wang, X., Anderson, G., Dillig, I., McMillan, K.L.: Learning abstractions for program synthesis. CoRR abs/1804.04152 (2018). http://arxiv.org/abs/1804.04152
36. Yang, W., Vizel, Y., Subramanyan, P., Gupta, A., Malik, S.: Lazy self-composition for security verification. In: Chockler, H., Weissenbacher, G. (eds.) CAV 2018. LNCS, vol. 10982, pp. 136–156. Springer, Cham (2018). https://doi.org/10.1007/978-3-319-96142-2_11

Open Access This chapter is licensed under the terms of the Creative Commons Attribution 4.0 International License (http://creativecommons.org/licenses/by/4.0/), which permits use, sharing, adaptation, distribution and reproduction in any medium or format, as long as you give appropriate credit to the original author(s) and the source, provide a link to the Creative Commons license and indicate if changes were made.

The images or other third party material in this chapter are included in the chapter's Creative Commons license, unless indicated otherwise in a credit line to the material. If material is not included in the chapter's Creative Commons license and your intended use is not permitted by statutory regulation or exceeds the permitted use, you will need to obtain permission directly from the copyright holder.

SMT-Based Deontic Reasoning for Åqvist Logics

Christian Köll, Agata Ciabattoni(✉), and Dmitry Rozplokhas

Institute of Logic and Computation, TU Wien, Vienna, Austria
{agata,dmitry}@logic.at

Abstract. Building on the small-model constructions for Åqvist's deontic logics introduced in [24], we present DEO-SMT, an SMT-based reasoner implemented in Z3 for checking validity and generating countermodels. DEO-SMT covers all four of Åqvist's logics (**E**, **F**, **F+(CM)**, **G**) and provides countermodel visualizations as text, matrices, and directed graphs. Our tool outperforms the existing Isabelle/HOL approach, while providing a lightweight and accessible interface for normative reasoning.

1 Introduction

Normative reasoning plays a central role in fields such as law, artificial intelligence, and ethics, where decisions must respect explicit or implicit norms. Norms prescribe, permit, or forbid certain actions or states of affairs, and are captured in terms of obligations, permissions, and prohibitions. Deontic logics provide formal tools for representing and reasoning about them [12,13]. Broadly speaking, these logics fall into two families: norm-based systems, which treat norms as inference rules, and preference-based systems, which interpret normative claims through an ordering of possible worlds. Among the most prominent representatives of the preference-based family are Åqvist's logics [1] **E**, **F**, and **G**, long recognized as foundational frameworks for modeling conditional obligation, denoted as $\bigcirc(\phi \mid \psi)$ (read as "ϕ is obligatory, given ψ"). Originally introduced to model Contrary-to-Duty (CTD) obligations, which are obligations that arise when other obligations are violated, Åqvist's systems interpret deontic modalities using a possible-worlds semantics with a preference (betterness) relation. **F+(CM)** [20] is a more recent extension of **F** that incorporates cautious monotonicity, a well-known principle from non-monotonic reasoning [11]; **F+(CM)** can be viewed as Preferential Conditional Logic $\mathbb{PCL}$ [5] supplemented with reflexivity and the absoluteness axiom, ensuring that the ranking is not world-relative; the shallow fragment of **F+(CM)** coincides with the KLM logic P [17]. **E**, **F**, **F+(CM)**, and **G** form a modular hierarchy of increasing deductive strength. At the top of the hierarchy, **G** coincides with $\mathbb{VTA}$ [14,18], one of Lewis's conditional logics, and its shallow fragment is the KLM logic R [17].

Åqvist systems have been extensively studied from semantic, axiomatic, and proof theory perspectives, e.g., [6–8,21]. However, these works do not directly

© The Author(s) 2026
A. Biere et al. (Eds.): IJCAR 2026, LNAI 16688, pp. 455–464, 2026.
https://doi.org/10.1007/978-3-032-32589-1_27

address practical questions such as whether, given a large body of norms and a set of factual circumstances, a particular obligation applies, fails to apply, or conflicts with others. Nor do they provide practical mechanisms for assessing the consistency of real-world normative systems, for example, determining whether provisions of the General Data Protection Regulation (GDPR) are consistent or contradictory.

As automated decision-making becomes more widespread, the need for tools that can reason with these logics has become increasingly pressing. A SAT-based tool for I/O logics [19], a prominent approach to norm-based reasoning, proposed in [26]. For preference-based systems, the available tools are based on embeddings into Higher Order Logic [2,3,22,23]; they support versatile experimentation but remain inefficient for object-level tasks like proof search and countermodel generation, since they encode the logic's semantics inside expressive, and potentially undecidable, higher-order frameworks.

In this paper, we build on the LEGO small-model constructions of [24] to introduce DEO-SMT, an efficient reasoning tool for all four propositional Åqvist systems. Following the ideas of Friedman and Halpern [10], the constructions assemble polynomial-size models from elementary components: chains, antichains, and cliques of worlds drawn from an arbitrary model. This yields NP-completeness for the logics and enables an encoding into classical propositional logic. Using these small-model constructions (LEGO for **E**, **F**, and **F+(CM)**, and the construction of [10] for **G** in its $\mathbb{VTA}$ reformulation), we design SMT-based decision procedures in Z3 for both validity checking and countermodel generation. DEO-SMT supports all four logics in Åqvist's family and provides countermodel visualizations in textual, matrix, and graph formats.

Empirically, DEO-SMT drastically outperforms existing approaches, achieving an average speedup factor of ×31.8 compared to the Isabelle/HOL encodings of Parent and Benzmüller [2,3,22,23]. This gain in efficiency reflects a different design trade-off: Isabelle/HOL-based approaches provide the strong guarantees of mechanically verified higher-order reasoning, whereas DEO-SMT prioritizes efficient object-level reasoning through SMT-based deduction and countermodel generation, together with an accessible interface for practical normative reasoning.

By combining the theoretical uniformity of the LEGO constructions with the efficiency of SMT solvers, our tool offers the first lightweight, scalable decision procedure for the full family of propositional Åqvist's preference-based deontic logics, making automated normative reasoning significantly more accessible.

DEO-SMT is available at https://lego.guest.logic.at/.

2 Åqvist's Systems in a Nutshell

Åqvist's systems are a family of modal logics for modeling conditional obligations. Building on the preference-based approach to conditional obligations proposed by [16], Åqvist introduced a hierarchy of bi-modal logics, combining the monadic alethic modality $\Box$ of **S5** and the dyadic deontic modality $\bigcirc$. The semantics of these systems is based on the following variant of preference models [18,25].

Definition 1. *A* preference model *is a triple* $\langle W, \succeq, \mathbb{V} \rangle$ *where* W *is a (non-empty) set of worlds, the preference relation* $\succeq$ *is a binary relation on* W*, and* $\mathbb{V}\colon \mathbb{P} \rightarrow 2^W$ *is a valuation function. We denote the set of worlds of* M *by* $W(M)$*, and write* $w \succ u$ *to denote that both* $w \succeq u$ *and* $u \not\succeq w$*.*

When evaluating a modal formula w.r.t. a preference model, $\Box$ is interpreted as a universal modality and $\bigcirc(\varphi \mid \psi)$ is true when φ holds in all *best* (i.e. $\succ$-maximal) worlds among the worlds satisfying ψ:

$$
\begin{aligned}
M, w \models \Box\varphi \quad &\text{iff} \quad M, u \models \varphi \ \forall u \in W(M) \\
M, w \models \bigcirc(\varphi \mid \psi) \quad &\text{iff} \quad M, u \models \varphi \ \forall u \in \text{best}_M(\psi) \\
&\text{where } \text{best}_M(\psi) = \{u : M, u \models \psi \text{and} \forall u' \succ u : M, u' \not\models \psi\}
\end{aligned}
$$

Definition 2. (Limit Conditions) *M is* limited *if for any formula φ satisfied in some world of M, $best_M(\varphi) \neq \emptyset$. M is* smooth *if for any φ and any world w satisfying φ, either $w \in best_M(\varphi)$ or there is $u \in best_M(\varphi)$ such that $u \succ w$.*

The weakest Åqvist logic, **E**, imposes no conditions on $\succeq$; **F** imposes only *limitedness* to rule out contradictory obligations; and the strongest system, **G**, assumes that $\succeq$ is a smooth preorder, as is standard for counterfactuals in the Lewisian tradition. Hence **G** coincides with Lewis' $\mathbb{VTA}$ [18], while **E** and **F** do not coincide with any known counterfactual logics due to the possible non-transitivity of $\succeq$. **F** + (**CM**) is a further addition to the Åqvist family that drops the totalness requirement from **G**, and thus lies strictly between **F** and **G** in deductive strength; in fact, it coincides with $\mathbb{PCLTA}$, a known extension of $\mathbb{PCL}$ [15]. All four Åqvist systems enjoy the finite model property [21]. Moreover, as shown in [24], for finite-model characterizations the limit conditions can be replaced by more natural frame conditions: for **F** + (**CM**) and **G**, smoothness is entailed by finiteness and transitivity, and for **F**, limitedness can be replaced by acyclicity. The Table 1 summarizes the semantic characterizations for the systems.

Table 1. Semantical characterizations of Åqvist's logics.

Åqvist's logic	Original characterization [21]	Finite-model characterization [24]
E	arbitrary models	finite models
F	limited models	finite, acyclic models
F+(CM)	smooth, transitive models	finite, transitive models
G	smooth, transitive, total models	finite, transitive, total models

To assess the computational complexity of conditional logics, [10] introduced *small model constructions* showing that every satisfiable formula is satisfied by some model of bounded (polynomial) size w.r.t. the size of the formula. In particular, they gave constructions for $\mathbb{VTA}$ (i.e., **G**) and $\mathbb{PCLTA}$ (i.e., $\mathbf{F} + (\mathbf{CM})$) with, respectively, a linear and a quadratic number of worlds. [24] extended this approach to all Åqvist logics, providing alternative constructions with a quadratic number of worlds. Our Deo-SMT will rely on these bounds.

3 Tool Description

The structure of Deo-SMT is in Fig. 1.

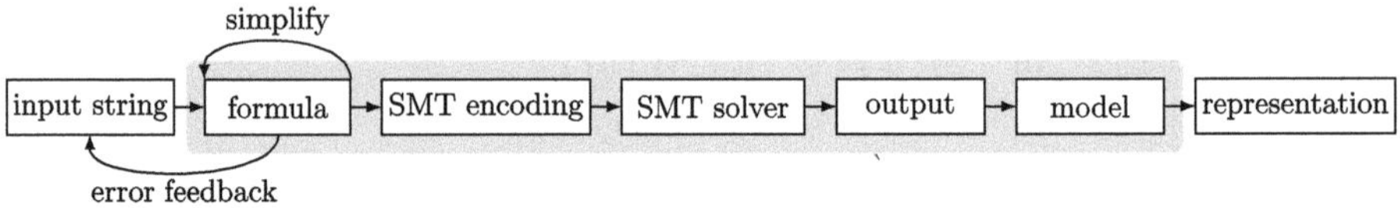

Fig. 1. Tool Structure

Parsing. The input text is translated into a logic formula using a custom parser for the obligation syntax, supporting infix notation with symbolic operators (e.g. `&`, `/`, `~`); syntactic errors are reported with their locations.

Formula Simplification. The parsed formula is simplified to minimize its size.

Model Encoding. The simplified formula is encoded into classical propositional logic. This encoding depends on the selected Åqvist logic and is then passed to the SMT-solver Z3 [9].

Minimal Countermodel Extraction. If the formula is not valid, a countermodel of minimal size is extracted from the model returned by Z3.

Countermodel Representation. The extracted countermodel is presented in a human-readable form. Different representations are used.

Formula Simplification. It reduces encoding size and eliminates semantic redundancies, improving performance and clarifying the formula structure. In particular, reducing modal operators lowers the upper bound on the number of worlds needed for a countermodel, achieving the largest reduction in encoding size. The syntactic and semantic simplification rules are applied bottom-up so that subformulas are simplified before their parents, avoiding missed opportunities in nested contexts. For example, $\neg\Box\top \wedge (\top \rightarrow \Box\Box\phi) \rightsquigarrow \bot \wedge \Box\phi \rightsquigarrow \bot$.

Model Encoding. The encoding into classical propositional logic, follows the approach in [24]. For any formula φ and Åqvist logic $\mathcal{L}$ define a propositional formula $F_{\mathcal{L}}(\varphi)$, which is valid iff φ is valid in $\mathcal{L}$. $F_{\mathcal{L}}(\varphi)$ encodes a countermodel M for φ with worlds $\{w_1 \dots w_{N(\varphi)}\}$, where $N(\varphi)$ is the size bound derived from the small model constructions (see below). The encoding uses the following variables.

- $p_{i,j}$ for $1 \leq i, j \leq N(\varphi)$ encoding $w_i \succeq w_j$
- v_i^{ψ} for $1 \leq i \leq N(\varphi)$ and $\psi \in Sub\mathcal{F}(\varphi)$, where $Sub\mathcal{F}(\varphi)$ denotes the subformulas of φ, encoding $M, w_i \models \psi$

If ψ is not a propositional variable, v_i^{ψ} depends on the v-variables for the immediate subformulas of ψ. The dependences are encoded by the following set of propositional equivalences:

$$
\begin{array}{rlll}
C^{ev}(\varphi) = & \{ \; v_i^{\neg\psi} \Leftrightarrow (\neg v_i^{\psi}) & \mid \; (\neg\psi) \in Sub\mathcal{F}(\varphi) & \}_{1 \leq i \leq N(\varphi)} \\
\cup & \{ \; v_i^{\psi_1 \wedge \psi_2} \Leftrightarrow (v_i^{\psi_1} \wedge v_i^{\psi_2}) & \mid \; (\psi_1 \wedge \psi_2) \in Sub\mathcal{F}(\varphi) & \}_{1 \leq i \leq N(\varphi)} \\
\cup & \{ \; v_i^{\psi_1 \vee \psi_2} \Leftrightarrow (v_i^{\psi_1} \vee v_i^{\psi_2}) & \mid \; (\psi_1 \vee \psi_2) \in Sub\mathcal{F}(\varphi) & \}_{1 \leq i \leq N(\varphi)} \\
\cup & \{ \; v_i^{\psi_1 \to \psi_2} \Leftrightarrow (v_i^{\psi_1} \to v_i^{\psi_2}) & \mid \; (\psi_1 \to \psi_2) \in Sub\mathcal{F}(\varphi) & \}_{1 \leq i \leq N(\varphi)} \\
\cup & \{ \; v_i^{\Box\beta} \Leftrightarrow (\bigwedge_{j=1}^{N(\varphi)} v_j^{\beta}) & \mid \; (\Box\beta) \in Sub\mathcal{F}(\varphi) & \}_{1 \leq i \leq N(\varphi)} \\
\cup & \multicolumn{3}{l}{\{ \; v_i^{\bigcirc(\gamma \mid \alpha)} \Leftrightarrow (\bigwedge_{j=1}^{N(\varphi)} (v_j^{\gamma} \vee \neg v_j^{\alpha} \vee (\bigvee_{t=1}^{N(\varphi)} (p_{t,j} \wedge \neg p_{j,t} \wedge v_t^{\alpha}))))} \\
 & & \mid \; \bigcirc(\gamma \mid \alpha) \in Sub\mathcal{F}(\varphi) & \}_{1 \leq i \leq N(\varphi)}
\end{array}
$$

To encode transitivity and totality of $\succeq$, we use the following sets of formulas:

$$
\mathcal{C}^{trans}(\varphi) = \{p_{i,j} \wedge p_{j,k} \Rightarrow p_{i,k}\}_{1 \leq i,j,k \leq N(\varphi)} \qquad \mathcal{C}^{total}(\varphi) = \{p_{i,j} \vee p_{j,i}\}_{1 \leq i,j \leq N(\varphi)}
$$

The relation $\succeq$ is acyclic if there exists a relation $\succeq^t$ that is transitive, irreflexive and contains $\succeq$. Using additional variables $t_{i,j}$ for $1 \leq i, j \leq N(\varphi)$ encoding the fact $w_i \succeq^t w_j$, we encode acyclicity with the following set of formulas.

$$
\begin{array}{rll}
\mathcal{C}^{acyclic}(\varphi) = & \{ \; (t_{i,j} \wedge t_{j,k}) \Rightarrow t_{i,k} & \}_{1 \leq i,j,k \leq N(\varphi)} \\
\cup & \{ \; \neg t_{i,i} & \}_{1 \leq i \leq N(\varphi)} \\
\cup & \{ \; p_{i,j} \Rightarrow t_{i,j} & \}_{1 \leq i,j \leq N(\varphi)}
\end{array}
$$

The encoding is then passed to the Z3 solver that determines whether a countermodel exists for the formula, thereby showing that it is invalid.

Size Bound Calculation The required number of worlds in a countermodel forms the basis for encoding formulas into propositional logic. The calculations of the size bound for each logic are based on the small model constructions in [24]. We introduce the notation: $\mathrm{Nec}(\varphi) = \{\Box\phi \in Sub\mathcal{F}(\varphi)\}$, $\mathrm{Obl}(\varphi) = \{\bigcirc(\psi \mid \phi) \in Sub\mathcal{F}(\varphi)\}$, $Cond(\varphi) = \{\alpha \mid \bigcirc(\gamma \mid \alpha) \in Sub\mathcal{F}(\varphi)\}$. Without determining for each subformula $\Box\phi$ and $\bigcirc(\psi \mid \phi)$ whether it is satisfied, we use the following upper bound on the number of falsifying worlds $\mathrm{Fal}(\varphi, M)$. $|\mathrm{Fal}(\varphi, M)| \leq 1 + |\mathrm{Nec}(\varphi)| + |\mathrm{Obl}(\varphi)|$

The small model constructions yield upper bounds on the size of countermodels in each logic, given by the following formulas.

$$sizeBound_E = 3 \cdot |Cond(\varphi)| + |Fal(\varphi, M)| \cdot (|Cond(\varphi)| + 1)$$
$$sizeBound_F = |Cond(\varphi)| + |Fal(\varphi, M)| \cdot (|Cond(\varphi)| + 1)$$
$$sizeBound_{F+(CM)} = |Fal(\varphi, M)| \cdot (|Cond(\varphi)| + 1)$$

For the logic $\mathbb{VTA}$ (i.e. **G**), Friedman and Halpern [10] use a different approach for constructing a countermodel. They take one world from the original model for each modality. This results in a linear size bound of the model and the following formula, which we use in our tool: $sizeBound_G = 1 + |\mathrm{Nec}(\varphi)| + |\mathrm{Obl}(\varphi)|$.

Finding a Minimal Countermodel. When reasoning about a formula, we call Z3 multiple times. To establish validity, we first attempt to construct a countermodel using the maximum number of worlds allowed by the encoding.

To encode the countermodels for all of Åqvist's logics, we combine the sets of formulas in the following way , adding $\neg v_1^\varphi$ to impose that φ is falsified in the model in the world #1.

$$F_{\mathbf{E}}(\varphi) = \neg v_1^\varphi \wedge \bigwedge C^{ev}(\varphi)$$
$$F_{\mathbf{F}}(\varphi) = \neg v_1^\varphi \wedge \bigwedge C^{ev}(\varphi) \wedge \bigwedge C^{acyclic}(\varphi)$$
$$F_{\mathbf{F}+(\mathbf{CM})}(\varphi) = \neg v_1^\varphi \wedge \bigwedge C^{ev}(\varphi) \wedge \bigwedge C^{trans}(\varphi)$$
$$F_{\mathbf{G}}(\varphi) = \neg v_1^\varphi \wedge \bigwedge C^{ev}(\varphi) \wedge \bigwedge C^{trans}(\varphi) \wedge \bigwedge C^{total}(\varphi)$$

If no countermodel exists at this upper bound, then no countermodel exists at all and the formula is valid. Since most formulas can be falsified with few worlds, we perform encodings and SMT calls with an increasing number of worlds, starting from 1, until a minimal model is found.

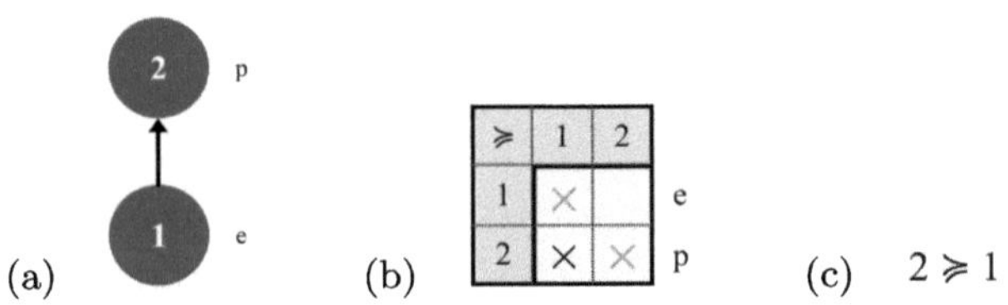

Fig. 2. Representations of the GDPR model. (a) Graph. (b) Matrix. (c) Text.

4 Countermodel Representation

To illustrate how DEO-SMT presents countermodels, following [4], we use the norms below from the GDPR (Regulation EU 2016/679) as a case study (we denote "processed lawfully" by p and "erase the data" by e):

1. Personal data shall be processed lawfully, i.e. $\bigcirc(\mathrm{p} \mid \top)$
2. If the personal data have been processed unlawfully, the controller has the obligation to erase the personal data in question $\bigcirc(\mathrm{e} \mid \neg\mathrm{p})$
3. It is obligatory to keep the personal data provided that it is processed lawfully $\bigcirc(\neg\mathrm{e} \mid \mathrm{p})$

Assume now that some data in the context of such an agreement has been processed unlawfully, i.e. ¬p. Norms 1 and 2 form a standard Contrary-To-Duty pattern, and norms 1-3 combined with the fact ¬p are inconsistent in the best known deontic logic: Standard Deontic Logic [27] (aka the normal modal logic KD). By contrast, in Åqvist systems 1-4 are consistent. E.g., in the logic **E**, the tool produces a two-world model $M = \langle W, \succeq, \mathbb{V}\rangle$ in which all four norms hold simultaneously. The formal definition of this model (see Definition 1) is: $W = \{w_1, w_2\}$, $\succeq = \{(w_2, w_1)\}$, and $\mathbb{V}(w_1) = \{\mathrm{p}\}$ $\mathbb{V}(w_2) = \{\mathrm{e}\}$.

DEO-SMT visualizes the model as (a) a directed graph, (b) a matrix, and (c) text only, as demonstrated in Fig. 2.

Directed Graph. In the graph view, worlds are nodes labeled by their number (i.e., node i representing world w_i), and an edge from i to j indicates $w_j \succeq w_i$. For larger models, and especially those with a dense preference relation, graphs are hard to read. For small models (up to three worlds), crossing-free layouts are used, either linear or triangular, with better worlds placed higher when possible.

Matrix. Countermodels can also be shown as a matrix with rows and columns indexed by worlds. An entry in column i and row j, indicates that $w_i \succeq w_j$, i.e. that world w_i is preferred over world w_j. We improve the readability of the matrix representation, especially for bigger models, by an interactive user interface. Indeed, hovering over a matrix entry or world number highlights the corresponding better and worse worlds and the true variables in the corresponding worlds.

Text Representation. The preference relation can also be presented textually by listing preference statements in formal notation. Instead of listing each pair separately, related statements are combined into compact expressions, e.g., merging $w_1 \succeq w_2$ and $w_3 \succeq w_1$ into $w_3 \succeq w_1, w_2$.

To construct these compact relations, worlds with identical sets of better or inferior worlds are grouped together, and their relations are listed jointly. For efficiency, the sizes of these sets are tracked to quickly identify and merge matching groups.

Remark 1. The most suitable representation for a countermodel depends on its size. For models with up to three worlds, all three representations are shown. For larger models with more than three worlds, the graph representation is omitted. The text representation of the preference relation remains useful for quickly identifying the most and least preferred worlds of a model.

5 Comparison to Existing Tools

We compare Deo-SMT to the existing automated approach by Parent and Benzmüller [2,3,22,23] using Isabelle/HOL. Their work embeds Åqvist's logics into higher-order logic via a shallow semantic embedding, enabling both automated and interactive reasoning about the logics and their properties. Isabelle/HOL, an interactive theorem prover based on classical higher-order logic, provides a suitable meta-logic for formalizing such complex systems. Their approach leverages this embedding to express and automatically verify properties and correspondences using higher-order reasoning.

The comparison below is carried out with respect to the following criteria:

- **Goals:** Conceptually, the two approaches pursue complementary goals. The Isabelle/HOL-based framework is designed for formal verification, correspondence theory, and meta-logical analysis of Åqvist's logics, whereas Deo-SMT targets efficient automated deduction, countermodel generation, and user-oriented feedback.
- **Supported Logics:** Our tool uniformly supports all Åqvist's logics: **E**, **F**, **F+(CM)**, **G**. In contrast, the Isabelle/HOL approach encodes each logic separately, each requiring a dedicated formalization.
- **Performance:** Deo-SMT uses finite model construction via propositional encoding and SAT-based solving. We tested both tools for the logic **E**, since most Isabelle/HOL implementations target it, on a benchmark of 10,460 formulas which are all possible formulas up to operator nesting depth at most 2, modulo equivalence under variable renaming, associativity and commutativity. On this benchmark, Deo-SMT reduces average runtime by a factor of ×31.8 compared to the Isabelle/HOL-based solver of Parent and Benzmüller [22], when performing validity checking and countermodel construction under the same formula-dependent size bounds.
- **Simplification:** Deo-SMT simplifies the input formula, which improves readability and also computational performance.
- **Model readability:** Deo-SMT provides countermodels in three human-readable formats (graphical, matrix, and text), while Isabelle/HOL uses Nitpick with lambda terms and explicit relation assignments.
- **Minimal models:** Our tool automatically finds a minimal model.
- **Input format:** Deo-SMT operates directly on formulas written in the logic's syntax. By contrast, Isabelle/HOL requires familiarity with formal proof environments and function syntax.

Acknowledgements. The work is partially supported by the European Union's Horizon 2020 research and innovation programme under grant agreement No 101034440, the FWF project I 6372-N (Grant-DOI 10.55776/I6372), and the WWTF project ICT22-023 (Grant ID: 10.47379/ICT22023).

Disclosure of Interests. The authors have no competing interests to declare that are relevant to the content of this article.

References

1. Åqvist, L.: Deontic logic. In: Gabbay, D., Guenthner, F. (eds.) Handbook of Philosophical Logic, vol. II, pp. 605–714. Springer, Dordrecht (1984)
2. Benzmüller, C., Farjami, A., Parent, X.: Åqvist's dyadic deontic logic E in HOL. FLAP **6**(5), 733–754 (2019)
3. Benzmüller, C., Parent, X., van der Torre, L.W.N.: Designing normative theories for ethical and legal reasoning: Logikey framework, methodology, and tool support. Artif. Intell. **287**, 103348 (2020)
4. Benzmüller, C., Parent, X., van der Torre, L.: A Deontic Logic Reasoning Infrastructure. In: Manea, F., Miller, R.G., Nowotka, D. (eds.) CiE 2018. LNCS, vol. 10936, pp. 60–69. Springer, Cham (2018). https://doi.org/10.1007/978-3-319-94418-0_6
5. Burgess, J.: Quick completeness proofs for some logics of conditionals. Notre Dame J. Formal Logic **22**(3), 76–84 (1981)
6. Ciabattoni, A., Olivetti, N., Parent, X.: Dyadic obligations: proofs and countermodels via hypersequents. In: Proceedings of the PRIMA 2022, pp. 54–71. Springer (2022)
7. Ciabattoni, A., Rozplokhas, D., Tesi, M.: GL-based calculi for PCL and its deontic cousin. In: Proceedings of the JELIA 2025 (2025)
8. Ciabattoni, A., Tesi, M.: Sequents vs hypersequents for Åqvist systems. In: Proceedings of the IJCAR 2024, pp. 176–195. Springer (2024)
9. De Moura, L., Bjørner, N.: Z3: An efficient SMT solver. In: Proceedings of the International Conference on Tools and Algorithms for the Construction and Analysis of Systems, pp. 337–340. Springer (2008)
10. Friedman, N., Halpern, J.Y.: On the complexity of conditional logics. In: Proceedings of the KR 1994, pp. 202–213. Elsevier (1994)
11. Gabbay, D.M.: Theoretical foundations for non-monotonic reasoning in expert systems. In: Apt, K.R. (ed.) Logics and Models of Concurrent Systems, pp. 439–457. Springer, Berlin Heidelberg, Berlin, Heidelberg (1985)
12. Gabbay, D.M., Horty, J., Parent, X., van der Meyden, R., van der Torre, L., (eds.): Handbook of Deontic Logic and Normative Systems. College Publications (2013)
13. Gabbay, D.M., Horty, J.F., Parent, X., van der Meyden, R., van der Torre, L. (eds.): Handbook of Deontic Logic and Normative Systems, vol. 2. College Publications, London (2021)
14. Giordano, L., Gliozzi, V., Olivetti, N., Pozzato, G.L.: Analytic tableaux calculi for KLM logics of nonmonotonic reasoning. ACM Trans. Comput. Log. **10**(3), 18:1–18:47 (2009)
15. Girlando, M.: On the Proof Theory of Conditional Logics. Aix-Marseille Universite; Helsinki University, Theses (2019)
16. Hansson, B.: An analysis of some deontic logics. Deontic Logic Introductory Syst. Readings, 121–147. Springer (1971)
17. Kraus, S., Lehmann, D., Magidor, M.: Nonmonotonic reasoning, preferential models and cumulative logics. Artif. Intell. **44**(1–2), 167–207 (1990)
18. Lewis, D.: Counterfactuals, blackwells (1973)
19. Makinson, D., van der Torre, L.W.N.: Input/output logics. J. Philos. Log. **29**(4), 383–408 (2000)
20. Parent, X.: Maximality vs. optimality in dyadic deontic logic. J. Philos. Log. **43**, 1101–1128 (2014)

21. Parent, X.: Preference semantics for Hansson-type dyadic deontic logic: a survey of results. In: Gabbay, D., Horty, J., Parent, X., van der Torre, L., van der Meyden, R., (eds.) Handbook of Deontic Logic and Normative Systems, vol. 2, pp. 7–70. College Publications, London (2021)
22. Parent, X., Benzmüller, C.: Automated verification of deontic correspondences in Isabelle/HOL-first results. In: Proceedings of the Automated Reasoning in Quantified Non-Classical Logics, 4th International Workshop (associated with FLoC and IJCAR 2022), pp. 92–108 (2022)
23. Parent, X., Benzmüller, C.: Conditional normative reasoning as a fragment of HOL. J. Appl. Non Class. Logics **34**(4), 561–592 (2024)
24. Rozplokhas, D.: Lego-like small model constructions for åqvist's logics. In: Ciabattoni, A., Gabelaia, D., Sedlár, I., (eds.) Advances in Modal Logic, pp. 631–651. College Publications (2024)
25. Shoham, Y.: A semantical approach to nonmonotic logics. In: Proceedings of the Symposium on Logic in Computer Science (LICS '87), pp. 275–279. IEEE Computer Society (1987)
26. Steen, A.: A reduction of input/output logics to sat. J. Appl. Non-Classical Logics, 1–34 (2026)
27. Von Wright, G.H.: Deontic logic. Mind **60**(237), 1–15 (1951)

Open Access This chapter is licensed under the terms of the Creative Commons Attribution 4.0 International License (http://creativecommons.org/licenses/by/4.0/), which permits use, sharing, adaptation, distribution and reproduction in any medium or format, as long as you give appropriate credit to the original author(s) and the source, provide a link to the Creative Commons license and indicate if changes were made.

The images or other third party material in this chapter are included in the chapter's Creative Commons license, unless indicated otherwise in a credit line to the material. If material is not included in the chapter's Creative Commons license and your intended use is not permitted by statutory regulation or exceeds the permitted use, you will need to obtain permission directly from the copyright holder.

Author Index

© The Editor(s) (if applicable) and The Author(s) 2026

A. Biere et al. (Eds.): IJCAR 2026, LNAI 16688, pp. 465–466, 2026.
https://doi.org/10.1007/978-3-032-32589-1

MIX
Papier aus verantwortungsvollen Quellen
Paper from responsible sources
FSC® C105338

If you have any concerns about our products,
you can contact us on
ProductSafety@springernature.com

In case Publisher is established outside the EU,
the EU authorized representative is:
Springer Nature Customer Service Center GmbH
Europaplatz 3, 69115 Heidelberg, Germany

Printed by Libri Plureos GmbH
in Hamburg, Germany